Black & Amber

A HISTORY OF THE GAA
IN THE PARISH OF DUNSHAUGHLIN,
1886-2014

Published by Dunshaughlin GAA

Black & Amber

A History of the GAA in the Parish of Dunshaughlin, 1886-2014

Jim Gilligan, Patsy McLoughlin

Far better it is to dare mighty things, to win glorious triumphs, even though checkered by failure, than to rank with those poor spirits who neither enjoy much nor suffer much, because they live in that grey twilight that knows not victory nor defeat.
Theodore Roosevelt, US President, (1901-1909), 10th April 1899.

Dedicated
To all those who, playing for Dunshaughlin, Drumree, Royal Gaels and St. Martins, dared mighty things, won glorious triumphs and experienced bitter defeat.

First Published in 2015 by
Dunshaughlin GAA

© Jim Gilligan and Patsy McLoughlin 2015

Jim Gilligan and Patsy McLoughlin have asserted their moral right
to be identified as the authors of this work.

All rights reserved.
The Material in this publication is protected by copyright law. Except as may be permitted by law,
no part of the material may be reproduced (including by storage in a retrieval system)
or transmitted in any form or by any means, adapted, rented or lent without the written permission
of the copyright owners. Applications for permissions should be addressed to the publisher.

ISBN No. 978-0-9933953-0-7

Design and typesetting by A & J Print, Dunshaughlin
Typeset in Sabon
Printed in Ireland by Anglo Printers, Drogheda.
Maps in Appendix 2 © Anú Design, Tara.

Dunshaughlin GAA Club acknowledges financial support by Meath County Council
under its Community Heritage Grant Scheme, 2015.

Contents

	Réamhrá	x
1.	Beginnings, 1886-91	1
2.	Revival, 1894-1906	17
3.	A Hurling Stronghold, 1902-1919	25
	Interlude 1: Dunshaughlin in the Early Twentieth Century	43
4.	Hurling Glory and Gloom . . .and Football Revived	51
5.	Patience Rewarded- Football titles at last, 1947-1958	69
6.	St. Martins and Underage Football	89
	Interlude 2: Dunshaughlin the 1950s	104
7.	In Seventh Heaven: Junior and Intermediate Titles, 1967 and 1977	117
8.	St. Martins' Revival, 1983-1998	139
9.	Hurling Revived	165
	Interlude 3: The Ban on Foreign Games	190
10.	Struggle to Achieve, 1978-1990	195
11.	A Second String to our Bow: The Eighties	213
12.	The Rocky Road to Intermediate Glory, 1992-1997	229
13.	Competing for the Keegan Cup, 1998-2000	251
14.	High Kings of Meath	279
15.	Fresh Fields: The Leinster Campaigns	305
16.	Going out in a Blaze of Glory: St. Martins 1999-2008	327
17.	Sowing the Seeds: Hurling in St. Martins, 1987-2008	353
18.	The Junior Challenge, 1995-2014	371
19.	The Royal Gaels	391
20.	New Century, New Challenges	423
21.	From Black and Red to Black and Amber: Underage Football 2009-14	439
22.	Highs and Lows of Recent Years, 2007-2014	463
	Achoimre as Gaeilge	482

Appendices

1.	Biographical Information, 1886-1950s	492
2.	Where We Sported and Played	510
3.	Part 1: The GAA in Drumree, 1887-1956	522
3.	Part 2: The GAA in Drumree, 1957-2014	536
4.	Handball	554
5.	Camogie	566
6.	Club Officers: Parish Clubs 1886-2015	578
7.	Dunshaughlin: Results of Championship Semi-Finals, Finals and League Finals	588
8.	St. Martins: Football and Hurling Results	610
9.	Drumree: Football and Hurling Results	626
10.	Royal Gaels: Results	634
11.	Titles won by Parish Clubs	639
11A.	Dunshaughlin Player Record: Intermediate Football Championship, 1983-1997	642
11B.	Dunshaughlin Player Record: Senior Football Championship, 1998-2014	644
12.	Winners of Leinster, All-Ireland Medals	648
13.	Senior Inter County Player Record, 1963-2014	650
14.	Hall of Fame and Other Awards	652
15.	Dunshaughlin Club Members as Officers of Meath GAA Boards	657
16.	Gaelic Games in the Schools in Dunshaughlin Parish	658
17.	GAA Clubs in the Parish and Locality, 1886-1900	690

Réamhrá

Cúis áthais dúinn stair Chumann Lúthchleas Gael i nDomhnach Seachnaill a chur ar fáil faoi dheireadh do gach duine a bhfuil suim aige nó aici sna heachtraí a tharla sa chumann ó thús. Tá súil againn go mbainfidh gach léitheoir taitneamh as an scéal. Ní heolas faoi na cluichí amháin atá luaite againn sa leabhar mar tá roinnt maith eolais faoi shaol na ndaoine i gcoitinne ann freisin. Tharla athruithe móra stairiúla i gcúrsaí polaitíochta, sóisialta agus eacnamaíochta i rith na mblianta ó bunaíodh an cumann i 1886 agus tá an scéal sin fite fuaite san insint.

This history is an update of the original Black and Amber published over three decades ago in 1984. We said then that the book was intended to be a simple telling of the club's story since its foundation. We attempted to entertain and inform and above all, to preserve in permanent form the story of the club. We have kept those aims to the fore in this revised edition also. The original volume attempted to set the club in its wider social, economic and political context and this time we have added sections called Interludes in the early part of the book to give more of this type of detail.

There has been extensive change and huge development in the club during the past thirty years. Whereas the first hundred years brought just three junior and one intermediate titles in football, since then the club has added three juniors, an intermediate, an historic three-in-a-row of senior titles and a Leinster crown. The hurling revival had just begun in 1984 and subsequently it expanded, declined and died in Dunshaughlin but was then taken up with dedication and commitment by the Drumree club and is currently thriving. The number of underage football and hurling teams being fielded has expanded as the population has increased and keeping track of the myriad of competitions was a daunting challenge. One of the most significant changes-one that was scarcely on the horizon in 1984-was the growth of ladies' football. From small beginnings in 1995 Royal Gaels has grown progressively and now occupies a central place in the GAA and the community.

In addition we have included a number of detailed appendices that record important information in narrative and statistical format. The history of where games were played, the story of handball and camogie, important championship results and team lineouts and records of club officers are included to give a comprehensive listing for reference. We have also included sections on the three primary schools in the parish, St. Seachnall's NS, Culmullen NS and Gaelscoil na Rithe as well as information on the GAA in Dunshaughlin Community College. We believe the history is unique for a club publication by the inclusion of individual adult player records for Dunshaughlin's premier team since the early 1980s.

In 1984 it was expected that Drumree would publish its own history, but, as this didn't transpire we have now included two sections on the Drumree club. This is an important feature of the book as it resurrects long lost details of the club and its antecedents, especially the era of the Pelletstown Reds.

When we researched the original black and amber we decried the fact that so many of the older players and officers had died before we commenced work on the book. Now, we realise how lucky we were to speak to those who were then still alive, as many of them could bring us back to the 1920s and 1930s and even earlier. Without their memories the early part of the book would be entirely dependent on newspaper coverage, which was always intermittent and often brief.

It would be foolhardy to attempt to acknowledge all who assisted us with information in 1984 and in recent times, as it would require another appendix to record them all. To each person who helped in any way we say a huge go raibh mile maith agat, we greatly appreciate your assistance, information and co-operation.

PREFACE

We wish to acknowledge the help we received from the following regarding photographs. Brendan Murray, who gave us permission to use some of his father PJ's unique pictures of the village and its people in our 1984 publication and in the current version. Declan Lynch of hoganstand.com and John Quirke of Navan have been unfailingly generous in giving us access to their portfolios while John Donoghue of the *Meath Chronicle* has been equally helpful. We also acknowledge permission from Waterford County Museum to use its unique picture of the early GAA goalposts, which can be seen in Chapter 1. Where possible we have noted the donor alongside the pictures used.

A huge word of thanks to the staff at Meath County Library, especially Tom French and Frances Tallon for their assistance, advice and access to their archives. Similarly we acknowledge the assistance of the staff at the National Library of Ireland, the National Archives and Louth County Library at Stockwell Lane, Drogheda.

The final stage of the work involved the typesetting, design and printing of the book. For the former we owe a huge debt of gratitude to Anne Gray and Tomas Korintus in A & J Print for their expertise, patience and understanding during a project that extended over a couple of years. Many thanks also to Karen Carty and Terry Foley of Anú Design, Tara for producing the unique maps of the area used in Appendix 2. Finally, our thanks to Anglo Printers, Drogheda for printing the final product.

We have not provided footnotes to record the sources of our information in the publication as to do so would have extended the book to unsustainable and unaffordable length without any benefit to the general reader. Instead, the summary below outlines the scope and range of sources consulted and used.

Newspaper accounts from the *Meath Chronicle, Drogheda Independent, Irish Independent, Sport, United Ireland, The Celtic Times, Dublin Saturday Post* and *Freeman's Journal*.

Special Branch files (Royal Irish Constabulary) for the 1880s and 1890s held in the National Archives.

Online versions of the census for 1901 and 1911.

Leinster Council minutes for the 1920s and 1930s, courtesy of Michael Reynolds, GAA Museum, Croke Park.

Club minutes 1957-1963 and 1976 to the present. Our thanks to Seamus Flynn for preserving the former. Dunshaughlin Hurling Club minutes 1982-1990 in possession of Paddy Ward, formerly club secretary. St. Martins' minute books, photocopied pages held by Linda Devereux. Unfortunately, most of the St. Martins' minutes have been mislaid despite the fact that the club is of relatively recent origin.

Notes of interviews with club members and players in 1984 and 2011-14 retained by the authors.

We hope that our combined effort has produced a comprehensive, balanced account that portrays the history of gaelic games in the area in detail and in depth. However, opinions expressed in the book are the authors' alone, and do not necessarily reflect the views of the individual clubs. We would be grateful if readers would draw factual errors to our attention so that at least one copy can be amended as necessary and kept safely for the next edition, if one is produced.

Le cúnamh Dé gheobhaidh gach léitheoir rud éigin suimiúil, rud éigin taitneamhach agus rud eigin conspóideach sa scéal! Bainigí sult as.

Jim Gilligan
Patsy McLoughlin
August 2015

CHAPTER 1: BEGINNINGS

Beginnings, 1886-91

'The Saints, true to the colours of their racing patron, and which they themselves have kept so well to the front, chose the well known black and amber.'

Sport, 7 November 1888

On the final Sunday in January 1887, Christopher Tallon and his Dunshaughlin Gaelic Football team faced their first game in the village under G.A.A. rules.

Near neighbours Ross provided the opposition and the game ended in victory for Tallon's men, 'in the presence of a great number of people' according to the weekly paper Sport. Dunshaughlin was one of the earliest, but by no means the first, club to be formed in Co. Meath.

By the time the game took place, the Gaelic Athletic Association had been in existence for over two years. Founded in Thurles in November 1884 by Michael Cusack, with Maurice Davin as President and Archbishop Croke of Cashel as Patron, the G.A.A. was much more concerned in its first few years with athletics than with games, and few football or hurling clubs were formed.

1886 was however, a year of major growth in club members. In March there were approximately sixty affiliated clubs nationally but none in Co. Meath, although there may well have been unaffiliated clubs in existence and active in the county. By August the figure had risen to 300 nationally while in Meath, Dowdstown, Kells, Kilmessan and Yellow Furze were among the first to form, with Dowdstown winning practically every game they played in 1886.

The Dunshaughlin club was probably formed in December 1886 and was called St. Seachnalls. It is not known who first suggested the idea of forming a club in the village. However, in May 1886 a sports' meeting under the rules of the G.A.A.

The Fingall Arms owned by Stephen Kelly, now the location of *Sherry Property Advisers*. Kelly's racing colours, black and amber, became the club's football colours. Count Stolberg, standing, is speaking to Edmund Morris, on horseback, early 1900s.
Photo copyright Brendan Murray.

CHAPTER 1: BEGINNINGS

was held at Ballina near the Hill of Tara. Among those who attended was none other than Michael Cusack himself and the idea of forming a club may well have had its inspiration at this meeting. It is highly probable that Dunshaughlin men like Patrick O Brien, John Finnegan and Thomas Delany were present at the sports as all were deeply interested in athletics.

The original founders and officers of the club are not known but eighteen months later the officers were as follows:

President: Patrick O Brien
Vice-President: Laurence F. Canning
Treasurer: Christopher Tallon
Secretary: John Finnegan

As these officers remained more or less unaltered until 1890 it is reasonable to assume that they were the founding members of the club. It is possible however, that James J. Connolly was Secretary for a period before Finnegan took over.

No record remains of the first meeting but it may well have taken place in The Fingall Arms run by Stephen Kelly, situated at the Navan end of the village. The building was later known as Gogans' Flats, and is currently occupied by Sherry Property Advisers. Kelly was also a racehorse owner and had a number of stables adjacent to the hotel. Some of the men who lined out for Dunshaughlin in the early years of the club worked in Kelly's stables as grooms and stable boys. At the time Kelly owned horses called Lagore, Barbrock, Liberia and one named Opponent, the winner of the Ulster Plate at Downpatrick in 1888.

Kelly's racing colours were black and amber and those were the colours adopted by the new G.A.A. club, probably from its foundation, but certainly from 1888 onwards. Apart from the fact that many of the club members worked in Kelly's, the choice of racing colours would not have been unusual at the time. In the early days few teams had a complete playing outfit but those who did must have borne a striking resemblance to jockeys. Many wore jockey-type caps, with a jersey, knee breeches and long stockings, while in some counties, the cap was the only article of football gear worn by juveniles (Under-16). Stephen Kelly himself appears not to have had any official connections with the G.A.A. club.

Patrick O Brien
Founder member of St. Seachnalls and its first President with his wife Mary Flynn on their wedding day in 1908. Patrick's sister Catherine married Christy Tallon, the club's first captain.

Early Games

The first two games played by Dunshaughlin were away fixtures. It is not known who their opponents were or how the black and ambers fared, but one of them was Ross. The other was probably one of the other local teams, most likely either Warrenstown or Merrywell.

The home tie with Ross was played on Sunday January 30th 1887 in what was described as a 'beautiful level field' which belonged to Mr. Patrick Delany. This field is most likely either the 'Cowbyre' down Rathill Lane or the Eight Acres on the Dublin Road.

According to a newspaper report, the Dunshaughlin team and its supporters were anxious during the game, as *it was the first public trial of the team on their own ground*. But they need not have worried, for although the visitors won the toss and were favoured with the wind in the first half, they could never get the ball near Dunshaughlin's goal, while in the second half, Dunshaughlin only once let the ball down to their goal. Meanwhile, at the other end, Dunshaughlin scored a goal after a *'grand struggle'* and also scored two forfeit points. Forfeit points were awarded in circumstances where a 45 metre free kick is awarded today.

Until 1892, a goal outweighed any number of points but goals were hard to come by in those early days. Teams were generally 21 a side and often crammed together on fields not of standard size. In addition, basic skills were probably lacking while footballs were often of poor manufacture. In any event, Dunshaughlin's first home game was a successful venture. The following are recorded as having played well, team captain Christy Tallon, Thomas Armstrong, Tom Reilly, T. Lynch, P. Mullen and Thomas Delany. Other names mentioned later in the year included J. Duffy, P. Everard, Con Sheridan and C. Skully.

During the remainder of the year, Dunshaughlin played numerous games against local opposition. On February 6th they were away to Warrenstown, while the following Sunday they suffered their first home defeat.

Appropriately the Seachnalls fell to their fellow parishioners, Merrywell, who were deserving victors by one point and six forfeit points to nil. The first half hour was scoreless but Merrywell, with the breeze to their backs in the second half, went on the attack and a shot for goal from M. Rourke was carried over the crossbar by the wind. Disaster now befell the home team and inside five minutes Merrywell scored six forfeit points. First the Dunshaughlin keeper missed the ball and then, in attempting to clear it, sent it through his own point posts for three forfeit points. A similar occurrence minutes later sealed Dunshaughlin's fate.

Before the end of the year, Dunshaughlin took the field against Warrenstown again, Ratoath twice, Ross, Rathfeigh Emeralds, Killana Shamrocks and Grange

> " The earliest rules, from 1884, ordained that games 'shall be decided by the greater number of goals. If no goal be kicked the match shall be deemed a draw.'

Geraldines. No results are available for the Ratoath games but Dunshaughlin was victorious in all the others. The game against Rathfeigh Emeralds was not finished as the Emeralds left the field twenty minutes before the end *'owing to some unaccountable reason'* in the words of a contemporary newspaper account.

A word on the rules of play and scoring may be in order here. The earliest rules, from 1884, ordained that games 'shall be decided by the greater number of goals. If no goal be kicked the match shall be deemed a draw.' There was no provision for points and it is likely that goal posts were similar to soccer goals. By 1886 there was still no mention of points but the 1888 rules provided for them. There were now two sets of posts at each end of the field, the goal posts, which were twenty-one feet apart with a crossbar eight feet high, and point posts twenty-one feet away from each of the goal posts. Goals were scored as today, while points were recorded by sending the ball anywhere between the point posts except under the crossbar. Initially, a goal had no equivalent in points, so it was only when no goals were scored or when teams scored an equal number of goals that the match was decided on the greater number of points. In 1895 a goal was deemed equivalent to five points and by 1900 its value had been reduced to three.

In the very early years forfeit points are mentioned in many newspaper reports of games. They seem to have been awarded in circumstances where a 45 metre kick, would result today, in other words when a ball was driven over the end line by a defender. However, there was no mention of forfeit points in the official rules. By 1888 it was clearly defined that when a ball was played over the end line by the defence a free kick forty yards out from the goal posts was awarded. In the Dunshaughlin v. Merrywell game referred to previously, six of the seven points conceded by Dunshaughlin were described as forfeit points, but they seemed to have been awarded due to defenders playing the ball between their own goal posts.

As can be imagined, when the end lines were not marked, and this was usually the case, there was great scope for disagreement. Although two field umpires assisted the referee, with the role of following play along the sideline and pointing out fouls to the referee, this only made matters worse. In practice, each team supplied a field umpire and they spent their time encouraging their own team, abusing the opposition and arguing with the referee. Referees were not always neutral either. In a game against Donacarney in 1888, Dunshaughlin complained that the referee wouldn't allow the umpires to say a word, telling them that they had no right to interfere at all and another time he cried out, 'Now for a goal Donacarney.' New rules in 1888 recommended that referees use whistles. It seems that prior to this referees called out instructions to players and of course spectators shouting comments often confused players who thought the referee was giving a decision.

 Dunshaughlin complained that the referee wouldn't allow the umpires to say a word, telling them that they had no right to interfere at all and another time he cried out, 'Now for a goal Donacarney.'

Christy Tallon
First captain and founder member of St. Seachnalls.

The referee's decision on all matters was final. He could send off a player for a given period or for the duration of the whole game, for pushing or tripping from behind, catching below the knees or butting with the head. Until the convention of 1886, wrestling was allowed if both teams agreed to it! In place of today's sideline kicks, the ball was thrown in, while at the commencement of play, the players stood in two ranks, each holding the hand of one of the other side. After the ball was thrown in they retreated to their positions.

Sports

When the GAA was founded, the main emphasis was on the word athletic. Cusack himself was a notable athlete and in the early years of the Association, the All-Ireland Sports were the high point of the year. At local level the same was true, the sports meeting involved weeks of organization and usually brought an influx of visitors.

The Dunshaughlin Sports were always well publicized in the national press and it was traditional for parties to come from Dublin *'in drags and other conveyances'* while *Sport* announced *'better prizes it would be difficult to find at any country meeting.'* Groups also came by train to Drumree Station, the return fare from Broadstone in Dublin being 1s 7d (10c).

In 1890, 4,000 were reported to be in attendance, coming from the adjoining counties and Dublin. The venue for these sports is not known but is described as being two miles from Drumree and *'in close proximity to the ancient and historic village of Dunshaughlin.'* Many of the local athletes to the fore in the early years were also members of the football team.

The chief performers were Thomas Delany and Patrick O Brien. Delany seems to have been a real flier in short sprints and the club President Patrick O Brien was the acknowledged expert in slinging the 56lb. (25½ kg) shot, achieving second place and 20 feet 6 inches (just over 6 metres) in 1887, and winning in 1890. In the following year, he was first in the Football Place Kicking contest, driving the leather 161 feet 0½ inches, almost fifty metres. Remember the footballs were very different to the modern streamlined ball! Other athletes of note were William Doran and Richard Swan.

From 1888 onwards, the Dunshaughlin Gaelic Sports were held under GAA rules. Those of 1887 were held under the rules of the rival Irish Amateur Athletic Association (IAAA) although the promoters wanted to run them under GAA rules. The main reason they were unable to do so was that the club was not then affiliated to the GAA, who opposed the suggested Handicapper. Correspondence with GAA headquarters in Dublin sheds some light on the standing of the GAA in the village six months after its formation.

'A Club chiefly composed of Poor Labourers'

James J Connolly as Secretary of the Sports' committee explained the club had about forty members and proposed to collect the club's affiliation fee of 10 shillings (63c) by a levy of 2½ pence (just over 1c) per member. But, he went on,

'yet so poor are they, and such dearth of work is here, that for two or three weeks many of them did not earn the 2½d necessary, and, of course, could not pay capitation.'

They then decided to pay the affiliation from club funds, which left them with just three or four shillings on hand (20 to 25 cent), insufficient to run the sports. In his own words,

'it was impossible amid so much poverty to get up sports with a club composed chiefly of poor labourers, and the football club committee had to invite the co-operation of the chairman, and of other men of means and influence in the locality.'

When the GAA was founded Dunshaughlin was a small village with a single long main street and no development off it. It was completely overshadowed by its neighbours, Navan and Dublin, and never developed as a business or commercial centre. By the 1890s there were six public houses, Brien's, Murphy's, Foley's, Blake's, Kelly's and Swan's, the last three of which doubled as grocery shops. The village had a hotel and a post-office while there were two bakers, a tailor, and a bootmaker.

The population of the village had declined from the pre-Famine figures of 524 to a low of 291 in 1891. There was a slight increase to 315 in 1901 but ten years later it hit its lowest level, 265 persons.

Population of Dunshaughlin Town, 1841-1911

1841	1851	1861	1871	1881	1891	1901	1911
524	422	403	362	354	291	315	265

The nearby townlands presented a similar picture with continuous population decline after the Famine. This was due, in the main, to the lack of employment on the grassland farms. Tillage farming, which was labour intensive, was rarely practised and a huge proportion of the farmlands were used for grazing cattle. Many townlands had only one or two houses and Bernard Carolan, club Secretary in its early years, complained in 1900 that the area was reverting to 'a howling wilderness' due to the large grazing farms, which required little or no farm labour. A *Celtic Times* writer on his way to Navan by train in May 1887 stated that, between Dunboyne and Kilmessan,

> Many townlands had only one or two houses and Bernard Carolan, club Secretary in its early years, complained in 1900 that the area was reverting to 'a howling wilderness' due to the large grazing farms, which required little or no farm labour.

Dunshaughlin Sports 1890
Drogheda Independent advertisement for the annual Dunshaughlin Sports, June 1890

BLACK & AMBER

CHAPTER 1: BEGINNINGS

Old Style Goalposts
The picture of a game in Dungarvan, Co. Waterford shows the point posts each side of the soccer style goalposts. The point posts survived until 1910 when the current uprights and crossbar came into use.
Image courtesy of Waterford County Museum.

'I did not observe six human habitations, and the houses that were discernible were the palatial mansions of the Lord of the manor.'

Many of the households were poor; about half lived in third-class or fourth-class housing and most sons were employed as farm servants or labourers, and daughters as domestic servants or housekeepers. They had very little disposable income and many in the area lived close to poverty. The number of players available for selection was small and fielding teams on an ongoing basis was bound to prove difficult. Looking at Dunshaughlin civil parish, that is the village and the surrounding twelve townlands, there were only 208 persons between the ages of 15 and 35, 120 males and 88 females. Very many of those probably had no great interest in gaelic games so the numbers available for selection were limited. Emigration, mainly to England, or migration to Dublin was a constant drain on the community.

The Mean Combination

Thomas Delany
Delany was a noted athlete during the early years of the GAA in Dunshaughlin. The club's first home game was played on land owned by his father, Patrick, and the club used the grounds for many years.

Though the committees in charge of football and the Sports were separate, membership overlapped and the prime focus was on football. 1888 saw even more activity than the previous year. The first County Championship began in 1887 but Dunshaughlin didn't participate and for them and most other clubs, the chief activity was local challenges and tournaments. Merrywell did enter the 1887 championship and drew Kilmessan who must have been victorious as they met Dowdstown in the second round.

The medals presented to tournament winners in the early years were usually described as silver crosses. Inscribed and intricately designed, they were vastly superior to today's mass produced trophies. In this area at least, the GAA has regressed over time.

In early 1888 the St. Seachnalls organized a tournament which led to some controversy. Dunshaughlin was inclined to blame the small entry on the timid local opposition, claiming that 'some of the neighbouring clubs, probably afraid to suffer defeat, didn't enter.'

On the first Sunday, before a crowd of over one thousand, Merrywell St. Martins, Ross and Crom-a-Boos of Maynooth were victorious. On the following Sunday the Crom-a-Boos defeated St. Martins to reach the final. Meanwhile, Dunshaughlin, organizing the tournament to their own advantage, reached the final by playing only one game.

The Croms, lining out for the final in their green, orange and black jerseys, were more than surprised to note that the black and ambers included on their team some of the St. Martins' men whom they had defeated the previous week.

Having travelled to Dunshaughlin on three successive Sundays the Croms were unhappy with this development- to put it mildly.

At first, Dunshaughlin denied they were playing St. Martins' men but finally admitted the offence. They claimed however, that they were not breaking any rules, as they were all from the one parish. The Croms played under protest and beat what they called the 'mean combination' by 2-1 to 0-3. They further claimed that the 'respectable people' of Dunshaughlin were thoroughly ashamed and that the man who had given his field on the previous two Sundays refused to give it when he learned of the 'disgraceful combination.'

The St. Seachnalls' Secretary, in a reply, claimed that the Seachnalls and St. Martins had decided to amalgamate and when they required a few men in the final, they believed it to be all right to include some of the St. Martins' men. He also denied the allegation about the field, claiming the committee had declined to play on it.

Those explanations don't really stand up under scrutiny. It is unlikely they would leave the field they had used in the earlier rounds, while we find that St. Martins themselves played a game three weeks later and no amalgamation took place. Thus, despite their best efforts, the 'mean combination' was thwarted in the effort to win its own tournament.

Despite this setback, Dunshaughlin was clearly a useful combination at this stage. Among the victories was one over Donacarney at Bellewstown Sports. This gave them *'the proud record of being the first club which succeeded in wresting a goal from Donacarney'* according to *Sport*. Donacarney were county finalists that year.

The Black and Ambers

In 1888 Dunshaughlin won the Moortown Tournament, an important one because of the nature of the prizes. The opposition in the final was provided by O Mahonys of Ardcath and at the final whistle the Saints were clear victors by 1-5 to 1-1, a victory *'which made them the conquerors of the fourteen clubs entered.'*

The reward for success was one that, nowadays, would be highly unusual, but was then common enough- a set of jerseys in the winning team's colours. *Sport* reported that

'The Saints, true to the colours of their racing patron, and which they themselves have kept so well to the front, chose the well known black and amber.'

This is the first reference to the club colours and it shows that the club had used them for some time prior to this tournament. The racing patron is Stephen Kelly, referred to earlier in this chapter.

Championship Debut

When the GAA was set up, it took some time for County Committees to be formed. The first Meath Convention took place on February 13th 1887, but the majority of clubs, including St. Seachnalls, failed to attend and did not take part in the 1887 championship.

Dunshaughlin's first championship outing was in the 1888 competition. Drawn against Crockafothas of Bellewstown they were victorious at Rathfeigh. There is no further information on the black and ambers' progress and it is not known who eliminated them. It appears that forty-three clubs entered and Dowdstown were the outright winners.

For the 1889 championships, Dunshaughlin's opponents were the Johnstown Faugh a' Ballaghs and the game was finally settled in the committee rooms. John Finnegan, in a letter to the County Committee, explained that the St. Seachnalls scored two points and the Faughs one point, which they claimed as a goal. This letter shows the difficulties with goal umpires referred to earlier, 'the Faugh's umpire giving a goal, the St. Seachnalls' gives it as a point, to the best of his belief.' Finnegan quotes the referee's precise words, 'I believe myself it is only a point' but he would not award the game to either side.

Finnegan's letter was in vain however. At the committee meeting, the referee stated that the disputed score was a goal and the committee awarded the game to the Faughs. Arguments of this nature were not unusual, for often the crossbar was merely a rope or a tape and could be easily manipulated by the goalkeeper.

St. Martins were also unhappy with their treatment in the championship. They complained that the referee harshly disqualified five of their men. The complaint, however, was ignored.

Decline and Fall

This championship game appears to be one of the few games played by St. Seachnalls in 1889. Their next recorded outing was a game against Kilmessan in December, which ended all square, 1-1 each. This decline in activity was part of a nationwide trend and was due to political developments in Ireland at the time.

Throughout the nineteenth century there was disagreement among the nationalist community in Ireland as to the best way to attain political independence from England, one group relying on peaceful constitutional agitation, the other advocating and using physical force and violence. Soon after its foundation, the GAA nationally became a battleground as representatives of the physical force persuasion tried to gain control of the organization.

County of Meath

List of G.A.A. clubs in above County & Officers of each club

No	Name of Club	Names of Officers	Position	Approximate N° of members in each club	Remarks
1	Athboy "Davitts"	Thomas Kiernan Jas. Casserly Edw.d Mathews	Capt. Treas. Secy.	60	
2	Balliver "Sir Chas. Russell's"	Pat. Gavigan Pat. Ryan Ths. Ryan	Capt. V.C. Treas.	40	
3	Dunshaughlin "St. Seachnall's"	Chr. Tallon Pat. Brien Pat. King L.J. Cuming	Capt. Prest. Secy. Treas.	40	
4	"St. Patricks" of Kilmessan	Henry Coady J.S.J. Tombe Henry Doran	Capt. Sec. Treas.	50	
5	Warrenstown of Warrenstown	Pat. Fox M. Kenny Jas. Cluskey	Capt. Secy. Treas.	45	
6	Killeg Volunteers	M. Tevlin Rev.d S. Kelly C.C. Wm O'Brien John Gaffney	Capt. Prest. Secy. Treas.	40	x

Extract from the 1891 report of the Special Branch of the Royal Irish Constabulary on the strength of the GAA in Meath, listing Dunshaughlin at number 3.

> priests in the diocese directed that 'in future, the young men who belonged to this Association should not go out of their own parishes to play matches against other clubs' as it led to drunkenness and many young men were being led into secret societies.

After the 1887 Convention in Thurles, the central executive of the GAA was controlled by a group sympathetic to, and in many cases members of, the Irish Republican Brotherhood (IRB), who favoured the use of physical force. Following the convention St. Seachnalls was one of hundreds of clubs from all over the country to pass a resolution condemning the IRB takeover. The split in the GAA was resolved in early 1888 but by 1889 the organization was again in IRB control, where it was to remain for some time.

Initially, the clergy had been enthusiastic supporters of the GAA following the lead of Archbishop Croke, who was its first patron. After 1889 many clergy left the organization and attacked it, mainly because of the power of the IRB within it. The GAA also came under fire from the clergy for other reasons; gambling and drinking at games was alleged to be common, serious injuries occurred and it was also claimed that games interfered with attendance at religious ceremonies.

Because of the IRB involvement the Special Crime Branch in Dublin Castle began to take a great interest in the GAA from 1887. The Association now joined the list of groups whose activities were seen by the government as subversive. The Castle authorities were always suspicious of large gatherings and the games and meetings of the GAA provided, in their eyes, an opportunity for the meeting of IRB men, the collection of funds and the general promotion of the national cause.

The Bishop of Meath, Dr. Thomas Nulty, was one of those most opposed to the GAA and numerous attacks issued from pulpits under his control. The Special Branch reported that on July 21st 1889, priests in the diocese directed that 'in future, the young men who belonged to this Association should not go out of their own parishes to play matches against other clubs' as it led to drunkenness and many young men were being led into secret societies. The Special Branch was happy with the effect of Dr. Nulty's sermons, claiming that 'The general prohibition is a great check upon the secret societies.'

A writer to *Sport*, under the pseudonym Meath Gael, refers to *'the suppression of the GAA by the ecclesiastical authorities throughout the length and breadth of the diocese of Meath.'* Special Branch figures show that, at the end of 1890 there were only fourteen clubs in Meath, compared to thirty-six a year previously. They attributed the collapse of these clubs to the opposition of Bishop Nulty and his clergy.

St. Seachnalls was one of the clubs then in existence. The Crime Branch, in its report, estimated the membership of the club in late 1889 as approximately forty, while the officers were:

Captain:	Christy Tallon
President:	Patrick O Brien
Secretary:	Patrick King
Treasurer:	L.F. Canning

According to the Crime Branch, none of the officers of the club was a member of the IRB. In the year prior to the clerical condemnation in the diocese, the Parish Priest of Dunshaughlin, Very Rev. James O Neill, was clearly sympathetic to the GAA. After a game against William O Briens of Clonee, both teams *'were treated to refreshments with generous cordiality by the popular parish priest of the Seachnalls.'* Whether his support for the local club survived his prelate's attack on the GAA is not clear, but in 1890 he was still a patron of the Dunshaughlin Gaelic Athletic Sports run under GAA rules.

The Special Branch officers were probably correct in their belief that St. Seachnalls was not under IRB influence. The name of the club and the colours chosen would support this. Numerous clubs chose clearly political or broadly nationalist names, such as Emmets, Davitts, O Mahonys, Campaigners etc. but Dunshaughlin chose a name associated with the history of the village, St. Seachnalls. Nor were the colours chosen to make a political point, as was the case with many clubs. They were based on the local racing colours.

This is not to say that the founders were not nationalists, they most certainly were. They would not have been in the GAA if they weren't. Indeed, in later years, many of the men who set up the club, especially Laurence Canning and Bernard Carolan, were deeply involved in nationalist politics but their involvement was with the constitutionalist wing and not with the IRB. However, even if the St. Seachnall's members were not involved in supporting secret societies, they were to suffer in the general decline.

The club was alive and well in December 1890 but seems to have played few games that year. They did not participate in the County championship, -only eleven teams entered-, and they were beaten by Lucan Sarsfields in the Warrenstown tournament. Secretary, John Finnegan, also left the club. It appears that other members left also but the reason for the departures is not known. Finnegan himself stated,

> 'along with others I left the branch to which I have always belonged, and left it with regret too, circumstances having arisen which made it impossible for me to longer remain a member with honour.'

His departure may have been connected with the Bishop's opposition to GAA clubs but it appears more likely that it was connected with an athletic dispute.

By mid 1891 St. Seachnalls had joined the list of lapsed GAA clubs. Patrick O Brien played at least one game for Warrenstown against the Dublin team, Sextons. Others may have played also and although the sports continued to be held under GAA rules, the football club had disbanded.

It had lasted for less than four years and this breakup was to foreshadow many more in the years to come.

> " Numerous clubs chose clearly political or broadly nationalist names...but Dunshaughlin chose a name associated with the history of the village, St. Seachnalls. Nor were the colours chosen to make a political point, as was the case with many clubs.

BLACK & AMBER

CHAPTER 2: REVIVAL

Revival, 1894-1906

The man mainly responsible for reorganizing county Meath was Richard Blake of Ladyrath, Rathkenny. Blake was not in the typical GAA mould.

The reasons for the break up of the Dunshaughlin club cannot be stated with absolute certainty. It was most likely due to the general decline of the GAA in the county, for, with widespread clerical condemnation and the gradual disappearance of many clubs, the few remaining clubs found themselves without opponents to play. According to the 1890 Crime Branch report there were only two other clubs adjacent to Dunshaughlin, those being Warrenstown and Kilmessan.

Warrenstown themselves did not survive 1891, and earlier the teams from Merrywell, Kilmessan and Ross, among others, had departed the scene. Some months after St. Seachnalls lapsed a team was formed in Drumree *'out of the remains of the Dunshaughlin and Warrenstown clubs.'* Formed in November 1891 the new club was known as Drumree Gaelic Athletic Club and its officers were President: Francis Hobson, Captain: P.J. Fox, Sub-Captain: Michael Brien, Hon. Secretary and Treasurer: James Griffin. Michael Brien is probably Patrick O Brien's brother, the former Dunshaughlin President. P.J. Fox, who had a public house known as *The Spencer Arms* where *Gilsenan's* is now, was previously captain of Warrenstown and appears to have been one of the chief movers in the formation of the club.

A number of games were organized locally, mainly with teams from The Hatchet, which had been 'comatose' since the previous February, and a reformed Kilmessan. Dunshaughlin men who lined out with Drumree included Patrick O Brien, ex-captain Christy Tallon and Bill Doran. The Drumree club recorded a draw and a victory against The Hatchet while a planned encounter with Kilmessan led to conflicting

Drumree Railway Station
Passengers in their Sunday best gather at Drumree to await the train to the races.
Photo copyright Brendan Murray.

17

BLACK & AMBER

accounts of the game. The revival didn't last and for the period 1892-93 there was little or no Gaelic activity in Co. Meath.

Parnellites and Anti-Parnellites

On top of the IRB infiltration and clerical condemnation the GAA suffered a further blow when nationalist Ireland split into Parnellite and anti-Parnellite factions.

Charles Stewart Parnell had gained widespread support in the 1880s due to his efforts to achieve land reform and Home Rule, so much so that he was popularly known as the Uncrowned King of Ireland. He was also one of the patrons of the GAA. However, his romantic involvement with Kitty O Shea, the wife of a political colleague, was to be his undoing.

In 1889 Captain O Shea sued his wife Kitty for divorce and named Parnell as the other man. By December 1890 the divorce case was the talk of the nation. After a bitter debate the Home Rule Party ditched Parnell as its leader. As a result the party and the country split up into Parnellite and anti-Parnellite groups.

Many in the GAA lined up behind Parnell but most of nationalist Ireland, including the majority of the Home Rule Party, the bishops and the clergy, opposed him. Approximately 2,000 GAA men attended Parnell's funeral in 1891, many with a hurley draped in black and held in reverse to resemble a rifle. After Parnell's death the GAA was the main national group that had stood against the anti-Parnellite majority. The result was that many GAA men, not sympathetic to Parnell, left the organization, clubs not already defunct went out of existence and in many counties the GAA simply died out. The association had been in decline prior to this, but the Parnellite split almost dealt it the death blow.

The St. Seachnalls' club had been in decline before the Parnellite controversy had reached its height and the club's disappearance does not appear to have been due to internal divisions on pro- and anti-Parnell lines. Nevertheless, a number of those involved in the club strongly supported the Anti Parnellite candidate, Jeremiah Jordan, in the 1893 election to represent the South Meath constituency. Among them were Bernard Carolan, Laurence Canning, Patrick King and Thomas Armstrong. Patrick Fox, the Drumree captain, was a strong Parnellite supporter. Jordan marginally defeated his Parnellite opponent JJ Dalton by just sixty-nine votes from a poll of 5,300. After 1892 the men responsible for building up the club in the 1886-1890 period, especially Bernard Carolan and Laurence Canning, devoted much energy to political activity. Politics appears to have taken over from Gaelic games as the main pastime of the nationalist population in Dunshaughlin and elsewhere. During 1892 and 1893 political meetings were regular fixtures, and meetings in the village attracted large crowds on both sides.

Bernard Carolan
Club Secretary, political activist, builder and bicycle shop owner. Carolan is shown checking a letter. The newspaper resting on his knee is the *Drogheda Independent*, a paper to which he regularly contributed.
Photo copyright Brendan Murray.

Revival

Meath was one of the counties most severely weakened by the Parnell split as Parnell had for a time been MP for Meath, and it was 1894 before the GAA began to re-organize effectively in the county. In December 1893 the Central Council issued a long circular suggesting that clubs be revived. The man mainly responsible for reorganizing county Meath was Richard Blake of Ladyrath, Rathkenny. Blake was not in the typical GAA mould. A Protestant and well-to-do farmer, totally opposed to the IRB, he was an extremely efficient organizer and was Chairman of the Meath County Board by 1895 and Secretary of the GAA nationally from 1895 to 1898. Mainly due to his efforts the GAA in Meath was revived.

By mid-1894 Dunshaughlin was again playing. Patrick O Brien was President once more, with Laurence Canning as Treasurer and Bernard Carolan as Secretary. The first report available is of an away game against Skryne Rangers. It was a return match and St. Seachnalls lost by 1-2 to 1-1. An early goal wasn't enough owing to *'their want of practice and the superiority of their adversaries.'* The reporter was obviously happy to see Gaelic games to the fore once again for he comments, *'This match would certainly remind one of the old times and it was admitted by all present to be one of the best played for a long time.'* There was still some dissatisfaction with the referees however; they needed to put an end to rough play, especially *'that old womanish habit of continually grabbing with the hands.'*

Few games appear to have been played in 1894, and some of those that took place often ended in disagreement. For example, St. Seachnalls defeated O Connells of Kilcock 2-2 to 0-1 but the O Connells left the field before time was up and *'refused to partake of the hospitality provided for them.'*

Dunshaughlin was among over twenty clubs affiliated for the 1895 championship and *Sport* reported that Meath was now practically the premier Gaelic County and the O Mahonys and Kilmessan were two clubs of whom *'all Irishmen are justly proud.'* The draws, under the influence of Blake, were extremely detailed. Dunshaughlin was drawn against Johnstown but no report of the game is available. It appears that Dunshaughlin didn't enter the championship the following year. Blake by now had resigned as Chairman of the County Committee. He was condemned by some of his colleagues for supporting the anti-Parnell candidate in North Meath in 1892 and after his departure the County Committee seems to have run the competition in a very inefficient manner.

Mr and Mrs Laurence F Canning. Canning was a founder member of the club and Treasurer for many years. He had a bakery where *Tara News* is at present.

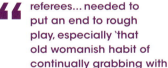

referees... needed to put an end to rough play, especially 'that old womanish habit of continually grabbing with the hands.'

Roadside Tactics

1897 was notable for two games between Newtown Round Towers of Trim and Dunshaughlin, the second of them in the junior football championship. Both games failed to run their full course. In the first outing Dunshaughlin, with the wind at their backs, led 0-2 to 0-0 at half time. In the second half Dunshaughlin adopted the novel tactic of constantly kicking the ball over the sideline and into the road! Thus time was lost, and as most of the play was near the sideline Newtown could only manage one point. *'Newtown,'* says the report, *'were simply perplexed'* by this play, which they found *'aggravating in the extreme.'* Finally, with the thirty minutes up Dunshaughlin left the field but the referee wanted to play an extra six minutes on account of the delays *'due to Dunshaughlin kicking the leather out of play into the road.'* Dunshaughlin, however, refused to continue and claimed the game. Who said tactics are new to Gaelic football?

A somewhat similar tactic was less successful in the junior championship. Ten minutes into the second half at Athlumney, with Newtown leading by 0-4 to 0-1, Dunshaughlin, *Sport* reported,

> 'acted in a very unsportsmanlike manner by walking off the field, simply because one of their players was very properly ordered off the field for deliberately kicking the Newtown goalkeeper.'

Thus Dunshaughlin's lack of success in championship games continued.

Death and Resurrection

The period 1899-1902 was yet another low point in the history of the GAA. Although 1898 was a year of great activity in many counties, with tournaments being organized to celebrate the centenary of the 1798 rebellion, there seems to have been few games in Meath. The annual Sports took place, but it is unclear if it was GAA controlled, while Dunshaughlin did play some games in 1898 but then disappeared until 1902. There was a general decline in many counties, including Meath, at the turn of the century.

Lack of organization and finance at Central Council level seems to have been partly to blame. Also, as many of the founders of the GAA were becoming less involved in the organization, there was very little young blood coming forward to take the reins of leadership. Emigration of players was always an issue and nationalist Ireland generally was in the doldrums following the political upheavals.

Cricket regained its popularity around the turn of the century and both the Chairman and Secretary of the Meath GAA County Committee, JL Timmon and Laurence Sheridan, played the game, as did the previous Chairman, Richard Blake.

Drumree regularly fielded a cricket team. Some of the players were men who had played Gaelic football in earlier years. PJ Fox the former captain of Drumree, Thomas Geraghty, Thomas Marley, Thomas Johnson, Patrick Muldoon, John Clarke, John Hughes, John Lynch, John Rooney, James Fox, F Kelly, John Mooney, Michael Fox, William Smith were among those who wielded the willow. Many of them lived in Knockmark and Drumree's opponents included Breemount, Kilmore, Ross and Grange. In 1900 there were also cricket clubs in the Hatchet, Warrenstown, Batterstown and further away in Kentstown, Newhaggard, Duleek, Robinstown and Slane. The Drumree club was very successful in what it seems were friendly encounters and a suggestion of a formal cricket league didn't take off. Some correspondents to the *Drogheda Independent* opposed cricket due to its status as a British game and by 1905 GAA rules subjected anyone playing 'foreign games' to suspension.

When the Meath County Committee was revived in 1902 it contained a number of men from hurling clubs. These hurling clubs were often associated with branches of the Gaelic league and they provided a badly needed influx of new members and renewed enthusiasm. The development of hurling will be outlined in the next chapter.

Plays and Replays

By 1902 the Dunshaughlin club was again active on the playing fields. A game against Castletown in the Senior Football Championship ended in a draw at 0-3 each but in the replay Castletown administered a severe *'trimming'* to the black and ambers, winning 1-11 to 0-1. Dunshaughlin fielded without the O Briens due to the death of a relative and failed to produce the form of the initial game. Castletown at this time was the strongest side in the county. Led by the famed, red-haired Joe Curran they were a match for any opposition and easily disposed of Julianstown in the final by 0-14 to 0-0.

The game with Dunshaughlin was in fact a county semi-final as only four clubs entered. The Dunshaughlin team was: Joe Downes, John Teeling, Jim 'Fish' Lynch, Paddy Lynch, J Marmion, F Murray, Mick Carberry, Patrick Hand, William Doran, Mickey Walls, John 'Dropper'

Details from the *Drogheda Independent*, 2 June 1900, of some games played by Drumree Cricket Club with a team list and scores v. local rivals, The Hatchet.

CRICKET.

ASHBOURNE V MULLAFIN (CO MEATH).—This match, played on Sunday last at Mullafin, proved rather interesting, and was witnessed by a large number of spectators. Time only allowed of one innings, and for this the score was: Ashbourne, 41; Mullafin, 32—the visitors thereby winning by 9 runs. For Ashbourne, Carty and Stoney batted well; while Kelly and C Tully did equally well for Mullafin. The visitors were most hospitably entertained during the evening. The return match will be played at Ashbourne on Sunday, June 10th.

ARDMULCHAN V DEANHILL.—This match was played at Deanhill on last Sunday, resulting in an easy victory for the visitors by 17 runs. For the home team Clarke and Lawlor played well. The fine batting of Moore, for the visitors, was highly appreciated by the vast concourse who witnessed the contest.—S DENVIR, Sec, Ardmulchan C C.

DRUMREE C C V HATCHET C C.—This match was played on the Hatchet ground on last Sunday, 27th May, and resulted in a win for the home team by one run and four wickets to fall. Score—Drumree, 24 runs; Hatchet, 25 runs. The visiting team was most hospitably entertained both before and after game; and, after a most enjoyable evening, the visitors returned home well pleased with their outing.

DRUMREE V DORHAMSTOWN will be played on Drumree ground on next Sunday, 3rd June.

MACETOWN V CORBALTON.—These clubs met for the first time this season on Sunday, 27th May, when Macetown gained an easy victory by an innings and 20 runs. The visitors collapsed before the bowling of Messrs R E and R J Sheridan. Messrs P Johnstone, S Doyle, and P Clarke scored freely for the winners. Return match at Corbalton on Sunday, 3rd.

HATCHET V DRUMREE.—This match was played on the ground of the former, on Sunday, and resulted in a win for the home team by one run and four wickets. Score :—

DRUMREE.

J Fox c by J Moy	3
J Rooney c by J Moy	0
J Cooney run out	6
J Marley c by Flynn	1
M Fox c by Flynn	4
T Johnston b M'Cann	0
T Marley c by Dillon	1
W Smyth b M'Cann	3
T Muldoon not out	1
J Clarke b by M'Cann	0
P Fox b by M'Cann	0
Extras	5
Total	24

HATCHET.

T M'Cann b by Smyth	4
L Mooney b by Fox	1
J Gorey b by Smyth	10
M Maloe b by Fox	1
J Mooney b by Fox	0
J Gorey not out	0
J Dillon l before	2
P Maleady not out	0
Extras	7
Total for 6 wickets	25

> James O Brien, the Dunshaughlin representative, claimed he was insulted and that a Navan player had said to a priest viewing the game, 'Get off the grounds with your wide hat.'

Mooney, P Bird, James 'Mebble' Ward, M Ward, Paddy Swan, Jack Clarke and Michael 'Jacob' Clarke. This, in a sense, is an historic team for it is the first full line-out to represent Dunshaughlin that it has been possible to trace.

By 1903 Dunshaughlin had affiliated a hurling as well as a football club and there appears to have been two separate clubs in the village. In the football championship Walterstown were defeated by 1-6 to 0-2 in the first round but Dunshaughlin fell at the next hurdle to eventual winners Kilmessan, 1-8 to 0-1.

The championship of 1904 was noteworthy for three tremendous games between St. Seachnalls and Navan O Mahonys. The first two games finished in draws and the third ended prematurely. Dunshaughlin was unlucky not to have won both of the drawn matches; by now new blood such as the Johnsons, Mickey Duffy and Willie Daly had arrived, and the team could match most opponents.

The third game led to prolonged controversy after it ended before half time with Dunshaughlin trailing by four points to two. Ratty of the O Mahonys refused to leave the field on being ordered off by the referee, who then declared the game at an end and awarded it to Dunshaughlin.

The referee reported that Ratty had used objectionable language- 'By God' were the words complained of. He also stated that six men had attacked him and their favourite expressions were 'You wh_ _ _' and 'You f _ _ _' and that only for the protection of the Kilmessan officials- on whose ground the game was played- he would have been assaulted.

O Mahonys claimed that the words used were 'Oh my God', which, in their view was not swearing. At the committee meeting James O Brien, the Dunshaughlin representative, claimed he was insulted and that a Navan player had said to a priest viewing the game, 'Get off the grounds with your wide hat.' O Brien joined the referee in demanding a 12-month suspension for six named O Mahonys' men.

Finally it was agreed to suspend the Navan team until September 1st and then replay the game. As it was now mid-August Dunshaughlin naturally were unhappy. O Brien and Patrick Martin walked out of the meeting, the club appealed to the Leinster Council and was awarded the game. There was a sequel, when O Mahonys, in a letter to the press, demanded that O Brien publicly apologize for the remarks made at the County Committee meeting. O Brien would have none of it and in a stinging reply advised O Mahonys that they would be better employed condemning 'the low actions and expressions' of their members who were 'a disgrace to the GAA.'

Dunshaughlin may have won the war of words but in the second round Castletown were again their masters on the field, winning 0-7 to 0-3. It was apparently a tough affair, one Castletown player was sent off and several players were *'grassed.'* The report blamed both Dan Killeen and the Dunshaughlin captain for losing the game for Dunshaughlin. Killeen allegedly missed ten scores and the Dunshaughlin captain was criticized for his *'blindness'* in not detecting that it was useless sending the ball to Killeen. The reporter was a strong admirer of Killeen obviously!

In this period it seems that defeating Dunshaughlin was a guarantee of winning the championship, for once again the conquerors of the black and ambers went on to take outright honours. The following did duty against Castletown, James O Brien, Capt., Patrick O Brien (goal), Jack Clarke, Owen Lynch, Jack Johnson, Paddy Johnson, Paddy Swan, Peadar Murray, Peter Lee, Patrick Hand, Patrick Mahon, Michael 'Jacob' Clarke, B McAuley, J Murray, Michael Duffy, Dan Killeen and William Daly.

Dunshaughlin participated in the 1905 championship without success and by 1906 had become inactive once again. This in fact was to be the end of football in Dunshaughlin for many years with the exception of short revivals in 1908-09, 1913 and 1920. A hurling team had been formed in 1902. For the next three decades it was as hurlers that Dunshaughlin would be feared and respected as the traditional black and amber went on to unprecedented success and glory.

BLACK & AMBER

A Hurling Stronghold, 1902-1919

It was at this time, September 1902, that a Hurling Club was established in the village. It was set up in connection with the Gaelic League and was separate from the football club initially. In the early years the club fielded under the name Na Fir le Céile - The United Men.

In the early years of the G.A.A. in Meath little or no hurling was played. Kilmessan may have formed a hurling team in 1887 while in 1888 two teams of hurlers from the Brian Ború Club in Clontarf gave hurling exhibitions during the Navan Harps and Shamrocks tournament.

Dunshaughlin appears to have been the next club to invite hurlers to the county, for in January 1889 as part of a football tournament in the village in aid of the National Monuments' Fund, Crom a Boos of Maynooth defeated Dauntless from Dublin by 2-4 to 0-0. A thousand people attended and there was *'considerable'* interest in the match, *'the first exhibition of our national pastime in that part of the country,'* according to *Sport*.

However, with the decline of the G.A.A. in the period 1889-1893 and again in 1897-1901 these efforts to establish hurling in the county failed. It was 1901-02 when the first Meath Senior Hurling championship was organized with four teams taking part, Navan Hibernians, Navan Young Irelands, Athboy Hurling Club and Kells Hurling Club. It was in 1902 also that a hurling club was formed in Dunshaughlin.

Aeridheacht in Dunshaughlin, 1903
An advertisement for the open air Feis (Aeridheacht) in Dunshaughlin following the establishment of Meath's first branch of the Gaelic League in the village. The event featured music, dancing, recitations and a hurling match with special excursion trains from Navan, Trim and Athboy.

The Gaelic League Link

The renewed growth of the G.A.A. in the early years of the twentieth century was helped by a timely influx of members from the Gaelic League. Eoin McNeill and Douglas Hyde had established the League in 1893 with the aim of reviving the Irish language. In many areas the local Gaelic League branch set up its own hurling club.

Meath was slow in forming Gaelic League branches but in November 1900 the first branch in the county, Craobh Naomh Seachnall, was founded in Dunshaughlin. Peadar Murray, *'the prime mover in the project'* was elected Secretary and among those present at the early meetings were many staunch G.A.A. men of the past and future, including Laurence Canning, James O Brien, Michael Duffy, Jack Clarke, Bernard Carolan, Christy Foley, senior and junior, P.J. Fox, Michael Gilmore and Michael Carberry.

PJ Murray, founder of the Gaelic League in Dunshaughlin, owner of Murray's public house and hardware shop. *Photo copyright Brendan Murray.*

Dunshaughlin's First Hurlers

In conjunction with the Gaelic League's Aeridheacht (open-air festival) of 1902 a hurling team from Navan played Athboy, on Thomas Delany's field, probably The Eight Acres on the Dublin Road. The Aeridheacht itself, with 1,500 in attendance, was held in a field belonging to Christy Tallon and among those present was Patrick Pearse, the future 1916 leader. It was at this time, September 1902, that a Hurling Club was established in the village. It was set up in connection with the Gaelic League and was separate from the football club initially. In the early years the club fielded under the name *Na Fir le Céile - The United Men*.

The hurlers were to play their first game on October 19th against Kilmessan but the earliest newspaper report of a Dunshaughlin game that could be traced refers to one played on November 9th. As this game was against Kilmessan it may in fact have been a return game. The report therefore is of some interest. *The Drogheda Independent* stated,

> 'The weather was fine. Although there was a strong breeze blowing the game was well and closely contested from start to finish, the Kilmessans playing with great dash, while Dunshaughlin showed their usual determination, the Kilmessans scored a minor shortly after the ball being thrown in. On the puck-out there was some up and down play, when the Kilmessans scored another point. Dunshaughlin then got on their mettle and soon equalized. Some very exciting play now following Dunshaughlin scoring a goal and Kilmessan responding with another and half-time found matters: Dunshaughlin 1-2 Kilmessan 1-2. No time was lost in resuming play,

and Kilmessan taking the lead, matters again became very exciting, the Dunshaughlin backs making a magnificent defence, but Kilmessan pressing very hard began to run up a majority.'

Kilmessan won by 1-6 to 1-2 with Laurence Canning as referee.

The first attempt on the championship was none too successful for Athboy humiliated Dunshaughlin by 4-12 to 0-2 in 1903. Unfortunately no record of an actual line-out is available for the early years.

O Growney's funeral... and Dunshaughlin's Death

In late 1903 the St. Seachnall's branch of the Gaelic League participated in an event of national importance, the funeral of Fr. Eugene O Growney. O Growney, a native of Ballyfallon, Athboy had been a leading figure in the language revival movement and his *Simple Lessons in Irish (Ceachta Beaga Gaedhilge)* were used by most branches of the League, including Dunshaughlin.

He had died in America in 1899 and in 1903 his body was brought home via Cobh for reburial in Maynooth. At the Pro-Cathedral in Dublin, and again at Maynooth, two members of the Dunshaughlin Gaelic League and hurling team, Michael Duffy and Michael Gilmore, and twelve from the Athboy and Kilskyre branches carried the coffin. Dunshaughlin Gaelic League members carried the first banner immediately behind the hearse in Maynooth whilst seventy-five members of the branch attended, including many hurlers.

In 1904 it was back to championship hurling and defeat by Dunboyne. Sometime during the next year the hurlers suffered the same fate as the footballers on previous occasions,- they disbanded. The Gaelic League branch also lapsed for a period, and this, combined with the lack of success was probably the reason for the disappearance of the hurling team. Many of the players however continued to play with Warrenstown Hurling Club, which was formed as part of the Warrenstown Gaelic League branch. Others played with Dunboyne, Ratoath and Greenpark.

Rallying Cry

By late 1907 moves were afoot to start a team in the village once again. A note in the *Drogheda Independent*, probably from Michael Duffy, spread the rallying cry.

'It is a shame that about Dunshaughlin where there is a lot of young men, that during the last couple of years they have allowed the practice of their National games to die away, while other places with not half the population, have gained distinction for their prowess in the field. But better late than never and we hope...that after the winter's practice we

will not be ashamed to enter the lists against any other team in the Royal County.'

The reformed club included a hurling and a football team and both participated in the 1908 championships at junior level. Michael Duffy seems to have been the driving force behind the club's rise to prominence in this period. Now in his prime as a player, at 24 he had already played for Meath in a Leinster Junior Hurling final.

Duffy's parents settled in Dunshaughlin about the turn of the century and Michael worked for Meath County Council from 1911 to 1922. He was equally at home in the committee room and debating chamber as on the playing field and represented the club at County Board level for many years. His organizational ability, first developed in the G.A.A., was such that he later became a member of the national executive of the Transport Union and was a Senator from 1922 until 1936.

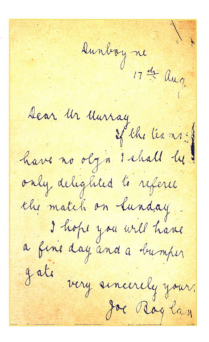

Joe Boylan Letter
Letter from Joe Boylan to PJ Murray agreeing to referee a hurling game, date c. 1903-07.

Success at Last

Success at county level finally came to Dunshaughlin in 1908, twenty-two years after the St. Seachnalls' club was formed. In the junior hurling championship semi-final Dunshaughlin defeated Navan Young Irelands by 6-6 to 0-1 and on November 15th at Dunboyne, captured the title when disposing of neighbours Ratoath by 7-14 to 3-3.

No report of the game is available but it is known that Ratoath objected on four grounds. It was claimed that Jack Johnson had played cricket with, and subscribed to, Corbalton Cricket Club but Duffy demanded that they produce evidence, observing:

'Everyone knows that is it is hard enough to get a man to subscribe to a football or hurling club without subscribing to a cricket club as well.'

This objection was disallowed, as were the three others, so Dunshaughlin were duly declared county champions. The team for this game is not known but the following definitely played: Michael Duffy, Jack Clarke, Michael Bruton, Jack Johnson, Ned Smith, Christy Smith, and Christy Foley. Undoubtedly, many of those who won medals in 1909 and 1910 played also but this cannot be confirmed conclusively.

Clearly this game led to a certain amount of local rivalry and when Ratoath later defeated Dunshaughlin in a friendly the winners reported the result in the *Drogheda Independent*. Duffy was unhappy with the report, for, in a letter to the paper he challenged Ratoath to put their 'superiority' to the test, saying Ratoath have been 'very careful to report only matches from which they had emerged

❝ 'Everyone knows that is it is hard enough to get a man to subscribe to a football or hurling club without subscribing to a cricket club as well.'

> 'When I go home and ask them to play senior I don't think they will do so!'

victorious', thus giving the public a false impression 'which Dunshaughlin are anxious to wipe out.' The challenge for a set of medals valued at £5 was accepted but unfortunately no account exists of the outcome.

The club was also playing football with a certain degree of success. Dunshaughlin took part in the 1909 Junior Football League, which had replaced the Junior Championship, and in the semi-final overwhelmed Kilbeg by 2-18 to 0-2 with the following team: John Rafferty, Jack Johnson, Jack Clarke, Peter Johnson, Pat Toole, John Curry, Peter Lee, Jack Lynch, William McDermott, Michael Duffy, Michael Bruton, Peter Kenny, Michael Carberry, William Corry, Tom Clusker, William Daly and Dick Doran. John Blake was appointed captain at the beginning of the year but doesn't seem to have played in the game. They lost the final to Navan Harps however, going under on a scoreline of 3-9 to 2-6.

Reaching the final was to be their undoing however, as it meant they would have to play at senior level in 1910. The County Board turned deaf ears to the claim to remain junior whereupon Duffy stated, 'When I go home and ask them to play senior I don't think they will do so!' He was correct in this, for Dunshaughlin took no part in the 1910 championship and it was to be a quarter of a century before the club again fielded a useful football team.

Glorious 1910

Yet 1910 was the most successful year ever in Dunshaughlin's history until then, for in that year two senior hurling championships were won. The 1909 final wasn't played until January 1910, when Dunshaughlin defeated Dunboyne by 2-7 to 1-3. *The Drogheda Independent* carried this short report:

'The final of the Meath Hurling championship was played on the Ratoath club grounds on the 8th inst. The day unfortunately was wet and cold, which prevented many lovers of the game from witnessing the match. Considering the slippery state of the ground it was marvellous how the players kept their footing so well, and especially during the last half-hour. Dunshaughlin played with wind and hill during the opening period, and when the whistle sounded the interval, Dunshaughlin had two goals and four points to one goal for Dunboyne. Dunshaughlin players in the second half worked with a dash and skill that fairly surprised the players, and especially their own followers who did not anticipate such a display of strength and skill on the part of their favourites. Dunshaughlin had added to their score at call of time three points, and ran out winners by two goals and seven points to one goal and three points for Dunboyne'.

The 1910 championship was the first for which goal posts as we know them were used. The point posts in use until then were abolished at the 1910 Annual

Convention. The changed scoring rules made no difference to the black and ambers who underlined their status as the premier club in the county. Eight teams participated on a knock-out basis, Dunshaughlin defeating Oristown by 4-6 to 1-1 and then disposing of Dunboyne.

A three-month delay before the final cannot have helped either team but it turned out to be no hindrance to Dunshaughlin, with Longwood no match for the champions. *The Drogheda Independent* reported:

'The game between Dunshaughlin and Longwood was a rather one-sided affair for the former team. Longwood however did better in the second half. The game could not be classed as a fine exhibition of hurling. Here and there some new play was witnessed but on the whole the match excited very little interest.

Dunshaughlin were the first to attack scoring an easy goal within the first ten minutes. Dunshaughlin kept up the running and the Longwood custodian was called on to save repeatedly. He had to yield however two further goals before Longwood transferred play with a nice exhibition of long passing. Dunshaughlin soon got the better of the play again and secured another goal. The light at this stage was not quite satisfactory, and the custodian did his work admirably under such disadvantageous circumstances. Longwood after some hard play succeeded in invading Dunshaughlin territory and amidst much delight they scored a lovely goal. Dunshaughlin maintained the upper hand however and scored two additional goals before the half-time whistle sounded when the teams stood Dunshaughlin six goals, Longwood one goal.

In the second half Longwood gave the Dunshaughlin men a better game and indeed if they had played half as well in the first half, Dunshaughlin would not have emerged from the contest with such a large margin to their credit. Both sides played well, the defence in each case being splendid. In the second half Dunshaughlin added two goals and one point to their credit while Longwood netted two goals. The game ended as follows: Dunshaughlin 8-1, Longwood 3-0'.

For the historic victory, their second senior title in the one year, Dunshaughlin fielded the following players: Jack Clarke, John Carty, Jack and Peter Johnson, Pat Toole, Michael Carberry, Michael Duffy, William Daly, William McDermott, Michael Bruton, Peter Lee, Jack Collier, Peter Kenny, Thomas Clusker, Patrick 'The Gah' Foley, Christopher Foley and Michael Clusker. (Teams remained 17-a-side until 1913).

BLACK & AMBER

CHAPTER 3: A HURLING STRONGHOLD

Dunshaughlin, Senior Hurling Champions, 1909 and 1910

Front: Toddy Clusker, Mick Clusker, Jack Carty, Patrick 'The Gah' Foley, William Daly, Gerry Kenny.
Middle: Ned Smith, Peter Johnson, Pat 'Toddler' Toole, Christy Foley, Jack Clarke, Mickey Carberry, Michael Bruton.
Back: Henry Foley, Jack Collier, Jack Johnson, Peter Lee, Paddy Duffy, Peter Kenny, Michael Duffy, William McDermott and R Brien.
Photo Copyright PJ Murray

BLACK & AMBER

CHAPTER 3: A HURLING STRONGHOLD

Dunshaughlin Football Team, c. 1905-10

Front: Lying on the ground: Bill Doran
Middle: Peter Lee, Not identified, Patrick 'The Gah' Foley, Christy Tallon, with ball, Paddy Lambe, Owen Lynch, Not identified.
Back: Jim Flynn?, Not identified, Peter Johnson, Jack Lynch? Mick Duffy, Not identified, Big Dick Doran, Not identified, Jack Clarke or a Johnson? Pat O Brien, Toddy Clusker.
There is a wealth of detail in this photograph. Note in particular: St. Seachnalls embroidered on the top stripe on the jersey of the first player on the left of the back row; the jerseys, hooped apart from one with vertical stripes; the caps; the heavy nailed boots; the trousers, either rolled up or tightened inside the stockings or the special jockey type trousers; shin guards on Peter Lee; the hunting horn held by Bill Doran. Top right hand corner missing from original glass negative.
Photo copyright Brendan Murray.

Dunshaughlin Senior Hurling Championship Medals
Peter Lee's Meath Senior Hurling Championship Winners' Medals 1909 and 1910. Presented to Dunshaughlin GAA club by Finian and Mary Englishby, May 2009. Inscriptions read: *Hurling C'ship na Mide '09 Domnac Seacnaill Wnrs* and *Hurling C' ship na Mide 1910, Dunshaughlin Winners.*

Leinster Finalists

As champions in 1909 the honour of representing Meath in the Leinster hurling championship (Division 2) rested with Dunshaughlin. The club had the right to select the county team and traditionally clubs chose a few men from other clubs to strengthen their team but the majority usually came from the champion club.

Meath disposed of Louth in the first round and in September 1910 at Jones' Road -now Croke Park- Kildare were no match for the men of Royal Meath, going under by 7-1 to 3-0. Thus Dunshaughlin reached the Leinster Final, which was played one month after the title-winning performance against Longwood. They either celebrated that title not too wisely but too well or met vastly superior opponents in the Leinster Final. At any rate they were crushed by Queen's County (Laois) by 12-2 to 2-2.

Nevertheless, to reach the final was an achievement in itself and indicates the tremendously high standard of hurling Dunshaughlin could play at this time. Eleven members of the Meath team were members of the Dunshaughlin club: John Carty, Michael Carberry, Pat Toole, William McDermott, Michael Bruton, Michael Duffy, Jack Collier, Thomas and Michael Clusker, Patrick and Christy Foley.

A third successive final appearance in 1911 didn't lead to a hat trick of victories as Dunboyne gained revenge for their defeat two years previously by 5-3 to 2-0. This was one of the best and most evenly contested finals for many years despite the score line. Duffy in particular played a stormer, but despite the advantage of the breeze Dunshaughlin led by a mere two points at the interval. In the second half they *'seemed to have lost all their early zest, and were evidently winded by their exertions.'* The score was not a true reflection of the play and Dunshaughlin should have recorded a bigger total, but this was of little consolation to the losers who had to finally relinquish the title.

CHAPTER 3: A HURLING STRONGHOLD

The period 1909-1918 was one of great rivalry, and at times enmity, between Dunshaughlin and neighbours Ratoath, and Dunboyne. In general, games and teams were rougher and tougher than now. Matty Wallace recalls attending games during that era as a young boy. Hurley sticks, he says, were usually home-made and indeed this was the case for many years afterwards. Billy Carberry recalls cutting young ash trees in the 1950s and bringing them to Bective Mill where they were shaped out roughly. It cost 3 old pence (about 2c) to shape each one and they were then filed down to a smoother finish at home. The young ash trees were cut near the roots for hurleys and the story is told that when asked 'When is the best time to cut a quick for a hurley?' the correct answer was, 'As soon as you see it.' This was because of the demand for hurleys and the cutting was often done at night when the owner was in no position to stop his property being removed.

It was an era of little fancy play and the Dunshaughlin team had no shortage of hard men, Willie Daly, the Johnsons, Mickey Carberry and Paddy Toole in particular were no altar boys.

At a tournament game in Dunboyne in 1915 played in thunder, lightning and rain Matty Wallace remembers a Dunshaughlin player saying before the match, 'I said I'd leave here with the ball or a man's head, so here goes for the man's head.' The game, though tough and hard, went off fine with Dunshaughlin emerging winners 3-2 to 1-0 according to the *Drogheda Independent*. Disagreements were often carried into County Board meetings where it was not unusual for Paddy Duffy and Sean Boylan to have 'words'.

The regular switching of players between their clubs didn't help matters. Hugh Mullally left Dunboyne and joined Dunshaughlin for a number of years after a split in the Dunboyne club. Toddy Clusker and Peter Lee among others played for both clubs at different times. Such transfers often led to humorous incidents also. Paddy Blake often recalled one such episode.

Toddy Clusker was cycling home after playing for Dunboyne and the local boys where waiting on the wall where Madden's Stores is now. The intention was to boo, jeer and clod Toddy as he passed. However seeing the 'welcoming party' in the distance Toddy got off the bicycle and rolled up his trousers to reveal a white pair of legs and then pedalled through the village. The boys seeing what they took to be a young woman coming down the street gave a series of calls and wolf whistles. By the time they realised this was no young woman Toddy had gone and escaped their wrath! In fact Toddy was one of the characters of the team. Whenever he scored Toddy would throw his cap in the air and shout *'They all love Pop'* much to the amusement of the crowd.

> **Whenever he scored Toddy would throw his cap in the air and shout 'They all love Pop'**

Michael Duffy
Secretary of Dunshaughlin Hurling Club in the 1900s and a Senator 1924-36.
Photo Copyright Brendan Murray

Unexplained Disappearance

The 1911 championship brought to an end Dunshaughlin's golden era of hurling, for although many of the players were young and at the pinnacle of their careers the club suddenly disappeared. Throughout its history the club has had a tendency to lapse and become dormant for short periods. Usually those lapses can be explained but the disappearance of the team in 1912 is inexplicable. Players were to be had in abundance, previously undreamed of success had been achieved, and probably could have been again, yet the village was now without a team. The break up of the club may have been due to personality conflicts and disagreements which seem to plague all clubs from time to time. However, most of the players were still playing. In the 1912 senior hurling final nine ex-Dunshaughlin players lined out on the losing Ratoath team and Peter Lee played for the winners, Dunboyne.

Whatever the upheaval that resulted in the club's disbandment, the disagreements were temporary. In February 1913 at a meeting in the *Fingall Arms* after last Mass the club was reformed with Paddy Duffy- Michael's brother- as Secretary and Willie Daly as President. In order to raise funds a sweep on the Liverpool Grand National was organized with prizes of £4, £2, £1 and 10 shillings (63 c) and five shillings (32 c).

Sport and Politics

It was not an auspicious time to reform as all clubs were now about to enter a decade of difficulty when football and hurling would take second place to the struggle for national independence, and many would forsake the hurley and the playing field for the gun and the battlefield.

By 1914 a Volunteer Corps had been founded in Dunshaughlin and in Drumree and many of the prominent GAA men were members. Time which was previously available for games, was now allocated to Volunteer activity. Drilling for the Dunshaughlin branch was held on Tuesday and Friday evenings and a Volunteer march to the ten mile Bush and back on a Sunday was not an unusual occurrence. Christy Tallon supplied a field for rifle practice, although the volunteers had few if any weapons.

A Fife and Drum Band was established in conjunction with the Volunteers and it performed at various events. It marked the passing into law of the Home Rule Bill in the British Parliament by performing a number of airs at a public meeting in Dunshaughlin featuring a huge bonfire. It also played at the 1914 Sports with all funds going to the band and performed at hurling and football games.

Despite the focus on the volunteers the hurling club was still active. Although

CHAPTER 3: A HURLING STRONGHOLD

1913 was an unsuccessful year, by 1914 the wearers of the black and amber bars were back in a semi-final again. The Dunshaughlin National Volunteers marched to the ground in Ratoath led by their Fife and Drum Band for the clash with the 'auld enemy' Dunboyne. The music and the colour however didn't affect the Dunboyne men and they emerged victorious by 4-2 to 2-0 in a foul ridden and bad tempered game. Four Dunshaughlin men- Carberry, Daly and Flood from the Dunshaughlin team and Toddy Clusker, then playing for Dunboyne- were sent off. The referee claimed he was assaulted and there was talk of the matter coming before the police courts. However, wiser counsel prevailed and the usual suspensions were imposed.

In 1912 the County Convention agreed to the establishment of a Middle Football League, with the Junior League to be confined in future to Under 20 players. Dunshaughlin took part in the 1913 Middle League and in 1914 performed well in a large group containing Enfield, Garlow Cross, Rathmolyon, Kilmore, Kilcloon, Summerhill and Bogganstown.

In late 1914 the Dunshaughlin and Drumree Volunteer Corps were amalgamated into one group, to be known as Dunshaughlin. The was part of a county-wide reorganization as the initial enthusiasm wore off with the prospect that they might have to fight in the Great War. The amalgamated volunteer group then formed a football team, to be known as Drumree Volunteer Club and the team played in the 1915 Middle League. It was the only team from the parish to enter so it is likely that it contained many of those who played with Dunshaughlin during the previous two years.

Meanwhile the hurlers redoubled their efforts to recapture the senior title. The 1915 competition was run on a league basis and a game against Ratoath indicates that they were now back to something approaching their form of old. Colour was the order of the day as Ratoath marched out to the strains of *The Wearing of the Green* immediately followed by Dunshaughlin, headed by the Fife and Drum Band.

At half time Ratoath were five points in front but early second half pressure led to 1-2 for Dunshaughlin and the teams were level. *The Drogheda Independent* takes up the story:

'Excitement reaches fever pitch, play waxes fast and furious, Ratoath dash down the field overcoming all opposition, the green flag signalling a major score. Play now baffles description. Dunshaughlin bombed the Ratoath posts, the latter's backs and goalkeeper are invulnerable, play is transferred to the other end but no further score resulted.'

Dunshaughlin later recovered to beat Dunboyne, but lost the game on an objection that Michael Moran, a former Dunboyne player, was not a registered Dunshaughlin player. Trim eventually defeated Dunboyne in the final, the club's first senior title.

> Colour was the order of the day as Ratoath marched out to the strains of *The Wearing of the Green* imnnediately followed by Dunshaughlin, headed by the Fife and Drum Band.

BLACK & AMBER

> 'Never in the annals of hurling in Meath has the game reached such a high standard of perfection... it has now almost become a science.'

1916 was not a year for undivided attention to the national games. After the Easter Rising some officers of the County Board were arrested and at a County Committee meeting it was stated, 'The teams are all disorganised.' Dunboyne suffered most, with a split in the club reflecting the divisions between members of the National Volunteers and those who joined the Irish Volunteers.

But this paled into insignificance compared to the loss suffered by PJ Fox, who had captained Drumree in 1891. The 1916 Rising in Dublin claimed the life of his sixteen-year old son, James. The youngster attended Culmullen NS initially and Dunshaughlin NS from 1908. The family moved to Dublin about 1912 and James joined Fianna Éireann. His father, who was a member of the committee of James Connolly's Irish Citizen Army, accompanied him to Liberty Hall on the morning of the Rising saying to Frank Robbins, a Sergeant in that army, 'Here is my lad; take him with you for the Irish Citizen Army. I am too old for the job.' James was stationed at Stephen's Green and was shot dead early in the morning of Tuesday 25th of April. He is buried in Knockmark Cemetery.

A Final Fling

The final fling for most of the old stalwarts came in 1916-17. With over half the men who had won the 1910 title still playing Dunshaughlin represented formidable opposition. The team was a potent mixture of youth and experience with names of the future like Mickey and Paddy Blake and Christy Doran to complement the guile and experience of Carty, Carberry, Duffy and Daly.

The standard of hurling was exceptionally high in the view of the commentators. In the 1916 semi-final Dunshaughlin overcame Ratoath by 3-5 to 3-2. The exhibition was such that a reporter believed that,

'Never in the annals of hurling in Meath has the game reached such a high standard of perfection... it has now almost become a science.'

A large crowd thronged Ashbourne for the game, there was a stream of vehicles from the small pony-cart to the taxi-cab, as well as 'innumerable velocipedes.' (Bicycles to you and me!) Two bands, and scouts from Trim viewing their final opponents also attended.

The scouts had a lengthy period in which to digest what they saw, nine months in fact, for it wasn't until June 1917 that the 1916 final was played. The delays in the main were caused by Trim.

When the final took place Trim toyed with Dunshaughlin in the first half, and after running rings around the defence led 6-3 to 1-0 at the break. The second half was a different story. Daly had an early goal and confidence rose as Dunshaughlin rediscovered their craft and style of old and a further three goals and four points brought them within striking distance of Trim. However, the concession of a simple goal in the last few minutes put the issue beyond doubt and a Clusker goal just at the end was too late. Trim deserved their 7-4 to 6-4 victory for *'there was little to pick and choose between the teams, but that little was in favour of Trim.'*

Dunshaughlin lined out as follows: John Carty, Nicky Moran, Michael and Paddy Blake, Michael Carberry, Michael Duffy, Jack Clarke, Hugh Mullally, Christy Doran, Michael Bruton, Gerry Kenny, Charles Curley, Thomas Clusker, William Daly and Paddy Kenny.

This game signalled the end of the most successful era in Dunshaughlin's hurling history. Many of the team were now past their prime and prior to the Trim game practice was non-existent. According to the *Dublin Saturday Post* 'unkind people were saying that the first thing necessary was that some of the forwards should learn that a goal post and a corner flag are absolutely distinct.'

Gaelic Sunday

Following the introduction of conscription to the British army and rumours of a German plot to invade Ireland the British government declared in July 1918 that all public meetings required an official permit. This applied to sports and games and the Dunshaughlin Aeridheacht that month had to be called off. In the words of the organizers

> 'The English Government deem this festival, a danger to their authority in Ireland, and consequently have proclaimed it. The promoters regret the disappointment to the public, but hope in happier times, when authority is based upon the consent of the governed to provide many a day's amusement.'

The GAA at national level moved quickly to call the government's bluff and directed clubs that Sunday 4th August would be Gaelic Sunday when matches were to be organized in every county and played without permits. Anyone seeking a permit would be automatically and indefinitely suspended. Numerous games were held on Gaelic Sunday and Dunshaughlin played Navan Gaels in a junior hurling game in Navan. The games highlighted the strength of the GAA and the inability of the authorities to thwart concerted action but it didn't secure Dunshaughlin's future.

A team was entered in the 1919 championship but seems to have made little progress and by 1920 Dunshaughlin Hurling Club was no more. The players dispersed and it wasn't until after 'the Troubles' that the club fielded a hurling team again.

BLACK & AMBER

Interlude 1

Dunshaughlin in the Early Twentieth Century

Dunshaughlin, c. 1914.
View of Dunshaughlin from the junction for Grangend and the Lagore Road looking towards the Dublin side of the village. The building on the left is the Old Toll House, now occupied by *Liam Keane and Company*. Large trees are growing where the *Bank of Ireland* and *Maddens* are currently located. Note the condition of the street.

Dunshaughlin was one of the most sparsely populated districts in the county when the black and ambers won the Meath Senior Hurling championship in 1909 and 1910. The whole parish consisted of 1,162 persons, down from a pre-Famine figure of 3,221, a massive drop of 64%. The Dunshaughlin end of the parish contained only 59 men between the ages of 20 and 30 so the manpower available to the club was very limited.

A land given over to the bullock

Bernard Carolan, one of the first officers of the GAA club, described the area in his flowery prose as 'a howling wilderness' due to the number of immense grazing ranches that needed little or no farm labour. Another political activist described leaving Dublin by train and entering

'a great green solitude, closely resembling the Sahara by reason of the lack of habitations and human beings, but quite dissimilar to the Sahara in its

undulating fertility and luxuriant pasture ... a rich soil totally untilled ... given over to the bullock.'

Work was scarce, many left, and life expectancy was low. While there was plenty of outward movement, there was very little inward traffic as 80% of the people had been born in County Meath. In the whole parish there were only six people of eighty years and older.

Of the 654 occupations listed in the 1911 census over half were agricultural related- farmers, herds, shepherds, agricultural and farm labourers. Reflecting the importance of horses, there were 26 grooms, ten blacksmiths and three saddle makers. The football and hurling clubs reflected this demographic. Of the twenty-two different players who featured in the 1909-1910 football and hurling finals the occupation of twenty can be identified. Five of them were farmers or farmers' sons, another five were farm labourers, four were described as labourers while there was also a blacksmith. The vast majority therefore had a link to farming and clearly would have difficulty getting time off to play or train, especially during the summer. Those in non-farm work were a rural postman, a shop assistant, a council employee and a domestic servant.

Only a limited number of club officers could be identified from the formation of the club to 1910. Nine are known and they tended to be less involved in manual labour and of a higher socio-economic status than the players. Many of them resided in or near the village. There were two publicans, a shopkeeper, a baker, a tailor, two court clerks and a farmer.

Transport

Transport for the majority of the population was the bicycle or a horse drawn cart. A report of a hurling match in Ratoath in 1916 refers to *'a stream of vehicles from the small pony cart to the taxi cab as well as innumerable velocipedes.'* (bicycles).

There was a cycling boom in Ireland in the 1890s and 1900s. It has been described as *'a craze for young sports' minded men of an athletic bent, as well as being a leisurely pursuit for the more adventurous element of the middle class, both male and female.'* PJ Murray, of *Murray's* public house, set up a local cycling club known as *The Buffalo Bills* with its own membership badge. He and a number of companions even cycled to Cork in June 1902 to visit the Cork Exhibition.

Murray and Bernard Carolan sold cycles, usually on an easy-pay system and advertised their wares extensively in the local press. Murray often advertised in Irish, reflecting his interest in the cultural revival of the time.

Regular traffic through the village consisted of horse drawn carts, both local

Peter Murray's shop, now Peter's.
The vertical advertising between the door and window lists Gilbey's Wines and Spirits, Guinness's Extra Stout, Drapery, Hardware, Oil, Paints, Coats etc.
Photo: Copyright Brendan Murray.

and through traffic on its way to and from Dublin, usually on Fridays. Carters with loads of hay for the Dublin markets passed through frequently and were often summoned, under a 1907 law, for not having lights on the carts. Occasionally, as happened twice in 1910, a load of hay was burned when a lamp set it on fire. Many of the carts had narrow, timber wheels with a metal band round the circumference that left tracks on the streets. In 1905 there were numerous complaints that timber carts were destroying the roads, especially the one to Drumree.

Cars were slowly beginning to appear on the scene. From 1904 identification marks such as a number plate, were required and a speed limit of 20 mph was imposed on public roads. By 1910 Bernard Carolan, was complaining about cars going through the village driven by

> *lunatics who endanger the lives of and limbs of the people traversing the street, scattering stones, gravel, and leaving an impenetrable cloud of dust in their wake.*

A report in 1913 noted that the street in Dunshaughlin was treated with what was described as 'tar paint' during May.

A railway station in Drumree provided easy access to Dublin, Navan or further afield for those who could afford it. The railway often brought large crowds to the annual Sports' meetings, the hunt or coursing. The *Drogheda Independent* claimed that four thousand people attended the Sports in 1890 '*from the adjoining counties and the Metropolis*'. Clearly, many arrived by rail, but a figure of such magnitude seems highly improbable.

Buffalo Bills Cycling Club
Peter Murray was part of a group of cyclists who went under the name of the *Buffalo Bills Cycling Club*. Note the two letter Cs inside the harp standing for Cycling Club.
Photo Copyright Brendan Murray.

BLACK & AMBER

Gaelic League Class
The picture shows a group of seven girls studying Fr. Eoghan O Growney's *Ceachta Beaga Gaedhilge* (Small or Simple Irish Lessons). They cannot be identified with any degree of certainty but the fourth from the left may be Florrie Carolan, daughter of Bernard, and the 6th Lena Murphy, daughter of Patrick, the Principal of the Boys' National School. Others in the picture are probably Janie Corcoran, Nora Gannon, Mary Murphy, Agnes Tugwell and … Woods, daughter of the local Royal Irish Constabulary Inspector.
Photo Copyright Brendan Murray.

Carolan's Bike Shop
Bernard Carolan, in white shirt, tie and waistcoat displaying his bicyles. The two adults are not identified. The child is probably Bernard's son Leo. Note the female type dress, a common feature with young boys. Bernard was Secretary of both the Dunshaughlin GAA club and the United Irish League which was a type of constituency organization for the Irish Parliamentary Party.
Photo Copyright Brendan Murray.

Culture and Sport

Gaelic League classes were popular in the early 1900s. PJ Murray and Patrick Murphy, the local publican and National Teacher respectively, established the Dunshaughlin branch of Conradh na Gaeilge, the Gaelic League. Known as Craobh Sheachnaill (Seachnall's branch), it was the first in County Meath. Sixty years later Michael Gilmore recalled his experience of learning Irish at the Gaelic League classes. After tuition they sang patriotic songs and listened to recitations. Andrew Mahon, the Workhouse Master, would relate historical incidents, Laurence Canning, the proprietor of the bakery, would recall *Rory of the Hill, Brave Michael Dwyer* and Bernard Carolan in a rich resonant voice gave rousing versions of *God Save Ireland* and *The Men of the West*.

In addition to language classes the League set up the first hurling team in Dunshaughlin, and organized dancing classes on Saturdays. Gilmore and his brother Tom cycled to numerous venues. In particular, he recalls a cycle trip to Longwood Aeridheacht (open air Feis), where he played hurling with Rathcore who were short a number of players, won a medal in a dance competition, danced for a crowd on his return journey at Rathmolyon and then attended a dance at Kilmessan before returning home in the early morning. With that level of activity there was hardly any need for training! Those representing the GAA club at meetings generally cycled to Navan.

Cricket was popular in Drumree and Warrenstown, with the Drumree club holding an annual reunion ball in 1904. Many of those who played football took to cricket when the GAA waned and this continued until the 1920s. A Coursing Club was established in 1905, and was favoured by the well-to-do. The club's officers included Count Stolberg, Lords Fingall and Dunsany and the local Parish Priest, Rev. Michael Kenny. The coursing club used land at Bonestown and Trevet, generally on farms owned by the Kellys of Creakenstown, Ratoath.

Other pastimes were an annual excursion to Warrenpoint and Rostrevor, organized by PJ Murray, costing three shillings by train. On such days *'Dunshaughlin and the adjacent villages will be as empty of people as are the lonely grazing ranches surrounding them,'* according to the *Drogheda Independent*.

Living Conditions

Sanitary conditions in the village were poor with regular complaints about the condition of the streets. Some houses on the main street had no back doors, none had piped water and, of course, there were no bin collections, so filth was thrown into the main street. James Gillic, who owned six houses, stated that putting in back doors could cause the houses to fall, so fragile were they. In Dunshaughlin civil parish, just over fifty percent of the private houses fell into the third or fourth class category and only seven per cent were deemed first class. Over half of the latter belonged to the substantial farmers, Daly in Clonross, Morris in Gaulstown, Morrin in Johnstown, Geraghty in Merrrywell, McEntee in Pelletstown and McDermott in Roestown.

The town contained a limited number of businesses. PJ Murray had opened a public house and shop in 1896, now *Peter's* public house, which, in addition to selling beer and spirits also provided groceries, drapery and hardware. Food available ranged from basic items such as tea, sugar, butter, loaves of bread, eggs and salt to more luxurious items such as sweet-cakes, biscuits, cakes and pots of jam. Many inhabitants clearly made their own bread, for flour and bread

BLACK & AMBER

Opening of *Gogan's Hotel*
Notice from The *Drogheda Independent* announcing the re-opening of *Murphy's Hotel* in 1902. The building is now occupied by *Bannon Auctioneers and Valuers*.

> **GOGAN'S HOTEL, DUNSHAUGHLIN.**
>
> Mr John Gogan announces the re-opening by him of the old and popular hostelry in Dunshaughlin known as "Murphy's Hotel," which, with the licensed premises attached, were purchased by him from the owner, Miss Murphy, who, owing to failing health, has retired from business.

soda were popular items. Tea was expensive, ranging in price from 2s 2d to 2s 4d (14c) per pound, while butter was also costly at 1s 2d (8c) per pound. Sugar and eggs on the other hand were relatively cheap. A pound of sugar cost a mere 2d while a dozen eggs could be had for a shilling (6 cent). Many of the poorer inhabitants kept hens and sold the eggs to Murray, or more often used them in part exchange for other food.

Murray had a wide selection of drink; stout, malt and porter are recorded but there is no mention of beer or lager. Many customers bought stout, mainly Guinness, by the bottle, at a cost of 1s 10d [11c] per dozen. Clothes and footwear was also on sale; boots, stockings, shirts, jackets, gloves, shawls, pinafores, corsets, handkerchiefs and belts could be had. By 1912 the shop sold farm implements, ranging from the simple spade, shovel and rake to more advanced machinery like mowers, reapers and wheel rakes and from 1909 he stocked bicycles, available on the hire purchase system. He even accommodated the slowly growing motor-car population by selling petroleum.

The majority of customers didn't pay for goods, especially groceries, at the time of purchase, but got them on 'tick,' meaning a record was kept in the shop and paid off at intervals when the customer had money. Farmers would settle accounts when cattle were sold, poor people might use eggs to reduce their debts but most customers rarely cleared bills in full. For Murray, a good day was one when accounts were settled rather than one when he sold a large amount of goods.

His diary refers to good days in 1901 when the Workhouse paid for goods and another great day's business as Mrs. Farnan paid £10. Local events such as sports' days, funerals or holidays could make the difference between a good and bad day. August 16th 1901 represented 'a pretty fair day's business owing to prizes having been bought for the sports', and, after a funeral in April there were 'a lot of Dunsany people in afterwards.'

By 1901 there were six public houses, including Brien's, currently the *Arch Bar,* whose owner, Patrick Brien was the GAA club's first President. In 1903 John Gogan took over what had been Murphy's Hotel and the Gogan family would have a major influence on the GAA club for the following century. Laurence Canning, Treasurer of the GAA club, described himself as a master baker and had his premises where *Tara News* is now. Charles Devitt ran the post office and there were two deliveries daily. Matthew Gilmore was a bootmaker, John Corcoran was a saddler and the police barracks was under the command of Stephen Lea, a Royal Irish Constabulary (RIC) Inspector. There was no bank apart from a branch of Ulster Bank that opened in Dunshaughlin from 1905 on fair days and on the second and last Tuesday of each month.

Patrick Murphy, a native of Waterford and a proponent of the Irish language, was Principal of the Boys' School and Brigid Mulligan headed the Girls' School, both in the relatively new schoolroom, erected in 1887, now St. Patrick's Hall. Each catered for about 60 pupils. An annual treat was an afternoon's entertainment in Dunsany Castle for the children from both schools, with '*a number of brakes and other conveyances sent to the school to bring the children,*' in 1906. This was deemed to be unusual '*in this part of the country where the classes wholly ignore the masses.*'

In summary, Dunshaughlin in 1910 was a small, unimportant village, with many depending on agriculture for limited employment. Housing, road and sanitary conditions were generally poor and until the old age pension was introduced in the 1908 budget older people must have experienced great poverty. Not that many in Dunshaughlin would benefit. In 1911 only twenty-three people were aged seventy and above, the qualifying age for payment. For the youth of the parish, the hurling club, the Gaelic League, the cycling club and sports' days probably presented a welcome diversion from the daily grind.

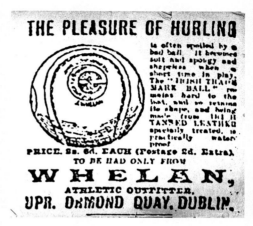

Hurling Advertisement, 1911
Advertisement for hurling balls costing 2 shillings and 6 pence (15c) from Whelan's in Dublin from the *Sunday Independent,* 5th February 1911.

BLACK & AMBER

Hurling Glory and Gloom ... and Football Revived

'Football is under a cloud in Meath' and there are *'half a dozen good senior hurling teams'* compared to three a few years previously.
Meath Chronicle, October 1925

Politics and Internment

In the period 1919-1921 politics and war became much more important than football or hurling.

For a time in 1921 parts of Meath were proclaimed by the British authorities, which meant that no games, fairs or markets could be held. Men who had run GAA clubs were in jail or on the run and Dunshaughlin, like many clubs, was dormant for much of the period.

Two of the most important men in the club, Paddy Blake and Paddy Kenny, were arrested, interned and not released until late 1921. Gaelic games continued even in prison and Paddy Kenny won the gold medal in a handball tournament in Kilmainham Gaol in 1921, beating a Longford opponent in the final. On their release they were met at Drumree Station by the local Volunteer Corps and Cumann na mBan representatives and welcomed home at formal receptions in Dunshaughlin.

A football team represented the club in the championships of 1921 and 1922 while a Hurling Club existed in Pelletstown from 1918. The Pelletstown Reds as it was known, entered a junior football and a senior hurling team in 1921. Its

BLACK & AMBER

Card produced by Paddy Blake while Interned, 1921
The Card reads: *Stand firm behind De Valera* with *Barbed Wire* in pencil underneath. The initials in the bottom left, *R.I.C.* stand for Rath Internment Camp, in the Curragh.

Secretary, JJ Wildridge was also interned and later released along with Blake and Kenny.

It wasn't until 1921 that the Dunshaughlin club was fully back in action again when Dunshaughlin and Garlow Cross objected to each other. The Garlow Cross objection was on three grounds: that Dunshaughlin had played three ex-soldiers, Michael Doran, Mattie Ryan and Augustine Gillic, that James Mahon, a member of Pelletstown, had played with the black and ambers, and that the Dunshaughlin keeper was not properly attired as he had no jersey and played with his coat on! Though Dunshaughlin was deemed illegal the game was refixed.

Dunshaughlin met their neighbours Pelletstown in what was effectively a divisional final of the 1922 junior championship in front of a huge crowd at Curraha. The Pelletstown Reds had an easy win by 1-5 to 0-1, but Dunshaughlin had more success on the social scene, promoting a dance in the Workhouse in 1922, -the British garrison had departed by now- to raise funds. Over 200 attended, making the club reasonably secure financially. The Black and Ambers were on the march again.

On the March Again

Paddy Blake appears to have been one of the men behind the moves to revive the hurling team and by March 1923 he was attending the adjourned County Board Convention. There was some opposition here to allowing Dunshaughlin field a junior hurling team. Many felt the team would be too strong, the Chairman declaring that Paddy Blake was looked on as one of the best men in the county. However, with the backing of Seán Newman of Bohermeen, Paddy persuaded delegates to his point of view and the club entered the junior championship.

Dunshaughlin soon proved that those who feared their strength were correct, by taking the title in their first year back in competition. Ten teams entered and the championship was run on a league basis. It has only been possible to trace five of the games played by Dunshaughlin but it appears that by the time they played the last of those they had captured the title and the other contenders had dropped out. However, recent county final programmes declare that there was 'no result' to the 1923 junior hurling championship. The following paragraphs prove that there was a result.

Dunshaughlin emerged as champions.

CHAPTER 4: HURLING GLORY AND GLOOM... AND FOOTBALL REVIVED

Dunshaughlin Hurling Team, c 1923

Make Sure You Dot the 'i'.

The campaign opened in June when the black and ambers overcame Kells by the slender margin of one goal. It was a game with a number of accidents and fouls and Nicholas Gogan, playing *'a dashing game'* retired early due to an injury. Victories over Ratoath and Curraha by more respectable margins followed. An objection from Kilcarne which went as far as the Leinster Council was also overcome and Dunshaughlin wrapped up the title by accounting for Athboy by 3-1 to 1-0 in October.

Modern programme compilers seem to rely on the Kilcarne objection when declaring there was no winner of the championship. Kilcarne's objection had two prongs; firstly, that James Kenny had played football with Pelletstown and secondly that a J Breen played against Kilcarne although no such player was registered. The first part was rejected as Dunshaughlin had affiliated to play football in 1923 but never fielded so Kenny was legal to play with Pelletstown. The second part was upheld and Dunshaughlin were deemed to have lost the points. It didn't benefit Kilcarne, as a Dunshaughlin counter objection was upheld and neither team got the points.

Front Right, kneeling: Harry Tugwell, with cap, Jack Reilly, Not identified.
Front: Anthony Coldrick, Paddy Huggard with bright hat, Matty Canning, Tommy Lynch, Arthur Tugwell, Paddy Kenny, Nicky Gogan, Matty Ryan, Johnny Lynch, Paddy McClorey, Paddy 'Or Or' Tugwell, Paddy Gogan, Not identified.
Middle, all on left: Christy Carey with cap, Young Peter Kenny? Not identified, Not identified.
Back: Paddy Carey partly hidden, Jim 'Fish' Lynch, Willy Dowd, Kit Brown, Not identified-partly hidden, Mick McKeon, Mick Blake in striped jersey, Jimmy Tallon, Jimmy 'Cheeser' Doran, Jack Tugwell, Jimmy Doran with upright hurley, Not identified, Not identified to rear, Leo Carolan, Not identified, Paddy Blake, Toddy Clusker with moustache, Peter O Brien, Gerry Kenny, J Flynn, Paddy Duffy, Not identified, Not identified, Johnny O Brien, Barney Carey, Willie Murphy, Jack Carey.

> 'Jesus ye'd win nothing at all, and all we won with a few auld lads and we had to wait for the gasoons to finish catechism.'

Dunshaughlin then appealed the decision regarding Breen to Leinster Council using the same argument they had used in Navan. Paddy Kenny explained that he had neglected to dot the 'i' on the list he handed to the referee so Brien looked like Breen on the team list. Leinster Council decided, as there appeared to be no doubt that Brien and Breen were one and the same person, to uphold the appeal of the Dunshaughlin club.

Finally, in March 1924, County Board Chairman, John Newman, handed the medals to Paddy Kenny at a County Board meeting in Navan, saying they well deserved them, and the club presented the players with their silverware at a dance in Dunshaughlin NS in April 1924. Presenting the medals Fr. O Farrell PP stated that it 'afforded him considerable pleasure to be present that evening to hand over to the club the coveted trophy which they had so deservedly earned in 1923.' Both events were recorded in the *Drogheda Independent* proving conclusively that Dunshaughlin won the 1923 championship, as many feared they would.

Further proof resides in Mickey Blake's championship medal held by the Blake family and reproduced later in this chapter.

The Dunshaughlin team that played in those games is not available. However, the list of players transferred to the club earlier in the year and other information indicates that the following probably won junior medals in 1923, Michael and Paddy Blake, Thomas Lynch, Thomas Clusker, Nicholas Gogan, Gerry Kenny, Paddy Kenny, John Lynch, Paddy Duffy, Tom and Paddy McClorey and Christy Doran along with most of those in the team photograph on the previous page.

The 1923 team was a combination of older experienced men who had played with Dunshaughlin up to 1917 and younger men who were now coming to the fore. Paddy Blake was never a man to speak at length about their deeds, but, in later years, when the then Dunshaughlin teams were not performing adequately his frustrations could break through. His son Pádraig recalls the occasional outburst on the way home from a game, 'Jesus ye'd win nothing at all, and all we won with a few auld lads and we had to wait for the gasoons to finish catechism.' In those days catechism classes after Mass on Sunday was the norm.

The gossoons were players like Paddy McClorey and Gerry Kenny. Of course the gasoons couldn't always be relied on to perform up to standard if the going got tough. To ensure that the younger players would be sufficiently motivated their older colleagues would often give them a dig of a hurley when melees developed and blame the opposition. In this way the gossoons would get the dander up and be all out for revenge.

The club won the Ashbourne Hurling Tournament in 1924 and organized a football and hurling tournament of its own in 1923-24 for the purpose of acquiring a field for practice while any balance was to be used to build a handball

CHAPTER 4: HURLING GLORY AND GLOOM... AND FOOTBALL REVIVED

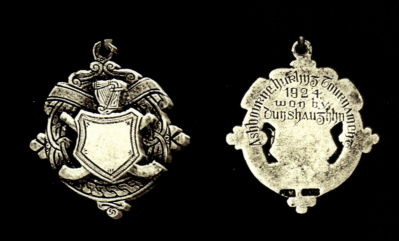

Advertisement for Tournament 1923
A notice advertising Dunshaughlin's Hurling and Football Tournament in 1923. It was planned to use the funds to get a field for practice and build a handball alley. The former wasn't achieved until the 1950s but the Handball Alley opened in 1930.

Hurling medal, front and back, won by a member of the Tugwell family with Dunshaughlin in the Ashbourne Tournament of 1924.

alley. A broadly based committee ran the tournament including the local clergy, PJ Mulvany, a Farmers' Party TD, who farmed where Kealys' farm is at present in Ballinlough, and Senator Michael Duffy. Ten clubs entered for the hurling competition with thirteen in the football section. The tournament appears to have been a great success, in particular the hurling game between Dunshaughlin, the 1923 junior champions, and Athboy, the 1923 senior title holders. Athboy won this contest but a large 'gate' must have made up for any disappointment. A practice field was never acquired but a handball alley was built beside the Garda Barracks, and opened in 1930. Its subsequent history is detailed in Appendix 4.

Dunshaughlin's Third Senior title

Near neighbours Kilmessan, who won the Dunshaughlin tournament, took the 1924 senior championship but 1925 was Dunshaughlin's year. At this stage hurling was the premier game in the county. *The Meath Chronicle* reported that *'football is under a cloud in Meath'* and that there were *'half a dozen good senior hurling teams'* compared to three a few years previously. Dunshaughlin it noted, *'has come on with a remarkable flash.'*

The championship operated on a league basis and in their first outing the black and ambers narrowly defeated

BLACK & AMBER

Dunshaughlin Hurling Championship Medals.
The Junior, first and second from left, and Senior, third and fourth from left, hurling championship medals, won by Mickey Blake in 1923 and 1925. The inscriptions read: Junior Hurling C'ship Na Mide, 1923 Dunshaughlin and Na Mide Sen. Hurling C'ship 1925 won by Dunshaughlin.

the reigning champions Kilmessan by 4-4 to 3-2 at the Navan Show Grounds, now Páirc Tailteann. John Lynch in goal made three wonderful saves and when he was beaten Paddy 'Or Or' Tugwell brought off a great save on the line. At the other end Paddy McClorey was in top form, banging home three goals, but with five minutes to go Dunshaughlin's lead was a mere point. Then with three minutes left defence was turned into attack and Nicky Gogan had a goal to which McClorey added another point before the final whistle. Dunshaughlin, the *Chronicle* reported, *'were meritorious if somewhat unexpected winners.'*

A further victory over Trim by the narrowest of margins, 2-0 to 1-2, in 'a rough and rather dangerous game' according to the referee's report, set Dunshaughlin up for a vital clash with Athboy. This game had practically the status of a county final, for victory would almost guarantee the title for Dunshaughlin. The *Drogheda Independent* reported as follows:

'The first wide went to Athboy who were pressing, but Dunshaughlin in turn attacked and after some repulses were rewarded with a point. A '70' to Dunshaughlin was well placed by Clusker and added another point to Dunshaughlin's score. In subsequent play a beautiful Athboy puck from midfield missed the net by inches. Following a free Athboy scored their first goal and lively play ensued with the balance in favour of Athboy. A fine puck by Blake from the mid-line narrowly missed the posts. Close up to half time Dunshaughlin scored another point, thus equalizing matters and within a moment they added another goal to their credit leaving the score Dunshaughlin 1-3 Athboy 1-0.
In the second half
Dunshaughlin maintained their superiority and P. Kenny with a good goal put his side on a safe lead. This was followed immediately after by a sharp shot, which put Dunshaughlin a further point up in the score. From a free Athboy scored another point and followed their success with another minor, but Dunshaughlin not to be denied replied with a flying major. Dunshaughlin to the end maintained their superiority.'

CHAPTER 4: HURLING GLORY AND GLOOM ... AND FOOTBALL REVIVED

Paddy, Nicky and Johnny Gogan and Ciarán Murray.
The Gogan brothers were stalwarts of Dunshaughlin hurling and football teams in the 1920s and 1930s while Ciarán Murray lined out for Drumree, Dunshaughlin and Meath before going on to mastermind the success of St. Martins in the 1950s.
Photo Copyright Brendan Murray

The Black and Ambers won by 4-5 to 2-3 and lined out as follows:

John Lynch

James 'Cheeser' Doran   Mick Clusker   Paddy 'Or Or' Tugwell

Gerry Kenny   Michael Blake   Paddy 'Gabby Ann' Duffy

Paddy 'Butcher' Blake   Nicky Gogan

Matt 'Doctor' Ryan   Christy 'Toes' Doran   Paddy Kenny

Thomas 'Muck' McClorey   Joe Kelly   Paddy McClorey

Others who played on the championship trail were Leo Carolan, John 'Fowler' Tugwell and Alex Ryan.

In the 1910s, 20s and 30s Dunshaughlin established for themselves the reputation of tough, hard hurlers and became great crowd pullers as people travelled from far and near to see the action. Paddy Huggard and Matty Wallace recall the shouts of 'Put off the Butcher!' from the crowds at almost every game in those years.

Paddy Blake in fact ran a butcher's shop and this was probably where the nickname came from originally. However, his performances on the field led many to conclude that the title referred to his style of hurling, for in a period when toughness and the ability to take care of yourself was essential Paddy Blake was well able to look after himself and his opponent! However, when he lost his temper he was much less effective as a hurler and crowds and opponents were only too happy to see him do so. Many old-timers claim that his brother Mickey, a short and stocky defender, was tougher than Paddy and more reliable in a crisis.

BLACK & AMBER

> 'Keep in the ducks Maggie, here come the Dunshaughlin blackguards!'

Much of Dunshaughlin's fame or notoriety, depending on your point of view, arose from the aftermath of the Athboy game. A row started in the field during or after the game and continued on the streets afterwards. It appears that some of the Dunshaughlin men celebrated too well, and didn't return home on the usual transport, Jimmy Blake's lorry. It is generally agreed that many didn't get back to base until almost mid-week, some sleeping along the Boyne on Sunday night.

It was about this period also that another oft-told incident occurred. The owner of a farm on the Navan Road, near Soldier Hill, was heard to exclaim when the Dunshaughlin hurlers were seen approaching on their way to a game, 'Keep in the ducks Maggie, here come the Dunshaughlin blackguards!'

During the 1920s Athboy replaced Dunboyne as Dunshaughlin's chief rivals on the hurling field. On one occasion before those opponents were due to play each other for a set of medals the Athboy men came to Carberry's window to view the silverware, which was on display there. Mrs. Carberry, seeing the crowd, came to the door and advised them, 'Take a good look at them now, because it's the last ye'll see of them.' It is not recorded if the medals remained in the village after the game.

Despite the long delay in getting home from Navan after the Athboy game the black and ambers were back again a fortnight later ensuring that the championship would be theirs by taming Killyon by 5-2 to 3-3. This game was *energetic enough to satisfy the most ardent searcher after excitement,* according to the *Drogheda Independent*.

The *Chronicle* felt the game was *vigorous to the point of roughness, excitement was intense and Killyon certainly gave a stomach full to the all conquering fifteen from St. Seachnall's parish.* In the first half Paddy McClorey had to retire as his head was cut and bleeding profusely. The enthusiasm of the spectators was at fever pitch and *'heat was engendered in the field and outside the playing pitch.'*

Dunshaughlin trailed by a point at the break but early in the second half a Gogan point levelled the scores and then 'The Butcher' pointed a 50 yard free. Another mix-up followed, but *the referee again got the parties to play the ball rather than indulge in another species of conduct,* the *Chronicle* reported. From then to the end Dunshaughlin held onto the lead and by the final whistle the players had confirmed their status as the champions.

Dunshaughlin was fixed to play Ratoath the following week and Ceannanus Mór in late November but it appears that neither game was played as the championship had already been decided. The following year the competition was changed to a knock-out format as Dunshaughlin's early victories virtually ended the competition long before its conclusion.

Decline and Fall

Dunshaughlin again reached the 1926 senior hurling final, which the County Board organized on a straight knock-out basis but only seven teams participated. Dunshaughlin beat Killyon in the first round and Ratoath in the semi-final to qualify for the final. In the decider the black and ambers had to give way to Athboy. Although the defeat was narrow, 5-4 to 4-4, were it not for the fine display of Mick Clusker at full back the margin would have been even greater. Athboy was now the best team in the county and went on to capture two in a row in 1928 and 1929.

Dunshaughlin never recaptured the form and spirit of 1925 and soon were no match for clubs like Athboy and Kilmessan. After a heavy defeat by Athboy in the 1928 championship a reporter noted, *'Evidently Dunshaughlin has not been practising.'* Later in the same year a full team couldn't be found against Trim and there was a danger of suspension by the County Board. Tom Lynch, a native of Limerick, the Principal of Dunshaughlin National School, was doing his best to keep the side together according to Jack Collier from Kilmessan while Séamus Finn of Athboy argued that to suspend them would destroy the team. The pleas were successful and no suspension was imposed.

But the end came anyway.

No Dunshaughlin team took part in the 1929 championship. Paddy Kenny joined Erin's Own of Kells and won a senior medal with them in 1930. Christy Doran joined Kilmessan, Mick Clusker rejoined the Faughs in Dublin and 'Or Or' Tugwell and Joe Kelly declared for Ratoath.

Meath's First All-Ireland Medals

However, before the breakup two Dunshaughlin men participated in Meath's first All-Ireland victory, and, in what must have been the highlight of their careers, won a coveted All-Ireland medal. This was in the 1927 junior hurling championship. The two were Mick Clusker and Christy Doran. Indeed, for the first round against Louth, Thomas McClorey and Nicky Gogan were in the panel also but it is unclear whether or not they won medals.

In the Leinster semi-final against Kildare Doran scored 1-4 while the Leinster final went to a replay before Meath triumphed by 4-6 to 2-2. The All-Ireland semi-final against Limerick involved a long trip to Thurles but Meath were clear winners by 5-2 to 3-0. Here Mick Clusker at full back came up against a man who was to become and remain a hurling legend, the giant from Ahane, Mick Mackey. Clusker played a sound, steady game and although Mackey posed problems for the defence, on his own he couldn't beat Meath.

Meath, All-Ireland Junior Hurling Champions, 1927

Front: Tommy Carrigy (Athboy), Ikey Madden (Kilmessan), Séamus Finn (Athboy), John 'Rack' Doherty (Athboy).
Middle Row: Seán Newman (Chairman), Jimmy Griffin (Trim), Bob Collins (Athboy), Mick Clusker (Dunshaughlin), Larry Mitchell, Capt., (Athboy), Martin Doherty (Athboy), Tom Browne (Athboy), Charlie Curley (Dunboyne), Ned Giles (Secretary).
Back: Players only: Willie Smyth (Kilmessan), Peter Moran (Dunboyne), Ned Giles (Erin's Own, Kells), Tom Irwin (Erin's Own, Kells), Christy Doran (Dunshaughlin), Joe Loughran (Kilmessan), Bosco Loughran (Kilmessan), Fr. Dinny Maher (Athboy).

Dunshaughlin Football Club, 1937

Front kneeling: Colm Delany, Paudge 'Poker' Morgan, Maurice Delany, Billy Carberry.
Middle: Paddy McClorey, Alfie Toole, Paddy Lynam, Ben Lynam, Dr. Dan O Brien, Fr. Willy Delany, Stephen 'The Blocker' Blake, John 'The Hackler' Flynn.
Back: Peter Reilly, Joe Carolan, Tommy Delany, Ikey Madden, Not identified, Johnny Gogan, John Murphy, ? Tugwell, Mickey Parr, Paddy Duffy with hat, Peter Doran, Mickey Carberry, Not identified, Ciarán Murray, Kevin Delany, Jim Shaw, Not identified, possibly a Johnson, Mickey Neill, Val O Brien with tie, Randall Carey, Pat Hand, partly hidden, Tony Coldrick, Joe Dowd.

CHAPTER 4: HURLING GLORY AND GLOOM ... AND FOOTBALL REVIVED

The All-Ireland final against Galway wasn't played until early 1928 and like the Leinster final it went to a replay. In the first game Meath played badly, equalized five minutes from time and deserved to lose. Clusker had to retire in the first half with a severely cut face after flinging himself at the Galway full forward to save what looked a certain goal. But in the second half he went back on again and '*did fine work notwithstanding a wealth of sticking plaster and a bandaged hand.*'

In the replay at Croke Park, Meath were a superior force and well deserved their 5-4 to 3-2 victory. Mick Clusker was back and '*better than we have ever seen him*' said the *Drogheda Independent*. Doran excelled himself, scoring 1-1 in the first half. Early in the second half with Meath a point behind a free was awarded to the Royal County. The *Drogheda Independent* takes up the story

'*Meath supporters knew Doran and wondered and wondered would he try for the goal and the lead, or the point and equality. There did not seem from the sideline much room for a major to penetrate, but Doran knew better and shot right into the net.*' A glorious goal and the lead. '*Men on the sideline and stands, staid phlegmatic men as a rule, shouted themselves hoarse. Hats, caps and even top coats were tossed as the game veered now one way, now the other.*'

But Meath did not let their slim advantage slip and before the end had two more goals. Thus Doran and Clusker gained the All-Ireland medals their ability warranted while Ikey Madden from Drumree, then playing club hurling with Kilmessan, was also a member of the all conquering team.

The following year Paddy Kenny was captain of the Royal County junior hurling team that defeated Louth in the first round before bowing out to Kilkenny while Christy Doran captained the county footballers in the championship defeat to Longford.

A Short-Lived Revival

From 1929 until 1932 Dunshaughlin fielded neither a hurling nor a football team. 1933 saw yet another effort to reorganize the club. What was described as the '*inaugural meeting of the St. Seachnall's hurling club*' was held on Monday, 6th February. Paddy Kenny took the chair and the redoubtable Paddy Blake was again appointed captain.

The earliest game played by the reformed club appears to have been in the Kilmessan tournament against Dunboyne and it ended in a draw. Victory in the replay went to Dunshaughlin by 6-3 to 3-4. Ikey Madden, now lining out for Dunshaughlin, was the best man on the team, while Mick Clusker was still playing a great game in the backs. Tom Everard was the forward ace, scoring four goals while Christy Doran was still good for a goal.

> '*Men on the sideline and stands, staid phlegmatic men as a rule, shouted themselves hoarse. Hats, caps and even top coats were tossed as the game veered now one way, now the other.*'

Original team list for Dunshaughlin v Kilcloon, at Clonee in July 1934.
This team may have played in a tournament as Dunshaughlin didn't take part in the 1934 championship. It shows the lack of regulation at the time as at least two of the players, John and Paddy Gogan, lined out with Culmullen in the Junior semi-final later in the year. Their participation in the July game would, if known, have rendered them illegal for the semi-final.

For Dunshaughlin 1933 was the best of years but also the worst of years. The best was qualifying for the county semi-final, the worst was the comprehensive hammering they received in that game. It is likely that the championship was on a league basis and Dunshaughlin didn't distinguish themselves in it. The initial outing against Erin's Own at Trim wasn't played due to a misunderstanding over time. Interestingly, for that game Jim Hurley the Cork All-Ireland hurler would have been on the Dunshaughlin team, if the game had been played.

The next game saw Dunshaughlin defeat old rivals Dunboyne by 2-3 to 1-0 and they lined out as follows: (Only 14 names were given in the report). Paddy Kenny, Christy Doran, Paddy Blake, Paddy McClorey, Nicky Gogan, Ciarán Murray, Matty Davis, Thomas Toole, Tom Everard, Jim Everard, Andy Everard, John Gogan, Johnny Lynch, Ikey Madden. In the following round Kilmessan led Dunshaughlin by 8-2 to 1-2 when the game was abandoned. The referee stated that James Maguire of Kilmessan struck one of the Everards and he had to retire with a serious head injury. Paddy Blake was alleged to have followed Joe Loughran around the field with a hurley and both Blake and Clusker failed to appear for the second half.

Despite all the setbacks Dunshaughlin were paired with Kilmessan in the semi-final. It resulted in an overwhelming Kilmessan victory, 8-8 to 0-0. Christy Doran was now in goals, Mick Carberry promoted from the minors played well in defence while others who attempted valiantly to stem the tide were Ciarán Murray and Andy Everard.

This crushing defeat spelled the end of Dunshaughlin as a hurling force. The attempted revival was not a success. Both the auld fellas and the gasoons of 1923 were past their prime. They had all grown up together, now they were growing old together and there was no ready-made supply of young hurlers available. Although the team participated in the 1934 Junior championship with reasonable success the club had to wait until 1957 for its next hurling title.

Hugh Isn't Hubert

In fact, it was at this period that Dunshaughlin began to revert to what they had started out as a half-century earlier, a purely football club. A number of men, who until then had played with Culmullen and Flathouse, transferred to Dunshaughlin when a junior football team was formed in the club. Men like the Gogans, John and Paddy, Peter Brady and Peter Doran who had reached a junior semi-final in the Culmullen colours in 1934 moved to the black and ambers.

The previous year, 1933, the Dunshaughlin minor footballers had reached a county semi-final and gave Erin's Own, Kells a good run for their money before

the registered list contained the name Hugh Byrd so the objection rested on the claim that Hugh and Hubert are distinct and different names.

Fiach Hartigan holds his great grandfather Paddy Blake's Dunshaughlin jersey from the 1920s. Fiach is also a great grandson of Hugh Byrne, GAA President 1961-64.

> **"** Some Dunshaughlin followers then came onto the field to 'inform' the referee and umpires of their errors while a Dunshaughlin player made the point in more dramatic fashion by grabbing the green flag and raising it in the air three times to signal the goal.

going down by 5-0 to 2-1. The *Chronicle* singled out Ciarán Murray for a faultless display of catching and long kicking from the centre half back position. He had also been outstanding in the Leinster minor championship against Dublin earlier in the year. Others who played against Erin's Own included Mickey Keogan, Matt Toole, Kevin Johnson, Mick Carberry, Christy Newman, a McCormick, Mick O Neill, John Gogan, Sonny Geraghty and Jim Farrell. The team had at least one 'wrong one', a Dublin lad playing under the name of Christy Dowd.

The Culmullen juniors and the Dunshaughlin minors provided the nucleus of a useful football team and inside two years Dunshaughlin featured in a junior county final.

The junior championship of 1936 was noteworthy, but not for what happened on the field. Dunshaughlin won the divisional final at Warrenstown against Flathouse by 1-5 to 1-1 to qualify for the county semi-final against Longwood, which they lost by two points 0-6 to 1-1. In the second half of the Longwood game Dunshaughlin appeared to have scored a goal after a melee but the referee did not agree, claiming that the ball had not passed through the posts.

Some Dunshaughlin followers then came onto the field to 'inform' the referee and umpires of their errors while a Dunshaughlin player made the point in more dramatic fashion by grabbing the green flag and raising it in the air three times to signal the goal. A spectator repeated the flag-waving procedure but despite all the interference the referee succeeded in completing the game.

Dunshaughlin felt they had been denied a legitimate goal and victory, and considered their options. An objection was formulated on the grounds that the Longwood team list included the name Hubert Byrd, whereas their list of registered players contained no such name. In fact the registered list contained the name Hugh Byrd so the objection rested on the claim that Hugh and Hubert are distinct and different names.

In retrospect such an objection seems both frivolous and unsportsmanlike. The club recognized this, but as Paddy Kenny said at the County Board meeting, 'We won the game on the field and did not get it. 90% of the Gaels in the county are in sympathy with us.' At the time objections on equally frivolous grounds were not uncommon. And Dunshaughlin, like other clubs, often observed the letter of the law but turned a blind eye to the spirit of the rules.

During the County Board meeting to consider the matter, Paddy Kenny opened a large parcel which had aroused a good deal of interest during the meeting. From inside he produced the *Chambers' Dictionary,* and opening it near the end drew the Chairman's attention to the names Hugh and Hubert given separately as two distinct names. Mr. Conway of Longwood claimed that as it wasn't an Irish dictionary it couldn't be recognized by the GAA. Ciarán Murray, though

CHAPTER 4: HURLING GLORY AND GLOOM...AND FOOTBALL REVIVED

not a member of the Dunshaughlin club at the time, had accompanied Paddy Kenny to Navan at the latter's request and he argued that whereas Hugh was an Irish name Hubert had no Irish equivalent. The Chairman upheld the objection, as did the Leinster Council and though Dunshaughlin were agreeable to a replay the County Board deemed them the winners.

Dunshaughlin lost a low-scoring final to Seneschalstown by 0-4 to 0-2. Points from Paddy Lynam and Matty Davis left Dunshaughlin ahead at the break and they lost numerous opportunities of going further ahead early in the second half. Finally Seneschalstown got moving, were level with ten minutes to go and in a final flourish peppered the Dunshaughlin defence and added two more points to their total. Packie Tully, later to become County Chairman, then a clerical student in Maynooth, played at midfield for Seneschalstown. In fact if the final had been played any later he would have been back at college and unable to play. Dunshaughlin was represented by Christy Newman; Peter Brady, Mickey Carberry, Thomas Toole; Paddy Gogan, Johnny Gogan, Peter Doran; John Sherry, Ben Lynam; Matty Davis, Peter 'Buston' Brady, Peter Kenny; Mick O Neill, Mickey Parr, Paddy Lynam.

A number of the players were from the Curraha area, as, at the time Dunshaughlin hurlers played with Curraha, while Curraha footballers assisted Dunshaughlin.

The Club in the War Years

During the war years, 1939 to 1945, or the Emergency as it was modestly termed in Ireland, some competitions and teams lapsed. Travel was difficult. In 1939 there were 7,480 private cars licensed in Ireland but that was down to 240 in 1941 as people could neither afford nor gain access to petrol. Emigration, which had declined in the 1930s due to the international depression, resumed with a vengeance from the mid-1930s with Britain as the main destination. Many of the emigrants were in their late teens or early twenties so their departure from rural areas decimated many clubs.

Dunshaughlin played in the intermediate grade in 1937 and 1938 but without ultimate success and were regraded junior in 1939. Ciarán Murray, who transferred from Erin's Hope in Dublin, was an invaluable acquisition. Ciarán played minor championship for Meath and lined out at senior level a number of times. In the 1936 National League campaign he played at centre half back against the great Mayo team of that era, in a victory during the early stages and in the final in March 1937. Mayo were All-Ireland champions in 1936 and winners of the National League six years in a row. The *Chronicle* described Murray as '*a magnificent centre half back, plucky, sure of his hands*', with '*an uncanny sense of position*'

Paddy Blake (top) and **Paddy Kenny** (bottom), two of the greatest servants of the GAA in Dunshaughlin.

and commented that he had definitely played himself onto the team. However, he never played in the championship, a decision probably due more to the politics of football and the predominance at senior level in the county of a very strong Navan Gaels outfit, than to judgment based on footballing ability.

Kevin Delany, the Gogans, Johnny and Paddy, were also fine footballers. Delany however lined out for Donaghmore in the 1940s, winning a senior championship in 1942, and finally gave up football to concentrate on athletics. Despite the availability of some fine talent the team failed to play consistently well. In 1938, victories over Duleek and Rathkenny left the side in with a chance of qualifying from the division but an unlucky one-point defeat by Seneschalstown and a bigger loss to Donaghmore, the eventual champions, put paid to any hopes of glory. The following lined out against Seneschalstown: Johnny Gogan; Alfie O Toole, Mick Carberry, Mick O Neill; Ciarán Murray, Mickey Parr, Paddy Lynam; Ben Lynam, Kevin Delany; Gerry Brady, Paddy Doyle, Willy Morgan; Paddy Brady, James Geraghty, Ikey Madden. Other regulars during the year were Thomas Doyle, Paddy Gogan, Joe Delaney, Peter Brady, Jack Reilly and Christy Dowd.

Many of the players 'double jobbed' during the 1930s and 1940s. Kevin Melia, Paddy and Ben Lynam among others, won Rowan Cup tournament medals with Garristown during the war years. Paddy and Ben played with Greystones on occasion while Christy Doran also turned out for a Wicklow side. Such double jobbing was of course frowned on by the powers that be, but a blind eye was turned to it as often as not.

A slight hurling revival occurred in the 1938-1940 period. In 1938 a junior hurling team was fielded with only limited success. The team defeated by Ratoath in mid 1938 was: John Gogan, Thomas O Toole, Ciarán Murray, Mickey Carberry, Alfie O Toole, Paddy Brady, Mickey Parr, Paddy Lynam, Johnnie Dowd, Paddy Dowd, Matty Davis, Mick O Neill, Patsy Crosby, Ikey Madden. Only fourteen names were given in the report. Others who played hurling during the year were Christy Doran, and Mick Clusker- Mick exchanged places in goals with Christy at half time in the game against Kilmessan- Pat Dwan, John Tugwell, Tom Kenny, Christy Snow and Paddy McClorey.

In 1939 the side lost narrowly to Oberstown, in the final divisional game with a place in the junior final at stake. Local rivalry was enhanced by the fact that both sides fielded a sprinkling of players from Ratoath. It was a close affair with Oberstown winning by 3-4 to 2-3. Mick Clusker was still playing and the team was: Mickey Carberry; Mickey Walls, Ciarán Murray, Pat Walls; Christy Foley, Tommy Foley, P O Toole; Mickey Parr, John Gogan; Mick O Neill, Alfie O Toole Paddy Brady; Pat Dwan, Mick Clusker, Ben Lynam.

CHAPTER 4: HURLING GLORY AND GLOOM... AND FOOTBALL REVIVED

In 1940 the only club team to perform well was the minor hurling side who beat Ratoath and Oberstown and fell narrowly to Navan de la Salles. The *Chronicle* believed that *'for alertness and intelligent anticipation'* Seán Kenny in goals couldn't be equaled while *'the backs and midfield were decidedly good.'* Brian Smith, later to win All-Ireland senior football medals in 1949 and 1954, was the prince of the forwards, giving, in the words of the *Chronicle*, *'a display equal to that of Christy Doran at his best.'* The following played minor in 1940: Billy Carberry, Francie Carberry, Paddy Lynam, Seán Kenny, Patsy Kenny, Vincent Clusker, Bill Doran, Paddy Dowd, Brian Smith, Kevin Melia, Tommy Reilly, Donald Moore, Tommy Melia, Tony Lynch, Paudge Morgan, Tossie Lynam, Kevin Darby, Mick Lee, Seachnall Murray, Dessie Delany and Jimmy 'Cuttler' Brien.

The club by now was in the doldrums once again. Paddy Lynam recalls having to make a door-to-door collection to raise 7s 6d (about 50 cent) to buy a football. In 1940 no adult team participated in the county championships. Ciarán Murray retired very young and Kevin Delany moved to Donaghmore. Paddy Lynam was seriously injured by a falling tree and travel difficulties and petrol shortages due to the World War exacerbated matters. An outbreak of foot and mouth disease also restricted fixtures in the early 1940s.

There was one further revival attempt in 1943 before the club lapsed once more. Again a modicum of success was gained as the junior footballers reached the county semi-final with Sergeant O Connell in charge of training.

Paddy Lynam remembers this is 'a ridiculous game' - there was a gale force wind blowing and despite winning the toss Dunshaughlin elected to play against the elements. The result was a heavy defeat for Dunshaughlin, 3-7 to 0-1, at the hands of an experienced Castletown fifteen. The score was somewhat unfair to Dunshaughlin, who fielded a young team and failed to make the most of the chances that came their way. The *Chronicle* believed that the Dunshaughlin lads possessed some excellent material and expected them to develop into a really first-class combination with experience. The black and ambers of 1943 lined out as follows: Vincent Clusker; Paddy Cosgrave, Billy Carberry, Rory Mahon; Kevin Johnson, Capt., Seán Kenny, Peadar Lynam; Paddy Lynam, Toss Lynam; Mickey Parr, Kevin Melia, Joe Gibney; Jimmy Allen, Jack Mahon, Seán Clusker.

A first-class combination was not immediately forthcoming however, and after over half a century in existence the club had not yet won a county football title. It lapsed again for a few years and when it was revived the initial success was at minor level. These minor players along with some of the stalwarts of 1943 were to lead the club into the 1950s and the most successful era yet in the club's football history.

BLACK & AMBER

Patience Rewarded - Football Titles at Last, 1947-1958

So here's to our champions in the years ahead
Now that you're senior you're the club each team will dread.
Extract from poem marking first football title.

In the years before and after the end of the Second World War, Dunshaughlin's involvement in championship football was practically nil. In fact, the popular sport among both young and old was boxing.

The St. Patrick's Boxing Club came into existence in the 1940s and under the guidance of Garda Sergeant Dan O Connell, Matty Russell, Brendan Murray and later Jim Cooney and Dickie O Brien, its members gained extraordinary success. Large crowds attended tournaments in the village. Open-air contests were held during the summer in Murphy's paddock and in winter the scene changed to a variety of indoor locations.

Many names that figured on the Dunshaughlin senior football teams of the 1950s boxed for the club including Larry O Brien, Billie and Tony Rattigan, Mickey Kenny, Seamus Foley and Kevin Melia. In the Meath Boxing Championships of 1946, Dunshaughlin captured five of the eight senior titles and six of the twelve juveniles. In the final of the six stone weight Tony Rattigan beat his brother Billie while the following year Larry O Brien won the all-Ireland juvenile championship. Christy Foley, undoubtedly the best boxer in the club, won the senior All-Ireland lightweight title and represented Ireland at that weight.

BLACK & AMBER

> "The referee claimed that only ten of the Dunshaughlin team wore the correct gear as 'some had no jerseys, others had wrongly coloured jerseys while others had neither togs nor jerseys.' At least one player appeared in a St. Martins' Athletic Club singlet!

Running was also popular. Under the banner of St. Martins and wearing black singlets with an amber sash, the club won the Meath novice, youth and juvenile cross-country titles in the one year. Among those involved were Mickey Kenny, Brendan and Aidan Murray, Kevin Johnson, Tommy Clusker, Billy Byrne, Kit Gannon, Charlie Bruton, Patsy McLoughlin, Fintan and Dermot Darby, Leo Reaper, Benny Foley, Patsy Crosbie and Kevin Lee.

Meanwhile the football club, although down, was not out for the count. In 1946 a number of locals who had been playing with various neighbouring clubs transferred back to the village club and Dunshaughlin once again fielded a junior football team. It was not a well organized or disciplined outfit if the referee's account of the divisional final against Batterstown in the Salesian College, Warrenstown is an accurate guide. The referee claimed that only ten of the Dunshaughlin team wore the correct gear as 'some had no jerseys, others had wrongly coloured jerseys while others had neither togs nor jerseys.' At least one player appeared in a St. Martins' Athletic Club singlet! Sometime in the 1940s circular black and amber hoops replaced the upright black and amber bars but the club didn't always have a full set of jerseys.

The referee also claimed that some of 'the Dunshaughlin players encouraged rough play and passed insulting remarks … against the referee and College officials' and he dismissed four of them. Dunshaughlin officials in turn were less than happy with the refereeing of 'Boiler' McGuinness, one of them telling the 'Boiler' after the game that he 'would surely get the plumbing job in the college now'.

Despite the disorder the club reached the county semi-final in 1947, but went under to Moynalty by 3-9 to 2-6. The team lined out as follows according to the *Chronicle*: Rory Mahon; Paddy Lynam, Ben Lynam, Billy Carberry; Patsy McLoughlin, Paudge Morgan, Seán Kenny; Aidan Morrin, Noel Downes; Toss Lynam, Benny Foley, Jimmy Geraghty; Tommy Clusker, Vincent Clusker and Paddy Dowd.

In fact, this line out is not quite accurate for Dunshaughlin fielded two 'wrong ones'! Two men from Dublin GAA club St. Margarets lined out for the club, both by the name of Billy Monks, one of whom- 'Little Billy'- later played with Dublin. It is likely that they played under the Cluskers' names. However, if Dunshaughlin was illegal, Moynalty was also at fault it appears. Some weeks after the game, a Moynalty player told Billy Carberry that he knew only seven of his team-mates that day!

1947 Minors

The real hope for the future rested with the minors of 1947 as Dunshaughlin powered through its section of the draw defeating Dunboyne and Salesian College among others.

At that time the majority of clubs never fielded a minor team, and so those who did could choose players from outside their own parish. The Dunshaughlin team included players from Curraha, Batterstown and Dunsany in addition to the locals. As divisional winners Dunshaughlin qualified to meet Julianstown in the county final. Julianstown was Julianstown in name only however, as it also included Duleek, Stamullen and other parts of East Meath.

The final wasn't played until 1948 and during the winter, under the watchful eye of Paddy Kenny, the Dunshaughlin boys prepared for the fray. Indoor training sessions took place where *Sherry's Property Advisers* is now and the drill consisted of running on the spot and skipping, using heavy, awkward ropes. The players also did laps of the Gráinsín- a circular route beginning where the *Village Grill* is now and going round by Christy Foley's to return to the starting point.

The final in 1948 ended all square, 2-1 for Dunshaughlin and 1-4 for Julianstown; Dunshaughlin conceded a goal from a 14-yard free in the closing stages, which forced a replay. A record crowd thronged Skryne for the second meeting, and they saw one of the best games in years. Against the breeze in the first half, a stubborn Dunshaughlin defence repelled numerous attacks and turned over a mere two points in arrears. Three times during the second half the sides were level and in a ding-dong struggle, Julianstown finally edged ahead to win by 0-9 to 0-7. The result was a great disappointment to the following Dunshaughlin team: John Mahon; Michael Morrin, John Ennis, Peter Tugwell; Patsy McLoughlin, Bill Delaney, Hugh Boyne; Percy McGuinness, Tom O Brien; Ernest Kenny, Dessie Smith, PJ McCluskey; Seán O Brien, Kevin Smith, Benny Foley. Sub: Mickey Regan.

Julianstown officials weren't entirely satisfied as to the legality of the Dunshaughlin team. At half time in the replay Sergeant Tuohy of Julianstown asked Patsy McLoughlin to sign his name but Paddy Kenny told him not to. 'If we lose this game we intend to object' said the Julianstown man. 'Win, lose or draw, I'd advise you to object,' replied Paddy. 'It's easy to object but not so simple to prove.' Julianstown were justified in their suspicion, for both Patsy McLoughlin and Benny Foley were over age.

> 'Win, lose or draw, I'd advise you to object,' replied Paddy. 'It's easy to object but not so simple to prove.'

BLACK & AMBER

Dunshaughlin, Minor Football Championship Finalists, 1947

Front: Benny Foley, Kevin Smith, John Ennis, Hugh Boyne.
Back: Peter Tugwell, Tom O Brien, Michael Morrin, Percy McGuinness, Patsy McLoughlin, PJ McCluskey, John Mahon, Unidentified.

A Football Title at last

Five members of the 1947 minor team had graduated to the adult ranks when Dunshaughlin finally won its first county title in football. This was in the junior championship of 1950. Football success was slow in coming as it was all of sixty-four years since the club had been founded. The competition gained notoriety at the time as the games leading up to the decider and their aftermath made the front pages of the local papers.

In 1949 Dunshaughlin had defeated Drumree by 2-6 to 2-5 in a divisional final but Drumree successfully o bjected on the grounds that Eddie Lyons had earlier played with Erin's Hopes. The following year the team was back determined to capture the title. In the divisional final Dunshaughlin defeated Stamullen by 1-5 to 1-2 to qualify for the county semi-final against Martry. However, the game against Stamullen was interrupted for lengthy periods as players and spectators allegedly engaged in a brawl. *The Drogheda Independent* sensationally headlined its report:

Spectators In Savage Fight At Ashbourne Game

Women And Children Flee From Field

The referee, Colm Walsh, claimed the game was one of the roughest he had ever witnessed,

'Both teams fought with fists and even boots, with spectators encroaching on the field like savages to make the fighting even 'better!'

Yet, only two players were sent off, one from each side.

The semi-final against Martry a week later produced a good game of football until, in the closing stages, an outbreak of fighting occurred. With the game drawing to a close Dunshaughlin trailed. Then Seán O Brien soloed towards the goalposts and parted to Maurice Delany who scored a goal. As the forwards turned their backs on the goals to return to their positions for the kick out a Martry player aimed a well-directed kick at Aidan Morrin's rear end. Aidan retaliated and bouts of fisticuffs broke out in a number of places on the field.

This was but a prelude. Trouble really began after the game and incidents of brawling and fighting took place on the field. The referee, John Clarke from Duleek, stated that both teams attacked each other violently and with savage fury. They kicked each other without reserve and turned Páirc Tailteann into a battleground, he alleged. Spectators also came on to the field to add to the mayhem but eventually peace was restored. For the record, Dunshaughlin won the game 3-5 to 2-5.

The County Board acted immediately but in their haste forgot to abide by the rules. At a meeting the following night, Aidan Morrin and Francis Rennicks of Martry were expelled from the G.A.A. and the Dunshaughlin, Stamullen and Martry teams were suspended for three months. In Dunshaughlin's case, the suspensions for the two games were to run concurrently.

In meting out these punishments, without giving the players and clubs adequate notice and the opportunity to defend themselves, the County Board was breaking Rule 25 of the Official Guide. Dunshaughlin immediately appealed the case to the Leinster Council, which held that the rule as to notification of the clubs had not been complied with, and ordered a rehearing of the case. The Council was also unanimous in its view that the referees' reports were extremely serious and directed the County Board 'to examine carefully all matters in the referees' report and deal with same rigidly.'

By the time the County Board met again in early January 1951, emotions had cooled somewhat. Maurice Delany for Dunshaughlin argued that the referee of the Stamullen game had made wholesale allegations, yet didn't name one guilty person, and if matters were as serious as alleged why didn't he call off the game? A proposal that no action be taken against the Dunshaughlin or Stamullen clubs was agreed by 29 votes to 19.

With regard to the Martry game, a proposal that Aidan Morrin and Francis Rennicks be suspended for two years was agreed after a motion proposing their expulsion failed to find a seconder. No motion proposing the suspension of Dunshaughlin or Martry was put to the meeting. Thus, Dunshaughlin no longer stood suspended.

> Leinster Council directed the County Board to examine carefully all matters in the referees' report and deal with same rigidly.'

The Chairman, Fr. Tully and the Secretary, Billy Eggleston were disgusted with these decisions. It was nothing less than encouraging unruly scenes declared Fr. Tully, while the Secretary announced his intention of resigning as the majority of delegates had not the slightest interest in the ideals of the Association. A month later Eggleston was prevailed upon to continue as Secretary.

The Leinster Council naturally was unhappy with the decisions of the County Board and set up a sub-committee to investigate the findings. The sub committee met in Barry's Hotel near Parnell Square in Dublin. At the meeting, Colm Condon, a future Attorney General, who had played for Dunshaughlin a number of times, convinced the delegates that to suspend the team would be a punishment out of all proportion to the crime. No suspension was imposed, so Dunshaughlin could now participate in the final.

On all other issues however, the sub-committee recommended a hard line, which was endorsed by the Council. Kevin Melia and J White of Stamullen received a six months suspension and Aidan Morrin was expelled from the Association. Thirteen of the Martry players were suspended for twelve months, as the club was reluctant to name its players who were involved in the unruly scenes, while Rennicks was suspended for two years. Regarding the Stamullen game the Council ruled that players did not take part in any scenes after the match and the spectators caused the trouble. A year later, the Leinster Council refused to reinstate Aidan Morrin despite a recommendation from the County Board that they do so.

Finally, in May 1951 Dunshaughlin played and defeated Carnaross in the junior final at Trim by 2-7 to 1-1. Dunshaughlin were never in danger of losing and had star performers in Seán O Brien, Eddie Lyons, Ben Lynam and sub Mickey Kenny. The team lined out:

Ben Lynam

Patsy McLoughlin   Ned Teeling   Barney Cooney

Larry O Brien   Paudge Morgan   Peter Tugwell

Eddie Lyons   Seán O Brien

Ernest Kenny   Maurice Delany   Paddy Lyons

Kevin Melia, Capt.   Billy Carberry   Benny Foley

Sub: Mickey Kenny for Maurice Delany, Johnny Lynch, Kevin Ryan.

Before the game began, the cross bar on one of the goals became dislodged and the Chairman of the County Board, Rev. Packie Tully marched down the field, hammer in hand, ready to carry out any necessary repairs. Seeing the hammer Ben Lynam quipped, 'Begod Father, ye must be expecting a row today!'

There was no row however and Dunshaughlin's reputation was probably exaggerated and certainly lost nothing in the telling. In the final, far from being ready for rowdyism and physical abuse, many of the younger Dunshaughlin players were in awe of, if not terrified by the referee, Patsy Ratty. Ratty was a top-class official who had a reputation for strict control and wouldn't allow any misdemeanour go unpunished. Dunshaughlin's reputation was probably also affected by the success of their boxers in this period.

It was unfortunate that the title was finally won amid such controversial and unseemly incidents. The newspapers even seem to have disapproved of Dunshaughlin's victory for they gave the game scant coverage. Nevertheless, the title was just reward for the years and years of effort and finally established Dunshaughlin as a senior club again. To Kevin Melia went the honour of captaining the first Dunshaughlin football team to win a county title.

This victory led to the appearance of a local ballad praising the deeds of the men in black and amber. It went as follows:

> The newspapers even seem to have disapproved of Dunshaughlin's victory for they gave the game scant coverage.

Dunshaughlin, Early 1950s

Front: Billy Byrne, Benny Foley, Ned Teeling, Seán O Brien, Ernest Kenny, Joe Foley.
Back: Larry O Brien, Bill Delaney, Ben Lynam, Mickey Kenny, Patsy McLoughlin, Eddie Lyons- partly hidden, Willie Carberry, Peter Tugwell, Barney Cooney, Paddy Lyons.

Black & Amber Victory, 1950

The game is over and the black and ambers they have won
So listen very carefully as I introduce them one by one.
Shake hands with Kevin Melia, the captain of our team
And Ben our great goalkeeper who's always razor keen.
This is Barney Cooney, the high fielder of the ball
And next we have the Poker, the daddy of them all.
Here's to McLoughlin, a corner back so sound
And young Peter Tugwell, a player of great renown.
When a high lobbing ball comes into the square
Ned Teeling our full back is sure to be there,
Here's to Larry O Brien our rising young star
And this is Billy Carberry who pops them o'er the bar.
We have the Lyons brothers, both Paddy and Eddie
And when a flare-up rises, the Bunch he's always ready.
Oh boys did ye ever see the Goofy play the game
He's like a roulette man, saying give us your name
He's so sure of his shot he'll say it's damn mean
If the white flag is hoist instead of the green.
Before the match was over, before the game was through,
Delany got the ball and like the wind he flew
He passed to Seán O Brien and Seánie's shot was true,
One more goal for Dunshaughlin before the whistle blew.
At half time Delany, he was forced to retire
And was replaced by Mickey Kenny who never seems to tire.
We had Aidan, the Hank Morrin, out behind the fence
Sure he had been suspended for an act of self-defence.
Here's to our selectors who were always loyal and true
Including our jersey keeper, the great McCarthy, Hugh.
At last our loyal supporters went wild with joy and glee
And when they returned on Monday the time had long gone three.
Bould Tommy Gogan said he didn't give a straw
But Sergeant Dan declared, 'You must obey the law.'
So here's to our champions in the years ahead
Now that you're senior you're the club each team will dread.

CHAPTER 5: PATIENCE REWARDED- FOOTBALL TITLES AT LAST

In 1951 also, Dunshaughlin won the Reid Cup, a prestigious tournament run by Skryne that attracted the cream of the senior teams in the county. In the final Dunshaughlin triumphed over Navan O Mahonys by 3-11 to 5-2 after trailing by eight points at the interval, with Mickey Kenny notching 2-1 in the second half. In the early 1950s the team had a tremendous run of success in tournaments, also winning those in Ratoath and Donaghmore. In the final of the latter Dunshaughlin defeated St. Margarets who fielded Billy Monks, the man who had illegally assisted Dunshaughlin in the 1947 semi-final.

The Senior Championship

1951 also saw the club reach the senior semi-final. Dunshaughlin lost the first round against Ballivor, 2-4 to 1-4, after missing many chances and playing the better football in the first half. Victories over Donaghmore and South Meath-an amalgamation of junior teams including Enfield, Rathmolyon and Summerhill- put the challenge back on the rails.

Dunshaughlin then faced Skryne and emerged victors by the narrowest margin, 2-6 to 2-5 at Ashbourne. As the game drew to a close with the black and ambers holding on to their lead, Skryne had a free kick just within scoring range. As the taker prepared to kick, Tommy Gogan waved a pound note in front of him saying, 'Betcha a pound you don't score.' The ball went wide and Dunshaughlin survived, but for the next game, the Reid Cup final, the players wore black armbands in memory of the same Tommy who had died suddenly.

The championship was running very late and it wasn't until March 1952 that Dunshaughlin defeated Trim 2-5 to 0-7. This victory put Dunshaughlin and Skryne level on points in the divisional group so a play-off, effectively a county semi-final, was necessary to decide who would qualify for the final. Dunshaughlin couldn't repeat the Ashbourne result of the previous year and went under by 1-11 to 0-6.

The following year, 1952, Dunshaughlin again reached the championship semi-final. Unfortunately, newspaper reports of the time are very inadequate, often neither scores nor reports of vital matches were given and recollections of the 1952 championship locally are very hazy. The divisional final, cum county semi-final, was played at Warrenstown in late December or early January 1953 with Skryne winning, by 2-7 to 1-3.

> As the taker prepared to kick, Tommy Gogan waved a pound note in front of him saying, 'Betcha a pound you don't score.'

Kevin Melia
Captain of the first Dunshaughlin football team to win a county title, the Junior title of 1950.

Hugh McCarthy
Committee Man Supreme in the 1950s and 1960s and Hall of Fame winner in 1997.

Dunshaughlin, Reid Cup Winners 1951

Front: Paddy Lyons, Ned Teeling, Capt., with cup, Ernest Kenny, Seán O Brien, Leonard Morgan, Phil Carey?
Middle: Raymond Morgan, Not identified, partly hidden, Paddy Togher, Joe Foley, Bill Delaney (Kiltale), Benny Foley, Larry O Brien, Peter Tugwell, Billy Byrne, Benny Carey.
Back: Tony Coldrick, Not identified- hidden, Frank Reilly, Ben Lynam with cap, Aidan Morrin, Tom Everard, Peggy Cooney, Billy Carberry, Not identified, Paddy Blake with tie, Patsy McLoughlin, Seán Kenny, Eddie Lyons, Billy Morrin, Barney Cooney, Not identified- hidden, Michael Morrin, Paddy Dowd-with cap, Mickey Kenny, Paddy McClorey-with hat, Lilly Mangan, Evelyn McInerney, Paddy Kenny-with cap, Bridie Lynam.

Skryne at this time was a powerful combination winning the senior championship in 1947, 1948 and 1954 and reaching the finals of 1951-53 with men of the calibre of Micheál O Brien, Paddy O Brien and Brian Smith. A great rivalry built up between the neighbouring parishes but in the crunch games Skryne generally got the verdict over their rivals. This was the case in both 1951 and 1952.

In the early fifties Dunshaughlin fielded one of the best teams to represent the club in its history. A number of the 1947 minors had developed into fine seniors, Ned Teeling joined the club from Killeen and from Drumree came two extremely talented footballers, Billie Rattigan and Larry O Brien and superb clubmen like Tony Rattigan, Patsy O Brien, Larry and Billy Byrne and Joe 'Little Sport' Byrne.

Larry O Brien won a Junior All-Ireland medal with Meath in 1952. He came on as a substitute in the semi-final replay against Donegal and was barely a minute on the field when he had a point to his credit. He didn't play in the 'Home' Final against Leitrim but lined out at right half forward in the final proper against London at Páirc Tailteann. Meath won without difficulty by 3-9 to 0-4. Larry was a stylish footballer, equally capable of performing in defence or attack. He was fast, a fine fielder with a safe pair of hands and a great man to lay on a pass to a better-placed colleague. However, for a player who was scrupulously clean himself, he came in for dog's abuse and an injury curtailed his career in later days. Larry was a member of the Meath panel that won the All-Ireland in 1954 but

Meath, All-Ireland Senior Champions, 1954

Front: Patsy Ratty (Navan O Mahonys), Jim Reilly (Dunboyne), Kevin Lenehan (Duleek), Tom O'Brien (Skryne), Mattie McDonnell (Ballinlough), Peter McDermott (Navan O Mahonys), Paddy Meegan (Syddan), Packie McGearty (Ballivor), Billie Rattigan (Dunshaughlin), Larry O'Brien (Dunshaughlin), John Clarke (Kells Harps), Mícheál O'Brien (Skryne).

Back: Paddy Brady (Navan O Mahonys), Ned Durnin (Donaghmore), Dick Mee (Trim), Jimmy Farrell (Trim), Brian Smyth (Skryne), Kevin McConnell (Syddan), Mícheál Grace (Kells Harps), Paddy Connell (Seán McDermotts), Tom Moriarty (Kilcloon), Bernard Flanagan (Kells Harps), Frankie Byrne (Navan O Mahonys), Gerry Smyth (Kells Harps), Paddy O'Brien (Seán McDermotts).

Photo: Copyright irishphotoarchive.ie

> Some of the off-the ball incidents continued at the Carnival in Dunshaughlin later that night when quick steps and foxtrots were not the only form of activity on the dance floor!

instead of an All-Ireland medal he received an inscribed gold watch, as he didn't play in the All-Ireland final or semi-final.

Billie Rattigan won the coveted senior All-Ireland medal in 1954. He lined out at left half forward when Meath beat Offaly by 4-7 to 2-10 in the Leinster final. In the All-Ireland semi-final he came on as a substitute but got no chance to enter the fray in the final as Meath powered their way to a famous 1-13 to 1-7 victory over Kerry.

Billie played for Dunshaughlin until 1956 and continued to give sterling service to Drumree into the 1970s. He was a master at carrying the ball and always put it to good use, either scoring or placing a colleague. Dunshaughlin's chief score getter in the 1950s, he was equally adept at taking points from play as from frees.

The year of Meath's All-Ireland victory was also the year of Dunshaughlin's last appearance in the senior championship for over twenty years. The club failed to reach the closing stages but again gave Skryne a good run for their money in Warrenstown. Skryne had full points and Dunboyne had dropped one so to remain in the race Dunshaughlin had to defeat Skryne.

Along with the usual neighbourly rivalry further 'needle' was added by the fact that Seán O Brien and Ernest Kenny, both of whom had been Dunshaughlin regulars, were now on the Skryne side. It turned out to be a close, tight-marking game during which a number of 'off-the ball' incidents occurred. Skryne led by a goal at half time and managed to retain that lead to the end to win 3-6 to 3-3. Some of the off-the ball incidents continued at the Carnival in Dunshaughlin later that night when quick steps and foxtrots were not the only form of activity on the dance floor! The Tara men later captured the title.

Intermediate Finalists

In 1955 Dunshaughlin was regraded to the intermediate grade and had two tremendous tussles with Duleek, the eventual winners of the title. The opening round of the championship resulted in victory for the Duleek men by 1-9 to 1-6. Ballinabrackey later defeated Duleek to bring Dunshaughlin back into the competition and the teams met in a divisional play-off at Skryne.

Once again Duleek triumphed by three points, 2-4 to 0-7. Billie Rattigan was in superb form and a large crowd saw a game brimful of excitement, particularly in the closing stages as Dunshaughlin pressed for an equalizing goal. But it was not to be, and though Dunshaughlin defeated their rivals in the Feis Cup a few weeks later, this victory couldn't compensate for defeat in the championship.

Games with Duleek were always tough, but honest and clean, and there was never a serious row. Devilment, however, was always likely, especially with characters like Benny 'Bunch' Foley and Joe 'Little Sport' Byrne on the team. In the second game with Duleek, as the players lined up at midfield for the throw-in, Benny shook hands with big Bartle Lenehan (later a brother in law of the O Dwyers) but continued to hold on to Bartle so he couldn't contest the throw-in.

'Little Sport' was a great goalkeeper and an even greater character. His advice to his backs was usually to 'spread out closer,' while if a penalty was awarded, he would attempt to unnerve the kicker with sarcastic comments, and it wasn't unknown for him to peg lumps of clay at the ball when it was placed for the penalty.

1956 was Dunshaughlin's best year of this era as the team reached the Feis Cup semi-final and the intermediate final. Ballinlough, with an attack spearheaded by Mattie McDonnell- then one of Meath's star forwards- and his brother Patsy, proved too good for Dunshaughlin in the Feis Cup. Ballinlough got the vital scores early on and ran out winners by 3-7 to 1-7.

Dunshaughlin defeated Clonard in the championship semi-final to qualify to meet Navan O Mahonys in the intermediate final. The game ended all square at 1-6 each but Dunshaughlin could have won at the end. As the game drew to a close with the teams level, Billie Rattigan coming through, passed low to Barney Cooney, who drew on the ball but drove it wide. The team lined out as follows:

Joe Byrne; Patsy McLoughlin, Br. Tom O Sullivan, Dickie O Brien; Patsy O Brien, Billy Byrne, Larry Byrne; Tony Rattigan, Peter Tugwell; Finian Englishby, Tom Nugent, Billie Rattigan; Benny Foley, Barney Cooney, Kevin Melia. Sub: Joe Foley for Larry Byrne.

Ned Teeling with Reid Cup
Ned Teeling receives the Reid Cup in 1951 from Tommy Mooney, Skryne Chairman. Paddy Blake is on the extreme right.

Seán McManus
Prime mover in the hurling revival of the late 1950s. Seán's son Enda captained the Meath Minor All-Ireland winning football team of 1990 and also won a senior All-Ireland in 1996.

It turned out that Dunshaughlin had missed the bus the first day, for the Navan men made no mistake in the replay, winning 3-6 to 0-5. Dunshaughlin's inability to score from close range, combined with a series of switches that didn't work out, cost them the title. Billy Byrne was switched to full back for the replay with Brother O Sullivan at centre-half. Billie Rattigan, who scored all of Dunshaughlin's five points, injured his knee during the game and had to be replaced. It was an injury that would plague him for the rest of his career.

O Mahonys followed up this victory with five senior championships in a row 1957-61, a record bettered only by the Bohermeen six in a row team of 1909-14.

During the 1950s Dunshaughlin went extremely close to capturing a major title on a number of occasions but could never produce that little extra, which would have seen them capture the senior or intermediate title. The gap between county honours and runners-up status is usually very narrow. But it is a gap that is extremely difficult to bridge, especially when teams are evenly matched, demanding a combination of above average ability, grim determination to succeed, concentration on the task in hand, confidence and maybe most of all, luck. Dunshaughlin had most of those qualities but they never seemed to combine them all on the big day.

The team often reserved its best performances for tournament games. The Kilbride Tournament final of 1956 was one of the best games the team played, defeating Dunboyne by 0-7 to 1-3 to win a set of gold medals. Tony Rattigan played a 'blinder,' marking county man Jim Reilly out of the game, while Noel and Bill Eiffe were also prominent.

Dunshaughlin also fielded a top-class seven-a-side team from 1954 onwards. In winning the Maynooth Tournament in 1957 the team ousted some of the best teams from Kildare, Meath and Dublin. The panel of nine players for these games was usually: Larry, Dickie and Patsy O Brien, Billie and Tony Rattigan, Billy and Larry Byrne, Seamus Foley and Peter Tugwell.

Hurlers Take Another Title

From 1957 onwards the players from the Culmullen part of the parish returned to play with Drumree.

There were a number of reasons for this. The defeats in the championship had been a blow to morale and it seemed as if Dunshaughlin was destined never to win senior or intermediate honours. Meanwhile a number of promising juveniles, many of them from Drumree, were coming through and it was felt that Drumree could make a successful assault on the championship on their own. This evaluation proved correct. Drumree captured the junior title in 1959 and intermediate

CHAPTER 5: PATIENCE REWARDED- FOOTBALL TITLES AT LAST

honours in 1961 and 1969 and in the early 1960s the team was a match for the best senior teams in the county. However, like Dunshaughlin a decade earlier they could never capture ultimate senior honours.

Another probable reason for the move was to guarantee players games. With just one parish team competition for starting places was intense, whereas with two clubs, fringe players had a better chance of a start. Another factor in favour of reviving a club in Drumree was that the playing field acquired in the early 1950s could be lost if there was no official team there.

Dunshaughlin agreed to the transfers to Drumree on the condition that those who were hurlers would throw in their lot with a revived Dunshaughlin hurling team. Seán McManus, -father of Enda, who won All-Ireland minor and senior medals with Meath in 1990 and 1996,- and worked in Gogan's Stores at the time, was the chief architect of the hurling revival. Matt Daly and Fr. Eamonn O Brien, when he came to the parish in 1957, aided McManus.

Dunshaughlin entered a hurling team in the 1957 Junior B championship. The competition was run on a league basis and apart from a game against Boardsmill, Dunshaughlin met with little opposition on the road to the title. Against Wilkinstown, Dunshaughlin was superior in every sector of the field, scoring 6-4 without reply. Billy Carberry and Tom Everard each had a brace of goals while John O Dwyer and Seamus Foley scored the others.

Dunshaughlin emerged victorious from the second last game against Boardsmill and finally annexed the title with a convincing victory over Kells at Kilmessan. The final score read 4-6 to 0-3 in favour of the black and ambers and so the village's hurling tradition was successfully revived. Roughly half the team members had never played the game seriously before, the only relatively experienced hurlers being Matt Daly, Benny Foley, Tony Rattigan, Dessie Johnson, Kevin Melia and a very youthful Tommy Troy. Billie Rattigan and John O Dwyer missed the final game due to illness and injury respectively.

The hurling revival was short lived however. In the junior championship proper of 1958 the team had a runaway victory over Trim in the first round, and then suffered a narrow defeat against Kilmessan and a heavy one at the hands of eventual winners Batterstown. The hurling team didn't survive much longer. It was decided not to field a team in 1960 and a note in the club minutes later in the year records that all the club's hurling sticks had been sold at a price of 8/- (51c) each.

> " a note in the club minutes later in the year records that all the club's hurling sticks had been sold at a price of 8/- (51c) each.

Dunshaughlin, Junior B Hurling Champions, 1957

Front: Kevin Melia, Eamonn O Donoghue, Tony Rattigan, Seán McManus, Capt., Séamus Foley, Dessie Johnson, Billy Byrne, Matt Daly, Barney Cooney.
Back: Bill Murphy, Hughie McCarthy, Tom Everard, Mickey 'The Barrett' Carberry, Larry O Brien, Billy Carberry, Patsy McLoughlin, Benny 'Bunch' Foley, Fr. Eamonn O Brien, Chairman, Ernest Kenny, Mannix Mangan, Tommy O Dwyer, Seán Kenny, Dickie O Brien, Tommy Troy, Paddy Melia.
Another version of this picture, used in the orginal *Black & Amber*, but no longer available, includes John O Dwyer and Patrick 'The Gah' Foley as an old man. Fifty years earlier Foley had played in the 1909 and 1910 senior finals, see picture in Chapter 3.

CHAPTER 5: PATIENCE REWARDED- FOOTBALL TITLES AT LAST

One Year: two Sets of Junior Medals

From 1957 onwards Dunshaughlin footballers fielded without the assistance of the Drumree men, and the team was regraded to junior status. At the 1958 AGM Fr. Eamonn O Brien, who had been appointed curate in Dunshaughlin, was elected Chairman of the club. He served in that position for twelve years, giving tremendous leadership and a sense of continuity to the club. In his first year as Chairman, he presided over the winning of a junior title and during the 1960s he was instrumental in completing the development work on the football field and building the clubhouse.

In 1957, their first year in the junior grade, the players were unable to make any impression. The team was more settled in 1958 and won the Junior B title and the Junior proper.

In the Junior B semi-final against Dunderry, Dunshaughlin had to come from behind and scored 1-1 in the final ten minutes to snatch a draw. The goal came from a penalty by Theo Joyce. The replay, as is often the case, turned out to be a one-sided affair, as Dunshaughlin experienced no difficulty in winning by 2-8 to 1-1. The final against Rathmolyon was played in deplorable weather conditions but that didn't prevent the black and ambers registering a 1-6 to 1-2 victory. Benny Foley was in top form, scoring as much on his own as all the Rathmolyon men managed while Ernest Kenny with two points, Mal Loughran and John O Dwyer notched the remainder.

The victory put Dunshaughlin into the junior final proper against the winners of the Junior A competition. However, this was a final destined never to be played, behind which lies a tale.

The A final rested between Curraha and Clonard and the former ran out victorious by 3-4 to 2-6. Benny Foley and Patsy McLoughlin attended the game to assess the likely opposition. Davy O Dwyer, then a minor, was with them. As the teams lined up for the start of the game Benny exclaimed, 'Jesus, that's Jim Farrell on the Curraha team.' Jim was a Donaghmore player and so playing with Curraha was illegal. He was wearing a cap and didn't stand in for the team photograph but Patsy McLoughlin wasn't convinced that it really was Jim. At the end of the game the Dunshaughlin 'scouts' went to the exit gate and satisfied themselves that it was indeed Jim Farrell.

Later that night Benny was going to the pictures in Finglas, with Rose Rafferty whom he later married, when he bumped into Jackie Maye of Donaghmore and said. 'There was one of your fellas playing with Curraha today.' Benny was sorry afterwards that he ever mentioned it for Donaghmore took a dim view of the affair. Clonard also had an inkling that the Curraha team wasn't completely above board, and asked the County Board to investigate the team.

Clonard wanted Patsy and Benny to give evidence but both were unwilling to inform on a neighbouring club. As a result of the investigation the Curraha team was declared illegal. However, Clonard was not awarded the game. For some reason they never objected to Curraha, they merely requested an investigation. If they had objected within seven days of the game and proven their objection they would have been awarded the game.

Thus, neither Curraha nor Clonard could become Junior A champions and Dunshaughlin became outright Junior winners. The players received two sets of medals in 1958, the Junior B medals and the Junior medals proper. It was unusual to receive two sets in the one year. Medals were awarded only to the Junior B winners and the outright winners, as it was generally the case that the A winners defeated the B winners in the final proper. However, it did happen that on a few occasions the B winners defeated the A winners in the final thus leaving the latter with no medals to show for all their effort. In the 1960s Ratoath, Enfield and Summerhill all lost Junior finals, beaten by the B winners.

The Dunshaughlin line out for the B final against Rathmolyon was:

Matt Ryan

Patsy McLoughlin   Jim O Neill   Dessie Johnson

Tom Everard   Peter Tugwell   Tommy O Dwyer

Finian Englishby   Theo Joyce

John O Dwyer   Benny Foley   Seamus Foley

Ernest Kenny   Michael Morrin, Capt.   Kevin Melia

Sub: Mal Loughran for Michael Morrin, Fergus Morrin.

This was a notable success that ensured intermediate grade football for the club in the following years. However, of more importance in the long run to both Drumree and Dunshaughlin, was the success of the juvenile footballers of St. Martins in 1957-59 to which we turn in the next chapter.

Reunion of Dunshaughlin's 1958 Junior Championship Winning Team

Reunion of surviving members of the Dunshaughlin Junior football championship winning team of 1958 pictured in The Black Bush Golf Club at a fiftieth anniversary presentation in May 2009.
Front: Ernest Kenny, Seamus Foley, Mal Loughran, Fr. Eamonn O Brien, Club Chairman 1958, Tommy O Dwyer, Matt Ryan.
Back: Patsy McLoughlin, Tom Everard, Fergus Morrin, Seán McManus, Michael Morrin.
No photograph of the team on the day of the final against Rathmolyon was found.

The men pictured above could not be present at the fiftieth anniversary presentation, or, in the case of Finian Englishby, was present but missed inclusion in the photograph.
Clockwise from top left, Dessie Johnson gets his memento from Patsy McLoughlin, Jim Smith accepts Peter Lee's 1909 and 1910 senior hurling championship medals from Finian Englishby and Jim O Neill gets his award from Patsy McLoughlin.

BLACK & AMBER

CHAPTER 6: ST. MARTINS AND UNDERAGE FOOTBALL

St. Martins and Underage Football

In 1956 a more positive step in the promotion of juvenile football was taken when St. Martins represented the parish. St. Martin is the patron saint of Culmullen and the church there is dedicated to him.

Cries of 'objection', swiftly followed by 'counter-objection' seem to have disfigured minor competitions from their inception. The playing of overage players was rife.

In his annual report to County Convention in 1928 the County Secretary, Seán Giles, stated that the minor competitions cannot be considered a success as 'there was nothing but objections to age.' The trend continued in the 1940s and 50s, and, as noted in the previous chapter Dunshaughlin was not immune, with two illegal players in the 1947 minor final.

After 1947 the parish had no success at under age level for a decade. Dunshaughlin entered a minor football team in 1948 and football and hurling teams in 1949 but for the following two years it seems the parish had no representation in Minor Board competitions. In years when Dunshaughlin or Drumree had no team, players from the parish could assist neighbouring minor sides. The Dunshaughlin 1947 team had featured lads from surrounding areas such as Curraha, Batterstown and Kiltale as well as Dunshaughlin and Drumree.

Juvenile competitions seem to have been infrequent and informal for many years, confined to tournaments, school games and friendlies. In 1936 Leinster Council recommended that all counties should promote juvenile competitions and

Drumree Under 16 Team, 1953

Front: John O Dwyer, Johnno Huggard.
Middle: Dinny Donnelly, Packie Doyle, Paul Strickland, Séamus Foley, Tommy O Dwyer, Joe McCann, Douglas Carberry, Jim Mahon.
Back: Des Englishby, Patsy O Sullivan, Leo Ryan, Cormac Englishby, Dan Donoghue, Joe Dowd, Peter Walsh, Fergus Morrin, Patrick Blount, Patrick 'Rah' Doyle.

some Council money would be available to support such an initiative. Initially, juvenile seems to have meant under 16 and a report to the council in 1937 indicated that such competitions began in Meath in 1936, nineteen teams playing football with four involved in hurling. The Council granted Meath £15 towards medals and expenses. A Schools' Hurling and Football Board existed in Meath in 1940 but it probably lapsed during the war years and in 1949 or 1950 a Juvenile Board was reorganized. It oversaw rural and urban competitions and was probably a successor to the Schools' Board.

In the early 1950s, Drumree took over from Dunshaughlin in the under age arena and entered teams at Under 14, Under 16 and Minor levels. This was probably due to the influence of Paddy 'The Rah' Doyle who was tireless in the promotion of Gaelic games, but not averse to stretching the rules at times!

The Under 16s reached a league semi-final against Kells in 1952 and the following year the Under 14s defeated Ballivor 2-6 to 1-7 in a league semi-final. Drumree never played the final as the bane of the GAA- illegal players, objections and boardroom battles- once again took centre stage.

Ballivor objected that Drumree included a player whose name was not on the team list and concluded by alleging that the Drumree team 'as a body and individually is illegal, playing players overage and non-resident in the parish.' The first charge was deemed proven and the club was debarred from further competition until such time as the Board was satisfied with the officials in charge.

In addition, two unnamed officials were expelled from the GAA but this proposed punishment seems not to have been enforced. The outcome was that no teams were entered for the next year or so.

The Drumree minor team of 1953 scored a completely unexpected victory against red-hot favourites De La Salle with an unknown midfielder dominating proceedings. It turned out he was Vinny Bell, a Dublin minor in hurling and football at fifteen. Nothing improper could be proven however. 'The Rah' Doyle denied any wrongdoing, and as Drumree won no further games the issue was forgotten.

Until the following year that is, when the same Vinny Bell helped the Dublin minors to a narrow 2-7 to 0-11 victory against Meath in the Leinster minor final. After the game 'The Rah' burst into in the Meath dressing room and loudly advised Minor Chairman Dick Snow, 'Object! Object! Bell is illegal-he played for Drumree last year!'

Though such events were humorous they did little to promote the long term health of the game.

A Crackpot Idea

Meanwhile, the Dunshaughlin end of the parish was also experiencing difficulty in putting underage teams on the field. After a particularly bad defeat at the hands of De La Salles at under 16 level, some committee members hatched the idea of playing a game between two sides which they jocosely named the *Inkpots* and the *Crackpots*. The unusual names were based on an annual fundraising charity game in Dublin between two sides involving personalities from the world of theatre and entertainment.

Posters advertising the game with details of the two teams were displayed in the village with many of the participants given nicknames. The appointed referee was described as 'P McLoughlin, the former Dunshaughlin star' to which one local wit added, 'That's the star that never shone.' Oliver Mangan led the pre-match parade with his accordion and Bobby Daly, a Dunshaughlin footballer, threw in the ball. The game ended in a draw, as did the replay.

After the initial game there were some complaints about the referee, one mother proclaiming, when told her son's side was in hard luck, 'Not at all, McLoughlin the hoor, he rode us!' John Ennis refereed the third game, which went to extra

> The appointed referee was described as 'P McLoughlin, the former Dunshaughlin star' to which one local wit added, 'That's the star that never shone.'

St. Martins, Juvenile Football Champions, 1957

Front: PJ O Rourke, Thomas Carty, Paddy Burke, Jimmy Walsh, Neil O Riordan, Noel Curran, David Cantwell, Joe Rattigan, Oliver Walsh.
Middle Row: John Murphy, Brendan O Shea, Brendan Cantwell, Val Dowd, Christy McCarthy, Arnold Blake, Stephen Mahon, Johnny Lynch, Ciarán Murray.
Back: Paddy Leonard, Jack Halford, Alec Hynes, Tommy Downes, James 'Sam' Mahon, Mick Walsh, Jimmy Carty.

time before a victor was found. Originally it was not intended to give any prizes to the teams but after the marathon effort it was decided to present the winners with biros and the losers with combs! The 'crackpot' idea succeeded in its aim of rekindling interest in underage football, and drew large crowds to the games. It also involved older members as each team was entrusted to a selection-cum-management committee.

St. Martins to the Fore

In 1956 a more positive step in the promotion of juvenile football was taken when St. Martins represented the parish. St. Martin is the patron saint of Culmullen and the church there is dedicated to him.

The name refers to St. Martin of Tours, a Frenchman, who lived c. 316-397 and joined the Roman army as a young man. He is noted for dividing his cloak in two with his sword to give it to a shivering half-naked beggar at Amiens. On leaving the army he became a hermit and was later made Bishop of Tours. The church in France has always considered him one of its greatest saints with numerous miracles recorded in his name. His feast day is 11th November. It is likely the name travelled with the Norman-French invaders who conquered Ireland after 1169. The present church in Culmullen features three large stained glass windows behind the altar showing scenes from St. Martin's life, including the incident with the beggar. The Marmion family from Bogganstown presented the glass in 1877.

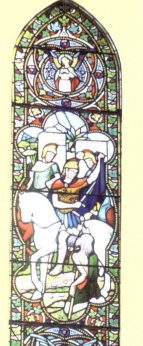

St. Martin from Window in Culmullen Church

CHAPTER 6: ST. MARTINS AND UNDERAGE FOOTBALL

In the years following the foundation of the GAA in 1884 teams appeared and disappeared with great regularity. Readers will recall from the earlier chapters that the first known reference to a St. Martins' GAA club is Merrywell St. Martins in 1888. The club, like most others of the era, didn't last long. In the 1940s an Athletic Club named St. Martins was formed and its runners wore black singlets with an orange sash. The club survived into the 1960s. Kit Gannon, Billy Byrne and Michael Kenny were all involved and the club was based in Culmullen Hall. The adult club in Culmullen/Drumree was also called St. Martins for a spell in the early 1940s.

Thus, when a number of men interested in the promotion of under age football in the parish decided to set up a club dedicated to juvenile football, it was no surprise that they named it St. Martins. Some believe that the Drumree Under 14s and 16s of the early 1950s were also called St. Martins but those teams were always referred to as Drumree in the press and it is probable that the St. Martins juvenile club didn't come into existence until the mid fifties. The club catered for players from both ends of the parish, Culmullen and Dunshaughlin. The initial steps in getting a combined team together seem to have been taken by Tommy Downes and Mick Walsh and they were later joined by Jack Burke, Jack Halford, Alec Hynes, Paddy Leonard, and Ciarán Murray from Drumree and Paddy Blake, Jim Cooney and Jimmy Carty from Dunshaughlin.

Juvenile football was now gaining a higher profile in the county with James Keaveney, a National Teacher in Carlanstown, as a very capable Secretary of the reorganized Juvenile Board. It is unclear if the St. Martins' club had a formal structure with elected officers and committee, but Ciarán Murray, then Principal of Culmullen NS, was described as Chairman on occasion and was certainly the chief organizer and mentor to the Under 14 team.

St. Martins achieved the holy grail of under-age football; they captured the Under 14 football title three years in a row from 1957 to 1959. A hat-trick of victories is extremely difficult at any level, but it is much more so at under-age where team building has to begin from scratch each year. Over the three years St. Martins used only thirty-seven players and Paddy Burke, Neil O Riordan, Johnny Lynch and Brendan O Shea featured in all three triumphs.

All home games were played in Drumree, across the field with wooden goalposts outside the sidelines. The football then was a brown leather size four, laced like a shoe where it was pumped. It was heavy at the best of times but in wet weather it absorbed the moisture and became a weighty soapy sphere of lead. Football boots were also heavy, and, like working boots supported the ankle. Before the first county final when the grass was wet, the mentors put resin on the players' boots so that the ball wouldn't slide off when kicking. Players togged out under

> The football then was a brown leather size four, laced like a shoe where it was pumped. It was heavy at the best of times but in wet weather it absorbed the moisture and became a weighty soapy sphere of lead.

St. Martins, Juvenile Football Champions, 1958

Front: Ulick McDonnell, Neil O Riordan, Syl McAuley, David Halford, Johnny Lynch, Paddy Burke, Capt., PJ O Rourke, Johnny Gilsenan, John Murphy, Andy Mahon. Back: Brendan O Shea, Joe Keogh, Charlie Johnston, Gerry Kearney, Leonard Morgan, Brendan Doyle, Tom Carty, Oliver Walsh.

the trees, as at that time no local ground had changing facilities. Clothes were rolled up and left in a heap, and, in the event of rain, play would come to a sudden halt and players would rush to the sidelines to put the clothes into one of the few available cars.

The team wore red, woolen, long-sleeved jerseys with buttons near the neck. Michael Walsh's wife, Sarah, was responsible for washing and providing fresh jerseys for each game. Very few people had cars and the players cycled to the home games in Drumree. Transport for away games was in Dan Donoghue's van, which was normally used for transporting food or animals to the Dublin markets and was cleaned out to accommodate the footballers. After away games, selector Tommy Downes would buy all the boys a four-penny wafer ice-cream, cut in the shop, and the team lined up dutifully behind Tommy for their treat. Molly Farrelly usually provided a half time treat of oranges, -a luxury unheard of during the war-, cut into segments, for the lads, while mentors had bottles of water.

The team's phenomenal run of success was due to a number of factors. For a small parish luck played a part, in that an extremely talented bunch of young players all appeared at the one time. The three-in-a-row team contained many top class footballers. Both Noel Curran and Jimmy Walsh went on to win All-Ireland senior medals with Meath in 1967. Val Dowd won a Leinster Junior in 1964 while Paddy Burke would surely have made it to the highest level had not

CHAPTER 6: ST. MARTINS AND UNDERAGE FOOTBALL

The Men Behind St. Martins
Front: Jack Halford, Jack Burke, Ciarán Murray, Mick Walsh.
Back: Paddy Blake, Paddy Leonard, Jim Cooney, Tommy Downes, Alec Hynes.

a knee injury ended his career prematurely. Neil O Riordan, Pádraig Blake and Andy Mahon, among others, became fine club footballers. In 1960 many of the 1957-59 St. Martins' juveniles were on the Kiltale team which lost the minor final by one point to Duleek.

But team management and organization were equally important. Practice games were played regularly. Ciarán Murray often arranged challenge games against Dublin teams through fellow teacher Tom Russell of Blanchardstown (after whom Russell Park is named). Games such as these, and games against slightly older opposition helped toughen up the St. Martins' juveniles and prepared them for the fray ahead. Some simple tactics were practised. The mentors created space in the centre of the field for star player Jimmy Walsh by having the other midfielder draw his man out of the middle, leaving room for Jimmy to gather possession and carry the ball forward. When St. Martins were awarded a free just outside of scoring range Paddy Burke and Syl McAuley worked a short free-kick routine that often led to scores. Ciarán waved a towel on the sideline to signal this tactic to his players!

Under 14 Champions, Three in a Row, 1957-59

In their first year in the competition, 1956, St. Martins lost a divisional play-off to Skryne after three closely contested games, but in 1957 the team qualified from its section without any difficulty. This included a comprehensive victory over previous year's conquerors Skryne, by 3-8 to 0-3 on the Blues' territory. Stamullen took them to a replay in the semi-final before the Reds won by a point, 2-5 to 3-1. St. Martins overcame Ballivor in the decider, 0-7 to 1-3, to take the club's first title. The *Chronicle* noted the superior teamwork of St. Martins who were the better team throughout.

The game was won at midfield where Jimmy Walsh dominated, ably assisted by Christy McCarthy. Most observers agree that Jimmy was one of the finest juveniles ever to grace a football field. He had the strength and skill to carry the ball from deep in his own defence into opposing territory against any opposition, and his presence at mid-field guaranteed a liberal supply of ball to his team mates. Val Dowd lined out in a variety of positions but in the final ended up at full back. Though small for the position, he had a safe pair of hands and once he got the ball he was very adept at avoiding opponents and getting space to clear. Arnold Blake in the left corner had a powerful kick-out for a juvenile, an invaluable asset at this level.

The *Chronicle* declared that St. Martins were the better team throughout with clearly superior teamwork but held a mere one point lead at the break despite wind assistance. Early points from Walsh edged St. Martins three points in front but then a Ballivor goal brought the sides level. Walsh pointed for the lead once more and Noel Curran added another two before the end while Ballivor registered a pair. However, it took a brilliant save by St. Martins' goalie PJ O Rourke to retain the advantage and capture the title. The team lined out as follows for the 1957 decider:

Arnold Blake applies full force on the kick out.

PJ O Rourke

David Cantwell   Val Dowd   Arnold Blake

Stephen Mahon   Paddy Burke   Neil O Riordan

Jimmy Walsh, Capt.   Christy McCarthy

Joe Rattigan   Noel Curran   Johnny Lynch

Oliver Walsh   Brendan O Shea   Brendan Cantwell

Subs: Thomas Carty, John Murphy.

In November the players attended a presentation of the winners' medals at a Céilí in Culmullen Hall. Fr. Eamonn O Brien, recently appointed to the parish

CHAPTER 6: ST. MARTINS AND UNDERAGE FOOTBALL

St. Martins, Juvenile Football Champions, 1959

Front: Joe Keogh, Pádraig Blake, Dinny McCarthy, Johnny Burke, Hughie Carty, Liam Carey, Michael Delany, David Halford, Brian O Sullivan, Jack Halford.
Middle: Pat Faherty, Michael Spillane, Andy Mahon, Neil O Riordan, Syl McAuley, Séamus Flynn, John Casey, Brendan O Shea, Paddy Burke, Johnny Lynch, Ciarán Murray.
Back: Alec Hynes, Tommy Downes, Fr. Eamonn O Brien.

and Chairman of Dunshaughlin from 1958, said he had not been in the parish long enough to be of any help winning the title but would 'do all in my power to help the team retain it.' Brendan Cahill, captain of Meath's first ever All-Ireland Minor winning side in 1957, was present with the Tom Markham Cup.

In 1958 St. Martins marched through the divisional stages, ousted Moynalty in the quarter-final and comprehensively defeated Ballivor 2-9 to 1-4 in the semi-final. The final, however, was a close run affair, with the Reds somewhat lucky to dispose of Bohermeen by 0-3 to 0-2 in treacherous conditions. St. Martins fielded six of the previous year's team but were without their 1957 trump-card, Jimmy Walsh. However, in Paddy Burke they had a ready-made replacement. His display in the final impressed all present. Juvenile Board Secretary, James Keaveney recorded in his annual report,

'If any player ever pulled a game out of the fire it was he. He was easily the best player of the thirty. His brilliant solo-run in the dying seconds of the game,

> 'If any player ever pulled a game out of the fire it was he. He was easily the best player of the thirty. His brilliant solo-run in the dying seconds of the game, when he brought the ball from his own half-back line down the right wing, to score the winning point was a treat to see.'

97

when he brought the ball from his own half-back line down the right wing, to score the winning point was a treat to see.'

Paddy also had a tremendous kick off the ground. Father Tully, the Chairman of the County Board, found it hard to believe a juvenile could drive the ball so far. After the 1958 quarter-final with Moynalty he said to Ciarán Murray, 'Between ourselves now, he's overage.' In fact Paddy played in all three victories, captaining the team in 1958 and 1959. The 1958 team was:

P.J. O Rourke

Andy Mahon   Johnny Lynch   Johnny Gilsenan

Thomas Carty   Paddy Burke, Capt.   Neil O Riordan

Gerry Kearney   Brendan O Shea

John Murphy   Syl McAuley   David Halford

Oliver Walsh   Leonard Morgan   Brendan Doyle

Subs: Charlie Johnson, Joe Keogh, Ulick McDonnell, Seamus Flynn, Brendan Cantwell.

In 1959 St. Martins had another close call in the semi-final before finally qualifying for the decider. The initial encounter ended in a draw but in the replay St. Martins edged out opponents Castletown by three points. The last leg of the treble was more easily achieved when St. Martins overcame Kilmainhamwood by 3-4 to 0-5 in the final at Páirc Tailteann. *The Drogheda Independent* called it *'an absorbing, if not brilliant, contest'* and added

'the winners had a powerful line down the middle in Lynch full-back, O Riordan centre half, Paddy Burke (captain) and McAuley, at midfield, the towering O Shea at centre forward and Flynn at full-forward. Kilmainhamwood were a much better team than the winning margin would suggest, but they lacked experience, team-work and the craft of the South Meath lads.'

St. Martins led at half time by 2-2 to 0-3 thanks to goals from a Brendan O Shea free and a well-taken effort by full forward Seamus Flynn. Kilmainhamwood piled on the pressure in the second half,

'but Lynch and his men stood fast and, after another great goal by Flynn and points by O Shea, St. Martins ran out easy winners. As well as those mentioned there were good displays from wingers Carey and Carty' said the *Drogheda Independent*.

Fr. Anthony Daly, then Chairman of the Juvenile Board, presented the cup to Paddy Burke. Ironically, Fr. Daly later became Catholic Curate in Culmullen and died in Dunshaughlin when he took ill while celebrating midnight Mass at Christmas 1977. He is buried in Culmullen.

St. Martins' Juveniles, 1957-59

The panel and mentors celebrate in Culmullen Hall
Front: Jack Burke, Pádraig Blake, Johnny Burke, David Halford, Liam Carey, John Casey, Brian O Sullivan.
Middle: Séamus Flynn, Dinny McCarthy, Louis McHugh, Syl McAuley, Hughie Carty, Joe Keogh, Noel Sheridan.
Back: Paddy Leonard, Mick Walsh, Jack Halford, Jim Cooney, Jimmy Walsh, Johnny Lynch, Stephen Mahon, Johnny Gilsenan,
Paddy Burke, PJ O Rourke, Michael Spillane, Gerry Kearney, Andy Mahon, Val Dowd-partly hidden, Thomas Carty, Not identified, Joe Rattigan,
John Murphy, Ciarán Murray, Noel Curran, Tommy Downes, Alec Hynes.

The following team probably represented St. Martins in the 1959 final. The line-out cannot be established with absolute certainty.

Andy Mahon

Pat Faherty   Johnny Lynch   Joe Keogh

John Casey   Neil O Riordan   Pádraig Blake

Paddy Burke, Capt.   Syl McAuley

Brian O Sullivan   Brendan O Shea   David Halford

Hugh Carty   Seamus Flynn   Liam Carey

Subs: Michael Delany, Dinny McCarthy, Michael Spillane.

It is unclear for how long St. Martins continued to field juvenile teams. However, it seems that Ciarán Murray resigned from his role when the County Board, in his view, failed to take adequate disciplinary action against a club strengthened by players from outside the county. At a time when many clubs saw nothing wrong with the odd illegal player, if they could get away with it, he abided by two steadfast principles during his period in charge of the juveniles- of never playing an overage player or a player from outside the parish boundaries.

The combined effects of the loss of Murray and a scarcity of young players probably resulted in the club lapsing sometime in the early sixties. 1962 seems to have been St. Martins' final year and the parish was not represented in juvenile competition for the following five years. In 1968 a Dunshaughlin team reached the semi-final of the Under 14 competition beating holders Ballivor in the quarter-final before going down in the next outing to Kilcloon. No record exists of the outcome or the line out but the team may have worn the original St. Martins' jerseys.

Minor Efforts 1972

From the mid sixties to the early eighties the organization of underage football in the area was haphazard. Most years the parish entered no juvenile or minor team and players of minor age continued to join other neighbouring clubs for the minor championship. When St. Martins put together the three in a row Under 14 team it was done on meagre resources. These teams rarely had more than three substitutes and when the players moved on to minor level in 1960-63 they joined other clubs for the minor championship, Skryne in 1959 and Kiltale in 1960-61. In 1960 for example, seven players from the parish featured on the Kiltale team that reached the minor final, Val Dowd, Stephen Mahon, Michael Walsh, Jimmy O Rourke, Jimmy Walsh, Noel Curran and Paddy Burke.

The parish continued to experience difficulty fielding underage teams throughout the 1960s. The total number of boys in fourth, fifth and sixth class in any given year in Dunshaughlin NS between 1955 and 1970 averaged out at twenty or less. Even if all of them played they would just about have made a minor team when they reached the age of sixteen, seventeen and eighteen. It was most unlikely all those pupils would play, as Gaelic football was never a high priority for the then Principal, Gerry Smith, so players had little experience of football. Culmullen school was even smaller and the combined numbers of the two schools were almost always insufficient to produce a minor team.

By the early seventies Dunshaughlin and Kilcloon were combining at Under 17 and minor levels. Kilcloon had strong juvenile teams during the 1970s and were runners-up in 1965. The Under 17s lost the 1971 decider to Seneschalstown while the minors fell at the semi-final stage to the same opposition. The following year, the combination, playing under the Dunshaughlin name and colours reached the Minor final. The side had a good semi-final victory against Parnells finishing in front 0-8 to 0-3 with five of the points coming from Ger Dowd and the remaining three shared among Joe McDonnell and Kilcloon representatives Tom Nolan and PJ Duffy.

The final against Trim was not played until November due to Meath winning the Leinster Minor title. Club officials, players and the press all agree that Dunshaughlin should have captured the title but defensive errors let Trim in for three goals. Dunshaughlin had a slight edge throughout and held the lead early on but a high lobbing ball deceived keeper Pat Jennings and dipped under the bar. Seconds later Trim hit a second goal after a goalmouth scramble to lead 3-2 to 0-4 at the interval. Despite these body blows Dunshaughlin dominated the second half with John Jennings playing his heart out at midfield, ably assisted by Tony Johnson. Kilcloon's Pat Callanan and Pat O Brien did well at the centre of the defence while Paddy Kenny and Ger Dowd impressed in a luckless attack. Trim could only manage two second half points to Dunshaughlin's five but the deficit proved too great and with Trim keeper, Frank Lynam, in outstanding form the losers were denied a goal on a couple of occasions. The team that lost out by 3-4 to 0-9 lined out as follows:

Pat Jennings; JJ Whitty, Pat O Brien, Jody Madden; Don McLoughlin, Pat Callinan, Pádraig Gallagher; John Jennings, Tony Johnson; Paddy Kenny, Dessie Fitzgerald, Andy Whitty; Joe McDonnell, PJ Duffy, Ger Dowd. Subs: Tom Nolan for Pat Jennings, Noel Mangan for Gallagher, John Madden for Duffy, Joe Donoghue, Seán Dunne, PJ Kelly, Seán Smyth, Bernie Snead.

The selectors who guided the Under 17s and minors to the threshold of success were Val Dowd representing Dunshaughlin, with John Kelly and Jack Fitzgerald from Kilcloon.

Culmullen, Under 14 Division 3 Champions, 1979

Front: Paul O Rourke, Séamus Magee, Vincent O Brien, Brendan O Rourke, Feargal O Brien, David Summerville.
Second Row: Cathal Gallagher, Martin Walsh, Martin McDonnell, Aidan Walsh, Kevin Kealy partly hidden, Michael Duffy, Patrick O Brien, Michael Boyle.
Third Row: Brian Duffy, Shane Holland, Paul Madden, Terry Foley, Richard Stoney.
Back: Patrick Summerville, Val McMahon, Egin Jensen, Ronan Morris, Tommy Byrne, Niall McCarthy, Pearse O Dwyer, Peter Tuite, Ger McDonnell.

Pat Jennings was Meath's minor goalkeeper when the Royal County captured its second Leinster crown in 1972, defeating Dublin by 3-8 to 1-10 before going out to Tyrone in the All-Ireland semi-final. He also had one outing in goals against Clare in the 1979-80 National Football League. Ger Dowd scored a point in Meath's first and only outing in the 1972 Leinster minor championship. He went on to play Under 21 for Meath in 1976 alongside Colm O Rourke and Gerry McEntee, scoring 1-1 against Louth, before the Royals exited to Dublin.

Under 14 Title, 1979

It was almost a decade after the three-in-a-row before a team from the parish again made an impact at juvenile level. In 1968 Dunshaughlin reached the Under 14 semi-final after a great win over defending champions Ballivor in the quarter-finals. The *Chronicle* deemed them favourites to qualify for the final with Johnstown but

CHAPTER 6: ST. MARTINS AND UNDERAGE FOOTBALL

neighbours Kilcloon came out on top in the semi-final. No score could be traced and memories of the game are extremely hazy, but clearly the team formed the nucleus of the minor sides of 1971-72 referred to above.

Although juvenile teams were fielded each year no further success was forthcoming until 1979. By now the Under 14s, registered as Culmullen, had been placed in Division 3 and with former Under 14 team mates Val Dowd and Jimmy Walsh in charge the team beat Enfield to take the title.

At one stage in the semi-final all seemed lost as United Gaels of Drumconrath built up a commanding lead. Culmullen responded to the challenge however, and in a whirlwind second half hauled down the deficit to win an extremely high scoring game, 7-7 to 3-14.

There were a few uneasy moments in the final also but Culmullen eventually triumphed by 4-10 to 1-6. This team had a liberal sprinkling of fine players who would make major contributions to Dunshaughlin and Drumree at adult levels during the 1970s and 1980s, the Walsh brothers, Aidan and Martin, Pearse O Dwyer, Kevin Kealy, Thomas Byrne, Seamus Magee, Michael Duffy, Michael Boyle, Val McMahon, Ronan Morris and Patrick O Brien.

The team lined out against Enfield as follows:

	Pearse O Dwyer	
Kevin Kealy	Thomas Byrne	Gerard McDonnell
Patrick O Brien	Michael Boyle	Val McMahon
Aidan Walsh, Capt.		Niall McCarthy
Martin Walsh	Martin McDonnell	Ronan Morris
Shane Holland	John Madden	Seamus Magee

Subs: Michael Duffy, Cathal Gallagher, Vincent O Brien, David Summerville.

As the century moved into its final two decades it seemed that under age success would continue to be sporadic and short lived. The halcyon days of the successful Under 14s seemed a distant memory, unlikely to be repeated. But change was afoot and the 1980s and 1990s would mark a return to the glory days. Chapter 8 charts that story.

Interlude 2

Dunshaughlin in the 1950s

Ireland in the 1950s is generally associated with unemployment, emigration and stagnation and viewed as the decade of the disappearing Irish. In 1958 close to 60,000 left Ireland, mainly to seek work. These trends were reflected in Dunshaughlin too, but it was not as badly affected by emigration as other areas while it was also an era when significant steps were taken to improve local facilities and infrastructure.

In 1949 one hundred and twenty pupils were enrolled in the National School. This was an increase on previous years and that trend continued to the mid fifties. This group grew into the teenagers of the 1950s and an analysis shows that, of the one hundred and eleven that could be identified, emigration claimed over a quarter of them. Slightly more females than males emigrated and the vast majority took the short boat trip to England. The shortness of the journey didn't entice them to return, for the vast majority settled away from home. Many of the women seem to have got office work, with some working as nurses.

There was little or no employment at home. Many worked on the larger farms, some got jobs linked to the equine industry, such as grooms and farriers, many worked in Dublin and a few earned a living as shopboys in local businesses. Gogans was one of the largest shops in Dunshaughlin, and, like most such establishments it stocked a variety of goods, with a bar, grocery, hardware and animal feed among its offerings. Guinness was bottled on the premises and the labels proclaimed this. The same was true of tea. It arrived in large tea chests and the staff then packed the loose tea into bags with *Gogan's Tea* emblazoned on them. People were enticed to buy the tea with the following jingle,

**If you buy tea by chance
You may by chance get good tea
But people who take no chances
Buy Gogan's Tea.**

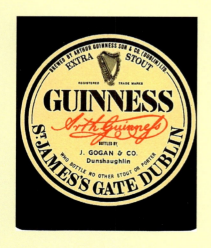

Gogan's Bottled Guinness
In the 1950s publicans usually bottled Guinness they bought in bulk and sold it bearing their own name on the label. This one is from Gogan's pub in Dunshaughlin.

The town the emigrants left behind lacked the facilities they would find in their new abodes. Many larger Irish towns had access to electricity from the 1930s but small settlements and rural areas didn't benefit until rural electrification began in the 1940s. When Dunshaughlin Parish Council was formed in 1948 electricity for the village was one of its priorities. The village probably benefited from its location close to Dublin but the vigour of the Parish Council in pursuing the issue was also a factor. Eventually, on Monday 20th March 1950, ESB current flowed to Dunshaughlin for the first time and the long awaited electric light was at last a reality in dwelling houses and business premises. Householders availing of the supply got a single light per room with a plug in the kitchen. In January 1952 public street lighting was introduced.

Even though Electricity Supply Board (ESB) officials gave a demonstration of electric apparatus in the Courthouse after the switch-on, for many people electrification brought electric light but no more modern conveniences. Indeed, not all homes took up the offer of electric power immediately, as they believed it was unnecessary and expensive. Two hundred and fifteen of the two hundred and ninety-six houses indicated an interest in electricity when it was first surveyed by the ESB but by August 1950 the actual number of consumers was estimated at one hundred and eighty six. The ESB held further demonstrations in 1957, at the Vocational School, and over a hundred persons attended the second evening with a 'marked increase in males' noted by the organizers. Their main interest was in grain grinders, water pumps and water heating as they saw the benefits of electric power to farming. They seem to have evinced less interest in easing the burden of the women, whose main interest was in the electric kettles and cookers.

There was no public water supply for most of the 1950s. Families depended on the public pumps located outside the primary school, at the Garda Barracks and Gallows' Hill. The population in the vicinity of Grangend relied on Paddy Ward's Well, on the Ratoath Road. There were private wells in *Morrin's Hotel*, now *Sherry Property Advisers*, and *Murray's*, now *Peters'*. Older residents recall the laborious chore of constantly ferrying water, generally in galvanized buckets, home from the pumps. The contents were quickly used and another trip was necessary almost immediately. It was the late 1950s before the first public water supply was installed. Arnold Blake recalls gangs of men digging a trench along the street by hand and laying the pipes. A well was dug in Johnstown and the water was pumped up to the newly built reservoir nearby before flowing, gravity assisted, to the village. The reservoir carried sufficient water for a week until new housing developments in the 1970s exposed its limitations. However, initially many houses didn't avail of the supply, as it was costly to take a pipe from the mains and install it in private houses.

Thus, throughout the 1950s few houses had running water and sanitary facilities were primitive. Most families relied on dry toilets, erected at the bottom of the garden. Until the new school opened in 1954 facilities there were no better.

New Schools for Dunshaughlin
Right: Mr. & Mrs. WJ Murphy outside the newly built Dunshaughlin NS in 1954. The Murphys donated the land for the school.

Below: Dunshaughlin Vocational School, early 1950s.

GAA Excursions
Though the railway through Drumree was closed to regular passenger trains during the 1950s it was used for GAA Specials to Croke Park for important championship games. This advertisement dates from the Leinster Semi-Finals of July 1953.

CIE SERVICE NEWS

EXCURSIONS TO DUBLIN: On Sunday, 5th inst., in connection with Leinster Football Semi-Finals —Senior, Meath v. Louth; and Minor, Louth v. Dublin—Special Trains will operate. Timetables and Day Return Fares will be as follows:—

Dep.	a.m.	s.	d.
Athboy	10.35	7	0
Trim	10.55	5	9
Kilmessan	11.16	5	0
Drumree	11.34	4	0
Batterstown	11.45	3	6
Dunboyne	12.02	2	6
Amiens Street arr.	12.30	—	

Passengers to return by 7.30 p.m. train from Amiens Street.

The newly erected school included a water tower that contained a water tank and it took water from the well that feeds the adjacent public pump.

By 1962 seventy-one per cent of homes in the Dunshaughlin Rural District continued to use a well or a pump and less than twenty per cent had hot water on tap. Similar figures applied for flush lavatories and for dry lavatories but a staggering forty-eight per cent had no special sanitary facilities.

In addition to efforts to procure electricity and water, the Parish Priest, Fr. Denis Mulvin, with Parish Council support, was intent on improving educational facilities also. The building now known as St. Patrick's Hall had housed the primary schools since 1887 but it was very small, and pupil numbers increased gradually in the early 1950s. Work on a new school began in 1953 and the Parish Council paid the substantial sum of £731 2s 3d (€930) to the Board of Works as the local contribution to the project. The Murphy family donated the site free of charge and pupils moved into the new building on 19th January 1955. Gerry Smyth, who had arrived in Dunshaughlin in 1932 was still Principal and remained in the post until 1973, a total of forty-one years. The vast majority of the pupils didn't progress beyond primary education with a few availing of the facilities offered by the local Vocational School.

Dunshaughlin had a Vocational School since 1933, based initially in the Workhouse until a new school was opened in October 1951. This was only a two-room structure and five years later a four-room extension was added. Numbers were very low in the early years, particularly in the mid 1940s, which the then Principal, Ciarán O Connell, attributed to transport difficulties and shortages of fuel. As it was based in an agricultural area the school focused on subjects pertinent to a rural community with Domestic Science, Agricultural Science and Woodwork receiving particular attention. Many of the boys later attended Warrenstown College and most remained in Ireland, taking up positions such as apprentice carpenters, builders' labourers, gardeners, farm labourers or working on the family farms. Some girls went on to St. Martha's Training College, a number trained as nurses in England but the majority, according to the Principal, remained at home initially or went into domestic service and emigrated later.

Despite the lack of work all was not doom and gloom. In late December 1948 the local Parish Priest Rev. Denis Mulvin set up a Parish Council and at its first meeting the Chairman stated its objectives as the erection of a new hall, opening of a new cemetery, electric light for the parish, a proper water supply, general improvement to the village, an extension of the primary school and the collection of funds for the church. The Council was neither a representative group nor a democratically elected one with business people, land owners, clergy, gardaí and teachers predominating, yet it proposed and achieved a number of improvements of benefit to all the people of the area. Although it lapsed in 1954, and wasn't resurrected until 1971, by then some of its initial aims had been achieved. Electric lighting was a reality, a new primary school had been built, grounds for a new cemetery were acquired, free of charge from Daniel Gilmore, in December 1953, but it wasn't blessed and dedicated until 1961. Other issues remained to be resolved, a new hall in the form of the Community Centre wasn't opened until 2000, proper water services had to wait until 2010.

Dunshaughlin remained a rural area in the 1950s but the traditional focus on rearing dry stock for the Dublin and English markets changed to an emphasis on dairy farming, with its guarantee of a consistent income. The regular cheque was a godsend to families who could then afford to settle their bills in local shops. In contrast, income from dry stock was uncertain and irregular, hence many farmers turned to the relative certainty of dairying. Most farmers, particularly those with small to medium sized farms, sent milk to creameries in Dublin, such as Merville or Lucan Dairies. Farmers from Lagore and Rathhill delivered their churns of milk to Madden's wall where Jim Darcy from Merville Dairies collected their produce.

The railway line through Drumree had provided easy access to Dublin and Navan and in the early part of the century railway companies garnered extra revenue by running popular day trips and seaside specials during the summer. However, by the 1950s the railways were struggling to survive. A bus service between Dublin and Kells, initiated in 1927, was much for convenient for Dunshaughlin residents and during World War II passenger services in Meath were suspended altogether. Service was restored on the Clonsilla-Navan line in 1946 but was suspended permanently the following year. The line continued in use for freight until its final closure in April 1963.

Despite its closure for regular passenger services the line was often used during the 50s for Football Specials as crowds flocked to Croke Park for Railway Cup finals on St. Patrick's Day and Leinster and All-Ireland semi-finals and finals later in the year. The late 40s and 50s were periods when the Meath senior team was a match for the best in the land and All-Ireland titles in 1949 and 1954 as well as Leinster crowns in 1947, 1949, 1951, 1952 and 1954 enticed many Royal County supporters to use the railways.

Car ownership had dropped during the World War due to fuel shortages, so that by 1945 there were only 7,845 licensed private cars on Irish roads. In the six years after the end of the war, the number of cars increased rapidly to 156,000 and as the motoring population increased the railways experienced a corresponding decline.

Dancing, Drama and the Silver Screen

The Parish Council was instrumental in initiating what became one of the highlights of the year for younger people, the annual carnival. The rationale was to raise funds for the parish, not to provide entertainment. Fr. Denis Mulvin initially opposed the idea in 1949 and his influence is tellingly summarized in the council's minutes, 'On the suggestion of Mr. P Kenny that a week's carnival be held in a marquee the Rev. Chairman said he strongly objected and the motion was dropped.' That didn't prevent it being raised again and in 1950 it took place on the national school grounds for a week with the minutes noting that, 'The Rev. Chairman complimented the committee on the very orderly way the carnival was run.'

Nevertheless, he did not relent in his opposition. He opposed the idea in 1951, arguing that the forthcoming Confirmation and a church mission would make it impossible to arrange definite dates and when it was raised at the next meeting he stated that members should already know his views on the matter. The minutes record that 'the matter was then dropped.' The following year he submitted to majority opinion, as 'all members present were in favour of a carnival [the] Chairman said he had no objection.' Carnivals were also held in Drumree, near the site of the current roundabout, in 1948 and 1949 and those were run by the fledgling Drumree GAA Club to pay for the GAA field. The carnival was not confined to dancing; it also included a film show, boxing contests and amusements ranging from swingboats and chairoplanes to slot machines and shooting ranges.

Dunshaughlin carnivals from 1951 were held in Madden's Lawn for a number of years and later relocated to the national school grounds. The GAA club took over the running of the carnival in the 1950s, sharing profits with the Parish Council, and organized a seven a side tournament in conjunction with it. At times the club ran the event under the pseudonym of Dunshaughlin Gaelic Football Supporters' Club, to evade the GAA's opposition to non-Irish music. It developed into one of the most popular dance venues in North Leinster and continued into the 1970s. When it transferred to the national school grounds St. Patrick's Hall was used for suppers and the event expanded from a week in April to a fortnight in July.

The first half of the fifties was the heyday of the big band orchestra, with up to a dozen musicians seated on stage playing their instruments and reading from music sheets on stands in front of them. Popular bands in Dunshaughlin during the fifties were the Del-Rio Dance Band, Maurice Mulcahy and the Regal Dance Band but these lacked the glamour and excitement that came with the Showbands in the 1960s. Dancing continued until the early hours, up to 3 a.m.,

Dunshaughlin Carnival
A Dance Card for the Dunshaughlin Carnival in 1956 running for three weeks in July-August. The Carnival took place beside the National School with St. Patrick's Hall used for refreshments.

SPOT PRIZES EACH NIGHT

★

Teas, Minerals, Ices and Cigarettes Available on Grounds

Valuable Prizes for
CARNIVAL QUEEN, FANCY DRESS
& TRAMPS' BALL

Ladies' Half-hour Each Night

★

Right of Admission Reserved

Proceeds in Aid of Parish Improvements

DUNSHAUGHLIN CARNIVAL

July 13 to August 5

Excellent Floor
Haunting Music
Genial Company

THE TEAMAIR PRESS, NAVAN.

DANCING PROGRAMME

Friday, July 13
SELECTION of CARNIVAL QUEEN
who is to be the Guest of the Committee for the remainder of the Carnival
Ralph Silvester and His Band
Dancing 10 to 3 — Admission 5/-

Sunday, July 15
COLLEGIANS DANCE ORCHESTRA
Dancing 9 to 3 — Admission 5/-

Wednesday, July 18
REGAL DANCE BAND
Dancing 10 to 2 — Admission 4/-

Friday, July 20
DEL-RIO DANCE BAND
Dancing 10 to 3 — Admission 5/-

Sunday, July 22
Jimmie Rabbitte and His 8-piece Orchestra
Dancing 9 to 3 — Admission 5/-

Wednesday, July 25
THE VINCENT LOWE TRIO
Ceili & Old-Time
Dancing 10 to 2 — Admission 3/-

Friday, July 27
FANCY DRESS and TRAMPS' BALL
Leo Singleton & His Orchestra
Dancing 10 to 3 — Admission 5/-

Sunday, July 29
JACK SILVER & HIS BAND
Dancing 9 to 3 — Admission 5/-

Tuesday, July 31
MAURICE MULCAHY
Dancing 9 to 3 — Admission 5/-

Friday, August 3
DES. FRETWELL
Dancing 10 to 3 — Admission 5/-

Sunday, August 5
GRAND FINALE
Del-Rio Dance Band
Dancing 9 to 3 — Admission 5/-

DRUMREE CARNIVAL

COME AND HEAR THE CREAM OF IRELAND'S BANDS.
Dancing in marquee, 3,000 ft. maple floor.

SUNDAY, 23rd October—Opening Dance, 9 to 3. Peggy Dell, stage and radio star, and her band. Admission 5/-.

MONDAY, 24th October—Film Show, "Come On George," starring George Formby. 8.30. Admission 2/-, 1/-.

TUESDAY, 25th October—Dance. Kit Kelly's Dance Band. 9 to 1. Admission 3/-.

WEDNESDAY, 26th October—Dance. Modernaires Dance Band 9 to 1. Admission 3/-.

THURSDAY, 27th October—Boxing Contests. 8.30. Admission 5/-, 3/-, 2/-. See posters.

FRIDAY, 28th October—Dance. Ralph Sylvester's Dance Band, the silver-voiced Irish tenor and saxophonist. 9 to 3. Admission 5/-.

Car and Cycle Park provided. Ice Cream and Mineral Bar. By special arrangement with "Webbs," sit-down supper 2/6.

Lighting and Effects by William Madden, Central Garage, Dunshaughlin. Spot Prizes. Novelties. Ladies half-hour each night.

McCORMACK'S AMUSEMENTS.—Buzz-Bombers, Chairoplanes, Swingboats, Slots, Shooting Range, Wheel-'em-in, Race Games, etc.

Drumree Carnival
Drumree also held a carnival in the late 1940s. This advert is for 1949. Note that a film show, boxing and various amusements were part of the bill.

INTER-COUNTY BOXING TOURNAMENT
MEATH v. WESTMEATH
in C.Y.M.S. Hall, Navan, Friday, 16th January, 1948

PROGRAMME.

Heavy — D. SULLIVAN v. P. McDERMOTT
(Westmeath Champion 1947-48) (Meath Champion 1947-48)

Cruiser — C. CAROON v. M. PENDER
(Westmeath Champion 1947-48) (Meath Champion 1947-48)

Middle — F. DEMPSEY v. T. BERGIN
(Westmeath Champion 1947-48) (Dunshaughlin B.C.)

Welter — J. McGAVE v. J. MULLALLY
(Westmeath Champion 1947-48) (Meath Champion 1947-48)

Welter — C. REYNOLDS v. SEAN FOLAN
(Runner-up to Champion 1947-48) (Athboy B.C.)

Light — J. MURPHY v. C. FOLEY
(Runner-up to Champion 1947-48) (Meath Champion 1947-48)

Feather — A. CLARKE v. B. FOLEY
(Westmeath Champion 1947-48) (Meath Champion 1947-48)

Bantam — F. FARRELL v. P. FOLEY
(Westmeath Champion 1947-48) (Dunshaughlin B.C.)

Fly — J. DOYLE v. M. MAGEE
(Columb B.C.) (Meath Champion 1947-48)

All contests will be of four two-minute rounds.
First bout commences at 7.30 p.m.

ADMISSION — 5/- (Ringside), 3/- and 2/-

Boxing Match
Boxing was popular in the post-war years.
The advertisement above is for a series of bouts in Navan in 1948 with the Meath team dominated by Dunshaughlin boxers.

St. Martins' Athletic Club
Many who played GAA were also involved in the St. Martins' Athletic Club.
Front: John Rafferty, Finian Englishby, Joe 'Sport' Byrne, Billie Rattigan, not identified- possibly a Dowdall.
Back: Not identified, possibly Johnny Cannon, Clonee, Patsy O Brien, Christy Barker, Billy Byrne, Tony Rattigan, Kit Gannon, Trainer, Tommy Manning, Alo Bruton, Not identified- possibly a Skelton, Joe Battersby, Clonee.

and admission varied from four to five shillings. The event featured a Carnival Queen contest, Fancy Dress and Tramps' Ball and a Ladies' Half Hour each night, where the ladies had the choice of partner. Otherwise, it was a male prerogative to invite a female to dance as the males charged across the floor hoping not to be rejected by their prospective partner. A refusal could spell doom and set off a spiral of rejections as second and third choices echoed the attitude of the first girl approached.

In common with such events throughout Ireland there were no dances during Lent, apart from St. Patrick's Day, as they were banned by the Catholic Church.

The fifties was also an era of travelling shows or 'fit-ups' when groups travelled the country bringing song, dance, comedy and drama to small towns. The arrival of travelling shows with their tents, caravans, strange accents and exotic costumes caused a stir. One of the most famous was Vic Loving with her 'Flash Parade.' She had a specially designed tent made so she could perform using fields rather than renting out halls controlled by clergy, who sometimes objected to her shows due to the amount of flesh on view! She stayed in Dunshaughlin for a few weeks, setting up in Brendan Murray's field where Gaelscoil na Rithe is now situated.

The arrival of such travelling shows probably provided the spur for the establishment of a drama group in the area. The first Meath Drama Festival took place in Navan in 1953 and a Dunshaughlin group consisting of Tommy Englishby, John Cullen, Tossie and Rosie Lynam among others, established a group in Dunshaughlin in the late 1950s. They used Carolan's shed, beside the *Arch Bar*, for performances. The group lasted for a short time, but was revived again and based itself in St. Patrick's Hall. The reincarnated group soon suffered the

BLACK & AMBER

Coursing Meeting
Group at a Coursing Meeting in the 1950s. Andy Everard, Dick Murphy from Grange, Maurice Davin, Carrick-on-Suir, Pat Murphy, from Grange, son of Dick, Johnny Gogan, Willie Murphy, Ivy House, Pat Murphy his son, holding a cap, Mick Horan, Newry, a greyhound slipper, Harry Everard, Kevin Delany, Gaulstown, Harry Everard, Senior.

fate of many Irish organizations, a split, apparently over the wisdom of entering competitive festivals such as Navan. One of the groups had minor success in Navan with John Cullen gaining a merit award there but the groups never qualified for the All-Ireland finals in Athlone. They did however establish a tradition that has been revived in recent times.

Though Dunshaughlin never had a cinema, films were shown by local entrepreneurs. Prior to the arrival of electricty Phonsie McEntaggart and Mickey Kenny used power from Madden's generator to set up a temporary picture-house in the Courthouse, but during the 1950s Bobby McDonnell, a Scotch man from Dunboyne, showed films in a temporary wooden-sided tent with tarpaulin over it. He used venues like Brien's garden, beside *An Síbin*, a garden at the back of Gillic's shop, which was later the site of Tommy O Dwyer's grocery store, Jack Carey's premises, now *Campus Oil* and *Dillon's Auctioneers*. Phil Sheehy vividly recalls the screams during a showing of *'The Clutching Hand'* but the fare on offer also evoked laughter when Charlie Chaplin or Laural and Hardy featured.

Showings were generally on Friday or Sunday nights and the audience consisted mainly of teenagers and youths. One GAA member Benny Foley, who was always game for some devilment got in under the tarpaulin free for years. On one occasion McDonnell got a friend, a Scotchman dressed in a kilt, to act as security. When Benny raised the tarpaulin to get in he saw the bare legs, disappeared and returned promptly with some nettles which he applied under the kilt, causing the Scotsman to flee his post!

Dunshaughlin Parish Council
Minutes of the first Parish Council meeting in December 1948 listing those in attendance. They are Rev. Denis Mulvin, P.P., Rev. Ulick Kyne, C.C., Gerry Smyth, Sergeant O Connell, Patrick Duffy, Andy Reilly, Jack Cuddy, Tommy McEntaggart, Paddy Kenny, Patrick McLoughlin, Jack Coldrick, Matt Daly, Kevin Delany, Patrick McMahon, Oliver Mangan, Patrick Blake, Aidan Morrin, Brendan Murray, Albert Lawless, William Madden, John Murphy, Michael Carberry, Thomas Farnan, Thomas Gogan, Patrick McLoughlin, Jun., Des Delany, Christy Foley, Michael Kenny, Daniel Gilmore, Eugene Englishby, William Murphy, Guard Cooney.

The Hibernian Bank, Dunshaughlin 1965, now *Bank of Ireland*. *Madden's* store is in the background.
Photo: Copyright irishphotoarchive.ie

The Sporting Life, Amateur Boxing: Athletics and the GAA

There were other organizations and clubs to attract the interest of the youth of the parish. The local garda Sergeant, Dan O Connell, established Dunshaughlin Boxing Club in the mid 1940s and the club held tournaments in the Courthouse, St. Patrick's Hall, the Workhouse, Madden's Garage, Ratoath and Kilmoon Halls and an open air one in Murphy's field. Mattie Russell was also involved in the training of the young pugilists. Christy Foley was its most successful product, becoming Irish Senior lightweight champion in 1950 but other family members also boxed successfully with the *Irish Independent* dubbing them the Fighting Foleys in 1951. Larry O Brien, more noted as a footballer, became Irish Juvenile champion.

The local athletic club, St. Martins, also flourished during the 1940s and 50s with its members, many of whom also played football, to the fore in cross country races. The junior cross country finals were held in Culmullen in 1951 when Billie Rattigan of St. Martins was first home, with Francis Gilsenan fourth and the club won the team event. The club also finished second in the novice competition in 1951. The same year Mickey Kenny won the Meath 220 yards championship with clubmate Fintan Darby winning the 880 yards event at Castletown.

Throughout the 1950s coursing was popular in Dunshaughlin. The Coursing club dated from 1905 and held meetings in October/November in Dick Murphy's farm at Grange. The club had over seventy paid up members in 1948 and Harry Everard was Secretary from the 1930s to the 1970s. A number of locals kept greyhounds for coursing and the event also provided financial reward for locals who acted as beaters. The beaters' job was to 'rise' the hares from the fields and the greyhounds would then chase them in pairs, with the best greyhound, in the opinion of the official judge, qualifying for the next round. As coursing took place in a large open field the greyhounds could run long distances and tire themselves. As a result when the finals came round it was often agreed to share the prize money rather than race again. Races were named the Dunshaughlin, Bonestown and Gaulstown Stakes and prize money was awarded to the winning owners.

Hunting was also popular locally with groups such as the Ward Union who hunted deer, the Meath Hunt who followed foxes and the Tara and Fingall Harriers who hunted hares. The hunt was an imposing spectacle with large crowds following its progress.

The 1950s saw the GAA in Dunshaughlin at its strongest since the 1920s. Meath captured its first senior All-Ireland title in 1949 with the victorious team stopping off in Dunshaughlin on its triumphant way back to Meath following the success. Bonfires and large crowds heralded the team's arrival and Fr. Packie Tully, Chairman of the County Board, introduced the players to the enthusiastic crowd. Another All-Ireland followed in 1954 while in the same decade Dunshaughlin captured two junior football titles and one in junior hurling, the junior of 1950 representing the club's first football title, sixty-three years after its formation. Although the Drumree club lapsed in the early 1950s it reformed in 1957 and won its first junior championship in 1959, following it with an intermediate title in 1961. St. Martins gave a huge boost to underage football with three successive Under 14 titles in 1957-59.

The post war period was also significant in expanding the GAA's facilities. Both Drumree, in the late 1940s, and Dunshaughlin, in the mid fifties, were active in procuring permanent grounds, although neither had proper dressing rooms. That would have to wait until the 1960s.

In the broader community other changes were afoot also. The Fire Service began in 1956. At first it consisted of a trailer pump, which was pushed around the village in cases of emergency, with a Bedford Fire lorry replacing it in 1959. The original members of the Fire Brigade were Station Officer Christy Foley, Sub-Officer Hughie McCarthy, Patsy McLoughlin, Oliver Mangan, Seán Kenny, Matt Daly and Seamus Foley.

This was the background to the GAA in the 1950s. A time of austerity, much manual labour, minimal education and the need for many to take the high road to Dublin or the high seas to England if they wanted guaranteed employment. Yet there were also premonitions of modernity, the arrival of electricity and public lighting, improvements in educational provision, the excitement of carnivals, athletics, boxing and the occasional visiting entertainer. It has been said that there was no colour in 1950s Ireland. That was not entirely true of Dunshaughlin, as here and there flecks of a more varied palette could be discerned amidst the monochrome backdrop.

BLACK & AMBER

In Seventh Heaven: Junior and Intermediate Titles, 1967 and 1977

An unusual feature of the 1977 team was that the whole full forward line had played in the half forward line in Dunshaughlin's previous championship win, the junior title of 1967.

After winning the junior football title in 1958 Dunshaughlin entered the intermediate grade once more but failed to make an impact and reverted to junior from 1963. The first year in the intermediate grade, 1959, was notable for three drawn games, two points each against Duleek and a similar score against Curraha. Against Duleek Davy O Dwyer saved a penalty while the meeting with Curraha with a needle affair, both teams seeing it as the junior final of 1958 that should have been. However, a drawn game failed to settle the question of who really deserved the medals.

Neighbourly Rivalry

By 1961 Drumree was the better of the two teams in the parish. Sporting many who had lined out for the black and ambers in the previous decade, Drumree took the intermediate title for the first time ever with victory against Slane in the final. Dunshaughlin went within an ace of meeting them in the decider. If such a final pairing had come about, it would have been most unusual for rarely can one parish

> Drumree took the intermediate title for the first time ever with victory against Slane in the final. Dunshaughlin went within an ace of meeting them in the decider.

field two teams, both capable of performing at the top of the intermediate grade.

Dunshaughlin faced Slane in the county semi-final. A month earlier the teams had met at Páirc Tailteann and the black and ambers, after a whirlwind start, ran out easy winners by 2-10 to 1-4. In the semi-final however, scores were almost reversed, the Boynesiders emerging on top by 3-8 to 1-6. This time it was Slane who ran in the early scores, getting 1-1 without reply.

Dunshaughlin were at sea without the steadying presence of John Holland at fullback, and it wasn't until Finian Englishby was moved to the edge of the square that the team settled. Tom O Brien, now at midfield, gave a great display in his new berth and Dunshaughlin managed to draw level. The *Chronicle* described the game as *'a thrilling, fortune swaying encounter.'* The black and ambers went from two points down to two ahead but Slane rallied well to win in the end. Peter Tugwell turned half chances to account at full forward to score 1-2, after refusing to play fullback, while Seamus Foley was in form with placed balls, notching 0-3. The other point came from Tom O Brien. Dunshaughlin took the field as follows: Davy O Dwyer; Benny Foley, Tom O Brien (0-1), Dickie Donnelly; Tom Morgan, Tom Everard, Tommy O Dwyer; John O Sullivan, Noel Curran; Seamus Foley (0-3), Finian Englishby, Seán O Brien; Val Dowd, Peter Tugwell (1-2), John O Dwyer.

Drumree disposed of Slane by 2-7 to 1-3 in the final and in the Feis Cup later that year, the intermediate final that might have been took place. Drumree easily defeated their neighbours by 1-11 to 0-5 in a tough sporting encounter where Larry O Brien excelled for Drumree and the Dunshaughlin forwards were too erratic.

Surprisingly, in the following year Dunshaughlin failed to make any progress in the championship. In the early 60s the Secretary, Seamus Flynn and the Chairman, Fr. Eamonn O Brien made regular references to the lack of practice and fitness among many of the players. Naturally, in the circumstances, success was bound to be elusive. The only noteworthy victory in 1962 was a revenge one over Slane in the Feis Cup by 3-5 to 2-3 with Con Kenny excellent in goals, Peter Tugwell, Arnold Blake and Dickie Donnelly playing well in defence and Seamus Foley the star off the attack with 1-3 to his credit.

Unorthodox Tactics

Dunshaughlin was regraded to junior the following year but even in this grade the club had to wait another five years before outright success on the playing field was achieved. They did gain a number of victories during the lean period, some of them achieved by unorthodox methods.

In the early 1960s in a tournament at Oldtown against Kilbride, who were then grooming their senior championship winning teams of 1964 and 1967,

Dunshaughlin were being beaten. As the ball went over the bar for another point Val Dowd caught the crossbar and unintentionally brought it down to head height. John Holland shoved it back into place intending to finish the game but Davy O Dwyer ran in from outfield is a slow loping pace, swung on the crossbar and brought it down with a crash saying, 'That thing is far too dangerous.' The game was called off and Dunshaughlin lived to fight another day. Davy's action only gained Dunshaughlin a temporary reprieve however, as Kilbride won the next outing.

In 1966, against Stars of the Sea, Dunshaughlin employed tactics reminiscent of those used against Newtown Round Towers in 1895, outlined in Chapter 2. In this game Dunshaughlin played with two footballs in the first half and one in the second! A gale was blowing and Dunshaughlin had it to their backs in the first half. During the initial half-hour Dunshaughlin kept a spare ball behind the Stars' goals so that when a ball was kicked wide the Stars' kicker-out was immediately given the spare ball. Thus no time was lost.

Yet Dunshaughlin could only manage to lead by two points at the break and the outlook seemed bleak. However, the spare ball was now stashed away in a car and the second half began with only one ball available. Whenever the Stars' kicked the ball wide there was a considerable delay before it was kicked out again by Dunshaughlin as the wind carried it well behind the goals. When asked for the second ball the Dunshaughlin players pleaded ignorance of its whereabouts. Dunshaughlin, with Noel Curran giving a tremendous second-half display, emerged narrow winners 0-4 to 0-3. At the County Committee meeting later, when someone said to the referee, 'I believe Dunshaughlin beat the Stars', he replied, 'They didn't beat them, they fooled them.'

The West of Ireland Factor

Over the years Dunshaughlin often faced difficulty in fielding teams due to the low population of the area. In the century following the Great Famine there had been a relentless decline in numbers. There was little or no employment in the village and the focus on cattle farming rather than tillage depressed the demand for labourers. The grazier farmers who dominated the rural hinterland of Dunshaughlin required, at most, a herd and one farm labourer to look after their cattle. They rarely kept cattle during the winter, thus saving themselves the expense of paying labourers to cut and harvest the meadows for winter feed. Emigration was commonplace and writers and the local press regularly highlighted the sparse population. The *Drogheda Independent* in 1907 described areas like Dunshaughlin where cattle farming dominated as

> At the County Committee meeting later, when someone said to the referee, 'I believe Dunshaughlin beat the Stars', he replied, 'They didn't beat them, they fooled them.'

little better than vast deserts ... of green grass on which there are no inhabitants of the human species, the magnificent fertility being given over to flocks and herds.

The policy of dividing up the large estates and turning them into compact farms had begun well before Irish independence in 1922 but it became a core policy of Eamonn de Valera's Fianna Fáil party, once in government from 1932. In 1937 a number of Irish-speaking families from the western seaboard settled in Rathcairn, near Athboy, giving up their home farms in return for new farms and homes in Meath. Other settlements took place in Gibbstown and Allenstown north of Navan and from the 1950s land redistribution in Dunshaughlin resulted in the arrival of a significant number of families.

The Duffys, Jennings, Joyces and Summervilles arrived in Rathill in 1952 and in the 1960s the McDonnells in Bonestown, McTigues, McHales, Corbetts, Nearys in Derrockstown, the Murphys and Fahertys in Leshemstown and Corrigans, Dixons and Mangans in Gerrardstown joined them. They brought business to the village, pupils to the schools and many of the family members played leading roles as players and administrators in the GAA club in the following decades. There seems to have been remarkably little hostility towards the newcomers who were allocated farms but any such ill-feeling quickly subsided as the newcomers integrated rapidly through the schools, sport and dances.

Another Junior Title

Despite the loss of players to Drumree in 1957, by the early sixties Dunshaughlin was able to field two junior teams, one in Junior A and a second in Junior B. Young players were coming through from the successful St. Martins' sides of the late fifties and the westerners also provided additional manpower. The second team wasn't just making up the numbers and remained unbeaten in the 1963 championship until July when Dunboyne punctured their ambitions. That team fielded as follows, Con Kenny; Ulick McDonnell, Joe Murphy, John Casey; Leonard Morgan, Jerry O Sullivan, John Murphy; Paddy Togher, John Neary; Hugh Carty, Bobby Daly, Dick Ryan; Brian O Sullivan, Johnny Ryan, Christy McCarthy.

After a number of years of inconsistent displays Dunshaughlin triumphed in the junior championship of 1967. En route the team defeated Dunderry by one point in the semi-final having earlier disposed of Shallon, Stars of the Sea, Bellewstown and Flathouse. Dunderry had been favorites for the title and Dunshaughlin took over that mantle for the final. They justified their ranking, edging out Athboy by 0-8 to 0-5 in a tough game at Páirc Tailteann. Val Dowd was adjudged man of the match by the *Chronicle*, which praised him for the way he marshaled his defence and lent a hand in attack. John Casey, then the team's brightest young

Dunshaughlin, Junior Football Champions, 1967

Front: Con O Dwyer, Hughie Carty, Pat O Hare, Paddy O Dwyer, John O Dwyer, Davy O Dwyer, Capt, Seamus Foley, Thomas Carty, Tom Everard, Seán Moran.
Back: Mossie Caffrey, Tommy O Dwyer, Brendan Johnson, John McNally, Pádraig Blake, Noel Curran, Val Dowd, John Casey, Andy Lynch, Brian O Sullivan.

BLACK & AMBER

> Brian O Sullivan achieved the extraordinary feat of getting a hat trick of goals by the 14th minute.

star, dominated midfield. The team was

Seamus Foley

Davy O Dwyer, Capt.   Mossie Caffrey   Seán Moran

Andy Lynch   Val Dowd   Tommy O Dwyer

John Casey (0-1)   Pat O Hare (0-1)

Con O Dwyer (0-1)   Noel Curran   Paddy O Dwyer (0-1)

John McNally   Pádraig Blake (0-1)   Brian O Sullivan (0-1)

Victory qualified Dunshaughlin for the junior final proper against 'B' champions Skryne. The game was a fiasco as the black and ambers annihilated Skryne by 5-3 to 0-4. After fifteen minutes Dunshaughlin led by three goals and at halftime were 4-2 to 0-1 in front. Brian O Sullivan achieved the extraordinary feat of getting a hat trick of goals by the 14th minute. After five minutes he swooped on a Con O Dwyer centre to fist the ball to the net, three minutes later he cracked home a low drive from the edge of the square and completed his hat trick by finishing a slick passing movement. Con O Dwyer and Pádraig Blake were the other goal scorers. Yet again the *Chronicle* singled out Val Dowd as,

'*the chief architect of his side's victory. Once again he proved that he is one of the best defenders in the county with a superb display of solid football.*'

Val had won a Leinster Junior medal as a substitute with Meath in 1964, although injury limited his participation after the first round. Despite recurring knee injury problems he was one of the mainstays of the Dunshaughlin team throughout the 1960s and 1970s. He was one of the greatest workers in the club, particularly at juvenile level, and was closely involved with practically every team that won county honours at adult and juvenile level. He also acted as Chairman for a number of years.

John Casey also played a blinder against Skryne while the forward line as a whole proved too hot for what was Skryne's second-team. The team lined out as for the Athboy game and the scores came from Brian O Sullivan 3-0, Pádraig Blake 1-1, Con O Dwyer 1-0, and John Casey 0-1. Davy O Dwyer captained the side and the selection committee consisted of Davy, Seamus Flynn, Benny Foley, Paddy Lynam and Joe Smith.

All-Ireland Success, 1967

To add further lustre to a glorious year for the club Noel Curran won an All-Ireland senior championship medal as Meath's full forward. In the first round of the championship against Louth Noel gave Doc Butterley the run around, scoring 2-5 of Meath's 2-9. In the All-Ireland semi-final he scored two points and his

CHAPTER 7: IN SEVENTH HEAVEN, JUNIOR AND INTERMEDIATE TITLES, 1967 AND 1977

Davy O Dwyer, Dunshaughlin Junior Captain and his wife Kitty with the Sam Maguire and Meath Junior Championship cups at the club's Dinner Dance.

ability in the air sorely troubled Mayo's Ray Prendergast, leading indirectly to two goals for Ollie Shanley. He landed another two points in the final as Meath overcame Cork 1-9 to 0-9. The first point was a gem. From the Hogan Stand side and without even looking at the posts, Noel calmly and coolly lifted the ball high over the crossbar.

He continued to play with Dunshaughlin until 1983, winning an intermediate medal in 1977. He was a magnificent clubman, regularly travelling up and down from Dublin and continuing to play junior or intermediate when he could have joined any of the glamour senior clubs in the county or in Dublin. He made a total of fourteen championship appearances for Meath, at a time when there was no 'back-door' in the form of qualifiers, and twenty-three National League appearances, during which he amassed 8-52 for the Royals. Jimmy Walsh also won an All-Ireland as a substitute in 1967 when he played his club football with Drumree. He had previously captained Meath to a Leinster and All-Ireland Junior in 1962.

The victorious Meath team stopped off in Dunshaughlin and Drumree with the Sam Maguire Cup. A crowd of 3,000 greeted the team in Dunshaughlin where the fire brigade siren announced the team's arrival. Curran and Walsh had the once-in-a-lifetime privilege of travelling to Australia with the Meath team in 1968, a visit that heralded the current Compromise Rules series between Ireland and Australia.

Meath, All-Ireland Football Champions 1967

Front: Tony Brennan (Enfield), Terry Kearns (St. Vincents, Ardcath), Peter Darby, Capt., (Trim), Seán McCormack (Kilmainhamwood), Mick White (Rathkenny), Pat 'Red' Collier (St. Patricks), Mick Mellett (Martinstown).
Back: Bertie Cunningham (Ballivor), Paddy Mulvany (Skryne), Noel Curran (Dunshaughlin), Peter Moore (Ballinabrackey), Jack Quinn (Kilbride), Mattie Kerrigan (Summerhill), Ollie Shanley (Duleek), Pat Reynolds (Walterstown).

Intermediates in the Late 1960s

For the remainder of the decade Dunshaughlin performed capably at intermediate level. One of the highlights of the 1960s was a series of four games against Dunderry in the 1968 championship. Early in the year Dunderry had been easy victors over Dunshaughlin but a later defeat for them brought the black and ambers back into contention. The luck of the draw brought Dunderry and Dunshaughlin into opposition once again and at Kilmessan they finished level, Dunshaughlin 0-6 and Dunderry 1-3.

The replay produced a scintillating game in scorching sunshine. Dunshaughlin, six points behind at one stage, clawed their way back and another draw resulted. The referee had been instructed to play extra time but he declined to do so saying, 'You couldn't ask those teams to play extra time after the performance they've given.'

Another replay was necessary before Dunshaughlin finally came out on top by the narrowest of margins, 1-9 to 2-5. This victory put the team through to the divisional final but the players could not maintain the momentum and collapsed against Bohermeen, intermediate runners-up the previous year. Dunshaughlin could only manage five points to Bohermeen's 2-11. The team, with Brian Smith

as trainer, lined out against Bohermeen as follows:
Seámus Foley; Davy O Dwyer, Val Dowd, Seán Moran; Tommy O Dwyer, Mícheál O Dwyer, Andy Lynch; John Casey, Michael Walsh (Mayo); Pat O Hare, Noel Curran, Paddy O Dwyer; Mosssie Caffrey, Colm Kane, Con O Dwyer.

In 1969 Dunshaughlin failed to make any headway in the championship, eventually won by neighbours Drumree, but Paddy O Dwyer at right half back and Pat O Hare as a substitute featured for the Meath team beaten by Wicklow in the Leinster Junior final.

From the Playing Field to the Boardroom

In 1952 the club procured the present grounds from the Irish Land Commission and in 1967 the club officially opened the playing field and clubhouse. Seán Ó Siocháin, General Secretary of the GAA, performed the opening ceremony and club Chairman Fr. Eamonn O Brien blessed the facilities. Meath easily defeated Kildare in a challenge game to mark the opening. Full details of the present facilities and the club's earlier playing fields are contained in Appendix 2.

During the 1960s the Dunshaughlin club made a significant contribution to the GAA at county, and indeed national level.

Nowadays goalkeepers must by rule 'wear a jersey which is distinctive from his own team's and the opposing team's colours.' Until 1963 that was not the case, with keepers lining out in the same jersey as the rest of the team. Séamus Foley hatched the idea of changing the rule following correspondence with then *Evening Press* columnist Joe Sherwood. His motion was passed at County Convention in 1962 despite the opposition of Chairman, Fr. Packie Tully, but it failed to get through Congress. However, Wexford successfully proposed the same motion in 1963 and from that year keepers wore a jersey that differed from those worn by the outfield players.

In 1966 the Dunshaughlin club was the originator of the idea that a coach be appointed to the Meath team. Meath had a trainer in the person of Fr. Tully but the club felt that someone who would give the team some idea of tactics was necessary. The idea was accepted and Peter McDermott was appointed. In the first year of the scheme Meath lost the All-Ireland final to Galway but won it the following year. Thus, the idea proved a worthwhile one and indeed it foreshadowed a trend in the 1970s and 80s when coaches like Mick O Dwyer of Kerry, Kevin Heffernan of Dublin and Eugene McGee with Offaly were essential to their teams' success.

A number of clubman also served at County Board level during this period. Patsy McLoughlin became Chairman of the Juvenile Board for four years, 1969-

Seamus Foley whose idea of the goalkeeper having to wear a jersey that differed from those worn by outfield players was adopted nationally.

72 and Deputy Vice Chairman of the County Board in 1979. Paddy O Dwyer acted as Assistant Secretary of the County Board from 1971 to 1973, was Leinster Council delegate in 1974-75 and went on to referee intermediate and senior finals in the following decade while Seamus Flynn became Secretary of the Intermediate Football League in 1970-71.

Intermediate Football: So Near and Yet . . .

Back on the playing field in the 1970s many of the 1972 minor team quickly developed into fine intermediate performers. Players like Pat and John Jennings, Pat O Brien, Don McLoughlin and Ger Dowd blended in effectively with the more experienced men like Val Dowd, the O Dwyer brothers, Con, Michael and Paddy, Noel Curran and Pat O Hare. The transfer of a number of Drumree players to the club in 1975 further strengthened the team. So did the acquisition

Long Serving Officers, 1950s – 1980s

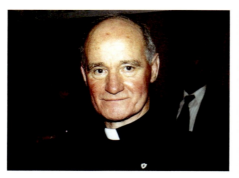

Fr. Eamonn O Brien, Chairman, 1958-69.

Tommy O Dwyer, Treasurer 1959-1982.

Patsy McLoughlin, Chairman or Vice Chairman in each decade, 1950-1980.

Davy O Dwyer, Junior Championship winning captain 1967 and Treasurer 1987-1990.

CHAPTER 7: IN SEVENTH HEAVEN, JUNIOR AND INTERMEDIATE TITLES, 1967 AND 1977

of Pat Farrell, formerly of Bellewstown, who came to live in Dunshaughlin in 1968 and began to play for the club in 1970 and Michael Wead who taught in Culmullen N.S for a couple of years. This combination presented formidable opposition in the intermediate grade from 1972 until 1977.

In 1972, captained by Pat Farrell, the team began with four victories on the trot before being shocked by near neighbours Ratoath. A draw with Bohermeen kept Dunshaughlin in the hunt but a comprehensive defeat at Summerhill's hands, 1-16 to 1-8 at Trim, finally put paid to all hopes of outright honours.

In 1973 Dunshaughlin reached the semi-final but not without a struggle. After victories against Drumree and Rathkenny the team fell to Moylough by two points. A draw, ten points each, with Enfield, meant the black and ambers had to face the same opponents the following week. Former Dunshaughlin clubman Finian Englishby was now an Enfield official but his erstwhile comrades did him no favours. Dunshaughlin had an easy 2-9 to 0-7 victory and then went on to beat Castletown 2-7 to 0-7 in the quarter-final.

Dunshaughlin, Intermediate Semi-Finalists, 1973

Front: Con O Dwyer, Noel Curran, Michael O Dwyer, Mossie Caffrey, Capt., Paddy O Dwyer, Ger Dowd, Brian Geraghty.
Back: Paddy Kenny, Val Dowd, Pat Jennings, Jody Madden, Michael Walsh, Pat Murphy, Derek Kenny, Pat Farrell.

BLACK & AMBER

> **"** In the second half 'dangerous tackling, petty retaliation and several stand up boxing matches substituted for the exhilarating football of earlier'

The semi-final resulted in victory for Bohermeen by the narrowest of margins 1-8 to 2-4 at Navan. Before half time Paddy Kenny had scored a great solo goal, splitting the Bohermeen defence wide open with a lightening burst through the centre before unleashing a chest-high shot which the Bohermeen keeper got his hands to but couldn't stop.

In the second half *'dangerous tackling, petty retaliation and several stand up boxing matches substituted for the exhilarating football of earlier'* according to *The Meath Chronicle*. The referee Dickser Dunne of Ardcath had arrived without umpires and two Kells men were drafted in to do the job. This had an unhappy outcome, for, when Paddy O Dwyer scored what seemed a legitimate goal in the second half the referee disallowed it after consulting 'his umpires'. Despite this setback Dunshaughlin continued to press and were rewarded with a goal from Brian Geraghty, which evened the scores once again. Before the end Bohermeen notched the winning point and Dunshaughlin then failed with a last minute free. Bohermeen later went on to take outright honours. The line-out for the 1973 semi-final was:

Pat Jennings; Con O Dwyer, Val Dowd, Jody Madden; Pat Farrell, Michael O Dwyer, Mossie Caffrey, Capt.; Michael Walsh (Mayo) (0-1), Pat Murphy; Derek Kenny, Paddy Kenny (1-0), Ger Dowd; Brian Geraghty (1-0), Noel Curran (0-1), Paddy O Dwyer (0-2). Subs: John Casey for Derek Kenny, Seán Mangan for Pat Farrell.

However, the promise of 1972 and 1973 was not fulfilled in 1974. The team suffered a shock defeat at the hands of St. Bridgets but nevertheless managed to qualify for the quarter-final. Opponents Rathkenny were somewhat lucky to come away with a draw in the first game, scoring 0-8 in reply to Dunshaughlin's 1-5. Joe Carberry scored the goal after Noel Curran, in brilliant form, had been fouled in the square. In the replay Joe wasn't so fortunate, his penalty hitting off the post midway through the second half. Dunshaughlin could only manage six points, as Rathkenny emerged victorious by two.

The One that Got Away

1975 is a year that many Dunshaughlin players and supporters would prefer to forget, for the title looked destined for the village when what seemed like certain victory suddenly transformed into bitter defeat.

The year had begun with a number of Drumree players transferring to Dunshaughlin as mentioned earlier. The possibility of the two parish clubs amalgamating was considered but not achieved. Drumree agreed to give transfers to those who wished to join Dunshaughlin and among those who availed of the opportunity were Paddy and Johnny Burke, Stephen Mahon, Neil O Riordan, Tommy Troy, Jimmy and Michael Walsh, Johnny Lynch and Seán Doyle. A number transferred back the following year but many remained to share the eventual victory of 1977.

Thus strengthened, Dunshaughlin seemed ideally placed to take the title in 1975. Indeed some clubs in the county were of the view that Dunshaughlin should have been regraded senior, such was the array of talent at their disposal.

The team lost only one of its games in the qualifying league when St. Vincents were easy 3-9 to 1-5 winners. St. Colmcilles were out of their depth in the quarter-final losing 4-12 to 0-5 but Castletown proved more of a problem in the semi-final. The north county combination had a fine first half and led by 0-6 to 0-3 at the break. The second half was a different story however. Pat Mooney of the Bush, Meath's centre back in the Leinster minor final defeat to Kildare in 1975, switched from the '40' to midfield and alongside Tommy Troy the pair dominated for the half. A goal by Ger Dowd, a dipping shot from forty yards that deceived the keeper, was the difference between the teams at the end, Dunshaughlin winning 1-7 to 0-7.

From Dunshaughlin's point of view the final against Moylough was a disaster. For forty-five minutes they dictated the trend of the game and led throughout this period. Faster to the ball and showing a greater appetite for the game the black and ambers led 0-8 to 0-2 at half time. John Jennings and Pat Mooney were well on top at midfield and Neil O Riordan at centre half back didn't give county man Pat Traynor an inch. A Jimmy Walsh point early in the second half stretched the lead but this proved to be Dunshaughlin's last score. The Moylough mentors then took action. Traynor was switched to the wing and the immensely strong Cooke came from full forward to the '40'. By this stage also the youthful midfield pairing of Pat Mooney and John Jennings was no longer dominant.

With ten minutes to go Dunshaughlin still led by seven points and seemed destined for victory even though now Moylough was the superior force. A point in the 20th minute was followed by two more. The introduction of a fresh man at midfield might have strengthened Dunshaughlin at this stage but the team still seemed in no great danger.

Suddenly it was too late. Moylough put together a three-man move that ended with a goal and left a solitary point between the teams. The northerners couldn't be stopped now and in a frantic finish a loose ball was hit towards the Dunshaughlin goals. Pat Jennings did well to parry, but it broke loose to Kevin Hanlon who shot to the net from close range. Dunshaughlin couldn't believe that the final whistle signaled their defeat. Moylough had, Lazarus–like, come back from the dead. For Paddy Clarke, Dunshaughlin's trainer, it capped an unfortunate

> With ten minutes to go Dunshaughlin led by seven points and seemed destined for victory

> *The concession of scores in the final quarter was becoming an ingrained habit and with half of the 1977 team over thirty very few tipped them as likely champions*

year as all three teams he trained lost their respective finals, Dunshaughlin the intermediate, Meath the minor football and Kilmessan the senior hurling. The Dunshaughlin team lined out: Pat Jennings; Michael Walsh, Val Dowd, Jody Madden; Michael Wead, Neil O Riordan, Michael O Dwyer, Capt.; Pat Mooney, John Jennings; Jimmy Walsh (0-5), Tony Kenny, Ger Dowd; Con O Dwyer (0-1), Noel Curran (0-3), Jimmy O Rourke. Subs: Paddy O Dwyer for O Rourke, Pat O Brien for Madden.

Despite this sickening set-back the team made the semi-final again in 1976. The game finished all square, Dunshaughlin 0-10 Castletown 2-4, and carried echoes of the previous year's final, for, with six minutes to go Dunshaughlin had a six-point lead. Kevin McConnell saved the day for Castletown with a 27th minute goal and the equalizing point in the last minute. The replay at Navan was a one sided encounter with Castletown winning 0-11 to 0-4. Dunshaughlin were level after twenty minutes but never led, and conceded three points in the last six minutes.

An Intermediate Title at Last

The games of 1975 and 1976 seemed to prove that this Dunshaughlin side, like its counterpart in the 1950s, didn't have that indefinable something so necessary for championship success. The concession of scores in the final quarter was becoming an ingrained habit and with half of the 1977 team over thirty very few tipped them as likely future champions.

A five points apiece draw with Summerhill's second team in the first round seemed to confirm this view. After the string of disappointments it was difficult to get the team to turn out. This was not surprising. In four years Dunshaughlin had lost a quarter-final, a semi-final and a final, and on three occasions had gone under to the eventual champions.

However, some important victories, albeit against poor opposition, gradually led to a build-up of team spirit and confidence once again. Three comprehensive victories in a row, over Ballinlough, Curraha and St. Vincents set up a meeting with the hitherto unbeaten Navan O Mahonys. Con O Dwyer was in fine fettle notching five points against the Navan combination as Dunshaughlin won 0-11 to 1-3 to confound many of the experts. After these easy victories Slane provided a rude awakening when only a late penalty goal from Jimmy Walsh saved an embarrassing defeat on a 1-7 to 0-8 scoreline.

In the final divisional game against Martinstown-Athboy the team suffered its only defeat 0-7 to 1-5. Martinstown had to win to remain in contention and their victory brought about a play-off between the same two teams on the following Sunday. This time it was Dunshaughlin that emerged victorious by a point, 2-4 to 1-6. Martinstown was the best team Dunshaughlin met during the campaign and

Dunshaughlin, Intermediate Champions, 1977

Front: Don McLoughlin, Paddy O Dwyer, Jimmy Walsh, Pat Jennings, Capt., Michael Walsh, Ger Dowd, Con O Dwyer.
Back: Seán Mangan, Noel Curran, Michael Wead, John Jennings, Val Dowd, Pat O Brien, Pat O Hare, Neil O Riordan.

had fine players in Mick Mellett, Eddie Mahon and Paddy Hanley, who missed the replay. Credit for the victory went to Pat O Hare, who despite an injured arm policed Mahon and denied him any score from play, and Val Dowd who played a stormer in the second half repulsing raid after raid, when Dunshaughlin looked in great danger. Jimmy Walsh scored the goals, one from a penalty.

For the replay with Martinstown and the remainder of the campaign Dunshaughlin had a new trainer-cum-coach in full back Val Dowd. Paddy Clarke, who had agreed to help out Dunshaughlin because of his association with Val as a county minor selector, was unable to attend the Martinstown game and didn't attend training on the following Tuesday either. He had expected Val to contact him, while Val thought Paddy would do the contacting. Thus, Val took over and team spirit was consolidated by short training sessions and open-ended discussion of the games over tea and sandwiches afterwards.

The more relaxed approach paid dividends. Donaghmore were strong favourites in the semi-final but Dunshaughlin had a commanding 3-6 to 0-10 victory. John Jennings and Pat O Brien gained the advantage at midfield over Pat McManus and inter-county minor Alan Tormey. With a good supply of possession the Dunshaughlin forwards gave the opposition the run around. Noel Curran and Con O Dwyer had goals in the first half and Con added another in the second to leave Dunshaughlin well ahead at the end.

Nobber, a team that had been playing Division 2 football in 1974 provided the final opposition. Despite the setbacks of the previous years, players and officials were confident of victory. The players were told to let the ball do the work, Ger Dowd being the only one who had licence to carry the ball, as this was his strength. To ensure that nothing interfered with preparations only officials and the team were allowed into the dressing room at half time.

Nobber's best player was Gerry McEntee and Dunshaughlin's plan was that Pat O Brien would draw him out towards the sideline on black and amber kick-outs, which would be directed away from McEntee. This worked for the first few kick outs but McEntee soon became wise to the ploy, stayed in the centre and O Brien realized he would have to outfetch his opponent. This he did to great effect and Dunshaughlin gained the upper hand around the middle.

In the event, Dunshaughlin proved much superior and won by 0-13 to 0-6. The full forward line in particular destroyed the opposition. The highlight of the game was Noel Curran's ability to pick off long-range points. Paddy O Dwyer in one corner scored two points, one of them a lovely forty yard shot, while brother Con in the other took his point as early as the fourth minute. Con's score was also a beautiful effort, kicked with the left foot from forty-five yards out on the right wing. *The Drogheda Independent* reported that *'the most adventurous*

Intermediate Final 1977

From top clockwise:
Panoramic view of the field on Intermediate Final day 1977. The Dunshaughlin players in the lighter jerseys, in positional order are Don McLoughlin, Val Dowd (3), Michael Walsh (4), Michael Wead (5, partially hidden), Sean Mangan (7), Pat O Hare running back towards the ball, Ger Dowd with hands on hips, Con O Dwyer in the distant right corner forward spot.

Pat Jennings holds the Intermediate Championship Trophy aloft.

Paddy O Dwyer soloes towards goal as Nobber's Shane McEntee, later a Meath East TD and Minister of State, moves in to tackle.

forward afield was the fleet footed Dunshaughlin No. 10 Ger Dowd.' It recalled two exhilarating runs from him

'one in the first half when, after gaining possession in his own half of the field, he careered towards the Nobber 21 yard line where he had his shot stopped by opposing goalie Pat Reilly. Then on one particular occasion he soloed about 70 yards down the field to set up Curran for a point.'

The report continued:

'one old stager who really made his experience tell was former Meath full forward, Noel Curran, who turned in a capital performance to shoot six points, a couple of these being really delightful efforts. Overall the Dunshaughlin attack did the team proud with the O Dwyer brothers, Con and Paddy, Jimmy Walsh and Neil O Riordan all using their experience to the best use. In the middle of the field, Pat O Brien turned in a good second half while the defence did very well all through. Veteran Val Dowd time and again caught the imagination of supporters with his catching and clearing. Behind him goal-keeper and captain Pat Jennings handled very confidently all through. Don McLoughlin, Pat O Hare and Seán Mangan were other defenders who were constantly to the fore.'

The defence in fact was rarely tested and at the end Pat Jennings accepted the Gaelic Weekly Cup on behalf of the club.

The victory was a relief after five years of frustration and defeat and represented the highest honour the club had attained in championship football. The selectors who shared in the triumph were Seamus Flynn, Paddy Lynam and Davy O Dwyer. Paddy had given over forty years service to the club so it was a fitting reward for his efforts. Joe Plunkett who was a selector for the previous eight years had stepped down for the 1977 campaign but he was on hand to see his work come to fruition. An unusual feature of the team was that the whole full forward line had played in the half forward line in Dunshaughlin's previous championship win, the junior title of 1967. The intermediate champions lined out as follows:

Pat Jennings, Capt.

| Don McLoughlin | Val Dowd | Michael Walsh |
| Michael Wead | Pat O Hare | Seán Mangan |

Pat O Brien   John Jennings

| Ger Dowd (0-1) | Neil O Riordan | Jimmy Walsh (0-3) |
| Con O Dwyer (0-1) | Noel Curran (0-6) | Paddy O Dwyer (0-2) |

Subs: Pat Farrell, Mossie Caffrey, Gerry Keane, Tony McConnell, Jimmy O Rourke, Tommy Reilly, John Forde.

Taking the Reins

Ger Dowd
Dunshaughlin star forward and Grand National Winning Jockey on Brown Lad in 1978.

Dunshaughlin GFC Committee, 1979
Front: Tommy O Dwyer, Seán Mangan, Val Dowd, Chairman.
Back: Tom Everard, Seamus Flynn, Patsy McLoughlin, Paddy O Dwyer, Mick O Keeffe.

On the team's arrival in Dunshaughlin with the cup, Oliver Mangan led the parade through the village on the accordion and a victory dance was held later in the County Club. Johnny McLoughlin, father of Don, used always tease Pat O Brien that he was no good, as his way of cajoling him to play better. After the victory over Nobber he said to Pat, 'Gasoon, I'm taking it all back. You were man of the match there today.' A week later the team played Duleek in a tournament, a week during which the only training was in the local public houses, and Pat had a less distinguished game. Afterwards Johnny approached him and declared, 'Gasoon, I'm taking it all back again!'

To cap a great year for the team it also won the Intermediate League, defeating Castletown by 2-9 to 2-5. This was a third consecutive league title, to go alongside victory in 1975 against Moylough and 1976 against Moynalty, underlining the fact that in this period Dunshaughlin had probably the best team in the intermediate grade.

The 1977 league victory was important in that it completed a double of league and championship and the victory was against a senior side. Early in the game Ger Dowd scored four points and Dunshaughlin led by 1-5 to 0-4 at the interval. By the tenth minute of the second half Castletown had drawn level and only a fine save by Pat Jennings prevented them taking the lead. *The Chronicle* reported this phase of the game as follows:

In repelling this Castletown pressure, Val Dowd was magnificent and grew in stature as the pressure increased. Inspired by his example and encouraged by Jennings' dramatic save, Dunshaughlin began to regain the initiative'.

A point from Jimmy Walsh and a Con O Dwyer goal put Dunshaughlin in a commanding position and they maintained the lead to the end. The team lined out as follows:

Pat Jennings; Jimmy O Rourke, Val Dowd, Michael Walsh; Michael Wead, Pat O Hare, Don McLoughlin; Pat O Brien, John Jennings; Jimmy Walsh (0-3), Gerry Keane, Ger Dowd (0-4); Con O Dwyer (1-0), Noel Curran (0-1), Paddy O Dwyer (1-1). Subs: Pat Farrell for Keane.

Victory in the championship brought to an end a successful ten years that had seen the field and clubhouse officially opened, a junior title claimed and now an intermediate win that entailed automatic promotion to the senior championship from 1978. How would the black and ambers fare among the big senior beasts? Chapter 10 will cover the outcome.

Ode to Seventy Seven

Twenty years after the championship victory Pat O Brien penned these lines in praise of the 1977 team.

Now, take me back to that great day
When we raised that silver chalice
Why on Nobber's fine we surely did dine
Without any fear or malice.
Proudly I stood in the centre that day
With John Jennings from Rathill
Twenty years can't dim the memories
When we left the two Macs cold and still.
The Jennings contribution
Was greater than at first it might seem
'Cos John's twin brother Pat
Was the Captain of our team.
The stories that could be told
About the Don at number two
'You'll not get past here you bas ___d
If you know what's good for you.'
The trainer of the team that year
Val, you now can take a bow
For a man's got to do what a man's got to do
Even if that means the odd row.
Many organizations then
Had a priest right at the core
Yes, we had our own that day
The Curate was at number 4.
That hardy annual at No. 5
Was a chap called Michael Wead
And often when in victory
It was he who sowed the seed.
Pat O Hare from Little Lagore
Has to be rated as one of our best
Any many's a forward's confirmation
Received the sternest test.
Tenacious through and through
And a man with plenty of pace
These are some of the reasons
Why Seán Mangan held down his place.
Did you know that Ger Dowd that day
Was the baby of our team?
Let it be Fairyhouse or Tailteann Park
He usually ruled supreme.
Neil O Riordan played the game with passion
He also played it with grace
He had style, he had speed, he had everything
Many's a footballer, his boot couldn't lace.
What can be said about the Dosser
That hasn't been said before
Whether footballer or hurler
He was a sportsman to the core.
From wedded bliss to come back to this
Con O Dwyer took it all in his stride
There was something very unusual that day
I don't think he kicked ere a wide.
When we speak of our team mate Noel Curran
Dunshaughlin's favourite son
It was because of his sheer class
That many of our games were won.
Football is a funny old game
And you need all your cylinders to fire
Free taking is a great art
He had it, Paddy O Dwyer.
To win the Gaelic Weekly Cup
It takes a very special team
But we had Tommy Troy and Pat Farrell
And from Mooretown, of course, Gerry Keane.
Mossie Caffrey and Jimmy O Rourke
They were both on the bench that day
John Forde, Tommy Reilly and Tony Mc
Ready and willing to join the fray.
Séamus Flynn is all that's left
From the selectors of '77
Davy and Paddy are gone now
To the dugout up in heaven.
The welcoming home party
Had every Dunshaughlin woman and man
With Oliver Mangan on accordion
Playing 'Kelly the Boy from Killane.'

Pat O Brien

BLACK & AMBER

St. Martins' Revival, 1983-1998

The organization of juvenile and minor football in the 1970s and 1980s was informal and the lack of a club to cater for young players in the parish militated against success at juvenile and minor level.

In early 1983 a meeting was held in Dunshaughlin Community College to overhaul the ineffective under age structures in the parish. Urgent action was needed.

The organization of juvenile and minor football in the 1970s and 1980s was informal and the lack of a club to cater for young players in the parish militated against success at juvenile and minor level. Neither adult club had responsibility for under age games. Instead, each year interested adults from the Drumree and Dunshaughlin clubs met to appoint selectors, and teams went under the name of Culmullen or Dunshaughlin in alternate years. With dedicated selectors teams might prosper, with uncommitted ones failure was certain. Preparation and coaching was at best haphazard, at worst non-existent. As there was no proper club structure there was neither back-up nor follow-up for mentors, and there was no accountability at an AGM.

The wider community was beginning to change. As the Irish economy grew, the town of Dunshaughlin finally cast aside its nineteenth century structure. New housing estates crept and then sprawled onto the green fields edging the main street. The population, static for a century, climbed upwards. Less than 300 in 1971, it rose to almost 500 in 1979, shot up to 884 by 1986 and rocketed to 1,275 in 1991.

> **"** With dedicated selectors teams might prosper, with uncommitted ones failure was certain. Preparation and coaching was at best haphazard, at worst non-existent.

BLACK & AMBER

Dunshaughlin, Under 13 Community Games Champions, 1983

Front: Declan Troy, Morty O Sullivan, Piaras O Connor, Dermot Kealy, Capt., Thomas Walsh, Brendan Kealy, Liam Holton.
Back: Ciarán O Connor, Karl Stoney, John Boyle, Stephen Lane, John Bacon, Paul Molloy, Garbhán Blake, Simon Conlon.

This represented a trebling of numbers in twenty years. The increase was replicated in Dunshaughlin National School where an enrolment of around 100 in the sixties tripled by 1980.

Now the GAA had the numbers, but needed modern administrative and coaching structures to harvest the benefits.

Changes were underway in the schools also. Until the late 1970s there was very little organized competitive football in the primary schools of Meath. There were occasional games at local sports' days or challenge games arranged by interested teachers. Local teams played during the annual Pony Races or at Macra na Feirme Field Days to boost attendances, while Dunshaughlin NS often competed against

CHAPTER 8: ST. MARTIN'S REVIVAL, 1983-1998

Rathbeggan NS. for the Tom O Brien Memorial Cup. With the arrival in the late 1970s of new teachers, Jim Gilligan in Dunshaughlin and Jimmy McGeogh in Rathbeggan, these games became more common. In 1980 those teachers organized a competition for the Instant Signs Cup including Dunshaughlin, Rathbeggan, Kilmessan, Ratoath and Summerhill.

At the same time moves were afoot to create a county-wide structure and by 1981 a Meath Primary Schools' Board, Cumann na mBunscol, was in operation, with Pat O Neill as its first Chairman. That year Dunshaughlin NS won the Cumann na mBunscol, Division 2 Championship for medium sized schools with Simon Farrell captaining the team. George Knightly entered Culmullen NS in the competitions, and the school made final appearances in 1984 and 1985, winning the latter. Practically all the players on those teams were from Dunshaughlin parish.

At post primary level Dunshaughlin Community College replaced Dunshaughlin Vocational School in 1973. There had been a long tradition of games there, but many of the students came from outside the parish and the promotion of Gaelic games in the college benefitted numerous clubs in south Meath. The Community College Principal, John Holland, who had played with Dunshaughlin in the 1960s, always promoted sport and the arrival of new teachers in the 1970s such as Vincent Lane, Pat Kenny, Mick O Keefe, Oliver Coogan and Tom Keegan gave Gaelic games a new impetus.

Underage Before St. Martins

Prior to the formation of St. Martins there were signs that the material for success existed, if it was carefully nurtured. In 1981 an Under 12 side, registered as Culmullen, made it to the championship final. The side played in the green jerseys of Dunshaughlin NS and Jim Gilligan, Dickie O Brien, and Tony Rattigan trained and selected the team. In compiling home and away victories against Moynalvey, Ratoath and Skryne no team came any nearer than seven points to the boys in green.

In the knock out stages similar victory margins were the norm until the final. Moynalty were quarter-final opponents and two slightly lucky goals early in the game gave Culmullen a lead they never relinquished, winning 3-9 to 2-5. Brian Duffy dominated midfield in a 3-5 to 0-3 semi-final victory over St. Colmcilles.

It was known however that final opponents Slane were in a class of their own. So it proved, as the Boynesiders won easily by 2-12 to 0-1, John O'Brien (Rathhill) scoring the solitary point. During the campaign Culmullen had some tremendous performers, none better than Pat Kealy on the '40'. He took some beautiful scores, never knew when he was beaten and could be relied on for an

BLACK & AMBER

individual effort when it was most needed. He got great support from Paul O Rourke and Michael Walsh, who began as a substitute but ended the year as one of the team's best forwards. Brian Duffy was an important cog in the machine, being the only one on the team with the size and strength so necessary for success at juvenile level. Dermot Kealy, then only 10 years of age, was never beaten at full back and got great cover from his corner men David Kane and Alan Doyle. John Davis, Simon Farrell and Niall Foley formed a solid half back line. Allen Foley suffered from an injury throughout which forced him to play in goals when he was required outfield. Shane Mahon who later developed into an excellent defender manned the full forward slot. This was the first Under-12 side from the parish to reach a final and the line out was:

Allen Foley (Capt.); David Kane, Dermot Kealy, Alan Doyle; John Davis, Simon Farrell, Niall Foley; John O Brien, Brian Duffy; Paul O Rourke, Pat Kealy, Michael Walsh; Vincent Moore, Shane Mahon, Ephrem Caffrey. Subs: Adrian Faherty, Richard Forde, Derek Jones, Derek Melia, Paul Molloy, Philip McCarthy, Alan O Dwyer, Karl Stoney, Morty O Sullivan, Colm Naughton.

Front: Declan Troy, Brendan Kealy, Philip Burke, Ciarán O Dwyer, John Boyle, Willie Brennan, Garbhán Blake, Martin Lynch, David O Neill.
Back: Colm Naughton partly hidden, Thomas Walsh, David Morgan, Liam Holton, Trevor Doyle, Andrew Tierney, Alan Boyle, John Bacon, Fiachra Page, Liam O Neill, Paul Molloy.

St. Martins, Under 12 Semi-Finalists, 1983

CHAPTER 8: ST. MARTIN'S REVIVAL, 1983-1998

This limited success was followed by the incredible decision that Drumree and Dunshaughlin would field separate teams at Under 12 in 1982. Such a policy was a recipe for disaster and a different template was urgently required if the under age potential was to be realized.

The star performers in 1983 were the boys on the Community Games Under 13 team. Anthony Gogan was the Community Games' organizer in Dunshaughlin while Pat Farrell and Jim Gilligan trained and selected the team. Though less competitive than the county championships, as fewer teams entered, the Community Games provided some thrilling matches and top class football. Against Skryne, they seemed to have the game wrapped up half way through the second half but were lucky in the end to equalize with a last minute free from Dermot Kealy. In the replay the boot was on the other foot for Skryne built up a good lead but were eventually over-hauled 3-8 to 3-4.

Duleek provided the semi-final opposition and defensive lapses almost lost the game but the black and ambers piled on the points in the second half to win 0-13 to 2-3. Kilcloon proved no problem in the final and were well beaten at the end, 5-13 to 3-3. The side exited to Newbridge in the first round of the Leinster competition. The line out v. Kilcloon was:

Stephen Lane

John Bacon   Simon Conlon   Ciarán O Connor

Garbhán Blake   Karl Stoney   Piaras O Connor

Liam Holton   Dermot Kealy, Capt.

Morty O Sullivan   John Boyle   Brendan Kealy

Paul Molloy   Thomas Walsh   Declan Troy

Subs. Neil McCarrick for Paul Molloy, Colm Naughton for Ciarán O Connor, Trevor Doyle, David Forde, Liam O Neill.

Potential was also evident in the Under 16 teams that reached the semi-final stages in 1980 and 1982 and the quarter-finals in 1981. Most of the players on those teams were part on the successful Under 14 team of 1979 detailed in Chapter 6. St. Colmcilles proved too good in the 1980 semi-final winning 3-10 to 0-9 with Aidan Walsh scoring seven of the nine points. In 1982 Dunshaughlin deservedly eliminated Slane, the U-14 champions of 1980 and strong favourites for the title, in the quarter-final. Bohermeen, however, proved too strong in the semi-final, particularly in the centre of the field where the absence of Val McMahon due to injury was sorely felt.

St. Martins, Under 12 Blitz, 1988

Front: John Cullinane, Ronan Curley, Aaron Fitzpatrick, Wayne Cottrell, Derek Doyle, Clive Dowd, Trevor Murphy, Graham Dowd.
Back: Caoimhín Blake, Micheal James O Rourke.

In 1982 the young footballers of the parish further underlined their ability by reaching the final of the U-15 seven-a-side Óg Sport blitz. This was an annual competition with the county champions qualifying for the All-Ireland finals in Gormanston. Final opponents were Carnaross, county U-14 champions of the previous year, powered by P.J. Gillic. Dunshaughlin on the other hand had no less than six of the eleven panel members under 14. Brian Duffy was switched from goals to the forwards for the final and the switch worked perfectly as he scored three goals in the first half dumbfounding the opposition with a combination of soccer and gaelic skills. Carnaross finally overcame a tiring Dunshaughlin team and emerged victors by 6-8 to 5-5. The panel of players that did duty was Kevin Kealy, Capt., Dermot Carey, Alan Cummins, Michael Duffy, Simon Farrell, Trevor Kane, Pat Kealy, Vincent O Brien, Brendan O Rourke and David Summerville.

The minors showed only limited promise. In the 1979-82 period minors from the parish fielded as a single team on one occasion but also linked up with Skryne in 1981 -playing only two games- and Moynalvey in 1982. There was an urgent need for a consistent policy on amalgamating with other clubs or adopting a go-it-alone policy.

St. Martins Reformed

It was against this background of informal structures and some signs of success that the 1983 meeting in the Community College took place. No record of the attendance exists but the twenty or so present included Val Dowd, Michael Walsh, Lena Doyle, Dickie O Brien, Joe Rattigan, Jim Gilligan and Patsy McLoughlin. The outcome was the revival of St. Martins. Val Dowd was elected as Chairman with Lena Doyle as Secretary. No Treasurer was appointed but Joe Rattigan took up the position in 1984 and Maura O Dwyer then gave nine years service until 1994. Tadhg Ó Dúshláine replaced Lena as Secretary in 1984 followed by Jim Gilligan from 1985 to 1988. Val served in the chair for five years and was succeeded by Pat Kelly who also put in a five-year stint. These appointments gave a sense of stability and continuity to the fldgling club.

St. Martins, Under 14 Division 2, FL Champions, 1987

Front: Paul Baker, Patrick Doyle, Evan Kelly, Richie Kealy, Ciarán O Dwyer, David O Neill, Barry Walsh, David Troy, Emmet Downes, Dermot Doyle.
Back: Kenny McTigue, Robbie McCarthy, James Walsh, Michael Keane, Willie Brennan, Hugh McCarthy, Alan Boyle, David Murray, Gary Baker, Aiden Kealy, David Faughnan, Seamus Flynn.

Presentation to Hugh Daly, St. Martins' Under 14 team trainer, by David O Neill.
Pictured from left: Brian O Rourke, Dermot Doyle, Ollie O Neill, selector, James Walsh, Alan Boyle, David O Neill, Gary Baker-hidden, Hugh McCarthy, Peter Rattigan, Hugh Daly, Willie Brennan, Emmet Downes, David Murray, Evan Kelly, Pat Kelly, selector, Barry Walsh, Paul Baker, Richie Kealy, David Troy, Robbie McCarthy.

David O Neill with Under 14 Trophy
Under 14 Captain, David O Neill, speaks after receiving the trophy. In the background are Benny Downes, girl not identified and Robbie McCarthy.

BLACK & AMBER

St. Martins, Under 14 Division 4 FL Champions, 1989

Front: Ian McTigue, Garreth Kelly, Clive Dowd, Michael James O Rourke, James Walsh, Capt., Keith Wickham, Dermot Doyle, Wayne Cottrell, Aaron Fitzpatrick.
Back: Kenny McTigue, Cathal O Connor, Brian Murray, Simon Duffy, David Power, Noel Burke, Paul Baker, Darragh Cannon, Mick Summerville,
Richie Kealy, David Troy.

> The meeting unanimously agreed that the club colours would be a combination of the red of Drumree and the black of Dunshaughlin.

GAA colours are always significant and often a source of contention. St. Martins in the 1950s wore red, echoing the Pelletstown Reds of the 1920s. The victorious Culmullen Under 14s in 1979 wore black and amber hoops but the 1981 Under 12s wore the green and white of Dunshaughlin NS. There was a lengthy discussion on club colours with various Drumree and Dunshaughlin combinations being suggested. Joe Rattigan shot down a suggested blend of Dunshaughlin's yellow and Drumree's white with the remark, 'There's no white (meaning surrender) in Drumree.' The meeting unanimously agreed that the club colours would be a combination of the red of Drumree and the black of Dunshaughlin. However, it wasn't until 1986 that sets of jerseys in St. Martins' colours were bought. The Drumree and Dunshaughlin clubs contributed £100 each for a set for Under 16 upwards while Dunshaughlin NS donated a set for Under 12 and Under 14 that the school won in a GAA competition.

St. Martins, Under 14 Football Championship Finalists, 1991

Front: John Cullinane, Graham Dowd, Garreth Kelly, Capt., Pádraic O Dwyer, Paul Doyle, Damien Fitzpatrick, Denis Kealy. Back: Ronan Power, Gordon O Rourke, Derek Doyle, Damien Spillane, Ronan Keating, Fionnán Blake, Ulick McDonnell, Shane Kelly.

After the first year in existence the club raised its own funds, with an annual eight-week draw the main source of finance. Table quizzes, tea parties and card games were also sources of funds. Scarce money was conserved by other economies. Players packed into mentors' cars for trips to away games, with buses used only when essential, while parents such as Cecilia Dowd, Kathleen Walsh, Patty Farrell, Ead Kealy, Mary Kelly, Maura O Neill and Róisín Blake washed the club jerseys.

St. Martins in the Eighties

At juvenile level the new club was soon celebrating success. In the five years, 1987-1991, the Under 14s won two leagues and finished as runners-up in another two. The first title came with the Under 14 Division 2 FL of 1987. Pat Kelly, Hugh Daly and Ollie O Neill selected and managed the side as it went on a successful league run of eleven games before defeating Kilmainhamwood by 1-8 to 0-1 in a play-off.

Despite an earlier loss to the same side St. Martins made a superb start, held the 'Wood scoreless in the first half and were 1-6 to 0-0 ahead before conceding the first score. David O Neill and Ciarán O Dwyer dominated midfield and provided plenty of opportunities for the attack with Emmet Downes grabbing the only goal before half-time. The 'Wood responded strongly in the second half but brilliant goalkeeping by Alan Boyle confined them to a solitary point.

The same squad had a good run in the championship, winning three games to reach the semi-final where they succumbed to Division 1 opponents Seneschalstown. The team featured two boys who would turn into All-Ireland senior winners, one an All Star and the other Meath Footballer of the Year. The former was Evan Kelly, the latter Richie Kealy, who lined out beside each other in the half-forward line. The line out for the final league game against Kilmainhamwood was:

Alan Boyle

Hugh McCarthy   Patrick Doyle   Dermot Doyle

Aiden Kealy   Gary Baker   Robert McCarthy

David O Neill, Capt. (0-1)   Ciarán O Dwyer (0-2)

Richie Kealy (0-1)   Evan Kelly (0-2)   Barry Walsh (0-1)

David Faughnan   Willie Brennan   Emmet Downes (1-0)

Subs: David Murray (0-1) for Patrick Doyle, Tiernan O Rourke, Kenny McTigue, David Troy, Seamus Flynn, Paul Baker, James Walsh, Michael Keane, Ronan O Dwyer, Noel Burke, Brian O Rourke, Jonathon O Connor, Peter Rattigan.

The following year's side went close to repeating the success of the '87 team. After leading at the interval by three points, St. Martins had their advantage reduced to a single point before a late breakaway goal gave Slane a two points victory in the final, 1-6 to 0-7.

A year later another success was registered. Though named Under 14 Division 4, it was in reality the second grade of the league, as teams were graded geographically to minimize travel. The team went through the league stages with just one loss, to St. Colmcilles. The victors soon became the vanquished as St. Martins reversed the result in the semi-final by 3-12 to 5-3. The final pitted St. Martins against Walterstown. Two years previously the team contested the Under 12 semi-final but the players continued to improve and ousted the Blacks by 1-7 to 0-5. Val Dowd, Jimmy Walsh and Paul Rattigan coached and selected the side which lined out in the final as follows:

CHAPTER 8: ST. MARTIN'S REVIVAL, 1983-1998

Noel Burke
Simon Duffy   Dermot Doyle   Kenny McTigue
David Power   David Troy   Aaron Fitzpatrick
        Paul Baker   Brian Murray
Richie Kealy   James Walsh, Capt.   Cathal O Connor
Clive Dowd   Darragh Cannon   Mick Summerville

Subs: Michael James O Rourke for Summerville, Keith Wickham, Garreth Kelly, Wayne Cottrell, Ian McTigue.

> Ronan Keating, who would go on to greater fame as the lead singer with *Boyzone*, lined out at midfield for St. Martins

Two years later, in 1991, the Under 14s again enhanced the reputation of the club by reaching both the league and championship finals. St. Martins operated out of Division 2 of the league but despite beating Skryne to reach the final, Yellow Furze (Seneschalstown) had too much artillery in the decider, winning by five points, 3-12 to 3-7.

The championship operated on an open draw format with all Division 1 and 2 teams included. St. Martins did well to progress to the final but any hopes of compensation for the defeat in the league looked slim as an exceptionally strong Oldcastle side lay in wait. Midfielder and team captain Garreth Kelly was just out of hospital after an accident but he took his place at centre field.

The Saints limited the north county side to five first half points but Oldcastle dominated the second half to win with ease, 2-18 to 0-1. Gordon O Rourke scored the solitary point and the winners amassed 2-13 after half time. Ronan Keating, who would go on to greater fame as the lead singer with *Boyzone*, lined out at midfield for St. Martins and had his well-struck penalty effort, awarded following a foul on Denis Kealy, equally well saved. His colleague Damien Fitzpatrick was described by the *Chronicle* as one of the best players on the field who performed heroically and whose skill and artistry was a joy to watch.

Despite the defeats the team fulfilled one of the main functions of a juvenile club, the preparation and development of adult players. Three of the team, Denis Kealy, Graham Dowd and Pádraic O Dwyer went on to help Dunshaughlin to an intermediate title in 1997 while the first two along with Shane Kelly and Fearghal Gogan played central roles in Dunshaughlin's three in a row of senior championships from 2000 to 2002. John Cullinane, a Drumree player as an adult, progressed to win Leinster senior, junior and Under-21 medals.

The championship team with Michael Boyle, Paddy O Dwyer, Tony Rattigan and Seán Spillane as selectors lined out as follows:
Damien Spillane; Ronan Power, Ulick McDonnell, Paul Doyle; John Cullinane, Fionnán Blake, Shane Kelly; Ronan Keating, Garreth Kelly, Capt.; Denis Kealy, Graham Dowd, Damien Fitzpatrick; Pádraic O'Dwyer, Gordon O Rourke (0-

St. Martins, Under 16 County Finalists, 1985

Front: Liam Holton, Brendan Kealy, Morty O Sullivan, John Bacon, Liam O Neill, Michael Walsh, Piaras O Connor, Shane Mahon, Paul O Rourke, David Kane, Vinny Moore, Pat Kealy.
Back: John Boyle, Derek Melia, Niall Foley, Simon Farrell, Brian Duffy, John Davis, Colm Naughton, Karl Stoney, Dermot Kealy, Allen Foley.

> 'It's very quiet around here mister, there's no helicopters or shooting.'

1), Derek Doyle. Subs: Dessie Keane for O Dwyer, Fearghal Gogan for Power, Brendan Killoran, Dominic Jones, Niall Kelly, Neil O Dwyer, Colm O Dwyer, Joseph Smith, Pádraig Herlihy, Niall O Connor, Andrew Neary, John Delany.

In 1991 and 1992 Meath hosted the All-Ireland Football Féile, a festival of football with the champion teams at Under 14 from each county and all the underage clubs in Meath competing over a weekend. The St. Martins' panel in 1991 was the same as that for the Under 14 final against Oldcastle while the 1992 panel comprised Damien Fitzpatrick, Capt., Damien Spillane, Niall O Connor, Paul Doyle, Brendan Killoran, Denis Kealy, David Crimmins, Ronan Power, Shane Kelly, Fearghal Gogan, Dominic Jones, Graham Dowd, David Tonge, Pádraic O Dwyer, Niall Kelly, Neil O Dwyer, Ronan Gogan, Pádraig McHale, Stephen Morgan and Rory O Sullivan. In 1991 St. Martins hosted Monaghan Harps with Mullaghbawn of Armagh the visitors the following year.

In addition to the games there were skill competitions, a massive Féile parade in Navan and social events for the players, mentors and host families. The reality of the conflict in Northern Ireland was apparent in the comment of one of the Mullaghbawn youngsters when Pat Kelly was transporting him to a family in rural Drumree, 'It's very quiet around here mister, there's no helicopters or shooting.'

St. Martins-Ratoath, Minor Football Champions, 1987

Front: Ciarán Byrne, Stephen Claire, Allen Foley, Capt., Brian Rooney, John Davis, Paul O Rourke, Dermot White.
Back: Dermot Kealy, Pat Kealy, Liam Eiffe, Derek Melia, Simon Farrell, Larry McMahon, Terry Rooney, Niall Foley, Derek Maher.

A Major Minor Force in the Eighties

From the time the minor championship began Dunshaughlin teams made occasional dents in the competition but could never manage a major impact.

At the time St. Martins was re-established in 1983 no team from the parish had ever won a minor title. (Salesian College, now Warrenstown College, based in the parish won the title in 1943 fielding players from various parts of the country who were students at the college). There had been only two final appearances by teams from the parish, in 1947 against Julianstown and 1972 versus Trim. From 1984 a consistent policy was pursued, as St. Martins combined with Ratoath and it was agreed to use the name Ratoath-St. Martins and St. Martins-Ratoath in alternate years. The selection committee consisted of two selectors from each club. From 1985 Jim Gilligan and Pat Farrell represented St. Martins with David Donoghue and Michael 'Skipper' Lynch from Ratoath. Dermot Rooney replaced Lynch in 1987.

Allen Foley and the Delaney Cup

1987 Presentation to Allen Foley by Pat O Neill, Chairman, Meath Minor Board. To the left of Allen Foley are, Oliver Gogan, Colin Foley, Fintan Ginnitty, County Board Chairman. To the right of Foley at rear, Jim Gilligan; in centre Ciarán Galvin, Denis Kealy and Ultan Fitzpatrick, Minor Board Secretary; foreground, Garreth Kelly.

CHAPTER 8: ST. MARTIN'S REVIVAL, 1983-1998

Before the 1987 minor campaign began St. Martins had another unsuccessful final day encounter with Slane, in the Under 16 championship of 1985. Though neither the game nor the result was as one-sided as the 1981 Under 12 meeting involving the same teams, the outcome was similar.

The Saints couldn't match Slane as Gerry Martyn controlled midfield and the constant pressure led to the concession of 1-4 without reply by the twentieth minute. A mini revival featuring two Michael Walsh points seemed to promise better to come but the losers could only add two more before the end. Michael Walsh scoring one and Pat Kealy the other as Slane went on to win 1-10 to 0-4 to add the Under 16 title to their Under 12 and Under 14 crowns. The following year they took the Under 17 league also- a clean sweep.

Thus, Slane held the red-hot favourites tag for minor honours in 1987 and the loss of Brian Duffy, one of St. Martins' best and most physically imposing players, following a car accident, made the path ahead more difficult.

The St. Martins' team was a good one, as Under 12 and Under 16 final appearances proved, but it had neither the strength in depth nor the physicality to match Slane. Amalgamation with Ratoath was the ideal solution, as all the Ratoath players were students at Dunshaughlin Community College and so were accustomed to playing alongside the St. Martins' boys.

Jim Gilligan recalls the outcome,

'From the beginning the combination worked well. We lost at quarter-final stage to Gaeil Colmcille by two points in 1986. That game started late, as due to my commitments as Minor Board Secretary, I didn't get to the grounds until the last minute with two players in tow. After that I decided it was either the Minor Board or the Minor Championship, so I stepped down as Secretary to concentrate on training the St. Martins' minor team.'

The team emerged from the group stages without difficulty, defeating Duleek, Wolfe Tones-St. Michaels, Gaeil Colmcille, Killough Gaels and St. Cuthberts before overcoming De La Salle, Navan in the quarter-finals. St. Cuthberts represented the last hurdle before a final encounter with Slane. With Dermot White in top form and scoring 0-3 from midfield and Simon Farrell adding 0-4, St. Martins recorded a convincing 1-14 to 2-5 victory in the semi.

The final in Walterstown was probably the lowest scoring minor final of all time. St. Martins-Ratoath fielded without influential midfielder and vice-captain Brian Rooney so regular full-back Liam Eiffe moved to the middle. Four of the Slane players were members of the Meath minor team eliminated in the first round by Laois, Gerry and Paddy Martyn, Gareth Downey and Colm Gough, while Fergus Gough was a substitute. St. Martins-Ratoath hadn't a single representative on the county panel.

Ratoath-St. Martins, Minor Football Championship Finalists, 1989

Front: Brendan Kealy, Pearse Fahy, Declan Troy, Garbhán Blake, Capt., Dónal Coyne, Terry Rooney, Robert McGuinness, Peter McCabe.
Back: Barry Donnelly, Robert Ennis, Liam Holton, Shane O Neill, John Boyle, Colm Naughton, Ciarán Byrne.

St. Martins had suffered too many hammerings from Slane to allow an open game; the team had to curb the influence of Gerry Martyn at midfield, prevent the Slane forwards from creating and taking scores and avail of any opportunities for scores. The plan worked to perfection and unbelievably only one point came from play, a Stephen Claire effort in the 55th minute. Referee Joe Harlin awarded Slane a last minute free, which he then moved closer to goal for dissent, but the effort went wide and St. Martins brought the first ever Minor title to the parish.

The *Chronicle* reported that the victory was carved out of tight marking, strong tackling and great commitment, which unsettled Slane. The St. Martins-Ratoath *'rearguard was particularly effective in the second half when they harried and hassled the losers' forwards and limited them to just a single point from a free.'* In the half back line Dermot Kealy was *'a tower of strength'*, Allen Foley *'quite magnificent'* while John Davis went through *'lots of effective work.'* Keeper Derek Melia was *'most impressive and brought off a magnificent save'* just before half time.

Slane led by 0-3 to 0-2 at the interval but the closeness of the score gave the players the belief that this was a game St. Martins could win. It was a new experience for Slane, as all previous clashes with them were as good as over by half time.

After the break Simon Farrell drew the sides level, Gerry Martyn scored Slane's only point of the half before Dermot Kealy equalized again. The intensity of the exchanges increased as both sides vied for victory with Stephen Claire's late point nudging St. Martins-Ratoath ahead. Despite the last minute drama the Saints held on to emerge victors by 0-5 to 0-4.

This was an overdue reward for a dedicated group of players. As the *Drogheda Independent* declared, '*Had Slane drawn or even won this match it would have been a rough injustice to St. Martins-Ratoath who fought with great determination and will to win for the entire match.*' Slane hadn't anticipated such an outcome as the team was aiming to complete a clean sweep of all titles from Under 12 to minor. The first ever title-winning team lined out as follows:

Derek Melia

Niall Foley   Derek Maher   Terry Rooney

John Davis   Dermot Kealy (0-3)   Allen Foley, Capt.

Dermot White   Liam Eiffe

Simon Farrell (0-1)   Stephen Claire (0-1)   Ciarán Byrne

Paul O Rourke   Larry McMahon   Pat Kealy

Subs: Brian Rooney for McMahon, Brendan Kealy for O Rourke, Michael Walsh, Karl Stoney, Philip Dolan, Pádraig Galvin. The following played in earlier rounds Alan Fahy, Dessie Donnelly, Vincent Moore, David Kane, Philip Dolan, Kevin Moroney.

The following year Duleek eliminated St. Martins 1-8 to 0-6 at the semi-final stage but in 1989 the team progressed to another Delaney Cup Final where Duleek awaited. The side's selectors were Ollie O Neill and John Holton from St. Martins with David Donoghue and Dermot Rooney continuing to represent Ratoath. The team had an abundance of natural ability but lacked the determination and commitment to training of the 1987 side. Ciarán Byrne, Terry Rooney and Brendan Kealy remained from the '87 champions and few sides could match Barry Donnelly and Colm Naughton at midfield. With players of the calibre of Garbhán Blake, Dónal Coyne, Pearse Fahy, Declan Troy and John Boyle also featuring, the side had every prospect of capturing the title.

The final turned into a three game saga, the first having to be abandoned due to the sudden, tragic collapse in the stand of the father of one of the Duleek players. At the time Duleek held a 0-6 to 0-4 lead. St. Martins were unlucky not to win the re-fixture, with Duleek's equalizing point coming from a free, awarded for an alleged pick-up in the final minute. St. Martins had recovered from a poor start, conceding two goals early on, but with Colm Naughton and Barry Donnelly in powerful form at midfield they forged ahead in the closing stages before Nigel McQuaile knocked over Duleek's equalizer.

BLACK & AMBER

In the final bout St. Martins had to give way on a 2-6 to 1-6 scoreline. Once again a shaky start left them with work to do, attempting to turn round a 2-4 to 0-4 deficit in the final twenty-five minutes. Despite the absence of David Moroney, with a collar-bone injury sustained in the second game, the team was almost up to the task, taking control in all sectors and gradually reducing the deficit. Declan Troy grabbed a Pearse Fahy free and netted to leave just a goal between the sides. In the closing stages Brendan Kealy blasted for goal only to see the ball go narrowly wide to end the chance of extra-time. Garbhán Blake was the unlucky captain of a side that left the title behind. The team for the replay was:

Robert Ennis; Ciarán Byrne, Garbhán Blake, Capt., Peter McCabe; Liam Holton, Terry Rooney (0-1), Dónal Coyne; Colm Naughton (0-2), Barry Donnelly (0-2); Pearse Fahy, Brendan Kealy, Declan Troy (1-1); Robert McGuinness, Shane O Neill, John Boyle. Substitutes: John Dollard for Boyle, Liam O Neill for Shane O Neill, Ivor Reilly for McGuinness, David Moroney, Alan Boyle, Evan Kelly, Tiernan O Rourke, Thomas Walsh, Paul Molloy, Martin Lynch.

St. Martins, Under 12, Division 2 Winners, 1995

Front: Bryan Duffy, Seamus Wallace, Alan Kenny, Seán White, David O Neill, John Brennan, Ray Maloney, Capt., Mark Devanney, Stephen Ward, JJ McCarthy, Liam Shanley, Caoimhín King.
Back: Pat Maloney, Selector, Paul Faherty, Joe McHale, John Crimmins, Ciarán Murray, Colm Finlay, John Murphy, Ronan Gilsenan, Stephen Burke, Seán Hayes, Gavin O Regan, Paddy Ward, Selector.
At rear, Macartan McGroder, Coach/Selector.

Gains and Losses: Progression of the 1992 and 1995 Under 12 Teams

Following the 1981 Under-12 defeat at the hands of Slane, a decade elapsed before a team from the parish reached another Under 12 final. In the intervening years teams were always fielded, with the 1984 side reaching the quarter-finals and the 1987 crew losing out at semi-final stage to ultimate winners Seneschalstown. Eventually, success at the Under 12 grade arrived in 1992 and 1995, albeit the former was a league rather than a championship success while the latter was not in the top grade.

1995 Team

The success of the Under 12 team of 1995 is noted first, as, unlike its 1992 counterpart, it didn't have any success at the older age levels. The team had a comprehensive win over Donaghmore in the final, inspired by nine points from Ciarán Murray, four from JJ McCarthy and a crucial goal from John Brennan as they romped to a 1-18 to 1-9 victory. Pat Maloney, Macartan McGroder and Paddy Ward were the selectors in charge of the following side:

		John Murphy		
Seán Hayes		John Crimmins		Caoimhín King
Mark Devanney		Ray Maloney, Capt.		Stephen Burke
	Colm Finlay		Ciarán Murray (0-9)	
Seán White		JJ McCarthy (0-4)		Stephen Ward (0-2)
Liam Shanley		John Brennan (1-1)		David O Neill (0-2)

Subs: Bryan Duffy, Joe McHale, Seamus Wallace, Alan Kenny, Gavin O Regan, Ronan Gilsenan, Paul Faherty.

1992 Team

In 1992 the Under 12s reached both the championship and league finals. The league competition had been introduced to dilute the ultra competitive nature of the championship and provide more games for young players. This panel continued to make an impact at Under 16 and minor level and its progress through the grades is outlined below.

St. Martins ended up with a share of the spoils at Under 12 level in 1992, losing the championship final in July and winning the league in August, with

St. Martins, Under 14 Division 2 Football League Champions, 1995

Front: Kevin Burke, Johnny Gilsenan, Brian Walsh, Colm Barber, Martin Duffy, Keith Mangan, Ray Maloney, David McNerney, Philip Doyle.
Back: Noel McNerney, Selector, Seán Jordan, Alan Spillane, Brian Kenny, Peter Smith, John Joe McDonnell, Capt., Christopher Carey, Barry Murphy, Christopher Doyle, Trevor Dowd, Noel Mangan, Selector.

Simonstown providing the opposition on both occasions. The Navan side won the championship encounter by 2-7 to 1-5 while St. Martins overturned the result in the league final, winning 3-11 to 3-8. Early scores were crucial in the win as the Navan side reduced, but couldn't overhaul, a 2-7 to 0-2 interval deficit.

The team featured a number of players who would go on to success at the highest level for Dunshaughlin- Trevor Dowd who scored 1-3 in the league final, David Crimmins who captained the side, Michael McHale and Niall Kelly. Macartan McGroder, Cyril Creavin, Noel Mangan and Joe Mahon were selectors and the 1992 league winners lined out as follows:

Barry Murphy
John Joe McDonnell   John McKiernan   Christopher Doyle
Alan Kenny   Vincent Cullinane   Conor Power
Gary Donoghue   David Crimmins, Capt. (0-2)
Michael McHale (0-2)   Niall Kelly (0-1)   John McKenna (0-1)
George Troy (1-0)   David Tormay (1-2)   Trevor Dowd (1-3)
Subs: Gerard Troy, Kevin Creavin, Robbie Kiernan, Keith Mangan, Brian Murphy, Conor Mahon, Philip Doyle, John Mulroy, Marcus Maloney, Neil Mooney.

Many of those players featured on the 1993 Under 13 Féile team that lost just two games in the campaign, the first and the last outings, both against St. Cuthberts. In between St. Martins compiled eight successive victories but had to bow out, 3-13 to 1-7, to a strong St. Cuthberts side in the final.

By 1995 four of the 1992 Under 12 team were still young enough to feature in the Under 14 Division 2 side that narrowly defeated Yellow Furze, 3-7 to 1-11 in the league final. Trevor Dowd scored a last minute goal to win the title and finished with a personal tally of 3-3.

A year later all the 1992 crew were back together at Under 16 and the team progressed to the Division 1 championship final. The road there was far from smooth. While the team recorded wins over Round Towers, Blackhall Gaels, Trim and Navan O Mahonys there were also losses to St. Cuthberts and Walterstown. Another victory over the Towers in the semi-final brought them face to face with earlier conquerors Walterstown, in the final in early July.

Like St. Martins, Walterstown had a number of players who would go on to successful careers at adult level, such as Gareth McGuinness, John Davis, Karl Reynolds, Charles McCarthy and Ronan Barry. This was a game St. Martins could, and probably should, have won. Despite conceding a score inside the first minute, they settled well with points from David Crimmins, John McKenna and Peter Smith helping to build a single point lead. A Walterstown goal midway through the half was but a minor interruption as the Saints dominated the remainder of the half and two points from Gary Donoghue, and one each from McKenna and Niall Kelly gave them a 0-7 to 1-2 advantage at the break.

If St. Martins had a dream first half they endured a nightmare second. Early on Vincent Cullinane was sent to the line for an off-the ball challenge and then the wides began to mount up, eight in all, with just a solitary point for the half-hour. As St. Martins squandered, Walterstown converted. The sides were level after forty minutes but Peter Smith's point restored hope and the lead. That was as good as it got. With the additional player the Blacks increased the pressure and in the closing stages Ronan Barry and Killian Kennedy kicked three points to give Walterstown a 1-7 to 0-8 victory.

Niall Kelly had an outstanding game at centre-back for St. Martins with the *Chronicle* deeming him worthy of a man of the match accolade. In a game where both defences took the honours the loss of a forward was to prove costly but ultimately the failure to convert a myriad of chances was the difference between two evenly matched sides. The following team represented St. Martins:
Christopher Carey; John Joe McDonnell, John McKiernan, Michael McHale; Gerard Troy, Niall Kelly, Capt. (0-1), John McKenna (0-2); David Crimmins (0-1), Gary Donoghue (0-2); Vincent Cullinane, Neil Reilly, Peter

> the failure to convert a myriad of chances was the difference between two evenly matched sides.

Fundraising 1985
The main source of funding in the early years of St. Martins was the annual Christmas Draw, usually run over eight weeks.

St. Martins, Committee 1997
Front: Frances Maloney, Mairéad Delaney (Secretary), Paddy Ward (Chairman), Gabrielle Kenny (Treasurer), Helen Murray, Catherine McHale.
Back: Noel Mangan, Peter Mooney, David Crimmins, Paul Barry, Pat Herlihy, Pat Maloney, Willie Shanley.

Smith (0-2); Alan Kenny, David Tormay, Trevor Dowd. Subs: Damien Minnock, Robert Harrington, Kieran Crimmins, Lee Watson, Jason Clarke, Brian Kenny, Colm Delany. Selectors: David Crimmins, Pat Reilly, Brendan Tonge. Trainer & Coach: John Boyle.

Less than a year later in 1997, four of the same players, Christopher Carey, John Joe McDonnell, Peter Smith and Trevor Dowd, along with sub Brian Kenny were back in another Under 16 championship decider. After overcoming Blackhall Gaels by five points in the semi-final, thanks to second half goals from John Joe McDonnell and Trevor Dowd and a penalty save from Barry Murphy, Navan O Mahonys awaited in the final. In one of the earliest conclusions to the championship the final was played in Walterstown in late May. O Mahony's corner forward Michael Reilly proved to be the match winner, scoring four points and setting up three more, as St. Martins struggled to overcome the town side.

The Saints went behind in the first minute and never held the lead. Full-forward Peter Smith kept them in touch with points from play and frees but had difficulty finding the range with other efforts on an evening when scores were at a premium. A three points interval deficit increased early in the second half and the game would have been over as a contest but for two stunning point blank saves from Barry Murphy, who denied Thomas Loughran from 15 metres and scurried back to his feet to foil David Hosie's effort from the rebound.

St. Martins improved in the final quarter, with Christopher Carey and John Joe McDonnell to the fore, but the bane of the previous year's side, inability to finish accurately, returned, with four wides in seven minutes. O Mahony's Reilly conjured three marvelous points from awkward positions late on to seal the result.

St. Martins: Officers during the early years

Chairmen

Val Dowd, 1983-1987

Secretaries

Lena Walsh, 1983

Secretaries

Oliver Gogan, 1989-1991

Treasurers

Joe Rattigan, 1984-1985

Pat Kelly, 1988-1992

Tadgh Ó Dúshláine, 1984

Cyril Creavin, 1992-1994

Maura O Dwyer, 1986-1994

Jimmy Walsh, 1993-1996

Jim Gilligan, 1985-1988

Peter Mooney, 1995-1996

Gabrielle Kenny, 1995-1998

The winners fielded a strong team and included two future Meath seniors, Stephen Bray and Shane McKeigue, and St. Martins could not complain about the 0-12 to 0-7 outcome. The team under selectors Noel Mangan and Noel McNerney lined out as follows:

Barry Murphy; Martin Duffy, Christopher Carey, Brian Walsh; Seán Jordan, Alan Spillane, Tristan Fahy; John Joe McDonnell (0-1), Brian Kenny (0-1); John Gilsenan, Trevor Dowd (0-1), David McNerney; Christopher Doyle, Peter Smith (0-4), Keith Mangan.

By 1998 the team had progressed to the minor championship and with all its top players available hopes were high of overturning the 1996 Under 16 defeat to Walterstown. The team recorded big scores against Summerhill, Ballivor and Dunboyne and progressed to meet its nemesis, Walterstown, once again. Their meeting in the group stages resulted in a high scoring draw, with the Reds hitting 3-13 to the Blacks 2-16. The semi-final showdown was set for Skryne but Walterstown with five players who were already playing senior championship football held all the aces.

Once Charles McCarthy scored the initial point Walterstown never lost the initiative. He ended the first half with five pointed frees, a figure matched by St. Martins' best performer, Trevor Dowd. David McNerney had the Saints only first half point from play, a superb effort from 35 metres after rounding his man. By the half way stage St. Martins had slipped to three in arrears but Gary Donoghue reduced it to two when placed by Dowd, immediately after the resumption.

Jersey Presentation
David Crimmins presents a set of jerseys to St. Martins in 1997. Pictured are, Paddy Ward, Chairman, Mairéad Delaney, Secretary, David Crimmins, Senior, David Crimmins, Junior and Ray Maloney.

CHAPTER 8: ST. MARTIN'S REVIVAL, 1983-1998

The next ten minutes belonged to the Blacks and they stretched the difference to seven points. David Crimmins trimmed one off the deficit but a Walterstown goal put the issue beyond doubt. The gap would have been greater but for two top drawer saves from Christopher Carey and a late goal and point from Trevor Dowd. Trevor displayed all his skill and accuracy to finish as the game's top scorer on 1-6.

The final score read 1-15 to 1-9 in favour of Walterstown who went on to claim the title and the St. Martins' team lined out as follows:
Christopher Carey; John Joe McDonnell, Brian Kenny, Kevin Moyles; Damien Minnock, Niall Kelly, John McKenna; Gary Donoghue (0-1), Gerard Troy; John Gilsenan, Christopher Doyle, David McNerney (0-1); Alan Kenny, David Crimmins (0-1), Trevor Dowd (1-6). Sub: Brian Murphy for McKenna. Team Manager Brendan Kealy. Selectors: David Crimmins, Pat Kenny.

A Solid Foundation

Fifteen years after the foundation of St. Martins, under age football in the parish was in a healthier state than ever before. At Under 12 level teams had reached the league and championship deciders of 1992, winning the former and losing the latter while the 1995 side won the league Division 2 title. The Under 14s had won Divisional titles in 1987 and 1989 and were also runners-up in championship and league in 1991. Three times the Under 16s reached the championship final, three times they lost, but getting there was an achievement in itself. The crowning glory was the minor title of 1987 while a second could have been added in 1989.

> The club provided a conveyer belt of talent to Drumree and Dunshaughlin whose first teams both took adult titles by 1998.

The increasing population, the work in the schools and the organization and leadership of the new club all contributed to the unprecedented success. The club provided a conveyor belt of talent to Drumree and Dunshaughlin whose first teams both took adult titles by 1998. In many cases the teams defeated in underage finals provided as many talented adult players as did the winning ones. Two of the 1987 minor champions featured on Dunshaughlin's title winning team of 1997 and two more were substitutes. The Under 16s who lost consecutive finals in 1996 and 1997 provided four who would be integral to Dunshaughlin's three consecutive senior crowns. The successful St. Martins' Under 14 sides of 1987-89 provided four players for Drumree's junior championship winning side of 1988, Evan Kelly, James Walsh, Dermot and Patrick Doyle while another two came from the unlucky 1989 minor side, Declan Troy and John Boyle.

St. Martins headed into the new century in fine fettle. The club had set a high standard in the first decade and a half but the best was yet to come.

163

BLACK & AMBER

Hurling Revived

The early '80's witnessed a general revival of interest in hurling with Galway and Offaly emerging from the wilderness to add a new dimension to the All-Ireland championship. Interest in the game was rekindled throughout Ireland.

Those who have read this far will know that hurling has had a long and honoured tradition in Dunshaughlin. The first appearance of a hurling team here dates back to the early part of the century and for over two decades the only team in the village was the hurling side which was then a match for the best in the county. After the revival of football in the mid-thirties hurling almost died out, apart from short-lived revivals in 1938-1940, 1949 and 1957-1960.

The early '80's witnessed a general revival of interest in hurling with Galway and Offaly emerging from the wilderness to add a new dimension to the All-Ireland championship. Interest in the game was rekindled throughout Ireland, so when Gerry Flanagan, chairman of Dunshaughlin G.F.C., invited Clann na Gael of London to Dunshaughlin in September 1981 it was decided that both a hurling and a football game would take place. Dunshaughlin won the hurling encounter and it was clear that the basis of a hurling team existed in the area.

In February the following year a general meeting was called to discuss the possibility of fielding such a team. Despite a small attendance of nine, it was decided to proceed and the following officers were elected: Gerry Flanagan as Chairman, Christy O Sullivan as Secretary-cum-Treasurer and John O Sullivan, Oliver Brooks and Tommy Troy as selectors. The committee consisted of the officers along with Pat Kenny and Oliver Brooks. John Davis, a winner of numerous senior hurling titles with his club Brownstown in Westmeath, but then resident

BLACK & AMBER

> As championship time drew near players and officials became obsessed with the number 15, all wondered would they have fifteen for the first round. As it transpired the 'bare 15' was available for the initial round against Baconstown.

in Dunshaughlin, was appointed team trainer while Dinny McCarthy looked after the team kit.

After a championship victory over Boardsmill, Gerry Flanagan was animatedly praising everyone for their contribution and commitment and how well they had taken their scores when Dinny piped up, 'We did well with the hurleys too, we've two more in the bag than when the game started!'

The fledgling club had limited finance but soon raised sufficient money to buy jerseys and pay for affiliation and insurance. Local people subscribed to an interest free £50 loan scheme, poker classics and other forms of card games were organized and Gerry Flanagan's participation in the Dublin City Marathon in 1983 added over £200 to the coffers with generous local sponsorship. Later, Peter Fahy, a member of the club who worked for Dermot Kelly of Kilcock, helped procure his employer's support for a hurling tournament. The competition for the Peter Kelly Cup attracted the best senior clubs in the county and realized £350 in 'gates'.

Initially, the hurlers used a set of jerseys donated by the football club but Gerry Flanagan wanted a new set and a committee meeting was held to discuss the matter. Pat Kenny was against spending a lot of money on jerseys when hurleys were a more pressing concern and convinced the committee not to purchase a set. After the meeting Flanagan accosted Kenny for opposing the plan concluding, 'F___ you Paddy Kenny, they're in the boot!' Flanagan with his customary efficiency and organization had already purchased a set and intended the committee meeting to rubber stamp the decision!

An early Hurling Club Fundraiser: Dublin City Marathon 1983
Dunshaughlin Hurling Club Chairman Gerry Flanagan on his way through the Phoenix Park in the Dublin City Marathon of 1983 to raise funds for the club.

CHAPTER 9: HURLING REVIVED

Dunshaughlin, Junior Hurling Champions, 1982

Front: Michael O Brien, Hugh Doyle, Tadhg Ó Dúshláine, Jimmy Walsh, Capt., Christy O Sullivan, Martin Walsh, Jimmy O Rourke, Gerry Keane, Frank Kelly, Pat Kenny.
Back: Peter Fahy, Gerry Flanagan, Maitias MacDonnacha, Bernard Jones, Pearse O Dwyer, Jim Condon, Mick O Keeffe, John Neville, Gerry Tuohy, Ollie O Neill, Tom Keegan, Tommy Troy, Aidan Walsh.

Have We Fifteen?

The most daunting obstacle was fielding a championship team. Men who had long retired from the game were persuaded to return to active service and all likely players were canvassed to see if they would line out. As championship time drew near players and officials became obsessed with the number 15, all wondered would they have fifteen for the first round. As it transpired the 'bare 15' was available for the initial round against Baconstown.

Defeat in this game was far from the start the team wanted and heads were low. However, with the championship being run on a league basis Dunshaughlin could still get back into contention and after a second round victory over Rathmolyon prospects were bright again.

The third game, against Trim, was crucial. Despite being seven points down at half time Dunshaughlin got back into contention with two Gerry Tuohy goals and a Frank Kelly 'special' and finished level, Jim Condon equalizing with the last puck of the game

By now the panel had grown to 20 and hope was on the rise. Jimmy Walsh was the scorer in chief, with 2-4 against Navan O Mahonys in the quarter-final and 1-6 in the semi-final with Boardsmill. Dunshaughlin emerged victorious by 2-10 to 1-5 in the semi and booked a place in the final against Killyon, then sweeping all before them in Meath hurling.

The final was a confrontation between youth and experience and in many people's books the youths of Killyon were favourites. The Dunshaughlin boys were now labeled Dad's Army and in the first quarter of the game the army looked like being overrun. However the team settled down and sheer determination and first time pulling soon put them on top. An 18th minute goal by Jimmy Walsh when he lobbed a free over the keeper's head was the boost the team needed and Mick O Keeffe rattled another off the underside of the crossbar soon after to give his side a seven point cushion at the interval.

O Keeffe went on to become the hero of the hour, adding two more goals to claim a hat trick of green flags. Mick O Brien pilfered one also as the full forward line accounted for all five goals. At the other end Martin Walsh made a number of important saves in the first half, one of them from a point blank John Rafferty shot. The final score was 5-4 to 2-4 in Dunshaughlin's favour. A feature of the team was that no player retained his position from the first game against Baconstown to the final. Pat Kenny was forced to miss the final owing to illness. Coach John Davis, with John O Sullivan, Oliver Brooks and Tommy Troy selected the following side to contest the final:

Martin Walsh

Ollie O Neill   Tommy Troy   Hugh Doyle

Gerry Flanagan   John Neville   Gerry Keane

Frank Kelly   Jimmy O Rourke

Gerry Tuohy   Jim Condon (0-1)   Tadhg O Dúshláine (0-1)

Jimmy Walsh, Capt. (1-2)   Michael O Brien (1-0)   Mick O Keeffe (3-0)

Subs: Maitias MacDonnacha, Pearse O Dwyer, Tom Keegan, Bernard Jones, Peter Fahy, Aidan Walsh, Pat Kenny, Christy O Sullivan, John O Sullivan.

Tommy Troy and John O Sullivan were links with the last Dunshaughlin team to win a hurling title, twenty five years earlier in 1957. Tommy was now a rock of strength in defence and had won a county medal in each of four consecutive decades. John was a substitute and did an important job as hurley repairer thus saving the club badly needed finance. By winning the junior championship Roscommon-born club Chairman Gerry Flanagan was achieving a remarkable feat, winning championship medals in four different counties in four different decades. His first was won in 1955 in his native Roscommon and following that he was on victorious championship sides in counties Kildare and Dublin. His collection also includes two All-Ireland Junior Hurling Championship medals with Roscommon.

CHAPTER 9: HURLING REVIVED

Junior Hurling Championship Presentation Night, 1982

Another Title

Victory in the junior championship qualified the club for the intermediate grade and at the 1983 A.G.M. it was decided that the club would field a junior and an Under-14 team also. Morale was high and with a few new players added to the panel all were confident the team would do itself justice in the higher grade.

A narrow victory over Donaghmore was followed up by a more decisive win over Killyon but Ratoath upset plans temporarily by defeating Dunshaughlin in the third round. Extra effort was put into training in preparation for a tilt with Athboy, for victory would ensure a final place. The Athboy men put up determined resistance but the black and ambers emerged victorious by two points to qualify for a final meeting with earlier conquerors Ratoath.

Dad's Army had now become Grandad's Army to the local press and the army was given little chance against the youth and spirit of Ratoath. To others, intent on denigrating a fine achievement, Dunshaughlin was The League of Nations for men from nine counties represented the club for the final. Fewer gave them credit for integrating such a diverse range of talent into a team capable of going from scratch to an intermediate final in less than two years.

County final day turned out wet and windy and ground conditions were testing to say the least. Dunshaughlin's band of loyal supporters did their best for the team by roaring encouragement but strong favourites Ratoath made a whirlwind start and it seemed as if all the predictions would be correct.

Ratoath, however, failed to translate out-field superiority into scores and were shocked by a Peter Byrne goal after twenty minutes which settled Dunshaughlin

DUNSHAUGHLIN HURLING CLUB

Presentation Social

in the County Club, Dunshaughlin
on Saturday 18th December, '82
Music By: THE PROFESSIONALS

Meal served at 10 p.m.   Presentation at 10.30 p.m.
Dancing until 1.30   Bar Extension 'til Midnight

TICKETS ... £6

From top left:
Celebrating Victory
Cathal Gallagher, Declan Brooks, Aidan Walsh, Ger Tuohy, Martin Walsh, Pearse O Dwyer, John Neville celebrate.

Players and mentors with trophy
Front: Gerry Flanagan, Chairman, Jimmy O Rourke, Jimmy Walsh, Captain, Christy O Sullivan, Secretary/Treasurer, John Davis, Coach/Trainer.
Back: Tommy Troy, John O Sullivan Selectors, Michael O Connor, Chairman Meath Hurling Board, Oliver Brooks, Selector.

Ticket to presentation 1982.

and gave them a two point interval lead. Captain Ollie O Neill and centre half Gerry Flanagan were playing brilliantly at the back, Peter Byrne was lording it at midfield while up front Jimmy Walsh and Jim Condon were increasing the pressure on the opposing defence. Mick O Brien, though not getting on the score sheet, gave the Ratoath full back a torrid afternoon in the rain.

For the second half the black and ambers continued to concentrate on ground hurling and slowly but surely wore down the Ratoath men, who long before the end became disheartened and disjointed. The conditions favoured defences and Dunshaughlin deserved to emerge victorious in a low scoring game, by 1-5 to Ratoath's 0-6. The successful final line out was:

		Martin Walsh		
Ollie O Neill, Capt.		Pat Kenny		Tommy Troy
Jimmy O Rourke		Gerry Flanagan		Gerry Keane
	Peter Byrne (1-1)		Ger Tuohy	
Frank Kelly		Jim Condon		Mick O Keeffe
Jimmy Walsh Jr.		Mick O Brien		Jimmy Walsh Snr. (0-3)

Subs: Tadhg Ó Dúshláine for J Walsh Jnr., Declan Condon for M O Keefe, Pearse O Dwyer for G Tuohy. Selectors: Oliver Brooks, Tommy Troy, John O Sullivan.

Martin Walsh capped a marvelous year for himself as he collected an All-Ireland Special Minor Hurling medal, a similar award in Leinster, and a Leinster minor league medal in addition to his intermediate medal. Martin was Meath's keeper throughout the All-Ireland campaign as the Royals defeated Kerry following a replay. In the final Martin had a relatively quiet hour but was called on to make one extremely vital save from a deflection towards the end of the first half. He was also chosen on the Meath team for the Christy Ring Hurling School and would have played in the final but it clashed with the Meath intermediate decider and Martin gave the club priority.

There were occasional moments of levity alongside the serious business of preparing for and winning titles. A video was made of the final and Brian O Sullivan in the role of interviewer asked Gerry Keane, originally from Kerry, for his views. True to his roots in the Kingdom, Gerry replied, 'Hurling to me is catch and kick!' On another occasion during a training match, Ollie Brooks called out after a dangerous tackle, 'For fuck sake ref, that's a free,' and a player had to remind Ollie that he was the referee!

The hurlers' two-in-a-row was celebrated in *The Boys of Dunshaughlin* penned by Tadhg Ó Dúshláine and set to the air of *The Boys of Kilmichael*.

Dunshaughlin, Intermediate Hurling Champions, 1983

Front: Gerry Tuohy, Pat Kenny, Gerry Flanagan, Adrian Flanagan, Michael O Brien, Martin Walsh, Ollie O Neill, Capt., Jimmy Walsh, Jun., Jimmy Walsh, Sen., Jimmy O Rourke.
Back: Hugh Doyle, Peter Byrne, Frank Kelly, Brian O Sullivan, Tommy Troy, Pearse O Dwyer, John O Sullivan, Gerry Keane, Mick O Keeffe, Tom Keegan, Gerry Campion, Maitias MacDonnacha.

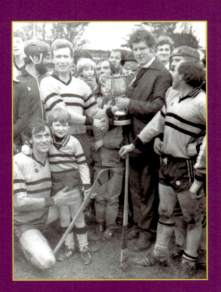

Intermediate Hurling Presentation, 1983
Michael O Connor, Chairman of the Hurling Board hands over the intermediate trophy to Dunshaughlin's winning captain Ollie O Neill. Also pictured front left, Gerry Flanagan and his son Adrian, front right Jimmy O Rourke.
At rear: Pearse O Dwyer, Tom Keegan with helmet and beard, Ollie O Neill, Brian Walsh, Jimmy Walsh Sen., James Walsh, partly hidden by handle of cup, Michael O Brien, unidentified man in hat, Michael O Connor, Hugh Doyle, Jim Condon, partly hidden, in helmet.

Among the Big Guns

Victory in the intermediate championship qualified the club to play at senior level in the centenary year of the G.A.A. This, however, was a daunting challenge.

The club had gone from formation to junior success within a year, followed immediately by intermediate honours. Many within the club doubted the team's ability to cope at senior level and poor attendance at training early in the year did not bode well. Any dreams of repeating the feats of the 1909-10 or 1925 teams by capturing the senior title were soon dashed by a nightmare debut when eventual champions Killyon annihilated the black and ambers 5-14 to 0-3 in the first game.

There was a slight improvement in performances in the later rounds but by mid July the side had played and lost three. The only success came in the final game when the team surprised everyone by overwhelming Trim on a 3-10

The Boys of Dunshaughlin

In Dunshaughlin a new team of old men
Was formed in the year '82
When the hurling championship began
'Twas said that they hadn't a clue;
For Baconstown sent them a-packing
The very first day on the field.
But every team thereafter
In their skill and their vigour believed.

Chorus

So here's to the boys of Dunshaughlin
Who won when not given a chance;
And brought to the great saints's homeplace
Once more, its due prominence.

The League of Nations they called them;
As juniors a flash in the pan.
After one intermediate battle

They'd never be heard of again
But Donaghmore, Killyon and Athboy
Can now sadly rue their mistake
While the young and the old of Dunshaughlin
The two in a row celebrate.

Chorus

On Sunday the 9th of October
Ratoath came to Trim in great joy
For they thought that the contest was over
And the boys of Dunshaughlin destroyed
But we waited determined and fearless
Most eager to enter the fray
When the final whistle was sounded
By two points we'd carried the day.

Chorus

By Tadhg Ó Dúshláine

CHAPTER 9: HURLING REVIVED

Intermediate Hurling Championship Presentation Night
Front: Gerry Flanagan, Chairman, Martin Walsh, Ollie O Neill, Captain, Dinny McCarthy, Michael O Connor, Meath Hurling Board Chairman.
Back: John O Sullivan, Gerry Tuohy, Hugh Doyle, Tommy Troy.

to 0-9 scoreline. Playing with great flair and enthusiasm the black and ambers notched three first half goals, two from Tadhg Ó Dúshláine and one from John Neville. The attack continued to impress in the second half, scoring a further goal and eight points, with Ger Tuohy and Peter Byrne prominent. Frank McCann, Trim's danger man in attack, was well marshaled due to impressive displays by Ollie O Neill, Tommy Troy and Paddy Ward.

For the only win in the 1984 championship the victorious side lined out as follows: Martin Walsh; Ollie O Neill, Paddy Kenny, Gerry Keane; Paddy Ward, Tommy Troy, Mick O Keeffe; Jim Condon (0-1), John Neville (1-0); Jimmy Walsh, Snr. (0-2), Peter Byrne (1-5), Ger Tuohy (0-1); Tadhg Ó Dúshláine (2-0), Gerry Flanagan, Jimmy Walsh Jr. (0-1).

Despite the victory it was obvious that Dunshaughlin could not hope to compete consistently at senior level. Club Secretary, Hugh Doyle, in his annual report was scathing on the lack of commitment from many players who 'will not emerge for training until the sun is on their backs or there is a championship match in the offing.'

He also wondered if they were just 'a collection of second-bite hurlers who still like to wield a stick?' The biggest problem was that the team was a blend, not of youth and experience, but of experience and more experience. The vast majority were in their thirties with only keeper Martin Walsh and John Neville in their teens. With no tradition of under age hurling in the club or local schools there were few if any home grown replacements.

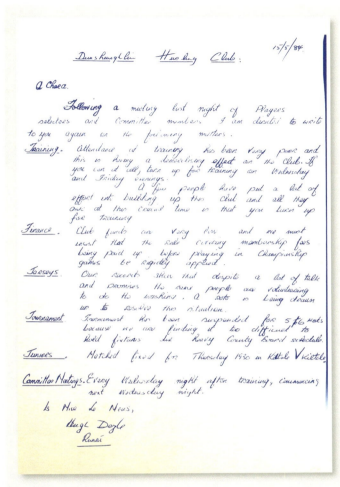

A Wake Up Call
In 1984 Club Secretary Hugh Doyle outlines the difficulties the club had to overcome to remain succesful.

Strengthening the Foundations

In the club's second year in existence, Gerry Flanagan began to address the issue by organizing juvenile coaching sessions on Sunday mornings. As the numbers in attendance increased, Ollie O Neill joined him and from 1983 the club entered teams in the Juvenile competitions at Under 11, 13 and 16 grades.

One hopeful sign on the horizon in September 1984 was the success of the Under 14s in winning Section C of the Féile na Mí festival of hurling at Boardsmill, even though many of the players had only started playing a few weeks earlier. Garbhán Blake recalls having to decide between a Wavin hurley given to him by Dickie Donnelly that vibrated on impact and a wooden one that was too big, while wearing a white helmet with string keeping one side of it in place.

This was the club's first underage success.

Dunshaughlin Hurling Club Committee, in 1984.
Front: Gerry Keane, Gerry Flanagan, Chairman, Hugh Doyle, Secretary.
Back: Oliver Brooks, John O Sullivan, Bernard Jones, Dinny McCarthy, Ollie O Neill.

In the semi-final Dunshaughlin beat Boardsmill 4-3 to 3-3 before overcoming Kildalkey in the final 5-6 to 1-4. A feature of the team was the skill and long range scoring of Vinny Moore and an outstanding performance from Shane Mahon.

The panel consisted of the following players: William Carey, Karl Stoney, Paul Davis, Trevor Doyle, Garbhán Blake, Liam O Neill, David O Neill, Vinny Moore, Shane Mahon, Thomas Walsh, Declan Troy, Declan Cottrell, Philip Burke, Trevor Conroy, James Farrell, Hugh McCarthy, David Walsh, Denis Burke and David Farrell.

The following year, 1985, there was further under age success when the club won the Under 14 B final. In the early rounds Rathmolyon were victorious by a point in a meadow on their own ground, but Dunshaughlin had revenge in a three-way play-off in Kiltale, 7-7 to 1-2, and hammered them again in the final by 6-3 to 3-0. Declan Cottrell and Fergus Summerville both grabbed a pair of goals while Liam O Neill, Martin Lynch, Garbhán Blake, John Bacon, Thomas Walsh and Trevor Doyle also played well. Patsy Curley and Ollie O Neill were the mentors for the championship success. The successful team was

David Farrell

Martin Lynch   Liam O Neill   Peter Rattigan

David O Neill   Garbhán Blake   James Farrell

John Bacon   Colm Naughton

Declan Troy, Capt. (0-1)   Thomas Walsh (1-1)   Liam Holton

Declan Cottrell (2-1)   Trevor Doyle (1-0)   Fergus Summerville (2-0)

Subs: Mark Rattigan, Hugh McCarthy, Darragh O Sullivan, Alan Boyle, Mark Cottrell, James Farrell.

By 1986 the groundwork for a better future was being established with teams entered at Under 11, 13 and 16 with mentors as follows:

U-11: Patsy Curley with Michael O Brien, Ben Fitzpatrick and Ollie O Neill.

U-13: Bernard Jones with Dinny McCarthy, John Gilsenan, Ollie Brooks, Anthony Gogan, Tommy Troy and Seán Doyle.

U-16: Tom Keegan with James Walsh, John Holton, Michael Bacon and John O Sullivan.

Presentation to Ollie O Neill for services to Juvenile Hurling.
Dunshaughlin Hurling Club Chairman Gerry Flanagan makes a presentation to Ollie O Neill in recognition of his work developing the underage players at the club.

Another hopeful sign for the future was that John Davis, Vinny Moore and Liam Neville were part of the Meath Under 16 team that reached the 1985 All-Ireland B Final where they lost out to Down. A year later compensation arrived for Davis and Moore as they were part of the panel that won the All-Ireland special Minor competition. In 1987, as St. Martins' players, John Davis recorded another success with the Meath minor team, which won the Leinster Special competition while Vinny Moore was also involved in the early stages. Liam O Neill was a member of the county panel beaten by Antrim in the All-Ireland Under 16 Special final while younger brother David represented Meath in the Tony Forristal Under 14 tournament in Waterford.

Dunshaughlin, Under 14 B Winners, 1985

This was the first underage hurling team in the parish to win a hurling title. The team wore a set of jerseys belonging to St. Seachnall's NS.
Front: David O Neill, Darragh O Sullivan, Alan Boyle, Declan Cottrell, Mark Cottrell, Peter Rattigan, Declan Troy, David Farrell, Patrick Doyle, Mark Rattigan, James Farrell.
Back: Patsy Curley, John Bacon, Thomas Walsh, Martin Lynch, Liam O Neill, Liam Holton, Colm Naughton, Fergus Summerville, Hugh McCarthy, Trevor Doyle, Garbhán Blake, Ollie O Neill.

Intermediate Again

This forward planning might secure the club in the longer term but it would not address the weaknesses of the existing senior team. The committee was well aware that another season of heavy defeats at senior level would hinder rather than help the team and it was agreed to apply to be regraded. This proposal encountered little opposition at County Board level and the club entered 1985 as an intermediate side.

However, before the championship began, tragedy struck. Peter Byrne, who had scored 1-5 in the club's final senior outing in 1984 and been the star of the intermediate win in 1983, suffered an accidental nose injury during a challenge game with the Meath junior side. The game was played at the request of the Meath hurling board and it was Peter's first game of the year. He retired injured, received medical attention at Navan Hospital and was then transferred to Dublin. Unbelievably, ten days later, while undergoing an operation, he died. Peter had played Under-21 hurling with his native Dublin before moving to Macetown, Tara, with his wife Mary.

Club members rallied round, and, under the leadership of Gerry Flanagan, extensive fund-raising began with the aim of completing the building of the couple's house. Support from individuals, clubs, eleven County Boards and provincial councils augmented the fund. Committee member Dinny Neville pulled off a notable coup when he persuaded Offaly and Galway to support the fund by playing a senior hurling challenge in Dunshaughlin on July 26th 1985 with both teams travelling at their own expense. Peter's mother visited both dressing rooms to thank the teams for their generous support. Six weeks later the same counties met in the All-Ireland final when Offaly emerged as champions.

Prior to the game a sudden thunderstorm flooded the playing surface rendering the game doubtful. Only the intervention of Dunshaughlin Fire Brigade, whose members pumped excess water from the field, enabled the game to go ahead.

A few weeks before the money was to be handed over in 1986, calamity was piled onto the initial tragedy when Peter's wife Mary died in a traffic accident. The funds raised, which amounted to almost £12,000, were then used to pay funeral and other expenses for the couple. Gerry Flanagan, on behalf of the committee, presented £500 to Michael Monagan of Skryne for under age football in the parish. Money from the fund was also used to purchase hurleys for the juveniles in Dunshaughlin and to erect a dugout on the Dunshaughlin grounds with John McSorley of Skryne carrying out the work free of charge, while individual, county board and provincial council subscriptions were returned.

To further dampen the spirits ahead of the 1985 championship, and prove that trouble rarely comes in single instalments, Jim Condon suffered severe eye injuries in a car accident and had to retire from the sport.

The 1985 squad featured, in the main, the men who had backboned the team since its formation but there were a couple of new recruits. The versatile Jim Rattigan from Drumree, who won a Leinster Under 21 football medal with Meath in 1985, added youth and scoring ability to the forward line, while JJ Keane and Nicholas Walsh were other capable additions up front. Keane showed his value in the championship opener when he claimed 1-1 of the team's 3-8 in an easy victory over Killyon's second string. A tougher outing against Baconstown followed with Dunshaughlin taking control only in the last twenty minutes. John Neville was outstanding at centre back, scoring 1-2, with Gerry Flanagan, Jimmy O Rourke, Mick O Keeffe, Jimmy Walsh, Snr. and Tommy Neville all playing well as the team recorded another victory by 4-7 to 1-4.

The week after the Peter Byrne Memorial game, neighbours Ratoath caused a major surprise when deservedly defeating the black and ambers by 2-7 to 1-6 at windswept Kilmessan. Only the accuracy of Frank Kelly from frees and an early second half goal, when substitute Mick O Brien brilliantly flashed JJ Keane's pass to the top corner of the net, kept Dunshaughlin in contention. The team needed to recover, and quickly.

Victory in the final round against old rivals Athboy was imperative to ensure a place in the final. Lining out against the wind the team went on an early offensive and after a highly productive first half held a 2-6 to 0-3 lead. Athboy couldn't take advantage of Dunshaughlin's failure to maintain this momentum during the second half and a place in the final was guaranteed after a double scores victory, 2-10 to 1-5.

Final Day Disappointments

There was a lengthy delay before the same two teams featured in the final in late October. This was a closer encounter in which Athboy made the better start, held Dunshaughlin scoreless for the first twenty minutes and seemed destined to lead at half time until JJ Keane's shot deflected off a defender past goalie Pat Ennis minutes before the break. To complete the turn-around Mick O Keeffe then notched a point to leave Dunshaughlin in front 1-2 to 0-3.

The revival didn't last however, and Athboy dominated the third quarter. They hit five points with only a JJ Keane point in response and then a late Pádraig Joyce goal gave them an unassailable five point lead as the game came to a close. Although Larry Kirwan netted on the stroke of full time the O Growney men would not be denied and at the final whistle Athboy laid claim to the trophy on a 1-8 to 2-3 scoreline.

Dunshaughlin could be pleased that they had arrested the apathy and poor form of the previous year but on the day the team never played to its ability and the *Meath Chronicle* reported that *'only Jimmy Walsh, Pat Kenny, John Neville and Frank Kelly produced any sort of worthwhile form for the hour.'*

The team line out read: Martin Walsh; Tommy Troy, Pat Kenny, Ollie O Neill; Tom Neville, Gerry Flanagan, Jimmy O Rourke; John Neville, Tom Finn; Jim Rattigan, Frank Kelly (0-1), Nicholas Walsh; Mick O Keeffe (0-1), JJ Keane (1-1), Jimmy Walsh, Snr. Subs: Larry Kirwan (1-0) for Finn, Michael Kennedy for Rattigan.

Another final defeat followed in 1986. This time Dunshaughlin faced up to Dunboyne, who like themselves had found the going too difficult at senior level and dropped to the lower grade. The sides had met in the first round with the Dunboyne men coming out on top by a goal. The game was notable for the impact of two seventeen year olds, Brendan Reilly for Dunboyne and John Davis for Dunshaughlin. Reilly was central to Dunboyne's victory while John Davis was the type of player Dunshaughlin needed if the club was to have a future- young, skilful and committed.

Dunboyne were the pundits' favourites with Reilly well supported by county

CHAPTER 9: HURLING REVIVED

full-back Paddy McIntyre and they justified their favourites' tag. This time the outcome was closer, with a single point separating the sides at the end, 0-11 to 1-7. Dunboyne's dominance in the first half produced eight points but they also hit thirteen wides and it seemed possible this profligacy would be their downfall as Dunshaughlin rallied early in the second period. Frank Kelly had given Dunboyne a lesson in the art of taking chances when he first-timed to the net in the second minute of the game and midfielders Denis Burke and Jimmy O Rourke supplemented it with early second half points as they took control of midfield.

Within five minutes of the interval the eventual losers had eased into a 1-6 to 0-8 lead. Burke hit three points, one a magnificent effort from 65 metres out on the right and O Rourke was on target with an equally spectacular shot from 70 metres. However, Dunboyne recovered. Reilly notched three points and Dunshaughlin's only response was a point from John Davis. The black and ambers could have won but in the *Chronicle's* view, '*If they had it would have been a triumph for economy and a cruel reversal of the Biblical story's ending for Dunboyne's prodigal sons.*'

The passing of twelve months had seen a substantial change in the make up of the team. Four men who had not featured in 1985 lined out in the 1986 final, the youthful John Davis and three newcomers, Denis Burke, a trainee farm manager from Cork, Fintan Delaney and Seán Minihane. Six who started in 1985 didn't feature on the starting fifteen the following year, Tommy Troy, Ollie O Neill, Tom Neville, Tom Finn, Nicholas Walsh and JJ Keane. It was a tribute to the club that it could sustain such a degree of change and still qualify for another final but in the long run the lack of continuity was bound to impede team cohesion and performance. The side that faced Dunboyne was: Martin Walsh; Gerry Flanagan, Pat Kenny, Mick O Keeffe; Jimmy Walsh Jr., John Neville, Larry Kirwan; Jimmy O Rourke, (0-1), Denis Burke (0-5); Frank Kelly (1-0), Fintan Delaney, John Davis (0-1); Seán Minihane, Gerry Tuohy, Jimmy Walsh Snr. Subs: Tom Moyler for Tuohy, Jim Rattigan for J Walsh Snr.

> The black and ambers could have won but in the *Chronicle's* view, '*If they had it would have been a triumph for economy and a cruel reversal of the Biblical story's ending for Dunboyne's prodigal sons.*'

Another Intermediate Title

Following two intermediate final losses the team hoped that 1987 would prove to be third time lucky. There were positive developments with the promotion of a number of younger players to the team; Jim Rattigan and John Davis were now regulars and were joined for some of the games by Liam Neville, Paul O Rourke and Vincent Moore, all in their teens. Martin Walsh played most of the games outfield and the arrival of PJ Townsend, living in Raynestown but originally from Kilkenny, and described by all as a gifted hurler, provided additional options in defence.

The team had a relatively smooth run to the final. Victories over Ratoath, Baconstown, Boardsmill and Athboy and a draw with Trim guaranteed the side a final place before the end of June. The league stages showcased a number of imposing displays, with comprehensive victories featuring impressive scorelines. Baconstown were dispatched by 4-7 to 1-5 with Gerry Flanagan using his craft and experience to set up John Davis for two well-taken goals while claiming 1-1 for himself.

The next outing against Boardsmill also featured four goals with thirteen points added for good measure. Jim Rattigan dominated midfield while scoring 1-3, captain John Neville was outstanding at centre back, Frank Kelly, back from retirement, netted two goals in as many minutes and the evergreen Jimmy Walsh raised an early green flag. The game against Athboy was over as a contest when Dunshaughlin led 2-8 to 0-1 by half time. The goals came from Gerry Flanagan and Vinny Moore while Pat Kenny, Liam Neville and PJ Townsend blotted out the majority of Athboy's rare attacks. The only concern was the failure to add more than four points in the second half. The high scoring of the earlier games was not repeated in the qualifier against Trim either, but eight points were sufficient to earn a draw and a final place.

Dunshaughlin, Intermediate Hurling Champions, 1987

Front: Liam Neville, Denis Burke, Jim Rattigan, Martin Walsh, Paul O Rourke, Larry Kirwan, Jimmy Walsh, Brian Walsh- mascot.
Back: John Neville, PJ Townsend, Mick O Keefe, Pat Kenny, Ollie O Neill, John Davis, Gerry Flanagan, Jimmy O Rourke.

CHAPTER 9: HURLING REVIVED

The decider at the end of July was a high scoring affair. Athboy corner forward John Doherty made a brave effort to win the title on his own, with 3-2, but Dunshaughlin played the more polished hurling and stamped their authority on the exchanges during the third quarter. Two men who made major contributions were centre-back PJ Townsend who bossed the centre of the defence and Jimmy Walsh who showed his magical stickwork hadn't dimmed with time.

Walsh had an early goal direct from a free to counter Doherty's second minute effort and John Davis claimed Dunshaughlin's second, the best score of the hour, when he won possession, turned sharply and blasted low past stranded keeper Anthony Leavy. It left the black and ambers with a narrow 2-5 to 2-2 interval advantage.

Victory was assured in the early stages of the second half as Dunshaughlin struck 1-4 without reply with Jim Rattigan notching the goal. Midway through the half the gap was an almost unbridgeable ten points but Athboy refused to bow to the inevitable. Doherty goaled from a penalty, then struck a magnificent point before John Davis and Jimmy Walsh had Dunshaughlin's final scores. Doherty repeated his earlier performance with another goal and point to reduce the margin to four but time was on Dunshaughlin's side and they eased to a deserved victory.

Fears of a third consecutive final defeat spurred the side on to victory and it was a relieved captain, John Neville, who accepted the Tommy Kane Cup from former Dunshaughlin clubman, and then Hurling Board Chairman, Finian Englishby. John Davis and Paul O Rourke went on to win a second championship medal three days later when both starred as St. Martins-Ratoath won the minor football championship.

John Davis, Senior, coached the following winning side along with selectors Oliver Brooks, Gerry Flanagan, John Neville and Paddy Ward:

Intermediate Championship Presentation, 1987
Hurling Board Chairman, Finian Englishby presents the TJ Kane Cup for the Intermediate Hurling Championship to Dunshaughlin captain, John Neville. In the background Brendan Johnson and Jimmy O Rourke celebrate.

Ollie O Neill
Larry Kirwan — Pat Kenny — Mick O Keeffe
Liam Neville — PJ Townsend — Paul O Rourke
John Neville, Capt. — Jim Rattigan (1-0)
Martin Walsh — Denis Burke (0-4) — John Davis (1-2)
Jimmy Walsh, Snr. (1-4) — Jimmy O Rourke (0-1) — Gerry Flanagan

Subs: Vinny Moore for Mick O Keeffe, Dermot Carey, Frank Kelly, Paul Davis, Declan Brooks, Tommy Troy, Fintan Delaney.

After a meal in Trim the team headed for Dunshaughlin and the traditional cavalcade with horns blowing. Then everyone assembled in the club's regular meeting place and watering hole, Gogan's public house, where the celebrations continued. Gogan's was an old style public house, with limited space, and outside toilets for the men with the women using facilities upstairs.

The Gogan family had a history of involvement with previous hurling clubs in Dunshaughlin as outlined in earlier chapters. This continued in the 1980s as the club used a room in Gogan's for committee meetings. It was an ideal solution as the committee was small, it was warm during winter when most meetings took place and participants could mix business with pleasure as Anthony Gogan ferried their drinks from the bar! Anthony supported the club financially through sponsorship of medals and jerseys while Mrs. Sheila Gogan often provided sandwiches when the hurlers played cards in the bar.

John Davis, Inspirational Manager
John coached the revived Dunshaughlin hurling team to junior and intermediate titles in the 1980s. He also coached the Meath hurlers to Kehoe Cup and National League titles while in recent years he has spearheaded a revival in Meath's camogie fortunes.

Second Team Second Best

Later in the year the club's second team, playing in the Junior Hurling Division 2 Championship, qualified for the final via a protracted route and the club had the enticing prospect of winning two adult championships in the one year. After defeating Trim twice, losing to Kildalkey and experiencing a win and a loss to Wolfe Tones, the team defeated Longwood in the semi-final, 2-8 to 0-7. The final pitted the black and ambers against earlier conquerors Kildalkey in Trim in early October.

The team consisted of a number of battle-hardened veterans but contained many younger, inexperienced players. John O Sullivan was selected in goals but a hand injury sustained at work ruled him out and Paddy Ward took over between the posts.

In a close encounter Dunshaughlin held the initiative for most of the first half. Brendan O Rourke could do little wrong at midfield and all the early traffic was towards the Kildalkey goal. The pressure told with two goals in the first five minutes. First Mick Farrell poked a loose ball over the line and O Rourke kicked the second in splendid style after catching a Tommy Troy free. With Kildalkey still in the doldrums O Rourke netted for a second time, this one direct from a free.

The lead amounted to ten points before the Kildalkey fight back began. In the closing stages of the half Dunshaughlin inexplicably faded out of the game and Kildalkey trimmed the deficit to a single point at the interval. The decline continued in the second half and Kildalkey were as dominant after the break as Dunshaughlin had been before it. The black and ambers could manage only a single point during the half hour and ended up at the wrong side of a 2-8 to 3-3 scoreline. Many of the players had limited hurling experience and skill and over the hour the team from the traditional stronghold of Kildalkey was able to overhaul Dunshaughlin's early lead.

CHAPTER 9: HURLING REVIVED

The team and subs were as follows:
Paddy Ward; Gerry Keane, Tommy Troy, Denis Hynes; John Bacon, Sean Walsh, Paul Rattigan; Michael Boyle, Brendan O Rourke; Dermot Carey, Tadhg Ó Dúshláine, Thomas Walsh; Declan Brooks, Mick Farrell, Johnny Leonard. Subs: Jimmy O Rourke, Colm Burns, Liam Holton, Declan Cottrell, Jeremy Cottrell, Michael Nixon, William Carey, Paul Davis, Derek Jones, Patrick Stoney, Mick O Brien, Tom Keegan, Tom Condon, David Walsh. John O Sullivan unable to play due to injury.

Stepping Down the Grades

The structure of the hurling championship in Meath suffered from an inherent weakness. Teams promoted from the intermediate grade often discovered that the standard of the top senior clubs was much higher than that encountered in the lower grade. Both Dunshaughlin and Dunboyne had won intermediate titles in the early eighties but their stay in the senior grade was short lived as they were unable to compete with the premier senior sides and both rapidly reverted to intermediate level. A similar prospect now faced Dunshaughlin once again.

Dunshaughlin, Junior Hurling Championship Division 2 Finalists, 1987

Front: Seán Walsh, Thomas Walsh, Brendan O Rourke, Paddy Ward, John Bacon, Tadhg Ó Dúshláine, Paul Rattigan.
Back: John O Sullivan, Mick Farrell, Gerry Keane, Declan Brooks, Tommy Troy, Michael Boyle, Dermot Carey, Denis Hynes, Johnny Leonard.

Dunshaughlin Panel, Junior Hurling Championship Division 2 Finalists, 1987

Front: Paul Rattigan, Paul Davis, John Bacon, John O Sullivan, Jeremy Cottrell, Declan Cottrell, Brendan O Rourke, Thomas Walsh, Jimmy O Rourke, Liam Holton, Michael James O Rourke, mascot, William Carey. Back: Mick Farrell, Colm Burns, Tadhg Ó Dúshláine, Tom Keegan, Johnny Leonard, Michael O Brien, Tommy Troy, Seán Walsh, Dermot Carey, Gerry Keane, Denis Hynes, Declan Brooks, Michael Boyle, Paddy Stoney.

Paddy Ward, on behalf of Dunshaughlin, had a proposal to address this issue. The club envisioned a Senior B Championship to consist of the weaker teams from the senior grade, the current intermediate sides and the Junior A winners, with the county committee entrusted with deciding which clubs would play Senior A or Senior B. It was a well thought out proposal, which would lessen the likelihood of one-sided fixtures and provide meaningful contests in the premier grade while ensuring a competitive second tier. To avoid the flaw in the existing system there would be no automatic promotion for the Senior B winners; the grading committee would decide whether or not the winning club should be promoted. This aspect of the proposal could have proven contentious but in the event the Hurling Board took offence at the airing of the proposal in the local press and the proposal never received the considered thought it deserved.

With participation in the senior championship on the horizon once again, some members at the AGM queried the club's readiness for the step-up, as a number of players intended to retire and emigration of younger players due to the economic recession of the 1980s was always likely. The alternate view, that competition in the premier grade would be beneficial to the younger players, prevailed.

However, before the senior competition could begin, controversy arose over entitlements to intermediate medals. Plans to award medals only to those who had played in the intermediate championship or were part of the panel for the final were opposed by others who held that any player who had been on earlier championship panels was also entitled to a medal. The disagreements eventually led to John Davis standing aside as coach while at an Extraordinary General Meeting following criticism of the club's officers and committee, Chairman Gerry Flanagan also stood down. To add to the chaos it was necessary to elect new selectors to replace Davis and Flanagan.

When the championship commenced in 1988 the club found the senior grade a supreme and insurmountable challenge. The outcome of the first outing didn't augur well. Matched with the previous year's runners up, Athboy, the black and ambers were on the wrong side of an 8-9 to 2-5 annihilation. The team had only one substitute and little support. Athboy corner forward Eamonn McGovern helped himself to five goals and only John Neville, Declan Brooks and Jimmy Walsh Snr. could be pleased with their endeavours. The game was played in the first week in May but the next round didn't materialize until late July.

The delay didn't prepare anyone for what the *Chronicle* described as the biggest shock in any of the hurling championships. Dunshaughlin out-hurled Navan O Mahonys to record a 1-11 to 1-8 victory with the maestro Jimmy Walsh claiming 1-6 of the total. O Mahony's however were no world beaters. Their only goal was scored by Martin Smith, forced out of retirement, with a jersey as his only item of sporting attire. The following round emphasized the reality. The team was again out of its depth and suffered a 5-9 to 1-2 reverse to Kildalkey who went on to contest the final.

On the positive side the club managed to field a second team that recorded victories over Trim and Moylagh and created opportunities for the younger players to gain competitive experience. However, regardless of the results, three outings in the senior championship spread out over four months betokened a poorly organized competition that benefitted no club. The senior finalists in 1988, Trim and Kildalkey, played three and four games respectively to reach the final,

BLACK & AMBER

Ollie Brooks, was the last Chairman of Dunshaughlin HC, 1988-90 and played football and hurling for the Black and Ambers. He also represented the area on Meath County Council and was Chairman of the Council in 2003-04.

Paddy Ward, was the last Secretary of Dunshaughlin HC, 1986-90 during which time he lined out for the club. He was also Chairman of St. Martins, 1997-2000 and Vice Chairman of Dunshaughlin, 2006-09. In recent year's he has been the club's delegate to the County Board. As a player Paddy won two Keegan Cup senior championships with Gaeil Colmcille in 1966 and 1968.

a statistic that indicates the championship was in need of reform.

Recognizing the futility of taking part in the senior championship the club returned to the intermediate grade in 1989. Even though the initial outing against Dunboyne clashed with a football league fixture, which meant some of the Drumree players were unavailable, the game went ahead. Junior players had to be promoted to fill the gaps and the side went down by 2-9 to 0-6. Only for the accuracy of John Neville from frees the deficit would have been even wider. The second round game against Longwood was fixed, then altered and then refixed at short notice and the club failed to field. Efforts to overturn the loss of the two points for failing to field were unsuccessful and the club played no further games in the championship.

The second team was hampered by the loss of the players promoted to the premier team for the clash with Dunboyne but secured a draw with Dunderry in the first game before losing to Donaghmore and Dunderry. A lack of players was the main cause.

In the league competitions the club's best team had an early victory over Longwood but lost to Dunderry and Dunboyne. The fact that the competition was spread out over eight months did little to maintain player interest. The second team had a more successful experience in Division 4 of the league with wins over Batterstown, Donaghmore and Moylagh in addition to two walk-overs and a defeat in the final game to Wolfe Tones. This grade was suited to the younger players and gave a reasonable level of competition.

However, many of the victorious panel of 1987 had now retired while two of the best younger players, Martin Walsh and John Davis, fulfilled their wish to play senior hurling by transferring to Kilmessan. In these circumstances the club had to assess its options.

CHAPTER 9: HURLING REVIVED

In view of the poor form and negative results in 1989 Dunshaughlin applied for regrading to junior hurling status. Paddy Ward declared at the Hurling Board's annual convention that neighbouring clubs were poaching their best players. He instanced the move of John Davis and Martin Walsh, to Kilmessan for 1989 and 1990 respectively, adding,

'now it seems the floodgates have opened. We are finding it difficult to field teams and in order to get the interest back and establish a solid base it was felt that a move to junior was best.'

He concluded

'Other players have been approached to move and, if this trend continues, it's going to be impossible to keep the club together.'

The Hurling Board acceded to Dunshaughlin's request so in three short years, 1988-1990, the team had a precipitous fall from the top to the bottom grade. The officers chosen to see the club into 1990 were Chairman: Oliver Brooks, Vice Chairman: John O Sullivan, Secretary: Paddy Ward, Treasurer: Mick O Keeffe and PRO: Bernard Jones with Jimmy Walsh, PJ Townsend and John O Sullivan appointed as selectors. Despite playing in the lower grade the outlook didn't improve, as the team made no impact and suffered a heavy loss to Trim by 5-10 to 1-2. At the end of the year the club bowed to the inevitable and decided not to affiliate hurling teams, leaving players free to transfer to other clubs, including a proposed new club in Drumree.

St. Martins was by now a successful, established club in underage hurling and Drumree men like Patsy Curley, Willie Shanley and Ben Fitzpatrick had been central to its success, as will be outlined in Chapter 17. In 1991 Patsy was Chairman of the Drumree club and it was clear to all that Dunshaughlin had run out of steam. As many of the Dunshaughlin players lived in Drumree it was decided to establish a club there. Dunshaughlin officials recognized the black and ambers couldn't field a team without Drumree players and a meeting involving Paddy Ward, John O Sullivan, Bernard Jones, Ollie Brooks and Jimmy Walsh, Snr., met Drumree representatives Paddy Curley, Joe Rattigan, Michael Boyle and Johnny Lynch.

It was agreed Drumree would take responsibility for the development and running of hurling in the parish as there were insufficient players to have two clubs. Drumree would affiliate at Junior Hurling Division 2 grade and Dunshaughlin players could play with them, or another club. Many of the Dunshaughlin players were by now of the vintage variety and opted for retirement. Others dispersed to a variety of clubs, John Neville joined Wolfe Tones, PJ Townsend went to Batterstown, Vinny Moore signed for Donaghmore while Paul and Brendan O Rourke, Liam and David O Neill opted for neighbours Ratoath. Paul later

Interprovincial Railway Cup Hurling Winner
David Crimmins receives his Railway Cup medal from Leinster Council Chairman Seamus Howlin in 2008. On left is sponsor Martin Donnelly.

transferred to Drumree while the O Neills played very little hurling afterwards. The remainder joined Drumree who went on to enjoy two successful decades of hurling triumphs, taking the Division 2 title in 1993 and 1996, the Junior title in 1998 and capped it with Intermediate victories in 2003 and 2010.

Retrospect

The idea of establishing a hurling club in Dunshaughlin seemed novel, if not revolutionary in 1982. In reality, it fitted into a century long tradition of intermittent hurling revivals, that brought initial but short-lived success. Thus, the glory days of 1908-11 were followed by almost a decade when the club alternated between achievement and absence. A revival in the early twenties brought a junior and senior championship followed by a lapse and temporary rebirths in the 1930s and 1940s. After another decade the tradition was revived and the club won the Junior title in 1957 but it was shorter lived than most and for a quarter of a century the sound of sliotar on ash was absent from the GAA fields in Dunshaughlin.

Each revival was driven by the enthusiasm and commitment of individuals, Michael Duffy, Paddy Kenny, Paddy Blake, Seán McManus, all single-mindedly messianic in furthering the cause. The revival of the 1980s fitted that pattern too. Gerry Flanagan was the inspiration and guiding light of the latest incarnation. He had an advantage the earlier revivals lacked, a gradually growing population, and the arrival of families from traditional hurling strongholds. Thus, once established and successful the club was able to attract newcomers to its ranks. The club however, faced a major problem, one that its predecessors had also faced and failed to address. That was the absence of an under-age structure that would guarantee the future of the club.

Valiant efforts were made to rectify this with the setting up of an under age structure in 1983 and the eventual delegation of responsibility for it to the newly re-established St. Martins from 1986. In the longer term this was an outstanding success but Dunshaughlin HC didn't survive long enough to reap all the benefits. Instead, Drumree became the standard bearers and building on the work at under age level has continued the hurling tradition to the present.

Players from Dunshaughlin continued to hurl at adult level with Drumree, among them Caoimhín King, Fearghal Delaney, David and John Crimmins, Paul and Brendan Walsh, Mark Devanney, Cillian Dennehy, Conal O Sullivan, Seán Gavin, James Rattigan, Daire Flanagan, and Alan Kenny among others. During 2008 David Crimmins was a regular at midfield on the Meath team that won the Kehoe Cup. *The Chronicle* praised his work rate in the final against Carlow and deemed one of his points to be *'out of the top drawer.'* He was rewarded with selection on the Leinster panel for the Inter Provincial competition, entering the fray in the semi-final victory against Connaught. He went on to garner what was formerly a Railway Cup medal as Leinster defeated Munster, the only Dunshaughlin man ever to gain the honour.

From the beginning the hurling and football clubs in Dunshaughlin were separate entities. Both had their own officers, committee and membership fee but shared the grounds on the Drumree Road. It was an unusual structure, as in most parishes a single GAA club caters for both football and hurling teams but a similar structure existed when hurling first made an appearance in Dunshaughlin in the early 1900s.

Co-operation on issues such as the upgrade of the clubhouse in 1985 and joint supper dances encouraged closer collaboration and there was discussion at the Hurling Club AGM in January 1990 of having a single GAA club with football and hurling sub-committees. Members of the hurling club felt that their membership fees didn't entitle them to the same rights as members of the football club, especially when tickets for All-Ireland finals were allocated, while many in the football club were unhappy about the hurling club's meagre contribution to the upkeep of the grounds and facilities. These conflicts, which are common in most dual clubs, would probably have been better dealt with within a single club rather than becoming a source of division between the two.

Thus, the revival of 1982 has had a more lasting impact than any of the previous ones. Though the name changed from Dunshaughlin to Drumree the parish has fielded teams without a break for over a quarter of a century. The work initiated by Gerry Flanagan, with sterling support from men like Paddy Ward, Oliver Brooks, John O Sullivan, Jimmy Walsh Snr., Jimmy Walsh, Jnr., Ollie O Neill, John Davis Snr. and Jnr, Tommy Troy, Dinny Neville, Dinny McCarthy, Hugh Doyle and Tadhg Ó Dúshláine has continued with much more success than the founders could probably have hoped for.

The short-term success was significant, intermediate titles in 1983 and 1987 and a junior championship in 1982 but the long term impact can only be appreciated by considering the success of St. Martins and latterly, Drumree.

Interlude 3

The Ban on Foreign Games

For almost all of its first 90 years, the Gaelic Athletic Association implemented a rule that anyone who played, promoted or attended 'foreign games', or who was a member of the British security forces, was prohibited from membership of the GAA. Foreign games included soccer, rugby, cricket and hockey. The GAA imposed the ban to counter what it saw as a process of anglicization of Irish society. Supporters of the rule regarded it as a practical expression of their support for native culture.

The events of the 1916-22 period strengthened the organization's determination to retain the ban but not all members approved and debate on the issue continued. In 1925 Paddy Kenny of Dunshaughlin Hurling Club unsucccessfully proposed at the Meath Convention that, as British soldiers and police had departed, it was time to remove the ban. Proposals to rescind the ban featured annually at Congress in the early 1920s until a rule limiting discussion on it to every third year was introduced. The vast majority of GAA officialdom approved of the Ban and in 1938 Ireland's President Douglas Hyde was removed as patron of the GAA for attending an international soccer game between Ireland and Poland!

County Boards enforced the rule by appointing Vigilance Committees, made up of men who attended banned games with the intention of reporting on GAA members who were either playing or watching these games. Anyone discovered in attendance or playing was suspended. The ban led to much hypocrisy, duplicity and cynicism. Players usually assumed false names when playing the forbidden sports and club officials generally knew when members were flouting the ban. Defeated clubs often reacted by objecting to the winner for fielding men who had flouted the ban rule while turning a blind eye to similar transgressions by their own members.

Cricket was still very popular into the 1920s, and in 1923 part of Dulane's objection to Pelletstown's junior semi-final victory was based on the claim that Michael Madden had played cricket and had not been reinstated. In 1924 Athboy objected to Kilmessan being awarded medals at the Dunshaughlin Tournament on the same grounds against the same player. During the 1920s the Leinster Council minutes contain regular references to players from its constituent counties being reinstated having been suspended for offences such as 'playing foreign games,' 'playing cricket,' 'attending Cricket Dance' 'witnessing soccer match' and 'playing rugby.'

In the 1960s concerted efforts were made to overturn the ban, but such attempts failed at Congress in 1962, 1965 and 1968. Many in the organization felt that the ban

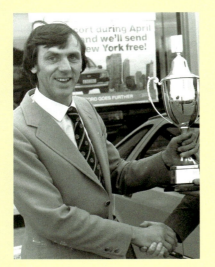

Gerry Flanagan
Gerry Flanagan, with the Dermot Kelly Cup, was central to the revival of hurling in Dunshaughlin in the 1980s. He was Chairman of the Football club 1980-82 and the Hurling club 1982-88, while he won Meath junior and intermediate hurling titles in 1982, 1983 and 1987. Gerry had previously won two All-Ireland junior hurling medals, three provincial juniors and one intermediate, all with Roscommon, as well as six senior hurling and three senior football championship medals in Roscommon. He had strong views on the use of Croke Park to accommodate other sporting organizations and on behalf of the Dunshaughlin club brought forward motions on the issue to Meath Convention.

was becoming increasingly irrelevant and indefensible as so called foreign games could now be viewed on television. The 1966 World Cup in England underlined this point.

A motion from Skryne was instrumental in removing the ban. It proposed that all clubs hold a special general meeting in November 1970, to consider the issue so that each club delegate would have specific instructions on his club's attitude to the ban. Colm Cromwell of Skryne described it as 'an attempt to put into practice the democracy we talk about in theory.' The motion succeeded and in an unprecedented exercise in grassroots democracy clubs throughout the country voted overwhelmingly in favour of abolition. Thirty counties supported the deletion of the rule while only two, Sligo and Antrim, voted to retain it.

Dunshaughlin was among many clubs voting to delete the ban at the Meath Convention and the proposal was carried there by 113 votes to 46. Patsy McLoughlin stated he believed it had outlived its usefulness whereupon, Seamus Murphy of Donaghmore declared him 'a renegade.' Peter McDermott, the Man in the Cap, proposed the motion stating that 'repressive rules and regulations were tried in the past and got them nowhere.'

With so many counties in favour of deletion the 1971 Congress in Belfast ended the ban on foreign games and eventually replaced it with a charter stressing that the aim of the GAA was 'the strengthening of the national identity in a 32 county Ireland through the preservation and promotion of Gaelic games and pastimes.'

British Soldiers and Police

Other aspects of the ban also caused controversy from time to time. British soldiers and police were banned from the GAA and this rule remained in place until 2001 as the RUC and British Army often harassed and abused GAA members during 'The Troubles' in Northern Ireland. It was removed in the context of progress towards peace based on the Good Friday Agreement of 1998.

During World War 1 many Meath men joined the British army, with about 350 losing their lives in the war. Urban centres and villages like Dunshaughlin often provided recruits for the British armed forces and in 1916, prior to the Easter Rising, Patrick Duffy of Dunshaughlin Hurling Club asked at a County Board meeting if they could do something to allow soldiers play Gaelic games. The Chairman retorted, 'Do you not think they ceased to be Gaels when they joined the army?'

Duffy stated that the club had discussed the matter and a Longwood delegate responded,

'If many of us brought it before our clubs we would not be here today.'

Irish Music and Dance

Non-Irish music was also outlawed. This rule was flouted more often than the ban on playing or attending foreign games. In Dunshaughlin, for example, the Carnival Committee organized the annual carnival during the 1950s and 1960s but in reality the promoter was the GAA club. The carnival programme consisted of some Ceilí music but in the 1950s bands and orchestras dominated while in the 1960s the showbands took over. At the County Convention in 1968 Dunshaughlin had a motion to delete the rule against foreign dances passed but it didn't find favour at annual Congress and the rule remained until it was swept away in 1971 also.

Foreign Games in Croke Park

Despite the removal of the ban on foreign games, Rule 42, which prohibited field games other than Gaelic football and hurling being played on GAA grounds, remained for much longer. Occasional exceptions were made, such as an American Football game between the American Navy and Notre Dame University in Croke Park in 1999 but it posed no threat to the GAA. Soccer and rugby were different however. They were viewed as foreign games and in competition with the GAA for the allegiance of the youth of Ireland.

Debate raged on the idea of allowing other field games in Croke Park during the 1990s, especially during Seán Kelly's term as GAA President. Yet, long before that Dunshaughlin became probably the first club in Ireland to propose this. Gerry Flanagan, the club's then Chairman proposed at the Meath Convention in 1982 that, the 'Gaelic Athletic Association authorities examine their position in relation to the playing of international soccer matches at Croke Park.' He declared that, 'We want a frank and friendly discussion as to why GAA grounds, eleven years after the removal of the ban, have not been made available for any of the games once banned.' County Chairman Brian Smith ruled the motion out of order but Flanagan returned the following year with a proposal that called for rugby, soccer and other non-Gaelic games to be played there. Proposing the motion he stated that money from the move could be used to update Croke Park and provide financial support for underage games, especially hurling, The argument wasn't based only on financial self interest, as, in what he described as an Ireland scarred by bigotry, the GAA should offer the hand of friendship. A Gaeil Colmcille delegate responded that it would be a sad day if a partitionist association was allowed into Croke Park and Hogan and Nally would turn in their graves if *God Save the Queen* was played there. The motion was rejected by 80 votes to 25.

Gerry Flanagan's proposal came to pass in February 2007, as first France and then England played Ireland in the Six Nations Tournament. The English team received a rousing reception and when *God Save the Queen* was played it was met with utter respect. No reports of underground movement by Hogan or Nally were recorded! GAA President Seán Kelly acknowledged Flanagan's foresight in his autobiography, *Rule 42 and All That*.

Speech to Convention, 1982
Draft of part of Dunshaughlin GAA Chairman, Gerry Flanagan's forward thinking speech to Meath County Convention in 1982 on the reasons for opening up Croke Park.

> Too often in the GAA we tend to fight shy of and run away from discussing subjects which some consider sensitive. This is a pity. One sure way of removing tension is by frank and friendly discussion. And that is the purpose of this motion. We want a frank and friendly discussion as to why GAA grounds 11 years after the removal of the ban have not been made available for any of the games once banned. Surely an initiative by the GAA leadership would, in addition to generating substantial revenue in rents, generate an amount of goodwill for the GAA as a bridge builder in the community. It is no harm to remind ourselves that the Charter, Rule in the Official Guide lays special emphasis on the obligation of the GAA-- I quote-- "in the development of a community spirit". I take it that when the Charter mentions "community" it means the whole community. I fear that some of our leaders haven't yet got round to accepting that definition. There is a greater need than ever today, with our society in this island deeply scarred by dissension, for a national body like the GAA to do its utmost to knit the different traditions that make up our society. This motion is put forward in that spirit.

BLACK & AMBER

Struggle to Achieve, 1978-1990

10

Like all championships the intermediate grade is a difficult competition to win, and the club soon realized that hopes of another title and a rapid return to senior ranks would not be easily achieved.

In 1978 Dunshaughlin footballers joined the senior grade, their reward as intermediate champions. It would turn out to be a short lived stopover.
At the time a team was guaranteed at least half a dozen games annually, as the senior grade consisted of two sections of seven or eight teams. Dunshaughlin's first outing was a victorious one, overcoming Ballivor by 1-8 to 1-7 in Páirc Tailteann, in a game dominated by the losers for lengthy spells. Paddy O Dwyer scored the goal while Jimmy Walsh notched six points. This, however, was the high point. The side recorded only one more victory, against former champions Kilbride who were now on the slippery slope to junior status. Defeats to Seneschalstown, Navan O Mahonys, Summerhill, Moylough and Castletown indicated that life in the senior grade would be difficult.

The 1979 draw was more favourable with Dunshaughlin avoiding the big guns until the later stages. Although the side went down to St. Patricks in the opening round, it recovered to record victories against Duleek, Harps and Ballivor. The core of the team consisted of the intermediate heroes of 1977 with a couple of additions such as John Forde, Mick O Keeffe, Gerry Flanagan, Dan O Sullivan and Ollie Bowe. Pat Jennings continued to star in goals, giving a brilliant performance against Harps, while John Forde contributed 1-5 in the opening four games.

Centenary Sunday, 29th July 1984

Pictured on Centenary Sunday, 1984 at the launch of the original *Black and Amber* in Dunshaughlin Community College.
Front: Paddy O Dwyer, Patsy McLoughlin, Róisín de Blacam, Seán Walsh, Davy O Dwyer.
Back: Tadhg Ó Dúshláine, Gerry Flanagan, Jim Gilligan, Val Dowd.

> It was abundantly clear that dropping down a grade was the only option and from 1983 the black and ambers were once more competing at Intermediate level.

Jimmy Walsh maintained his form as the main score getter, notching 2-5 in the same period.

When the big guns arrived Dunshaughlin had no answer. Seneschalstown blasted aside a weakened team, registering seventeen points to a mere goal and two points. The black and ambers were missing Michael Wead, Pat O Hare, Ger Dowd, Pat O Brien and Seán Mangan due to a combination of holidays, injuries and suspension. The defeat took its toll. The club failed to field in the next round against O Mahonys and then withdrew from the competition. Secretary Seán Mangan in his report to the AGM stated that the team showed 'a total lack of dedication to training which was clearly evident in all the matches' while selectors Val Dowd and Seán Walsh rarely missed a night's training.

Despite this setback a new year always brings renewed hope and the team made a bright start to the 1980 championship. Reversing the previous year's result against St. Patricks, the side followed up with a single point win over Colmcille Gaels of Kells. It was a close run victory with Ollie Bowe equalizing two minutes from time before Con O Dwyer's last minute free earned victory.

The side however, was no match for the real championship contenders in the

CHAPTER 10: STRUGGLE TO ACHIEVE, 1978-1990

Centenary Sunday, 1984, Present v Past

later rounds. The *Chronicle* declared that the boxing rule, where a bout is stopped to prevent unnecessary punishment, could have been used against Skryne. The Blues won by 3-8 to 0-3 and this was followed by defeats to Seneschalstown and O Mahonys, both by smaller margins. Dunshaughlin performed well against reigning champions O Mahonys at rain-soaked Kilmessan. With John Jennings and Dan O Sullivan in control at midfield, John Forde and Mick O Keeffe netted twice before the interval. Pat O Brien hit a third goal in the second half but it wasn't enough as a failure to score points and a late O Mahonys' surge left the champions victorious by 1-13 to 3-2.

The encouraging performances of 1980 didn't continue the following year. The side recorded but one victory and scores were almost as scarce as hen's teeth. Against St. Patricks, Seneschalstown and All-Ireland Club finalists Walterstown the black and ambers recorded a mere combined total of seven points while conceding a massive 9-31. The club chanced one last throw of the dice in 1982. Four defeats were shipped before the end of June, and, although none of them mirrored the margins of the previous year, by now morale was low and the club failed to field against Skryne in July. It was abundantly clear that dropping down a grade was

Present and past selections that played each other on Centenary Sunday, 1984:
Front: Gordon O Rourke, Denis Kealy, Shane Kelly, Neil O Dwyer, Pádraic O Dwyer, Jerry O Donoghue, Pádraig Gallagher, Derek Kenny, Jimmy Walsh, Martin Walsh, Patsy McLoughlin, Seán Walsh.
Middle: Jimmy O Rourke, Seán Mangan, John Jennings, Con O Dwyer, Michael Walsh, Pat Jennings, Paddy O Dwyer, Don McLoughlin, Neil O Riordan, Pat O Hare, Tom Finn, Mick O Keeffe, Aidan Walsh, John Summerville, Martin Everard.
Back: Michael Wead, Pat O Brien, Tommy Troy, Mossie Caffrey, Noel Curran, Matt McEntaggart, Val Dowd, Gerry Keane, Pat Farrell, Oliver Brooks, Michael O Brien, Niall McCarthy, Pearse O Dwyer, Dominic Moran, Tommy Byrne, Martin Summerville, Pat Donoghue, Joe McDonnell, Seamus Magee.

Centenary Sunday, 1984
Paddy O Dwyer speaks to a group in the GAA grounds on Centenary Sunday. Young children unidentified, Oliver Mangan, Hugh McCarthy, Josie McCarthy, Winnie Melia, Kevin Melia, John O Dwyer, Matt Hollywood, Dessie Johnson, Mannix Mangan, Joe McDonnell.

Centenary Sunday, 1984
Jim Gilligan presents a copy of the original Black and Amber to Colum Cromwell, Chairman, Meath Centenary Committee.

CHAPTER 10: STRUGGLE TO ACHIEVE, 1978-1990

Dunshaughlin Intermediate Panel, 1984

Front: Jimmy Walsh, Dominic Moran, John Summerville, Don McLoughlin, Kevin Doherty, Jerry O Donoghue, Gerry Keane, Mick O Keeffe, Pat Jennings, Paddy Kenny, Aidan Walsh.
Back: Pat O Hare, Tommy Byrne, Pádraig Gallagher, John Kelly, Pat O Brien, Jimmy O Rourke, Michael O Brien, Pearse O Dwyer, Dan O Sullivan, John Jennings, Tom Finn, Capt.
Absent from photograph Matt McEntaggart and Martin Summerville.

the only option and from 1983 the black and ambers were once more competing at intermediate level. Ironically, the final senior championship game was against Nobber, the same club Dunshaughlin defeated in 1977 to gain admission to the senior ranks, and the line out in that 1-11 to 1-4 defeat at Seneschalstown read: Pat Jennings; Matt McEntaggart, Michael O Brien, Paddy Kenny; Dominic Moran, Dan O Sullivan, Gerry Keane; John Jennings, Pat O Brien; Jerry O Donoghue (1-0), Ger Dowd, Kevin Doherty; Aidan Walsh (0-4), Noel Curran, Mick O Keeffe.

Intermediate Again

Like all championships the intermediate grade is a difficult competition to win, and the club soon realized that hopes of another title and a rapid return to senior ranks would not be easily achieved.

In fact the club struggled to qualify from the group stages during the remainder of the decade and had to rest content with an annual victory or two at group level. Life in the intermediate grade began, as the experience of senior football had ended, in defeat, with losses to Oldcastle and Moynalvey. Two victories followed, firstly an unexpected one point win against Slane and then another, by five points,

The Cup That Never Was
Brian Smith, Chairman, Meath County Board, presents the East Meath League Cup to Dunshaughlin Captain, Pat O Brien before the final in 1985. He had to leave prior to the game, so presented the cup to both captains! Unfortunately, Ratoath won the game so Pat didn't take the cup home. Also pictured on left is Owen O Sullivan of host club Donaghmore.

> 'Bring that fucking linesman with you, it's the only way ye'll win any other games.'

against Donaghmore. A defeat to Wolfe Tones in a low-scoring final round put paid to hopes of further progress.

During the Centenary Year of the GAA defeats to St. Marys, St. Colmcilles and Duleek eliminated the side from the race for honours. The only consolation was a great victory over St. Michaels in Páirc Tailteann by 1-8 to 0-6, with Pat O Brien giving a storming performance and recording a goal and three points. A line ball decision, given incorrectly in Dunshaughlin's favour, led to the goal and afterwards Paddy O Connell of St. Michael's berated Pat O Brien advising him to 'Bring that fucking linesman with you, it's the only way ye'll win any other games.' If results are the yardstick then obviously the linesman decided not to appear at the following games!

Results in 1985 gave even less cause for optimism following the loss of all five championship games. After three years at intermediate level the club had won three of the fourteen championship games played, an average of one game in every five.

Despite the gloom there were small rays of hope on two fronts. The team was in transition. By 1986 only four of the intermediate title winning side from almost a decade earlier were left, Pat Jennings in goals, Michael Wead in defence, Pat O Brien at centre field and Ger Dowd up front. The vacancies were being gradually filled, partly by the arrival of new players in the area, such as Dan O Sullivan, Tom Finn, Kevin Doherty, Jerry O Donoghue and Gerry O Leary, and partly by younger players who had come up through the ranks. Among the latter were Michael O Brien, Martin Summerville, Pádraig Gallagher, Tommy Byrne, Michael Duffy, Alan Cummins, Matt McEntaggart, Kevin Kealy and Aidan and Martin Walsh. This gradual intermingling of youth and experience gave hope that the transition would be successful.

Secondly, despite the poor championship performances, the team was building up an impressive record in the East Meath League. Meath County Board ran Winter and Spring Leagues at the time but these were poorly supported and badly planned so local clubs organized the East Meath League to ensure regular competition. The current structure of All County Leagues did not commence until 1986. After finishing in the upper reaches of the East Meath table in 1984 the side went through the league undefeated the following year but lost the final

Dunshaughlin Intermediate Panel 1986

to Ratoath, then one of the contenders for the intermediate title.

The final in Donaghmore saw Dunshaughlin shred their dismal championship form as they forced Ratoath to fight all the way. Dunshaughlin gained the edge at midfield where team captain Pat O Brien played superbly, outcaught the skillful Stan Gibney on several occasions and linked effectively with partner Jimmy O Rourke to open up the Ratoath defence. Seán Boylan selected Aidan Walsh as Man of the Match after he ended with a tally of 1-4, the goal coming just before half-time when he converted a penalty following a foul on himself.

The underdogs went ahead early in the second half when Mick Rawdon goaled and Ratoath didn't regain the lead until five minutes from the end when Martin Mockler netted. Even then Dunshaughlin fought back and it took a last minute Kieran Gaughan point to assure Ratoath of a 1-12 to 2-7 victory. The run of victories gave the team an injection of self-belief, which carried over into the following year's championship.

The runners-up lined out as follows: Pat Jennings; Matt McEntaggart, Michael O Brien, Michael Wead; Martin Summerville, Dan O Sullivan, Tom Finn; Pat O Brien (0-1), Jimmy O Rourke (0-1); Derek Kenny, Jerry O Donoghue (0-1), Aidan Walsh (1-4); Mick Rawdon (1-0), Joe Carberry, Don McLoughlin.

The only squad to qualify for the knock out stages of the Intermediate championship in the 1980s pictured prior to the final group game v Athboy in Summerhill. The side lost the subsequent quarter-final to Navan O Mahonys.
Front: Seamus Magee, Kevin Kealy, Brian Duffy, Aidan Walsh, Pat Jennings, Jerry O Donoghue, Martin Walsh, Ger Dowd, Noel Devanney, TP Toolan.
Back: Gerry Keane, Pat O Brien, Tommy Byrne, Alan Cummins, Michael O Brien, Paddy Kenny, Michael Duffy, Martin Summerville, Michael Wead, Matt Shortt, Gerry O Leary.

Some Championship Progress

> 'Hans Christian must have scripted the second half as the east Meath side made the Ugly Duckling story seem almost credible'

Two early victories over fancied opposition, St. Michaels and Dunderry, gave Dunshaughlin an ideal start to the 1986 championship. St. Michaels had completely dominated the first half but after the break Pat O Brien and substitute Gerry O Leary were in complete control at midfield. The *Chronicle* suggested that

'Hans Christian must have scripted the second half as the east Meath side made the Ugly Duckling story seem almost credible' while *'the skill of the Walsh brothers and Jerry O Donoghue was revealed in all its glory, and the roving of Ger Dowd completely unsettled the Mikes.'*

So much so that at the final whistle Meath star Martin O Connell booted the ball into the next field in frustration!

Against Dunderry, Dunshaughlin didn't take the lead until two minutes from time when a clearance broke to an unmarked Aidan Walsh who carried the ball for thirty metres before belting a superb shot to the roof of the net. The ecstacy of two narrow victories was followed by the bitter pill of a narrow one-point loss to Oldcastle in the next round and Dunshaughlin needed victory in the final outing against Athboy to make it to the knock-out stages. The defence was almost non-existent in the first half as seven different Athboy players pointed but two cracking second half goals from Jerry O Donoghue, the second a brilliant solo effort that left five defenders in his wake, gave Dunshaughlin a narrow 2-10 to 1-12 victory.

On the last Sunday in August the blue and white hoops of Navan O Mahonys proved too strong for the black and amber stripes in the quarter-final in Athboy. O Mahonys opened with an early goal but an Aidan Walsh penalty brought Dunshaughlin back into contention. In a low scoring game Dunshaughlin leveled early in the second half but the final quarter belonged to the Navan side as they dominated midfield and edged in front by 1-7 to 1-4. The following team represented Dunshaughlin:

Pat Jennings; Matt McEntaggart, Michael O Brien, Michael Duffy; Michael Wead, Gerry O Leary, Tom Finn; Pat O Brien, Alan Cummins; Martin Walsh, Kevin Kealy, Jerry O Donoghue (0-1); Ger Dowd, Mick Rawdon, Aidan Walsh (1-3). Subs: Gerry Keane for Cummins, TP Toolan for Kealy, Thomas Byrne for M Walsh.

David Carty from Skryne, Meath captain in 1966 and an All-Ireland winner in 1967, coached the team with Val Dowd, Michael Walsh and Seán Walsh the selectors.

Viewing a video of the game one is struck by the stop-start nature of games at the time. The free kick from the hand would not come into being until 1990 and every free kick was preceeded by the careful placement of the ball, three or four steps backwards, a moment for the taker to compose himself before play eventually resumed. Even then O Mahonys were slicker. For free kicks they sometimes placed the ball on the ground and struck it directly without a run-up. This often caught out the defending team, but the game was still pedestrian.

Dunshaughlin suffered from two weaknesses. Firstly, the team was very dependant on Aidan Walsh for scores, both from play and frees. In the 1986 championship he accounted for 3-18 of the team's 5-41, almost fifty per cent of the side's scores. Against O Mahonys the team managed only two points from play. Without an increased scoring input from the other forwards it was difficult to build up match winning scores while such a high level of dependency on one man meant that the opposition knew who to focus attention on.

Secondly, the side was imbalanced in terms of age and experience. It featured four or five old hands with experience of the previous successful intermediate campaign and a number of players not long out of the under age ranks. Apart from a couple of players, it lacked men in their mid to late twenties at the peak of their ability. There were a couple of reasons for this. The under-age structure in the parish during the 70s was haphazard. There was no organized under-age club until St. Martins was reestablished in 1983. Instead, an informal sub-committee of the Drumree and Dunshaughlin clubs looked after the juveniles from the parish, so there was no continuity or structure for the promotion of games between Under 12 and minor.

Nor were there any organized competitions in the county at primary level so football in St. Seachnall's NS was confined to a few challenge games or one-off encounters on sports' day. Dunshaughlin Vocational School, a Community College from 1978, was better organized and participated in various county and provincial competitions but it catered for many of the surrounding clubs as well as those from Dunshaughlin. For example, the team which reached the Leinster Vocational Schools' Final in 1978 had Michael O Brien at full back and John Forde at midfield but no others who would go on to play for the local club.

Quarter-final qualification in 1986 seemed to signal better times ahead. It wasn't to be. Another six years would elapse before the side returned to the knock-out stages. The false dawn of 1986 was followed by the dark nights of 1987 and 1988 when the team failed to emerge from the group stages.

In 1987 the black and ambers were unable to overcome Bellewstown in a play-off to decide the winners of the group. The AGM at the end of the year discussed the possibility of dropping down to the junior grade but wiser counsel prevailed and it was agreed that the club needed to retain its intermediate status.

Results improved in 1988 with two victories and a draw before the crucial final game against St Marys. Despite a spirited rally in the final twenty minutes

BLACK & AMBER

From top:
Aidan Walsh: Dunshaughlin star forward and scorer in chief in the 1980s and 1990s.
Seán Walsh: Vice Chairman 1984-86, Chairman 1987 but died in office. Regular intermediate selector.
Pat Farrell: Club captain 1972, Chairman and Secretary in the 1980s and selector with the Minor Championship winning team in 1987.

Dunshaughlin could not recover lost ground and went under by 2-7 to 1-8. The following year was similar; two victories and a loss were recorded early on but the final group outing against Kilmainhamwood was a bridge too far and the north Meath side emerged victorious by 0-10 to 0-7.

Further disappointment followed in 1990. The championship started brightly with a spectacular first half goal from Stephen Claire helping to dispose of neighbours Dunsany in Round 1.

A late Aidan Walsh point salvaged a draw against Syddan before Ballinlough administered a severe nine-point defeat in the next round. A heavy loss to O Mahonys ended the team's interest in the championship for another year.

Despite the poor championship record Dunshaughlin had been performing well in the All County League and after an easy first round championship victory against Moynalty in 1991 the *Chronicle* believed that Dunshaughlin '*must be fancied to go a long way in the intermediate championship.*' But the team spluttered to an unconvincing draw against St. Marys before two great goals by Ger Dowd and Pat Kealy secured victory over Athboy.

The level of performance began to tail off in the latter part of the year. The media, and followers generally, expected Dunshaughlin's meeting with Dunboyne in the final round to be closely contested but the *Chronicle's* headline, *Dunshaughlin's Day of Woe,* told the story. Missing Simon Farrell and Pat and Dermot Kealy the team struggled throughout and despite the great efforts of Francis Darby, Dunboyne emerged merited victors by 0-12 to 0-5.

Changing Times

By 1990 only Pat O Brien and Ger Dowd remained of the 1977 stalwarts. A new team was gradually taking shape, as the minors of the late 1980s graduated onto the side. Players like Derek Melia, David and Trevor Kane, Derek Maher, Pearse and Alan Fahy, Stephen Claire, Simon Farrell, Francis Darby, Niall Foley, Garbhán Blake, Ciarán Byrne, Alan Duffy, Pat, Dermot and Brendan Kealy, Tiernan O Rourke and Colm Naughton began to feature but they were still young and inexperienced and would face many bitter disappointments in their quest for the intermediate title.

By 1990 scores were more evenly spread among the forwards. Aidan Walsh was still the provider in chief with 0-14 in the 1990 championship but Stephen Claire chipped in with 2-4, while Alan Duffy contributed 0-6. However, the loss through emigration due to the levels of unemployment in Ireland, of Michael Duffy (Australia), Kevin Kealy (England) and later Pat Kealy and Trevor Kane (USA) put a brake on progress.

CHAPTER 10: STRUGGLE TO ACHIEVE, 1978-1990

Dunshaughlin Intermediate Team v. Bellewstown, 1987
Front: Ger Dowd, Michael Wead, Pádraig Gallagher, Paddy Kenny, Martin Walsh, Francis Darby, Tom Finn, Aidan Walsh.
Back: Pat O Brien, Matt McEntaggart, Pat Jennings, Kevin Kealy, Mick Rawdon, Michael O Brien, Gerry O Leary.

Trevor Kane was one of the brightest prospects in the club in the late 80's. He won a Leinster Minor medal as a substitute with Meath in 1985 and in 1988 a Leinster and All-Ireland Junior at midfield. His performance against Cork in the Home Final made him the *Meath Chronicle's* selection as Man of the Match, which described his performance as '*majestic*' and '*a pleasure to watch*.' After a short spell in Australia in the early 90s he returned to play a central role up to 1993 before a knee injury and permanent emigration to the USA ruled him out. Kevin Kealy, after departing in the late 1980s and lining out with Tara in London, also returned to join the team from 1993. Neither Michael Duffy nor Pat Kealy returned, both settling abroad, while Stephen Claire had spells overseas on peace-keeping missions as an officer with the Irish army.

Olé, Olé, Olé

The 1980s was a period when soccer ballooned in popularity. Jack Charlton was appointed Irish manager in 1986 and with players of the calibre of Liam Brady, Ronnie Whelan, Paul McGrath, Packie Bonnar and David O Leary at his disposal Ireland qualified for the 1988 European Championships in Germany. A Ray Houghton goal against England was the highlight of a tournament that

BLACK & AMBER

Half-Time Worries
Ger Dowd, Tom Finn and Garbhán Blake in pensive mood at half time in the All County Football League, Division 3 Final v Ballinlough, 1988.

> 'Italia '90,' Meath star Bernard Flynn declared, 'had brainwashed the country. The GAA people had gone over to soccer.'

went on for three weeks and attracted massive media coverage.

Christy Moore helped make the adventure part of popular culture with his tale of *Joxer Goes to Stuttgart*. Ireland also qualified for the World Cup- for the first time- in 1990, emerged from the group stages and defeated Romania in the second round before exiting to hosts Italy in the quarter-final. Half a million people welcomed the team on its return to Dublin.

'Italia '90,' Meath star Bernard Flynn declared, 'had brainwashed the country. The GAA people had gone over to soccer.' This was only partly true. Soccer was popular from the early 80s in Meath and the Mid-Meath League, later the Meath and District League (MDL), was well organized and expanded to eighty-two teams in 1985. A Dunshaughlin club was one of the eight founder members but left the following year to join the Leinster Junior League. A new club known as Dunshaughlin Dynamoes replaced them and Archers later joined. By 1985 the Dynamoes and Archers were both in Division 2 of the MDL. Archers clinched the title and promotion to Division 1 in 1987, and the line-outs read like a roll call of Dunshaughlin GFC. Later, clubs called Dunshaughlin Rebels and Dunshaughlin United participated in the leagues.

There were other reasons, apart from the success of the Irish team, for the growth of soccer throughout the country. Players were sure of regular games each week, they knew in advance when they would be playing and postponements were rare. In contrast, the GAA in Meath had no proper league structure to complement the championships. There were senior leagues, junior leagues, winter leagues and spring leagues but many of the stronger clubs didn't bother to participate in those, preferring to enter club tournaments that attracted large crowds and substantial 'gates'.

The East Meath League was an attempt to give GAA players a regular schedule of games and the Meath County Board finally addressed the issue in 1986 by organizing an All County Football League in five divisions. Meath GAA clubs soon had another advantage in promoting their games as the county senior team entered an era of unprecedented success with All-Ireland titles in 1987, 1988 and 1996 and final appearances in 1990 and 1991, the latter after four monumental tussles with Dublin in the first round.

CHAPTER 10: STRUGGLE TO ACHIEVE, 1978-1990

Dunshaughlin, All County Football League Division 2 Finalists, 1991

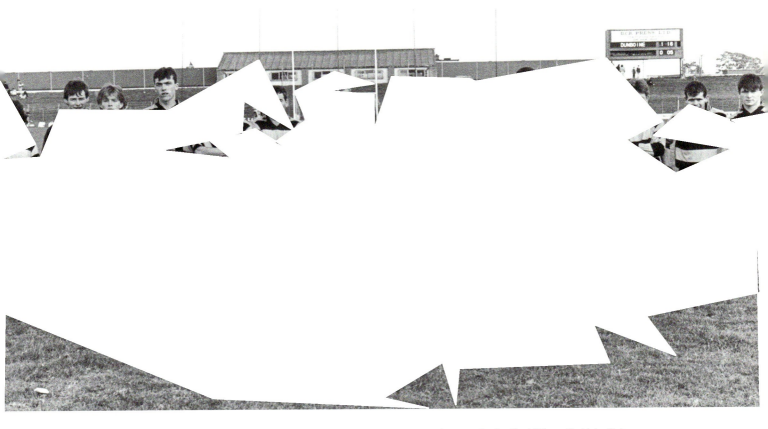

Front: Allen Foley, Pádraig Gallagher, Kevin Kealy, Dermot Kealy, Ger Dowd, Francis Darby, David Kane, Garbhán Blake, Aidan Walsh, Brendan Kealy, Alan Fahy.
Back: Pat Kealy, Donnchadh Geraghty, Pearse Fahy, Tiernan O Rourke, Ciarán Byrne, Matt McEntaggart, Pearse O Dwyer, Niall Foley, Derek Maher, Paul Hession, Trevor Kane, Pat O Brien, Alan Duffy, Derek Melia, Aiden Kealy.

When the All County League was organized Dunshaughlin was placed in Division 3. Parallel to the poor championship performances in the eighties the team began compiling an impressive league record and gradually moved up the divisions. A successful first year ended with a semi-final loss to Oldcastle in 1986. More wins than losses were recorded in 1987 but the Secretary's annual report spoke of difficulties in fielding teams at the end of the year.

Moving up the Ladder of the All County Leagues

The following year's league form was a major improvement, with only two losses, to Dunderry and undefeated Ballinlough, both on home ground. There were good victories against An Gaeltacht, Kilcloon, Ballinabrackey, Athboy, Ratoath, Donaghmore, Simonstown Gaels, Wolfe Tones, Carnaross and Cortown. The team's leading scorer was the excellent Aidan Walsh who recorded 3-43 over eleven games.

Sam Tours Dunshaughlin, 1987

Pictured clockwise from top:

After Meath's All-Ireland victory in 1987 the Sam Maguire Cup toured Dunshaughlin.

Front: Denis, Maria, Fiona and Richie Kealy.
Back: Kevin, Aiden, Brendan and Dermot Kealy and Garbhán Blake.

Patty, Elaine, Simon and Tracey Farrell.

Kenny McTigue, Paul Baker and Ian McTigue.

Trevor, Clive, Tommy and Graham Dowd.

Dunshaughlin GFC Management, 1980s

Dunshaughlin GFC Committee and Presidents, 1984
Front: Seán Walsh, Mick Togher, Harry Everard, Pat O Brien, Chairman, Con O Dwyer, Tommy Dowd, Joe Plunkett, Patsy McLoughlin.
Back: Shaun McTigue, Pearse O Dwyer, Michael Walsh, Tossie O Rourke, Matt McEntaggart, Martin Everard, Kevin Kealy, Davy O Dwyer, Aidan Walsh, Ollie Brooks.

Stephen Burke, All-Ireland Clubman of the Year, 1988
GAA President John Dowling, on right, presents Stephen Burke with the All-Ireland Clubman of the Year award in 1988. Also in the picture is a representative of sponsors CIBA-GEIGY.

Dunshaughlin GFC Committee, 1989
Front: Michael Walsh, Paddy O Dwyer, Stephen Burke, Donnchadh Geraghty, Davy O Dwyer.
Back: Shaun McTigue, Chairman, Aidan Walsh, Patsy McLoughlin, Pat Farrell, Dermot Kealy, Jim Gilligan.

Second place in the league led to a place in the final and another tilt at earlier conquerors Ballinlough. Mutual misunderstanding often attended games between clubs from the north and south of the county. Northern sides saw their opponents as soft city types, who were unfamiliar with real football and could be easily intimidated by a touch of steel, while the southerners viewed their counterparts as playing a crude unsophisticated style of football. Before one previous game when Dunshaughlin took on Ballinlough the latter's mentor began his team talk by advising, 'Now look here, these are an ignorant shower!' It was a mutual feeling!

This time the outcome was a comprehensive victory for the simpler northern virtues with Ballinlough triumphing by 5-5 to 1-10. Although missing Trevor Kane and Michael Duffy, Dunshaughlin held a narrow 1-7 to 2-3 lead at half time with Simon Farrell hitting the goal. However, Ballinlough engineered three second half goals to take the honours, but gaining the runners-up position meant promotion to Division 2 and the opportunity to cross swords with the stronger teams. The team that faced Ballinlough lined out as follows: Derek Melia; Matt McEntaggart, Michael O Brien, Garbhán Blake; Donnchadh Geraghty, Derek Maher, Tom Finn (0-1); Ger Dowd, Pádraig Gallagher; Pat Kealy, Pat O Brien (0-1), Aidan Walsh (0-4); Dermot Kealy (0-3), Pat Flanagan (0-1), Simon Farrell (1-0). Sub: Martin Walsh for Pat Kealy.

The players discovered they weren't out of their depth at the higher level and finished the 1989 Division 2 league in a respectable mid-table position after winning five and losing five games, with one drawn. Dunshaughlin's league record of steady progress from Division 3 to Division 2 featured some fine performances against the top teams in the county. Whereas in the mid 80s junior, or poor intermediate clubs, like Bellewstown or An Gaeltacht could derail the team, by 1990 the side was a match for the much stronger Kilmainhamwood, Walterstown, Gaeil Colmcille and Dunboyne, among others. In 1991 the team blazed a trail of glory in the early stages of the league. With many of the top clubs unable to use their county players for league games, the black and ambers were a match for even the best-rated sides. By August they were undefeated in ten games, with eight wins and two draws and were guaranteed a place in the decider.

That final against Dunboyne was an opportunity for rapid revenge for the earlier championship defeat. It was not to be. Dunshaughlin were once again the bridesmaids, losing on a 0-11 to 0-9 scoreline. The team started atrociously but in the second half rocked Dunboyne *with a blistering spell of all out attack which was a far cry from their feeble efforts in the first half.* Simon Farrell was denied by the woodwork from two frees in the final quarter but Dunboyne's Tony Byrne, a leading light in Meath's All-Ireland Minor victory of 1990, was the difference between the sides, recording eight of their eleven scores. Despite the disappointment of adding a loss in the Division 2 League final to the previous Division 3 failure, the silver lining was promotion to the premier grade. In six years the team had risen from an also-ran in Division 3 to a place at the top table. John Davis coached the team and his selectors were Mick Fennell and Don Kane with the team that met Dunboyne lining out as follows:

Pearse O Dwyer; David Kane, Derek Maher, Garbhán Blake; Ciarán Byrne, Kevin Kealy, Niall Foley; Trevor Kane, Pat O Brien; Simon Farrell (0-3), Francis Darby (0-1), Pat Kealy, Capt. (0-1); Aidan Walsh, Pearse Fahy (0-2), Ger Dowd (0-1). Subs: Brendan Kealy (0-1) for Walsh, Alan Duffy for Dowd, Alan Fahy for Darby, Derek Melia, Matt McEntaggart, Tiernan O Rourke, Paul O Rourke, Donnchadh Geraghty, Michael O Brien, Colm Naughton, Dermot Kealy, Allen Foley, Paul Hession.

One of the missing cogs in the wheel slowly being assembled was Dermot Kealy. He would anchor and inspire the team from mid-field in the future but in the early 1990s he missed a number of crucial games due to a cruciate knee injury. Even when he did play he never got a chance to commandeer one position as his versatility saw him switched to plug every gap. In his early career he oscillated between centre back, midfield and centre forward but also manned both wing back and corner back positions as well as cameos in the full forward line. When he finally slotted into midfield from 1999 he became the engine that would drive the team to new heights.

Early arrivals for the 1991 league final got a preview of the future as the St. Seachnall's National School team won the Cumann na mBunscol Division 2 title with a 5-6 to 0-4 victory over Oldcastle. The team featured players who would be centre stage with the black and ambers in the following decade, Michael and Paddy McHale, Ronan Gogan, David Crimmins, David Tonge, Niall Kelly, Denis Kealy and Trevor Dowd.

As we have seen the team was unable to transfer its league form to the championship. This was probably due to the youth and inexperience of the panel but the relative success in the league undoubtedly contributed to the team's ability to compete effectively in the championship from the early 1990s. From 1992 the club played in the premier grade of the league and gradually championship results began to reflect league form.

BLACK & AMBER

A Second String to our Bow

11

From 1987 to 1994 when the club's intermediate side was gradually improving but winning no silverware, the juniors were laying claim to a range of trophies.

While the period from 1980 to 1996 was a barren one for the club's premier side the opposite was true for the second team. Even when the main team was struggling to compete at senior and intermediate level in the early eighties the seconds were often competitive in Junior Division 2. Indeed, at times, players were reluctant to move up to a first team that was never in contention for outright honours, whereas the seconds were always in with a realistic chance of reaching the final stages. From 1979 to 1982 the team reached two quarter-finals and two semis.

Walterstown were the opponents in the 1980 semi-final and a late goal gave them a two-point victory, 1-5 to 0-6. Throughout the game the Dunshaughlin defence was in superb form with Michael O Brien at full-back more than a match for his Walterstown namesake. The most spectacular defender was Michael Wead whose catching was first class, but Joe McDonnell, until injured, Michael Walsh, Pat Farrell and John Kelly were just as effective.

Though Walterstown had plenty of possession it was a tribute to the Dunshaughlin defence that the Blacks only managed six scores over the hour. Three of Dunshaughlin's points were gems from Oliver Brooks, Paddy O Dwyer and Tommy Kane with Jimmy O Rourke laying on accurate passes in each case. Kane had another beauty following a well-worked move involving Paddy O Dwyer

Dunshaughlin Junior Team 1984

Front: Pat Kenny, Pádraig Gallagher, Derek Kenny, Jimmy Walsh, Seán Mangan, John Jennings, Pat Donoghue.
Back: Joe McDonnell, Ken Magee, Pearse O Dwyer, John Summerville, Joe Carberry, Seamus Magee, Cyril Everard, Martin Everard, Oliver Brooks, Capt.

and Fergus O Rourke. However, five minutes from time with Dunshaughlin a point ahead, Eamonn Ward shot through a forest of legs for the vital goal and the black and ambers were defeated.

The team lined out as follows: John Summerville; Joe McDonnell, Michael O Brien, Michael Walsh; John Kelly, Pat Farrell, Michael Wead; Ollie Brooks (0-1), Pat O Hare; Tommy Kane (0-2), Jimmy O Rourke (0-1), Derek Kenny; Tommy Troy, Fergus O Rourke, Paddy O Dwyer (0-2). Subs: Aidan Walsh for Brooks, Val Dowd for McDonnell, Paddy Kenny for Troy.

The team lost at the quarter-final stage to Castletown in 1981 and went a step further in 1982. Having won the division by defeating Kilcloon, Ratoath, Skryne and Donaghmore they qualified for a quarter-final with Oldcastle. The game went to a replay before Dunshaughlin outclassed their opponents. The semi-final against Syddan was a different story. Dunshaughlin started well and were five points up and looking good. However, they soon lost their grip on the game and a youthful Syddan side wrapped the game up early in the second half and finally earned a comprehensive victory, by 1-12 to 1-3. The 1982 team was as follows: Martin Everard; Don McLoughlin, Joe Carberry, Matt McEntaggart; Jimmy O Rourke, Pat Farrell, Seán Mangan; John Kelly, Christy O Sullivan; Michael Wead,

CHAPTER 11: A SECOND STRING TO OUR BOW

Dunshaughlin, Under 21 Football Finalists, 1988

Martin Summerville, Derek Kenny; Con O Dwyer, Jimmy Walsh (1-3), Paddy O Dwyer. Subs: Michael Walsh for O Rourke, Neil O Riordan for P O Dwyer, Joe McDonnell for Mangan.

Those sides consisted mainly of experienced men, many of whom were playing at intermediate level in the 1970s, but also provided opportunities for younger players to gain championship experience. Michael O Brien, John Kelly, Matt McEntaggart, Derek Kenny, Tommy Kane, and John and Martin Summerville were among the younger group.

It was the 1990s before the club's second team would win a title but during the 1980s solid foundations were being laid at under age. St. Martins had been revived in 1983 with the remit of catering for underage football in the parish and that development is covered in detail in Chapter 8. Gradually, those players and others from St. Martins progressed to the Dunshaughlin Under 21 and Junior sides.

Front: Brendan Kealy, Garbhán Blake, Michael Walsh, Alan Fahy, Dermot Kealy, Pat Kealy, Kevin Kealy.
Back: Colm Naughton Paul Hession, David Kane, Derek Maher, Alan Cummins, Simon Farrell, Stephen Claire, Derek Melia, Michael Duffy, Niall Foley, John Davis, Trevor Kane.

Under 21s 1985-1993

In the 1980s there was only one competition at Under 21 level and results were very poor with a loss to junior side St. Vincents in 1985 and a heavy defeat to Dunboyne the following year. A three point loss to Dunderry in 1987, champions the previous year, with a team backboned by that year's minor title winning side held out hope of better things to come.

The following year the team reached the final against Gaeil Colmcille, after good victories over Dunboyne and Seneschalstown following a replay. Against Dunboyne Garbhán Blake, only out of the Under 16 grade, recalls the efforts of then Meath minor Alan Geraghty to intimidate him but the aggression ended after Niall Foley threatened, 'If you touch him again I'll f____ing bust you!'

The opposition from Kells was exceptionally strong with seven of them playing the previous Sunday in a narrow senior semi-final loss to Navan O Mahonys. Before the game started Dunshaughlin faced a huge handicap with the losses of Trevor Kane, injured in the replay against Seneschalstown, and Vinny Moore, sent off in the same game.

However, the most disappointing aspect was the failure of the team to perform to its ability and the side shipped a heavy 0-9 to 0-1 defeat. Simon Farrell claimed the only score but the tactic of using Stephen Claire in a roving role, which worked so well in the minor championship, backfired on this occasion. Yet, many of the players would make a huge contribution at adult level in the years to come.

The team lined out as follows: Derek Melia; David Kane, Derek Maher, Garbhán Blake; John Davis, Michael Duffy, Capt., Niall Foley; Alan Cummins, Kevin Kealy; Pat Kealy, Stephen Claire, Alan Fahy; Michael Walsh, Simon Farrell (0-1), Dermot Kealy. Subs: Brendan Kealy for Cummins, Colm Naughton for Claire, Paul Hession for Foley. The selectors were Jim Gilligan, Val Dowd and Paddy O Dwyer.

Over the next few years Under 21 teams would often go close but would not reach another championship final. In 1989 Dunshaughlin once again went under to the Kells outfit, this time at the quarter-final stage, but only after a rousing contest when Dunshaughlin's ten points were not enough to deny the holders. Trevor Kane and Simon Farrell- who recorded six points- were outstanding.

St. Patricks replaced Gaeil Colmcille as the bogey team for the next two years. With players from the minor championship winning team of 1987 backboning the side many observers expected Dunshaughlin to claim the Under 21 title in 1990. Victory over Skryne, after a replay, and Ballinlough set up a semi-final meeting with the Stamullen side. It was a close encounter but Martin Kirk inspired St. Patricks to a two point victory, 1-11 to 1-9. Stephen Claire had a first half goal

Dunshaughlin, Reserve League Finalists, 1990

1990 Reserve League Team beaten in a replayed final v Skyne, played in December 1991.
Front: Allen Foley, Niall Foley, Pat Kealy, Alan Fahy, Pat O Brien, Kevin Kealy, Alan Duffy, Paul O Rourke, Ciarán Byrne.
Back: Tiernan O Rourke, Pearse Fahy, Noel McTigue, Aiden Kealy, Paul Hession, Pearse O Dwyer, Alan Cummins, Donnchadh Geraghty, Michael O Brien.

Dunshaughlin, Under 21 Semi-Finalists, 1993

Panel that played Seneschalstown in 1993 and who reached the semi-final following Seneschalstown's expulsion from the competition following the water incident. See text.
Front: Hugh McCarthy, David O Neill, Aiden Kealy, Clive Dowd, Ronnie Yore, Ollie McLoughlin, Richie Kealy, Kenny McTigue, Cathal O Connor.
Back: Tiernan O Rourke, Mick Summerville, Michael Keane, Andrew Keane, Brendan Tuite, Brian Murray, Alan Claire, Fionnán Blake, Caoimhín Blake, David Faughnan, Robbie Keane, partly hidden.

Missing from photo: Brian O Rourke, Brendan Kealy and Denis Kealy.

> **Though success at this level eluded the club between the mid eighties and early nineties the pattern of early elimination had been replaced by progress to the latter stages of the competition.**

but, when Dunshaughlin seemed like taking control the Saints' Peter Sullivan netted from a penalty.

Both sides returned for another semi-final tilt the following year, but the end result was the same although the scoreline was more emphatic, 2-10 to 1-5 for the Stamullen lads.

Another appearance in 1993 came about as much by default as ability. The initial round was abandoned when a Seneschalstown player emptied the contents of a bottle of water over referee Joe Harlin. Seneschalstown held a 0-7 to 0-4 lead at the time but were eliminated from the competition by the County Board, who declined a Dunshaughlin offer of a replay.

The 'victory' resulted in Dunshaughlin meeting Moynalvey in the semi-final. With time almost up Moynalvey held a slender one-point lead. Then, Meath All-Ireland winning Under 21 captain Cathal Sheridan scored a goal and though Alan Claire replied almost immediately with a similar strike at the other end Moynalvey held on to the minimum margin and progressed to the final. That team read: Kenny McTigue; Hugh McCarthy, Ronnie Yore, Brian Murray; David Faughnan, David O Neill, Robbie Keane; Aiden Kealy (0-3), Michael Keane; Clive Dowd, Tiernan O Rourke, Alan Claire (1-0); Brian O Rourke, Brendan Kealy (0-3), Cathal O Connor. Subs: Fionnán Blake for McCarthy, Mick Summerville for O Connor, Denis Kealy for Dowd, Richie Kealy, Ollie McLoughlin, Brendan Tuite, Andrew Keane, Caoimhín Blake.

Though success at this level eluded the club between the mid eighties and early nineties the pattern of early elimination had been replaced by progress to the latter stages of the competition. Thus, the nineties began with renewed optimism that the work at underage, Under 21 and junior levels would soon provide a team capable of matching, and maybe surpassing, the achievements of the seventies' team. However, the road ahead proved to be rocky and uneven and the trip was to be far from smooth.

A Reserve League Title

With numerous new players emerging from St. Martins, a third team was entered in league and championship. A team captained by Niall Foley, with Jim Gilligan and Aidan Walsh as selectors, won the 1989 Reserve League, with a semi-final victory over Castletown, and a comprehensive final victory over Kilmainhamwood by 1-15 to 0-5. Because the final stages were delayed until 1991, the team contained many intermediate players and it marked their first success at adult level.

Apart from the 1987 minor title most of the young players had experienced numerous defeats as minors and Under 21s and were beginning to wonder if they would ever win anything. In late 1990 some of the players won a bottle of champagne at a karaoke competition in a Navan nightclub and it was agreed that it would be used to celebrate the intermediate title when it arrived! However, such was the relief at having won something that it was opened in the dressing room in Kilberry after the Reserve League victory and sprayed around the room in celebration.

The winning team read: Pearse O Dwyer; David Kane, Donnchadh Geraghty, Niall Foley, Capt.; Ciarán Byrne, Dermot Kealy, Garbhán Blake; Colm Naughton, Alan Cummins (0-1); Pat Kealy (0-2), Francis Darby (0-1), Brendan Kealy (0-2); Pearse Fahy (1-3), Simon Farrell (0-4), Paul O Rourke (0-2). Subs Aiden Kealy for Byrne, Alan Duffy for Fahy, Martin Summerville for Kane.

The 1990 reserve team went close to replicating that achievement when reaching the final against Skryne. It took a replay to separate the neighbours, with two late Alan Fahy goals forcing a draw in the initial encounter. The replay was a closely contested affair, with Pearse Fahy and Tiernan O Rourke scoring Dunshaughlin's goals. Points were scarce however, O Rourke had one and Pat Kealy recorded four but that left the black and ambers one short of the Blues' total, 2-6 to 2-5.

Both of those teams were backboned by graduates of the 1987-89 minor sides. The 1989 Reserve team featured eleven and the 1990 side started with seven of them. In addition, the arrival in Dunshaughlin of players like Donnchadh Geraghty, John Considine, Val Gannon and Alan Duffy formerly of Navan De La Salles, Walterstown, Cavan Gaels and St. Pauls respectively added further experience and depth to the club's resources. While the intermediate side embarked on a slow, circuitous voyage to the title, success arrived more rapidly at junior level.

A Championship at Last: Junior Kingpins 1991

Val Dowd, Stephen Burke and Jim Smith took charge of the club's second team for the Junior Division 3 competition in 1991. The team disposed of St. Marys in the quarter-final with two goals from Ciarán O Dwyer and eliminated Carnaross in the semi-final by 2-6 to 1-5. Liam O Neill scored the first goal, with his replacement Alan Claire, bagging the second. Kevin Kealy, the side's second highest scorer on 0-16, missed the final due to his promotion to the intermediate side earlier.

It took two games to decide the outcome of the title, with a last gasp Alan Duffy free giving Dunshaughlin a replay in the first meeting. St. Michaels from north Meath were final opponents and on a wet and windy November day Dunshaughlin

> While the intermediate side embarked on a slow, circuitous voyage to the title, success arrived more rapidly at junior level.

Dunshaughlin, Junior Football Division 3, Champions, 1991

Front: Alan Fahy, John Considine, Allen Foley, Alan Cummins, Capt., Ciarán O Dwyer, Paul O Rourke, Val Gannon.
Back: Stephen Claire, Alan Duffy, Colm Naughton, Derek Melia, Michael O Brien, Aiden Kealy, Donnchadh Geraghty, Pádraig Gallagher.

Junior Selectors 1990s
The successful Junior selectors of the 1990s sporting a Cecilia Dowd creation in Black and Amber, Val Dowd, Stephen Burke and Jim Smith.

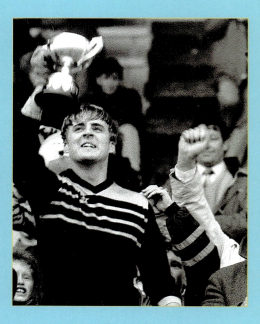

Captain Cummins and Cup
Alan Cummins raises the cup after victory in the 1991 Junior Division 3 final. On left of photo, partly hidden is a young Michael McHale.

CHAPTER 11: A SECOND STRING TO OUR BOW

was the better team throughout, seeming to have the title in their grasp as the game entered its closing stages. But opposition midfielder Jimmy Farrelly struck late with two goals, the first, a lob under the bar that eluded Derek Melia in the goals, and the second, a scrappy affair poked over the line with time almost up.

Team manager Val Dowd, frustrated with the unexpected turn around, appeared near the end-line as the second goal went in and thumped the ground with his umbrella in disgust. Disillusioned, he made his way to the dressing room and missed one final effort to retrieve the situation. Corner-forward Alan Duffy, like the cavalry in the best westerns, rescued the situation at the death. He gained possession and went on a run deep into the St. Michaels' half where he was fouled. He then held his nerve to send over the equalizing point from the resultant free.

The replay confirmed Dunshaughlin as the better team, with captain Alan Cummins celebrating his twenty-third birthday when leading the side to an emphatic victory by 1-8 to 0-4. Conditions were again poor and the winners held a slender 0-2 to 0-0 half time advantage after completely dominating play but coming up short on the scoreboard.

In the final half-hour Dunshaughlin made no mistake and Val Gannon notched the only goal of the day. When Paul O Rourke surged out of defence and delivered a long ball that St. Michael's keeper Noel Clarke could only parry, Val was on hand to fist the breaking ball to the net. Moments later Val and Jackie Lynch were dismissed by referee Barney McCluskey after a melee broke out.

Alan Duffy was in top form from frees and set up substitute Alan Claire for another with a well crafted pass. Michael O Brien, who had returned from London that morning, was outstanding at full-back in a defence that was always on top. Other top class performances came from Aiden Kealy and Paul O Rourke in the corners, and Donnchadh Geraghty at centre back. David O Neill, who came on as a substitute, played superbly in the half back line while John Considine marked his first championship medal with a fine late point and a very effective performance in defence.

Pádraig Gallagher was unfortunate when an injury in the early minutes forced his departure. Val Dowd had reminded the panel at a meeting prior to the replay to have everything in order, in particular boot laces. When Liam O Neill got the call to replace Gallagher and went to check his boots, the laces snapped and frantic, furtive efforts were made to replace them in the hope Val wouldn't notice. Val, however, detected the commotion and Liam was dispatched to the field of play with benedictions ringing in his ear!

This was the first championship victory for the club since 1977 and was celebrated in style. Val Dowd in particular, could take great credit for moulding the team into a unit. In the words of co-selector Jim Smith, 'Val Dowd will be crowned King of Dunshaughlin.' The line out for the replay was:

> Team manager Val Dowd, frustrated with the unexpected turn around, appeared near the end-line as the second goal went in and thumped the ground with his umbrella in disgust.

BLACK & AMBER

Dunshaughlin, Junior B Football Finalists, 1992

Neighbours Batterstown defeated the above team in the 1992 Junior B final in Páirc Tailteann.

Mascots at front: Amy Considine, Duncan Geraghty.

Front: David O Neill, Alan Fahy, John Considine, Ger Dowd, Aidan Walsh, Matt McEntaggart, Ciarán O Dwyer.

Back: Brian O Rourke, Noel McTigue, Alan Cummins, Michael O Brien, Derek Melia, Colm Naughton, Donnchadh Geraghty, Kevin Kealy.

Derek Melia
Paul O Rourke   Michael O Brien   Aiden Kealy
Allen Foley   Donnchadh Geraghty   John Considine (0-1)
Alan Cummins, Capt.   Colm Naughton (0-1)
Stephen Claire   Pádraig Gallagher   Alan Fahy (0-1)
Alan Duffy (0-4)   Val Gannon (1-0)   Ciarán O Dwyer

Subs: Alan Claire (0-1) for O Dwyer, Liam O Neill for Gallagher, David O Neill for Foley, Martin Summerville, Brian O Rourke, John Joe McDonnell, TP Toolan, Noel McTigue, Martin Walsh, David Faughnan, Robbie Keane.

The following year, 1992, the panel made a brave bid for further honours. Now promoted to the Junior B Championship, the omens did not look good after a heavy first round defeat to neighbours Batterstown. Meath minor star Paul Nestor had a tally of 3-2 from corner-forward. Not daunted by this setback the

CHAPTER 11: A SECOND STRING TO OUR BOW

team and management ploughed on to emerge from the section as runners-up after victories against Walterstown and St. Ultan's and a walkover to Ballinabrackey. Slane provided little opposition in the quarter-final as Dunshaughlin recorded a comprehensive 3-6 to 1-5 victory. The semi-final was a more closely contested affair but Dunshaughlin registered a well-deserved 1-10 to 2-5 win against Seneschalstown. Substitute Michael Keane scored the decisive goal when he fielded a free outside the square, turned and shot to the net.

This set up a reprise of the first round, for Batterstown had progressed, unbeaten, to the final. Dunshaughlin knew the first round game had little relevance to the final, as players like Matt McEntaggart, Ciarán O Dwyer, Kevin Kealy and Ger Dowd who had missed the initial meeting were available for the decider.

Dunshaughlin fielded a strong team, with Aidan Walsh, who had moved down from intermediate level, the side's top marksman on 5-18 from five games prior to the final. Ger Dowd was a handful at corner-forward and the team contained eight players from the previous year's winning side. Derek Melia, Michael O Brien, Donnchadh Geraghty and John Considine were still in defence, the midfield pairing of Alan Cummins and Colm Naughton was the same but Alan Fahy was the only forward who started both finals. Ciarán O Dwyer who featured in attack in 1991 was a wing back in 1992. The same selectors were at the helm as Dunshaughlin, with wind assistance, led 0-7 to 0-6 by the interval.

The outcome was decided by two goals soon after the restart. Paul Nestor, a member of that year's Meath Minor All-Ireland winning team, was hauled down three minutes into the second half and although Derek Melia saved his penalty shot, Nestor followed up to slide the rebound past the keeper. Three minutes later Darragh Smith combined with Nestor for a second goal. Despite Dunshaughlin's efforts there was no way back and Batterstown deservedly went on to take their first title since 1972.

For the losers Alan Cummins had a superb first half at midfield, John Considine, Michael O Brien and Donnchadh Geraghty gave nothing away at the back and Aidan Walsh was in superb form up front, with a marvelous point from play and four frees. Substitutes Diarmuid Leen and Pádraig Gallagher also contributed a point each, as did David O Neill, Alan Fahy and Ger Dowd. Noel Farrell captained a Batterstown side that won by 2-8 to 0-10. A feature of the final for the 'fashion' conscious was the appearance of all three selectors kitted out in newly knitted black and amber jumpers- a Cecilia Dowd creation.

> **"** A feature of the final for the 'fashion' conscious was the appearance of all three selectors kitted out in newly knitted black and amber jumpers- a Cecilia Dowd creation.

In 1992 Dunshaughlin and Batterstown played a repeat of that year's Junior Final to raise funds for the victims of the Somalia Famine. Donnchadh Geraghty accepted the Bank of Ireland sponsored trophy from bank representative Brendan Dowd. The trophy was subsequently presented annually to the club's Hall of Fame winner between 1995 and 2012.

A Saga in Three Acts

Many of the same players were playing league football for the club's second team in Division 5 of the All County Football League. The team had a very successful 1992, qualifying for the final with Gaeil Colmcille, but it would take three games and over a year to get a result. The team combined intermediate and junior players and victory could have gone either way in the initial meeting at Castletown as the lead changed hands in the closing stages. An Alan Fahy goal early in the second half put Dunshaughlin in the driving seat but the Kells men gradually hauled back the lead and went one point ahead close to time. An Aiden Kealy point from 50 metres rescued Dunshaughlin and the game ended 1-7 to 0-10.

The replay didn't take place until a year later, but in the meantime incidents during the game made all the news. Dunshaughlin's Ger Dowd and Michael Rennicks of Gaeil Colmcille were sent off in one incident and Tomás McQuaid of Kells was also dismissed near the end. Following McQuaid's departure a row erupted on the sideline during which a Gaeil Colmcille supporter attacked and injured Val Dowd. For Dunshaughlin the outcome was lengthy suspensions for Val and for John Considine who had been involved in an altercation with McQuaid prior to his sending off.

The issue led to conflict and dissension in the club that continued for almost a year with Val believing the club had failed to support him adequately and had colluded with the County Board in his suspension. Leinster Council reduced the suspension on appeal and Val was able to return as a team mentor for the long delayed replay. Club Secretary, Jim Gilligan, resigned at the following annual meeting due to the controversy.

A whole year elapsed before the second replay took place. It also ended in a draw, in Páirc Tailteann, with a last minute goal giving the Kells side a draw, 0-9 to 1-6. Extra time wasn't played as the Division 2 league final between Carnaross and Simonstown was scheduled to follow and in the gathering gloom it was clear there would be insufficient light to cater for extra time as well as the second game.

Finally, Dunshaughlin emerged victorious in episode three in Rathkenny a few weeks later by 1-9 to 2-5. Given the history of the fixture a hullabaloo was inevitable. This time it revolved around Castletown referee Paddy Smyth, who initially claimed Gaeil Colmcille had won. Dunshaughlin's officials insisted that the black and ambers had recorded a one-point win and as Gaeil Colmcille backed up this view the referee finally accepted he was in error. Val Dowd, Con O Dwyer and Joe McDonnell were the mentors of the following team that finally emerged victorious:

Derek Melia; Donnchadh Geraghty, Capt., Michael O Brien, David O Neill;

Dunshaughlin, Junior B Champions, 1994

Michael Keane, Aiden Kealy, Stephen Claire (0-1); Alan Cummins (0-1), Colm Naughton; Richie Kealy (0-4), Diarmuid Leen, Alan Fahy (0-2); Ger Dowd (1-1), Tiernan O Rourke, Aidan Walsh. Subs: David Faughnan for O Rourke, Brian O Rourke for Walsh, Ronnie Yore for Michael O Brien, Paul O Rourke, Garbhán Blake, Thomas Walsh, Alan Duffy, John Considine. (Two points unaccounted for).

Front: Eric Yore, Liam O Neill, Niall Foley, Stephen Kelly, Matt McEntaggart, Mervyn Ennis, Thomas Walsh, Alan Duffy with Duncan Geraghty in front and Daniel Geraghty to his left, John Considine with Rebecca Considine, Mick Summerville. Back: Cathal O Connor, David Faughnan, Ronnie Yore, David O Neill, Michael Keane, Brian Murray, Alan Cummins, Michael O Brien, Noel McTigue- partly hidden, Kenny McTigue, George Ennis, Capt., Clive Dowd, Alan O Dwyer, Pat O Brien, Donnchadh Geraghty, Martin Summerville.

Another Junior Title, 1994

Following the championship defeat to Batterstown in 1992 Dunshaughlin remained in the Junior B grade. The team reached the quarter-final in 1993, losing out to Slane, but in 1994 returned to Páirc Tailteann for another tilt at the title. It took a play-off against Simonstown to reach the semi-finals where Dunshaughlin overcame St. Patricks by 2-13 to 2-6. A cracking 25-metre goal from Clive Dowd was the highlight of the hour- he also added three points to his tally- and another goal from Michael Keane late on, ensured victory.

George Ennis with Junior Cup, 1994
George Ennis, captain of the victorious Junior B championship winning team of 1994, raises the trophy aloft.

Breen O Grady, formerly with Navan O Mahonys, joined selectors Val Dowd, Con O Dwyer and Derek Kenny before the semi-final to hone the team for the final stages of the campaign. North Meath side Syddan provided the opposition in the final in late November. Of the fifteen who started the 1991 final replay against St. Michaels, only four lined out in 1994. Surprisingly, all four retained the same positions. Michael O Brien and Donnchadh Geraghty manned central defence, Alan Cummins took his place at midfield while Alan Duffy wore the number thirteen jersey. John Considine who played in defence in 1991 was a substitute three years later. Diarmuid Leen, a former Galway Under 21 player, then living in Dunshaughlin, was a newcomer to the team and the Ennis brothers, Mervyn and George occupied the left wing of the attack.

It took a rousing final quarter display to capture the title. Although the sides were level at half-time Dunshaughlin slipped into arrears early in the second half and with twenty minutes remaining Syddan were 1-6 to 0-5 to the fore. The introduction of David O Neill and Niall Foley and the move of team captain Donnchadh Geraghty from defence to centre forward paid dividends as the black and ambers took control of the game.

Eight minutes from time Geraghty was on hand to score a crucial goal, which proved the difference between the sides. After a move involving Stephen Kelly, Alan Duffy and George Ennis, Geraghty forced the ball over the line at the second attempt for a vital goal. A super point from play by Mervyn Ennis, a pointed free from the same player and a further point from brother George completed Dunshaughlin's recovery and guaranteed them the title on a score of 1-9 to 1-6.

The team lined out as follows:

Kenny McTigue

Matt McEntaggart   Michael O Brien   Brian Murray

Stephen Kelly   Donnchadh Geraghty (1-0)   Thomas Walsh

Michael Keane   Alan Cummins

Clive Dowd   Diarmuid Leen   Mervyn Ennis (0-6)

Alan Duffy (0-2)   Pat O Brien   George Ennis, Capt. (0-1)

Subs: David O Neill for Cummins, Niall Foley for P O Brien, Noel McTigue for Leen, Brian Murray, Ronnie Yore, Alan O Dwyer, John Considine, David Faughnan, Cathal O Connor, Martin Summerville, Raymond Yore, Liam O Neill and Mick Summerville.

Due to promotion to the intermediate team the junior side lost its first two captains, Derek Melia and Alan Fahy. George Ennis successfully took over the role after their departure and captained the side in the final. It was a remarkable achievement for a man who had the use of one arm only and who, despite this, developed a level of skill in the sport that many could only aspire to.

The same year the club won the inaugural McCarthy-Duffy Cup, which commemorated young players Robert McCarthy and Simon Duffy who died tragically in a car accident in Dunshaughlin in June 1993. A team captained by Hugh McCarthy defeated Skryne 1-8 to 0-5 lining out as follows: Kenny McTigue; Martin Summerville, Matt McEntaggart, Robbie Keane; Allen Foley, Brian Murray, David O Neill; Larry Smith, Michael Keane (1-0); Alan O Dwyer (0-1), Noel McTigue (0-1), Clive Dowd (0-3); Vinny Moore (0-1), Cathal O Connor (0-1), Hugh McCarthy, Capt. (0-1).

Thus, from 1987 to 1994 when the club's intermediate side was gradually improving but winning no silverware, the juniors were laying claim to a range of trophies. Between them St. Martins and Dunshaughlin had captured championships at Minor (1987), Junior Division 3 (1991) and Junior B (1994) as well as a Reserve League (1989) and All County Division 5 league (1991). In addition the club finished as runners-up in the Minor (1989), Under 21 (1988) and Junior B (1992) championships. These victories paved the way for success for the club's first team in the late 1990s and into the new millennium.

ent_inter-e#d;B> # BLACK & AMBER

CHAPTER 12: 1992-1997

The Rocky Road to Intermediate Glory, 1992-1997

From the lows of the 1980s through the disappointments of the early 1990s the club had finally reached the promised land after almost as many tribulations as Moses.

From 1992 onwards the intermediate team moved out of the pack of also-rans and took its place among the front-runners for the championship.
Whereas, during the eighties the best performance was a quarter-final appearance in 1986, during the nineties the team invariably reached the semi-final. Operating out of Division 1 of the league the team was always up against the best teams in the county and this provided top class championship preparation.

    The arrival of Colum Bracken also boosted the side. He had almost a decade of senior experience with St. Oliver Plunketts in Dublin and won a Leinster Under 21 title with the Dubs in 1984, prior to moving to Australia for two years. There he played at state level and captained New South Wales against a Victoria side who had Trevor Kane and Jim Stynes at midfield. He also partnered Trevor on an All-Australian team against the visiting Bank of Ireland All Star side. When he returned to Ireland Colum relocated to Dunshaughlin and was pleasantly surprised to find himself again partnering Trevor in the centre of the field.

    After winning promotion from Division 2 in 1991 the team soon established itself firmly in the top grade, finishing in fourth place in 1992. Bracken recalls his first game for the club, against St. Michaels in Carlanstown, when his welcome to

> Dunshaughlin 'were kicking wides as if scores weren't allowed,'

football in the Royal County was a fist to the jaw from an opposition midfielder on the throw-in. 'Brack' noted that this was a once-off, commenting that, 'The game in Meath was more physical compared to Dublin but there were never any nasty blows or dirty play, apart from the first day.' Maybe opponents quickly realized that Colum wasn't to be trifled with! Medical facilities were still primitive, however. Later in the same game Francis Darby suffered an injury and in the absence of a stretcher was carried off on a toilet door!

The first of many semi-final appearances occurred in 1992. The initial round of the intermediate championship pitted the black and ambers against regular opponents, St. Marys, who often had the upper hand in clashes. A 1-13 to 2-7 victory was a promising start, but the concession of two goals set what was to become a worrying trend. A narrow victory against Carnaross was followed by a scare against Dunsany when only a late goal from Francis Darby retrieved a game that seemed to have slipped away. This guaranteed the squad a place in the knock-out stages but a defeat to St. Patricks meant progression as runners-up rather than winners.

A comprehensive quarter-final victory against Ballinabrackey, 2-16 to 2-5, set up a semi-final meeting with neighbours Dunboyne. Early in the quarter-final Dunshaughlin *were kicking wides as if scores weren't allowed,*' but with Francis Darby *'scoring three fine points from play and using his strength to telling effect'* the team drew level at half-time. In the second half the losers were run off their feet, Colum Bracken was a tower of strength and goals from Pearse Fahy and Stephen Claire left the black and ambers comfortable winners.

The *Chronicle* described Dunshaughlin as *'one of the best organized and most consistent teams in the county'* in a preview of the semi-final, but the game was a complete mismatch. Bracken had moved to centre-forward during the Ballinabrackey game to counter the influence of their centre back Aidan Coffey, but his selection there against Dunboyne gave the winners the advantage at midfield and an early Dunboyne blitz put them eight points ahead at half time. Already missing Simon Farrell and Brendan Kealy before losing Stephen Claire during the game, all due to injury, Dunshaughlin could make little impact and finished 0-13 to 0-5 in arrears and exited the championship.

Nevertheless, 1992 was a successful year, for, in addition to reaching the Junior B final, as outlined in the previous chapter, the Division 1 league team recorded seven victories to four losses. There were a number of other positives.

The usual midfield pairing of Trevor Kane and Colum Bracken was a match for any in the county. When he performed at his best Trevor was a spectacular fielder and a consistent scorer, with 0-16 in league and championship in 1992. He was outstanding in Meath's All-Ireland junior victory in 1988, and again in 1992 when Wexford proved too strong for the Royals in the Leinster final. Bracken complemented Kane, bringing strength, intelligence, calmness and determination to the side and such was his impact that he was appointed captain in his first year with the club.

The forwards did reasonably well; the points tally was impressive but goals were scarce. Alan Duffy and Brendan Kealy shared the scoring honours in league and championship on 0-36 and 2-27 respectively, Simon Farrell recorded 0-24, Francis Darby 1-16 and Tiernan O Rourke 1-15. One of the biggest problems was the absence of a recognized centre half back. After an injury to Dermot Kealy a different player was used in each of the three championship games. A consistent performer was essential here while more penetration was required up front.

The Carnaross Saga

Appointing a coach or trainer to the team often proved drawn out and problematical. In 1993 John Davis had taken on the role but was also busy guiding the Meath senior hurlers to the All-Ireland B title and was thus unable to oversee the Dunshaughlin intermediate side. It was mid-August before Anto McCaul, a member of Dublin's All-Ireland winning panel in 1983, arrived.

He watched Summerhill defeat the black and ambers in a league game before agreeing to manage the team. It was an ideal game, in that Dunshaughlin's performance didn't match the team's potential and the side looked leaderless and disorganized. McCaul saw the talent, decided that the team had the ability to win the title and took on the job with the intention of correcting the deficiencies and boosting fitness.

A demanding regime was put in place. Players had to be on time for training and ready for one hour's intensive work. Training was all about everyone giving total commitment and everything was done on a competitive basis. In group sprints the slowest runner's time counted as the group's time so participants had to support each other. Lots of supporters attended training to view the strict regime, one observing, 'I don't know if they're training for a football match or a marathon.'

Challenge games against Dublin sides were also a feature of the regime. In one, against Oliver Plunketts on their Navan Road grounds, a major fracas broke out after a couple of fouls on Dunshaughlin players and the referee blew the whistle and walked off! Afterwards McCaul commended the team on its 'one in-all in' approach and the willingness to stand up for each other.

A week later, during a challenge against Lucan, a posse of Dunshaughlin players waded in to sort out the transgressor after a foul and McCaul had to remind the players that while he admired solidarity he didn't mean the players were to go

> 'Full credit to Dunshaughlin for grabbing the chance but if I was told they had spent the week prior to the game in Lourdes I'd be tempted to believe it.'

looking for opportunities to display it! Experiences like this, and the huge effort required at training, moulded the team into a unit, dedicated to each other. Aidan Walsh, by now a regular for a decade, believed that the team improved its fitness by forty per cent, to levels not previously experienced.

Prior to McCaul's arrival the team had no difficulty progressing to the knock-out stages with victories over Donaghmore, Moynalty, Castletown and St. Ultans. After his arrival the team played Civil Service from Dublin, a side peppered with county players, and in front of a massive crowd drew the match after a cracking game.

In the *Arch Bar* afterwards all the talk was of a county championship. Later, a narrow two-point victory over St. Marys put Dunshaughlin through to the semi-final for the second successive year. This time the opponents were Carnaross, backboned by current and future Meath stars PJ Gillic and Ollie Murphy. It took two games and extra time to separate the sides.

The *Chronicle* headed its report on the initial encounter, '*What a Shambles as Carnaross Blow It!*' going on to comment, '*Full credit to Dunshaughlin for grabbing the chance but if I was told they had spent the week prior to the game in Lourdes I'd be tempted to believe it.*' Dunshaughlin had started well, with Garbhán Blake outstanding, and led at half time, but with less than ten minutes remaining Carnaross held a one-goal lead. Dunshaughlin's Tiernan O Rourke and Colum Bracken had already been sent off, David Kane was replaced due to injury and all the aces seemed to be with Carnaross. However, against the odds, Dunshaughlin rallied for a draw with a Brendan Kealy free, a super score from substitute Simon Farrell and an injury time Alan Duffy free making seven points to Carnaross' 1-4.

The club formally objected to Paddy Kavanagh's appointment to referee the replay in the light of his two sendings off in the first game and also asked for a deferral of the replay for a week. No response was forthcoming and he duly took charge of the second encounter the following week. Further controversy erupted prior to the game when Kavanagh upbraided Anto McCaul and selector Paddy O Dwyer for allegedly condoning rough play and a further formal complaint was lodged. By then it was immaterial.

The replay was the opposite of the original game with an under strength Dunshaughlin playing some outstanding football to carve out a six point lead in the second half after Pat O Brien set up Aidan Walsh for a goal. Now it was Carnaross' turn to rally and their pressure told when two penalties were conceded, both of which PJ Gillic converted. A free edged them ahead, but again, Alan Duffy, as so often in his career, came to the rescue with a pressure point from a '45 three minutes into injury time.

Extra time followed but an early goal gave Carnaross the initiative, which they held to the end to emerge victorious, 3-15 to 1-17. Seamus Reilly, who lined out at wing-back, was a pivotal member of the winning team. He later moved to Dunshaughlin where he became heavily involved in under-age coaching before succumbing to illness in 2011.

The team for the replay read as follows:

Pearse O Dwyer; Dermot Kealy, Derek Maher, Garbhán Blake; Ciarán Byrne, Aiden Kealy, Kevin Kealy; Trevor Kane, Colm Naughton; Aiden Walsh (1-8), Francis Darby, Brendan Kealy (0-2); Alan Duffy (0-5), Pat O Brien (0-1), Ger Dowd (0-1). Subs: Michael O Brien for Darby, Darby for Blake, Blake for M O Brien.

The semi-final outcome was a disappointing end to a year that had promised much, made all the more frustrating when, like Dunboyne the previous year, Carnaross went on the win the championship. Injuries to key players were a feature of the year, especially during the semi-final, and the departure early in the year of Stephen Claire on United Nations' duty with the Irish Army didn't help matters. This was balanced by the return of Trevor Kane from Chicago at the quarter-final stage but he suffered a critical injury in the semi-final replay in what transpired to be his last game for the club.

The quality of the team was underlined by the number of players who were featuring at inter-county level at the time.

Trevor Kane won a Leinster Minor championship medal with Meath in 1985 before going on to feature in three Junior triumphs. Four of the Kealy brothers featured on the Meath Junior team at various stages with three of them, Aiden, Dermot and Richie on the team that won Leinster championship honours in 1997. Richie would eventually lay claim to three Leinster medals while Aiden and Dermot both won a brace. Derek Maher won a Leinster championship as an Under 21 in 1990 but suffered a broken jaw in the semi-final against Kildare. Yet, he was back the following year as part of the Meath junior panel that took Leinster honours after a replayed victory against Dublin in Croke Park.

Both Francis Darby and Stephen Claire were members of the county junior team in 1993 but the selected fifteen never played. The junior selectors resigned when the county board's fixture list led to a clash between club games and the junior inter-county game. As a result, Meath fielded a weakened side and lost to Laois.

Brendan Kealy was an outstanding half-forward on the Meath Minor All-Ireland winning team of 1990. His determination was reflected in his recovery from an appendicitis operation in late April of that year to make the county minor team in June and play a central role in the All-Ireland triumph in September. He possessed an uncanny ability to win possession in congested contests, burn opponents with pace and skill and kick vital scores, but injuries had limited his

Success at County Level

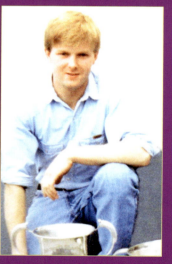

Clockwise from top left:

Action shot of Brendan Kealy, from Leinster Minor final 1990.

Pictured in Dunshaughlin in 1992 with the All-Ireland Minor Football trophy, the Tom Markham Cup, are panel members Brian O Rourke and Aiden Kealy, with Amy Considine grabbing a ringside seat.

Trevor Kane winner of All-Ireland Junior 1988, Leinster Junior 1988 and 1991 and Leinster Minor medals 1985.

Derek Maher winner Leinster U21 medal in 1990 and Junior title in 1991.

The Kealy family, Ead, Richie, Aiden, Dermot and Patsy, celebrate the Leinster Junior title in 1996.

participation in 1993 for club and county. He played Under 21 for Meath for three consecutive years following the Minor win in 1990, winning two Leinster and one All-Ireland in that grade. Younger brother Richie won a Leinster Minor championship medal in 1993, having played against Louth in the first round, only to be inexplicably excluded from the panel for the final stages.

Dermot Kealy earned a Leinster Under 21 medal in 1991 while Aiden Kealy and Brian O Rourke were members of the Meath panel that won the All-Ireland minor title in 1992. Aiden played at centre back in the first two rounds but a recurring knee injury limited his appearances thereafter. Brian joined the panel following impressive form with St. Martins in the minor championship and played in the Ulster minor league.

With such a reservoir of talent it seemed an intermediate title would not be long delayed. It transpired that the delay was much longer than most observers expected.

Another Semi-Final Tilt

Cecilia Dowd
Dunshaughlin club's Fixtures' Secretary during the 1990s and dedicated supporter of the club's teams.

If McCaul had been appointed earlier in the year he would have had a longer time to improve fitness. In the event, the heavy training probably told against Dunshaughlin in the semi-final replay as they faded out in extra time. Many people hoped that 1994 would prove third time lucky but engaging a coach continued to be an ongoing saga. McCaul seemed the logical choice but despite taking a number of training sessions he was unable to commit to the position.

The lack of certainty led to dissension among the panel early in the year with poor turn outs at training and mediocre results. The *Chronicle* noted that *'internal problems haven't helped their early preparations, but once they settle down and get into the right frame of mind they should be knocking on the door.'* This proved correct and victory over St. Patricks in the quarter-final sent the team into its third semi in a row. St. Patricks could only manage two second half points as Colum Bracken dominated midfield, Ciarán Byrne, Derek Maher, Garbhán Blake and David Kane were on top in defence and Richie Kealy notched a goal in the opening minute.

Liam Harnan, the former Meath centre back was recruited to assist with preparations late in the campaign as Kilmainhamwood stood between Dunshaughlin and the dream of a final place. There was to be no third time lucky, as the 'Wood triumphed 0-10 to 0-7. The *Chronicle* was critical of Dunshaughlin's physical approach and claimed that Kilmainhamwood were far better and concentrated on their task.

The black and ambers were in front by one point at half time and held a 0-7 to 0-6 lead entering the final quarter when the 'Wood lost a man after a high challenge on Garbhán Blake. However, the advantage was short lived. Within minutes a free was moved closer to goal due to a defender's dissent and the sides were level. Players on the field were soon equal in numbers also when Francis Darby was sent off. The eventual winners pulled clear in the closing stages and even though veteran substitute Ger Dowd almost grabbed a dramatic equalizing goal Dunshaughlin were again denied a final appearance.

Once more the black and ambers had faltered close to the winning post. The 1993 performance suggested the team was improving but defeat after such a huge effort meant many faced into 1994 in pessimistic mode. The difficulty in maintaining the progress of the previous year and the defeat to Kilmainhamwood caused doubts to take root and many commentators declared that the side would never win a championship. Trevor Kane's absence throughout the year was a big blow and his departure for the USA meant the strong centre field partnership with Colum Bracken was at an end.

The forwards had not made the requisite improvement from the previous year. Apart from a big score against a poor Moynalty outfit the side struggled to compile decent totals. In four championship outings with Simonstown Gaels, Donaghmore, St. Patricks and Kilmainhamwood the team amassed a mere 2-30, and the seven points recorded against the latter was never going to win a semi-final. Aidan Walsh, who was in and out of the team in 1993, played in all championship games in 1994 and was the side's leading scorer on 1-17. Apart from Simon Farrell with eleven points, nobody else made a regular, significant scoring contribution and until that was rectified championship success was unlikely.

Matters deteriorated in 1995 when, for the first time since 1990, the team failed to emerge from the group stages. A coach was in position early in the year with Kevin Kilmurray, an All-Ireland winner with Offaly in 1971 and 1972 and an All Star in 1972 and 1973, in charge. The year started well with championship wins against Moynalty and St. Patricks and big wins against St. Ultans and St. Brigids but an unexpected loss to Castletown brought St. Patricks back into the reckoning and forced a three-way play off. Preparation for those was inadequate, turn out at training was inconsistent and the coach was unavailable for the final play-off games.

First up was an opportunity to reverse the Castletown result with the losers entitled to a second chance against St. Patricks. In a low scoring encounter at headquarters Dunshaughlin fell a point short in the end. Ger Dowd fisted an early goal after superb work by Colum Bracken and Brendan Kealy and then he had another goal effort excellently saved. Castletown could make no headway in the first half and Dunshaughlin held a 1-4 to 0-1 advantage early in the second. The referee dismissed two Castletown players and Aiden Kealy followed soon after, but despite the numerical disadvantage Castletown rallied as Dunshaughlin wilted. A goal and two points for the north county men in the closing stages, saw them emerge victorious by a solitary point, 1-5 to 1-4.

In the early nineties Dunshaughlin always seemed to perform badly in Páirc Tailteann, a venue later teams would regard as home. There was a war of words in the tunnel after the game with taunts from Castletown of 'Go on back to Dublin!' and an unhappy sulphurous dressing room after the game compounded matters. A meeting with St. Patricks at Walterstown was to be the last chance saloon but the change of venue didn't improve matters.

The recovery time was too short and the team was probably defeated before it took the field as the loss to Castletown hung like a pall over the panel. Simon Farrell, Aiden and Dermot Kealy missed the encounter and a lack of accuracy in the forward line limited the team's tally to 1-6. It wasn't enough to trump St. Patrick's 0-11, which included three points from centre-back Cormac Murphy, and the black and ambers were out of the championship for another year.

Emerging Talent

The only bright spot in 1995 was reaching the Under 21 Special final against Slane. This grade was a level below the championship proper and Dunshaughlin had an impressive semi-final victory over neighbours Blackhall Gaels by 3-6 to 1-9. New young players who would have a long and successful career at intermediate and senior level such as Kenny McTigue, Denis Kealy, Fearghal Gogan, Graham Dowd and David Tonge featured on the side. Nevertheless, the final outcome was a crushing blow.

Dunshaughlin led from the 2nd to the 59th minute and even the *Chronicle* described the result as *'harsh justice'* and that *'it seemed somewhat unfair that the inspirational Richie Kealy ended up on the losing side.'* David Tonge scored with a powerful shot to the corner of the net early on, and in a tightly contested final quarter Dunshaughlin led by two points on three separate occasions only for Slane to snatch a last minute goal. A despairing last effort by Robbie Keane drifted wide to leave the black and ambers unlucky runners-up on a 1-9 to 1-8 scoreline.

In 1996 the Under 21s repeated the achievement. A quarter-final victory over Blackhall Gaels after a replay and a semi-final win against St. Ultans put the team into the final against Carnaross. It wasn't played until February 1997 and the absence of Niall Kelly for the final, following his sending off against Ultans a fortnight earlier, was a huge loss. Despite his absence Dunshaughlin dominated the early stages but missed a number of gilt-edged goal chances in the first half.

BLACK & AMBER

Eventually, Meath star Ollie Murphy's sheer brilliance was the primary reason for Carnaross' comfortable victory. Dunshaughlin held a single point advantage early in the second half but the team had no answer when Murphy paraded his brilliance in the second period and went down 1-15 to 0-9 at the final whistle.

In 1996 some of those players began to graduate on to the intermediate side and the club benefited from the incoming transfers of Brendan Mooney and Barry Doyle. Mooney was a tight marking, tenacious and committed defender while Doyle, a former Clann na nGael, Roscommon player added much needed scoring ability up front.

The club's representation on county teams continued with Richie Kealy especially prominent. He won a Leinster Under 21 championship in 1996 along with provincial junior honours in 1996 and 1997, a prelude to a senior All-Ireland in 1999.

Dunshaughlin, Under 21 Special Finalists, 1995

Front: David Tonge, Pádraic O Dwyer, Denis Kealy, Aiden Kealy, Capt., Richie Kealy, Kenny McTigue.
...an O Rourke, Michael Keane, David Faughnan, Fearghal Gogan, Clive Dowd, Robbie Keane, Graham Dowd.

Another Semi, Another Defeat

For 1996 there was once again a change in the coaching set up, the club opting for internal management with Paddy O Dwyer as team manager, Jim Gilligan as trainer and Mick Fennell as the third selector. Fennell was a former Laois star who represented his club in three finals and his county in five in 1964, including the All-Ireland Under 21 football decider against Kerry and minor hurling final against Cork. He won a Laois senior football championship with Graigecullen in 1965, scoring 1-2 in the final.

Many of the usual suspects turned up again as group stage opponents. The first outing featured 1-5 from Simon Farrell, the goal from a penalty after Graham Dowd was pulled down, in a 2-13 to 2-9 revenge victory over St. Patricks. Victory over regular opponents Moynalty followed before a Rathkenny goal in the last minute resulted in a drawn match in the next round. With a comprehensive victory over Athboy, 6-17 to 0-5, and a walkover to Ballinabrackey, the team progressed straight through to the semi-final.

There was a huge delay of thirteen weeks before the semi-final in late September, as Meath's progress to the All-Ireland title led to a hiatus in club fixtures. Dunshaughlin spent some of the long summer evenings training on the beach and sand-dunes in Bettystown to add variety to preparations and boost fitness.

The semi-final opponents were Duleek, junior champions the previous year, with Eamonn Barry as their coach. Despite dominating exchanges around the centre Dunshaughlin couldn't make it count on the scoreboard and mid-way through the second half Duleek led by a goal. Brendan Kealy's introduction in the closing stages added *'much needed life to a lethargic attacking brigade'* reported the *Chronicle* and he grabbed three points to leave the sides all square on 0-11 to 1-8.

In the replay, Bracken and Naughton were again on top at midfield but after a few half-hearted surges Duleek suddenly snatched a goal to remain in touch. Dunshaughlin remained in control for much of the second half but another Duleek goal in the final quarter gave them victory by 2-5 to 0-9. Although the team had improved on the previous year's efforts to once again reach a semi-final this was the fourth semi-final defeat in five years, two of them after replays. The question was could Dunshaughlin take the step to the final or were they destined to be always the bridesmaids and never the bride?

In the period from 1993 to 1996 a strong consistent defence had been established but scoring remained a problem. David Kane was a regular corner back until 1995 when Brendan Mooney took the number two jersey and in the other corner Garbhán Blake was ever present until his departure to the USA in 1996. Ciarán Byrne played at right half back for an even longer period, wearing

Dunshaughlin, Intermediate Semi-Finalists, 1996

Front: Dermot Kealy, Alan Duffy, Francis Darby, Barry Doyle, Kevin Kealy, Denis Kealy, Ciarán Byrne.
Back: Kenny McTigue, Aiden Kealy, Derek Melia, Colm Naughton, Colum Bracken, Brendan Mooney, Derek Maher, Simon Farrell.

the number five jersey in twenty-four out of the club's twenty-six championship games between 1993 and 1996. Aiden Kealy was usually the first choice full back while Derek Maher and Dermot Kealy shared the pivotal centre back role.

Up front an inability to maximize opportunities and in particular to hit the net in tight championship encounters often proved costly. Although six were scored against Athboy in 1996 such outings were no preparation for games against genuine contenders. In the same year no goals were scored against Moynalty or Rathkenny, neither of whom featured among the leading lights of the championship, while between the original semi-final and replay Duleek grabbed three goals but Dunshaughlin couldn't manage even one.

There were some promising developments. Players from the Under 21 sides of 1995 and 1996 were gradually claiming a place on the intermediate team. Both Graham Dowd and Denis Kealy made their debuts in 1996, Graham against St. Patricks when he scored two points and Denis against Rathkenny. Significantly both were forwards. Kenny McTigue initially replaced Garbhán Blake at number four and Brendan Mooney was also a valuable addition to the defence.

Finally, The Title

For the 1997 campaign there was yet another change of team management with Val Dowd taking over as team manager and appointing Don Kane, Matt McEntaggart and Seamus Magee as his co-selectors. There was the usual difficulty appointing a coach. Pending a permanent replacement John Davis took charge initially, and in March, Martin Coyne, a former Summerhill player, was appointed. By the end of April he had departed, citing unspecified reasons on and off the field. The selectors decided to continue without an official coach pending qualification from the section. In July Don Kane invited Philip Phelan on board as team trainer. Philip brought expertise from his army career and later went on to train the Louth senior side. Then, in late July Colm O Rourke came on board as coach after an approach via his nephew, Dunshaughlin keeper Brian O Rourke. Colm was reluctant to become involved but agreed to take a few sessions if Dunshaughlin qualified from the group stages.

Prior to this the team had drawn Donaghmore-Ashbourne, Moynalty, Syddan, Ballivor and Drumconrath in the group stages of the championship. Drumconrath, the previous year's junior champions, were novel opponents and the north Meath side dominated the first half to lead 1-6 to 0-3 at half-time. Inspired by Graham Dowd, Dunshaughlin fought back in the second half; he laid on a goal for Francis Darby and scored five points himself as Dunshaughlin came out on top by 1-10 to 1-7.

Next up was another new side, Ballivor, who also dominated the first half and Dunshaughlin went in at half time five points in arrears. The situation looked bleak but Colum Bracken recalls a determination not to be beaten. 'We just decided we wouldn't be beaten and went out determined to win in the second half'.

Nevertheless, Ballivor hit the first point after the restart and five minutes elapsed before Simon Farrell scored Dunshaughlin's first of the half,- an outstanding score from a tight angle. Two pointed frees from Graham Dowd either side of a great Colum Bracken point reduced the deficit to two. Despite the dismissal of Barry Doyle, Dunshaughlin continued to press. Kenny McTigue launched a foray into enemy territory after taking a pass from Bracken before knocking over an inspirational point. Richie Kealy then edged Dunshaughlin in front, a lead the side held to the end to engineer a single point victory, 0-10 to 0-9, with outstanding displays from Brendan Mooney, Colum Bracken, Richie Kealy, Simon Farrell and Graham Dowd.

The third round clash at Skryne against neighbours Donaghmore-Ashbourne was even closer. Numbers were depleted and Paul O Rourke had to be drafted in from the Junior C team to play at corner-back. Dunshaughlin with wind advantage had a narrow two-point lead at half time and when this was quickly overhauled they looked in trouble. However, the team rallied to regain the lead but had to settle for a draw when Donaghmore-Ashbourne equalized in the final minute. An easy victory over perennial opponents Moynalty by 6-10 to 1-10 followed and a narrow 0-14 to 1-9 victory over Syddan put the team straight into the semi-finals.

'We just decided we wouldn't be beaten and went out determined to win in the second half'

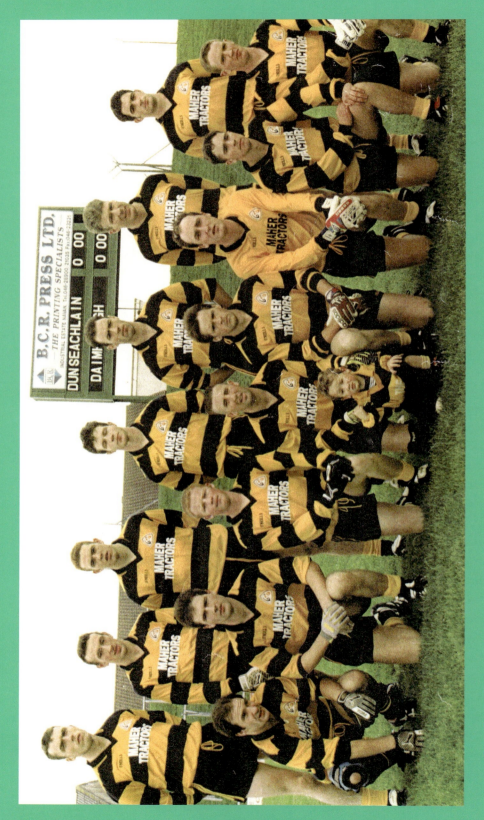

Dunshaughlin, Intermediate Football Champions, 1997

Front: Dermot Kealy, Brendan Mooney, Pádraic O Dwyer, Francis Darby with mascot Patrick Darby, Ciarán Byrne, Capt., Brian O Rourke, David Tonge, Ronnie Yore.
Back: Tiernan O Rourke, Kenny McTigue, Graham Dowd, Richie Kealy, Colm Naughton, Colum Bracken, Denis Kealy.

By now Dunshaughlin were veterans of intermediate semi-finals, all of which had turned sour and the outlook seemed bleak once again when Blackhall established a seven-point lead. The *Chronicle* declared that *'Character is Key Factor'* in its report as Dunshaughlin pegged back the deficit. Graham Dowd's accuracy kept Dunshaughlin ticking over during troubled times and he scored four first half points, one of them a super effort from play. Just before half time a Tiernan O Rourke shot was saved and Pádraic O Dwyer followed up to force the ball into the net to leave Blackhall with a mere two points advantage despite their early supremacy.

O Rourke himself netted early in the second half and the dismissal of Paul Nestor added to Blackhall's woes. Finally Dunshaughlin, wearing Skryne jerseys to minimize a clash of colours, had made it back to the intermediate final, twenty years after their previous appearance. Near the end the referee sent Barry Doyle to join Nestor on the sideline and this ruled him out of the decider.

Duleek, winners of the previous year's semi-final meeting, provided the opposition. A final was a new experience for Dunshaughlin, but, having finally laid the semi-final bogey to rest, the team management and players were confident they could win. Despite the long record of near misses the team was very young. Two seventeen year olds and a nineteen year old made up the half forward line on a team whose average age was twenty-three.

Colm O Rourke presided over a number of training sessions where all the focus was on ball work, attacking scenarios involving two on one or three on two. His arrival was a huge boost, as he was one of Ireland's most famous players. His approach was to keep it simple and direct, letting the ball do the work and everyone must be good enough to win his own ball before moving it on to a better-placed team-mate.

Both wing forwards, David Tonge and Denis Kealy- in their first and second year on the team respectively- were crucial to the team. They had pace, scoring ability and a willingness to act as defenders by tracking back to help the defence when necessary. Brian O Rourke's lengthy kick out was another significant factor. He was always capable of landing the ball into the centre of the field on restarts, which suited the high-fielding Colum Bracken and Colm Naughton. In Brian's view Colm O Rourke brought a great sense of calm to the sideline that filtered on to the pitch.

The week before the decider Dunshaughlin played a challenge against Arles of Laois and the whole team was moving as smoothly as a well-oiled machine.

The final was a case of saving the best wine till last. In the *Chronicle's* words *'years of frustration and unfulfilled potential were brought to an end'* as the black and ambers made a whirlwind start. *The Weekender* reported that they were

> **Despite the long record of near misses the team was very young. Two seventeen year olds and a nineteen year old made up the half forward line.**

Intermediate Action Shots, 1997

Clockwise from top left:
Graham Dowd in Skryne colours in action against Blackhall Gaels in the semi-final.

Colum Bracken outfields Blackhall's Stephen Nally and Nigel Nestor to gain possession in midfield.

Francis Darby has time and space to consider his options.

David Tonge keeps the ball at arm's length from the opposition in the intermediate final against Duleek.

'brilliant in the opening quarter at the end of which they led by 0-8 to 0-1. Richie Kealy and David Tonge were especially impressive making their presence felt in attack where Pádraic O Dwyer made his mark with two points and Graham Dowd kicked some lovely points from frees.'

Duleek's attack was restricted to scraps, as, in the words of the *Chronicle* *'The winner's defence and in particular Dermot Kealy, must take the plaudits for Duleek's lack of attacking creativity, the tight marking of [Michael] O Connor was not the only impressive aspect of Kealy's play. His presence inspired those around him and captain Ciarán Byrne and Francis Darby were also outstanding in a terrific defensive display.'*

Duleek reduced the margin to six points as half time approached but the game looked over as a contest when Richie Kealy laid the ball off to his brother Denis who blasted to the net from 20 metres before the break. There was initial bedlam in the dressing room at half time with back-slapping and players asking for thirty minutes more, but the frenzied atmosphere changed when Colm and Val entered. Mistakes were calmly highlighted, culprits were criticized and players were refocused on the game with O Rourke ruthlessly imparting the message that the team go out and double its advantage in the second half.

Soon after the restart Tiernan O Rourke put an end to a mini Duleek revival when he collected a Dowd pass and volleyed to the net after his initial effort was blocked. Graham Dowd was accuracy personified from frees and before the end added to his tally with a delicate chip over the keeper for his side's third goal. When the referee Seamus McCormack signaled the end each forward had scored at least twice, with Dowd leading the way on 1-5 as the rampant black and ambers clocked up 3-14 to Duleek's 1-6.

Brian O Rourke was faultless between the posts. Kenny McTigue had worn the number three jersey in each of the earlier rounds but for the final moved to the corner to accommodate the return of Dermot Kealy. McTigue and Brendan Mooney in the corners were solid throughout while Kealy held his man scoreless from play. Colum Bracken and Colm Naughton had the better of the midfield duels and in a game short of high fielding got the vital touches that enabled the half backs and half forwards pick up a regular supply of breaking ball.

The half back line consisted of three determined defenders. Ciarán Byrne and Francis Darby had experienced many narrow defeats before the ultimate victory and both were outstanding in a terrific defensive display. Ronnie Yore had catapulted himself from the juniors to a regular spot on the top team. He made three championship appearances in 1995 and one in 1996, but missed just one game in 1997 and his tenacious tackling made life difficult for the most talented forwards. Ronnie went on to produce sterling displays with the seniors in the glory years that followed.

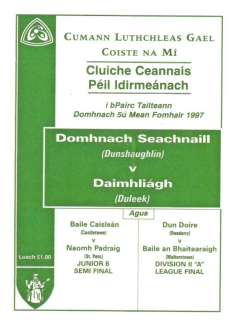

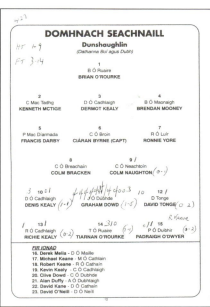

Intermediate final programme, 1997

BLACK & AMBER

We've Finally Got It!
Ciarán Byrne raises the Mattie McDonnell Cup after eventual Intermediate Championship success in 1997.

The half forward line of Denis Kealy, Graham Dowd and David Tonge scored 2-8 between them in the final with Dowd the leading scorer of the campaign on 1-33. Richie Kealy, -who along with brother Dermot, won a Leinster Junior championship earlier in the year with final victory over Louth- missed a number of earlier games. In the final, however, he was a constant threat, scoring a magical point early on, setting up Denis for a goal and foraging for possession all over the field. Pádraic O Dwyer who lined out in defence in the earlier rounds moved up front for the final and semi-final and amassed an impressive 1-3 between the two games.

Inevitably, time brings changes and many of the young players who experienced early success were replacing older lads who had given outstanding service to the club, but weren't on the field on the day of ultimate glory.

Ger Dowd provided the only playing link with the successful 1977 team, as he was still training with the panel. His comrade in arms, Pat O Brien, had soldiered on until the Carnaross semi in 1993, acting as a selector in 1994-95. Simon Farrell, who was the team's second highest scorer prior to the final, on fourteen points, and a mainstay of the forwards throughout the nineties was unfortunate to suffer an ankle injury in the semi-final that ruled him out of selection for the decider. David Kane, who had featured in the semi-final win, Derek Maher, who had played thirty-three consecutive championship games for the team between 1992 and 1996 and Derek Melia, the regular keeper for many years, were among the unlucky ones. Aidan Walsh's scoring prowess had carried the team in lean times, but by 1997 he had left the panel, but another with an accurate eye for the posts, Alan Duffy, was part of the successful panel. Others like Pearse O Dwyer and Michael O Brien had moved on before the title arrived.

A few of the stalwarts of the early to mid 1990s had departed for foreign fields. Pat Kealy headed for the United States, eventually settling in Los Angeles, after the 1992 campaign, Trevor Kane left for Chicago after the 1993 defeat, and Garbhán

CHAPTER 12: 1992-1997

Intermediate Cup on Tour
The morning after the Intermediate triumph in 1997 the following group brought the cup to St. Seachnall's NS.
Front: Colum Bracken, Graham Dowd, Robbie Keane, Simon Farrell.
Back: Cormac Delaney (pupil), Val Dowd, Pádraic O Dwyer, Francis Darby, Orla Power (pupil), Denis Kealy, Caoimhín King (pupil).

Blake departed to Milwaukee in mid 1996. Blake, however, would return to share in the senior successes of the following decade.

Thus, the quest for the Mattie McDonnell Cup came to an end and when Ciarán Byrne triumphantly raised the trophy it was well overdue. For team manager Val Dowd it crowned a series of successes with the juniors in the nineties. He and the other selectors were rewarded for placing their trust in youth. Val was one of two links with the 1977 side. He lined out at full-back on the earlier intermediate winning team and his son Graham followed in his footsteps in 1997. Paddy O Dwyer, team manager in 1996, provided the second link with the 1977 team. Both he and son Pádraic wore the number 15 jersey and ended up with two points each in county finals twenty years apart.

Between 1992 and 1997 Dunshaughlin had played in seven intermediate semi-finals, including replays. Two players played in all seven, Francis Darby in five different positions and Ciarán Byrne who lined out at right half back in six consecutive semis, switching to centre back for the 1997 game against Blackhall Gaels. Ciaran played every single minute of the seven games, a testament to his fitness and dedication. He would go on to play in four consecutive senior finals in the number four jersey.

Those games and the juniors covered in the previous chapter were played during an era before clubs engaged paid physios to minister to players and dry cleaners to provide fresh jerseys. Instead, the club depended on Majella Considine's voluntary expertise as physio during the 1990s and Kathleen Walsh's dedication in presenting newly washed and folded jerseys for all games in the 1980s and 90s.

> **Thus, the quest for the Mattie McDonnell Cup came to an end and when Ciarán Byrne triumphantly raised the trophy few could have begrudged the club the title.**

The winning team lined out as follows:

Brian O Rourke

Kenny McTigue   Dermot Kealy   Brendan Mooney

Francis Darby   Ciarán Byrne, Capt.   Ronnie Yore

Colum Bracken   Colm Naughton (0-1)

Denis Kealy (1-1)   Graham Dowd (1-5)   David Tonge (0-2)

Richie Kealy (0-2)   Tiernan O Rourke (1-1)   Pádraic O Dwyer (0-2).

Subs: Robbie Keane for O Dwyer, Michael Keane for Yore, Kevin Kealy for Denis Kealy, Derek Melia, Clive Dowd, Alan Duffy, David Kane, David O Neill.

The following were not listed on the county final programme but had played or were members of the panel during the year: Simon Farrell, injured for the final, Barry Doyle, sent-off in the semi-final, Derek Maher, David Moroney, Paul O Rourke, Declan Rock, Ger Dowd, Michael O Brien and Niall Kelly.

The scores throughout the campaign were compiled as follows: Graham Dowd 1-34; Simon Farrell 0-14; Richie Kealy 1-7; Tiernan O Rourke 2-4; Pádraic O Dwyer 2-3; Barry Doyle 2-2; Colum Bracken 1-4; David Tonge 1-4; Denis Kealy 1-1; Francis Darby 1-0; David Moroney 0-2; Colm Naughton 0-2; Robbie Keane, Kevin Kealy, Kenny McTigue 0-1 each.

Looking Back, Looking Forward

From the lows of the 1980s through the disappointments of the early 1990s the club had finally reached the promised land after almost as many tribulations as Moses. The series of near misses caused some to doubt the club's ability to ever win the title. However, it was a period of intense competition at intermediate level with a number of capable sides emerging from the grade that would later make a significant impact in the senior championship.

Dunboyne, victors in the 1992 semi-final went on to win the intermediate title that year and by 1998 were senior champions. Carnaross, after their extra time victory in 1993, also captured the Mattie McDonnell trophy. The frustrating pattern continued the following year when Kilmainhamwood, having eliminated Dunshaughlin at semi-final stage, went on the win the title. They followed it with a senior title two years later. In 1995 Dunshaughlin seemed to be suffering withdrawal symptoms after making the last four for three consecutive years but they were back in the semi-final the following year before going under to Duleek after a replay. This time defeating the black and ambers didn't guarantee the championship, as Cortown ousted Duleek in the decider. It is doubtful if the intermediate grade ever contained so many outstanding sides.

Other factors were at work also. The team was gradually evolving as younger players emerged from the ranks of St. Martins. Over the half decade spanning the semi-final defeat to Dunboyne to the final victory against Duleek the team had undergone a major overhaul. Only five of those who played in the 1992 semi also played in the 1996 semi while four of them remained for the 1997 final, a huge change in a few years. The four were the 1997 captain, Ciarán Byrne, Francis Darby, Colum Bracken and Tiernan O Rourke.

In the early part of the decade the team produced many outstanding league or Feis Cup displays and had the measure of teams like Dunboyne, St. Patricks or Kilmainhamwood. But when it came to serious championship fare or a league decider the team often underperformed. Thus, there was a league final defeat to Ballinlough and a league and championship loss to Dunboyne. As early as 1991 Dunshaughlin ran Walterstown to two points in the 1990 Feis Cup semi-final in Skryne. It was played on a fine summer evening, and featured some great football with two spirited comebacks in the second half. Dunboyne players and mentors were impressed and worried.

However, in the 1991 championship in Navan, Dunboyne were overwhelming victors. It was prior to the arrival of Colum Bracken and Dunboyne's Tony Byrne pulled Trevor Kane out to the sideline for their kick-outs and crowded the centre on Dunshaughlin restarts, thereby neutralizing Kane's influence. They also exploited a weakness in the full-back line by isolating players and disposed of the black and amber challenge by 0-12 to 0-5. They had their homework done, and were more determined and street-wise, whereas Dunshaughlin lacked composure, inner belief and the tactical awareness to respond.

The team didn't always function as a unit, often it was a collection of talented individuals. At times the side lacked the discipline it later developed and crucial games were sometimes lost due to the dismissal of players or the concession of vital ground due to dissent. With experience the team became stronger physically and mentally and once they got out of the intermediate bear-pit and acclimatized to the senior grade the team became more assured and confident.

Another factor during the nineties was the lack of continuity in team management. Not only were different coaches appointed almost every year, selectors also tended to have short terms. Apart from Paddy O Dwyer, who was a selector from 1993 to 1996, most served for a year or two at most before being replaced. In retrospect, it may have been as well that the title was delayed. A championship win in 1992 or 1993 would have been very welcome but it is doubtful if the club then had the resources to compete seriously at senior level.

When the team did finally make the long delayed breakthrough in 1997 with a confident display, full of skill and flair the *Chronicle* concluded its report by observing that if the team could repeat this type of form on a regular basis they would prove difficult to beat at senior level. The next decade would validate that prediction.

> In retrospect, it may have been as well that the title was delayed. A championship win in 1992 or 1993 would have been very welcome but it is doubtful if the club then had the resources to compete seriously at senior level.

BLACK & AMBER

Competing for the Keegan Cup, 1998-2000

During the close season the club took a decision that was to have a huge impact in the following years. After a decade of difficulty in attracting coaches, Eamonn Barry was appointed for the 1999 season.

There were some similarities between the 1978 and 1998 sides as they entered the senior championship after winning the intermediate title but there was also one significant difference. Both sides had struggled for the better part of a decade to emerge from the intermediate grade. The 1978 side had lost a final in 1975, a semi-final in 1973, and another in 1976, after a replay, before emerging as champions in 1977. The 1998 panel suffered four semi-final defeats, -two after replays,- in 1992, 1993, 1994 and 1996 before capturing the title. Both sides were written off after many of those defeats with the phrase, 'sure when they couldn't win it this year, they'll never win it.'

Both sides proved the skeptics wrong.

In terms of age profile the sides couldn't have been much different. The seventies side had soldiered together for many years, half a dozen of them were close to their mid-thirties and the average age of the team lining out at senior level was 30 years. Pat and John Jennings, Ger Dowd and Don McLoughlin provided the youthful element but there were very few players coming through from under-age teams to join them. In contrast, the 1998 side averaged out at just over 25 years, and, more importantly, there was a regular supply line of young players from St. Martins who would reduce the age profile even further in subsequent years.

The first year at senior level in the nineties provided little encouragement

BLACK & AMBER

> **The intermediate winning selectors were retained but once again the appointment of a coach proved difficult.**

that the latest campaign would be more successful than the previous ones. The intermediate winning selectors were retained but once again the appointment of a coach proved difficult. The club minutes record that twenty people had been approached without success before joint trainers Tadhg Fallon and David Foran were appointed. Foran was a former Dublin senior player, while Fallon, a member of Dublin Fire Brigade, had partnered him previously in club coaching. In the event, Fallon eventually became sole trainer. The year didn't start well as the team lost the first three league games and went under to Simonstown in the first round of the championship by 1-7 to 0-6 in what the *Chronicle* claimed *'would figure high among the nominations for most unexciting encounter of the year.'*

By the next championship outing matters had disimproved. A dressing room row after the first outing between a player and team management was referred to the committee for resolution but no solution or compromise was forthcoming. A second championship defeat, after dressing room dissension on team selection, to Gaeil Colmcille, followed. Meanwhile controversy over the possibility of moving the club grounds from the Drumree Road to a greenfield site on the Ratoath Road caused dissension among, and resignations from, the committee.

Finally, an extraordinary general meeting was scheduled and new officers, committee and team management were put in place. Paddy O Dwyer was elected as Chairman while Tadhg Fallon continued to train and coach the senior team. His new co-selectors were TP Toolan and Martin Summerville.

At the end of May the side recorded a league victory over Gaeil Colmcille but went down to Kilmainhamwood in the Feis Cup before finally recording its first senior championship victory when disposing of Ballinlough. A poor first half display was further blighted by a career-ending broken collar bone for Colum Bracken early in the game.

The second half ushered in a vastly improved display as Dunshaughlin scored five unanswered points to win by 1-12 to 0-9 with a late Graham Dowd goal. Another victory, over Moynalvey, meant the team went into the final championship game with qualification hopes still alive. That outing, against neighbours Skryne, was to foreshadow more important contests between the sides in future. On this occasion, a Blues' side missing many regulars, emerged victorious 0-12 to 0-10 despite an outstanding performance from Stephen Claire who notched four points.

Dunshaughlin Supremo
Eamonn Barry, Senior Coach and Selector, 1999-2004.

CHAPTER 13: COMPETING FOR THE KEEGAN CUP, 1998-2000

A New Coach and High Hopes

During the close season the club took a decision that was to have a huge impact in the following years. After a decade of difficulty in attracting coaches, Eamonn Barry was appointed for the 1999 season. Barry had an impressive record as player and manager, winning five Meath senior titles, two Leinster club medals and playing in two All-Ireland club finals as a Walterstown forward. As manager he had coached the Meath juniors to Leinster success and piloted St. Peregrines to a Dublin junior championship. He had experience of the Dunshaughlin side when managing Duleek, winning the 1996 semi-final and losing the 1997 decider against them.

Dunshaughlin had approached Barry in 1998 but he had already committed to Duleek. He did, however, indicate that he would be interested in the position the following year if there was a vacancy, so when the opportunity arose in 1999 he accepted enthusiastically. Eamonn believed that Dunshaughlin had immense potential. He had witnessed their prowess in the intermediate final and worked with a number of the players as Meath junior coach. On a personal level it was a new adventure as it catapulted him into senior management, having worked with junior and intermediate teams prior to this.

An ambitious manager and a talented panel made for an ideal marriage.

Eamonn's co-selectors, chosen at the club's AGM, were TP Toolan and Brendan Kealy. Toolan was a native of Roscommon who won an intermediate championship with Boyle before settling in Dunshaughlin and lining out with the black and ambers for a number of years. Kealy, an All-Ireland winner with Meath at minor and Under 21 level in 1990 and 1993 respectively, was also a member of the club's senior panel. A serious back injury had curtailed his playing career but hadn't prevented him from coaching the St. Martins' minors and the Dunshaughlin Under-21s. He gained the respect of those young players and brought a deep knowledge of their strengths and weaknesses to the new management team.

From the beginning all were impressed with Eamonn's professional, structured approach. He met with the club officers, his fellow selectors and later the players. Training began on Sunday 10th January in Dunshaughlin with locations varying thereafter, including Coolmine, Drumree Hall, Warrenstown, the Hill of Tara, Donabate Beach and Tara Athletic Club. In the early stages Eamonn had a simple philosophy, firstly get fit to play and secondly improve the basic kicking and handpassing skills. Initially, turn-outs were in the low twenties but gradually numbers increased. A weekend trip to Castlebar in March was an opportunity to play a challenge game against the locals and for selectors to discuss options.

BLACK & AMBER

> "there would be 'no ICA meetings around every free kick.'

As the year progressed so did the training and the methodical approach. Eamonn was ahead of many inter-county coaches with innovations such as video analysis. Players viewed and analyzed their own performances, how often they had possession, how they used it, the quality of the passing. Over time Eamonn focused on developing individual and team strengths and emphasized the importance of attempting to score only from a defined scoring zone, no more than 30m from goal, and eliminating hopeful shots from hopeless positions.

A distinctive style of play began to emerge, with quickly taken frees central to keeping the ball moving. In selector TP Toolan's words there would be 'no ICA meetings around every free kick.' Prior to the quarter-final in 1999 Eamonn called 7 a.m. Sunday morning training sessions when few counties, never mind clubs, were doing so. A Drumree mentor seeing the early morning activity commented, 'The Drumree lads were only coming home from the disco when the Dunshaughlin boys were out training.'

Given the previous year's form the local press didn't rate the team's chances too highly, calling them 'very dark horses' at odds of 25 to 1 and predicting they would finish with the wooden spoon in a group containing Walterstown, Dunboyne and Trim. Barry's goal was to emerge from the group stages and qualify for a quarter-final. Ironically, his first championship game in charge pitted Dunshaughlin against his original club, Walterstown. For most of the first half Walterstown *'played second fiddle to an impressive Dunshaughlin side'* but a goal conceded just before half time left Dunshaughlin trailing and they failed to recover, going down 2-9 to 0-8.

Before the next round Eamonn and the selectors focused on rectifying Dunshaughlin's greatest weakness, an inability to profit sufficiently from possession. The team displayed an impressive work ethic but was not getting the reward in terms of scores after all the graft. Elementary errors, such as shooting from poor angles, dropping the ball into the opposing keeper's hands and making poor use of set plays had to be eliminated. The coach continued to work on shot selection in the scoring zone and developing some simple set-piece plays.

A Dynamic Duo
Cyril Creavin, Club Secretary, 1994-2005 and Paddy O Dwyer, Club Chairman, 1999-2005 who guided the club through its most successful era.

CHAPTER 13: COMPETING FOR THE KEEGAN CUP, 1998-2000

More traditional approaches were not neglected and a routine that became legendary among the players developed. It involved six timed laps around the field, outside the wire perimeter so corners could not be cut. Each lap was a gut-wrenching 500 metres and it became an ultra-competitive challenge for all, as much a mental as a physical challenge. Ronnie Yore, Richie and Denis Kealy generally posted the fastest times.

The work on the training ground bore fruit as outside of the championship the team maintained the club's good league record and by June held third place, having won four of six games played. A draw with Navan O Mahonys in the Feis Cup also augured well.

A Turning Point

Round two of the championship was a defining game.

For years Dunshaughlin lived in the shadow of Dunboyne. Beaten in a league final in the early 90s, beaten in the race between the clubs to be the first to win the intermediate title and now Dunboyne were senior champions after besting Oldcastle in the 1998 final. They enjoyed flaunting their championship medals. 'What's that rattling in my pocket?' some of them would taunt at local discos. Dunshaughlin had beaten them in the 1999 league opener after providing a guard of honour and applauding the champions onto the field. Outwardly respectful, inwardly the team was determined to change that relationship in future.

The championship meeting between the two black and ambers in Summerhill on a warm Monday evening in June was a do-or-die affair. Both sides had lost their opening game and defeat for either would eliminate them. Dunshaughlin wore Oliver Plunketts' maroon jerseys to avoid a clash of colours while Dunboyne switched into Meath gear. The game was among the best of the championship, with two penalties, a sending off and a nail biting climax.

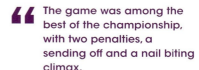
"The game was among the best of the championship, with two penalties, a sending off and a nail biting climax.

Dunshaughlin held a 1-4 to 0-4 half time lead, the goal from a Denis Kealy penalty *'struck brilliantly into the top left corner of the net'* after David Moroney was fouled. Mid way through the second half the old order seemed to be imposing itself once again when Andy McEntee's penalty ended up in the net after first hitting the post and then keeper Brian O Rourke. Five minutes into injury time and the teams were level, a result neither side wanted. McEntee was dismissed for a foul as Dunshaughlin pressed but the maroon clad men couldn't unlock the Dunboyne defence.

Then a set play gave Dunshaughlin a final chance of victory. A simple Denis Kealy line ball found brother Dermot and before he could return the pass he was fouled 30 metres from the post. Eamonn Barry directed Denis Kealy to strike the

Dunshaughlin, Senior Football Finalists, 1999

Front: Ciarán Byrne, David Moroney, Denis Kealy, Dermot Kealy, Capt., Fearghal Gogan, Brian O Rourke, Kenny McTigue.
Back: Tiernan O Rourke, Niall Kelly, Shane Kelly, Aiden Kealy, David Crimmins, Richie Kealy, Stephen Claire, Graham Dowd.

Three members of the Blake Cup winning St. Seachnall's NS team of 1991, Graham Dowd, Shane Kelly and Fearghal Gogan who all featured in the senior county final eight years later. See team picture above.

free. Impervious to the pressure he slotted it home and in the process kicked the holders out the championship.

Now Dunshaughlin could really believe.

Trim provided the opposition in the final group game and while Dunshaughlin won by six points this was a close encounter. The sides were level seven times in total but it was always Dunshaughlin playing catch up. It was the best championship performance to date with eighteen points shared by nine players. At midfield Niall Kelly and Dermot Kealy formed a solid partnership that eclipsed the opposition, Denis Kealy was again outstanding as an attacking half back and Tiernan O Rourke proved to be a great target at full-forward. Trevor Dowd, just turned eighteen, who was to be a lynch-pin of the team in the years ahead, made his senior championship debut as a substitute and promptly scored two points. For the

CHAPTER 13: COMPETING FOR THE KEEGAN CUP, 1998-2000

first time since 1952 the club had reached the knock-out stages of the senior championship, which were delayed until early October due to Meath's success in claiming the Sam Maguire.

In a further sign of the club's progress Richie Kealy established himself as a member of the county senior panel. After marking his first league start with a goal against Laois in 1998 he made his championship debut, as a substitute, against Wicklow in 1999 and entered the fray for the final fifteen minutes of the All-Ireland final against Cork. His courage and bravery in winning a ball he had no right to claim earned the Royals a vital free that Trevor Giles pointed and Richie joined former St. Martins' colleague Evan Kelly in helping to bring Sam to the Royal County.

Into Knockout Territory

After All-Ireland fever died down Dunshaughlin faced into the Meath quarter-final and the *Chronicle* headed its report *Denis The Menace Blows Away Simonstown Gaels*. Despite conceding an early goal, Dunshaughlin steamrolled aside a Simonstown team studded with inter-county players, and led by six points near the end. *The Menace* notched six points, five frees, from half back. It was not just his scores that impressed the press as *'his strength in the tackle was excellent as were his sense of positioning and determination.'*

Full back Kenny McTigue also came in for praise, frequently thwarting the Simonstown forwards and making a number of vital interceptions. Tiernan O Rourke thundered a powerful drive off the underside of the crossbar for a goal before half time and the winners added to the advantage throughout the second half including a masterful effort from Niall Kelly from fifty metres, equaled for skill and audacity by a Graham Dowd point from the right touchline. Some late Simonstown scores couldn't dent the black and ambers' victory on a 1-10 to 1-7 scoreline.

Dunderry were most people's favourites in the semi-final but Dunshaughlin were worthy winners in a low scoring game, 1-8 to 2-2. Although dominant for long periods, Dunshaughlin found it hard to put Dunderry away. A Tiernan O Rourke goal created a half time lead and despite moving five ahead mid-way through the second half the issue was in doubt to the end as Dunderry scored a late goal and pressed hard for another to force a replay. It was not to be, and the black and ambers, after over one hundred years in existence, had reached their first ever senior championship final. There they would meet near neighbours Skryne, one of the most formidable of senior clubs.

> the *Chronicle* headed its report *Denis The Menace Blows Away Simonstown Gaels.*

Singing the Blues

In retrospect, there was a fairytale approach to the final despite the best efforts of the team management to maintain focus on the game. There was unprecedented local interest in the final with a carnival atmosphere on the streets decorated with bunting, flags and good luck signs. Players were given tracksuits, slacks and T-shirts and a bus with a garda escort took the team to Navan. It even did a circuit of the village prior to departure.

Skryne had reached the final in impressive style and were most pundits' favourites for the title. If Simonstown and Dunderry had underestimated Dunshaughlin, Skryne would not do so. Even Eamonn Barry admitted he was surprised to have reached this stage as his main aim had been to emerge from a tough division. He pinpointed the team's weakness as an inability to take the many scoring chances they created and acknowledged that a score of 1-8 might be good enough to win a semi-final but would be inadequate against Skryne. The main dangers on the Skryne side were Meath stars Trevor Giles and John McDermott as well as Mick O Dowd and Brian Smith. Barry stated that Dunshaughlin would take a straightforward approach,

> 'Our aim is plain and simple. We want to get the ball up the field as quickly as possible and score as often as possible. I'm more hopeful than confident.'

Despite the intense build up, final day nerves didn't worry the underdogs in the early stages and Dunshaughlin played the better football for most of the first half. Denis Kealy opened the scoring with a pointed free and Graham Dowd followed up with a point from play. With Dermot Kealy and Niall Kelly having the better of the midfield exchanges, Dunshaughlin created enough opportunities to build up a half time lead but the forwards were unable to convert possession into scores and could only add two more pointed frees before the break. Meanwhile, from less possession, Skryne recorded a similar score and the sides went to the dressing rooms at half time all square. A crucial save by Skryne goalkeeper Philip Kinsella denied David Crimmins when the teams were tied on 0-3 each and the Blues retired the happier at half time.

Dunshaughlin left the dressing room early after the interval but hopes of a second half improvement soon unravelled, for although another Kealy free edged them in front, Skryne, and in particular Trevor Giles, turned on the style early in the second period. Selector TP Toolan, standing behind the goal line, recalls seeing his hopes fall apart and being unable to do anything about it. Two quick points put Skryne back in front and then John McDermott and Giles each added a point. Giles followed up his score with a goal Eamonn Barry described as one

Camera, Lights, Action, Senior Championship 1999 and 2000

Clockwise from top left: Ronnie Yore with eyes on the ball; Shane Kelly in charge; Trevor Dowd has big brother Graham as backup against Syddan

Tiernan O Rourke shoots goalwards against Cortown.

of the best he has seen. Running backwards he got a fist to a Mick O Dowd cross and the ball nestled in the far corner of the net.

It was a killer blow. In less than ten minutes Skryne had turned a one-point deficit into a six-point advantage.

The misery didn't end there for Dunshaughlin. The winners added a further four points before the final whistle and while two points from Denis Kealy and one from Tiernan O Rourke kept Dunshaughlin in touch, the early second half Skryne onslaught was not to be overhauled and there could be no complaint about the final outcome. Eamonn Barry summed it up succinctly in his after match comment,

> 'In the end, class told and you have to take your hat off to Skryne for the way they played at the start of the second half. Trevor Giles and John McDermott turned it on and they simply destroyed us in the space of 10 minutes.'

He also ruthlessly analyzed Dunshaughlin's failings, commenting,

> 'I was disappointed that we weren't four or five points up after the first-half because I felt we were much the better team, but our problem all year has been a failure to turn possession into scores and it happened again on Sunday.'

Although the team had improved substantially during Barry's first year in charge Dunshaughlin's championship outings during the year rarely yielded more than 1-8. Only twice was that exceeded, against Trim and Simonstown. Leading scorer by a huge distance was Denis Kealy who played as a half forward in the first round without scoring and always lined out in the half back line thereafter. The vast majority of his 1-22 came from frees. The leading forward scorer was Richie Kealy, who scored in all games except the final, with twelve points in total, followed by Tiernan O Rourke on 2-4. Apart from the Trim game there was rarely a good spread of scorers and this failing was emphasized in the final when only three players scored and only one of the eight points came from play, that honour falling to Graham Dowd.

Defensively the team was solid throughout. It conceded an average of eight points per game but leaked at least one goal in all outings except against Trim. The defence and midfield was settled, Brian O Rourke, Kenny McTigue and Aiden Kealy were ever present in goals, at full-back and centre-back respectively as were Dermot Kealy and Niall Kelly at midfield. Ciarán Byrne wore the number four jersey in all games bar one and would remain one of the team's most effective defenders while Ronnie Yore was beginning to develop the form that would later guarantee him a regular starting place. TP Toolan had admired Fearghal Gogan's ability as an Under 21 player to shadow his opponent without committing impetuous

CHAPTER 13: COMPETING FOR THE KEEGAN CUP, 1998-2000

fouls and he was promoted to the senior team in 1998. He developed into one of the most outstanding defenders for the next decade and after missing the first round in 1999 went on to play twenty-nine consecutive championship matches.

In contrast the only forward to start in the same position in all games was Richie Kealy at number 11. It was clear that an improvement was needed up front. Either the existing forwards would have to be more incisive and accurate or additional players would have to make the step up to senior level.

There was no disgrace in defeat, just an illustration of the difference between peak and potential.

Another Tilt at the Keegan Cup

The same selectors and coach took charge once again in millennium year. The public consensus was that Dunshaughlin had exceeded expectations and would find it difficult to repeat the feats of 1999. However, the team management did not concur. Eamonn Barry believed that with such a young panel the team was only going to get better and there was room for an improvement of at least twenty per cent.

The draw for the group stages offered an early opportunity for revenge when Dunshaughlin was drawn alongside Skryne, as well as Blackhall Gaels and Cortown.

There were no major changes in the line out for the first round against Blackhall. Ronan Gogan had replaced Australia-bound Brian O Rourke in goals and Graham Dowd moved to partner Dermot Kealy in the absence of Niall Kelly, who had suffered a cruciate knee injury in the 1999 final.

An outstanding performance from David Tonge created havoc in the Blackhall defence and the youthful Trevor Dowd, taking over the free taking duties from Denis Kealy, benefitted. Ten of his hugely impressive tally of eleven points came from frees. In defence Ciarán Byrne marked the Gaels' Nigel Nestor out of game. Dunshaughlin scored twenty-one points in total, treble their opponents tally, to send a warning to all the group teams, especially Skryne, on whose grounds the game was played.

The Skryne game didn't take place until mid June as the Meath team progressed to the National Football League final where they lost out to Derry after a replay. Soon afterwards a surprising defeat to Offaly in the Leinster championship paved the way for the club championship to resume. Richie Kealy featured at left half-back for Meath but he was still playing his club football at centre forward.

He didn't remain there for long against Skryne, as, following an early injury to Graham Dowd, the selectors moved him into midfield where he made a big

Kevin Kealy escapes Cortown clutches with Paddy McHale in support.

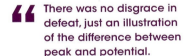

> There was no disgrace in defeat, just an illustration of the difference between peak and potential.

impact, scoring four points. Trevor Dowd was again in excellent form, with a first half goal and a final total of 1-4, but it was not enough and the Taramen came out on top once again, 2-12 to 2-9. Soon afterwards Dunshaughlin gained some small element of revenge with a comprehensive league victory over the Blues by 2-15 to 0-9.

Some of the elements missing in 1999, particularly in the forwards, were beginning to slot into place. David Crimmins was now staking his claim for a permanent role on the side and having scored 1-1 in the championship tussle with Skryne he claimed 2-3 in the league encounter. Trevor Dowd was continuing his consistent scoring form at corner forward and Richie Kealy had moved into the number 13 jersey to complete a line that in time would be feared throughout the county. Graham Dowd's ball winning capability, strength and scoring rate from midfield perfectly complemented Dermot Kealy's leadership and work ethic. The defence had retained its basic, reliable structure from the previous year and the only line that experienced regular change was the half forward trio.

A Performance of Sheer Class

The *Chronicle* described the final outing of the group stage against Cortown as *'absolutely awesome.'* Carlo Divito purred that it was *'the most impressive display I have witnessed in this year's championship'* as he described a performance of *'sheer class'* and a second half where Dunshaughlin *'overwhelmed the opposition with a performance of high energy and clinical finishing.'* He was reluctant to single out individuals in a superb team display but had to mention the brilliance of Trevor Dowd, Richie and Aiden Kealy and Kenny McTigue. Dowd with three goals

> *'proved yet again that he is one of the most outstanding attacking prospects in the county. Richie Kealy showed that he is even more effective in attack with 1-3 while his brother, Aiden and McTigue played leading roles in a superb defensive display.'*

The defence conceded a meagre 0-8 while the attack compiled a cricket like score of 6-11, with Trevor Dowd on a hat trick of goals and points, Richie Kealy on 1-3 and new centre-forward Paddy McHale grabbing two points. Kevin Kealy at wing forward gave an outstanding display, his use of the breaking ball setting up numerous scores.

The victory guaranteed Dunshaughlin entry to the quarter-final stages where the team recorded a 0-17 to 1-6 victory over the previous year's intermediate champions, Syddan. Despite trailing early on, following the concession of a goal, this was an emphatic victory as the winners outscored Syddan in the final forty minutes by fifteen points to three. Graham Dowd retained his midfield berth

County Final Day, 2000

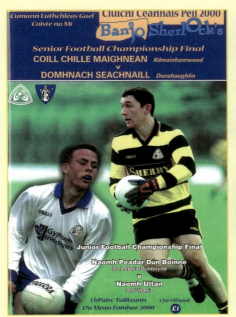

Clockwise from top left:

Match Day Programme Cover.

Patsy Throws in the ball, Never the Towel!

Pre Match Pleasantries as match referee Seamus McCormack oversees the ceremonial handshake between the opposing captains, Liam Shankey and Dermot Kealy.

On Parade. Dermot Kealy, (No 8) leads the black and amber squad.

despite Niall Kelly's return but Kelly was the driving force behind the victory. His reappearance was a major boost to the side. Though playing in the number ten jersey he acted as a third midfielder and provided an additional target for Ronan Gogan's kickouts. He was, said the *Chronicle*, '*in a different class*' and overwhelmed three separate markers during the hour. He frequently gained possession deep inside his own half and

> '*managed to stay with the play and provide vital support as he displayed a tremendous workrate and fitness level. His ability to pick out a colleague with a long pass of 60 or 70 metres is extremely difficult to defend against and that contributed to many of the thirteen points from play.*'

The report concluded that Dunshaughlin was '*a team to be feared.*'

The semi-final on the first weekend in September proved to be a much sterner test. Town side Trim provided the opposition in Páirc Tailteann and they had the better start, recording an early four points advantage that Denis Kealy reduced with a penalty goal. Ronan Gogan had to make a spectacular save to prevent a Trim goal soon after, but in the 25th minute the black and ambers struck a crucial blow when David Crimmins won possession around midfield, advanced on goal and combined with Dermot and Brendan Kealy before Richie Kealy netted. Dunshaughlin had only five points in the half to Trim's eight but went in at the break 2-5 to 0-8 in front.

Trim pressed hard on the resumption and reduced the deficit to four and could have goaled after a mazy Benny Murray run, but the ball struck the woodwork. Once again Niall Kelly was inspirational and responsible for Dunshaughlin's recovery from their early setbacks, while the full forward line embellished its growing reputation with 1-8 of the total.

The result seemed to pave the way for another showdown with Skryne but in the second semi-final, Kilmainhamwood, the champions of 1996, shocked the Tara men, by 3-12 to 0-13, and thus set the scene for a North Meath v. South Meath final. In the run-up to the big day Stephen Burke with club members, supporters and local businesses once again decorated the streets of Dunshaughlin in black and amber bunting, flags and banners but the team avoided the distractions and focused on the essentials. The local schools contributed to the colour and neighbouring clubs, including Skryne, erected 'Good Luck' displays.

And the Game is On!

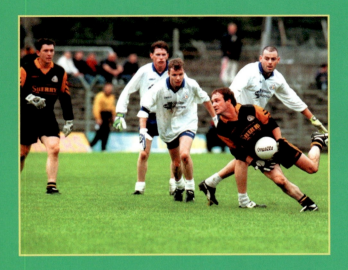

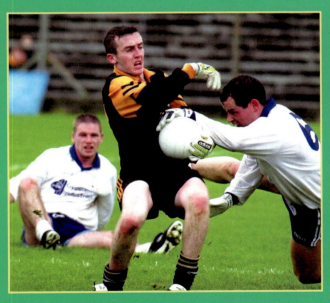

Action from the 2000 Senior Final, clockwise from top left:

1. Midfielder or Scrum-Half?
Dermot Kealy lays off the ball as David Crimmins watches on.

2. Fearghal Gogan, Leader of the Pack!
Fearghal Gogan emerges from the crowd as Brendan Kealy, Graham Dowd and Ciarán Byrne prepare to support.

3. Missile on Target!
Niall Kelly launches his trademark left footed rocket into Kilmainhamwood territory.

4. It's Mine!
Trevor Dowd refuses to yield despite the attention of Kilmainhamwood's Ray Madden.

'it is doubtful if any previous Keegan Cup winners gave an exhibition to compare'

Dunshaughlin deservedly held the favourites' tag prior to the final. The performance against Cortown had shown the potency of the side, especially up front where Trevor Dowd and Richie Kealy were identified as the championship's most feared attacking duo. According to the *Chronicle* they were *'awesome all through and have scored for fun on almost every occasion.'* Whereas Trevor made few appearances, and scored only two points in 1999, he was ever-present in 2000 and had amassed a phenomenal 4-23 from five games before the final while Richie Kealy had scored 2-21. Between them they had already scored more in the run up to the final than the whole team had managed in the previous year's full campaign.

In addition, the defence and midfield had been a model of consistency. In each of the six games the goalkeeper, the complete full back line, centre half back and midfield was the same for every championship game. The only changes were at wing back and here it was confined to Denis Kealy and Ronnie Yore switching the number five and seven jerseys between them. Within that structure there was great flexibility. Eamonn Barry often deployed players, especially Denis Kealy, to man-marking roles, and nominal positions weren't always adhered to. Excluding the Skryne game the defensive record was excellent, with an average of nine points conceded per game.

Barry was totally convinced Dunshaughlin would win. The required improvement from the previous year had been made, especially the ability to take scores. The biggest danger was complacency as everyone had expected to face Skryne in the final and there was a danger that players might believe the game was won before it started.

Patsy McLoughlin had the honour of performing the ceremonial throw-in and when the real action began the black and ambers made a lively start that featured points from Paddy McHale and Richie Kealy and an opportunistic goal from Graham Dowd when he fisted a Richie Kealy centre to the net in the sixth minute.

Then Kilmainhamwood star and Meath county player, Ray Magee, turned the game around. As the Dunshaughlin defence failed to deal with a long free he nipped in to finish smoothly to the net. Worse was a follow a couple of minutes later when Magee repeated the medicine after availing of a long sideline delivery. Now it seemed as if the 'Wood might tear up the form book and frustrate Dunshaughlin's best efforts.

Panic could have ensued as Dunshaughlin's lead was so suddenly wiped out, but the team recovered its composure and the sides were level after twenty minutes.

Dunshaughlin, Senior Football Champions, 2000

Front: Brendan Kealy, Kenny McTigue, David Crimmons, Denis Kealy, Fearghal Gogan, Ronnie Yore, Trevor Dowd.
Back: Aiden Kealy, Niall Kelly, Richie Kealy, Paddy McHale, Ronan Gogan, Dermot Kealy, Capt., Graham Dowd, Ciarán Byrne.

> Before half time Dunshaughlin launched attack after attack and the Weekender wondered if there was a magnet placed directly behind the town goals as seven points in a row were posted between the uprights.

Before half time Dunshaughlin launched attack after attack and the *Weekender* wondered if there was a magnet placed directly behind the town goals as seven points in a row were posted between the uprights with Richie Kealy kicking three and setting up another three. David Crimmins, Trevor Dowd and Dermot Kealy availed of his assists and Niall Kelly added one of his own to a solitary reply from the 'Wood and so the favourites went in at half time 1-11 to 2-2 in front. The turn around emphasized the character, commitment and calmness of the team. Few sides could concede two goals and still lead by six points at the break.

Kilmainhamwood introduced the great Brian Stafford soon after half time but nothing could halt the black and amber momentum. Another eight points were added with Richie Kealy claiming some superb scores to end up with a total of seven points and the Man of the Match award. Sean Wall in the *Drogheda Independent* wrote that he was

> '*simply awesome with his accuracy, pin-point passing, and ball winning ability out of the top drawer. He gave a succession of opponents a roasting and seemed at ease shooting from either the left or right wing.*'

Even the sending off of Ciarán Byrne as the game entered the final quarter and Denis Kealy missing a penalty late on couldn't halt Dunshaughlin's relentless progress as they just increased their workrate and coasted to the title by 1-19 to 2-6.

The *Weekender's* Noel Coogan declared that, '*it is doubtful if any previous Keegan Cup winners gave an exhibition to compare*' and praised their '*terrific teamwork, blinding pace and magnificent point taking enabling them to serve up a feast for their supporters and admiring neutrals.*' He highlighted the performance of Dermot Kealy who '*was the midfield general of the team, stamping his authority on proceedings in Roy Keane fashion around the half way line.*'

Dermot had the honour of becoming the first Dunshaughlin man to raise the Keegan Cup and quipped 'I have no speech ready. I had one last year and didn't get to use it.' He didn't forget to pay tribute to Eamonn Barry's role, praising his ability to get through to the players and impart his knowledge of the game. Eamonn himself told the press that,

> 'The team has developed a never-say-die attitude and we play for each other in an intelligent way. We have learned a lot from last year and today we chased and hassled for every ball.'

The whole team contributed to an outstanding display. Graham and Trevor Dowd scored 1-4 between them. Trevor, the youngest member of the side, finished as the top championship scorer with an impressive 4-27. Kenny McTigue and Aiden Kealy were ever present at full back and centre back respectively, in 1999 and 2000 and anchored the defence, both using their superb distribution to launch many an attack.

CHAPTER 13: COMPETING FOR THE KEEGAN CUP, 1998-2000

Ronan Gogan in his first year in goals couldn't be faulted for either of Magee's strikes and his placement of kick outs helped the team establish supremacy around the middle. Fearghal Gogan and Ciarán Byrne were both solid in the corners and half back Ronnie Yore gave a tenacious performance based on incessant tackling and ball winning ability. In Eamonn Barry's estimation, Denis Kealy had been a real star during the year, marking some of the best players in the county and having the unenviable task of curtailing Magee in the final.

Paddy McHale made the number 11 jersey his own as the championship progressed and he performed his dual role of curtailing opposition defenders from moving into attack while also creating openings for his colleagues. Brendan Kealy, in addition to acting as selector, used his pace, aggression and determined ball retention to set up the lethal inside forwards while Niall Kelly on his return to the side was central to the victories against Syddan and Trim and contributed three points on final day.

David Crimmins occupied the full-forward position after the second round, scored a vital point to start the recovery in the first half and was a handful with his ability off his right and left. Tom O Sullivan came off the bench in the semi and the final to claim a point in each while Kevin Kealy's appearance in the final brought to six the number of Kealys on the field. Garbhán Blake had returned to the panel for 2000 and made a number of championship appearances as substitute, including the final when he replaced Fearghal Gogan.

The historic team lined out as follows:

Ronan Gogan

Fearghal Gogan   Kenny McTigue   Ciarán Byrne

Denis Kealy   Aiden Kealy   Ronnie Yore

Dermot Kealy, Capt. (0-2)   Graham Dowd (1-0)

Niall Kelly (0-3)   Paddy McHale (0-1)   Brendan Kealy

Richie Kealy (0-7)   David Crimmins (0-1)   Trevor Dowd (0-4)

Subs: Tom O Sullivan (0-1) for McHale, Kevin Kealy for Trevor Dowd, Garbhán Blake for Fearghal Gogan, Damien Eames, Shane Kelly, David Tonge, Stephen

Dermot Kealy triumphantly raises the Keegan Cup after Dunshaughlin's first senior football championship title with brother Richie holding the Man of the Match trophy in the background.

BLACK & AMBER

> The following day those who weren't too 'tired and emotional' made the traditional visits to the schools and in the evening welcomed and entertained the Kilmainhamwood club in the *Arch Bar*

Claire, David Moroney, Pádraic O Dwyer, Kevin Moyles, Christopher Carey, Declan Fahy, David McNerney, Ulick McDonnell. Tiernan O Rourke, Michael McHale

The welcome in Dunshaughlin surpassed the players' expectations. Traditionally Dunshaughlin's support has been loyal but limited but on 17th September the village was thronged as the team progressed to the church and back to the centre on Graham Faughnan's *Height for Hire* lorry. Eamonn Toal serenaded the team as *Simply the Best* and a convoy of passing lorries blowing their horns added to the atmosphere, before all wedged into Anthony Gogan's licensed premises to begin the celebrations. The following day those who weren't too 'tired and emotional' made the traditional visits to the schools and in the evening welcomed and entertained the Kilmainhamwood club in the *Arch Bar* for a night and morning of prolonged revelry.

An All County League Title that Escaped

The club reached two other finals in Millennium Year, the All County A League and the Under 21 A deciders.

In 1999 the senior team finished joint second in the League and missed the final by losing a play-off to Walterstown. Despite the focus on the championship in 2000 the side amassed fifteen points from a possible twenty in the league to qualify automatically for a final tussle with St. Patricks. The team had suffered only two losses in the league, one of them ominously to St. Patricks, but the newly crowned senior county champions were red hot favourites to master their intermediate counterparts when the sides took to the field under the floodlights at Simonstown.

By half time Dunshaughlin looked in complete control, leading 0-7 to 0-2. Apart from a top drawer save from an Ivan Curran effort, keeper Ronan Gogan and his defensive colleagues were rarely troubled. David Crimmins, Trevor Dowd and Brendan Kealy had early points before St. Patricks managed a score and such was Dunshaughlin's control that corner back Fearghal Gogan got on the scoresheet before the break.

But the black and ambers were as ineffective in the second half as they had been efficient in the first. Selector TP Toolan recalls the team departing the dressing room after the interval with an over-confident, casual attitude. The combination of winning the Keegan Cup, the substantial half time lead and the fact that St. Patricks were only out of the intermediate grade lulled the team into a false sense of security and when the tide turned in the second half Dunshaughlin were as ineffective as Canute in holding it out.

CHAPTER 13: COMPETING FOR THE KEEGAN CUP, 1998-2000

The First Keegan Cup
Top left: TP Toolan, Eamonn Barry and Patsy McLoughlin celebrate victory in Millennium Year.
Above: Club sponsor Pádraig Sherry raises the Keegan Cup supported by Niall Kelly, Paddy McHale and Declan Fahy.
Left: Happy Dunshaughlin supporters, Catherine McHale, Joan Gogan, Cecilia Dowd and Ead Kealy.

Within five minutes the deficit was down to three points, midway through the half it was reduced to a single score before Trevor Dowd's free put two between the sides again. Incredibly, that was Dunshaughlin's only score of the second half. It didn't halt the relentless effort of St. Patricks to chip away at the lead. Cormac Sullivan from a '45' and Daithi Whyte drew the sides level with over ten minutes remaining before Ivan Curran slotted over the lead, an advantage the Saints retained to the end.

Three weeks after the Keegan Cup triumph and a week before the Leinster Club championship commenced, it was a reminder that success is temporary, and uneasy lies the head that wears a crown. The team whose crown tumbled by 0-9 to 0-8 was Ronan Gogan; Fearghal Gogan (0-1), Kenny McTigue, Garbhán Blake; Denis Kealy, Aiden Kealy, Ronnie Yore; Dermot Kealy (0-1), Graham

271

Dowd; Niall Kelly, Paddy McHale, Brendan Kealy (0-1); Richie Kealy (0-1), David Crimmins (0-1), Trevor Dowd (0-3). Subs: David Tonge for Graham Dowd, Kevin Kealy for Kelly, Stephen Claire for Crimmins, Michael McHale for P McHale.

Garbhán Blake, lining out at left corner back in the final, was completing a unique record, his fourth league final lining out in the same position, a dozen years after his first! He occupied the same slot in the Division 3 final in 1988, the Division 2 decider in 1991 and the Division 5 Reserve contest in 1992 prior to donning the familiar number four against St. Patricks in Millennium Year!

Under 21s Over the Moon

> In the three previous games Dunshaughlin had recorded a total of 7-41 with scores spread among the forwards and midfield. In contrast on final day only two players scored,

Graded in the A section of the Under 21 competition, just below the championship proper, Dunshaughlin recorded easy initial victories over Donaghmore-Ashbourne and Syddan.

It was December before the semi-final was played. Dunshaughlin controlled the game throughout but poor first half shooting and two late St. Ultans' goals made the passage more difficult than it should have been. Keith Mangan scored some excellent points from play and second half goals from David Crimmins and substitute Declan Fahy ensured that the Bohermeen side's late fight back was in vain.

Fittingly, the final against Ballivor provided the tightest contest of the campaign. Dunshaughlin built a half time lead of 1-5 to 0-3, the highlights of which were an exquisite goal from David Crimmins after Trevor Dowd provided him with a pin-point pass though under pressure and a Ronan Gogan penalty save. The second half started promisingly with Crimmins rifling to the net in the fourth minute followed by a Dowd free to put the black and ambers nine points clear.

It looked over but it was another long seventeen minutes before they would hit the target again. Meanwhile Ballivor were in the ascendant. Another Ballivor penalty, -this time Ronan Gogan was beaten-, and three quick points revitalized the game as a contest. When Paddy McHale was dismissed after an off-the ball altercation Dunshaughlin were in real trouble with twelve against thirteen in the wide-open spaces of Páirc Tailteann.

In the closing stages Seán Corrigan had a gilt-edged Ballivor goal chance but fired over to leave the minimum between the sides. Dunshaughlin's defence was now under incessant pressure and finding it difficult to lift the siege. When Trevor Dowd engineered a rare break to set up David Crimmins the keeper kept out his goal bound effort. Ballivor then counter-attacked but the raid was repulsed and, with excitement at fever pitch, Crimmins finally claimed the goal he had been

Dunshaughlin, Meath U21 A Champions, 2000

Front: John McKenna, Piaras Delany, Declan Fahy, Denis Kealy, Capt., Paul Hendrick, David McNerney, David Tonge, Christopher Carey, Trevor Dowd.
Back: David Crimmins, Niall Kelly, Michael McHale, David Tormay, Paddy McHale, Ronan Gogan, Ronan Murphy, Keith Mangan, John Crimmins, Ray Maloney, Kevin Moyles, John Joe McDonnell.

On left: Denis Kealy with the Under 21 trophy after final victory against Ballivor.

Faces in the Crowd
Dunshaughlin supporters linger in Páirc Tailteann following the 2000 senior final.

denied a minute earlier. Victory was now assured.

In the three previous games Dunshaughlin had recorded a total of 7-41 with scores spread among the forwards and midfield. In contrast, on final day only two players scored, David Crimmins with his hat-trick of goals and two points and Trevor Dowd who had five points. Another senior, Niall Kelly, was dominant throughout at midfield with good support from David Tonge. This was Dunshaughlin's first ever success at Under 21 level. The team management consisted of Fergus O Rourke, Pat Maloney, Graham Dowd and Jim Gilligan and Denis Kealy captained the following side that had a 3-7 to 1-9 victory in the final.

Ronan Gogan

Kevin Moyles   Denis Kealy, Capt.

Christopher Carey   Michael McHale   Paul Hendrick

Niall Kelly   David Tonge

David McNerney   Paddy McHale   Keith Mangan

David Crimmins (3-2)   Trevor Dowd (0-5)

Subs: JJ McDonnell for Hendrick, Ray Maloney for Mangan, Declan Fahy for Moyles, David Tormay, Ronan Murphy, Piaras Delany, John McKenna, John Crimmins, Brian Murphy.

Could it Possibly Continue?

The Under 21 victory brought the curtain down on the club's most successful ever year. To acknowledge the success, a party of forty-five players, officials and partners departed for a holiday in the sun in Playa Des Ingles, Gran Canaria. Shane Kelly and his committee organized a highly successful fund-raiser for the holiday with the support of 140 patrons who contributed £17,000 to cover the costs.

The medal presentation was celebrated with panache at a Dinner Dance in the Ardboyne Hotel when the whole panel, in formal evening wear, entered to rapturous applause from the three hundred and twenty assembled supporters. County Board Chairman, Fintan Ginnitty, presented the senior medals and the club also honoured the surviving members of the junior side who brought the first ever football title to the village half a century earlier.

The team could chill out and ponder on a first senior championship, just three years after winning the intermediate title, a first Under 21 title, runners-up in the senior league and an exciting and controversial Leinster club campaign, covered in Chapter 15. It was a level of success that once seemed the stuff of dreams. Could it possibly continue?

Enjoying Success

Footballer of the Year 2000. Top left.
Richie Kealy, Meath Footballer of the Year 2000, receives his award from Peter McDermott. Also shown are Barney Allen and Fintan Ginnitty, Secretary and Chairman of Meath County Board.

Dunshaughlin GAA Committee 2000. Top right.
Front: Neil Halpin, Cyril Creavin, Paddy O Dywer, Fergus O Rourke, Lally McCormack.
Back: Brian O Rourke, Jim Smith, Oliver Gogan, Pat Maloney, Shaun McTigue, Shane Kelly.

1950 Junior Winners. Centre left.
Surviving members of the 1950 Junior Football Championship winning team celebrate the Golden Jubilee of the title.
Front: Kevin Ryan, Patsy McLoughlin, Paddy Lyons.
Back: Mickey Kenny, Larry O Brien, Seán O Brien, Johnny Lynch.

Gone to the Dogs!
Even the Dogs in the Street are celebrating as Jack Yore and Misty sport the black and amber.

BLACK & AMBER

High Kings of Meath

Within six years the team went from intermediate winners to senior kingpins and Leinster club champions.

When January comes teams all over Ireland dare to believe once again. Whether champions or also-rans the future holds the prospect of success.

A new coach, a player transferring in, or the 'brilliant' minor from last year might just make the difference between success and failure. Even the loss of a league game or two doesn't dampen enthusiasm for the championship draw. The local press adds to the expectation with previews that attempt to dissect the hopes and dreams of contestants. The sense of anticipation is heightened by the live broadcast of the draws on LM/FM radio.

Monday 19th February 2001 and Dermot Kealy as captain of the defending champions has the honour of making the senior draws. With just four teams to a group, championship hopefuls can ill-afford to drop any points. Dermot put Dunshaughlin in what the *Meath Chronicle* named *'The Group of Death'*. He picked out beaten finalists Kilmainhamwood, perennial hopefuls Simonstown Gaels, coached by Colm O Rourke, and the expected also-rans, Ballinlough. Dunshaughlin's first outing would be against the latter.

The club had, naturally, retained the same coach and selectors. The team management added another arrow to their quiver when Martin Reilly transferred from St. Brigids in Blanchardstown. He was formerly a Dublin minor, but had been resident in Meath for a decade and was a contemporary of most of the team in Dunshaughlin Community College. His unerring accuracy from frees was to be a crucial factor as the year progressed. Apart from Martin, Dunshaughlin would rely on the panel and management that had brought unprecedented success in the

Black and Amber Cats
The black and ambers having made the Keegan Cup their home intend to keep it for another year!

BLACK & AMBER

David Crimmins and Niall Kelly after Meath's victory in the 2001 Leinster Under 21 final against Dublin.

> **By the time the championship commenced Dunshaughlin were a long way from firing on all cylinders.**

millennium year. 2000 had been an extremely demanding season and ended in the Leinster championship defeat to Moorefield after a three game marathon with Rathnew.

By the time the championship commenced Dunshaughlin were a long way from firing on all cylinders. This could be partly accounted for by the regular absence of David Crimmins and Niall Kelly who formed the attacking spine of the Meath Under 21 side that captured the Leinster title in April. The Royals defeated Dublin in the final with Kelly scoring two points and Crimmins one. Richie Kealy was similarly occupied on senior county duty.

Meanwhile, Dunshaughlin had stuttered and stumbled through four league games, drawing the first three before a 2-11 to 2-8 victory against Dunderry in mid-April. The local press was divided in its view of who would eventually triumph in the championship, the *Chronicle* deemed Skryne to have the best credentials while Noel Coogan in the *Weekender* gave the vote, not a confident one he emphasized, to Dunshaughlin. Anyone prepared to gamble on Coogan's tentative vote of confidence could have got 8/1 at the local bookies, with Skryne, Kilmainhamwood, Dunboyne, Dunderry, Simonstown and Walterstown all on lower odds. Clearly, the betting fraternity didn't like the black and ambers' early season form.

CHAPTER 14: HIGH KINGS OF MEATH

Defending Champions

The outcome of the first round on a Friday evening in late April didn't cause a rush of new bets for Dunshaughlin. Unfancied Ballinlough provided a stern test. The champions would have lost but for Richie Kealy. He repeated his seven white flags of the previous year's county final, with four from play and three from frees. His three consecutive unanswered points gave Dunshaughlin a four-point advantage early in the final quarter but Ballinlough pressure resulted in a Jody Devine goal. Martin Reilly proved his value with a pressure free and though Devine hit another superb point they couldn't find a way through during eight minutes of injury time. A late Graham Dowd point gave Dunshaughlin a little more breathing space and at the final whistle the scoreline read 0-12 to 1-7.

A league defeat, to Cortown, the following week emphasized the side's frailties, even if the absence of David Crimmins, Niall Kelly, Brendan and Richie Kealy, could be adduced in mitigation. Brendan Kealy's absence was a long term one for he had been stretchered off against Ballinlough and the diagnosis was a cruciate ligament injury.

A large crowd gathered for the second round bout with Simonstown Gaels on a sunny, sultry evening in Dunsany. Dunshaughlin had two changes from the victory over Ballinlough, Garbhán Blake replacing the injured captain Ciarán Byrne at corner back with David Tonge coming in for Brendan Kealy at number ten. This was a crucial game for Simonstown after going down to Kilmainhamwood in the previous round. Simonstown had joined the senior ranks in 1996, two years before Dunshaughlin, and their line out had a liberal sprinkling of county players. Colm Brady, Hank Traynor, Ronan McGrath, Seamus Kenny and Ned Kearney had all represented Meath at various levels while Gareth O Neill had seen service with Louth. With Colm O Rourke, Dunshaughlin's 1997 coach, in charge they were well placed to thwart the black and ambers.

When it was over there were major question marks hovering over Dunshaughlin's continued reign as champions. Simonstown bolted from the starting stalls to hit four points inside the first six minutes. The whirlwind start rocked the holders back on their heels but they got a lifeline at the end of the quarter when Denis Kealy converted a penalty after Graham Dowd was taken down. This, added to a great point from Michael McHale earlier in the proceedings, left the teams all square 1-1 to 0-4. It was a false dawn however. The Dunshaughlin rearguard was having difficulty curtailing the rampant Simonstown forwards and had to resort to fouling. As a result the light blues kicked two frees and a '45' and Ronan Gogan had to pull off a fine save from John Lunney to prevent an even worse outcome.

Teams with the initiative often lose their momentum during the interval as it

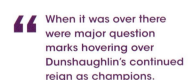

> When it was over there were major question marks hovering over Dunshaughlin's continued reign as champions.

281

gives opponents time to analyze the situation and regroup. But Simonstown had no intention of easing off. They maintained the pressure on the restart and could have had three goals in the opening minutes before, seven minutes in, they struck the killer blow. Substitute Eric O Reilly dispossessed Denis Kealy and lobbed the ball into John Lunney. The lethal corner-forward glanced up, saw Ronan Gogan advancing off his line and gently chipped the ball over the keeper's head into the net. The Navan side finished deserving winners by 1-13 to 1-6.

To outsiders, Dunshaughlin looked a side in decline but the players now had a calculated approach to games. In Ronnie Yore's words, 'We could afford to lose, Simonstown couldn't' and the attitude was you just had to win the next game. Three teams went into the final round of games with a chance of qualification. Kilmainhamwood had four points, Dunshaughlin and Simonstown two each and Ballinlough none. Simonstown seemed a certainty against Ballinlough. If so, then Dunshaughlin would need a victory over Kilmainhamwood to remain in contention while a loss would place them in the relegation zone, if Ballinlough confounded predictions. Surprisingly, Ballinlough did upset the form and set Simonstown's great victory over Dunshaughlin at naught. The black and ambers improved significantly on their earlier form and overcame the previously unbeaten 'Wood by 2-13 to 1-10.

The selectors reshuffled the pack, switching Richie Kealy to wing back to counter Cavan senior Raymond Cunningham and moving Denis Kealy into the full-back line to keep tabs on the 'Wood's most lethal forward, Ray 'Smoothie' Magee. The tactics worked a treat. Magee was confined to a point, Cunningham failed to score from open play while Richie Kealy's counter attacks from defence put severe pressure on the 'Wood's rearguard. Six of the North Meath side's points came from frees whereas Dunshaughlin had eleven from play.

This performance was the closest the side had yet come to reproducing the form of 2000. It featured direct, clinical attacking play based on the dominance of Niall Kelly and Graham Dowd in the centre. Dowd was a major player with a hand in both goals. He blasted to the net early in the first half after a surging run by Kelly and a pass from brother, Trevor, and six minutes after the break he provided a perfect cross for Kelly to crash the ball past keeper Mark Kiernan. The champions were then nine points ahead. Though Kilmainhamwood rallied and reduced the gap to five points, Trevor Dowd, Martin Reilly, Dermot Kealy, David Tonge and Reilly again had points for the free flowing black and ambers to stretch the advantage to eleven. A late rally only served to enhance the respectability of the scoreboard.

Martin Reilly had an outstanding game, roasting two different opponents and finishing with six points. Ronan Gogan had an inspired outing, making a super save early in the game, while Niall Kelly's strength, vision and long range passing highlighted his inexplicable omission from the Meath team. The result was enough to send Dunshaughlin into the quarter-finals and convert them once more into serious championship contenders.

In both the quarter and semi-finals Dunshaughlin built up early leads but had to dig deep to hang on at the death. Oldcastle provided the quarter-final opposition but two goals from Richie Kealy and another from Fearghal Gogan before half time cushioned Dunshaughlin when the late revival began.

Semi-final opponents Walterstown were unbeaten prior to their tussle with the black and ambers. However, the game seemed as good as over mid-way through the second half when the champions held a 1-10 to 1-2 lead. The *Meath Chronicle* described it as a forgettable encounter that was littered with frees and stoppages and produced more pulls and drags than a wrestling bout while Dunshaughlin were too fond of getting involved in skirmishes and conceded too many frees.

Richie Kealy finished as the game's top scorer with 1-5, while Trevor and Graham Dowd both notched two points. The early productive spell kept Dunshaughlin ahead when Walterstown's rally began with a looping Joey Farrelly shot for a point that ended in the net. Their total of 2-7 fell a point short of Dunshaughlin's 1-11 but the single point was as good as a dozen as the black and ambers stumbled over the line into a third consecutive final.

Showdown with Skryne

In the build up to the decider the players were aware of the challenge that confronted them. Skryne, the aristocrats of the game, waited in the wings and in three championship meetings since 1998 Dunshaughlin had never beaten the Tara men. Skryne had missed out on the previous year's final when surprisingly defeated by Kilmainhamwood at the semi-final stage. Many had belittled the significance of Dunshaughlin's title as the final was so one sided. Players and mentors were intent on overturning the 1999 final result between the same two teams but also knew that victory would transform them from a good team to a great one. Retaining titles was increasingly difficult in Meath, no club had done so since Skryne in 1993, so while Dunshaughlin had the incentive of matching that achievement Skryne were equally determined to prevent the neighbours encroaching on their records.

As Niall Kelly said after the game, 'If we lost today it would be three years of hard work down the drain.' Eamonn Barry put it more bluntly in his eve of game talk to the players, 'If ye don't win tomorrow, ye can fuck last year's medals into the Boyne.' This was not just a motivational ploy, he believed that many in the county

 'If ye don't win tomorrow, ye can fuck last year's medals into the Boyne.'

Showdown with Skryne, 2001

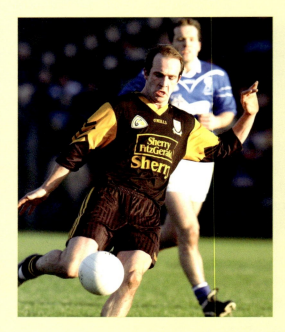
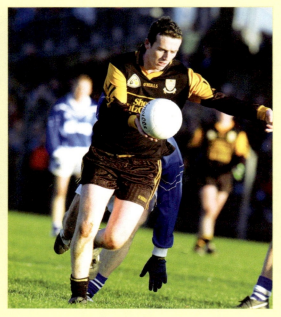

Clockwise from top left:
Team captain Dermot Kealy drills the ball forward.
Trevor Dowd on the move.
Martin Reilly evades three Skryne opponents to initiate another attack.

would not accept Dunshaughlin as real champions until they defeated Skryne.

There had been a subtle change in Dunshaughlin's approach compared to previous years. The team still used the ploy of the quickly taken, long free from Niall Kelly or Aiden Kealy into the full forward line but there was an increasing emphasis on having the half-backs, midfielders and half forwards run at defenders to draw frees. Martin Reilly had a near-perfect record from free kicks so it made sense to capitalize on his talent.

Dunshaughlin had started well against Skryne in 1999 but couldn't defeat them. Now they started poorly, conceded two early points and with the first quarter over had failed to raise a flag. Worrying times. Eventually an increasingly influential Graham Dowd ran on to a great Richie Kealy pass and kicked the champions' first point. Within a minute Skryne nullify it when Denis Kealy late tackles John McDermott and Mick O Dowd extracts maximum punishment with a pointed free.

Two points in three minutes nudge Dunshaughlin back to parity. The black and ambers' best attacking move sees Niall Kelly and Richie Kealy combining before setting up Graham Dowd for his second point and Martin Reilly soon adds another with his first touch of the ball in open play. Bryan McMahon fists a Skryne point before the champions win a free that could have gone the other way. Dunshaughlin's launcher of long-range Exocet missiles, Niall Kelly, steps up and directs the ball over the bar from 60 metres, leaving the sides sharing eight points.

In the dressing room at half time Dunshaughlin's management decide that they must be more direct and pressurize the Skryne defence. From half-back upwards players are under clear instructions to run at the opposition. This, they believe will result in scores or force Skryne into costly fouls.

It bears early fruit. Dermot Kealy and Michael McHale are fouled in the opening five minutes and Martin Reilly slots the opportunities and the black and ambers have a two-point lead. Then disaster for Dunshaughlin. Against the run of play Bryan McMahon gets in on goal and shoots. Ronan Gogan does well to smother the shot but Ken O Connell rifles home the rebound. Advantage Skryne.

But Dunshaughlin remain calm and adhere to the game plan. Within a minute Richie Kealy restores parity with a point after Trevor Dowd is fouled. Then Dermot Kealy drives forward from midfield, is hauled back and Martin Reilly steps up to confidently land the point. A single point lead. Advantage Dunshaughlin.

The pressure on the Blues continues with another surging run out of defence into Skryne territory. Raider Ronnie Yore parts to Martin Reilly who is upended and calmly converts the free himself. Reilly now seems to draw frees like a magnet. After receiving a pass from Dermot Kealy he makes ground, is again fouled and metronomically claims the point. Dunshaughlin lead by three and Reilly already has six points to his credit. Looking good!

Keeping the Keegan
Dunshaughlin captain Ciarán Byrne is delighted to keep the Keegan Cup for a second year after the 2001 victory over Skryne.

 Reilly now seems to draw frees like a magnet.

Dunshaughlin Senior Panel and Team Management
Meath Senior Champions, 2001

Front: Damien Eames, Kevin Kealy, Keith Mangan, David McNerney, Garbhán Blake, Martin Reilly, Denis Kealy, Ciarán Byrne, Capt., Fearghal Gogan, Ronnie Yore, Dermot Kealy, David Tonge, Trevor Dowd, Brendan Kealy, Kevin Moyles.
Back: Tiernan O Rourke, Paddy McHale, Christopher Carey, Niall Kelly, Aiden Kealy, Richie Kealy, Michael McHale, Ronan Gogan, David Crimmins, Kenny McTigue, Graham Dowd, Ray Maloney, Shane Kelly, Stephen Claire, Tom O Sullivan, Eamonn Barry, TP Toolan.

But the contest is not over yet as Trevor Giles is unerring from a 40 metre free and Skryne switch him from his starting berth at centre back to attack in a last ditch effort to rescue the game. Still plenty of time. With six minutes remaining Giles gets an opportunity from the left wing and shoots for a point. The umpire waves the white flag but referee Eugene McDonnell emphatically declares it wide. Still two points between the sides. Now Dunshaughlin's composure wobbles, as Richie Kealy, David Crimmins and Niall Kelly all have chances but can't find the target. With a minute on the clock that man Reilly claims another point, languidly placing the ball between the uprights after yet another foul, this one on Trevor Dowd.

As the game drifts into injury time Dunshaughlin hold a solid three points' advantage, with 0-11 to the Blues' 1-5. Skryne come raiding with a goal in mind. Instead, two poor efforts sail wide. With the clock having drifted four minutes past the sixty, Ronan Gogan is about to take a kick-out when Eugene McDonnell's three blasts on the whistle signal the end. Champions Again! Two in a row! Unbelievable!

In 2000 the outcome was clear long before the final blast of the referee's whistle. This time the closeness of the game meant that there was a sudden release of pent-up emotions, and players, mentors and supporters were ecstatic at the outcome. Suddenly the pitch was a heaving mass of black and amber as supporters poured out of the stand and terraces to savour the moment. Ronnie Yore, Graham Dowd and Dermot Kealy were all contenders for Man of the Match but it went to the sharp-eyed shooter, Martin Reilly, for his immense contribution of seven points. Incredibly, he didn't touch the ball until the 22nd minute of the first half but after that he wreaked havoc. The man who had lifted the intermediate trophy in 1997, Ciarán Byrne, was back on the podium to accept the Keegan Cup.

It was a very different game to the free flowing display against Kilmainhamwood a year previously. Of the seventeen scores registered by the teams only five came from play and just one of those arrived in the second half. In Niall Kelly's words, 'We didn't want to be considered a team that won an easy championship and we proved it today by winning a hard one.'

The foundations for victory were laid at centre-field where Graham Dowd and Dermot Kealy outshone a previously rampant John McDermott. Dunshaughlin gained control between the two 45s and forced Skryne into conceding frees. All the black and amber second half points were kicked following fouls, a vindication of the half time instructions. Skryne erred in delaying Trevor Giles' move into the attack until the closing stages, but, while it might have reduced the ultimate deficit it was unlikely to have changed the result. Just as Skryne had taken a stranglehold on the 1999 final after half time Dunshaughlin dominated the second period in

> 'We didn't want to be considered a team that won an easy championship and we proved it today by winning a hard one.'

BLACK & AMBER

Richie Kealy celebrates his goal against Dublin in the 2001 Leinster Final.
Photo: Damien Eagers, Sportsfile.

2001. They were clearly the better team and but for Skryne's goal strike against the run of play the margin would have been even more emphatic. The potential of 1999 had finally been transformed into peak.

The champions lined out as follows:

Ronan Gogan

Fearghal Gogan   Kenny McTigue   Ciarán Byrne, Capt.

Ronnie Yore   Aiden Kealy   Denis Kealy

Dermot Kealy   Graham Dowd (0-2)

Niall Kelly (0-1)   Michael McHale   Martin Reilly (0-7)

Richie Kealy (0-1)   David Crimmins   Trevor Dowd

Subs: Christopher Carey, David Tonge, Garbhán Blake, Shane Kelly, Tiernan O Rourke, Paddy McHale, Kevin Kealy, Brendan Kealy, Stephen Claire, Damien Eames, Keith Mangan, David McNerney, Kevin Moyles, Ray Maloney, Tom O Sullivan.

At county level 2001 was a stand out year also. Meath's Leinster senior championship winning side contained four Dunshaughlin clubmen, Richie Kealy, Dermot Kealy, Niall Kelly and David Crimmins. Martin Reilly in his debut year with the club just missed out on a Leinster junior medal when Offaly defeated the Royals by a single point in the Leinster final. The highlight was the Leinster senior final victory against Dublin with Richie finishing as joint top scorer courtesy of a crucial goal. Midway through the second half he won possession twenty-five metres from the posts and fed Nigel Nestor who returned the compliment with a magnificent hand pass which left Kealy in the clear and his stunning strike gave Dublin keeper David Byrne no chance. He already held an All-Ireland medal from 1999 after his early introduction against Cork but Meath couldn't repeat that feat two years later when Galway proved too strong in the final.

Richie came into the 2001 campaign as Meath Footballer of the Year, the only clubman ever to earn the accolade. He would conclude his career as the most decorated footballer ever to represent the black and ambers. Starting with his Meath debut at minor level in 1993 against Louth, he won Leinster championship medals at all grades, minor, Under 21, junior and senior as well as an All-Ireland senior. He collected one Leinster club, an intermediate and three senior championship medals and was the clear Man of the Match award winner in the 2000 final with seven points. At his peak he was unrivalled in the scoring stakes but his versatility, dedication and commitment enabled him to play with equal facility in defence or attack and when a regular defender with Meath he was Dunshaughlin's shining forward. He made his club debut against Castletown in the 1993 intermediate championship and featured in the senior final against Summerhill eighteen years later. In between he made twenty-four intermediate and eight-eighty championship appearances for the club. For loyalty, dedication and achievement his record is likely to stand the test of time.

Further recognition for a stand-out year came when Dunshaughlin shared the award of Club of the Year with Blackhall Gaels.

Any Chance of Three in a Row?

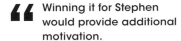
Winning it for Stephen would provide additional motivation.

When Dunshaughlin embarked on the 2002 campaign they had ample motivation. Three in a row is a rarity in any sport but setting it as a target can be a two-edged sword. It may be the spur to victory or the albatross that leads to failure. The team and management fervently believed that the side should have done, and could still do, much better in Leinster. (See Chapter 15). Setting such a distant target however, could divert attention from the immediate task of qualifying for the knock-out stages of the county championship. More immediate motivation came with the sudden, untimely death of club stalwart Stephen Burke. The team was on its annual end of season holiday in Tenerife when selector TP Toolan had the unpleasant task of passing on the devastating news. Winning it for Stephen would provide additional motivation.

But could they summon up the hunger and dedication necessary for a third successful campaign? Selector and player Brendan Kealy had no doubt that the hunger for more success remained. He had his own personal motivation, a searing memory from the also-ran days, 'I was on Dunshaughlin intermediate teams that lost six championship semi-finals, including replays, so any opportunity you get to win something, you try to take it and enjoy it.'

In 2001 the side had displayed true grit to recover from humiliation at the hands of Simonstown Gaels to go on and retain their crown. That game was played in Dunsany and the 2002 campaign commenced at the same venue on 21st April. From there to Páirc Tailteann in November was a long and winding road. As in the maps of old denoting dangerous and unexplored territory the journey could be signposted 'Here be dragons.'

No dragons appeared to upset stage one of the journey. Though Summerhill stayed in step with the champions well into the second half Dunshaughlin then resurrected the power, pace and precision of old. Richie Kealy fisted to the net, then booted another past Tony McDonnell while substitute Ray Maloney cracked in a third to ensure a safe passage by 3-12 to 0-8.

The next two rounds revived the doubts. Dunboyne forced a late draw in May and more worryingly Gaeil Colmcille repeated the feat in August. The black and ambers could only score eight points in the first outing and that fell to six in the second, with Trevor Dowd accounting for five of the half dozen. With two teams qualifying from four, the results were enough to see Dunshaughlin through to the quarter-finals, but a red card for David Crimmins against Gaeil Colmcille ruled him out of the clash against Blackhall Gaels. Also ruled out was the Gaels' inter county star, Anthony Moyles. He had been sent off against Ballinlough the previous week.

> **it was the beginning of delays, debates, disputes and distraction.**

They'll hardly play him

Rumour circulated prior to the clash with Blackhall in Dunboyne that Moyles would play despite the sending off. It transpired that the referee had misunderstood his lineman's instruction when dismissing the Gaels' man. Meath County Board, adhering to a directive from GAA President Seán McCague, that a red card results in automatic suspension unless video evidence is available to clear a player's name, informed Blackhall that Moyles was not eligible to play.

The truth of the rumour was confirmed when Moyles appeared in the number fourteen jersey but it didn't seem to matter, as Dunshaughlin controlled the early stages. Trevor Dowd and Brendan Kealy scored first half goals but the side hit eight costly wides before half time. Blackhall improved in the second half; two early points, a Mark Crampton goal and three more unanswered points gave them a commanding lead and the late dismissal of Richie Kealy seemed to herald Dunshaughlin's dismissal also. Instead it was the beginning of delays, debates, disputes and distraction.

The Three Wise Men:
Dunshaughlin's selectors during the three in a row: TP Toolan, Eamonn Barry, Brendan Kealy.

Where it Began:
St. Seachnall's NS, winners of the Meath Primary Schools' Championship in 1991. Seven of them played in the club's first senior championship success, Graham Dowd, Pádraig McHale, David Crimmins, Fearghal Gogan, Niall Kelly, Ronan Gogan and Denis Kealy, another three- Pádraic O Dwyer, Shane Kelly and David Tonge were subs, while Neil O Dwyer served as Club Chairman, 2013-15.
Front: Niall Kelly, Brendan Killoran, Neil O Dwyer, Pádraic O Dwyer, Shane Kelly, Capt., Ronan Gogan, David Tonge, Denis Kealy.
Back: Graham Dowd, Pádraig McHale, David Crimmins, Niall O Connor, Fearghal Gogan, Fintan Lawlor, Dominic Jones.

The Kealy Brothers:
Brendan, Dermot, Denis, Richie, Kevin and Aiden.

Action from the 2002 Senior County Final

Pictured clockwise from top left:

David Crimmins has eyes for the ball only as he prepares to shoot.

Denis Kealy makes for the opening with brother Richie ready to assist.

An attacking Niall Kelly forces the Trim defence to retreat.

Ronan Gogan prepares to clear his lines with Ciarán Byrne available for the pass.

Dunshaughlin objected to Blackhall on the basis that they played a suspended player and were thereby illegal. At a County Board meeting on September 12th the objection was considered. Delegates gave their views in the packed meeting room under Páirc Tailteann and speaker after speaker expressed their sympathy with Blackhall. When Dunshaughlin Chairman, Paddy O Dwyer proposed the objection he had to rely on clubman Cyril Creavin, an officer of the board, as a seconder. However, County Board Chairman, Fintan Ginnity was not swayed by popular sentiment. He upheld the rules and imposed a four-week ban on Moyles for the red card and a further twenty-four weeks for playing while suspended. As the *Chronicle* noted Dunshaughlin were cast *'undeservedly as villains of the piece.'* Blackhall appealed to Leinster Council but it rejected the appeal. When Meath County Board proposed to arrange the Dunshaughlin v Seneschalstown semi Blackhall threatened to seek a court injunction and the fixture was deferred.

Meanwhile, efforts were proceeding behind the scenes to resolve the issue with Board officers meeting both clubs to broker a compromise. The outcome was a proposal that the original game should be declared null and void and that the clubs meet again to settle the issue. Blackhall agreed, delegate Noel Farrell stating, 'we feel that we won the match against Dunshaughlin fairly and deserve to go through, but we do not want to be responsible for holding up the championship.' This ignored the fact that they won while fielding an illegal player. Paddy O Dwyer agreed to take the proposal back to the club and Dunshaughlin accepted the compromise.

As the original game was now deemed null and void Anthony Moyles was clear to play in the re-arranged quarter-final and duly took his place when the sides met in Páirc Tailteann. The *Meath Chronicle* declared that Dunshaughlin

'must be applauded for the manner in which they conducted themselves throughout the debate in which they were completely innocent bystanders in an exchange between Blackhall Gaels and the County Board. Football matters, where possible, should be resolved on the pitch, and Dunshaughlin made a significant contribution behind the scenes towards a resolution to this matter.'

The champions were handicapped by the loss of captain Aiden Kealy and Trevor Dowd, both of whom had received suspensions arising from the Kilmacud All-Ireland Sevens. Matters worsened when Graham Dowd had to depart in the first quarter with a recurrence of a knee injury. Damian Burke, originally from The Downs club and a former Westmeath senior player, was a ready-made replacement. Luckily, David Crimmins was once again eligible and had a major impact on the game. He hit a goal mid-way through the half after a sweeping move beginning with Ronan Gogan was carried on by Niall Kelly and Ray Maloney. Though Dunshaughlin dominated the half they could only add three points, two from Richie and one from

Three County Finals, Three Award Winners

Man of the Match Awards clockwise from top left.

Richie Kealy 2000, Martin Reilly 2001, David Crimmins 2002.

Dunshaughlin supporters in the background behind Martin Reilly include: in red, Brendan Tonge and Frances Maloney, while lower down Christy Purcell and Vincent Clusker look on. To the right in blue headgear beside the garda is Alan Fahy, a regular on Dunshaughlin teams during the 1990s.

Happy Dunshaughlin spectators as David Crimmins accepts his award are Patty and John Holland, with cap and rosette, and Brendan Murray in Dunshaughlin baseball cap. John Holland, former Principal of Dunshaughlin Community College, played with Dunshaughlin in the 1960s, while his wife Patty is a brother of noted former Roscommon keeper Aidan Brady. Brendan's father, PJ Murray, was involved in the club from the beginning of the twentieth century, while his brother Ciarán played with Dunshaughlin and Drumree and was the inspiration behind the establishment of St. Martins in the 1950s.

Brendan Kealy while Crimmins and Burke both missed good goal chances.

Blackhall began the second half with a Mark Crampton point, matched by a superb solo effort from Niall Kelly. Minutes later Burke and Maloney combined to set up Crimmins for a second goal and the black and ambers led 2-6 to 0-3. It seemed as good as over but Blackhall responded with six unanswered points as well as hitting the post twice. Then the lethal combination of Burke and Maloney intervened and set up Crimmins again for his hat-trick of goals. Anthony Moyles managed a Blackhall goal before the end and Ronan Gogan had to dramatically come to his side's rescue at the death as he grabbed Crampton's net bound fisted effort. When the final whistle blew Dunshaughlin had done enough on and off the field to record a narrow 3-7 to 1-10 victory.

Seneschalstown powered by Graham Geraghty and Joe Sheridan provided a new foe in the semi-final. In vile weather conditions Dunshaughlin failed to impose themselves on the scoreboard until the closing stages. Geraghty grabbed 1-3 and also hit seven wides but none of his forwards registered a score. In contrast Dunshaughlin had five

That Winning Feeling
Dunshaughlin players and mentors celebrate in the dressing room after defeating Trim in the 2002 final.
Front: Shane Kelly, David Tonge, Dermot Kealy, John Crimmins, Kevin Moyles.
Back: Denis Kealy, Kevin Kealy, Stephen Claire, Brendan Kealy, Fearghal Gogan, Keith Mangan, Declan O Dwyer, Michael McHale.

scorers and this greater balance, combined with experience, enabled them to move clear in the final ten minutes. Dermot Kealy was outstanding around the middle, driving his side forward at very opportunity as well as assisting in defence. With ten minutes remaining Geraghty brought the sides level at 0-7 to 1-4 and Seneschalstown looked likely winners. However, the dismissal of Colin Clarke didn't help their cause and Martin Reilly proved his value to Dunshaughlin by pointing a free. Geraghty missed two opportunities to level before Reilly thumped a ball high between the uprights from 45 metres and then set up Richie Kealy for the final score. Dunshaughlin had negotiated the dragons thus far and were into their fourth consecutive final.

Trim, like Dunshaughlin, had a less than smooth run to the final. In between victories over Cortown and Skryne they fell to Kilmainhamwood and only overcame Walterstown at the quarter-final stage by virtue of a late Darren Fay goal. A semi-final victory over Dunboyne put them into their first Keegan Cup final since 1997. The favourites' tag rested with the black and ambers, based on Trim's lack of consistency and the champions' experience, but it was a hesitant vote. A look at the respective scoring records suggested that there was little between both sets of forwards with Trim averaging fourteen points to Dunshaughlin's twelve but the defending champions had the meaner defence, conceding an average of less than ten points per game to Trim's thirteen.

A Drama in Three Acts

> **"** The game could be described as a performance in three acts.

Seven months after the opening round the sides faced each other on Sunday 10th November, on a beautiful day on an immaculate surface. The game could be described as a performance in three acts. The first saw Dunshaughlin display their best form either side of the half time break to build up a substantial six points lead. The second part belonged to Trim who clawed back the lead to draw level with three minutes remaining. The climax came in the third act, the most dramatic and exciting part of the game.

Trim opened with an early goal when Michael Lowther opportunistically punched a Brendan Murphy '45' past Ronan Gogan, and Dunshaughlin got their challenge underway when Martin Reilly converted a free. Before half time the black and ambers added another five points before a solitary Trim reply deep in first half injury time. Brendan Kealy had a fine point from play, Reilly converted another free, David Crimmins added an impressive effort from play, Denis Kealy broke out of defence to shoot over and Richie Kealy converted a free awarded to Damian Burke.

Soon after half time David Crimmins from play and Reilly from a free improved the interval score of 0-6 to 1-1. Michael Lowther managed to dispossess Fearghal

CHAPTER 14: HIGH KINGS OF MEATH

Gogan for a Trim point but then Trevor Dowd, who had been replaced and later brought back on, pounced to score a crucial goal. Trim keeper Mark Daly had done well to keep out a shot from Ray Maloney but he had no answer to Dowd's accuracy and opportunism. The champions with a 1-8 to 1-2 lead seemed impregnable and the reduction of both sides to fourteen men when Martin Reilly and Kevin Walsh incurred the referee's wrath looked unlikely to change that.

But there was a second act.

Trim scored a point but failed to add to it for almost ten minutes. Then, a long Darren Fay free caused confusion in the Dunshaughlin square. Michael McHale rose to grab it but the ball slipped off his fingers past a helpless keeper and a minute later Eoin McGrath reduced the lead to the minimum. Ray Maloney gave Dunshaughlin some breathing space with a point while being tightly marked, but Trim's riposte was effective. Two Paul Gilsenan points in four minutes, both from distance, one from play and one from a free, brought equality with three minutes of normal time remaining.

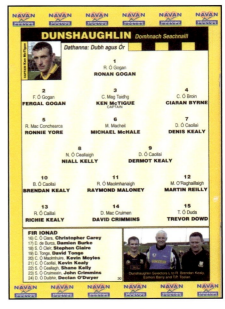

Dunshaughlin line-out and substitutes against Trim from the 2002 county final programme.

For the final act the initiative seemed to have swung to the challengers. Fresher looking and on the attack they seemed the more likely to score. Ronan Fitzsimons carried the ball towards goal, looked up and shot for the winner but the ball drifted left and wide. Paul Gilsenan had an equally good chance but an underhit effort dropped short and Dunshaughlin breathed again. The clock had ticked well into injury time when Trim's Seán Murphy drove the ball over the sideline to seeming safety, 45 metres out from his goal. A line ball and Niall Kelly stepped up to take it.

Moments earlier he had a similar opportunity, decided to go short, got the return and drove the ball towards goal only for Murphy's despairing clearance to provide this second chance. Too far out for a score and everyone waited for it to drop in around the goal.

But Kelly had different ideas. Having tried the percentage game he now opted to go for broke. A quick spin of the ball from one hand to the other, three strides and the left boot drills through the ball, sending it spinning towards the hospital end posts. Time seems to stand still as the ball spirals towards the goal, too high for any human intervention. Its destination is in the lap of the Gods. As it arcs downwards it is clearly on target. It clears the bar, stopping only on contact with the netting behind the goal. Trim supporters slump in their seats while the Dunshaughlin crowd leaps for joy. A point ahead and over two minutes of injury time played.

There is still time for a kick-out but the demoralized Trim players can hardly comprehend what has happened. Ray Maloney takes possession from a Damian Burke pass and rattles the crossbar with his shot. The ball rebounds into play, David Crimmins pounces on it and calmly slots over a classy insurance point. The hat-trick of titles is complete on a score of 1-11 to 2-6. Twelve scores to eight is

297

A Triple Triumph in 2002

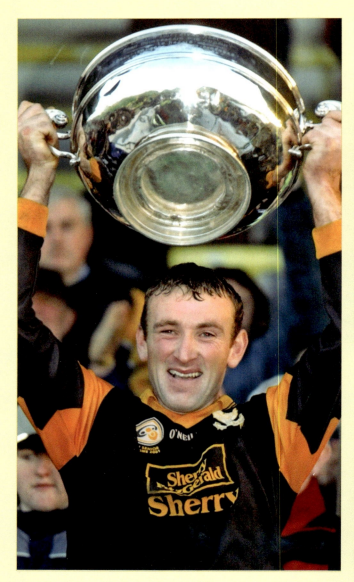

Kenny McTigue raises the Keegan Cup as Dunshaughlin retain the title in 2002.

Kenny McTigue accepts the Mooney Cup from County Board PRO Barry Gorman after Dunshaughlin won Division 1 of the All County Football League.

Ronnie Yore accepts Dunshaughlin's first ever Feis Cup from Cyril Creavin.

a gauge of Dunshaughlin's superiority but the final act could easily have ended in tragedy for the black and ambers.

David Crimmins, with three points from play was Man of the Match and captain Kenny McTigue in his acceptance speech remembered Stephen Burke and club captain Aiden Kealy. Eamonn Barry summed up the game succinctly,

'We made things difficult for ourselves by losing our concentration a few times during the match. Admittedly Trim's first goal was an excellent example of opportunism, but the second goal was a mistake on our part.'

Nevertheless, the final result cemented the side's place alongside the greatest Meath club sides of all time. As Eamonn Barry later declared from the top of the Mound of the Hostages on the Hill of Tara, 'Look around you. You're the High Kings of Meath!'

The historic line out was,

We've Done It.
Niall Kelly and Michael McHale embrace following the final whistle to signal the three in a row.

Ronan Gogan
Fearghal Gogan   Kenny McTigue, Capt.   Ciarán Byrne
Ronnie Yore   Michael McHale   Denis Kealy (0-1)
         Niall Kelly (0-1)   Dermot Kealy
Brendan Kealy (0-1)   Ray Maloney (0-1)   Martin Reilly (0-3)
Richie Kealy (0-1)   David Crimmins (0-3)   Trevor Dowd (1-0)

Subs: Damian Burke for Dowd, Dowd for Yore, Stephen Claire for B Kealy, Chris Carey, David Tonge, Kevin Moyles, Kevin Kealy, Shane Kelly, John Crimmins, Declan O Dwyer, Keith Mangan, Caoimhín King, Graham Dowd, Aiden Kealy.

Another brace of trophies

Training that began on 10th January with two nights indoors and Sundays in Tara was not at an end as the Keegan Cup made the now familiar journey along the N3 to Dunshaughlin. The Leinster Championship awaited and the side had also reached the League and Feis Cup finals. The provincial campaign would continue until Christmas so it was January before the local competitions concluded.

First up was the Division 1 final. Dunshaughlin had shipped only one defeat in the eleven league games and gave a reprise of their best form when disposing of Dunboyne in the final at Donaghmore by double scores, 4-12 to 2-6.

A slow start was followed by a pedigree performance featuring 3-8 in the twenty minutes before half time. In the centre of the park Dermot Kealy tackled and worked like a terrier and Niall Kelly fielded superbly to give the county champions complete control. Both got on the scoreboard, Kealy forcing David Gallagher to cough up possession, then combining with brother Richie before pointing while Kelly hit two points, both from distance, one a free and the other from play. Eight different players contributed to the score and four forwards, David Tonge, David Crimmins, Trevor

Dowd and Ray Maloney shared the four goals.

The winners rarely gave an inch in defence where Fearghal Gogan, Kenny McTigue, Denis Kealy, Ciarán Byrne and Michael McHale excelled. The forwards, in addition to compiling a comprehensive score card with everyone contributing, impressed by their work ethic, fighting for every ball and defending from the front. Dunshaughlin emptied their bench before the end with one of the substitutes Keith Mangan notching a point. Another substitute Damian Burke was unlucky to be sent off with Dunboyne's Tomás O Connor, for what the *Chronicle* described as '*nothing more than horizontal waltzing.*' Kenny McTigue once again stepped forward to accept the silverware, the Mooney Cup, named in honour of Skryne stalwart, Tommy Mooney.

The successful team and substitutes read,

Ronan Gogan

Denis Kealy Kenny McTigue, Capt. Ciarán Byrne

Fearghal Gogan Michael McHale Richie Kealy

Niall Kelly (0-2) Dermot Kealy (0-1)

Brendan Kealy (0-1) David Crimmins (1-1) David Tonge (1-2)

Martin Reilly (0-4) Ray Maloney (1-0) Trevor Dowd (1-0)

Subs: Damian Burke for Reilly, Declan O Dwyer for B Kealy, Kevin Moyles for F Gogan, Kevin Kealy for Tonge, Keith Mangan (0-1) for Dowd.

Following a ten-day team holiday in California the side returned to face intermediate side Castletown in the Feis Cup final. The Feis Cup was the oldest trophy on offer in Meath and had never been won by Dunshaughlin. Played on a simple knock-out basis the black and ambers had reached the final courtesy of victories over Walterstown, Donaghmore-Ashbourne, Dunderry and Trim.

With an All-Ireland club semi-final ahead the team management reshuffled the pack, leaving Ronan Gogan, Denis Kealy, and David Tonge in reserve and moving regular centre-back Michael McHale to full forward. He proved just as resourceful in his new posting, finishing with three points, two of them superbly executed in the early stages. Martin Reilly contributed seven points, six from frees, and Dunshaughlin held a 0-10 to 1-1 interval advantage.

With ten minutes remaining Damian Burke forced the Castletown keeper into an error and David Crimmins had the simple task of placing the ball in the empty net. Dermot Kealy and Niall Kelly once again ruled the roost in the middle with Kealy making little of an ongoing knee injury to cover all areas of the pitch and Kelly providing his trademark point from a 50m free. Ronnie Yore was given the honour of collecting the cup, which left the club in possession of the senior championship, All County Division 1 league, Feis Cup and Leinster club titles.

Dunshaughlin, Meath Senior Champions, 2002

Front: Andrew Barry- mascot, Caoimhín King, David Tonge, Kevin Moyles, Keith Mangan, Brendan Kealy, Kenny McTigue, Capt., Denis Kealy, Martin Reilly, Fearghal Gogan, Trevor Dowd, Ronnie Yore, Christopher Carey, Kevin Kealy, Stephen Claire.
Back: Gerry Keenan, Physio, Declan O Dwyer, John Crimmins, Shane Kelly, Niall Kelly, Aiden Kealy, Michael McHale, Richie Kealy, Ray Maloney, David Crimmins, Ronan Gogan, Dermot Kealy, Ciarán Byrne, Damian Burke, Graham Dowd, Eamonn Barry, Coach.
Photo: Matt Browne, Sportsfile.

The winning Feis Cup line out was

Christopher Carey

Fearghal Gogan — Kenny McTigue — Ciarán Byrne

Ronnie Yore, Capt. — Richie Kealy (0-1) — Kevin Moyles

Niall Kelly (0-1) — Dermot Kealy

Brendan Kealy — Ray Maloney — Martin Reilly (0-7)

David Crimmins (1-2) — Michael McHale (0-3) — Trevor Dowd (0-3)

Subs: David Tonge (0-1) for B Kealy, Caoimhín King for Byrne, Shane Kelly for Reilly, Damian Burke for McHale, Kevin Kealy for Dowd.

The three in a row of senior titles, victory in the league and Feis Cup finals and the heroics in the Leinster championship entitle this team to a place alongside the greatest club sides in the history of the GAA in Meath. In the previous fifty years only O Mahonys, twice, Kilbride, Summerhill and Walterstown have managed three in a row while in the dozen years since Dunshaughlin's last title no club has managed to win two consecutive titles. In recent decades the pool of possible winners has widened making such dominance even more difficult to achieve.

Within six years the team went from intermediate winners to senior kingpins and Leinster club champions. It was in the main a home-grown team, progressing from St. Seachnall's National School, onto Dunshaughlin Community College and St. Martins. Fourteen of the side that started the 2000 final were past pupils of St. Seachnall's and all of them attended the Community College. All had played at under-age level with St Martins. Dermot Kealy, Ciarán Byrne and Brendan Kealy had won Minor Championship medals with St. Martins-Ratoath in 1987 but the majority had won no underage championships. They had, however, always been competitive and St. Martins provided a regular conveyer belt of talent for the adult club.

From the beginning Eamonn Barry was impressed by the team's dedication and commitment. Attendance at or performances in training was never a problem, whether early in the morning or late in the evening, whether locally in Dunshaughlin or as distant as Donabate. Swathes of time was dedicated to video analysis. It was not unusual for the panel to spend up to two hours after training viewing and analyzing videos of games, often on Saturday nights when contemporaries were socializing. The fact that many of the players were single enabled them to dedicate so much time to preparation but as the years advanced and players assumed family responsibilities there was no diminution in their dedication to training and preparation.

Dunshaughlin's Three in a Row

On the tenth of November in 2002
All went to Páirc Tailteann, the great deed to do
With two Keegan Cups already in tow
Dunshaughlin was playing for three in a row.
Trim met our heroes in senior football
And the men in red shirts tried to plot our downfall.
Ronan Gogan, our keeper, a stopper supreme
He's number one always, on our outstanding team.
Fearghal, his brother, can play left or right
When he wins the ball the outlook is bright.
Our brave captain Kenny, a full back without peer
He'll win every tackle, each ball he will clear.
Ciarán Byrne in the corner will stop any attack
The forward who rambles he'll constantly track.
Attackers who try to outwit Ronnie Yore
Are quickly subdued and retire sick and sore,
We've big Mick McHale, on his back number six
He can counter all forwards and their bags of tricks.
Young Kealy, that's Denis, with his strength and his speed
Will attack from all angles, it's part of his creed.

Out in the middle there's no one to beat
Dermot Kealy, Niall Kelly, for their play is a treat.
Dermot you'll find him both upfield and down
He was our captain when we won our first crown.
Niall scores many points with his long booming drive
Where's the man who can match him, dead or alive?

Our forwards are lethal, they never stand still
And without any warning they're in for the kill.
Brendan Kealy he plays a demanding dual role
As player or selector winning is always his goal.
Martin Reilly he joined us just one year ago
From his lethal right boot points constantly flow.
Our county star Richie, goals and points he will snatch
Seven points v the Wood made him Man of the Match.

At number eleven Ray Maloney is set
He can carry the ball and rattle the net.
Trevor Dowd in the corner, he's the best man to score
If the team needs a boost he'll supply even more.
With right foot or left foot Crimbo's skill is sublime
He keeps fooling poor keepers time after time.
David Tonge in the forwards has incredible pace
When he enters the field we are playing an ace.
Graham Dowd and Aiden Kealy with two medals to date
Missed out on the final, a most terrible fate.

And on our subs bench Burke is part of the crew
While Carey, Claire and Mangan all know what to do.
A Kealy called Kevin, a Kelly, that's Shane
All add to our talent, it's clear and it's plain,
Kev Moyles, John Crimmins, Kingsy, Declan O Dwyer
Ensure that in future we'll go higher and higher.

Tom Sullivan played a part on our earlier teams
With Dec Fahy, Dave Moroney and sub keeper Eames,
P McHale at 11, Garbhán Blake in defence
And Tiernan with goals when the going was tense.
There was Ulick McDonnell and Pádraic O Dwyer
And young Dave McNerney, an out and out flyer.

TP Toolan our selector can make a masterful move
And switch round a player till he enters the groove.
Our coach Eamonn Barry is the best in the land
With training and tactics all our moves are well-planned.
We've beaten them all, the Wood, Skryne and Trim
Your chances of beating us are very slim.
Here's a health to our heroes, the men you all know,
They brought glory to Dunshaughlin with the three in a row.

Jim Gilligan

BLACK & AMBER

Fresh Fields: The Leinster Campaigns

As Meath senior champions, participation in the Leinster club championship beckoned. Teams from the Royal County had an undistinguished record in the competition with only two Meath clubs winning it from its inception in 1970.

Winning the Keegan Cup for the first time ever was an end in itself. But it was also a new beginning.

As Meath senior champions, participation in the Leinster club championship beckoned. Teams from the Royal County had an undistinguished record in the competition with only two Meath clubs winning it from its inception in 1970. Summerhill were victors in 1977 and Walterstown captured the title twice, in 1980 and 1983, with Eamonn Barry central to the Blacks' successes. Reaching the final proved beyond the resources of practically all Meath champions; only Seneschalstown, in addition to Summerhill and Walterstown, qualified for the final during the three decades, 1970-2000. In the same thirty years the Meath senior team played in eighteen Leinster finals, winning eight titles.

Meath clubs were certainly punching below their weight.

The competition had its origins in a motion passed at the GAA's Annual Congress in 1969. It proposed provincial competitions between the champion clubs in each county culminating in an All-Ireland final. Initially opposed by many, the competition grew in popularity and prestige especially once the All-Ireland finals were scheduled annually for Croke Park on St. Patrick's Day. The competition gave club players the honour of representing the basic unit of the GAA, the club,

BLACK & AMBER

at the highest possible level, and, as it was played after the conclusion of inter-county competitions it became the focus of press and public attention.

Episode One

On Sunday 22nd October 2000, one month after the Keegan Cup win over Kilmainhamwood, Dunshaughlin returned to the same venue as representatives of Meath. Dermot Kealy had the honour of leading his black and amber troops into battle against the red and green clad Wicklow champions, Rathnew. The Wicklow men had just won their fifth consecutive county title and were experienced campaigners at provincial level. It turned out to be the first instalment of a saga that endured for three years. It developed from friendly rivalry to naked hostility before ending in gradual, grudging mutual respect.

On a raw autumn day Dunshaughlin's direct brand of football unsettled Rathnew. Trevor Dowd grabbed a long accurate pass from Aiden Kealy in the tenth minute and rifled a bullet-like shot to the net. A second goal arrived five minutes before half time when Dermot Kealy raced menacingly into opposition territory before being halted illegally in the square. Keeper Tommy Murphy brilliantly saved the resultant penalty only for the taker, Denis Kealy, to drill the rebound to the roof of the net. Dunshaughlin held a 2-2 to 0-3 lead at the break and Trevor Dowd with three points maintained that five-point lead as the game entered its final ten minutes.

By then Rathnew's Mark Coffey had been dismissed for a full-frontal assault on Richie Kealy, who had to retire injured as a result. Dunshaughlin should have wrapped up the game but the loss of a player seemed to inspire Rathnew and they began to reel in the deficit. The Dunshaughlin defence came under sustained pressure and conceded frees which the accurate Tommy Gill converted. The dismissal of Aiden Kealy, with time almost up, evened up the numbers and by the end of seven minutes of injury time Gill had tied up the scores also, with Rathnew finishing on eleven points to Dunshaughlin's 2-5.

The game was extremely physical throughout, the foul on Richie Kealy being the most serious incident. At the end the players bundled down the tunnel, spent and exhausted, exchanging mutinous words and trading blows. Carlo Divito of the *Meath Chronicle* declared,

'Never before have I witnessed such exchanges on a football field and although some may accuse me of biased reporting, the simple fact is that the Rathnew players, mentors and supporters were mainly responsible.'

He blamed the *'over-zealous'* Rathnew supporters for adding fuel to the fire by

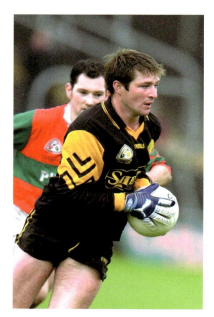

Aiden Kealy gets out in front against Rathnew

shouting *'several verbal obscenities during the game and they continued outside the dressing room when the contest concluded.'* He declared that their *'idea of tackling would be better suited to a wrestling ring.'*

Next stop Aughrim. A fortress of Wicklow football and a venue most counties prefer to avoid. Rathnew had won their five consecutive Wicklow titles here and used the venue for all their home games in the Leinster championship. A week after the Battle of Navan would there be another Battle of Aughrim?

On a miserable day gusts of wind and sheets of driving rain made for a soft, heavy pitch. Two sets of partisan supporters roared on their teams but the only similarity to the earlier encounter was the result, another draw, after extra time. Five Rathnew yellow cards and two for Dunshaughlin were due to the deplorable conditions rather than evil intent.

This time Dunshaughlin had to do the reeling in. Rathnew's Tommy Gill was in imperious form, scoring ten points, seven of them from play. The Wicklow side, with wind advantage, took a 0-8 to 0-3 lead to the break. Richie and Brendan Kealy and Trevor Dowd accounted for Dunshaughlin's first half total. Prospects didn't look too bright early in the second half as Rathnew added an early point and Dunshaughlin struggled to find their form. Points from David Crimmins and Richie Kealy reduced the deficit to four before Michael McHale took advantage of defensive fumbling to shoot to the net. Finally Trevor Dowd sent the sides into extra time with a dubiously awarded free, but Dunshaughlin weren't objecting.

Rathnew carved out a three-point advantage after the first period of extra time but the black and ambers responded superbly with early points from Michael McHale and Richie Kealy and a late booming 50 metre free from Niall Kelly ensuring deadlock. Dunshaughlin were happy to escape from the lion's den with a draw and another chance but on a day when they found it difficult to play their normal free flowing football they could thank Ronan Gogan for thwarting three Rathnew goal efforts with outstanding stops.

Seven days later all roads led to Navan for the third encounter. In the meantime there was no improvement in the weather. Another rain-lashed, grey day was lit up by three stunning Dunshaughlin goals. Richie Kealy hit the first a mere two minutes in, as Dunshaughlin played a possession game against the elements. It came at the end of a multi-man move featuring slick inter-passing and speedy interplay with David Crimmins and Dermot Kealy setting up Richie.

By half time Rathnew held a slender one-point lead but Crimmins' two lethal strikes after half time gave Dunshaughlin a comfortable lead. Trevor Dowd set up his first with a pass and Crimmins again displayed his predatory instincts for his second when he took advantage of a breaking ball to unleash a vicious left-foot shot to the top corner of the net. Rathnew couldn't match the three goals as the

> their 'idea of tackling would be better suited to a wrestling ring.'

BLACK & AMBER

> *'Dunshaughlin were in their traditional black and amber jerseys but, considering they were handing out gifts like Santa Claus, perhaps they should have been in red and white.'*

black and ambers marched to victory on a 3-8 to 1-6 scoreline. It was a tough, uncompromising encounter but without the venom of the first meeting. Rathnew had two players red carded by referee Brian White while Dunshaughlin lost Niall Kelly to a straight red midway through the second half. His loss would be felt in the next encounter against Kildare champions Moorefield.

Over the three games Dunshaughlin were the better-balanced side and the team more likely to poach goals. Rathnew were very dependant on the excellent Tommy Gill for scores. In the final game he scored all their points, accounted for almost seventy per cent of their scores in the three-match saga and was their only player to score in each game. Dunshaughlin had a much bigger spread of scorers. The side had three major marksmen, Trevor Dowd, Richie Kealy and David Crimmins but another seven players also contributed. Finally Rathnew's single goal over the series was totally eclipsed by their opponents return of six.

Dunshaughlin's line out for the third game was: Ronan Gogan; Fearghal Gogan, Kenny McTigue, Ciarán Byrne; Denis Kealy, Aiden Kealy, Dermot Kealy (0-1); Niall Kelly, Graham Dowd; David Tonge (0-2), David Crimmins (2-0), Brendan Kealy; Richie Kealy (1-1), Michael McHale, Trevor Dowd (0-4). Subs: Paddy McHale for Graham Dowd, Ronnie Yore for Gogan.

Next up was Moorefield in a quarter-final in Páirc Tailteann on the following Sunday. Like Dunshaughlin they were newcomers to the Leinster club scene. They had recently captured their second Kildare title and were not one of the traditional powers. The black and ambers went into the game handicapped by the loss of two of their most influential players, Niall Kelly due to suspension and Richie Kealy from an arm injury. It turned out to be an afternoon to forget for the Meath champions.

Against the wind in the first half, Eamonn Barry's men had plenty of possession and confined the opposition to four points and a lead of two. However, Moorefield confounded expectations as the second half began with a goal in the first minute rapidly followed by a long-range point. Regular scorers Trevor Dowd and David Crimmins were struggling to create openings up front but then blunders in defence sank all hope of a revival. Noel Coogan in *The Weekender* declared that

Dunshaughlin were in their traditional black and amber jerseys but, considering they were handing out gifts like Santa Claus, perhaps they should have been in red and white.

Ronan Gogan who had been a saviour against Rathnew couldn't hold an under-hit point attempt and Moorefield's Brian McGrogan tapped in off the post. Two minutes later the same player got his fist to a cross to net once again and Dunshaughlin's hopes were in tatters. Though the team battled hard and introduced five substitutes, the loss of Kelly and Kealy was huge. Four games

Action from the Leinster Campaigns

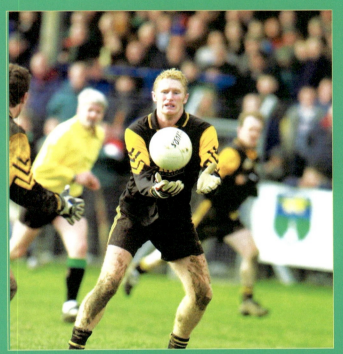

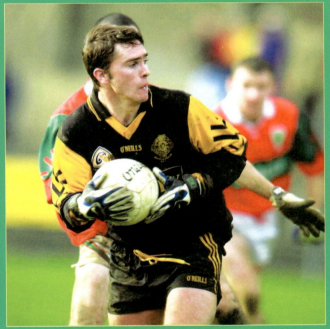
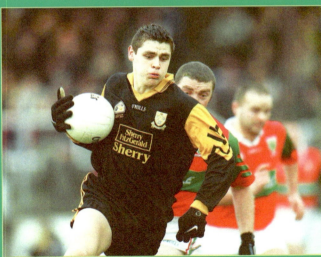

From top Left, clockwise:
Michael McHale prepares to distribute the ball to a team mate.
Graham Dowd considers his options.
David Tonge in control against Rathnew.
Ray Maloney accelerates away from the Rathnew's Eamonn White.

and 270 minutes of tough, uncompromising championship football in twenty-one days had taken its toll and Moorefield were deserving victors.

Episode 2

A year later, on Sunday, 4th November, Dunshaughlin retained their Meath title at the expense of Skryne. Meanwhile, the draw for the 2001 Leinster club championship had put Dunshaughlin straight through to the quarter-finals. Louth champions Newtown Blues were pitted against perennial Wicklow winners Rathnew in a preliminary round with the Garden County men emerging victorious. Fate ensured that the rivalry of 2000 would be re-visited and the Meath and Wicklow representatives prepared to renew hostilities. The game was scheduled for Aughrim just one week after the county triumph but Eamonn Barry was keen to downplay the role of the venue,

'Aughrim is no different than any other place and it's fifteen players against fifteen. If we are to make an impression on the Leinster Championship we cannot afford to get involved in a three-match battle like last year. We will have to win it the first day and go on from there.'

They didn't win it the first day.

Incredibly, it ended in another draw. Both sides displayed their ability to recover from deficits. Rathnew took a 0-5 to 0-1 first quarter lead but in a blistering eight-minute spell Dunshaughlin hit five excellent points and held a single point advantage at the break. With six minutes remaining the black and ambers had established a four-point lead and a string of Rathnew wides seemed to signal victory for the Royals. In a storming finale however, the green and reds took control of midfield and two points from play, book-ended by two Tommy Gill frees, left the sides all-square at the finish. Eamonn Barry acknowledged that Dunshaughlin could have lost, 'Rathnew played great football in the second half and really, if they hadn't shot so many wides, we were gone.'

Twice during the replay in Navan, a clear resolution to the tie was in prospect, only for last-gasp scores to leave the sides facing into a third meeting. The game was played at a frantic pace and with ten minutes of ordinary time remaining, Dunshaughlin, similar to the previous week, held a four-point advantage.

Inevitably, there was a comeback. Points from Barry Mernagh, Trevor Doyle, a Gill goal and another point by Leighton Glynn thrust the red and green side into a two-point lead. With the clock running down Niall Kelly lobbed a point. Two minutes into injury time and a free to Dunshaughlin. Regular free taker Martin Reilly had been substituted five minutes earlier. Up steps Trevor Dowd. His shot falls agonizingly short. Out of the crowd, Richie Kealy emerges to win

> 'Rathnew played great football in the second half and really, if they hadn't shot so many wides, we were gone.'

the ball and shoot. Over the bar. Equalizer. Joy unconfined among the black and amber supporters and referee Eamonn Whelan's long blast on the whistle brings temporary respite.

Rathnew started better in extra time and Dunshaughlin looked in real trouble when Shane Kelly got his marching orders just after scoring a stunning point. Once again the dismissal served to galvanize the disadvantaged side. Dunshaughlin edged two points to the fore at the next changeover. Wing back Fearghal Gogan weighed in with a point before David Tonge, put through brilliantly by Crimmins, opted for a point with a goal possible and the Meath representatives were four ahead again.

By then both sides were down to fourteen men with Leighton Glynn taking an early shower during the second half of extra time and Dunshaughlin looked home and hosed. Cue another comeback. With the game in injury time Mark Coffey latched on to a short, low Tommy Gill free and fisted to the net. Goal. Just a point between the sides. Rathnew win the kick out and Trevor Doyle races downfield. A shot. Up with the white flag. Another draw. Dunshaughlin 0-16 Rathnew 2-10. Now plans are put in place for another trip to Aughrim.

The Dunshaughlin management had a couple of issues to concern them. In both games the side had established good leads only to fritter away the advantage. Teams usually pay for an inability to seal the deal. More worryingly, goals, which were a feature of the 2000 run, were proving hard to come by. None in the two games to date, whereas Rathnew had filched two. On the positive side sixteen points was a huge return, especially so late in the year, and eight different players contributed to the total.

The third scene of the 2001 production, in Aughrim, provided another roller-coaster contest. It was a far cry from the memorable encounter a week earlier, however, as off-the-ball skirmishes and some rough challenges made for a stop-start contest. Longford referee John Bannon issued seven yellow cards, three to Dunshaughlin. Rathnew, despite playing against a stiff wind and a blinding sun went in at the break 1-3 to 0-4 in front. A further point early in the second half upped the ante.

Then for fifteen minutes Dunshaughlin took over. At midfield Dermot Kealy and Graham Dowd went through a purple patch and the black and amber forwards, aided and abetted by wing backs Ronnie Yore and Fearghal Gogan, swarmed the Wicklow goal. Martin Reilly set up Trevor Dowd who finished clinically to the net and David Crimmins forced a stunning save from the opposing keeper. Other opportunities went a-begging and entering the final ten minutes Dunshaughlin were in front by two-points. In Eamonn Barry's words,

'We had very little to show for five or six point chances and two goal chances that we had in the second half.'

By now spectators expected a twist in the tail and the Garden County men provided it. Tommy Gill leveled the scores, Robert Dignam grabbed the minimum lead and Anthony Mernagh squeezed the ball over the Dunshaughlin goal line at the end of a sweeping move. Rathnew were now rampant and went on to win by 2-9 to 1-6.

It was a bitter end to another glorious adventure for Dunshaughlin. There was little between the sides, with Dunshaughlin in pole position in each game but failing to stay in front to the chequered flag. When Rathnew went on to overcome Edenderry and Na Fianna to take the Leinster title they had the support of all Dunshaughlin players and supporters. Their success however, only served to underscore how close the black and ambers were to ultimate glory.

That would be the spur if another opportunity presented itself.

Episode 3

After a circuitous route to the Keegan Cup final in 2002, involving defeat to Blackhall Gaels before a refixture, Dunshaughlin narrowly defeated Trim in the decider in Navan on 10th November. The side seemed to have lost its impressive form of 2000 and press and neutrals had low expectations for the Leinster campaign.

However, players and management were quick to switch focus from their third county title to the provincial campaign. Selector and player Brendan Kealy told the press after the county final, 'We'll go out and enjoy ourselves tonight and then prepare for next Sunday. It's important that we do well in the Leinster club championship.' Midfielder Niall Kelly, who had just scored a wonder point from a line ball to snatch the title, was also focusing on Leinster.

'There's no point in winning in Meath if you're not going to apply yourself to another level. To win three Meath titles is great but we'd like to have another cup on the mantelpiece.'

The quarter-final represented a novel challenge, a meeting with Carlow kingpins, Rathvilly, in Dr. Cullen Park, Carlow. Dunshaughlin fielded without Martin Reilly and Aiden Kealy but still overpowered the Carlow side by 1-11 to 0-2.

Niall Kelly gave a man of the match performance. His surging runs through the Rathvilly defence resulted in two points for himself and his phenomenal work rate ensured a plentiful supply for his forwards. He initiated the move that ended with Ray Maloney palming the ball to the net for a substantial half-time lead of 1-6 to 0-2. Michael McHale at centre-back ran Kelly close for the top award

> "There's no point in winning in Meath if you're not going to apply yourself to another level. To win three Meath titles is great but we'd like to have another cup on the mantelpiece.'

CHAPTER 15: FRESH FIELDS: THE LEINSTER CAMPAIGNS

Ray Wrecks Rathnew!
Ray Maloney turns outfield after his goal assures Dunshaughlin of a place in the Leinster final.

Go Damian!
Damian Burke in action in the Leinster Championship.
Photo: Ray McManus, Sportsfile.

and his high fielding and effective clearances cut off any Rathvilly threats. Denis Kealy, Ciarán Byrne, Ronnie Yore and Kenny McTigue proved impenetrable in defence and Richie Kealy deployed at wing back and midfield had a superb outing. In addition to twelve scores the winners dominance was reflected in their total of twelve wides.

Thoughts immediately turned to the semi-final but there was a wait of a fortnight before the University College Dublin (UCD) v. Rathnew game was played. UCD featured a crop of inter-county stars but with Dunshaughlin waiting in the wings there could only be one outcome! Rathnew scraped home by a single point and set the scene for a renewal of old rivalries.

Prospects of another Dunshaughlin v Rathnew epic once again attracted national media attention. Six previous outings resulted in four draws and one victory each, so for such an evenly balanced saga it was fitting that the seventh showdown was fixed for the neutral surroundings of Newbridge. Rathnew held a slight advantage having defeated UCD at the same venue but there was plenty of talk of stalemate in the week before the game.

The game evolved as if following a preordained script. The contest see-sawed one way then the other, and, as in previous encounters one side seemed to have victory secured only for the other to summon up a late rally. On this occasion the black and ambers were slow to start while Rathnew roared out of the blocks. After fifteen minutes the red and greens held a five point lead, including four Trevor Doyle points, before Dunshaughlin reduced the margin to one during seven minutes of successful raids. Just before half-time Rathnew's Mark Doyle was put clean through and slipped the ball to the net and early in the second half Tommy Gill pointed a free to hand the initiative to Rathnew again.

Now it was time for Dunshaughlin to dictate terms. A David Crimmins point

> **The game evolved as if following a preordained script. The contest see-sawed one way then the other, and, as in previous encounters one side seemed to have victory secured only for the other to summon up a late rally.**

313

> 'Both team have guts, bags of guts. Both teams have what they call bottle in another code. And if they play hard, they also play fair. Every man afield last Sunday was a credit to his parish, to his club, to his county and to the GAA. It was heartwarming on a cold winter's day'.

was sandwiched by two from Martin Reilly and Niall Kelly then thumped a 50m sideline kick between the posts for the lead for the first time. Substitute Damian Burke added another, the ball bouncing off the bar on the way over. Two ahead. Mark Doyle reduced the lead to the minimum again. Sixty minutes up and a 65m free. Too far out surely? But not for Niall Kelly. The ball sails between the posts. Two ahead again. Another attack from the kick-out. Fearghal Gogan hits the post. The ball breaks and Trevor Dowd hits the crossbar.

That must be it. But it's not! Rathnew win a kick out. A free to Tommy Gill. Sixty-three minutes gone. A goal seems the only hope but he puts it over the bar. There is still time for the kick out. Rathnew come looking again. Ciarán Byrne drives the ball to the safety of the sideline. But no final whistle. There's still time! Trevor Doyle hits the ensuing kick towards the Dunshaughlin goal. Inevitably it drops over the bar. Another draw!

As the darkness descended after yet another thrilling encounter Dunshaughlin reflected on a game that could have gone either way. Eamonn Barry admitted that,

'After fifteen minutes, when we were five points down, if I was asked would I take a draw, I'd have grabbed it with two hands and ran out of Newbridge back home.'

Yet, as the end approached he acknowledged that,

'I would be telling a lie if I said I didn't think we had it in the bag. I was as sure as I could be that we had it won, but at the same time we were only two points in front and a goal could have cost us the game.'

In the dressing room Eamonn was livid. Once again the side had relinquished a winning lead. Once again they had failed to close the deal when the opportunity arose and a return trip to Newbridge was the only consolation.

Long before this latest replay the ongoing clashes had produced acres of newsprint and no scarcity of pathetic puns. Cormac MacConnell writing in *The Irish Examiner* was fulsome in his praise of both sides.

'This was a hard game but a clean one, very clean indeed on a treacherous sward. You can actually see the respect that the players of Dunshaughlin and Rathnew have, quite literally, shouldered and clattered into each other over the last three years. Both team have guts, bags of guts. Both teams have what they call bottle in another code. And if they play hard, they also play fair. Every man afield last Sunday was a credit to his parish, to his club, to his county and to the GAA. It was heartwarming on a cold winter's day.'

Odds of 13/2 were available on another draw the following Sunday but anyone taking the offer was to be disappointed. The two previous victories had been clear cut, Dunshaughlin by eight points in 2000 and Rathnew by six in 2001. That pattern was repeated with Dunshaughlin winning by six, 1-7 to 0-4, in a game

Leinster Final Action, Dunshaughlin v Mattock Rangers, 2002

Clockwise from top left:
David Crimmins goes for the ball as his opponent tackles the man.
Dermot Kealy emerges with the ball as Ronnie Yore provides support.
Martin Reilly embarks on a solo run into Mattock territory.
Niall Kelly and Ronan Gogan defend the goal line as Michael McHale maintains cover.

Cover of Leinster final programme, Dunshaughlin v. Mattock Rangers, in Páirc Tailteann on 22nd December 2002.

that contrasted sharply with the previous week's draw.

This time the Dunshaughlin defence shackled the Rathnew attack throughout. Michael McHale was outstanding at number six. He restricted Trevor Doyle to a single point, made numerous spectacular catches and launched attacks with his accurate distribution. Denis Kealy gave another superb performance, quelling the threat of Tommy Gill. Kenny McTigue and Ronnie Yore also excelled and severely limited Rathnew's chances. Dermot Kealy and Niall Kelly ruled the roost at midfield and when Rathnew lost midfielder Declan Byrne with a recurrence of a hamstring injury early in the game the Wicklow side could not cope round the centre.

Dunshaughlin were prodigal in attack, hitting twelve wides over the hour and as a result held a slender 0-2 to 0-1 half time lead. Rathnew did level early in the second half but failed to score again until injury time. By then Dunshaughlin had added 1-5. The goal was a wonderfully worked move involving David Tonge and David Crimmins before full-forward Ray Maloney made no mistake from close range. The only dangerous moment came when Ronan Gogan did well to reach a Trevor Doyle shot and divert it past the post. The football didn't match the high calibre on display the previous week and despite relatively good conditions referee Michael Monaghan issued eleven yellow cards to the sides, and one red, for Rathnew's Robert Dignam.

Thus after eight games, five draws, two victories and one defeat Dunshaughlin had the upper hand. It was the end of one of the most remarkable rivalries in the history of Gaelic football. The black and ambers had amassed 8-75 to Rathnew's 6-73 over the series of games and provided spectators with over 500 minutes of competitive, combative football.

Leinster Champions

The Leinster final took place in Páirc Tailteann on the last Sunday before Christmas with Louth's Mattock Rangers from Collon providing the opposition. Mattock were first time winners of the Louth senior title and fielded a young and upcoming team. They surprised many by reaching the provincial final. After needing a replay to oust Starlights of Wexford in the first round they had scored an impressive 2-11 and 3-13 in the quarter-final victory against Tullamore and semi-final wins against Moorefield.

Eamonn Barry had viewed Mattock's semi-final win and had no doubt Dunshaughlin had greater strength in depth and the ability to capture the title. Most observers agreed, yet the early signs weren't promising. Within three minutes of the throw-in Mattock's David Reid had two points on the scoreboard and their attacking brand of football looked like it could pay dividends. Dunshaughlin's first attack, a surging burst from defence by Richie Kealy, ended with Martin Reilly pointing from a free. Kealy himself with a free and David Crimmins from play then gave the black and ambers a narrow lead, an advantage they would not lose.

Throughout the game Richie Kealy continued to push forward, earning himself the Man of the Match award, while alongside him Ronnie Yore and Michael McHale had fine games. They formed the most solid line on the field and the rock on which Mattock foundered. The Louth men could only manage one more point before half time while Dunshaughlin tagged on a further five to go to the dressing room at the break with a 0-8 to 0-3 lead.

Mattock started the second half as they began the first, with an early point. However, Dunshaughlin soon resumed their relentless progress. Niall Kelly added a masterly point, Richie Kealy converted another free and David Tonge pushed the lead out to seven points at the three quarter stage. Mattock had to work hard for a single point after two goal openings were blocked. Their most productive period followed, and Christy Grimes had a brace of points to reduce the gap to a bridgeable four.

Dunshaughlin were not to be denied however, and Niall Kelly pointed brilliantly from close to the sideline while Martin Reilly added a late free to leave the black and ambers clear winners by 0-13 to 0-7.

It was a clear-cut win, but more comfortable than it should have been. Inexplicably, Mattock played into Dunshaughlin's hands by agreeing to play in Navan, effectively conceding home advantage to the black and ambers. Then, the Louth men squandered two golden goal opportunities when dominating possession in the second half that, if scored, would have made for a nail-biting finish.

Dunshaughlin had winners all over the field. After David Reid's early scores Kenny McTigue dealt comfortably and calmly with a succession of full forwards. As usual his ball-winning ability was complemented by excellent distribution. Ronan Gogan conceded just one goal during the campaign, denied Mattock in the second half with a timely block and was on the alert to tip a Robert Brennan effort over the bar in the first half. Brother Fearghal displayed his versatility by playing in both corner back positions and at wing back on the road to the final and was never in trouble. Denis Kealy, having earlier tamed Rathnew's Tommy Gill produced another top class display in the corner with a performance of disciplined aggression.

Michael McHale, as was the case all through the campaign, was an outstanding anchor in the centre and Yore's sterling defensive qualities complemented Kealy's attacking instincts.

Niall Kelly and Dermot Kealy bossed the midfield sector. Kealy, despite playing

Leinster Senior Club Medal, 2002.
The rear reads Club Peil Sinsir 2002 Dhomhnach Seachnaill.

through the campaign with a knee injury, won vital possession and his work rate was unparalleled while Kelly claimed three points in addition to bombarding opposing defences with quality ball. His displays earned him the Leinster Club Player of the Year Award to go alongside two Man of the Match awards, against Rathvilly and Rathnew. Wing forwards Martin Reilly and Brendan Kealy foraged ferociously out the field and Reilly was consistency personified from frees. Kealy had one of his best games. He defended from the front to snuff out Mattock attacks at source, and his menacing attacks forced the Wee County men to commit fouls resulting in two converted frees. David Tonge and David Crimmins both finished with two points while Trevor Dowd contributed a point before half time and earned a second half free, converted by Richie Kealy. In his debut year Ray Maloney was at the centre of the attack for all the Leinster games and proved to be an effective target man. His goal against Rathnew copper-fastened the semi-final victory.

The gap in scores reduced the tension of the closing stages but the final whistle nevertheless heralded an invasion of Páirc Tailteann. First the ecstatic mentors, club officials and subs, followed by a mass incursion of supporters. It seemed like the whole town of Dunshaughlin swarmed the pitch, hugging the players, congratulating the mentors and barely able to believe it was true. Not just Meath champions, but Leinster champions. Achieving what no Meath club had done for eighteen years. And while pandemonium reigned all round, Kenny McTigue, captaining the side in place of Aiden Kealy, accepted the Sean McCabe Cup from Leinster Council Chairman Nicky Brennan with the same calm, understated style that marked his performances on the field. Always in control, rarely wrong-footed and consistently doing the simple things well.

The historic Leinster winning team lined out as follows:

Ronan Gogan

Fearghal Gogan   Kenny McTigue, Capt.   Denis Kealy

Ronnie Yore   Michael McHale   Richie Kealy (0-2)

Niall Kelly (0-3)   Dermot Kealy

Martin Reilly (0-2)   David Crimmins (0-2)   David Tonge (0-2)

Brendan Kealy   Ray Maloney (0-1)   Trevor Dowd (0-1)

Subs: Damian Burke for Maloney, Ciarán Byrne for F Gogan, Christopher Carey, Kevin Moyles, Kevin Kealy, Shane Kelly, John Crimmins, Declan O Dwyer, Keith Mangan.

The first stop on the way home was the Clubhouse and then by lorry to the town centre. Veteran club President Patsy McLoughlin was attired in a Santa Claus suit

Leinster Champions: Bringing Home the Title

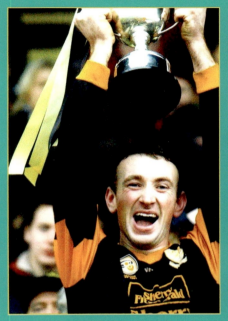

Pictured clockwise from left
Kenny McTigue announces, We're Leinster Champions.

Ho! Ho! Ho! Santa Claus, alias Patsy McLoughlin, addresses the crowd at the homecoming with club Chairman Paddy O Dwyer and Dinny McCarthy alongside.

Clamour in the Clubhouse as the Leinster champions celebrate. Front: Kevin Kealy, partly hidden, Richie Kealy, Keith Mangan, Ray Maloney, David Tonge, Ciarán Byrne, Fearghal Gogan, Martin Reilly, Michael McHale.
Back: Patsy Mcloughlin as Santa, Gerry Keenan, physio, Damian Burke, Declan O Dwyer, David Crimmins, John Crimmins, TP Toolan, Caoimhín King, Graham Dowd, Dermot Kealy at rear, Niall Kelly, Shane Kelly and Christopher Carey.

Dunshaughlin, Leinster Senior Champions, 2002

Front: Brendan Kealy, Trevor Dowd, David Tonge, Denis Kealy, Martin Reilly, Kenny McTigue, Capt., Ronnie Yore, Fearghal Gogan.
Back: Niall Kelly, Richie Kealy, Michael McHale, Ray Maloney, Ronan Gogan, David Crimmins, Dermot Kealy.

as a Garda escort with black and amber colours attached led the triumphant team. Past the crowded *Arch Bar*, owned by the O Brien family, whose ancestor Patrick was the club's first president in 1886. Past *Catty Ned's*, previously PJ Murray's, instrumental in setting up a hurling club in Dunshaughlin in 1902 and who had captured the first picture of a Dunshaughlin team on camera in the 1900s. Past *Sherry Auctioneers*, the sponsor of the team and based in what was the *Fingall Arms* where the club was founded in 1886 using the then owner, Stephen Kelly's black and amber racing colours. Now the street and Mac's Corner were a sea of black and amber flags and jerseys as Eamonn Toal, Ireland's representative in Eurovision 2000, led the crowd in '*Simply the Best*.'

Club Chairman, Paddy O Dwyer, introduced the team, 'three in a row Meath senior champions, and now, Leinster club champions.' He recalled the long year of training and preparation starting in January, commiserated with Graham Dowd and Aiden Kealy who had missed the final and thanked the crowd for their support in distant Carlow, Aughrim and Newbridge. Coach Eamonn Barry, selector TP Toolan, team captain Kenny McTigue, Niall Kelly and Richie Kealy all addressed the crowd before Santa Claus was invited to speak. 'Ho, ho, ho' declared the club president and with that the Christmas and Leinster celebrations kicked off.

> the street and Mac's Corner were a sea of black and amber flags and jerseys as Eamonn Toal, Ireland's representative in Eurovision 2000, led the crowd in 'Simply the Best.'

Surfin' USA

Prior to contesting the All-Ireland club championship as Leinster representatives, Dunshaughlin combined business with pleasure. The business was the All County Football League final in which they disposed of Dunboyne 4-12 to 2-6 and the Feis Cup final where they overcame Castletown 1-18 to 1-3. The former was played in January and the latter in February 2003 and are covered in the previous chapter. The pleasure was a team trip to California between the two games.

Travel to the United States presented a much bigger obstacle and costs amounted to over €40,000. Within a month a small committee chaired by Eamonn Dunne netted €47,000. This was achieved with the backing of local businesses and supporters who sponsored advertisements in a *Meath Chronicle* Special Supplement. Former club player Pat Kealy organized the American end of the venture and between January 17th and 19th on two separate flights twenty-two players departed Dublin Airport, visiting Los Angeles, San Diego, the Grand Canyon and Las Vegas on the trip of a lifetime in a whirlwind ten days.

The All Star football teams of 2001 and 2002 were in San Diego at the same time and they were stunned to learn that while their trip consisted of a visit to San Diego, a mere club team was travelling throughout the south west of the USA, all thanks to the phenomenal support of the community back home.

Eamonn Dunne
Eamonn spearheaded the fundraising drive that financed the three in a row team's holiday in the USA in 2003. He was a senior selector in 2005 and first Chairperson of the Under Age section in Drumree when it was decided in 2009 that Dunshaughlin would look after juvenile football and Drumree would cater for under age hurling.

Enjoying a boat trip on San Diego Bay during the club's holiday in the USA in 2003.
Front: Ronan Gogan and David Tonge.
Middle: Fearghal Gogan, Brendan Kealy, Keith Mangan, John Crimmins, Kevin Moyles, Trevor Dowd, Declan O Dwyer.
Back: Ray Maloney and Michael McHale.

Pictured in San Diego are Eamonn Barry, Armagh's Kieran McGeeney captain of the 2002 GAA All Stars, Shaun McTigue and TP Toolan.

Jim Cable, an award winning journalist with cable TV channel ESPN, was also in San Diego that week for the Super Bowl final between the Tampa Bay Buccaneers and the Oakland Raiders. Used to covering the professional game he was amazed to discover a bunch of amateurs who played only for their local parish team and who continued to play long after they left high school, a total contrast to the scene in America. He mused,

'Wouldn't it be better if we focused more of our attention on playing our own games than devoting it to an overhyped game on TV the final Sunday of each January? Wouldn't it be better if we rooted for teams whose players truly represented their local community?'

Sometimes it takes an outsider to see the wood from the trees.

The All-Ireland Series

Once back in Ireland training commenced for the semi-final with Mayo's Crossmolina. The western representatives had an impressive blend of experience and talent. Three Connaught titles in four years and an All-Ireland in 2001 provided the former, while talent oozed from Kieran McDonald and James Nallen, both All-Stars. John Maughan, Mayo's former manager, was Eamonn Barry's counterpart for the westerners. Eamonn Barry was well aware of the challenge,

'I am quite hopeful that we can get over this hurdle. But the team will need to play to something close to their best if that is to happen.'

He wasn't blind to his side's failings,

'The passing could be improved, fifty per cent of possession is being wasted. The forwards need to get more scores, some might say the backs have been doing well but they could have conceded a couple of goals in the Leinster final.'

The semi-final began brilliantly for Dunshaughlin. Twenty minutes in and the black and ambers had a stunning 1-6 to 0-1 lead. All over the field Crossmolina were in trouble and Croke Park on St. Patrick's Day was a real prospect. David Crimmins put on his own exhibition, kicking two early points, while alongside him Ray Maloney, Richie Kealy and Martin Reilly were also plundering points. When Brendan Kealy, suspiciously close to the square, got a hand to a Trevor

CHAPTER 15: FRESH FIELDS: THE LEINSTER CAMPAIGNS

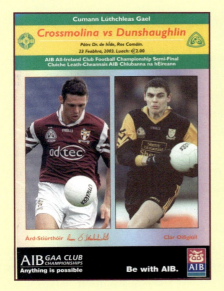

Dowd delivery, to score the first goal of the game Dunshaughlin appeared to be in the driving seat.

However, one minute before Martin Reilly slotted Dunshaughlin's sixth point from a free, came the turning point of the game. Niall Kelly, yellow-carded earlier for an innocuous foul, incurred a second yellow and automatic dismissal. It was a massive blow. As a result Crossmolina clawed their way back into contention. A crucial goal before half-time reduced the lead to 1-8 to 1-5. The changes necessary after Kelly's departure disrupted Dunshaughlin. David Crimmins switched out the field and his predatory instinct close to goal was missed. John Maughan admitted that his side was outclassed in the first twenty minutes, 'Nothing to do with complacency at all, they just covered us all over and gobbled us up.'

Any hopes of holding onto the slimmed down lead as long as possible and then hitting Cross on the counter attack evaporated within four minutes of

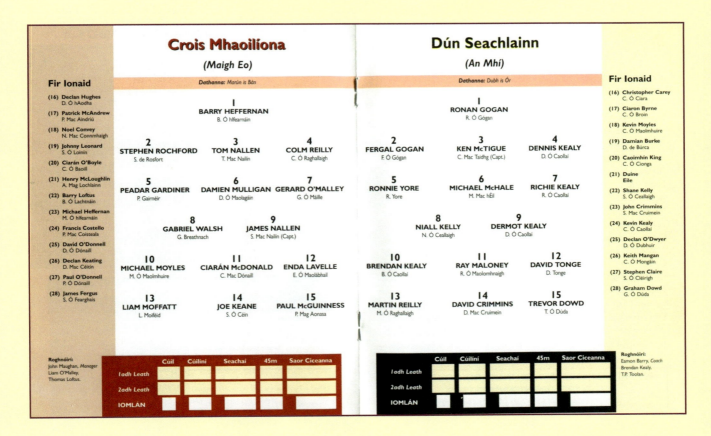

the restart. First Michael Moyles hit a second Cross goal to draw the sides level. There was no hope of holding the maroon-clad men now. With fifteen players it was difficult to counteract their fast running game, with fourteen it was well nigh impossible. A McDonald '45' and a Leo Moffatt point from play put them two points ahead. Though Martin Reilly halved the lead with a pointed free Cross responded with three of their own and when Moffatt shot a third goal the outcome was inevitable.

Dunshaughlin, true to their hallmark, continued to battle. Four frees that would normally be converted were missed but the black and ambers accounted for the final three points from frees, two from Reilly and one from Richie Kealy. By then the outcome had been decided and Crossmolina cruised into the winner's enclosure by 3-10 to 1-12. They eventually fell to Cork's Nemo Rangers in the final. Representing Dunshaughlin in the All-Ireland semi-final were:

Ronan Gogan; Fearghal Gogan, Kenny McTigue, Denis Kealy; Ronnie Yore, Michael McHale, Richie Kealy (0-2); Niall Kelly, Dermot Kealy; Brendan Kealy (1-0), Ray Maloney (0-1), David Tonge; Martin Reilly (0-6), David Crimmins (0-3), Trevor Dowd. Subs: Aiden Kealy for Yore, Ciarán Byrne for Dowd, John Crimmins for Brendan Kealy, Christopher Carey, Kevin Moyles, Damian Burke, Caoimhín King, Shane Kelly, Kevin Kealy, Declan O Dwyer, Keith Mangan, Stephen Claire, Graham Dowd.

Kelly's dismissal was crucial to the outcome. Eamonn Barry felt that with a full complement Dunshaughlin had every chance of reaching the All-Ireland final. The sending off was inexplicable, the second yellow would not normally merit even a free. The selectors had to unexpectedly reconfigure the formation and Barry deemed the decision to relocate David Crimmins to defence as one of the biggest mistakes in his Dunshaughlin career. Crimmins had run the Cross defence ragged in the early stages but was less of a threat after his switch.

Despite the understandable disappointments, the 'might have beens' and the 'what ifs'

Niall Kelly, Leinster Club Footballer of the Year 2002, receives his award from Seán McCague, GAA President, and Billy Finn, Managing Director, Ark Life, the award sponsor.
Photo: Ray McManus, Sportsfile.

Dunshaughlin could look back on 2002 as a season of phenomenal achievement, the high-water mark of the club's existence. Leinster champions, county champions, All County league champions and Feis Cup winners represented a roll of honour never previously matched. Eventual victory over Rathnew gave all involved quiet satisfaction. It was the perfect culmination of three years' work. Winning the Leinster title is rarely a one-year project and Dunshaughlin gradually built up the expertise and self-belief needed to come out on top.

The campaigns brought out the best in players and supporters. The success of the team was a source of immense pride in the community whose support for the team was phenomenal. That support ranged from funds for the holiday in the US to vocal encouragement in Aughrim, Carlow, Navan, Newbridge and Roscommon. Whole families devoted their autumn Sundays to adventurous forays outside the county, to Sunday dinners in Lawless's of Aughrim or the County Club on the return journey. Generously supporting the team throughout was local sponsor Pádraig Sherry who ensured that the team was as well looked after as many county outfits.

At the time the mere mention of Dunshaughlin led to a discussion on football. Locals who were previously indifferent to the club's existence became avid supporters while there was widespread support and admiration for the team throughout Meath. The manner in which the club agreed to a refixture with Blackhall added to the respect accorded the team.

In addition to the astute management of the team on the field of play the club had an impressive background team. Club Chairman and Secretary Paddy O Dwyer and Cyril Creavin had sought out and appointed Eamonn Barry as coach and they steered the club expertly during the glory years. Behind the scenes work by Shane Kelly and Fearghal Gogan resulted in full colour newsletters and a club website that placed the club amongst the most progressive in the country, impressing national GAA reporters such as Seán Moran of *The Irish Times* and Mark Gallagher of *The Examiner*.

For the players the longest lasting impact was the friendships that were created and the respect for each other that will endure. Players recall the camaraderie and the honesty between the players. Many had gone to school together and had grown up together and this created a team spirit more characteristic of a small rural club.

Could the team sustain the performance and remain at the peak? Time would answer that quandary.

> **Dunshaughlin could look back on 2002 as a season of phenomenal achievement, the high-water mark of the club's existence.**

BLACK & AMBER

Going Out in a Blaze of Glory, St. Martins 1999-2008

The decade ahead was to be one of unparalleled success as title followed title but it would all end abruptly, unexpectedly, and, for many, bitterly.

After a decade and a half in existence St. Martins headed into the new century with a solid background of achievement. The decade ahead was to be one of unparalleled success as title followed title but it would all end abruptly, unexpectedly, and, for many, bitterly.

Minors 2002

In 2002, St. Martins captured the Minor Division 2 title with a team that, unlike many of the club's winning sides, had no notable success in the lower age groups. The closest the team had gone to outright victory was in the Under 13 Division 2 league in 1998 when it was at the wrong end of a sixteen point hammering, 3-12 to 1-2, against Summerhill. Many of the same players manned the Under 14 side that Dunsany eliminated in both league and championship and the team that exited the Under 16 campaign at quarter-final stage in 2000.

Consequently, there was no great expectation of making an impact in the minor grade in 2002. A placement in Division 2 gave the side a sporting chance, as the top

St. Martins, Under 13 Division 2 Runners-Up, 1998

Front: Rory Bowe, Cathal O Dwyer, Cormac Delaney, Ciarán Hoary, Shane Kelly, David Murphy, Liam Barber, David Devereux.
Back: Robert Lyons, Jamie Minnock, Colin Murphy, Paul Cosgrove, Caoimhín King, Owen Herlihy, Ciarán Kenny, David McMahon, John Kieran, Ronan Gilsenan, Kevin Ward.

teams in the county were in the higher division. The players who were on the Under 13 side four years previously had continued to play and develop despite the lack of silverware. More importantly, a cohort of younger players like Michael Ahern and David Devereux were talented enough to earn central starting places.

The competition dragged on into the closing months of the year and wouldn't finish until January 2003 as the Meath minors, with Caoimhín King holding down a regular place, reached the All-Ireland final. Dee Rangers, a Syddan and Nobber combination, provided the semi-final opposition. St. Martins trailed at half time and snatched a draw with a point from the last kick of the game. The replay was equally tight. The sides were level at the interval but an outstanding display from Rory Bowe, who scored 1-3, gave the Saints a two-point victory, 2-11 to 2-9.

Ratoath provided the final opposition and the initial meeting failed to separate the sides. Conditions for the replay didn't augur well as heavy overnight frost left the Donaghmore ground rock hard in places and potentially dangerous. Yet the sides served up a performance that ensured the spectators forgot the bitter cold and enjoyed a display of skill and style.

Ratoath drew first blood with a Dónal Kirwan point but St. Martins' response was incisive and instant. First Rory Bowe, Jamie Minnock and Diarmuid Delaney combined before Cathal O Dwyer fisted to the net. A minute later a ground pass from Delaney released Minnock who, in soccer style dispatched a rocket-like shot to the top corner and Ronan Gilsenan further punished an already shell-shocked Ratoath with a point immediately afterwards. Ratoath recovered their composure to forage 1-2 before half time, but just before the break Stephen Caffrey poached time and space to shoot to the net, giving the Saints a substantial lead of 3-2 to 1-3.

Ratoath won the battle for possession during the second period and though they outscored their opponents they had difficulty converting the possession into

CHAPTER 16: GOING OUT IN A BLAZE OF GLORY, ST. MARTINS 1999-2008

St. Martins, Minor Football, Division 2 Champions, 2002

Front: Rory Bowe, Jamie Minnock, Diarmuid Delaney, Cathal O Dwyer, Ciarán Hoary, Owen Herlihy, Kevin Ward, Paul Cosgrove, Mark West, Stephen Caffrey. Back: David Devereux, Conor Gallagher, Gavin O Regan, John Crimmins, Capt., David McMahon, James White, Michael Ahern, Pádraig Smith, Ronan Gilsenan, David Donoghue, Caoimhín King. Missing from photo: Paul Sheehy.

> Up front Cathal O Dwyer with a total of 1-2 used his pace and skill on the thawing ground to leave defenders trailing in his slipstream

enough scores to overhaul the deficit, and at the death couldn't conjure up the vital point to force extra time as the St. Martins' defence refused to yield.

Caoimhín King in the number three jersey, but playing at centre-back, repeatedly cut out moves and invariably got lengthy clearances away that relieved pressure. Michael Ahern at full back, -still eligible for Under 16 the following year- gave a storming display, fielding high balls and making frequent vital interceptions. He had stepped in to replace regular midfielder Paul Sheehy who incurred a serious knee injury in the semi-final. The tenacious tackling of Ciarán Hoary, Kevin Ward and Owen Herlihy kept Ratoath out in the closing stages. Up front Cathal O Dwyer with a total of 1-2 used his pace and skill on the thawing ground to leave defenders trailing in his slipstream while David Devereux contributed two points and created others with his incisive passing.

This was the first minor title the club had won on its own. The only previous title, in 1987, had, ironically, combined St. Martins and Ratoath. The winning team, with Gabriel King, Pat Herlihy and David Crimmins selecting, lined out per jersey numbers as follows:

James White
Ciarán Hoary   Caoimhín King   David Donoghue
David McMahon   Kevin Ward   Owen Herlihy
John Crimmins, Capt.   Michael Ahern
Ronan Gilsenan (0-1)   Rory Bowe   Jamie Minnock (1-0)
Diarmuid Delaney   David Devereux (0-2)   Cathal O Dwyer (1-2)

Subs: Gavin O Regan for Delaney, Stephen Caffrey (1-0) for Minnock, Mark West for Donoghue, Conor Gallagher, Pádraig Smith, Paul Cosgrove.

John Crimmins, 2002 minor captain, lifts the trophy after St Martins' final victory over Ratoath.

St. Martins, Under 13 Féile Champions, 2001

Front: Fionán O Kane, Shane Toher, Mark Caldwell, Martin Cosgrove, John Coleman.
Middle: Macartan McGroder, Conor Staunton, Paul Kiernan, John Coffey, Shane Kelly, Stephen McGroder, Ian Hand, Cathal O Reilly, Keith Byrne, Tom Finn.

Back: Tim O Kane, James Gaughan, Patrick Doohan, David Wallace, Christopher Dixon, Adrian Toolan, Michael Ahern, Brian Coughlan, Alan McLoughlin, David Devereux, Ciarán Farrelly, Cillian Finn, Don McLoughlin.

Féile Fortunes by Four

The years 2001 to 2006 were to be the most successful in the history of the club, with the achievements in Féile taking centre stage. Every year the best Under 14 team in each county took part in the annual Féile Peile na n-Óg (Youth Festival of Football). Qualification in Meath, via the previous year's Under 13 competition, was highly competitive with traditional strongholds such as Simonstown Gaels, Navan O Mahonys, Dunboyne and Kells dominating. St. Martins had made the final only once, when St. Cuthberts outscored a strong side in the 1993 final. Yet, between 2001 and 2006, St. Martins qualified to represent Meath on four occasions, initially in 2001 and then for the glorious three-in-a-row of 2004-06.

Féile 2001 Team

Around 1987 something was obviously temporarily added to the water in Dunshaughlin and Drumree and a uniquely talented bunch of Gaelic footballers was produced. Certainly, in previous years there had been sporadic appearances of very skilful players but rarely in sufficient quantity.

The 2001 Féile team had lost heavily to Round Towers in the 1999 Under-12 final, their solitary defeat during the year, but in the first round at Under 13 level against the same opposition they displayed a steely resolve to reverse that result.

CHAPTER 16: GOING OUT IN A BLAZE OF GLORY, ST. MARTINS 1999-2008

This was a trait of the team all the way to minor level.

The Féile final again pitted them against Round Towers. St. Martins' team management instructed David Devereux, by now a marked man due to his scoring feats, to lay off any ball he got to his support forwards. Not having lost a game all year the Saints were in no mood for an upset and the plans worked to perfection. Devereux gave a 'man of the match' performance but only scored two points, while the other forwards reaped the harvest. Shane Kelly and Conor Staunton both recorded two goals and a point while Mark Caldwell had three points. The outcome, a 4-9 to 1-5 victory, brooked no argument.

Tipperary hosted Féile 2001 and St. Martins, in Division 2, were based in Holycross-Ballycahill. The team won all the divisional games, holding their hosts scoreless. They easily defeated Loughmore, despite fielding a weakened team to mislead the watching Bundoran mentors. The Donegal side thought the Meath representatives were only mediocre and were stunned when a full strength St. Martins raced into an early lead against them and finished up 5-9 to a single point in front. The massive total was compiled in thirty minutes, as all games were half an hour long.

Victory brought a semi-final place against Down representatives An Ríocht whose star player was Martin Clarke, a future All-Star and Australian Rules player with Collingwood. Preparation for the semi-final was hindered by a delay in getting to the venue and the absence of ace forward Conor Staunton on soccer duty in Northern Ireland. St. Martins started slowly, then recovered well and a late goal effort from Christopher Dixon rebounded off the butt of the upright. An Ríocht held on to emerge victorious by 1-6 to 1-2, and went on to a convincing final win against Tullamore. David Devereux was the top scorer overall with 5-6, while Adrian Toolan narrowly missed out on a place in the skills' final. Team manager Macartan McGroder remains convinced that if St. Martins ousted An Ríocht they would have won the final and been crowned All-Ireland champions.

On their return to Meath the team reignited its drive for Under 14 honours. David Devereux had been the regular midfielder at Under 12 level but a year later the selectors had made a significant switch. They moved him to the edge of the square with Christopher Dixon moving to the centre of the park in a challenge with Baconstown and this configuration was to wreak havoc on many defences in subsequent years.

In the Under 14 championship the side powered through the quarter and semi-finals with stunning performances and clinical accuracy, running up scores of 2-17 and 4-14 against Blackhall Gaels and Summerhill respectively. In the final the Round Towers defence escaped a repeat of those bombardments but they were still vanquished by 1-8 to 0-3. A mediocre first half with wind advantage segued

St. Martins, Under 13 Division 2 Champions, 2002

Front: Tadhg Ó Dúshláine, Keith Commons, Cillian Dennehy, Conor Ennis, Dermot McGreal.
Middle: Don McLoughlin, Thomas Evans, James Kelliher, James Horgan, Ciarán Clusker, Danny Logan, Robert Kane, Fearghal Delaney, Duncan Geraghty, Keith Caffrey, Paul Logan.
Back: Des Boyhan, Paul Caffrey, Joe Boyhan, Dara Devereux, Paul Barry, Seamus White, Colm McLoughlin, Des Dolan, Mark Coffey, Kieran Murphy, Conor Hegarty, Seán Doyle, Donnchadh Geraghty, Tommy Clusker.

> **Ciarán Farrelly** *'took a pass from David Devereux before embarking on a mazy 30 metre run, evading several challenges and cutting in from the left wing before side-footing the ball with his right boot into the opposite corner of the net.'*

into a superb second half display based on the midfield dominance of Michael Ahern and Christopher Dixon.

With the inspirational David Wallace at its hub the parsimonious defence conceded only one point from play. David Devereux and Conor Staunton were outstanding in attack while Ciarán Farrelly displayed a great array of skills and capped a memorable performance with a stunning late goal. To quote the *Chronicle*, he *'took a pass from David Devereux before embarking on a mazy 30 metre run, evading several challenges and cutting in from the left wing before side-footing the ball with his right boot into the opposite corner of the net.'* Former St. Martins' Secretary, Mairéad Delaney, who was then Meath Juvenile Secretary, had the honour of presenting the trophy to Alan McLoughlin, the winning captain. The championship winning team was:

Brian Coughlan
Stephen McGroder   James Gaughan   John Coffey
Alan McLoughlin, Capt.   David Wallace   Adrian Toolan
Christopher Dixon   Michael Ahern (0-1)
Shane Kelly   Ciarán Farrelly (1-1)   Conor Staunton (0-2)
Cillian Finn   David Devereux (0-4)   Patrick Doohan

Subs: Ian Hand for McGroder, Mark Caldwell for Finn, Fionán O Kane for Staunton, Martin Cosgrove for Coffey, John Coleman for Doohan, Shane Toher, Paul Kiernan, Cathal O Reilly, Keith Byrne.

CHAPTER 16: GOING OUT IN A BLAZE OF GLORY, ST. MARTINS 1999-2008

St. Martins completed the double by taking the league title in equally stunning style. In the semi-final Conor Staunton's tally of 3-3 was sufficient on its own to overwhelm Summerhill's 1-7 but the other forwards were in similar lethal form, running up 6-9 before the final whistle. Simonstown Gaels provided the final opposition but they too drowned in a tsunami of scores. Ten St. Martins' players contributed to the 3-18 total, with David Devereux topping the individual charts on eight points.

This was the first Under 14 Division 1 Championship for the parish since the three in a row of 1957-59. It can be argued that the 2001 team surpassed the achievement of their illustrious predecessors who did not have to overcome teams from the large towns as they competed in the rural championship at the time. The 2001 side also took the league title, as well as winning the Under 13 league with the consequent right to represent Meath at Féile. They stood supreme within the county as juvenile champions, no side could cope with their lethal forward formation or score with ease against a tight marking, niggardly defence.

The successful mentors were Macartan 'The Maestro' McGroder, Tim O Kane, Don McLoughlin, and Tom Finn. The management was always a team effort. Sometimes hard decisions were required. Sons were dropped or taken off in vital matches and the collective good was always elevated above individual needs. Tim O Kane coached the players from the time they were eight, and with Tom Finn assisting, the group won the Kilcloon Under-11 tournament in 1998. Don McLoughlin joined the team at Under 12 level while Mac had been involved with legions of St. Martins' Under 12 teams prior to joining the group as coach, selector and sage.

The club under the chairmanship of David Crimmins, Secretary Mairéad Delaney and Treasurer Angela Reilly raised over £8,000 to cover the costs of the Football and Hurling Féiles, with the players on both panels collecting over £2,500 of this. There were two main sources of funding; the players sourced contributions with sponsorship cards and over seventy local benefactors, both business and private, contributed donations.

Two years later, in 2003, the same group again faced Summerhill, this time in the Under 16 Division 1 final. The previous year a number of the players featured on the Under 16 team, which

> **The management was always a team effort. Sometimes hard decisions were required. Sons were dropped or taken off in vital matches and the collective good was always elevated above individual needs.**

Under 14 Captains 1957 and 2001
Jimmy Walsh, captain of the first St. Martins' team to win the Under 14 championship in 1957 with the club's 2001 captain Alan McLoughlin, following St. Martins' Under 14 championship success in 2001.

St. Martins, Under 16 Football Champions, 2003

Front: Stephen Fox, John Coffey, Mark Caldwell, Conor Staunton, Fionán O Kane, Bryan McKeown, Adrian Toolan, John Coleman, Stephen McGroder, Emmet O Callaghan.
Back: Shane Kelly, James Gaughan, Michael Ahern, Alan McLoughlin, David Devereux, Christopher Dixon, David Wallace, Cillian Finn, Brian Coughlan, Ciarán Farrelly, Shane Toher.

First Ever Under 16 Championship Title
Michael Ahern, St. Martins' Under 16 captain, accepts the cup from Eugene Comaskey, Meath Minor Board.

won the Division 2 final. A narrow two points semi-final victory over Skryne booked a place in the Division 2 decider against St. Colmcilles and two first half goals from Conor Staunton and Cathal O Dwyer created the foundation for victory. Between them they accounted for all of St. Martins' tally of 2-6, apart from a single point scored by centre back David Wallace. Players like Wallace, Staunton, James Gaughan, Alan McLoughlin, Christopher Dixon, Michael Ahern, Ciarán Farrelly and Adrian Toolan would go on to backbone the championship side of 2003.

While the Division 2 title was welcome the club had one glaring absentee in its list of honours. No side had ever won an Under 16 Championship proper. Only once before had the club contested the Under 16 final, in 1985, when Slane were the victors. Now, just as they made club history when winning the first Féile in 2001, the same group of players was on the trail of another club first.

CHAPTER 16: GOING OUT IN A BLAZE OF GLORY, ST. MARTINS 1999-2008

They got their campaign off to a poor start when old rivals Round Towers were too good for a weakened side. Subsequent victories over Summerhill, Dunboyne, Skryne and Simonstown and a loss to Duleek were sufficient to set up a rematch with the Towers in the semi-final. The Kells side was never in with a chance of replicating the earlier victory as St. Martins cruised to a 1-14 to 0-4 win. The winners ran riot after the interval chalking up 1-10 in thirty minutes.

The final was a close affair and, unusually, most of the plaudits went to the defence. Countless vital blocks and several crucial interceptions frustrated Summerhill who could only manage three points in the first period, a figure St. Martins doubled. Summerhill made a spirited second half rally but the crucial score came early in the half when Brian Coughlan netted after Cillian Finn's pass found him in space.

St. Martins managed to retain the advantage despite persistent pressure, the highlight being a brilliant save by Christopher Dixon from Michael Gorman. When the final whistle blew St. Martins had its first Under 16 title, Coughlan's goal being the difference, on a 1-9 to 0-9 scoreline. David Devereux was outstanding, playing in practically every position on the pitch and covering acres of ground while Coughlan was a serious threat in possession. The defence excelled where James Gaughan, John Coffey and Bryan McKeown were always in front of their opponents and the half back trio of Alan McLoughlin, David Wallace and Adrian Toolan were relentless in crowding out anyone in blue and gold and depriving them of the space and time to launch attacks.

Michael Ahern captained the victorious side. He, and Alan McLoughlin, Ciarán Farrelly, Adrian Toolan and Conor Staunton, were members of the Meath Under 16 panel that won the annual Gerry Reilly inter-county tournament. David Devereux captained the Meath side and was named Man of the Match after the final against Cavan which copper fastened his reputation as the finest Under 16 player in the Royal County. Team mate David Wallace was county captain for the Under 16 hurlers.

The championship winning team was

Man of the Match.
Meath captain David Devereux receives the Man of the Match award following Meath's victory in the 2003 Under 16 Gerry Reilly Tournament final against Cavan.

                     Christopher Dixon
      John Coffey   James Gaughan   Bryan McKeown
      Alan McLoughlin   David Wallace   Adrian Toolan
           Conor Staunton (0-1)   Michael Ahern, Capt. (0-2)
      Shane Kelly (0-1)   David Devereux (0-2) Ciarán Farrelly (0-1)
      Cillian Finn (0-2) Brian Coughlan (1-0) John Coleman

Subs: Emmet O Callaghan for Kelly, Mark Caldwell for Coughlan, Kelly for Coleman, Stephen Fox, Fionán O Kane, Stephen McGroder, Shane Toher. Patrick Doohan was unavailable as he was in St. Finian's College Mullingar.

This cohort of players hoped to conclude their under age careers and further burnish their reputation with a Minor title in 2005. The team reached the 2004 Under 17 League final where Round Towers got the better of the Saints but the team easily topped its group once the minor campaign commenced and then disposed of Na Fianna in the quarter-final. The semi gave an opportunity for rapid revenge on the Towers, and, in a game that Mac McGroder calls 'one of the best he remembers', the team obliged with a 3-11 to 1-14 victory. It was a costly one though, as keeper Christopher Dixon was sent off.

This set up a repeat of the 2003 Under 16 final but St. Martins were at a huge disadvantage before a ball was kicked. Having to field without captain Adrian Toolan, keeper Christopher Dixon, full back Brian Coughlan and forward Paddy Doohan due to a combination of suspension, injury and illness left the panel with a mountain to climb. It proved to be too much against the defending champions, fielding ten of their successful side from 2004. St Martins struggled to keep in touch with a fast, confident and disciplined opposition that led by 1-10 to 1-3 at half time. Conor Staunton unlocked the Summerhill defence to score the goal, a brilliant effort, after David Devereux set him up.

For a period during the second half it seemed that St. Martins might emerge triumphant as a lively attack reduced the lead to four points. However, Summerhill soaked up much of the pressure before Caolan Young struck a second goal to put the game beyond St. Martins' reach. Late on Conor Staunton cannoned a penalty

St. Martins, Under 12 Division 1 Champions, 2002

Front: Paul Walsh, David Fitzmaurice, Eamon Bowe, Conor Ennis, Eoin Hagarty, Niall Murphy, Barry Jordan, Tadhg Ó Dúshláine, Robert Crosbie, Danny Logan.
Middle: Bill Reilly, Dara Devereux, Shane Troy, Ciarán Clusker, Mark Coffey, Stephen Clusker, James Horgan, James Kelliher, Joe Boyhan, Colm McLoughlin.
Back: Brendan Murphy, Paul Logan, Tommy Clusker, Des Boyhan.

CHAPTER 16: GOING OUT IN A BLAZE OF GLORY, ST. MARTINS 1999-2008

off the post and Mark Caldwell netted, before being red carded, but it only added respectability to a final scoreline of 2-16 to 2-9. In its final outing together the team comprised of: Seán Doyle; Bryan McKeown, James Gaughan, Cathal Moore; Alan McLoughlin, David Wallace, Emmet O Callaghan; Cillian Finn, Michael Ahern; Ciarán Farrelly, Shane Kelly (0-1), Conor Staunton (1-2); John Coleman, David Devereux (0-6), Mark Caldwell (1-0). Subs: Dara Devereux for Moore, Stephen McGroder for McKeown, Shane Toher for Farrelly, Christopher Dixon, Duncan Geraghty, Fearghal Delaney, John Coffey, Brian Coughlan, Paddy Doohan.

This group of players was the most successful ever produced by the club. An Under 13 title, Under 14 championship and league titles, an Under 16 championship and defeats in the Under 12, Under 17 and minor finals betokens an extraordinary level of consistency. Over six years St. Martins, Round Towers and Summerhill vied for supremacy, as the sides met regularly in finals. The desire for victory never strayed into foul play nor the wish for revenge into retribution and the teams gave their supporters and mentors half a dozen glorious years of spills and thrills and unprecedented honours.

One of the vital members of that team was Paddy Doohan, his presence in the dressing room a great source of inspiration and fountain of fun to all the players. His death in January 2006 was a huge loss to all his teammates, family and friends. He played in the first round of the minor championship against Summerhill and left hospital to attend the minor semi-final and subsequent final.

> This group of players was the most successful ever produced by the club. An Under 13 title, Under 14 championship and league titles, an Under 16 championship and defeats in the Under 12, Under 17 and minor finals betokens an extraordinary level of consistency.

Féile 2004 Team

The Féile team of 2004 gave early notice of its intentions when powering to the Under 12 Division 1 league title in 2002. Martins annihilated Simonstown in the decider with an avalanche of goals. The lethal attack struck seven times with Shane Troy claiming the lion's share, four, leaving Eamon Bowe, Danny Logan and Stephen Clusker to feast on the remaining three. Colm McLoughlin and Ciarán Clusker co-captained the side as Ciarán missed the final due to injury. Five points in addition to the goals tally was more than sufficient to overcome Simonstown's 2-11, a tally that would win most finals.

The 2002 reserves almost made it a unique double but this time another Navan town side, O Mahonys, registered the goals to win by 4-6 to 0-5.

Féile 2004 would take the team to Tyrone. The mentors made qualification for Féile their number one priority. To earn the right to represent the Royal County, St. Martins gained a narrow 1-4 to 1-2 semi-final victory over St. Cianans, Duleek before the team produced its best performance of the year. In the final against

A Féile Treble, 2004-2006

St. Martins, Under 13 Féile Champions 2004
Front: Paul Walsh, Danny Logan, Conor Ennis, Eamon Bowe, Barry Jordan, Daniel Geraghty.
Middle: Robert Crosbie, Niall Murphy, Cillian Dennehy, David O Rourke, David Fitzmaurice, Tadhg Ó Dúshláine, Eoin Sheehy, James Horgan, Stephen Clusker.
Back: Bill Reilly, Joe Boyhan, Colm McLoughlin, Conor Devereux, James Kelliher, Ciarán Clusker, Shane Troy, Dara Devereux, Mark Coffey. Missing from picture: Eoin Hagarty.

St. Martins, Under 13 Féile Champions, 2006
Front: Frankie Lally, Liam Ormsby, Stephen McCarthy, James Beattie, Gavin Byrne, Leon Everett, Keith Doherty, Aidan Boswell, Jeff Flanagan, Eimhín Kinsella, Eoin Hannon, Andrew Kiernan, James Reilly, Gary Flanagan.
Back: Henry Komolafe, David Baggott, Neil Ridgeway, Alastar Doyle, Michael McCarthy, Joe O Brien, Conor Devereux, Conor O Brien, Niall Clusker, Fergus Toolan, Niall Hannon, Ian Donoghue, Alan O Brien.

CHAPTER 16: GOING OUT IN A BLAZE OF GLORY, ST. MARTINS 1999-2008

St. Martins, Under 13 Féile Champions 2005
Front: Daniel Geraghty, Gavin Byrne, Brian Woods, James Doolan.
Middle: Luke Briody, Seán Joyce, Eamon Bowe, Barry Jordan, Cian Christie, Fergus Toolan, Alan O Brien, James Rattigan, Shane Connolly.
Back: Niall Murphy, Stephen Clusker, Conal O Sullivan, Eoin Hagarty, Michael McCarthy, Stephen Doyle, Conor Devereux, Emmet Staunton, Conor O Brien, Neil Ridgeway.

Round Towers in late November 2003 Shane Troy was in superb form from frees and Mark Coffey goaled on the stroke of half time. Two more goals from James Horgan and Danny Logan and a penalty save, allied to several outstanding blocks by James Kelliher assured victory by 3-8 to 0-5.

With qualification secured, off the field arrangements began and parents and committee members immersed themselves in the preparations with relish. A complication arose when the competition was brought forward by one week, limiting the side's dual players to only five days' recovery time after the Hurling Féile. Fatigue, injuries and restrictions on preparations due to the hurling event would be factors but the selectors and panel still managed to squeeze in a preparatory away trip to Roscommon representatives Clann na nGael.

Eventually, Friday 2nd July arrived. Having come through bag packing, raffles, race nights, measuring and fitting, flag making, meetings, birth certs, photos, form filling, accommodation arrangements, host presents, presentation night and codes of conduct, the players enjoyed a 7.30 a.m. team breakfast at *The Village Grill* prior to departure. The squad looked resplendent in the club tracksuit, runners and T-shirt together with club gear bags. The coach was bedecked with flags and banners and the all-important video machine for the two and a half hour journey to Coalisland. An entourage of parents and supporters followed in convoy.

Five minutes into the second half against hosts Coalisland, St. Martins were five points in arrears with only ten minutes to recover. Supporters were getting anxious and expectations were fading but then the old magic kicked in and the Meath representatives finished with a three-point victory, 1-7 to 1-4.

Coalisland managed to camouflage the disappointment of their defeat and their warmth and hospitality came to the fore. Gerry Mc Stravick took the soaking St. Martins' jerseys at one o clock that night and the next morning at nine arrived with them washed, dried, pressed and folded. After the magnificent spectacle of the parade it was back to the clubhouse to dispatch the players to their host families and then hospitality was focused on the adults. Suffice to say a good night was had!

The following morning the team was again slow to start and trailed Ardboe at half time 2-2 to 3-0. Despite the deficit the side was playing good football and the second half performance, ending in a 4-5 to 3-1 victory, sent out the message that the team from Meath would be hard to beat. After two tough games, paramedic Dolores Murphy was earning her stripes and getting fit in the process! It was clear that every member of the squad would have to play an active role as the injuries mounted up. The final group game against Armagh champions, Cullyhanna, was a cracker. Level at half time, the second half was end to end and that old spirit, guts and skill, combined with the wearing of the Royal County's green and gold jerseys gave St. Martins a slender 1-5 to 0-7 victory.

The mood was positive for the semi-final even though it was obvious that Galway champions Corofin had height and weight advantage in most positions. Leading by a point at halftime, 1-1 to 0-3, St. Martins were fifteen minutes away from an All-Ireland final. With two minutes remaining the game was level for the third time. St. Martins failed to convert two chances to snatch victory and then in injury time Corofin hit the winning point, emerging victorious 0-6 to 1-2. The defence had performed magnificently with Conor Devereux to the fore. Corofin went on to win the final, 2-4 to 0-6, against Kilmacud Crokes.

Devastation followed as the final whistle blew and the inconsolable players trudged to the silent dressing rooms away from the clamour and tumult of the victorious westerners. But mentors - Des Boyhan, Donnchadh Geraghty, Tommy Clusker, Paul Logan, Brendan and Dolores Murphy - and players soon recovered and after another evening of partying with the Coalisland hosts the crew departed on Sunday evening satisfied that they had represented Meath with honour.

The side failed to qualify for the knock-out stages of the Under 14 championship prior to Féile but reached the semi-final of the league where St. Cianans had a two point victory. An injury time goal from Tommy Johnson, who went on to play for St. Martins and Dunshaughlin later, was crucial in giving the Duleek side a narrow win.

Two years later, in 2006, the side progressed to the U-16 championship semi-final but injuries and a hectic schedule of games resulted in defeat to the eventual winners, Donaghmore-Ashbourne. The team's litany of near misses continued with a two-point defeat to Walterstown in the Minor Football League of 2007 and in their final year at minor level the side failed to emerge from the group stages.

The side was expected to make a greater impact at Under 16 and minor level but a combination of factors prevented that. As was natural in such a successful group, many of the players were talented in other sports. A number played soccer with Dunboyne, others lined out with Dunshaughlin Youths and Barry Jordan had a spell with Home Farm. In addition to soccer and gaelic Mark Coffey played schools' rugby with Castleknock College. The multiplicity of demands led to persistent injuries, regular unavailability of key players and a constant need to rearrange fixtures. In combination these factors caused the panel to lose the focus and direction of earlier years.

Féile 2005 Team

Victory over Navan O Mahonys in November 2004, in a match that was competitive until half time, earned St. Martins the right to go to Féile as Meath champions for the second year running. Both sides scored eight points but St Martins' ability to filch goals, five in all, gave the holders a comfortable win. Daniel Geraghty and Stephen Clusker each goaled before the break and Emmet Staunton, Eamon Bowe and James Rattigan shook the net after the interval.

With Féile qualification assured St. Martins faced into the 2005 Under 14 championship and league with confidence. After a comprehensive 3-15 to 0-8 championship semi-final victory against Simonstown Gaels, the final opposition was provided once again by O Mahonys. The game took place on a June evening when the heat of a glorious day lingered in the air, cooled by a stiff breeze. Perfect conditions produced a contest of skill and commitment at GAA headquarters in Páirc Tailteann. The town side dominated the first half, grabbed 1-8 before the interval and held a five point advantage that would have been eight but for Stephen Clusker's goal.

As in the Féile final St. Martins saved the best wine till last. Within five minutes the deficit was a single point with a Fergus Toolan goal the major contributor. A couple of astute switches, Eoin Hagarty to full forward, with Clusker on the forty and captain Emmet Staunton to midfield, shifted the balance of play in favour of the reds and a goal and six points followed without reply. The goal climaxed the move of the match. Seán Joyce won possession and moved the ball from defence, Fergus Toolan devoured ground before releasing to Emmet Staunton who bore down on goal and fired low to the net. Another goal from Alan O Brien put St. Martins 4-13 to 1-11 ahead but O Mahonys refused to concede and in a blistering finish hit a goal and a point, blasted off the woodwork twice and forced keeper

Michael McCarthy into a point-blank save.

Despite the late wobble, when the final whistle blew, St. Martins had a second title of the decade on a 4-13 to 2-13 score with the following team:

Michael McCarthy

Seán Joyce   Joe O Brien   Shane Connolly

Conor O Brien   Stephen Doyle (0-1)   Barry Jordan (0-1)

Eoin Hagarty (0-4)   Conor Devereux (0-3)

Eamon Bowe (0-1)   Emmet Staunton, Capt. (1-0)   James Rattigan

Fergus Toolan (1-2)   Stephen Clusker (1-0)   Niall Murphy

Subs: Alan O Brien (1-1) for Bowe, Alastar Doyle, Daniel Geraghty, James Doolan, Cian Christie, Brian Woods, Neil Ridgeway, Gavin Byrne, Luke Briody, Conal O Sullivan.

After the championship victory, a trip to Bettystown Beach for the squad on a brisk Sunday morning was the final ingredient to having a fit, united team for Féile in Limerick. Ranked in Division One, the group captained by Stephen Doyle under the charge of Donnchadh Geraghty, Don McLoughlin, Harry Clusker, John O Brien and Brendan and Dolores Murphy headed to Abbeyfeale, whose football grounds are just inside the Kerry border. The journey was shortened by Stephen Doyle and Ronan Geraghty's renditions of *It's so Lonely Round the Fields of Drumree!*

The first match against the hosts, Father Caseys, was won easily in wet and windy conditions but a lengthy journey, tired limbs and a festival parade followed by a long night meant very little sleep for players and mentors. The next morning the weather had a change of mind and a hard earned victory over Newcastlewest in sunny conditions resulted in a decider against Austin Stacks of Kerry. With a semi-final place at stake, a hard, tough, physical battle ensued but tired limbs were no match for the strong skilful Kerry team. However, Eamon Bowe cheered everyone up by winning the Division One skills' competition. A great night followed in Father Caseys' Clubhouse and back at the hotel, the parents' base, Fran Doolan's guitar playing entertained those that could stick the pace.

At Under 16 level two years later the side progressed to the championship semi-final where after a titanic struggle and an impressive tally of 2-16 they went under to Skryne's even more imposing 4-12. When they fielded in the Minor championship in 2009 huge changes had taken place in club structures in the parish. St. Martins was no more and the side lined out in the name and colours of Dunshaughlin. The outcome is considered in chapter 21.

Féile 2006 Team

Before Féile 2006 commenced it was clear that St. Martins had another fine team in the making. There were signs of this when, as Under 12s in 2004, the side captured the Division 1 League, seeing off the Ratoath challenge in the final. A goal in each half from Niall Clusker was crucial. The first arrived when he grabbed possession of a long delivery before firing a shot to the roof of the net to haul back a three-point deficit. The sides were still all-square at half time but Clusker poached the second goal immediately after the restart. The winners stretched the lead to eight points with a Michael McCarthy goal and although Ratoath battled back before the end the Saints had five to spare when the final whistle sounded.

In the autumn of 2005 St. Martins attempted to earn the right to represent Meath for the third consecutive year. The final showdown featured a repetition of the Under 12 meeting with neighbours Ratoath on a wet surface in windy conditions and the holders took advantage of the elements in the early stages. Inside a minute Conor Devereux had the ball in the net and five points in a row in the middle of the half gave them a decent cushion at the break, 1-6 to 0-3.

St. Martins limited Ratoath's ability to benefit from second half wind advantage with short passing and calm retention of possession. By the tenth minute only one point had been chipped off the deficit. The middle of the half proved crucial as St. Martins conjured up three points in reply to a similar total from Ratoath. Ian Donoghue with two and Conor O Brien were the marksmen. The final ten minutes stretched to fifteen with additional time and Ratoath dominated at this stage. They were unable to find the net as the winner's defence held firm and keeper Aidan Boswell ensured victory with two fine saves from close range shots in a congested goalmouth. A stand out display by midfielder Conor Devereux, featuring an insatiable work ethic and a goal and four points, was crucial in the win.

Before the trip to Wicklow for Féile the team had an Under 14 championship title to defend and an Under 14 league to aim for also. Despite the Féile success, manager Tommy Clusker and selectors John O Brien and Dominic Devereux decided to continue light training with the emphasis on the basics of catching, kicking and scoring. Tommy highlighted the side's assets as its strength in depth and willingness to play as a team.

'There's a good balance in the squad, as there is nobody hogging the limelight or trying to carry the ball 50 yards. If there is a player in a better position they always give it. They respect each other for that.'

The extra training put them in pole position in the league. The closest they came to defeat was in the league semi-final when Na Fianna held a two points

St. Martins, Under 14 FC and FL Winners, 2006

Front: Frankie Lally, Stephen McCarthy, Keith Doherty, James Beattie, David Baggott, Aidan Boswell, Niall Hannon, Eoin Hannon, Eimhin Kinsella, Henry Komolafe, Leon Everett, Gary Flanagan. Back: Gavin Byrne, Alastar Doyle, Jeff Flanagan, Fergus Toolan, Alan O Brien, Niall Clusker, Conor Devereux, Capt., Joe O Brien, Ian Donoghue, Conor O Brien, Michael McCarthy, Liam Ormsby, James Reilly, Neil Ridgeway.

Conor Devereux displays the Meath Under 14 Football Championship trophy, 2006. (First picture on right).

Neil Ridgeway with the Under 14 Football League trophy, 2006. (Second picture on right).

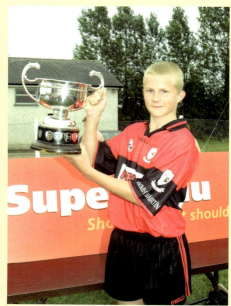

lead with five minutes remaining. The team always had an uncanny ability to unravel the best defences with crucial goals and the killer instinct was in evidence here with three in as many minutes. The game ended on the surreal scoreline of 8-10 to 5-11.

The prelude was much more difficult than the final, for Round Towers proved no match for the boys in red and black. The game was over long before half time as St. Martins blitzed the Kells side with 2-16 in thirty minutes and in a leisurely second half increased it to 2-24 to Towers' 0-6. Conor O Brien had the first goal when he finished off a trademark passing movement while James Beattie notched the second before half time.

In late June the team was back for the championship decider and Na Fianna, who had been such a handful in the league semi-final, stood between them and the title. The game was played at a helter-skelter pace with the sides trading scores. Na Fianna goaled early on to put the pressure on the holders. With the advantage of a stiff breeze St. Martins attacked in droves and both corner backs, Keith Doherty and Niall Hannon, surged forward to claim early points. Mid way through, Conor Devereux bore down on the Na Fianna keeper Ciarán Brennan who saved well but Devereux was quick onto the loose ball to whip it to the net. Points from James Beattie, Michael McCarthy and Joe O Brien consolidated the lead, which amounted to 1-10 to 2-2 at half time.

The concession of two first half goals was a worry but surprisingly the pace of the game dropped after the interval and Na Fianna could only muster another two points. Conor O Brien and Fergus Toolan were superb in defence while Devereux and Joe O Brien controlled midfield, denying their opponents possession time and again. With ten minutes remaining Alan O Brien wrapped up the title when he goaled after initially hitting the upright. The final team captained by Conor Devereux read:

Aidan Boswell

Keith Doherty (0-1)　　Alastar Doyle　　Niall Hannon (0-1)

David Baggott (0-1)　　Conor O Brien　　Fergus Toolan

Joe O Brien (0-1)　　Conor Devereux, Capt. (1-2)

Eimhín Kinsella　　Ian Donoghue (0-1)　　James Beattie (0-1)

Alan O Brien (1-0)　　Niall Clusker　　Michael McCarthy (0-5)

Subs: Gavin Byrne (0-1) for O Brien, Liam Ormsby for Beattie, Eoin Hannon for Toolan, Stephen McCarthy for Donoghue, Frankie Lally, Neil Ridgeway, Jeff Flanagan, James Reilly, Henry Komolafe, Leon Everett, Gary Flanagan.

Féile 2006 was less demanding in terms of travel than the previous two years, but no less competitive, as the champions of each county decamped to Wicklow

St. Martins, Under 16 Football Champions, 2008

Front: David Doherty, Andrew Kiernan, Gavin Malone, Liam Ormsby, James Reilly, Conor Devereux, Aidan Boswell, Niall Hannon, Alan O Brien, Tommy Clusker, Manager.
Back: TP Toolan, Coach, Dominic Devereux, Selector, Stephen McCarthy, Conor O Brien, Robert Connolly, Alastar Doyle, Michael McCarthy, Joe O Brien, Keith Doherty, Neil Ridgeway, Niall Clusker, Eoin Hannon, Henry Komolafe, John O Brien, Manager.
Missing from picture and shown as insets at top: Sam Duggan, Eimhín Kinsella, David Baggott, Fergus Toolan.

in early July. The opening game in the competition against St. Kevins of Wicklow proved to be the perfect start with St. Martins winning easily and all players on the panel getting a taste of the action. The next game against Killarney flowed from end to end and provided some of the best football of the tournament. Both teams gave their all, with St. Martins eventually gaining revenge for the previous year's defeat by a Kerry side when they pulled away near the end to win by eight points.

This set up a quarter-final match against St. Endas of Tyrone. Their mentors had viewed the game with Killarney and were aware that, to win, it would be necessary to stop St. Martins playing the open, flowing type of game that accounted for the Kingdom's representatives. St. Martins got dragged into an over physical, stop-start type of game and came out on the wrong side of a six points loss. However, spirits were soon lifted, mainly thanks to the girls from Warwickshire at the disco on Saturday night! The players' parents put an amount of hard work into preparing for Féile but it paled into insignificance in comparison with the effort they put into enjoying themselves over the weekend!

Overall, it was a disappointing end to a great twelve months. The Féile finalists were Celbridge, a team St. Martins had easily beaten many times over the previous two years, and the eventual winners were Kilcoo from Down, who had defeated St. Martins by a mere three points in the An Ríocht tournament a year earlier. Conor Devereux established the incredible record of having played in all three Féiles.

CHAPTER 16: GOING OUT IN A BLAZE OF GLORY, ST. MARTINS 1999-2008

Captain Conor Devereux and team mates celebrate the Under 16 FC Division 1 title, 2008
St Martins' players included from left are Alastar Doyle with arms raised, Stephen McCarthy Conor Devereux, Michael McCarthy and Henry Komolafe on extreme right. The officials are Pat O Reilly and Ultan Fitzpatrick.

The Under 14 double winning crew of 2006 set its eyes on emulating or surpassing the feats of the 2001 Under 14s who went on to add an Under 16 title two years later. At Under 15 level the team reached the league final but lost out to Ratoath by four points in a muddy Curraha on the first day of December.

The weather and form improved by mid 2008 when the Saints overturned the Under 15 result to reach the Under 16 championship final. Opposing them were perennial challengers Round Towers. St. Martins grabbed an early brace of goals and it seemed as if the Kells lads would once again be clinically and ruthlessly put to the sword. However, once the Towers settled, they provided a determined challenge and caused some anxious moments before the end.

The main difference between the sides was Conor Devereux. The St. Martins' captain started as a wing-back, but he covered every blade of grass in a power packed performance that bamboozled Round Towers and earned him the man of the match accolade. He posted 1-5, with three points coming from his less favoured left foot, and when the Towers did threaten in front of the posts it was often Devereux or the outstanding Alastar Doyle who cleared the danger.

A superb early goal from Niall Clusker and a penalty goal from Devereux contributed to St. Martins' two-goal interval advantage. The third quarter was the Devereux show. He took control of the game, kicking five points from play to boost St. Martins to a 2-8 to 0-3 lead.

> **The main difference between the sides was Conor Devereux. The St. Martins' captain started as a wing-back, but he covered every blade of grass in a power packed performance that bamboozled Round Towers and earned him the man of the match accolade.**

BLACK & AMBER

> **The Féile successes deserve to be recorded as the high water mark for the club. The only other contestants for the accolade were the all-conquering Under 14 sides of 1957-59.**

Just when Towers looked down and out they conjured up their best form. This yielded them a brace of goals from Carry either side of a Barry Farrelly point to reduce the deficit to four. But it was a false dawn. St. Martins once again imposed their authority, a rampant Michael McCarthy settled the side with a point, Liam Ormsby denied Carry with a brilliant block and then the irrepressible Devereux kicked an outstanding point to put the game out of reach. In the closing stages McCarthy clinched a magnificent goal that put the icing on the cake for a superb St Martins' side that triumphed by 3-11 to 2-4.

Alastar Doyle gave a masterful display at fullback and Liam Ormsby chipped in with a number of crucial tackles and excellent blocks. Niall Hannon and Joe O Brien ensured the winners dominated midfield for lengthy stretches and while Devereux took most of the scoring plaudits, McCarthy contributed handsomely and took his late goal brilliantly. Neil Ridgeway impressed with numerous forays along the wing while Conor O Brien, who missed the Ratoath game, returned to dominate the centre half back position. Alan O Brien, who scored 1-4 against Ratoath, continued his rich vein of form with the opening point, one of three.

The team management consisted of Tommy Clusker, John O Brien, TP Toolan and Dominic Devereux. Tommy had been a selector with the Féile teams of 2004 and 2006, had guided the Dunshaughlin team to an Under 21 'A' title in 2007 and was also involved with the Meath Under 16s in 2008. His death, just three months after the club's success in the Under 16 final, was a major loss to the club, dwarfed only by the loss to his family.

The victory over Round Towers was the second Under 16 title for the club and further proof of the talent of a team that lined out as follows

	Aidan Boswell	
Keith Doherty	Alastar Doyle	Liam Ormsby
Conor Devereux, Capt. (1-5)	Conor O Brien	Neil Ridgeway
Joseph O Brien (0-1)		Niall Hannon
Alan O Brien (0-3)	Eoin Hannon	James Reilly
Henry Komolafe	Niall Clusker (1-0)	Michael McCarthy (1-2)

Subs: David Doherty for J O Brien, J O Brien for Reilly, Robert Connolly for Komolafe, Andrew Kiernan, Gavin Malone, Sam Duggan, Eimhín Kinsella, David Baggott, Fergus Toolan.

A number of those players lined out on the side that played in the Under-17 semi-final defeat to Skryne later in the year. They would not go on to play minor football under the St. Martin's banner, as 2008 marked the club's final year in existence.

The Féile successes deserve to be recorded as the high water mark for the club.

St. Martins, Under 12 Reserve Football League Winners, 2008

Front: Paddy Maher, Adam Kealy, Ronan Kingston, Martin Keane, Mark Galvin, Anthony Fildes, Curtis Rattigan, Seán O Neill, James Logan.
Back: Pádraig Scurry, Andy Quinn, Selector, Niall Swan, Ben Conlon, Senan O Muirí, Conor Mooney, Gavin Maher, Capt., Seamus Doyle, Mark Phelan, Conor McEvoy, Conor Huijsdens, James Swan, Aaron Kealy, Kevin Kealy, Team Manager.

Community Games: Meath and North Leinster champions 2008.
Photo on left.
Enda Kennedy, Luke Shannon, Darren Beattie, Dylan O Brien with raised hands, Cian Lynch, Conor Jones, Conor Oliver, Neil Byrne, Shane Claire, Andrew Leneghan to rear, Paddy Maher, Jack Hetherington, Conor Keena, Adam Kealy, Tom Watté, Cian Gallogly, Pádraig Clinton.
Selectors at rear: Paul Hetherington, Kevin Kealy (Team Manager), Seán O Neill.

The only other contestants for the accolade were the two all-conquering Under 14 sides of 1957-59 and 2001. The former took three Under 14 rural titles but didn't have to compete against town teams. They had to work with much smaller panels and four players featured on all three title-winning teams, Paddy Burke, Neil O Riordan, Johnny Lynch and Brendan O Shea. In addition PJ O Rourke and David Halford both featured on two of the triumphs. There were few subs so it was a tremendous achievement to capture three titles.

All sides had top class mentors. Ciarán Murray was the guru behind the 1957-59 successes and his role is outlined in detail in chapter 6. No one mentor directed the 2001 and 2004-06 sides and the selectors altered from year to year but men like Macartan McGroder, Donnchadh Geraghty, Des Boyhan, Tommy Clusker, John O Brien, Dominic Devereux, Don McLoughlin, Brendan Murphy and Harry Clusker were guiding lights for the teams. The earlier and the recent sides lacked nothing in preparation and coaching.

The modern three in a row side had a much bigger selection to choose from and only Conor Devereux was good enough to feature on all three. The opposition was more demanding in 2004-06. St. Martins had to overcome all the top clubs in the county to represent Meath and when they did progress to the All-Ireland stage they more than held their own, reaching the semi-final in 2004 and the quarter-final in 2006. The 2005 side also went on to capture the minor championship, the first time a St. Martins' team took the Delaney Cup without amalgamating with another club. That overall, consistent level of performance and achievement entitles them to claim to be the best ever St. Martins' crew.

However, success at underage is no guarantee of adult achievement and to date the underage success of the 2004-06 sides has not translated onto similar achievements on the adult scene. The 1957-59 side produced men who went on to win Leinster and All-Ireland senior medals in Noel Curran and Jimmy Walsh. Val Dowd and Walsh also won Leinster junior medals and many of the players successfully represented Drumree and Dunshaughlin in junior and intermediate finals. While many of the 2004-06 panels have worn the Royal green and gold at championship level they have not made a substantial impact on the senior club team. Bridging the gap between underage and adult still seems to be problematic, despite the creation of a single club from Under 8 up to adult level in 2009. With emigration and players moving away to study at third level there is a need to track players, meet their needs and keep them attached to the club.

CHAPTER 16: GOING OUT IN A BLAZE OF GLORY, ST. MARTINS 1999-2008

Lower Age Grades in Recent Years

In the last decade there has been a revolutionary change in the GAA's approach to games at Under 11 level and below. The previous ultra competitive, fifteen a side game has been replaced by *GAA Go Games* with a philosophy of small-sided contests, modified rules and meaningful participation by all players. Thus, coaching at Under 8 level concentrates on skill development and enjoyment.

The Under 12 competition has long since dropped the championship element but leagues are still promoted. St. Martins had a successful start to the decade taking Division 1 titles in 2002 and 2004 and reaching an Under 12 Reserve final in 2002 also. Those achievements have been outlined earlier in this chapter.

The club remained competitive for the remainder of the decade without being able to maintain the previous litany of success. In 2007 the Under 12s reached a semi-final against Donaghmore-Ashbourne after six league games, featuring three wins and three losses. A year later the reserves had a successful league run, defeating Kells in the final. Kevin Kealy managed the side with Andy Quinn as selector and the players are listed in the accompanying photograph of the panel.

The Community Games has not entirely eschewed the original competitive aspect. Once played at Under 13 level, of which St. Martins were winners in 1983, it has been an Under 10 competition in recent years. St. Martins, and later Dunshaughlin, had a significant run of success in the event from 2008. Kevin Kealy managed, while Paul Hetherington and Seán O Neill selected the 2008 side that defeated Skryne in the Meath final in Dunboyne. The group went on to record a Leinster quarter-final victory against Shannon Gaels of Longford before exiting to Emo of Laois at Leinster semi-final stage.

The players involved with this successful group were: Enda Kennedy, Luke Shannon, Darren Beattie, Dylan O Brien, Cian Lynch, Conor Jones, Conor Oliver, Neil Byrne, Shane Claire, Andrew Leneghan, Paddy Maher, Jack Hetherington, Conor Keena, Adam Kealy, Tom Watté, Cian Gallogly and Pádraig Clinton.

The Under 13s also featured in the concluding stages of the leagues in 2008 with the first team losing to Seneschalstown after a replay while the reserves went under to Dunboyne in the final of that grade. The Under 13 side was the last to play in the black and red of St. Martins when they had to give way to Seneschalstown by 0-10 to 0-8 at Walterstown in November.

As 2008 waned major change was in the offing for underage teams in the parish. That episode is covered in Chapter 21.

BLACK & AMBER

Sowing the Seeds: Hurling in St. Martins, 1987-2008

The Secretary's report cautioned on the need for additional mentors to assist the man who was the driving force behind the coaching and the success, Patsy Curley.

In February 1987 at the request of Dunshaughlin Hurling Club the fledgling St. Martins took over responsibility for hurling, as well as football. Those in attendance at a meeting to organize the handover were Club Chairman Val Dowd, Vice Chairman Pat Kelly, Secretary Jim Gilligan, Treasurer Maura O Dwyer with Derek Melia, Simon Farrell, Pat Kealy, Kathleen Walsh, Patty Farrell, Aidan Walsh, John O Sullivan, Patsy McLoughlin, Dinny McCarthy, Paddy Ward, Gerry Flanagan, Oliver Brooks, Oliver Gogan, Frank Egan, Joe Rattigan, Patsy Curley, Seán Doyle, Ben Fitzpatrick, Seán McKiernan and Pat Farrell.

From the beginning the club fielded teams at Under 11, Under 13, Under 14 and Under 16, and the following coaches and mentors looked after the first St. Martins' hurling teams.

Under 11:	Gerry Flanagan, Patsy Curley, Ben Fitzpatrick, Seán McKiernan and Oliver Gogan.
Under 13:	Bernard Jones, Seán Doyle, Joe Rattigan.
Under 14:	Ollie O Neill, Seán Doyle, John O Sullivan.
Under 16:	Patsy Curley, Oliver Brooks, Tom Keegan, Frank Egan, Dinny McCarthy.

St. Martins, Under 11B Champions, 1987

The first St. Martin's team to win a hurling title.
Front: Jonathon Farrell, Derek Davis, Peter Egan, Joseph Smith, Damien Fitzpatrick, Seán Curley, Patrick Burke, Paul Doyle, Noel Doyle, Cathal Smith, Ian Rattigan, Alan McCarthy.
Back: Gerry Flanagan- almost fully hidden, Barry Jones, Ross Geraghty, Ronan Coffey, Aaron Fitzpatrick, Enda Lynch, Garreth Kelly, Shane Kelly, Adrian Flanagan, Ronan Curley, Wayne Cottrell, Derek Doyle, Eoin Coffey, Ben Fitzpatrick. At rear Patsy Curley.

The first year was a successful one with the Under 11s taking the B Championship. Starting from scratch the selectors built a panel of thirty players that defeated Navan De La Salle, Boardsmill and Wolfe Tones. The final pitted St. Martins against the Tones once again and they were always on top with a 2-2 to no score advantage at half time. By the end, the Saints had a comprehensive 5-2 to 0-0 victory, the first ever hurling title for the club, with Ronan Curley, Aaron Fitzpatrick and Derek Doyle giving stand-out displays. The selectors with the following historic team were Patsy Curley, Gerry Flanagan and Ben Fitzpatrick.

CHAPTER 17: HURLING IN ST. MARTINS: SOWING THE SEEDS, 1987-1996

Garreth Kelly
Enda Lynch   Wayne Cottrell   Eoin Coffey
Noel Doyle   Ronan Coffey   Paul Doyle
Ronan Curley (1-0)   Aaron Fitzpatrick (1-0)
Damien Fitzpatrick   Derek Doyle (1-2)   Shane Kelly
Barry Jones   Adrian Flanagan (1-0)   Patrick Burke (1-0)

Subs: Ross Geraghty, Derek Davis, Peter Egan, Joseph Smith, Seán Curley, Cathal Smith, Ian Rattigan, Alan McCarthy, Jonathon Farrell

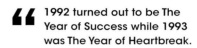

> 1992 turned out to be The Year of Success while 1993 was The Year of Heartbreak.

That year the Under 14s defeated Rossin and Wolfe Tones and lost to De La Salle to reach the semi-final where Boardsmill emerged convincing winners. This team also took part in the Meath Under 14 Hurling Festival in June 1987 and hosted the Aughrim club from Wicklow. Playing in Division 3 the team defeated Rathmolyon and lost to Kildare side Broadford. This put St. Martins into a Runners Up Final but a superior Clontarf team won 1-2 to 0-1. The panel also visited and played Patsy Curley's home club, Killimor from Galway.

It was a very successful start to hurling in the club but the Secretary's report cautioned on the need for additional mentors to assist the man who was the driving force and inspiration behind the coaching and the success, Patsy Curley. Willie Shanley and Jimmy Walsh, Junior joined him as the main promoters of under-age hurling over the next few years. Indeed, many a tale could be told about teams traveling in Willie's van to away-matches. Seat-belts were unheard of in those days. If you survived the journey you were declared fit for the match!

When Patsy retired from training duties others came on board, such as Paddy Ward, Jimmy Walsh Snr., Peter Mooney, Michael Wallace and Paul Barry. Gradually, hurling began to thrive at under-age level in St. Martins. Although minor teams were affiliated from 1988 the younger age groups remained the most successful for a number of years. In 1988 the Under 14s lost a B semi-final to Rathmolyon and the following year went a step further, defeating Trim in the semi-final before finishing as runners-up to Dunboyne.

A Year of Success and A Year of Heartbreak

1992 turned out to be *The Year of Success* while 1993 was *The Year of Heartbreak*. In 1992 the Under 14s won the Division 2 Féile final with victory against Kildalkey while practically the same team won the Under 14B championship later in the year. After losing the opener to Killyon, St. Martins recovered to post victories against Navan O Mahonys, Wolfe Tones, Batterstown, Kiltale and Gaeil Colmcille. That title came after an extremely low scoring final where St. Martins got the upper hand on Gaeil Colmcille again, by four points to one. Keeper Gary Donoghue was in superb form and was well supported by Eoin Coffey, Noel Doyle, Mick O Brien and David Crimmins.

The team that captured St. Martins' first championship at Under 14 level lined out as follows:

Gary Donoghue

Eoin Coffey   Noel Doyle   Mick O Brien

Alan Kenny   Rory O Sullivan, Capt.   David Crimmins

Paul Doyle   Gerard Clarke

Pádraig Shanley   Seán Curley   Damien Fitzpatrick (0-2)

Jason Clarke (0-1)   Brendan Boyle (0-1)   Paddy Boyle

Subs: Paddy Burke for Curley, GT Troy, Gerard Troy.

The Under 13s matched their older counterparts when they brought the first title to the club at this level. After starting out with a draw to Killyon, the two teams met again in the decider where St. Martins took the honours. The Under 15s reached the league final but lost out to Baconstown in late October and this turned out to be an omen for results to come the following year.

In 1993, *The Year of Heartbreak*, the club lost four finals, three of them in hurling. Killyon beat the Under 11s, due to an own goal off a deflected clearance when they looked to be in command. The Under 16s had a good victory against Baconstown in the semi-final but had no complaints when well beaten, 2-7 to 0-1, by a superior Boardsmill side in the final. In addition the Under 13s lost out at semi-final stage by a point, 2-2 to 2-1 versus Rathmolyon.

The minors were the unluckiest of all three finalists. They overcame Kildalkey in the semi-final and drew with Kiltale in the final, 2-2 to 0-8. The second encounter featured a substantial increase in the scoring rate and Kiltale made the greater improvement, finishing 5-4 to 2-3 in front. The Saints were not ten points inferior on the overall balance of play. Influential defender Mick Summerville had to be replaced due to an injury and substitute Brendan Tuite, who was also making an impact, had to be withdrawn. Keeper Ronan Curley moved outfield after Summerville's injury and his first half goal kept St. Martins in contention at the break. Two quick Kiltale goals after the interval ensured victory and St. Martins only score was a goal from brilliant centre-back Dermot Doyle. Many of the team had featured in the club's first success in 1987 at Under 11 level and the side lined out as follows:

Ronan Curley (1-0); Noel Burke, Wayne Cottrell; Mick Summerville, Dermot Doyle (1-0), Roy Sheridan; James Walsh, David Troy (0-3); Paul Doyle, Seamus Smith, Aaron Fitzpatrick; Alan Egan, Derek Doyle. Subs: Noel Doyle for Summerville, Brendan Tuite for Smith, Ronan Coffey for Tuite.

St. Martins, 1994 Féile Winners

Front: John Crimmins, Neil Mooney, Stephen Ward, John Gilsenan, Brian Walsh, Keith Mangan, Jason Keogh, Liam Shanley, Martin Duffy, Kevin Burke, Christopher Doyle, Ciarán Murray, Philip Doyle.
Back: Christopher Carey, John Joe McDonnell, Vincent Cullinane, John McKiernan, Gary Donoghue, Brian Kenny, David Crimmins, Gerard Troy, Neil Reilly, GT Troy, Alan Kenny.

Two Years of Success, 1994-95

The disappointments of 1993 were forgotten when the following year brought success on a number of fronts.

In May the Under 14 side won the Féile competition with a runaway victory in the final against Rathmolyon by 6-5 to 0-3. Full forward Christopher Carey took the scoring honours with three goals. Rathmolyon were at the receiving end of two further final defeats to St. Martins, the Under 14 B final won by St. Martins by 1-7 to 1-3 and the inaugural Rural Championship where a late Johnny Gilsenan goal sealed the issue. The side went on to win the Leinster Hurling Council's mini Féile with three victories against Naas, O Tooles of Dublin and Kilmessan followed by a victory in the final against Navan O Mahonys on a 2-1 to 0-3 scoreline after a thrilling game. The loss of the Under 11B and the Under 13B deciders didn't take from a productive year.

The venue for the mini Féile was Wexford and the team combined two victories and one loss to reach the final. The Wexford representatives, Ballyfad, were too strong in the decider and recorded a 3-3 to 1-1 victory over St. Martins.

After two final defeats at Under 11 level the 1995 side made it third time lucky when defeating Blackhall Gaels, a newly formed amalgamation of Batterstown and Kilcloon. Managed by Paul Barry and Jimmy Walsh Jnr. St. Martins took control in the second half to record a 3-3 to 2-0 victory with Ciarán Murray

BLACK & AMBER

> After a decade of catering for under age hurling St. Martins could claim that the small ball game in the parish was in good hands and rude health.

outstanding, alongside other top performers, the Delaney brothers, Cormac and Diarmuid, John Crimmins, Fergal Moore, Paul Sheehy and David O Neill. It was the second title in the grade and the winning side lined out as follows:

Ronan Gilsenan
Joseph Coffey   Caoimhín King
Diarmuid Delaney   John Crimmins   Fergal Moore
Paul Sheehy   David Donoghue
David O Neill   Ciarán Murray (2-2)   Paul Cosgrove
Cormac Delaney (1-0)   Mark Devanney (0-1)
Subs: Emma Doyle for O Neill, John Crosbie for D Delaney.

The following year the club captured the Under 11 Grade 1 Ground Hurling title with a 2-1 to 0-0 victory over Kilmessan.

After a decade of catering for under age hurling St. Martins could claim that the small ball game in the parish was in good hands and rude health. It has been said that there were three reasons for the success, Patsy Curley, Willie Shanley and Jimmy Walsh, Junior. It is an over-simplification, for many others assisted also, but it is an accurate précis of the genesis of the success. Four Under 11 finals

St. Martins, Under 11 Ground Hurling Grade 1 Champions 1996

Front: Fionán O Kane, Paul Coffey, Mark Coffey, Alan Carey.
Middle: Pauric Smith, Brian Coughlan, Séamus White, Stephen McGroder, Caoimhín King, Fergal Moore, Cormac Delaney, John Coffey, David Quinn, David Wallace, Joseph Coffey.
Back: Caroline Duffy, Orla Power, John O Callaghan, John Kieran, Ronan Gilsenan, Edel Walsh, Breda White, Aileen White, Robert Lyons.
Team Management at rear: Willie Shanley, Jimmy Walsh, Jun., Paul Barry.

with two victories, the same number of titles from three finals at Under 14 level and a close run Minor final in 1992 ensured St. Martins were no longer neophytes in the hurling pool. The club's status was underlined when Aaron Fitzpatrick and David Troy represented the club on the Meath Minor team in 1993 and six players represented the Royals in the 1996 Under 16 All-Ireland Hurling Final against Kerry, Gary Donoghue, John McKiernan, Neil Reilly, GT Troy, Gerard Troy and David Crimmins.

In 1996 the club took another progressive step in the promotion of hurling with the introduction of a Schools' Coaching Project. John Davis Jnr. was employed as hurling coach in the local schools, Culmullen N.S., Gaelscoil na Rithe and St. Seachnall's N.S., during school time. This project was highly successful as was evident by the increase in the number of new young players joining the club and the participation of the schools in Cumann na mBunscol competitions. The project endured until 2000.

Consolidation, 1996 - 2008

First Minor Title, 1997

The club would be well over a decade old when the first minor hurling title arrived. The 1996 side was unable to follow up a comprehensive semi-final victory against Blackhall Gaels with a repeat performance in the final. Though superior to Killyon for much of the game, St. Martins couldn't seal the deal on the scoreboard.

Many of the players were still eligible in 1997 and with most of the Under 14s who had captured the Féile title in 1994 progressing to minor level the club was well placed to record a first Minor hurling title. This was probably the best group of players to represent the club until then and the team exacted some measure of revenge for the previous year with a convincing semi-final victory, scoring 3-11 to Killyon's 3-5.

Waiting in the final was Rathmolyon but a blistering opening, featuring three first half goals, Gary Donoghue with one and GT Troy with a brace, killed off their challenge. The winner's slick, fast moving and accurate play was a feature of the success.

St. Martins' half time lead of 3-3 to 0-1 looked insurmountable but Rathmolyon dug deep in the early stages of the second half as they attempted to make an impression on the deficit. However, their all-out attacking left weaknesses at the back and Seán Curley exploited the space to grab the Saints' fourth goal. Even then Rathmolyon refused to surrender and hit back with two goals but Curley and David Crimmins eased St. Martins' worries with well-taken points. The Drumree-Dunshaughlin lads captured the trophy with a 4-8 to 3-1 victory with

> Waiting in the final was Rathmolyon but a blistering opening, featuring three first half goals, Gary Donoghue with one and GT Troy with a brace, killed off their challenge.

BLACK & AMBER

Minor Captain and Cup, 1997.
Seán Curley, captain of St. Martins, receives the Minor Trophy from TJ Reilly.

Pádraig Shanley, Paddy Boyle and Gary Donoghue outstanding on the following team, while the team management consisted of Willie Shanley, David Crimmins and Peter Mooney.

John Gilsenan

Kevin Burke   Gerard Troy

Neil Reilly   Paul Doyle (0-1)   Brian Kenny

Pádraig Shanley   Paddy Boyle

GT Troy (2-0)   David Crimmins (0-3)   Gary Donoghue (1-1)

Cathal Smith   Seán Curley, Capt. (1-3)

The club ensured the players got due recognition for their efforts with a medal presentation ceremony where Meath Hurler of the Year Nicky Horan from Kilmessan presented the silverware. Also receiving medals were the members of the Under 11 team that won the ground hurling shield.

Building to More Minor Titles, 2001-03

The first Minor hurling success of 1997 was the prelude to a couple of years of impressive performances at that level. Promoted to the A Grade the following year the side progressed to the semi-final before losing to a Boardsmill-Kildalkey combination by 2-9 to 2-4.

Meanwhile the club was building from the ground up and a core group of players equal to any in the county progressed through the grades. Two talented Under 13 teams came along in successive years. The 1998 side overcame Boardsmill to capture the B title on a score of 2-9 to 4-0.

After waiting four months for the game to be played the team couldn't have got off to a worse start, conceding four goals in the first half. However, the physically stronger St. Martins gradually imposed themselves on the game after the break with Ronan Gilsenan, John Kieran, Caoimhín King and Cormac Delaney impressing. Gilsenan was the leading scorer with 1-5, ably supported by John Kieran's 1-1 while David Wallace and Stephen McGroder with two points and one point respectively completed the total. Paul Barry, Willie Shanley, Michael Wallace and Jimmy Walsh, Jnr. were in charge of selection and training. The following year many of the same players progressed to another Under 13 final but on this occasion Blackhall Gaels held the upper hand, winning 4-10 to 2-8.

2001 was the year of two Minor finals. The 2000 final was greatly delayed and not played until April 2001 when Killyon overcame St. Martins. The 2001 side was as good as the 1997 outfit and went in pursuit of the club's second title at this level. Many of the players were exceptionally young for the grade and

CHAPTER 17: HURLING IN ST. MARTINS: SOWING THE SEEDS, 1987-1996

the team's genesis was in the winning Under 11 and Under 13 sides of 1995 and 1998 respectively. Between them those two sides produced seven of the minor panel, Caoimhín King, Ronan Gilsenan, Cormac Delaney, David Wallace, Paul Sheehy, Rory Bowe and Peadar Smith. The side's quality was emphasized by the presence of Caoimhín King at full-back on the Meath team that won the 2001 All-Ireland Under 16 Hurling Championship, the first such title since 1989. Rory Bowe and Ronan Gilsenan were both panel members as Meath defeated Carlow by 4-10 to 0-6 while Brendan Walsh, Seamus Wallace and Seán White were on the Meath minor panel in 2001.

In the 2001 competition St. Martins defeated Moylagh in the semi-final to set up another final meeting with Killyon. The sides had drawn during the league stages when a last minute Seán White goal leveled a high scoring game 5-8 to 4-11. It took two games to separate the sides in the final, and there was no sign of the earlier high scoring as defences dominated the initial meeting and both sides finished with a mere five points.

The replay produced another closely contested encounter with Killyon looking likely winners when they held a two-point advantage at the interval and seeming certain victors after an early second half goal. St. Martins refused to surrender and Seamus Wallace gave a man of the match exhibition, picking off points from all angles to finish with ten to his name. While Wallace's efforts hauled the Saints into contention others to shine were John Crimmins, Paul Sheehy, Peadar Smith, Caoimhín King and Brendan Walsh. With time ebbing away Seán White again pounced for a late goal that was sufficient to clinch the title on a 1-12 to 2-7 scoreline, with 1-6 coming in the second half. The side that captured the second minor title was:

Cormac Delaney

John Crimmins   Paul Sheehy

Peadar Smith   Caoimhín King   David Donoghue

Seán White (1-1)   Brendan Walsh

Ronan Gilsenan   Seamus Wallace, Capt. (0-10)   Liam Shanley (0-1)

John Brennan   David Wallace

Subs: Rory Bowe, John Kieran, Pádraig Smith, Eoin Reilly, Brian Coughlan, John Crosbie, Ciarán Gilsenan.

The following year St. Martins could make no impact in the higher grade, having lost five of the top performers from 2001,- White, Walsh, Shanley, Brennan and captain Seamus Wallace. In addition it was difficult to recruit mentors with the economy booming and many people under pressure at work. As a result attendance at training was poor and games were postponed. A concerted effort

St. Martins, Minor Hurling B Champions, 2001

Front: Seamus Wallace, Brendan Walsh, Brian Coughlan, Seán White, John Crosbie, David Wallace, Liam Shanley, Ciarán Gilsenan.
Back: Rory Bowe, Eoin Reilly, Peadar Smith, David Donoghue, John Crimmins, Pauric Smith, Cormac Delaney, Ronan Gilsenan, Caoimhín King, John Brennan, Paul Sheehy.
Missing from photo: John Kieran.

was made to improve matters in 2003 and the outcome was a return of the success of two years previously.

St. Martins played neighbours Blackhall Gaels in the final in October. Five of those who had played in the 2001 final lined out against Blackhall, Cormac Delaney, Caoimhín King, Ronan Gilsenan, David Wallace and Rory Bowe.

The teams produced an entertaining encounter, featuring quality hurling that was in sharp contrast to the scrappy affair in the Minor A Championship decider at the same venue, in the *Chronicle's* view. St. Martins made the better start with points from Wallace and Cormac Delaney before Blackhall struck the only goal after twelve minutes. As the game wore on, midfielders Ronan Gilsenan and Ciarán Kenny came more to the fore while Rory Bowe also played impressively for the winners. Two other key men for St. Martins were Caoimhín King, who started in defence, but moved forward and contributed a well-struck second-half point, and Cormac Delaney with three crucial points.

St. Martins trailed by two points at the interval and the second half was a close affair. The Saints' win was all the more exemplary as they trailed for long

CHAPTER 17: HURLING IN ST. MARTINS: SOWING THE SEEDS, 1987-1996

St. Martins, Minor Hurling B Champions, 2003

spells, yet character, persistence and the switching of David Wallace into the full-forward line paid off handsomely. With only three minutes of normal time remaining Wallace finally edged St. Martins in front. But this wasn't the final action as Blackhall responded with an equalizer from the impressive Jonathan Meyler a minute later.

A replay looked a cast-iron certainty until the referee awarded St. Martins an injury time free, forty-five metres out. David Wallace, still only sixteen, had been the hero of the hour as he weaved his magic throughout. At Féile in 2000 and 2001 he won the individual skills award so he was nerveless when faced with the last minute challenge. His puck split the posts for the most important of his six points, over half the winning total, and it gave St. Martins a 0-10 to 1-6 victory and their third minor title.

Front: John O Callaghan, Caoimhín King, Rory Bowe, Ronan Gilsenan, Capt., Pauric Smith, David Wallace, Ronan Cleary. Back: Robert Lyons, James Gaughan, Joseph Coffey, Eoin Reilly, Brian Coughlan, Ciarán Kenny, John Crosbie, Cormac Delaney, Stephen McGroder, Christopher Dixon, Thomas O Regan.

> David Wallace… was nerveless when faced with the last minute challenge. His puck split the posts for the most important of his six points, over half the winning total,

Ronan Gilsenan with Minor B Hurling Trophy, 2003
Ronan Gilsenan raises the cup after captaining St. Martins to victory in the 2003 Minor Hurling B final against Blackhall Gaels.

Seán Delaney, Gabriel King and Michael Wallace managed the successful team that lined out as follows:

John Crosbie

Eoin Reilly　　　Caoimhín King (0-1)

James Gaughan　　　Brian Coughlan　　　Joseph Coffey

Ronan Gilsenan, Capt.　　　Ciarán Kenny

Pauric Smith　　　David Wallace (0-6)　　　Cormac Delaney (0-3)

Ronan Cleary　　　Rory Bowe

Subs: Stephen McGroder for P Smith, Christopher Dixon for Cleary, Robert Lyons for McGroder, John O Callaghan, Thomas O Regan.

The successes at under age level and especially at minor grade soon fed into adult level. Dunshaughlin Hurling club had disbanded in 1990 with Drumree taking over as the adult hurling club in the parish. The training and coaching work with St. Martins soon bore fruit with Drumree winning the Meath junior hurling championship in 1998. The side sported many who had developed their craft with St. Martins, among them Declan Troy, Pádraig Shanley, David Crimmins, Gary Donoghue, Ronan and Seán Curley, David Troy, Gerard Clarke and Dermot Doyle. By then David Troy was also a member of the Meath senior panel. Meath VEC awarded St. Martins the Sports' Club of the Year in 2002 for its work promoting hurling in the area.

The 2003 minor victory completed a spectacular week for the Wallace family and Caoimhín King. Michael Wallace had the honour of coaching both the minor champions and the Drumree side that won the intermediate hurling final the previous Sunday. David Wallace and Caoimhín King played central roles in both finals while Seamus Wallace, a minor winner in 2001, lined out on the forty for the victorious Drumree side.

Many of the players were making an impact at county level. David Wallace captained the Meath Under 16s who reached the All-Ireland final with Brian Coughlan and James Gaughan also on the panel. At minor level, Caoimhín King and David Wallace represented the club while Brendan Walsh, Seán White and Seamus Wallace featured on the Under 21 panel. The victorious Meath junior side that won a Leinster title saw David Troy among the medal winners while Seamus Wallace became a regular on the senior side, winning a Kehoe Cup medal in 2004. By then Seán White and Brendan Walsh had joined Wallace on Meath's National Hurling League panel.

Reflecting on the successes Michael Wallace recalled that,

'The work of the underage coaches with St. Martins was beginning to bear fruit as men like Willie Shanley, Seán White, Paul Barry and Joe Rattigan had done so much for the club in recent years. For these men it was as big an honour to win the championship as anyone.'

St. Martins, Division 1 Féile Winners 2001

Front: Duncan Geraghty, Martin Cosgrove, Emmet O Callaghan, Val Gannon, Stephen McGroder, Seamus White, Fionán O Kane, Fearghal Delaney, Bryan McKeown, Timmy O Regan, Shane Troy.
Back: Paul Barry, John Coffey, David Bracken, Adrian Toolan, Liam Mulvihill, Director General, GAA, Paul Kiernan, Shane Kelly, Brian Coughlan, Ciarán Farrelly, David Wallace, Paul Coffey, Christopher Dixon, James Gaughan, Mairéad Delaney, Michael Wallace.

An Established Club, 2003-08

Féile Fortunes in the Millennium

In the early years of the new century St. Martins embellished its reputation as a club capable of producing skilful hurlers and teams able to compete with the best. In terms of skill they were the best in the Royal County in 2000 and 2001, winning both team and individual honours in the Under 14 Féile Skills Competitions. David Wallace won the individual award in both years.

The All-Ireland Hurling Féile, a festival of hurling for Under 14 teams, was scheduled for a northern county in 2001 but ended up in Cork due to a foot and mouth outbreak. The previous year St. Martins had valuable preparation for the outing to Cork, capturing the Meath Under 14B championship and Under 14 B Féile crown. Fergal Moore was the hero of the hour in the championship final against Wolfe Tones, helping himself to 1-4, with Brian McEntee getting another goal and Adrian Toolan contributing a vital three points. St. Martins dominated throughout but the Tones' backs defended well to limit the half time deficit to four points. In the second period Ciarán Kenny controlled midfield and combined well with David Wallace, Eoin Reilly, Cormac Delaney and Adrian Toolan as St. Martins converted possession into scores to establish a commanding ten-point lead. Tones grabbed a brace of goals near the end but the Saints were deserving winners by 2-8 to 3-1.

The same side overcame Boardsmill in the Under 14B Féile final and ended the two campaigns unbeaten in Meath.

> **Paul Barry was a driving force with the St. Martin's hurlers for almost a decade.**

The panel went on to represent Meath in a poorly organized B Féile in Westmeath where St. Martins recorded one win and one loss.

In 2001 St. Martins went a step further and won the A Féile and the right to represent Meath in the Rebel County. Completed in blitz format over a weekend in May, St. Martins topped their group, defeated Trim in the semi-final and outscored Kilmessan 4-4 to 2-2 in the final with captain David Wallace contributing a goal and a point. The victory completed a unique double for the club as the Under 14 footballers were also representing Meath in the football Féile in Tipperary.

Aghabullogue hosted the hurlers in late June but didn't extend their hospitality to the playing field where the home side was victorious. Yet St. Martins came away with a notable scalp, victory over the famed St. Finbarrs in the initial game. A second defeat, to Antrim champions, Gort na Móna, eliminated the Saints. The side was coached, trained, coaxed and driven by Paul Barry and Michael Wallace ably assisted by Mairéad Delaney. The players are listed in the accompanying photograph of the panel.

The same side advanced to the championship Grade A semi-final where Navan O Mahonys proved too strong.

Meath part hosted Féile 2003 and 2004 with St. Martins, captained by Dara Devereux, exiting at the semi-final stage of Division 5 to Coill Dubh of Kildare in 2004.

Paul Barry was a driving force with the St. Martin's hurlers for almost a decade. He had a distinguished underage hurling career with his native Delvin, captained them to an Under 14 championship and also won Under 16 and minor championship medals. He represented Westmeath at Under 16 and minor level and later served as secretary of the Delvin club. After settling in Dunshaughlin he threw himself wholeheartedly into the promotion of the game at all under age levels. He was also PRO of the Meath Juvenile Board as well as PRO and team manager of Drumree's second team and his sudden death in 2002 was a huge loss to his family, St. Martins and Drumree.

Under 16s, Dual Runners Up, 2006-2007

Despite St. Martins' success in promoting hurling in the parish its hurlers had the same difficulty as the footballers in capturing an Under 16 title. The closest was the defeat to Boardsmill in 1993. It often proved difficult to recruit selectors for the Under 16 and minor grades while Sunday morning games also presented problems. Fixtures regularly clashed with soccer commitments, and, as many of the players were sitting their Junior Certificates, hurling often took second place.

In 2006 training commenced in early March but bad weather resulted in a deferral of the competition until late April. Though St. Martins defeated Moylagh 5-7 to 3-11 it was with the minimum number of players. Valuable points were garnered with victory against Donaghmore-Ashbourne but the sequel was a heavy defeat to O Mahonys and a scarcity of players once again. A walkover from Dunderry was sufficient to guarantee a semi-final place against Na Fianna and after the performance of the year the Saints emerged victorious by 3-6 to 1-1.

The reward was another clash with O Mahonys with the previous outcome casting its shadow over the encounter. The first half offered a glimmer of hope as the Saints matched the Navan side in skill and determination and at the interval a single point separated the sides. Second half injuries disrupted a team that needed maximum outcomes from minimum resources and O Mahonys took advantage of the losses to take the title by 1-10 to 0-5.

The 2007 Under 16 championship was an eleven a side competition in response to clubs' difficulties fielding full sided teams. Victories over Rathmolyon and Wolfe Tones sandwiched a loss to Na Fianna but it was enough to earn a play-off against Kildalkey for a final place. Saint Martins proved equal to the demands and earned a second chance against earlier conquerors Na Fianna, a combination of Enfield and Baconstown.

It was a game St. Martins could and should have won. They dominated the game for long periods and hit the target more often than the opposition but four of Na Fianna's scores were goals. It was the failure to limit the concession of goals that undermined St. Martins' challenge.

The Saints had the better of the first half with a goal just before the break giving them a half time lead of 1-3 to 1-2. Prospects looked even brighter early in the second half with three pointed frees to Na Fianna's one and the title seemed within their grasp when St. Martins netted for the second time. The seven-point lead looked unassailable and even when Na Fianna pulled back two goals St. Martins seemed to have the upper hand. However, Na Fianna's Daniel Queeney with a goal and a point in the closing stages snatched victory from the jaws of defeat and left the reds to rue the concession of goals.

Under 11s and 12s Back in the Spotlight, 2003-2008

There has always been a strong tradition favouring the promotion of Gaelic football in the primary schools in the parish. Hurling, however, finds it more difficult to flourish and as a result it falls to the club to ensure that the more demanding skills of the game are developed. The South East Hurling Development Drive, with John Davis Jnr. as hurling coach working in the local schools, previously

St. Martins, Under 11 C Hurling Runners Up, 2008

Front: Senan Ó Muirí, Niamh Gallogly, Brona Gavin, Mark Galvin, Lorcan O Reilly, Cian Gallogly, Conor Jones.
Back: Ciarán O Muirí, Stephen Ennis, Ciara Jones, William McCarthy, Aaron Keane, Niall Gavin, Alan Reilly, Martin Keane, Robert Smith, Roy Horan, Michael O Regan.

referred to, was a visionary scheme but lack of finance put an end to it by 2000.

Another scheme aimed at developing the hurling skills of young players was the introduction of indoor hurling. Initiated by Mairéad Delaney and Paul Barry, it started originally in Drumree Hall and later transferred to Dunshaughlin Community Centre. A number of stalwarts, such as Martin Kennedy, Jim Reynolds, Niall McCarthy, Jimmy Walsh, Conor Gavin, Ciarán Ó Muirí, Nuala Gavin, Maureen Kennedy, Maura Reynolds, Edward O Riordan, Frank Bawle, Willie Hanley, Cathy Casey, Helen Ó Muirí, Kim Slater and Mairéad McMahon ensured it continued over the years. The venture catered for boys and girls aged six to eleven and has been an important conduit in supplying players for St. Martins, and later Drumree, juvenile teams. It also helped in the establishment of a camogie team in St. Martins.

By the middle of the decade juvenile hurling was thriving with large numbers of children and youths actively involved from Under 7 to minor level. In 2004 the club welcomed Kilkenny maestro and multiple All-Ireland winner Eddie Brennan to Drumree where he demonstrated some of the skills of the game to over 90 players before signing autographs and partaking in a question and answer session with the children.

In this period the club consistently qualified for the concluding stages of the juvenile competitions, especially Under 11 and Under 12, even if they failed to gain outright honours. In 2003 St. Martins contested two juvenile finals, at Under

CHAPTER 17: HURLING IN ST. MARTINS: SOWING THE SEEDS, 1987-1996

St. Martins, Under 13 B, Runners-Up, 2006

Front: Sam Houlihan, Killian Gavin, Kevin Sweeney, David Moore, David Reilly, Gary Commons, Darragh Kennedy, Leon Everett, Ruadhán O Riordan, Seán Gavin. Back: Oliver Killoran, Alan Keane, James Reilly, Niall Hannon, David Baggott, Eoin Hannon, Stephen McCarthy, Keith Rooney, Kristina Troy, Oisín de Bhál, Caimin Dunne. Missing from picture Andrew Kiernan.

11C and Under 12B, in addition to the minor title described earlier. Both juvenile sides had to give way to the traditional hurling stronghold of Killyon.

For the following three years the Under 11s reached the semi-final of the championship, losing out on each occasion. All of those teams emerged from the indoor training and with up to forty participants in the sessions St. Martins was able to field a reserve team in the county leagues at times. Finally in 2008 the Under 11s went a step further and reached the final, this time in grade C, but victory eluded this group also.

One of the unluckiest crews was the Under 13 team of 2006. The Saints overcame Dunderry in the semi-final on a 1-8 to 1-4 scoreline with Niall Hannon scoring the goal and Stephen McCarthy recording four points. The final against Kilmessan had a dramatic finale. St. Martins held a 3-1 to 1-2 interval advantage and extended it to a seemingly impregnable eight-point lead with six minutes remaining. However, Kilmessan produced a whirlwind finish, scoring 3-1, to deny St. Martins by two points, 4-3 to 4-1. A school colleague of the players, Fergal Cleary, was one of the tormentors in chief as he hit two goals during the game. The panel for the final is listed under the accompanying photograph.

From 2009 hurling teams in the parish played as Drumree following the demise of St. Martins as outlined in chapter 21 and details of successful teams in the 2009-12 period are listed in Appendix 9.

BLACK & AMBER

The Junior Challenge, 1995-2014

In a club with a successful first team the seconds and thirds are usually populated with young players on the way up or older men on the way down. Akin to the Senate, full of aspiring hopefuls and retiring elder statesmen.

The club's first team is always the number one priority.

In theory.

In reality, if your first team is not remotely close to winning championships or leagues then the club's second team assumes an added importance. Thus, in the decade from the early eighties to the early nineties, junior titles were celebrated with gusto as the intermediate side struggled to make an impact on the championship. Players with the ability to play at the higher level might prefer to forego the dubious pleasure of almost certain defeat at intermediate level for the possibility of a medal and glory at junior. After Reserve League titles in 1989 and 1991, a Junior C and Junior Division 2 championship in 1991 and 1994 respectively and a final appearance in 1992 the juniors had almost exhausted all the titles on offer. After 1992 it was clear that the first team could win an intermediate in the not too distant future and so the juniors were relegated in importance.

The composition of any club's second team is dependent on the first team's demands for players. In the early rounds the second team may have all except the best fifteen available for selection but as the year progresses the top team will have to call on extra players due to injuries, suspensions or loss of form. The bane of junior team management is this loss of the best players to the first team, and

> Men who have long retired are cajoled back into the fold, the corner back who hasn't been seen since last year's defeat is persuaded to return and the handy Under 16 or minor jumps at the chance to play adult football.

if the club qualifies for the knock-out stages it is bound to be much weaker than initially. This is a major difficulty facing a club whose second team takes part in the Junior A Championship.

In a club with a successful first team the seconds and thirds are usually populated with young players on the way up or older men on the way down. Akin to the Senate, full of aspiring hopefuls and retiring elder statesmen. Playing games is a priority, serious training is only for the first team. Men who have long retired are cajoled back into the fold, the corner back who hasn't been seen since last year's defeat is persuaded to return and the handy Under 16 or minor jumps at the chance to play adult football. The team will have its fair share of lads who were 'great minors' until injury or the social scene or both intervened and the fella who 'hasn't played for years' but 'was a great one.'

The Art of Managing the Juniors

Managing the junior teams, and in particular the thirds, is an art mastered by few. It is often a role people are reluctant to undertake for it brings with it unique challenges, but one man who has an expert understanding of the role is Lally McCormack. From the late 1990s through the first decade of the new century he took charge of numerous Junior C championship teams as well as the third league team while also performing the role of PRO in an affable, efficient manner. As he describes it, the role of junior team manager requires patience, perseverance and persistence.

Usually there is a core group of eight to ten players committed to the cause. They might not be prepared to train consistently, but they do like to play regularly. Most of them want to stay at the level they are at. They are in it for the enjoyment and have no ambition to graduate to a higher level. If the team reaches the knockout stages of the championship or has a crucial game in the league, turn out at training will improve and commitment will increase.

If you implement a strict regime you won't have a team. A selector can't take the approach that players who don't train or don't turn up regularly won't get their place. If you do you will soon run out of personnel.

A big challenge is recruiting younger players for the teams. At the beginning of the year Lally always got details of the previous year's minor players from the super efficient club Secretary, Caroline Malone, contacted the parents to explain the workings of the junior teams and obtained permission to text or e-mail details of games to the players. On average around half a dozen players will be enlisted annually via this process. Soccer was once the GAA's main rival for players but currently rugby presents an equally potent attraction. The success of Irish sides

Lally McCormack
Junior team manager supreme and club PRO 1998-2006.

in the Heineken Cup has given the game a much higher public profile and players with experience of the sport at schools' level often continue to play it, albeit not always for their club's first team.

Players enjoy the camaraderie and craic and the younger selectors need to be ready to don their boots in the event of a shortfall. In a junior game against St. Brigids in Cortown, team manager Neil Halpin was called upon when just fourteen players could be mustered. His position of choice was in goals and after giving his team talk he geared up for the action in track suit and runners. In the huddle before the game commenced he removed his dentures and offered a final few words of wisdom, slurring his speech in their absence. Then Niall Foley, called on as captain to say a few words, announced, 'Ye mightn't learn much about football here tonight, but at least ye'll all learn to make sure to brush yer teeth!'

In an outing against St. Vincents, Lally himself had to line out in wellington boots in the number 13 jersey. His marker advised him to 'stay over in the corner out of harm's way' which he did, even when his son David came charging through the centre. As David was about to pass the ball to him Lally remembered his marker's advice and roared 'Keep going.' Dunshaughlin won the game with the ball-shy corner forward claiming that his role as a decoy runner was crucial in the victory!

> 'Ye mightn't learn much about football here tonight, but at least ye'll all learn to make sure to brush yer teeth!'

Junior A and B, 1995-2014

From 1995 the second string played in the Junior A competition but it was at least a grade too high. Up to 2000 teams generally won no more than a game or two in the group stages and often toyed with relegation. In 2002 and 2004 demotion was avoided after play-offs yet the Secretary's annual mantra that the club should drop to Junior B was ignored until four losses and a draw in 2005 precipitated the inevitable drop. There was an immediate boost in fortunes in the more congenial surroundings of Junior B as the side contested semi-finals in 2006 and 2009 with quarter-final appearances in the intervening years, 2007 and 2008.

In the first year in Junior B the team had seven fixtures to fulfil, against opposition from all four quarters of the county, to qualify for the knock-out stages. Despite a loss to Blackhall Gaels and a draw with Moynalty good wins over Cortown, Navan O Mahonys, Donaghmore-Ashbourne and Bellewstown and a walk over to Na Fianna propelled them into the quarter-final.

The black and ambers emerged victorious after a low scoring encounter with Seneschalstown at Walterstown. The teams were level on three points after half an hour but Paul Sheehy edged Dunshaughlin in front soon after the resumption. Though Seneschalstown soon leveled, half forward Shane Kelly pointed to restore

Dunshaughlin, Junior Panel, 2009

Front: Mark Caldwell, Declan O Dwyer, Tadhg Ó Dúshláine, Eamon Bowe, Conor Devereux, Alan McLoughlin, Ronnie Yore, Fearghal Delaney, Kevin Moyles, Niall Murphy, Neil O Dwyer.
Back: Duncan Geraghty, Paul Sheehy, Paddy McHale, Eoin Hagarty, James Kelliher, Stephen Clusker, Cillian Finn, David McMahon, Brian Murphy, Christopher Carey, Dara Devereux, John Coleman.

the lead. Pádraic O Dwyer and David McCormack added two more points and that was enough to see Dunshaughlin home on a 0-7 to 0-5 scoreline. The semi-final matched them against St. Brigids and the north Meath side had an easy 1-16 to 1-8 victory. St. Brigids extended their three point half time advantage as Dunshaughlin could only muster two second half scores, a goal from Simon Farrell and a point.

Opponents St. Brigids fielded their first team whereas by now Dunshaughlin's senior team had already used twenty players. It was a team populated in the main by young players; only Shane Kelly and Kevin Moyles had experience of senior championship football with the legendary three in a row side. So it was a creditable result, adding fuel to the argument that the club should have dropped down a grade a couple of years earlier.

The 2009 outfit went closest of all to progressing to a final. With four wins from four in the group stages the team eliminated Ratoath in the quarter-final by the minimum margin, 1-11 to 1-10. Semi-final opponents Duleek-Bellewstown had two or three players whose talent entitled them to a place on their senior side but they managed to elude the privilege. By the time the semi-final took place Dunshaughlin had lost three crucial players to the senior side. Their departure was significant for the trio, Cillian Finn, Conor Devereux and Paddy McHale, had scored 1-5 between them in the first junior outing.

The sides had to meet twice to decide the outcome. The initial encounter went to extra time as Duleek matched Dunshaughlin's 3-10 with 2-13 of their own. The early loss of the dominant Graham Dowd through injury was a severe blow but his replacement Duncan Geraghty gave an outstanding performance in the centre of the field. Despite this, Dunshaughlin struggled to stay in touch and as injury time beckoned Duleek-Bellewstown held a five point lead. David Devereux shaved two points off the deficit before, deep in additional time, wing back Fearghal Gogan pushed forward in support of the attack, grabbed a pass from Niall Murphy and finished to the net to make it all-square.

Extra time was equally dramatic. Dunshaughlin keeper Christopher Carey couldn't field due to a freak injury incurred while celebrating Gogan's strike and replacement netminder Stephen Clusker's first task was to pick the ball out of his net after an early Duleek raid. David Devereux responded with a goal at the other end and then Niall Murphy netted with style to hand the initiative to the black and ambers. It wasn't enough as the east Meath combination dominated the final ten minutes, reduced the lead to two and replicated Dunshaughlin's achievement earlier by grabbing an equalizer at the death.

The replay was almost as close at the end but Duleek-Bellewstown held the upper hand in the third quarter and had built up a six point lead with as many minutes remaining. The black and ambers engineered a late scoring spurt with an Eamon Bowe point and a David Devereux goal from a penalty. With time almost up and persistent pressure on the Duleek defence Bowe tapped over another free kick believing there was enough time left to grab an equalizer. The final whistle sounded on the kick-out however, and Duleek emerged winners by 1-9 to 1-8, later going on to defeat Moynalty in the final. The team selectors were Michael McHale, Don McLoughlin and Noel McTigue and they choose the following team for the replay:

Stephen Clusker; Kevin Moyles, Brian Murphy, Fearghal Delaney; Fearghal Gogan, Ronnie Yore, Tadhg Ó Dúshláine; Paddy McHale (0-1), Duncan Geraghty (0-1); Dara Devereux, David Devereux (1-2), Ciarán Clusker; Eamon Bowe (0-2), Eoin Hagarty (0-1), Niall Murphy (0-1). Subs: David McMahon for Delaney, Alan McLoughlin for Dara Devereux, Shane Kelly for Hagarty, Mark Devanney for McMahon.

In 2007, 2008 and 2011 the team's interest in the championship ended at the quarter-final stage. Apart from a five-point loss to Walterstown in 2007 the other defeats were by margins of one and two points, St Vincents' first team winning by the minimum amount in 2008 and Ratoath's seconds by two points in 2011. Thus, in the years since being regarded to Junior B in 2006 the side had reached three quarter-finals and two semis, failing to make the knockout stages once only, in 2010.

Dunshaughlin, Junior B Winners, 2012

Front: Shane Kelly, Cillian Dennehy, David Tonge, Seán Doyle, John Joe McDonnell, Capt., with Ulick McDonnell, Jnr., Daniel Geraghty, James Rattigan, with Evan Darby, David McMahon, Kevin Ward, John Coleman, Liam Ormsby.
Back: Martin Reilly, Niall Kelly, David Fletcher, Michael Ahern, Eoin Farrelly, Ciarán Clusker, Ulick McDonnell, Mark Devanney, Stephen Ward, David Crimmins, Graham Dowd, Patrick Darby, Stephen Doyle, Emmet Staunton, Simon Farrell, Gavin Malone, Gary Flanagan, Duncan Geraghty. Missing Michael McHale, Team Manager.

> James Rattigan was the hero of the hour notching all but one of the winners' scores. His accuracy from frees punished the Saints' indiscretions and the crucial score was his goal direct from a forty-five during the second quarter.

The saga of good, but not good enough, came to an end in 2012 when the Bs powered their way to the final. Victories in the early rounds against Gaeil Colmcille and St. Marys and in the final two outings against St. Patricks and Moynalvey more than compensated for a shuddering defeat by Donaghmore-Ashbourne in the third round. The results were good enough to place the team on top of the group table and propel it directly into a semi-final meeting with St. Vincents.

The Saints were fielding their first team as the sides met under lights in Ashbourne and were most people's favourites for the county title. They had ample opportunities to reach the final but a combination of great goalkeeping from Seán Doyle and some good luck favouring the black and ambers kept Dunshaughlin in front at the end. James Rattigan was the hero of the hour notching all but one of the winners' scores. His accuracy from frees punished the Saints' indiscretions and the crucial score was his goal direct from a forty-five during the second quarter. It enabled Dunshaughlin carry a five-point lead to the dressing room at half time and it was needed in the final half hour when St. Vincents took command.

They gradually whittled the lead away as Dunshaughlin failed to score until the closing five minutes but the crucial move of the game was the introduction of Michael Ahern, just back from Singapore. He used his senior experience and fitness to hold St. Vincents at bay while Rattigan converted another free and Kevin Ward surged into attack before slotting the ball over the bar. The Vins reduced the margin to the minimum but in a dramatic finale couldn't force extra time. The black and ambers

CHAPTER 18: THE JUNIOR CHALLENGE, 1995-2012

emerged victorious by 1-7 to 0-9 to qualify for the final for the first time since the 1994 victory over Syddan.

Training which had been haphazard and optional prior to the semi-final suddenly became popular as the final loomed. The side was boosted by the return of Niall Kelly from honeymoon and the continued presence of Michael Ahern while others adding their senior experience were the two Davids, Crimmins and Tonge. Graham Dowd would have made a fourth from the three in a row era but injury ruled him out.

Opponents St. Marys were more than a match for Dunshaughlin in the intermediate grade during the 1990s but they had fallen on hard times later, dropping down to Junior A and then into the B grade. Nevertheless, Dunshaughlin would be facing the East Meath's side's first team so the outcome was difficult to predict. A second round meeting of the sides that resulted in a fortuitous three-point victory for Dunshaughlin pointed to a close contest.

On the day, Dunshaughlin's greater strength in depth swung the contest in their favour. St. Marys remained in contention until the closing stages but their inability to score from play proved to be their Achilles' heel. Surprisingly, Dunshaughlin's reliance on James Rattigan for scores, which was so marked against St. Vincents, wasn't evident in the final and Michael Ahern, Niall Kelly, Stephen Ward and David McMahon joined him on the scoreboard.

Dunshaughlin held a narrow interval advantage, 0-6 to 0-5 and a brace of early second half Rattigan points, one from play and one from a free, pushed his side three

Dunshaughlin captain, John Joe McDonnell, addresses the crowd following his side's Junior B triumph in 2012. Also shown are James Rattigan, Mark Devanney- partly hidden holding the trophy aloft, John Coleman and Ciarán Clusker. Supporters behind the players include Pat Maloney and Patsy McLoughlin, wearing cap, and behind them Linda and Dominic Devereux.

A Penny for Your Thoughts?
Selectors Martin Reilly and Simon Farrell in deep thought during the 2012 Junior B Final.

 Training which had been haphazard and optional prior to the semi-final suddenly became popular as the final loomed.

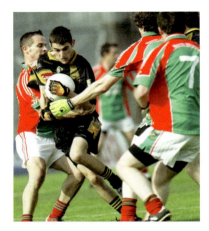

James Rattigan
'No one is going to stop me'.

Stephen Ward
A study in style against St. Marys.

ahead. St. Marys' best period followed and three successive pointed frees drew the sides level entering the final quarter. The Saints then had an opportunity to seal the deal but Seán Doyle diverted Robbie Callaghan's well-struck low drive onto the base of the upright and Dunshaughlin worked the ball out of the danger zone. The miss seemed to deflate St. Marys and Dunshaughlin struck for three vital points in the closing stages.

Wing-back Mark Devanney made a key interception and set up Stephen Ward for the lead, James Rattigan doubled the advantage with an outstanding point following a pass from David Crimmins and Niall Kelly revived memories of the glory days with a trademark point off a lengthy free kick. There was still time for a desperate St. Marys to lay siege to the Dunshaughlin goal but resolute defending from John Joe and Ulick McDonnell, Mark Devanney and Kevin Ward ensured victory by 0-12 to 0-9. Michael Ahern gave a man of the match performance at centre field and in defence while Stephen Ward displayed his formidable repertoire of skill in the number eleven jersey, setting up scores while grabbing three points for himself.

John Joe McDonnell accepted the Larry Kearns Cup on behalf of the following team managed by Michael McHale with Simon Farrell and Martin Reilly as selectors.

Seán Doyle

John Joe McDonnell, Capt.   Ulick McDonnell   Kevin Ward

Eoin Farrelly   Niall Kelly (0-2)   Mark Devanney

Michael Ahern (0-1)   Ciarán Clusker

David Tonge   Stephen Ward (0-3)   David McMahon (0-1)

Daniel Geraghty   David Crimmins   James Rattigan (0-5)

Subs: Emmet Staunton for Clusker, John Coleman for Geraghty, Duncan Geraghty for Tonge, Shane Kelly, Graham Dowd, Cillian Dennehy, Patrick Darby, Liam Ormsby, Stephen Doyle, David Fletcher, Gavin Malone, Gary Flanagan.

By winning the championship the two Geraghtys, Daniel and Duncan, were replicating the achievement of their father, Donnchadh, in the same grade in 1994 while Graham Dowd's brother Clive also featured on the victorious side eighteen years previously.

Victory in the championship elevated the team to Junior A status for 2013, a grade that has always proven a step too steep in recent years. Nevertheless, the team rose to the challenge, advancing to the quarter-finals where Kilmainham's first team proved too strong. James Rattigan gave an outstanding display of score taking, recording one hundred per cent of Dunshaughlin's total, an imposing 1-8. Despite this initial flourish the club will probably find it difficult to maintain A status in the longer term and a single victory in 2014 doesn't augur well.

CHAPTER 18: THE JUNIOR CHALLENGE, 1995-2012

Junior C, 1995-2014

From 1995 to 2011 the club's third team participated in the Junior C championship and getting sufficient bodies on the field was the biggest initial challenge. Usually, about forty players who play senior or Junior B are ahead of the Junior C players in the pecking order. It can be a test of gargantuan proportions to source eligible players and persuade them to turn out. Since entering a third team in the 1990s the Junior Cs have reached two quarter-finals and a semi. The quarter-final appearances came in successive years, 2001 and 2002, when the senior team was in its pomp and there were few kudos for managing or playing on the most junior side.

The 2001 team had a circuitous route to the knock-out stage. Captain Mick Summerville noted that despite losing the first game, 'more lads dusted off their boots and started back training' and they benefitted from working along with Eamonn Barry and the seniors. In addition the team wasn't depleted as much as usual with the higher teams using fewer players that year.

Two wins and a draw following the first round loss to Dunboyne set up a play-off between the Duns. This time Dunshaughlin overturned the earlier result to qualify for a preliminary quarter-final. Mick Summerville, writing in the Club Newsletter in August 2001 upped the ante by announcing that 'Lally has promised us an all-expenses trip to Thailand should we make the quarter-finals' and added "I'd say a round the world trip would be in order were we to win the championship!!'

The team recorded a comprehensive victory against Kilmainhamwood and qualified for the quarter-final proper. Starting without the club's first forty-seven players, a side managed by Lally McCormack, Oliver Gogan and George Ennis finally met its match as Simonstown Gaels triumphed by 3-18 to 3-5. The proposed trip to Thailand had to be abandoned!

The following year the team again emerged from its group and faced Boardsmill's first team. Dunshaughlin held a six-point interval lead and a Stephen Ward goal extended it to an unassailable looking nine on the resumption. The black and ambers failed to score again however, and Keith Hamilton salvaged a draw with eight of his side's nine points.

The second meeting was close throughout. Boardsmill established a four-point lead late in the second half but near the end Stephen Ward closed the deficit to three, and then on the stroke of full-time Rory Bowe fired a dramatic goal to force extra time. Boardsmill took control in the additional half hour, outscoring the black and ambers 0-9 to 0-3 to give them a deserved victory by 0-21 to 2-9 and went on to capture the title. The replay capped a series of very creditable

> 'Lally has promised us an all-expenses trip to Thailand should we make the quarter-finals' and . . . "I'd say a round the world trip would be in order were we to win the championship!!'

performances from a young Dunshaughlin team, among them future Meath senior star, Caoimhín King. Ollie Gogan and Georgie Ennis again assisted Lally McCormack with team management and the following team faced Boardsmill in the quarter-final replay:

James Whyte; Brian Murphy, Fionnán Blake, Pearse Fahy; Declan Fahy, Caoimhín King, Owen Herlihy; Robbie Keane (0-1), Paul Sheehy; Kevin Ward, Dessie Keane (0-1), Rory Bowe (1-1); George Ennis, Stephen Ward (1-5), Mick Summerville. Subs: David Tormay for Summerville, Eoin Farrelly for Dessie Keane, Gavin O Regan for Whyte, Mark West for Stephen Ward, Damien Minnock for Ennis, Ciarán Hoary (0-1) for Tormey.

With a number of the young players moving up to the higher grade the following two years brought no success but in 2005, the Junior Cs again made good progress with Mick Summerville, Pat Herlihy and George Ennis making up the managerial team. Four wins and just one defeat was the outcome of the group stages. It included impressive displays against Dunboyne, Skryne and Seneschalstown, and qualified the side to meet Wolfe Tones in the quarter-final.

The sides were evenly matched throughout, including at the interval by which stage they shared eight points. The crucial score arrived midway through the second half when Ciarán Hoary slotted home a penalty to put his side two points in front. A late goal from Declan Fahy gave Dunshaughlin a safety margin of four points and almost guaranteed victory. However, it turned out to be a vital score, as when the Tones goaled in injury time Dunshaughlin's margin was down to the minimum. The black and ambers held on and won by 2-7 to 2-6.

The semi-final turned out to be an insurmountable challenge. Though the first half was close and Dunshaughlin were level early in the second, once St. Colmcilles scored their first goal the outcome was never in doubt. The seasiders had five points to spare at the end, 2-11 to 1-9, but Dunshaughlin's goal from Simon Farrell didn't arrive until the closing stages.

Since then the main achievement has been fielding a team throughout the championship. Emigration of young players has taken a severe toll on the club and many who would normally man the Junior C team have had to move up to Junior B level to fill the vacancies. This has significantly weakened the third team and at the end of 2011 the club dropped down to the Junior D grade. The best year at the lowest grade was 2013 when three victories put the team into a quarter-final where they fell four points short of Seneschalstown.

Dunshaughlin is one of the few clubs able to field a third team in the championship and getting a team on the field is a significant achievement with great credit due to Shane Kelly and his selectors.

All County B Football League, Higher Divisions, 1995-2014

As outlined in Chapter 10, competitive, well-organized league structures with promotion and relegation date from 1986. Soon after a Reserve league was instituted for clubs willing and able to field two teams and Dunshaughlin won the 1989 league and were runners-up in 1990 as recorded in Chapter 11.

In the 1990s such was the demand from clubs for a subsidiary league that a single Reserve League wasn't adequate. Instead an All County B League began with three divisions initially, expanding to six by 2011. Teams participating had to name their fifteen best players for the A League. Such players were confined to playing in the A League and all other players were then eligible to play in the B League. Clubs could put two teams into the B Leagues, and if so doing, had to name a second fifteen who could not play for the lowest graded team.

From 1998 Dunshaughlin always entered two teams in the B Leagues, the stronger side in Division 1 or 2 and the weaker team in Division 3 or 4. The leagues suffer from a number of defects. In particular, they often provide a surfeit of games early in the year and a scarcity later with finals nevertheless often taking place in the depths of winter.

Despite this, they provide a regular diet of competitive football for all abilities, the relegation and promotion system ensures interest is maintained throughout the year and clubs have the opportunity of winning a league title. The subsidiary championships on their own do not provide sufficient football, especially for young developing players. The GAA's Strategic Review recommended in 2002 that each adult player should expect a minimum of twenty games

Dunshaughlin, All County B League, Division 1 Winners, 1999

Front: David Crimmins, Pádraic O Dwyer, Kevin Kealy, Declan Fahy, Brendan Kealy, Fearghal Gogan, Shane Kelly, Capt., David McNerney, Trevor Dowd, Neil O Dwyer, Simon Farrell.
Back: Neil Halpin, Team Manager, Kevin Moyles, Michael McHale, Ulick McDonnell, Brian Murphy, Paddy McHale, Ronan Gogan, Garbhán Blake, George Ennis, Christopher Carey, Niall Foley, Alan O Dwyer, Fergus O Rourke, Selector. Missing from picture: John Davis and selector Martin Summerville.

> With Neil Halpin, Fergus O Rourke and Martin Summerville in charge of operations the side powered its way to the final.

per annum. The leagues go some way towards fulfilling this obligation.

In the early years of the B League Dunshaughlin usually finished in mid-table but in 1999 reached the final having finished near the top of the table. The first outing in the league hadn't been very auspicious as the selectors struggled to put fifteen on the field against Trim but managed to eke out a four-point victory. The side featured a host of young players, all under twenty, who would go on to play prominent roles in the three in a row side, Ronan and Fearghal Gogan, Michael and Paddy McHale, David Crimmins and Trevor Dowd. There was also a dash of experience with four players from the successful St. Martins' minor sides of 1987-89, John Davis, Simon Farrell, Garbhán Blake and Brendan Kealy. With Neil Halpin, Fergus O Rourke and Martin Summerville in charge of operations the side powered its way to the decider.

Summerhill shaded the first half of the final with Billy Shaw accurate from frees but Dunshaughlin dominated the second, drew level at the end of the third quarter and moved ahead when the impressive Trevor Dowd netted from a penalty. Victory looked assured after David McNerney added a second two minutes later but Shaw continued to knock over points and narrowed the gap to three. The decisive score came when Paddy McHale struck Dunshaughlin's third goal for a 3-9 to 0-9 victory. The team lined out as follows:

Ronan Gogan
John Davis   Ulick McDonnell   Shane Kelly, Capt.
Kevin Moyles   Fearghal Gogan   Garbhán Blake
Simon Farrell   Kevin Kealy
David Crimmins (0-1)   Brendan Kealy (0-1)   David McNerney (1-0)
Paddy McHale (1-1)   Michael McHale (0-1)   Trevor Dowd (1-5)
Subs: Pádraic O Dwyer for Crimmins, Christopher Carey, Declan Fahy, Niall Foley, Alan O Dwyer, Neil O Dwyer, Brian Murphy, George Ennis.

Unlike championship teams, league teams can change substantially from year to year as the better players move up to the higher levels and players on the way down move to lower grades or retire. Many of those who lined out against Summerhill were earmarked for the senior league and championship and in the period 2000-05 the B team won an average of half their games each year and hovered round the middle of the table. Results disimproved in 2006 and the team dropped to Division 2 where they enjoyed a short sojourn before ascending upwards again.

It took the team a year to adjust to its reduced status as it finished mid-table with three wins and a walkover balanced by four losses. There was a huge improvement in 2008 with just one loss during the league stages, to Donaghmore-

CHAPTER 18: THE JUNIOR CHALLENGE, 1995-2012

Dunshaughlin, All County B League, Division 2, Winners, 2008

Front: Pádraic O Dwyer, Eamon Bowe, Fearghal Delaney, Ciarán Farrelly, Trevor Dowd, Tadhg Ó Dúshláine, Michael Johnson, Ciarán Hoary, Kevin Moyles, Donnacha Lloyd, John Coleman.
Back: Brian Murphy, Neil O Dwyer, Dara Devereux, Tommy Johnson, Stephen Clusker, David Devereux, Alan McLoughlin, Niall Dundon, Eoin Hagarty, Graham Dowd, Capt., Seán Doyle, Paddy McHale, Mark Devanney, Shane Kelly.

Ashbourne. As often happens, the sides renewed acquaintance in the final, under lights in Ashbourne in early November. It was a case of venturing into the lion's den as weather conditions ruled out the original venue, and in the interests of a speedy conclusion to a very long campaign Dunshaughlin agreed to play on their opponents' home patch.

Spectators enjoyed a close encounter with Dunshaughlin establishing an early lead and Donaghmore-Ashbourne reducing it as the game drew to a conclusion. Highlights of the first half included a miraculous Stephen Clusker save, three successive points from Trevor Dowd and a triple save by the Ashbourne keeper from a Dowd penalty. It all added up to a solid seven points to two lead when the half ended.

It wasn't an impregnable shield as Donaghmore returned in a more determined mood and gradually reduced the deficit, point by point. Though David Devereux pointed early on, Dunshaughlin's scoring prowess faltered and with the countdown to the long whistle well under way the sides were deadlocked on ten points. Enter super sub Shane Kelly. A man equally at home in defence or attack, he took a sublime pass from Mark Devanney, raced clear of the despairing defenders and, forty metres from the Donaghmore posts, steadied himself and with his trusty left peg drilled the ball in a looping arc between the uprights. It was a score worthy of a final and enough to earn his side the trophy, 0-11 to 0-10. Shane's colleague from the three in a row side, Graham Dowd, captained the following team, managed by Don McLoughlin with his co-selectors Simon Farrell and Noel McTigue.

Captains and Finals

Captains and Finals
Above: Dunshaughlin's Kevin Moyles and O Mahony's Ian Matthews meet before the Division 1 B League final in 2009.

Graham Dowd, captain of the 2008 B League, Division 2 winning team, accepts the trophy from Brian Carberry.

                    Stephen Clusker
Donnacha Lloyd   Tommy Johnson   Fearghal Delaney
Alan McLoughlin   Kevin Moyles   Tadhg Ó Dúshláine
        Graham Dowd, Capt.   Ciarán Farrelly
Dara Devereux   Trevor Dowd (0-6)   Ciarán Hoary
Eamon Bowe (0-2)   David Devereux (0-1)   Michael Johnson (0-1)

Subs: Niall Dundon for Dara Devereux, Brian Murphy for Lloyd, Shane Kelly (0-1) for Ó Dúshláine, Mark Devanney for Delaney, Seán Doyle, Eoin Hagarty, Duncan Geraghty, Mark Caldwell, John Coleman, Paddy McHale, Neil O Dwyer.

Qualification for the final also brought promotion back up to Division 1 in 2009, a daunting prospect after relegation three years earlier. A huge loss to Skryne in the first outing seemed to presage a difficult campaign. Instead, six victories catapulted the team into contention for a place in the final and victory over Wolfe Tones in the final game in late November achieved it.

Prospective opponents Navan O Mahonys inflicted an eight-point defeat on Dunshaughlin earlier in the year so the final posed a major challenge. Although Dunshaughlin gave a determined, dogged display, it was not sufficient to contain the Navan side. Stephen Clusker was forced into action on a number of occasions, the highlight being a first half finger-tip save that turned a goal-bound effort over the bar.

O Mahonys held a two point lead by half time and in a closely contested second half they extended it by a further point to win 0-11 to 0-8. It was a double disappointment for many of the players as they had already lost the Junior B championship semi-final to Duleek-Bellewstown after a replay, as described earlier. Dunshaughlin's league team against Navan O Mahonys read:

Stephen Clusker; Kevin Moyles, Capt., Brian Murphy, Fearghal Delaney; Fearghal Gogan, Ronnie Yore, Tadhg Ó Dúshláine; Ray Maloney (0-1), Cillian Finn; Eoin Hagarty (0-1), Paddy McHale (0-1), Conor Devereux (0-2); David Devereux (0-1), John Crimmins (0-1), Niall Murphy (0-1). Subs: Eamon Bowe for Hagarty, David McMahon for Niall Murphy.

The team maintained its good form in 2010 finishing fourth in the table and topped that in 2011 winning six of the nine league games, which, along with a walkover, was enough to tie Dunshaughlin and old rivals Donaghmore-Ashbourne at the top of the table. As in 2008, the final venue was Ashbourne but this time the home side got the upper hand in a high quality game. A goal midway through the second half, when Tony Morgan tipped in the ball after Stephen Clusker had made an outstanding save, was the crucial score. Behind by 1-8 to 0-4, Dunshaughlin threatened a recovery with points from Emmet Staunton and

Richie Kealy either side of a brace from Martin Reilly to reduce the deficit to four. Donaghmore-Ashbourne were not to be denied however, and stretched the lead to five points before the end, 1-10 to 0-8. The starting team, with Graham Dowd, Michael McHale and TP Toolan as selectors, read:

Stephen Clusker; Kevin Moyles, Kenny McTigue, Mark Devanney; Kevin Ward, Fearghal Delaney, Anthony Johnson (0-1); Paddy McHale, Capt., Eoin Hagarty (0-1); Niall Kelly, Emmet Staunton (0-2), James Horgan; Ciarán Hoary, Martin Reilly (0-2), James Rattigan (0-1). Subs: Richie Kealy (0-1) for Hoary, Alan McLoughlin for Johnson, David McCormack for Rattigan, Daniel Geraghty for Moyles, Jamie Minnock.

The 2012 team seemed set for another tilt at a trophy after an opening run of three wins but could add only two more for the remainder of the year to finish in a respectable mid-table position. Similar placings resulted in 2013 and 2014.

All County B Football League, Lower Divisions, 1995-2014

From 1998 the club entered two teams in the Reserve League, later known as the B League, in Divisions 1 and 4A. The third team initially operated in Division 4A of the B League before dropping to Division 5. Teams generally lost more games than they won between 1998 and 2001 before turning in a good year in 2002 with five victories, and an outstanding one in 2003. With seven wins from nine games they finished level on points with Carnaross and those two top-dogs met in the final.

Dunshaughlin compiled a portfolio of impressive totals on their way to the decider, 3-14 against Donaghmore-Ashbourne, 3-18 against Summerhill and 5-17 against St. Marys. They put 1-11 past Carnaross in the league stages for a five point win so were warm favourites for the re-match in Bective. Captained by Dessie Keane, the black and ambers delivered for the bookies with another substantial total, 2-14, whereas Carnaross could only raise eight white flags. Cathal O Dwyer, as he was to do frequently at senior level in later years, topped the scoring charts with 1-7, though his cousins Neil and Ciarán would claim that the quality of the ball they supplied him made it possible! With his brother Pádraic coming on to score two points and brother-in-law Shane Byrne in goals it was a day to remember for the O Dwyer Fliers.

It wasn't just a one-clan show. Stephen Ward with four points and David McCormack with 1-1, the goal from a penalty just before the break, contributed to the final total. Carnaross were still in with a chance at the three-quarter stage but

> *Cathal O Dwyer, as he was to do frequently at senior level in later years, topped the scoring charts with 1-7, though his cousins Neil and Ciarán would claim that the quality of the ball they supplied him made it possible!*

CHAPTER 18: THE JUNIOR CHALLENGE, 1995-2012

Captain Keane Captures Cup
Dessie Keane captain of the Dunshaughlin Reserve League Division 5 team in 2003 accepts the cup from Cyril Creavin.

Wardie on the Ball
Kevin Ward in action against Carnaross in the Reserve League Division 5 final in 2003.

the superior Dunshaughlin full-forward line posted 1-6 to no reply in the closing fifteen minutes to wrap up the title by 2-14 to 0-8. When the club's premier team left the Division 1 title behind the following month, after a controversial end to the final with Walterstown, the Division 5 team had the distinction of being the only team in the club to bring home some silverware. After the avalanche of trophies between 2000 and 2002 failure to win anything could have produced severe withdrawal symptoms, so the league victory was a welcome success. Thirty-seven different players played for the side during the year and the team for the final was:

Shane Byrne
Brian Murphy   Noel McTigue   Neil O Dwyer
Ciarán O Dwyer   Hugo Lynch   Francis Darby
Owen Herlihy   Pearse Fahy
Dessie Keane, Capt.   Kevin Ward   John Joe McDonnell
David McCormack (1-1)   Stephen Ward (0-4)   Cathal O Dwyer (1-7)

Subs: Pádraic O Dwyer (0-2) for JJ McDonnell, Ciarán Hoary for Keane, Eoin Farrelly for Darby, Jamie Minnock, Alan Fahy, Ronan Murphy, Ronan O Dwyer, Alan O Dwyer, Derek Bevan, Paul Sheehy, Kevin Brennan, Gavin O Regan,

Dunshaughlin, B League Division 4, Runners Up, 2007

Front: Gerard O Brien, Pádraic O Dwyer, Martin Duffy, Fearghal Delaney, Ciarán Clusker, Mick Summerville, with Cathal McCormack, Mark Caldwell, Eoin Farrelly, Cathal Moore, Shane Kelly, Paul Hendrick, Christopher Carey, Pat Gargan, Selector. Back: Lally McCormack, Team Manager, Hugh Lynch, John Joe McDonnell, Tadhg Ó Dúshláine, Tadhg Woods, Gerry Keenan, Niall Dundon, Mark Devanney, Owen Herlihy, Ray Yore, Ronan Murphy, Simon Farrell, George Ennis. Philip Bevan, Declan Fahy, Joseph McHale. Selectors: Lally McCormack, Oliver Gogan and Hugh McCarthy.

Victory ensured automatic promotion to Division 4 and the team coped exceptionally well in the higher grade. In fact four years later the club qualified for the Division 4 final. This time the winning scores in the league stages were more modest but the team didn't drop a point en-route to the final. As in 2003, the 2007 side got the better of its final opposition in the league stages, defeating Rathkenny on the latter's home turf by 1-11 to 0-9.

The defects of the league mentioned earlier were evident in the run-up to the final. Dunshaughlin's first outing was in late March and the team had qualified for the final by late August. There was then a long delay until the decider in mid October and the momentum built up during the summer was interrupted by the two-month interval. During those two months Rathkenny had a couple of games including a must-win tie with Moylagh and probably entered the final the sharper of the two sides.

Despite the disadvantages Dunshaughlin saw possible victory plucked from them in the closing stages. It was close throughout with Rathkenny's ability to score points balanced by Dunshaughlin's facility for crucial goals. A Pádraic O Dwyer penalty put his side ahead but Rathkenny leveled by half time. The North Meath side then stretched two clear before the introduction of Gerard O Brien paid dividends when he pounced on a long delivery and finished to the net. Niall Dundon added to the advantage but Rathkenny methodically hauled back the lead and edged in front.

In the closing stages Pádraic O Dwyer pointed and Mark Caldwell seemed to assure victory with a late point. Unfortunately for Dunshaughlin there was time for another twist in the tale. Rathkenny substitute Emmet Martin calmly slotted the equalizer with three minutes of play remaining and then Richie Timmons claimed his sixth point, the lead and victory on a final score of 0-13 to 2-6. Lally McCormack with co-selectors Hugo Lynch and Pat Herlihy managed the following team:

Christopher Carey; Ray Yore, Martin Duffy, Eoin Farrelly; Ciarán Clusker, Owen Herlihy, Mark Devanney; Shane Kelly, Simon Farrell; Fearghal Delaney, Gerry Keenan, Mick Summerville, Capt.; Niall Dundon (0-1), Pádraic O Dwyer (1-3), Mark Caldwell (0-2). Subs: Tadhg Ó Dúshláine for Summerville, Gerard O Brien (1-0) for Keenan, Cathal Moore for Duffy, Paul Hendrick for Devanney.

By reaching the final the team progressed to Division 3 for 2008. This however, was a step too far as the club had gone from Division 5 to two grades higher in five years. Though able to compete at the higher level in 2008 and 2009, by 2011 the team was struggling against other club's second teams. The loss of all games that year resulted in a return to Division 4 for 2012, a milieu more suited to the introduction of new players and an environment that provides more competitive encounters. Although finishing second last in 2013, the team has usually attained comfortable mid-table status. Ominously however, emigration, as well as the usual call of the Leaving Certificate and other exams in early summer can create difficulties fielding a third team in the league at certain times during the year.

BLACK & AMBER

The Royal Gaels

Various names were considered, but Ollie's own suggestion of Royal Gaels found favour with the vast majority. The inspiration for his choice was the title of Peter McDermott's book about Meath's trip to Australia in 1968, Gaels in the Sun.

In July 1974 the Ladies' Gaelic Football Association was officially formed in Hayes' Hotel, Thurles with four counties, Tipperary, Offaly, Galway and Kerry represented. Later in the year Tipperary defeated Offaly by 2-3 to 2-2 to become the first All-Ireland Ladies' champions.

Ladies' football did exist before this, but, it was only in the 1960s that the sport became popular. The late development of the game is surprising, given that camogie dates back to 1904 and while that sport had its peaks and troughs it survived throughout the century.

Many in authority frowned on ladies' sport. The GAA made no provision for games involving females in its early years and the Catholic Church often expressed its disapproval of girls playing in public. Pope Pius XI declared in 1928 that sport was 'irreconcilable with women's reserve' and 'unbecoming that they should flaunt themselves and display themselves, before the eyes of all.' John Charles McQuaid, later Archbishop of Dublin, fulminated against mixed athletics in 1934, declaring that 'Mixed athletics and all cognate immodesties are abuses that right-minded people reprobate, wherever and whenever they exist.' Two decades later he was of the same view expressing his 'grave disapproval of the practice of permitting young women to compete in cycling and athletics in mixed public sports.'

His reactionary views were soon overtaken by events, however. During the

> Many in authority frowned on ladies' sport. The GAA made no provision for games involving females in its early years and the Catholic Church often expressed its disapproval of girls playing in public.

1960s carnivals and festivals were common throughout the country and organizing committees were always looking for novel methods of boosting attendances. Thus, challenge games were organized between local schools as they would attract the children's parents. Ladies' football provided another attraction and local teams played each other in front of curious spectators. Reports of such games can be found in newspapers published in Galway, Offaly, Waterford, Tipperary, Cork and Kerry, among others. In the late 1960s a competition began in Meath involving eight clubs, among them Fyanstown, Moynalty, Cormeen, Moylagh, Bellewstown and Simonstown but it appears to have been short lived.

Prior to this there were two ladies' teams in the Dunshaughlin area. The first to be formed was The Red Devils. The team flourished in the late sixties and consisted of Nora Carty, Lena Doyle, later the first Secretary of St. Martins, Nuala Walsh, Ann Coyle, Maggie Hughes, Margaret Brady, Ann Tugwell, Miriam Sheridan, Imelda Coyle and Ann Lynch. The team trained in Drumree alongside the males and the trainers included Hughie, Raymond and Thomas Carty. Nobody knows precisely why the team was called the Red Devils, but it was probably linked to the Drumree colours. Initially the team was seven a side but with more recruits it later developed into fifteen a side and wore red and white knitted tops.

The team took part in a number of tournaments, winning most of them, including the Rolestown Tournament in 1968. The Devils defeated St. Margarets, Ballyboughal and Garristown and overcame Ardcath in the final, 1-8 to 1-3. The team also played a game against Clane, as a curtain raiser to a Meath v. Kildare championship game.

A second side was associated with the Macra na Feirme club formed in Dunshaughlin in April 1965. Macra is a rural youth organization, aimed primarily at young people involved in agriculture, but open to all, and providing a social scene incorporating drama, debating, sport and travel. In 1968 the Dunshaughlin branch set up a ladies' football team that competed at sports' days and carnivals in south Meath and Dublin.

Initially the team wore ordinary clothes and leggings but later bought a set of jerseys. A proposal that participants be allowed wear football boots was vetoed at a meeting of Macra in Navan so the ladies in the main wore runners. Shaun McTigue trained the side that included his future wife Margaret Carty, her sisters Carmel (now Yore), Joan (now Caffrey), Anne, (now Gray), Breege Monaghan (mother of champion jockey, Barry Geraghty), Rita and Olivia O Hare, (now Fleming and Darby) Julieanne Flynn (now Clinton), Breege and Phil McDonnell, (both married to Colgan brothers), Josie Blake (now Mrs. McDonnell), Josie Neary (Edward Veith in Colorado, USA).

Dunshaughlin Macra Ladies' Team, 1968

Front: Olivia O Hare, Josie Neary, Margaret Carty, Carmel Carty.
Back: Breege Monaghan, Josie Blake, Joan Carty, Rita O Hare, Julieanne Flynn.

Red Devils' Ladies' Team

ANNUAL SPORTS will be held in G.A.A. Grounds, Dunshaughlin, on Sunday, 30th June
Commencing 6.30 p.m. sharp.
1st Item: LADIES' FOOTBALL CHALLENGE
Dunshaughlin Macra Na Feirme v. The Red Devils.
Programme Includes:
BOYS' CHAMPIONSHIP RACE FOR TRADERS' CUP.
Other Races for Boys and Girls, Youths and Men. Also Sack, Wheelbarrow and 3-Legged Races.
ADMISSION 2/-.   CHILDREN 6d.
Competitors pay at gate.   Minerals, Ices, etc. available.

Local Rivalry, Macra v. The Red Devils
Advertisement for Dunshaughlin Sports, June 1968 with the ladies' football game between the Macra team and the Red Devils as the centrepiece.

Red Devils' Ladies' team pictured at a soccer competition.
All the players played Gaelic Football also.
Front: Ann Power, Vera Gantley, Nora Carty.
Back: Olive Clusker, Nuala Burke, Lena Walsh.

> By the late sixties both ladies' teams had disbanded. There was no organized competitive league or championship for the teams and as the ladies retired or married there were no replacements to maintain the teams.

Training took place in McDonnell's field in Bonestown, on the Ratoath Road. Games were usually against other Macra clubs as many of them held annual field days during the summer and autumn and the ladies' games provided the centrepiece of the action. The team even featured on national television, performing on *The Riordans*, the most popular 'soap' of the day.

The Macra team played at Garristown, Skryne, Bohernabreena, the Mullagh and Athboy. The two local clubs eventually had a showdown when the Red Devils played the Macra in the GAA grounds. There was huge rivalry between the sides and a large crowd turned out to see the game, which the Macra side won.

By the late sixties both ladies' teams had disbanded. There was no organized competitive league or championship at the time and as the ladies retired or married there were no replacements to maintain the teams. An effort was made to reestablish a ladies' team in 1976 when Anne Power and Peggy Cottrell sought permission to use the GAA field for practice and games. Verbal consent was granted but the GAA club baulked at giving written permission, as this would imply the ladies were insured when using the grounds. A number of players, all adults, took part in training but an injury to one of them led to a rethink and the idea was abandoned. This was at the same time that properly structured ladies' competitions commenced in Meath and Cormeen became the first ever Meath champions in 1975. It would be almost twenty years before a club was again established in Dunshaughlin.

St. Martins' Ladies

In late 1993 Mary Kelly suggested the idea of an underage girls' team to the St. Martins' Committee. She and Ann Power, with help from Siobhán Cartúir, began coaching sessions on Friday evenings and large numbers of girls, ranging in age from nine to fourteen, turned out. Membership money was collected but no games were played, as it was late in the year. The following year Gabriel King assisted as a mentor while St. Martins provided footballs and jerseys. By this stage a number of underage girls' teams had been established in the county, including Ratoath, where Mary Kelly's daughter Siobhán initially played, Dunsany, featuring Karen Ward, and Blackhall Gaels.

The club founders were intent on registering the club with the Meath Ladies' Football Board and compiled a list of girls who paid a membership fee of £5 per family. The historic group that formed the core of the club was: Jennifer Duffy, Laoise Kinsella, Edel Walsh, Rachel Barrett, Christine McManus, Sarah Morgan, Caroline Duffy, Angela Byrne, Orlaith Duffy, Karen Bowe, Lorna Brady, Áine McKenna, Gráinne Kelly, Fiona Murray, Olivia O Neill, Emma Russell, Sarah

Mary Kelly, organizer of a Girls' Under 14 team with St. Martins in 1993 that predated the formation of Royal Gaels.

Dunshaughlin NS Girls' Team, 1994-95

The earliest known picture of a Girls' GAA team in Dunshaughlin NS. This picture predates the founding of the Royal Gaels.
Front: Elaine Fagan, Edel McDonnell, Karen Ward, Siobhán Gogan, Glenda Faughnan, Lynda Fairbrother.
Back: Cora McTigue, Caoimhe Delany, Angela Flanagan, Gillian O Regan, Karen McManus, Karen Daly.

Boland, Lorraine Tallon, Deirdre Kane, Sylvia Brennan, Maria Kealy, Aoife Tallon, Olivia Power, Caroline Curran, Ciara McHale, Rachel Mahon, Donna Brennan, Orla Power, Siobhán King and Caroline King. The only team fielded was an Under-14 side as there was no Under 12 competition until 1997.

However, efforts to formally affiliate the club as St. Martins fell foul of the Meath Ladies' Football Board. For reasons still not entirely clear the Board refused to accept an affiliation, apparently on the grounds that they could not affiliate boys and girls under the one banner. Thus, the team's activities were confined to training and playing challenge games but the most significant development was the arrival of Ollie Bowe as coach. Ollie had played underage with Drumconrath and Kilberry and with Dunshaughlin at senior and junior level and he was to be instrumental in the establishment and growth of a new club.

In view of the obstacles to affiliating as St. Martins, Ollie decided in 1995 that a new approach was needed. The girls were growing restless with the lack of progress and he suggested a completely new club. The girls' parents arranged a meeting on 12th August to consider the future and the outcome was the formation of Royal Gaels. Various names were considered, but Ollie's own suggestion of Royal Gaels found favour with the vast majority. The inspiration for his choice was the title of Peter McDermott's book about Meath's trip to Australia in 1968, *Gaels in the Sun*.

> efforts to formally affiliate the club as St. Martins fell foul of the Meath Ladies' Football Board.

BLACK & AMBER

The First Ladies
Official list of the girls it was hoped to affiliate as St. Martins in 1994, signed by club Secretary Cyril Creavin.

Thus, the Royal Gaels came into existence. Those in attendance at the meeting were Mary Kelly, John Morgan, Ead Kealy, Maura O Neill, Doris Tugwell, Mary McConnon, Anita King, Catherine McHale, Róisín Farrell, Angela Donnelly, Marian Kane, Ann Power and Ollie Bowe. Joint Chairpersons were elected, Catherine McHale and Ead Kealy sharing the role, with Ann Power chosen as Secretary and Maura O Neill and Marian Kane as Treasurer and PRO respectively. The club elected to use the Dunshaughlin colours, black and amber, and local butcher Karl McEnroe sponsored the first set of jerseys.

Though the club was up and running, controversy and confusion continued to dog it. In its first full year in existence Ollie Bowe steered the fledgling club to an Under 14 county final only for an objection to scupper the girls' chances. The Gaels recorded a 5-3 to 0-9 semi-final triumph but opponents Moylagh objected to the presence of Kathryn Farrell and Ailish Byrne on the team. Both girls attended primary and secondary school in Dunshaughlin and resided in Lagore just outside Dunshaughlin, but in Ratoath parish. Moylagh objected on the grounds that the players should play with the parish in which they resided and the County Board upheld their objection.

Though Royal Gaels received what they described as 'a sympathetic hearing' from Leinster Council, the provincial body ruled against them and the girls missed the opportunity of a final appearance. The controversy overshadowed the achievement of reaching a decider so early in the club's history, an achievement that augured well for the future.

The victorious Gaels' side against Moylagh read: Ciara McHale; Gráinne Kelly, Olivia O Neill; Maria Kealy, Ailish Byrne, Siobhán King; Karen Bowe, Deirdre Kane; Kathryn Farrell, Fiona Murray, Shona Donoghue; Caroline King, Aileen Creavin. Subs: Sarah Morgan, Sharon Tugwell, Olivia Power.

Nevertheless, the club was establishing a pedigree with four players selected on the Meath Under 14 panel that won the 1996 All-Ireland final at the expense of Monaghan, Siobhán King, Ciara McHale, Deirdre Kane and Karen Bowe. During the late nineties many others featured on Meath teams at provincial and All-Ireland levels. In 1998 the Under 14s, including Caroline King, Maria Kealy and Deirdre Mooney, missed out on adding an All-Ireland title to their earlier Leinster victory when losing by a point to Waterford in the decider. Ollie Bowe was also involved with the team management. In the same year the Under 16s also took the Leinster title against Louth, with Karen Bowe and Lorna Duffy featuring in the green and gold.

In 1997, as part of the drive to improve standards and performances, Ollie

Bowe arranged for a group from the club to attend a weekend coaching clinic in Gormanston. Seventeen girls travelled and for many of them it was their first time away from home on their own. Ollie convinced them that the Royal Gala apples were named especially in their honour! The participants recall a brilliant weekend, but not just for the coaching! A young male Italian group and an Irish volleyball team were also present, and some of the Royal Gaels' girls went to great lengths to become acquainted with the 'Italian Stallions,' including setting off the fire alarms that brought everyone together outside the building!

1997 was notable also for a first-ever final appearance. The Under 14s bagged a significant scalp when getting the better of Simonstown Gaels in a thrilling semi-final, 1-8 to 1-6 before giving way to an all-conquering St. Ultans' side in the decider, where goals proved decisive in a 5-12 to 0-12 outcome. The historic side that reached the final was Sarah Morgan; Deirdre Mooney, Sharon Tugwell; Gráinne Kelly, Maria Kealy, Caroline King; Sharon Mahon, Aileen Creavin; Karen Bowe, Fiona Murray, Fiona McCabe; Shona Donoghue, Donna Brennan. Subs: Orla Power for Brennan, Catherine McDonald for McCabe.

All-Ireland Winners.
Dunshaughlin GAA Chairman Paddy O Dwyer makes a presentation to Maria Kealy and Caroline King to mark their part in Meath's All-Ireland Under 16 championship victory in 2000. Maria captained the side.

Glory Days at Adult Level

By the beginning of the new century the club was well established and becoming increasingly prominent. Ollie Bowe, with the support of a progressive committee that he describes as the best he ever worked with, had transformed a small underage group into a vibrant club that would go on to become one of the most successful in the county, with many girls representing Meath at various levels. Bowe, along with John O Brien, continued to provide the coaching and managerial expertise as the girls graduated to adult level. By July of 2000 the team, based on the girls who had formed the club's Under 14 side half a decade earlier, was top of the Junior League and unbeaten in the championship.

Later in the year Maria Kealy and Caroline King played pivotal roles on the Meath team that won the All-Ireland Under 16 title, defeating Galway 3-11 to 1-8. Kealy captained the side, on the same weekend that her brother Dermot led Dunshaughlin to its first Keegan Cup. The girls went on to win a Leinster minor championship in 2002 as Meath overcame Longford in the final. In addition Lorna Duffy and Ciara Byrne played for the Meath Under 12s while Gillian Flanagan and Áine Ryan were successful at inter county Under 14 level. Karen Bowe represented the club when Meath won a Leinster Minor in 2000 and was on the team that went under to Waterford in the All-Ireland minor final a year later and Shona Donoghue was lining out for the Royal County seniors by 2002.

> **"** Ollie Bowe, with the support of a progressive committee that he describes as the best he ever worked with, had transformed a small underage group into a vibrant club that would go on to become one of the most successful in the county,

The youthful junior side was unable to maintain its early season form of 2000, eventually losing to Blackhall in the championship semi-final. However, by 2001 the team had matured further and reached that year's league and championship finals under the new management team of Seán Walsh and Peter Mooney. Though the outcome was a disappointment, a defeat in both deciders, it unveiled prospects of a better future. Early victories against Syddan, Seneschalstown and Donaghmore secured a semi-final tilt with Navan O Mahonys where the Gaels edged the honours by two points to qualify for a final day encounter with Boardsmill.

The game went to extra time before Boardsmill took the crown by 3-10 to 4-5. After a lethargic start and the concession of 1-2 in the opening ten minutes the Gaels rapidly recovered to hold a 2-2 to 1-3 half time lead and added another goal early in the second half. Prospects looked bright but the black and ambers wouldn't score again in normal time as Boardsmill used their greater experience and physique to eat into the lead. Nevertheless, it took a last minute penalty to square the scores and produce extra time. The Gaels recovered their scoring boots in the early stages, hitting another 1-2 without reply, before Boardsmill once again dominated the second period to leave the losers pondering what might have been.

The Division 3 league final piled further misery on the Gaels' ladies as Navan O Mahonys took the title by four points, 1-11 to 2-4. Once again the Gaels held an interval advantage that they could not retain and good opposition goalkeeping denied them crucial second half scores.

The panel of players that went so close to ultimate success was Aileen Creavin, Fiona Murray, Ciara McHale, Mary McHale, Sorcha O Dwyer, Charlene McAuley, Caroline King, Blaithín Brennan, Katie Brennan, Shona Donoghue, Leona Gilchrist, Karen Bowe, Fiona McCabe, Deirdre Kane, Jane Everard, Suzanne Colgan, Tracey Redmond, Gillian Flanagan, Orla Power, Maria Kealy, Olivia O Neill, Gráinne Kelly, Siobhán Gogan, Deirdre Mooney, Aoife O Donoghue, Brenda McTigue, Anne Swaine and Sharon Mahon.

Seán Walsh demanded a dedicated approach to training and games. Excuses for not attending training, such as Dunshaughlin or Drumree playing at the same time, were brushed aside with the mantra that the Gaels had to focus single-mindedly on their own preparation. Training, generally on the Drumree or Community College grounds, was increased in frequency, duration and intensity and the girls' fitness levels rapidly overtook that of their rivals. Seán arranged strenuous challenge games against Man O War and Garda, with whom he had been previously involved, preparing the team for the rigours of championship football. The dedication reaped dividends when he steered the club to its first adult success.

Double delight in 2002 countered the double disappointment of 2001. The team was now on an upward curve and the championship and league titles were

Royal Gaels, Junior Finalists, 2001

Front: Leona Gilchrist, Mary McHale, Olivia O Neill, Ciara McHale, Aileen Creavin, Sorcha O Dwyer, Maria Kealy, Charlene McAuley.
Middle: Brenda McTigue, Gillian Flanagan, Siobhán Gogan, Deirdre Kane, Fiona McCabe, Katie Brennan, Gráinne Kelly, Orla Power, Bláithín Brennan.
Back: Tracey Redmond, Aoife O Donoghue, Ann Swaine, Jane Everard, Suzanne Colgan, Caroline King, Deirdre Mooney, Shona Donoghue, Karen Bowe, Sharon Mahon.
Missing from photo: Fiona Murray, Emma Donoghue, Ciara Byrne.

Above: Mary McHale accepts the 2004 Football League trophy from Paddy Brady while supporters watching approvingly are, left to right: Adam Kealy, Vivienne Power, Micheal Beagan, Pádraig Redmond, Anita King, Vera Creavin, Paddy McHale.

Royal Gaels, League Division 2 Winners, 2004

Pictured on left:
Front: Ciara O Dwyer, Siobhan Kiernan, Tara Ryan, Niamh O Sullivan, Tracey Redmond, Clíona Ní Dhúshláine, Sorcha O Dwyer, Charlene McAuley, Angie Doyle, Ciara Byrne, Maureen Bowe, Maria Kealy, Fiona O Sullivan.
Back: Sinéad McGroder, Mairéad Kiernan, Lorna Duffy, Gráinne Kelly, Róisín Ní Dhushláine, Brenda McTigue, Caroline King, Fiona Murray, Mary McHale, Shelley Macham, Aileen Creavin, Blaithín Brennan, Ciara McHale, Gemma Flanagan, Fiona McCabe, Lisa Redmond, Suzanne Colgan, Orla Power, Fiona Kealy.

Royal Gaels, Intermediate Winners, 2007

Front: Maria Kealy, Shona Donoghue, Niamh O Sullivan, Sorcha O Dwyer, Róisín Ní Dhúshláine, Charlene McAuley, Rebecca Considine, Bronagh Tinnelly, Cliona Ni Dhúshláine, Aisling O Donoghue, Laura Ryan, Ciara O Dwyer, Robyn Kinsella.
Back: Maureen Bowe, Tara Ryan, Karen Bowe, Sinéad McGroder, Mary McHale, Gemma Flanagan, Ciara McHale, Orlagh McLaughlin, Gráinne Gallogly, Blaithín Brennan, Aileen Creavin, Eimear O Sullivan, Fiona Murray, Sinéad Ennis, Louise O Regan.

Royal Gaels, Victory Celebrations after Intermediate Final, 2007

Front: Tara Ryan, with cup, Orlagh McLaughlin.
Centre: Laura Ryan, Robyn Kinsella, Gemma Flanagan, Karen Bowe, Niamh O Sullivan, Shona Donoghue, Róisín Ní Dhúshláine, Sinéad McGroder, Rebecca Considine, Sorcha O Dwyer.
Back: Maria Kealy, Ciara O Dwyer (partly hidden), Maureen Bowe, Louise O Regan, Mary McHale, Ciara McHale, Gráinne Gallogly, Bronagh Tinnelly, Sinéad Ennis, Charlene McAuley, Blaithín Brennan, Eimear O Sullivan, Fiona Murray, Aileen Creavin.
Note re colours: Royal Gaels lined out in the black and red of St. Martins but for the official team photo, top of page, wore the black and amber colours.

captured in stunning style. The Gaels were the better team in the first half of the Junior B championship decider against Moynalty and built up an interval advantage of 1-5 to 0-2. They were even better after the break as they overwhelmed the north county girls by a comprehensive 3-12 to 0-4. A month later they disposed of a fancied Boardsmill side in the league decider, once again going in ahead at the break and stamping their authority on the game in the second half to emerge victorious by 1-7 to 0-4. Orla Power came on the claim the only goal of the game.

The championship winning side read:

<blockquote>
Ciara McHale

Suzanne Colgan   Maria Kealy   Fiona Murray

Karen Bowe   Aileen Creavin   Deirdre Mooney

Charlene McAuley   Shona Donoghue

Sarah Weld   Fiona McCabe   Sorcha O Dwyer

Blaithín Brennan   Mary McHale   Caroline King

Subs: Gemma Flanagan, Katie Brennan, Tracey Redmond, Brenda McTigue.
</blockquote>

> "Double delight in 2002 countered the double disappointment of 2001. The team was now on an upward curve and the championship and league titles were captured in stunning style."

The step up to a higher grade the following year, Junior proper, meant it was a year for consolidation on the playing front. The loss of players to injury and travel overseas militated against further progress and the team suffered a number of heavy defeats, especially in the league against senior grade opposition.

By 2004 prospects were brighter. The team reached the junior championship final and the Division 2 league decider, coming out second best in the former but winning the latter. Na Fianna were too strong in the championship but the Gaels gained a measure of consolation with a 1-11 to 1-10 victory against Donaghmore-Ashbourne in the league.

Recognition for the club's effort in developing and nurturing the ladies' game came in 2006 with the award of Club of the Year by Meath Local Sports' Partnership.

2007 Intermediate Title

The year 2007 was the most successful ever in Royal Gaels' history. In existence for just a dozen years the club had progressed from the acorn of a small dedicated Under 14 panel to an oak tree of many branches, Under 12, Under 14, Under 16, Minor and Under 21 as well as adult intermediate grade.

By July the intermediates had qualified for the semi-final of the championship where they met neighbours Dunsany, who had dropped down from senior level. The Gaels grabbed the initiative early on via a goal from Robyn Kinsella and

BLACK & AMBER

Royal Gaels, Dinner Dance Presentation, January 2008

Front: Robyn Kinsella, Maureen Bowe, Shona Donoghue, Karen Bowe, Cliona Ni Dhúshláine, Sorcha O Dwyer, Niamh O Sullivan, Louise O Regan, Sinéad McGroder, Tara Ryan.

Back: Blaithín Brennan, Maria Kealy, Ciara O Dwyer, Rebecca Considine, Bronagh Tinnelly, Aisling O Donoghue, Gráinne Gallogly, Sinéad Ennis, Seán Walsh, Aileen Creavin, Gemma Flanagan, Dan O Sullivan, Orlagh McLaughlin, Peter Mooney, Róisín Ní Dhúshláine, Fiona Murray, Ciara McHale, Laura Ryan, Mary McHale.

points from Gráinne Gallogly, and with Blaithín Brennan, Maria Kealy and Eimear O Sullivan in superb form they amassed a 1-6 to 0-3 interval lead. Second half possession was more evenly distributed and this was reflected on the scoreboard with both sides adding three points, enough to leave the black and ambers comfortable six point winners.

A wait of six weeks for the final with Na Fianna, who had won an earlier encounter between the sides by a point, couldn't halt the Gaels' momentum. Preparation was the key to the Gaels' success. Seán Walsh prepared meticulously for the big day, even doing a run through of final day procedures on two occasions in Drumree. Each element was timed and rehearsed, togging out, departing the dressing room, setting up and going through the pre-match drills and the team talk. Thus, when final day arrived there were no surprises, each player knew her role.

As in the semi-final the Gaels took an early lead and stubbornly refused to relinquish it. Karen Bowe was the tormentor in chief of Na Fianna's defence with a number of surging runs from midfield. Her partner Blaithín Brennan gave a

CHAPTER 19: THE ROYAL GAELS

match winning display while Charlene McAuley used her pace to sail serenly past opponents. The Gaels' goal before half time typified the team's skill and confidence. McAuley picked up a wayward clearance, nonchalantly side-stepped a few challenges before passing accurately to Karen Bowe who smashed the ball to the net from close range. Niamh O Sullivan immediately added to Na Fianna's woes with a long-range point, one of six from the unerringly accurate forward.

An interval lead of 1-9 to 1-2 proved too great an obstacle for Na Fianna. They could only add three second half points whereas the Gaels, though playing into a stiff breeze, recorded double that. At the back the Gaels were solid and sturdy with Cliona Ni Dhúshláine, Maria Kealy and Sorcha O Dwyer forming a formidable last line of defence.

The Gaels were not to be denied the title and Gemma Flanagan had the honour of accepting the Brian McKeown Memorial Cup.

Seán Walsh coached the side to victory with Peter Mooney and Dan O Sullivan as his selectors. They decided to play with the wind in the first half, the coach stating that, 'We believe you should play with every advantage you can', particularly after the earlier loss to the same opposition. He noted that the team came through a tough semi-final with Dunsany due to the strength of the panel as a number of players were on holiday. 'To win a title you need a panel, it's not just about fifteen players any more,' stated the happy coach.

The victorious team lined out as follows:

The founder members of Royal Gaels pictured at the club's inaugural dinner dance in January 2008.
Front: Anne Power, Ollie Bowe, Maura O Neill.
Back: Ead Kealy, and Catherine McHale.
Photo courtesy of John Quirke.

Orlagh McLaughlin
Cliona Ní Dhúshláine   Maria Kealy   Sorcha O Dwyer
Eimear O Sullivan   Aileen Creavin   Rebecca Considine
Blaithín Brennan (0-2)   Karen Bowe (1-2)
Róisín Ní Dhúshláine (0-1)   Gemma Flanagan (0-1)   Sinéad McGroder
Niamh O Sullivan (0-6)   Charlene McAuley (0-1)   Tara Ryan (0-1)

Subs: Shona Donoghue for McGroder, Robyn Kinsella for Ní Dhushláin, Gráinne Gallogly for Ryan, Fiona Murray for Considine, Ciara McHale, Sinéad Ennis, Mary McHale, Ciara O Dwyer, Louise O Regan, Maureen Bowe, Bronagh Tinnelly, Aisling O Donoghue, Laura Ryan, Áine Nestor, Heidi Carty, Lisa Redmond.

Bláithín Brennan later represented the Royal County in the TV *Underdogs* series, and after nailing down the number six jersey played on the victorious Underdogs team against the US All Stars in Gaelic Park, New York.

In an echo of the 2002 double, the girls captured the Division 2 league title in November with victory over another side from the west of the county, Summerhill. Though the 'Hill competed in the senior championship the Gaels' ability to hit the net proved to be the difference between the sides. One goal before half time from a Tara Ryan penalty gave them an interval lead and it was only in the closing stages that two more, one from Maureen Bowe and a second from Ryan left Royal Gaels the victors by 3-8 to 0-9. The winning line out read, Orlagh McLaughlin; Cliona Ní Dhúshláine, Maria Kealy, Shona Donoghue; Róisín Ni Dhúshláine, Blaithín Brennan, Rebecca Considine; Gemma Flanagan, Niamh O Sullivan (0-4); Tara Ryan (2-2), Karen Bowe (0-1), Sinéad McGroder; Gráinne Gallogly, Robyn Kinsella (0-1), Maureen Bowe (1-0). Subs: Sinéad Ennis, Fiona O Sullivan, Bronagh Tinnelly, Ciara McHale.

The game gave Shona Donoghue an insight into the demands of playing in defence. Accustomed to attacking roles at the opposite end of the field she often teased her defenders about how easy their job was compared to the forwards. Her initial response to her new role was, 'What the effing hell am I doing in here?' but she proceeded to give an outstanding display, always first to the ball and at one stage upending two of her own defenders as she emerged from a goalmouth scramble with the ball. Afterwards she declared, 'I take it back, all I said about ye doing nothing in defence!'

Success in the championship gave the team entry to the Leinster competition where Eadestown of Kildare proved far too strong in the quarter-final. The club also played in the All-Ireland Sevens, losing the semi-final by a solitary point to Portmarnock, the eventual champions.

The intermediate championship capped a wonderful year for the club that was celebrated with an inaugural Dinner Dance attended by over two hundred, including founder members Ollie Bowe, Ead Kealy, Catherine McHale, Ann Power and Maura O Neill, in The Ardboyne Hotel in January 2008. Three of the players made the *Meath Chronicle's* Green Stars team, Maria Kealy at corner back, Blaithín Brennan at centre field and Karen Bowe at wing forward. Three others featured on the Meath minor team defeated by Dublin in the Leinster championship, Orlagh McLaughlin in goals, Niamh O Sullivan in defence and Tara Ryan in attack while Rebecca Considine was a regular on the county Under 16 side. Blaithín Brennan, Niamh O Sullivan, Tara Ryan and Karen Bowe lined out with the Meath seniors as did Maria Kealy and Orlagh McLaughlin the following year with Rebecca Considine a panel member.

You Win Some . . . You Lose Some

Royal Gaels' First Under 12 Title, 2004

Front: Pat O Regan, Niamh Donnachie, Rebecca Considine, Laura O Toole, Clare Duffy, Shiobhra Delaney, Leanne McMorrow, Laura Ryan, Nicola Bowen, Rachel Lord, Shauna Moore, Fionnuala Kane, Stephen McMorrow.
Back: Charlotte Coquet, Avril Tormey, Tara Matthews, Louise O Regan, Sarah Corrigan, Amy Ennis, Alex Swan, Jenny Kelly, Kristina Troy, Sinéad Kelly, Aoife Moore, Megan Holohan, Mary Fitzmaurice.

Royal Gaels, Under 13 Féile Finalists, 2006

Front: Rebecca Keane, Katie Lavery, Laura McMahon, Jenny Kelly, Louise O Regan, Maeve Scanlon, Laura Murray, Emma Kennedy.
Back: Caitríona Kennedy, Louise Griffin, Nicola Bowen, Kate Jennings, Orla Bracken, Kristina Troy, Alex Swan.

Royal Gaels, Under 15 Blitz Winners, 2006

Front: Tara Ryan, Niamh O Sullivan, Niamh Beagan, Capt., Kristina Troy, Lisa Redmond.
Back: Aisling Reilly, Sarah McBride, Leah Russell, Orlagh McLaughlin, Laura McMorrow, Sinéad Beagan, Zoe Baggott, Carol Gregan, Shauna Moore.

Under 12 Presentation 2004

Aoife Moore accepts the trophy after Royal Gaels defeated Moynalvey in the 2004, Under 12 Division 2 final.

Royal Gaels, Under 13, 2008

Front: Aoife O Shea, Cara Usher, Aisling Traynor, Ciara Murray, Niamh Gallogly, Maeve Scanlon, Róisín Bruce, Niamh Bedford, Cliodhna O Riordan, Alannah Chalkley.
Back: Bevin Usher, Laura Murray, Gemma Donoghue, Bronagh Walsh, Karen O Regan, Claire O Brien, Siobhán O Riordan, Emma Kennedy, Niamh Kennedy, Amy Mulvaney, Hannah O Brien.

Royal Gaels, Under 14 Division 1 Finalists, 2006

Front: Kristina Troy, Laura Ryan, Laura Murray, Laura O Toole, Karen O Regan, Jenny Kelly, Maeve Scanlon, Emma Kennedy, Shiobhra Delaney, Laura McMahon.
Back: Eve Mahon, Louise Griffin, Katie Lavery, Niamh Donnachie, Kate Jennings, Alex Swan, Shauna Moore, Rebecca Considine, Aoife Moore, Nicola Bowen, Tara Matthews, Amy Ennis, Niamh Kelliher, Louise O Regan, Sinéad Kelly.

Royal Gaels, Under 16 Winners, 2006

Front: Shauna Moore, Laura O Toole, Shiobhra Delaney, Tara Ryan, Niamh O Sullivan, Laura McMorrow, Kristina Troy, Rebecca Considine.
Back: Áine Nestor, Lucy Shirren, Sarah McBride, Jenny Kelly, Gráinne Gallogly, Aoife Moore, Leah Russell, Zoe Baggott, Orlagh McLaughlin, Lorna O Connor. Karen O Regan holding flag.

Royal Gaels, Under 16 Finalists, 2008

Front: Laura McMahon, Laura Murray, Karla O Callaghan, Laura Ryan, Rebecca Considine, Amy Ennis, Shiobhra Delaney, Leanne McMorrow, Clíona Murphy, Bevin Usher, Maeve Scanlon.
Back: Jenny Kelly, Nicola Bowen, Orla Bracken, Rebecca Keane, Kate Jennings, Karen O Regan, Kristina Troy, Louise Griffin, Méabh Gallogly, Saoirse Conlon, Louise O Regan.

Under 16 Joint captains, 2006, Niamh O Sullivan and Laura McMorrow.

Surviving the Senior Scene... but for how long?

> Despite the unprecedented level of county representation there were fears that the senior grade would prove too demanding for the club.

Despite the unprecedented level of county representation there were fears that the senior grade would prove too demanding for the club. Those worries were soon dispelled with victory over reigning champions Seneschalstown in the first round, 2-8 to 1-9. Orlagh McLaughlin gave an outstanding performance in goals and Niamh O Sullivan contributed 1-3. A comprehensive victory over Summerhill continued the fairy tale start that came to an end when Dunboyne recorded a third round victory by 2-8 to 1-5.

The earlier results were sufficient to set up a quarter-final with Boardsmill who eked out a single point victory to eliminate the Gaels. It was a frustrating defeat, for the Gaels kicked it away, but, in reality, while they should have won that game they could easily have lost the earlier outings that they won. The team also faced the challenge of league football in Division 1 and ended the year with a couple of victories while also reaching the quarter-final of the Feis Cup where Na Fianna proved too strong.

In the following years the club struggled to cope with the demands of senior football. In early 2010 the side retained Division 1 status when recording a comprehensive play-off victory against St. Michaels by 5-14 to 0-2. However, remaining at that level proved a more demanding challenge and heavy defeats were soon shipped against Boardsmill and St. Ultans. Despite a deserved victory against Donaghmore-Ashbourne the Gaels dropped down a grade for 2011.

In the championship the club retained senior status in 2010 with a play-off victory over Blackhall Gaels but by 2011 there had been a significant turnover of players from the intermediate winning side of four years earlier, with half the successful side having to be replaced due to retirements, injury and emigration.

It was time to rebuild from the bottom up and the Gaels had plenty of under age success to suggest that the future could still be rosy.

2014 was a year of consolidation and progress. The team managed by Hugh McCarthy and Michael McHale shot out of the blocks in Divison 3 of the league to register substantial scores and post consecutive victories against Wolfe Tones, Ballivor, St. Patricks, Skryne and Walterstown. By May the side had qualified for the final but a three-way play-off to decide their opponents deferred the final until September. The Gaels couldn't replicate their early season whirlwind and St. Michaels cantered to a 4-10 to 0-9 victory.

Games were much more competitive in the championship but once again the Mikes proved to be a thorn in the Gaels' side. Two losses, including a defeat to Michaels, forced a three-way dogfight for a semi-final slot. The Gaels had two bites at the cherry but Michaels emphasised their superiority with another victory that left the Gaels needing to overcome Summerhill to advance to the final. In a close, high scoring game the Hill had four points to spare but the Royals could still reflect on a year that promised a brighter future.

Underage Achievements: 2004-08

The Royal Gaels started life as a juvenile club, only entering adult teams once the initial crop had progressed through the underage grades. Consequently, the club always retained a focus on the young girls without whom there would be no adult success.

In 2004 the club captured its first Under 12 title with Aoife Moore captaining the team to victory against Moynalvey, and recorded success at Under-15 blitz level when Niamh Beagan's panel overcame Dunboyne in the final by 1-5 to 1-4.

Success wasn't always on the menu and for a time it seemed as if the Gaels were beginning to develop an unwelcome habit of occupying the runners-up position. Oldcastle, who were then beginning to establish a strong presence at underage level came out on top in two consecutive Under 14 finals, 2006 and 2007, as well as thwarting the Gaels' effort to win the Under 13 Féile final in 2006.

Despite the setbacks, a number of players represented Meath in 2007. Maeve Scanlon, Kate Jennings, Laura Murray and Orla Bracken won Leinster medals as the Under 14 Royals defeated Laois in the final. At Under 12 level Karen O Regan captained Meath to success in the Leinster Blitz and was joined on the team by Emma Kennedy.

Sweet Sixteens . . . . and some not so Sweet!

Though victory was proving elusive at under 14 level, Royal Gaels teams have been consistently strong in the under 16 grade. The first title at this level arrived on St. Patrick's Day 2004 when the club captured 2003 B honours. After a semi-final victory against Seneschalstown in February, the Gaels overcame Boardsmill in the final with Suzanne Colgan and Brenda McTigue as joint captains. The semi-final team was Orlagh McLaughlin; Aisling Reilly, Ciara Byrne, Niamh Beagan; Lisa Redmond, Eanya O Brien, Laura McMorrow; Suzanne Colgan, Brenda McTigue; Sinéad Beagan, Lorna Duffy, Fiona O Sullivan; Niamh O Sullivan, Maureen Bowe, Kristina Troy. Subs: Zoe Baggott for McMorrow, Sarah Murphy for Reilly, Leanne McMorrow for Redmond, Tara Ryan for Sinéad Beagan, Sinéad Kennedy, Lucy Shirren, Lorna O Connor, Sarah McBride, Carol Gregan, Leah Russell.

In 2006 the Gaels annexed a second title, this time in the Division 1 grade, when disposing of neighbours Ratoath by 4-7 to 1-7 in the final. In the initial stages it

Royal Gaels, Under 19 Champions, 2009

Front: Maria Kealy, Maeve Scanlon, Rebecca Considine, Niamh O Sullivan, Leanne McMorrow, Amy Ennis, Shiobhra Delaney, Laura McMahon, Caitríona Kennedy, Saoirse Conlon.
Back: Orla Bracken, Laura Murray, Laura Ryan, Aimee McQuillan, Laura McMorrow, Gráinne Gallogly, Orlagh McLaughlin, Méabh Gallogly, Fiona Traynor, Emma Connolly, Louise O Regan, Jennifer Kelly, Tara Ryan, Colum Bracken.

Club and University Success for Niamh O Sullivan

Above: Royal Gaels' Captain Niamh O Sullivan with the Giles Cup as NUI Maynooth captain after the Ladies' Colleges All-Ireland Final in 2010 and below, receiving the Under 19 trophy from Meath County Board Chairperson Geraldine Sheridan.

Celebrating Under 19 Success, 2009
Front: Laura McMorrow, Tara Ryan, partly hidden, Louise O Regan, Gráinne Gallogly, partly hidden, Niamh O Sullivan with cup, Jenny Kelly, Laura McMahon, Leanne McMorrow.
Back, right: Orlagh McLaughlin, Orla Bracken, Amy Ennis.

Royal Gaels, Under 16, Sevens, 2014

Panel that reached the semi-final of the All-Ireland Under 16 Seven-a-Side Finals in 2014.
Front: Tara Scanlon, Sarah Kelly, Sadhbh Ní Muirí, Ava Fox, Rachel Huijsdens.
Back: Rachel Ennis, Hayley Reynolds, Laura Quinn, Saoirse Patchell, Jessica May, Ailis Bruce.

seemed an unlikely outcome, as the eventual winners had an early goal disallowed and trailed by 1-5 to a point at the interval. The second half saw a complete turn around, as a flurry of points and a goal from Kristina Troy restored parity. Niamh O Sullivan and Gráinne Gallogly gave outstanding displays, surpassed only by the magnificent Troy who went on to complete her hat trick. Niamh O Sullivan and Laura McMorrow jointly captained the following side:

Orlagh McLaughlin

Lucy Shirren   Laura McMorrow   Aoife Moore

Alex Swan   Rebecca Considine   Jenny Kelly

Tara Ryan   Leah Russell

Zoe Baggott   Áine Nestor (0-1)   Shauna Moore (1-0)

Niamh O Sullivan (0-4)   Kristina Troy (3-1)   Laura O Toole

Subs: Gráinne Gallogly (0-1) for Baggott, Shiobhra Delaney for Swan, Sarah McBride.

The club contested its third Under 16 final in six years in 2008 as Pat O Regan and Colum Bracken guided the team to four victories in the league stages and an exciting semi-final triumph against Donaghmore-Ashbourne. Three finals didn't turn into three titles as Oldcastle repeated their Under 14 victory of the previous year. By half time in the decider at Donore a stronger and more powerful north county side had a stranglehold on the game. Despite their best efforts the youthful Royal Gaels couldn't turn the game round in the second half and Oldcastle went on to take the title.

The club had to wait another five years for the next Under 16 crown. A loss to Skryne in the 2012 final was the prelude to a convincing final day performance in 2013.

After an unbeaten run through the league stages the Gaels took on Gaeil Colmcille in the final at Martry. First half goals from captain Niamh Gallogly, Rachel Huijsdens and Aideen McCabe gave the black and ambers a seven-point half time lead and the look of winners. Though the Kells' girls reduced the lead to three points early in the second half it was a false dawn for them as the Gaels replicated the first half goal fest with Gallogly, Alannah Chalkley and Ailis Bruce netting. Not satisfied with half a dozen goals the black and ambers also racked up sixteen points to emerge victorious by 6-16 to 5-0.

The outstanding Niamh Gallogly who helped herself to 1-10 later went on captain the Meath Under 16 side that won the Leinster championship but fell at the final hurdle to Waterford. The victorious Under 16 team was

Lara Reynolds

Sarah Kelly   Sarah Darby   Kate Hanley

Saoirse Patchell   Gemma Donoghue   Sadhbh Ó Muirí

Niamh Gallogly (1-10)   Cara Usher

Rachel Huijsdens (1-2)   Alannah Chalkley (1-0)   Tara Scanlon

Louise Nevin (1-0)   Ailis Bruce (1-3)   Aideen McCabe (1-0)

Subs: Niamh Curtin (0-1) for Nevin, Katie Usher for Kelly, Eimear Traynor for McCabe, Jessica May for Bruce, Laura Costello.

The 2014 crew was also successful, albeit in the Shield final when a 2-11 to 2-4 victory was recorded against Donaghmore-Ashbourne. They had an exceptional run in the All-Ireland Under 16 Sevens in Clare when three victories and a loss propelled them to a semi-final tilt with Glenamaddy. Down to a panel of eight for the game due to earlier injuries the Gaels eventually lost out to the Galway girls. The panel consisted of Jessica May, Sarah Kelly, Saoirse Patchell, Laura Quinn, Sadhbh Ó Muirí, Ailis Bruce, Ava Fox, Rachel Ennis, Rachel Huijsdens and Tara Scanlon.

Under 19s

In 2008 and 2009 the club made an impression at Under 19 level as many of the successful Under 16s graduated to the older grade. In the 2008 competition Royal Gaels and Donaghmore-Ashbourne were the last two clubs remaining as the championship persisted into April 2009. The final at Ratoath was competitive

Royal Gaels, Under 13 Division 2 Winners, 2010

Front: Juliette Wall, Katie Usher, Sadhbh Ó Muirí, Ailis Bruce, Saoirse Patchall, Louise Nevin, Gemma Donoghue, Tara Scanlon, Emma Murray.
Back: Tara Ryan, Siobhán Duffy, Jessica May, Sarah Kelly, Tara Hurley, Amy Mulvaney, Alannah Chalkley, Cara Usher, Kate Hanley, Niamh Hetherington, Sarah Darby, Niamh Gallogly, Ian Bruce.

Royal Gaels, Under 11 Winners, 2010

Front: Katelyn Doherty, Ava Foley, Orlagh Keane, Niamh Curtin, Kelly O Dwyer, Ava Fox, Rachel Ennis, Orlaith Moyles, Megan Reilly, Ciara Galvin.
Back: Molly Regan, Caoimhe Rooney, Rachel Huijsdens, Sophie O Connor, Lara Reynolds, Eimear Traynor, Laura Quinn- partly hidden, Hayley Reynolds, Saoirse Carey, Shaughna Gibney, Kevagh Slater, Katelyn O Neill, Hope O Dwyer- partly hidden, Georgie Benson.

Royal Gaels, Under 16 Division 2 Winners, 2013

Front: Niamh Curtin, Louise Nevin, Cara Usher, Tara Scanlon, Niamh Gallogly, Ailis Bruce, Sadhbh Ó Muirí, Saoirse Patchell, Kate Hanley, Eimear Traynor.
Back: Niamh O Sullivan, Aideen McCabe, Rachel Huijsdens, Alannah Chalkley, Sarah Darby, Sarah Kelly, Amy Mulvaney, Lara Reynolds, Niamh Hetherington, Gemma Donoghue, Katie Usher, Jessica May, Laura Costello, Laura Quinn, Ian Bruce.

> The final proved a much easier challenge as Clanna Gael had no answer to a rampant Gaels' side that posted 3-10 and conceded just six points.

and entertaining but the Gaels were behind from an early stage and it took sterling work and four points by captain Niamh O Sullivan to keep them within range. At the other end of the field the determined defending of Orla Bracken and Laura McMorrow confined the Dons to 1-7.

Two penalties in the second half, both clinically dispatched by O Sullivan, kept the Gaels' hopes alive but a strong finish from Donaghmore-Ashbourne gave them a merited 1-14 to 2-5 win. O Sullivan was outstanding throughout and accounted for all her sides scores while her midfield partner Jenny Kelly also impressed.

The Gaels' line out was: Orlagh McLoughlin; Laura Murray, Laura McMorrow, Louise O Regan; Laura Ryan, Orla Bracken, Rebecca Considine; Jenny Kelly, Niamh O'Sullivan (2-5); Shiobhra Delaney, Gráinne Gallogly, Cliona Murphy; Heidi Carty, Sinéad Ennis, Leanne McMorrow. Subs: Karla O Callaghan for Ennis, Rebecca Keane for Leanne McMorrow, Catríona Kennedy for Gallogly, Tara Matthews for O Callaghan, Maeve Scanlon for Carty, Emma Connolly, Méabh Gallogly, Saoirse Conlon, Amy Ennis, Fiona Traynor.

With Maria Kealy and Colum Bracken in the management role many of those players featured once again the following year and exacted sweet revenge, first on Donaghmore-Ashbourne in the quarter-final, and later on perennial conquerors Oldcastle with a hard earned 3-11 to 2-11 semi-final triumph. The final proved a much easier challenge as Clanna Gael had no answer to a rampant Gaels' side that posted 3-10 and conceded just six points.

Royal Gaels, Under 14 Division 2 Winners, 2010

Front: Hannah O Brien, Catherine Kennedy, Cara Usher, Sarah Darby, Veronica Conlon, Róisín Bruce, Alannah Chalkley, Marissa Horan.
Back: Gemma Donoghue, Claire O Brien, Aisling Traynor, Ciara Murray, Niamh Gallogly, Niamh Kennedy, Amy Mulvaney, Cliodhna O Riordan, Niamh Hetherington, Aoife O Shea, Mary O Regan.
Missing from photo, Hannah Duggan, Siobhán Duffy.

The Gaels started the final at a blistering pace, slotting over three points in the opening ten minutes before Rebecca Considine and Caitríona Kennedy combined to set up Laura McMahon who shot to the net from close range. Before half time McMahon registered another goal when she gathered a Tara Ryan cross-field pass, cut inside and fired to the net. There was still time for Amy Ennis to shoot home a third when another Ryan effort came off the woodwork. Additional points from Rebecca Considine, Jenny Kelly, and Maeve Scanlon gave the Gaels an impregnable 3-7 to 0-2 half time advantage.

Though the Clann defence limited the Gaels' attacks after half time and outscored their opponents, the black and ambers were never in any danger and a top class save from Orlagh McLaughlin when she superbly tipped over a shot from Laura Gilsenan frustrated any dreams of a recovery. Team coach Maria Kealy commented after the victory, 'The team suffered a sore loss last year. When we defeated Donaghmore-Ashbourne this year in the quarter-finals and then went on to get the better of Oldcastle we knew we could win it if we kept working. ' The Gaels' team spirit, fitness and self-belief was evident throughout as the following side, captained by Niamh O Sullivan, powered its way to the title:

	Orlagh McLaughlin	
Leanne McMorrow	Aimee McQuillan	Gráinne Gallogly
Shiobhra Delaney	Laura McMorrow	Laura Ryan
	Niamh O Sullivan, Capt.	Rebecca Considine (0-2)
Caitríona Kennedy	Jenny Kelly (0-1)	Maeve Scanlon (0-2)
Amy Ennis (1-0)	Tara Ryan (0-5)	Laura McMahon (2-0)

Subs: Orla Bracken for Delaney, Louise O Regan for Bracken, Saoirse Conlon for Kennedy, Laura Murray, Fiona Traynor, Emma Connolly, Méabh Gallogly.

Niamh O Sullivan had already achieved another honour as captain earlier in the year when she led NUI Maynooth to victory in the All-Ireland Ladies' Final for the Giles Cup.

BLACK & AMBER

Mary O Regan
Long Serving Secretary of Royal Gaels, 2006-2015 and Secretary Meath Ladies' Board, 2009-15.

Ollie Bowe receives his Hall of Fame award for 2014 from Aisling Clery, Meath Ladies' Board Chairperson.

Successes in Recent Years

In recent years the club has maintained its traditional competitive form at underage and recorded a number of successes, with 2010 being a particularly rewarding one.

The Under 14s displayed outstanding consistency throughout a long campaign before taking the title. After eight straight victories in the league stages, the semi-final against Skryne turned into a nail biting, extended affair. The sides were evenly matched and it took extra time to produce a result. A magical goal from Hannah O Brien and a point from Niamh Gallogly in the second period of extra time was enough to defeat the Blues and two days later the Gaels faced Clanna Gael in the final.

This produced another high quality game between two well-matched and equally determined sides. Despite Niamh Hetherington's haul of a goal and two points in the first half the Royals were two points in arrears at the break. Hetherington rattled the net once again early in the second half as the black and ambers gradually asserted control. Yet, it took some excellent defensive work by Sarah Darby, Cliodhna O Riordan and Gemma Donoghue to snuff out several Clanna Gael attacks. Niamh Gallogly and Alannah Chalkley were rock-solid in the back line and also surged into attack to contribute valuable scores. Gallogly's goal nudged Royal Gaels in front near the end and Cara Usher chipped in with the final score of the game to seal the victory that enabled captain Róisín Bruce to claim the silverware on a final score of 4-5 to 3-6. The winning team was:

Amy Mulvaney
Cliodhna O Riordan   Sarah Darby   Aisling Traynor
Niamh Gallogly (1-0)   Alannah Chalkley   Gemma Donoghue (0-1)
Róisín Bruce, Capt.   Marissa Horan
Hannah O Brien (1-0)   Niamh Kennedy   Ciara Murray
Aoife O Shea   Claire O Brien   Niamh Hetherington (2-3)

Subs: Cara Usher (0-1), Hannah Duggan, Siobhán Duffy.

The early weeks of November 2010 brought two underage titles in rapid succession.

The under 11s took the Division 2 title with an exceptional display that featured 4-7 from the forwards while the defenders completely shut out Clanna Gael, refusing to concede a single score during the game. After an early scare when the eventual losers rattled the cross bar, Royal Gaels assumed complete control. Kelly O Dwyer and Niamh Curtin opened the scoring with fine points

Royal Gaels, Under 14 Féile Winners, 2015

Front: Shauna Summerville, Michelle Sherry, Sarah Oliver, Aoibhinn Bracken, Ellie McCarthy, Ava O Brien, Sonia Leonard, Molly McNamara, Rebecca May.
Middle: Sarah Benson, Áine Lawless, Katie Reilly, Jane Larkin, Petra Reilly, Mary McDonagh, Tara Hetherington, Maria Borgnolo, Kayleigh Fox.
Back: Méibh Reilly, Katie O Brien, Liadan O Neill, Ciara Gorman, Megan McCarthy, Katelyn Doherty, Méadhbh Byrne.
Photo by Des O Neill.

BLACK & AMBER

Gaelic for Mothers and Others at Blitz in 2014
Front: Catherine Clinton, Jenny Barry, Edel McTigue, Anne Marie McHugh, Sharon Ennis, Orla Rafter.
Middle: Sam Oliver, Elaine O Brien, Martina Allen, Dee Ennis, Kate Ahern, Nuala O Riordan, Ursula Summerville, Mr. Motivator.
Back: Shirley O Connor, Trudy McCarthy, Teresa Smithers, Kathleen Naughton, Mags Reilly, Naoise Hartigan, Ger Reilly- partly hidden, Dee Reilly, Ger Reid, partly hidden.

and with Caoimhe Rooney, Georgie Benson, Ava Fox, Orlagh Keane and Rachel Ennis impressing, the title went to the Dunshaughlin girls.

The victorious side read:

Saoirse Carey
Molly Regan   Rachel Ennis   Orlagh Keane
Kevagh Slater   Caoimhe Rooney   Rachel Huijsdens
Eimear Traynor   Laura Quinn
Niamh Curtin   Kelly O Dwyer   Ava Fox
Georgie Benson   Orlaith Moyles   Hope O Dwyer
Subs: Caitlin O Neill, Sophie O Connor, Ciara Galvin, Shaughna Gibney, Lara Reynolds, Megan O Reilly, Ava Foley, Lauren Slater, Katelyn Doherty.

A week later the Under 13s repeated their younger clubmates' success. After losing the Under 13 Division 2 final in 2009 the Gaels shipped just one defeat en route to the 2010 decider with Skryne. After a slow start the Gaels were always in control of the final. Sarah Darby and Saoirse Patchel dominated midfield and limited the Tara girls' possession, confining the Blues to a single first half point. Meanwhile Tara Scanlon, Niamh Hetherington and Ailis Bruce notched points

One Club Model

Caroline Malone, Secretary Dunshaughlin GAA, Colum Bracken, Chairperson Royal Gaels, Jim Smith, Chairperson Dunshaughlin GAA, Mary O Regan, Secretary Royal Gaels.

to give the Gaels a narrow half time lead. The black and ambers were even more dominant after the break and doubled their first half scores to win by 0-9 to 0-2.

The winning panel read: Amy Mulvaney, Kate Hanley, Sarah Darby, Sadhbh Ó Muirí, Gemma Donoghue, Saoirse Patchel, Katie Usher, Niamh Gallogly, Cara Usher, Emma Murray, Tara Scanlon, Alannah Chalkley, Louise Nevin, Niamh Hetherington, Ailis Bruce, Juliette Wall, Sarah Kelly, Tara Hanley, Siobhán Duffy, Jessica May, Kevagh Slater.

2013 and 2014 were stand-out years for the younger age groups.

In 2013 the Under 12s recorded a significant achievement by reaching two finals; the first team met Dunboyne in the Division 1 decider while the reserves' opponents in Division 5 were St. Colmcilles. Dunboyne thwarted a unique double by emerging victorious in the former by 3-2 to 1-5 but the reserves had the better of the Seasiders, winning by 4-9 to 2-3.

The Under 14s endured a see-saw contest in their Division 2 final against Na Fianna. The Gaels started in generous mood conceding 3-1 in the first quarter but in the remaining fifteen minutes Michelle Jibowu plundered three for the black and ambers to restore the balance. Early in the second half roles were reversed as the Gaels' Rachel Huijsdens hit the net first, only for Na Fianna to counter with a similar score. Soon after the Gaels put an end to the equilibrium. They recorded a rapid fire 2-2, Orlagh Keane netting first followed by Jibowu's fourth green flag. The half dozen goals and five points outbalanced Na Fianna's 5-4 to give the Gaels the title. The winners lined out as follows:

Shaughna Gibney

Caoimhe Rooney   Laura Quinn   Rachel Ennis

Orlaith Moyles   Eimear Traynor   Ava Foley

Rachel Huijsdens   Olivia Flanagan

Lucy Kelly   Kelly O Dwyer   Ava Fox

Niamh Curtin   Michelle Jibowu   Lara Reynolds

Subs: Ellen Byrne, Caitlin O Neill, Megan Reilly, Kyra Synnott, Orlagh Keane, Ciara Galvin. Teresa Ennis and Séamus Traynor managed the side.

A year later the Under 12s captured the Divison 1 Shield against Simonstown and on the same day the under 14 reserves, fielding some of the girls fresh from their Under 12 triumph, ousted St. Colmcilles in the Under 14 Reserve cup final. This was but a prelude to the most important success, victory in the Under 13 Division 1 league final. Its importance was reflected in the fact that it was against arch-rivals Dunboyne, whom the girls had not previously defeated.

A 4-5 to 2-3 victory buoyed up the team and they entered the blitz to decide the Royal County representatives for Féile 2015 full of confidence. The black and ambers chalked up four wins from four in the league stages and then eliminated Seneschalstown in the semi-final.

It was almost pre-ordained that regular nemesis Dunboyne should make the decider also. When it mattered most the girls stamped their authority and confidence on the final, and, after an even first half resulted in equality on the scoreboard, they streaked to a convincing victory in the second, recording 3-6 to Dunboyne's single goal. This qualified the club, for the first time in its two decade history, for the national Féile finals in Wexford in June 2015.

The successful panel, with scorers in the final, consisted of Ellie McCarthy, Jane Larkin, Michelle Sherry, Ava O Brien, Ciara Gorman, Sonia Leonard, Molly McNamara, Petra Reilly (1-0), Mary McDonagh, Katie O Brien, Tara Hetherington (1-0), Megan McCarthy, Sarah Oliver, Katelyn Doherty (0-5), Katie Reilly, Shauna Summerville, Aoibhinn Bracken (0-1), Méibh Reilly, Méadhbh Byrne, Áine Lawless, Liadan O Neill (1-0), Kayleigh Fox, Rebecca May, Sarah Benson and Maria Borgnolo. The team management comprised Hugh McCarthy, Colum Bracken, Niamh O Sullivan and Alan Reilly.

The team went within an ace of taking the All-Ireland title in Wexford. Hosted by the Kilmore club the Gaels recorded victories over St. Patricks of Wicklow and the home side and finished all-square with Offally's Seir Kieran. A semi-final victory against Taghmon-Camross of Wexford set up another encounter with St. Patricks, this time for the title. Despite a nervous start and the concession of two early goals the Gaels salvaged a draw with a Ciara Gorman free dipping into the net almost on the call of time. Two additional five minute periods of extra time resulted in another nerve wracking conclusion but the black and ambers fell a point short on a score of 3-5 to 2-7. It was a cruel conclusion to an epic effort but players, mentors and parents could bask in pride on a glorious effort.

The recent degree of success at under age grades suggests that the club has the playing resources to develop a strong adult side in the coming years and replicate the success of the early years of this century. The club has also changed its structure becoming integrated into the broader entity that is Dunshaughlin GAA club while retaining its name and separate officers. Thus, it will have full access to Dunshaughlin's current playing fields and the new clubhouse. The move towards integration is in line with the GAA's policy known as the One Club Model.

The pioneers of the Royal Gaels two decades ago who began with a single Under 14 team can be well pleased at the current state of their vision.

> **The pioneers of the Royal Gaels two decades ago who began with a single Under 14 team can be well pleased at the current state of their vision.**

The Royal Gaels' Crest

The Royal Gaels' crest features the Lagore Brooch, representing the Dunshaughlin part of the parish and the ruins of Knockmark church steeple to symbolize Drumree. The third element is a football and the inscription reads *Ar Scáth a Chéile a Mhaireann na nDaoine*, meaning *People live in each other's Shadows*. It emphasizes the necessity for teamwork. The crest dates from 2009 and prior to that the club used the Dunshaughlin crest.

BLACK & AMBER

New Century, New Challenges

20

Both 2003 and 2004 were era ending years. The former brought down the curtain on a run of championship success that placed Dunshaughlin among the elite of Meath club teams. The latter brought to an end the reign of the club's most successful ever manager, Eamonn Barry.

From the summit of the mountain there is only one direction.
Down.
You may linger at the top for a time, enjoying the view and your superior status but eventually someone else will take your place. After three years at the top Dunshaughlin were displaying signs of wear and tear, fraying at the edges. Injuries had begun to accumulate and the hunger for success may have begun to wane.

By 2003 many of the players were veterans of demanding intermediate and senior campaigns for close on a decade. Dermot Kealy, probably the club's best ever, and assuredly most important ever, player, had first lined out in the intermediate championship in 1988. Ciarán Byrne, intermediate and senior winning captain of 1997 and 2001, had made his debut in 1991, while Brendan Kealy had started a year earlier. Graham Dowd, who had been at the centre of a lethal half forward line and was the leading scorer in the intermediate triumph of 1997, had developed into an ever-present midfield powerhouse for the first of the two senior titles but suffered a serious knee injury in 2003 that initially limited and later ended his career with the senior team. Aiden Kealy, a fortress at centre back for a decade, played in a variety of positions in 2003, but 2004 was his final year at senior level.

> **"** After three years at the top Dunshaughlin were displaying signs of wear and tear, fraying at the edges.

BLACK & AMBER

Cillian Finn
Meath midfielder in the Leinster Minor championship victory, 2006.

Trevor Dowd
Leinster Junior medalist with Meath in 2006 and Dunshaughlin's leading all-time scorer in senior championship games, accumulating 20-158 in eighty games between 1999 and 2014.

None of those players was easily replaced. All had central roles in the glory years and their absence would be felt in the campaigns to come. There were some ready-made replacements. Ray Maloney had burst onto the senior team in 2002, winning a senior championship and a Leinster medal in his first year. Once on the team, he quickly made the central forward positions his own with a direct approach, combining natural ball carrying and scoring skills. Later he would go on to anchor midfield.

Caoimhín King, who had captained Meath at minor and Under 21 level, became a regular fixture in defence from 2003. He was one of the most naturally talented players to ever wear the Dunshaughlin jersey. His versatility enabled him to man any position, while his balance, coolness under pressure, confidence on the ball and especially his vision and ability to deliver accurate passes marked him out as a special talent.

In the middle of the decade Cathal O Dwyer appeared on the scene and lit up the forward line. He won a Hogan Cup Colleges medal with St. Patricks, Navan in 2004, and a Dublin senior football championship with University College Dublin in 2006. After two outings as a substitute for the black and ambers in 2004 he made thirty-three consecutive championship appearances, scoring in twenty-eight of them. His pace, accuracy and skill confounded and bamboozled defenders who invariably discovered they were up against more than they bargained for.

Despite the gradual changing of the guard many of the central characters

CHAPTER 20: NEW CENTURY, NEW CHALLENGES

from the three in a row team continued to wear the black and amber during the decade. The lethal full forward line of Richie Kealy, David Crimmins and Trevor Dowd continued to destabilize defences. Trevor Dowd was ever present in attack, apart from a year in Australia in 2005, and took over the role of leading scorer by the middle of the decade. Richie Kealy, Meath Footballer of the Year in 2000 and the club's most decorated player, alternated between defence and attack in a sterling club career that began in 1993 and culminated in a cameo county final appearance in 2011. David Crimmins, two-footed and skillful to his finger tips, filled a variety of roles from centre back to full forward while also pursuing a hurling career that featured an Inter Provincial Railway Cup medal with Leinster in 2008.

Niall Kelly, Leinster Club Player of the Year in 2000, made the centre field slot his own. His ball winning and carrying skills were crucial in gaining possession, while one long delivery could turn desperate defence into productive attack in an instant. Though at times his long distance frees could go awry, more often than not he converted slim chances into vital scores and his iconic point in the 2002 final against Trim was the mould for many equally stunning replicas.

In defence Kenny McTigue continued to hold the number three jersey, going on to create a club record of 107 senior championship appearances by 2013 and was undoubtedly the outstanding club full back in the county during the decade. Younger players such as Ronan Gogan, who had taken over from Brian O Rourke between the posts in 2000, his brother Fearghal, Denis Kealy, Michael McHale, Martin Reilly, David Tonge and Ronnie Yore formed the core of the team well into the new century.

Struggling to Retain the Keegan Cup

After three years atop the mountain, staying there in 2003 was a prolonged, but ultimately unsuccessful battle. The side mixed the good with the bad. Trevor Dowd contributed 1-2 to a promising start against Summerhill but Walterstown got the upper hand in the second round and St. Patricks took a point off the champions in the fourth series of games. In between was a good win against Dunboyne but when Trim exacted some revenge for the 2002 final defeat the black and ambers looked also-rans. Five points dropped in as many games wasn't championship winning form.

The up-and-down performances continued in the next two games. Four goals and thirteen points against Kilmainhamwood, two of the goals from David Tonge and one each from David Crimmins and Trevor Dowd, sent out the message that Dunshaughlin could not be written out of the script. A fortnight later the script

> After three years atop the mountain, staying there in 2003 was a prolonged, but ultimately unsuccessful battle.

was being revised and obituaries penned after a draw with Cortown. The see-saw pattern was sufficient to see Dunshaughlin scrape into a quarter-final with Skryne and in a display reminiscent of the previous three years the obituaries were once again shelved after a 3-8 to 1-12 victory.

Trevor Dowd was in outstanding form with goals from play and a penalty in addition to three points. Dermot Kealy, battling injuries and lack of training, was back to spearhead midfield where his work rate and economical use of the ball created numerous opportunities for the forwards. His work was complemented by the outstanding performance of Niall Kelly that left Skryne clutching at straws. His long-range distribution, by now a trademark of Dunshaughlin's style, had the opposing defence at sixes and sevens. The side was still so strong that Roscommon inter county player Mick Ryan couldn't make the starting fifteen during the knock-out stages.

The semi-final scoreline was almost the direct opposite of that recorded in the quarter-final. This time Dunshaughlin mustered 1-12 but it was insufficient to match Blackhall Gaels' 3-9. Dunshaughlin were knocked from their Meath and Leinster perch, sent tumbling from the heights into exile by impressive opponents. Dermot Kealy was unable to field after his heroics against Skryne and with Michael McHale, Richie and Brendan Kealy able for substitute roles only, Dunshaughlin struggled to secure a fifth successive final ticket. The losers could only manage a single point from play and Ronan Gogan was forced to make two fine saves to prevent a bigger defeat.

Although the championship trail ended at semi-final stage the team reached the final of the All County League, bidding to retain the 2002 title won in early 2003. Walterstown provided the opposition, but Dunshaughlin, despite looking the better side for most of the game, conceded a costly three goals and the Blacks took the title by the minimum margin, 3-4 to 1-9. Former Dublin player Senan Moylan proved a match winner for Walterstown when he came on as a substitute and scored 2-1. Dunshaughlin were level at half time and again midway through the second half when Kelly showed his power and strength, fielding a ball from David Crimmins and in one movement turning and blasting a superb goal.

A two-point advantage late in the game turned out to be the most dangerous of leads when Moylan produced a brilliant catch and rifled the ball to the net. There was still time for Justin McCarthy and Niall Kelly to exchange points and in a final onslaught Kelly rattled the crossbar, Paddy Reynolds cleared a follow up off the line and as the pressure mounted the defence fouled Brendan Kealy within scoring range. Before Niall Kelly could knock over the equalizer referee Noel Martin changed his decision and threw the ball in, deeming Dunshaughlin over zealous in their efforts to get the ball. Inevitably the whistle went moments later and the clean sweep in 2002 was followed by the bare cupboard in 2003.

The team lined out against Walterstown as follows:

Ronan Gogan; Fearghal Gogan, Kenny McTigue, Ciarán Byrne; Ronnie Yore, Michael McHale, Caoimhín King; Aiden Kealy (0-1), John Crimmins; Brendan Kealy, David Crimmins (0-1), Martin Reilly (0-2); Richie Kealy, Niall Kelly (1-3) Trevor Dowd (0-2). Subs: Ray Maloney for Richie Kealy, Mick Ryan for Yore, Andy Quinn for Dowd, Damian Burke for John Crimmins, Denis Kealy for McHale.

Both 2003 and 2004 were era ending years. The former brought down the curtain on a run of championship success that placed Dunshaughlin among the elite of Meath club teams. The latter brought to an end the reign of the club's most successful ever manager, Eamonn Barry. When two younger members of the panel, Caoimhín King and Stephen Ward, applied to play in the United States during the summer the club decided not to stand in their way. Eamonn, however, was unhappy at their loss and resigned as coach. Attempts to resolve the impasse failed and though there was a possibility of his return the players made it clear that they wanted a change and there was no way back.

One Year, Three Managers

2004 had started out promisingly with a narrow victory over Dunboyne and a comprehensive one against Gaeil Colmcille. The next outing, Eamonn Barry's last in charge, against a Ballinlough side facing their third straight defeat, proved that there is no certainty in sport. The favourites hit fourteen wides and only managed eight points as a late Jody Devine score gave the reds victory.

Former Meath star and Monaghan manager, Colm Coyle, replaced Barry and Dunshaughlin boosted their chances of making the knock-out stages with victory over Simonstown Gaels and a draw with Navan O Mahonys. Skryne dented those hopes with a single point victory in Ratoath and in the final game Trim seemed to have dealt a critical blow to the black and ambers' prospects when they finished a goal in front. Despite dropping seven points, other results favoured Dunshaughlin and they found themselves facing into a quarter-final showdown with Blackhall Gaels. This was an opportunity to reverse the previous year's semi-final result while also depriving the new champions of their title.

The managerial change over had not been entirely smooth. Colm Coyle had missed the Skryne clash due to holidays and then came news that he was unavailable for the Blackhall game also. Brendan Kealy stepped into the coach/manager role in his absence. Following the poor qualifying performances few gave the side much chance against the holders. Instead, as had happened so often

> *'It must have been demoralizing for Blackhall, when one Kealy goes and another appears.'*

in the past, Dunshaughlin kept the best wine for the concluding stages and they dictated matters throughout before recording a merited 0-16 to 0-14 victory after extra time.

The heavyweights of Meath football slugged it out for over an hour in a tough, tense encounter. Substitutions were critical as the combined effects of cramp and physicality took their toll. The *Chronicle* declared that

The Kealy factor had a big bearing on this result. Denis Kealy at centre back, hobbled off towards the end of normal time, but also answered the call during an extra time crisis when another hero, Caoimhín King was struggling with cramp. Aiden Kealy formed a solid midfield partnership with Niall Kelly until he too was called ashore as the batteries needed recharging in the final quarter. Another Kealy, Dermot, proved an adequate replacement. It must have been demoralizing for Blackhall, when one Kealy goes and another appears.

Cathal O Dwyer terrorized Blackhall down the left wing and a return of three points from play was scant reward for expended energy, but, his ability to carry the ball and wrong foot defenders created plenty of opportunities for others. Caoimhín King was a towering influence in defence, but was equaled by the tigerish Kevin Ward who excelled in the half back line.

Unlike the previous year when they couldn't buy points from play this time they had ten, five in extra time indicating the reserves of energy and determination possessed by the side. In the gathering gloom of extra time two O Dwyer points and another brace from Michael McHale and Trevor Dowd pushed Dunshaughlin in front. Robert Cox and Tadhg Brosnan countered before

Blackhall were dragged reluctantly to the guillotine where Kelly and Dowd finished the job despite some more resistance from Crampton and Cox. It was exhausting just watching it. Bring on the next victims' recorded the *Chronicle*.

Now back on the semi-final stage the team took matters into its own hands. For a crew used to the professional approach and meticulous organization of Eamonn Barry it was unacceptable that a coach would miss a qualifier and then compound it by going absent for the quarter-final. They demanded that Colm Coyle be dispensed with and Brendan Kealy stay on in the role of coach. Though some committee members viewed this as player power run riot it was sanctioned. While playing with and coaching Dunshaughlin, Kealy was also coaching Ratoath and would guide them to the Meath junior championship and the Leinster junior tournament titles before the end of the year.

Skryne provided the semi-final opposition and it took two games and extra time to produce a result. In the initial meeting Dunshaughlin were always playing catch-up and only got on terms, 0-12 to 1-9, deep into second-half injury time when Cathal O Dwyer converted a free. That point sent the Dunshaughlin supporters into raptures and a minute later they were in seventh heaven when Niall Kelly's booming point gave them the lead for the one and only time.

Skryne retrieved the situation with a late point that sent the tie into extra time. That couldn't separate the sides either, for two early Skryne points were matched by two from Niall Kelly, one in each additional half. Both teams exited to a standing ovation in appreciation of the quality and intensity of the contest.

In the replay Dunshaughlin started brightly, and Trevor Dowd rifled the ball to the net as early as the tenth minute. Cathal O Dwyer, Aiden Kealy, Trevor Dowd and Niall Kelly added points as Skryne started the slower of the two. Shortly before half time the goal was still the difference, 1-4 to 0-4, when two players were dismissed. First Ray Maloney received a second yellow card and on reaching the sideline threw his gloves into the stand in frustration. This diverted the crowd's attention from the incident that led to Trevor Giles being red carded to reduce both sides to fourteen men.

Skryne fared better after the dismissals. They reduced the lead to a point before half time and had four more early in the second half with substitute Kevin Mulvany running riot. When Dunshaughlin re-awoke they grabbed three points in a few minutes but despite plentiful possession never looked like threatening Skryne who continued to clip over points to win 0-15 to 1-7.

In the knock out stages in 2003 Dunshaughlin had defeated Skryne and lost to Blackhall. Now the order was reversed, beating Blackhall and losing to Skryne but the outcome was the same. There was to be no final appearance for the black and ambers and in both years their conquerors went on to claim the title.

Despite the red card Trevor Giles did line out in the final the following week. Meath County Board decided to rescind the card and overrule referee Jimmy Henry's decision on the basis of what it deemed 'authentic evidence.' The Referees' Administrator, Joe Harlin, stated, 'To say that referees were dumb struck at the decision would be an understatement' as he questioned how the County Board could be sure the 'authentic witnesses' were at the game and claimed that neither the referee nor umpires were called to give evidence.

Thus Trevor missed no games as a result of the red card. This was in ironic contrast to Aiden Kealy, who, two years earlier, missed eight championship games in 2002, four in Meath, four in Leinster, in addition to a Feis Cup and All County League final in early 2003. This was as a result of drawing the attention of a linesman to an off-the-ball injury to a Dunshaughlin player in the Kilmacud Sevens. The referee reported Aiden for interfering with the linesman and despite the best efforts of club mentors a six-month suspension wasn't reduced until January 2003.

The contrasts in treatment left a bitter taste.

> 'Blackhall were dragged reluctantly to the guillotine where Kelly and Dowd finished the job despite some more resistance from Crampton and Cox. It was exhausting just watching it. Bring on the next victims'

Mairéad Delaney
Mairéad was the first female to hold an elected position with Meath County Board at juvenile and adult level. She was PRO of Meath Juvenile Board in 2001, Secretary 2001-04, Development Officer of the County Board 2009-12 and is currently Assistant Secretary, 2013-15. She was also Secretary of St. Martins, 1997-2001 and Dunshaughlin, 2006-09.

Dunshaughlin, Under 21 A Champions, 2004

Front: Cormac Delaney, Alan McLoughlin, David Devereux, Conor Staunton, Cathal O Dwyer, Ciarán Hoary, Eoin Farrelly, Caoimhín King, Jamie Minnock.
Back: Kevin Ward, Paul Sheehy, Gavin O Regan, Owen Herlihy, Stephen Ward, Ray Maloney, Capt., Michael Ahern, Shane Kelly, Ciarán Farrelly, Adrian Toolan, Colin Murphy.

Under 21s Provide some Cheer

> On the day Dunshaughlin's artillery was always superior but its inaccuracy left the issue in doubt till the end.

While progression to the final was beyond the senior team in 2004, the Under 21 side was up to the task. The competition didn't get underway until after the senior semi-final and it was December before it reached a conclusion.

After winning the title in 2000 the club spent three unsuccessful years in the championship proper before settling for the A grade once more in 2004. The side had a sprinkling of established senior performers, Ray Maloney, Caoimhín King and Kevin Ward, and a clutch of players who had been successful at under-age with St. Martins.

The initial outing was of little value to the victors or the vanquished, as Dunshaughlin put six goals and eighteen points past Nobber, with Conor Staunton accounting for 3-2 of the total. Skryne's Under 21s couldn't emulate their adult counterparts in the semi-final meeting as they shipped 3-13 against a rampant Dunshaughlin side. Staunton again headed the scoring charts with a pair of goals and points.

Na Fianna provided the ultimate opposition. On the day Dunshaughlin's artillery was always superior but its inaccuracy left the issue in doubt till the end. Sixteen wides, evenly shared between both halves, made for a laboured victory. The black and ambers spurned three first half goal chances, including a Conor Staunton penalty, deflected over the bar for a point, yet contrived to lead by eight points to three at half time. Keeper Michael Ahern had to depart with a serious injury but Gavin O Regan capably manned the breach with some good saves.

Cathal O Dwyer and Conor Staunton were Dunshaughlin's liveliest forwards,

CHAPTER 20: NEW CENTURY, NEW CHALLENGES

but didn't get the opportunity to wreak the havoc of earlier rounds. Nevertheless, O Dwyer and David Devereux both scored three points as centre forward Stephen Ward used his vision and skill to create numerous openings. Once Dunshaughlin stretched the lead to six early in the second half, Na Fianna faced an uphill battle and though they eventually reduced the deficit to two they were unable to punish Dunshaughlin's poor conversion rate.

When the game ended 0-11 to 1-6 in Dunshaughlin's favour, former club Secretary Cyril Creavin had the pleasant task of presenting the cup to captain Ray Maloney. The successful team lined out as follows:

Under 21 Trophy Presentation, 2004
Ray Maloney, Dunshaughlin Under 21 Captain and Cyril Creaven, Meath County Board Assistant Secretary.

Michael Ahern

Caoimhín King   Ciarán Hoary

Alan McLoughlin   Kevin Ward   Eoin Farrelly

Ray Maloney, Capt. (0-2)   Owen Herlihy

Ciarán Farrelly   Stephen Ward (0-2)   David Devereux (0-3)

Cathal O Dwyer (0-3)   Conor Staunton (0-1)

Subs: Gavin O Regan for Ahern, Cormac Delaney for Farrelly, Shane Kelly for Devereux, Paul Sheehy, Adrian Toolan, Diarmuid Delaney, Jamie Minnock, Brian Murphy. Team Manager: Gabriel King, Selectors, Pat Herlihy, David Crimmins. Coach: Denis Kealy.

With ten of the 2004 side still eligible in 2006 the team reached the semi-final where Gaeil Colmcille surprisingly proved too strong in Dunganny as Dunshaughlin missed numerous goal chances. Dunshaughlin had more scores, fourteen, all points, whereas the Kells' side's eleven scores amounted to 2-9, enough for a single point victory. The goals all arrived at vital stages of the second half and overcame Dunshaughlin's interval advantage of four points.

The following year, 2007, six of the 2004 starters were still Under 21, when, for the third time in the decade Dunshaughlin took the A title. The campaign was a sharp, short one beginning in mid October and concluding within a month. The team got off to a stuttering start, edging past Duleek before annihilating Nobber in Round 2.

The semi-final produced the game of the year, a thrilling shoot-out with Na Fianna at Summerhill. Despite posting an early lead Dunshaughlin couldn't retain it and did well to reel in a dominant Na Fianna side before the full time whistle and force extra time. Fortunes continued to oscillate as goals from Mark Caldwell and Cathal O Dwyer seemed to assure victory but Na Fianna hit the net near the end to set up a nail-biting climax. A late Conor Staunton goal assured victory after a high scoring contest by 3-16 to 2-15.

> **The black and ambers had the lion's share of possession throughout but wayward shooting, thirteen wides to complement thirteen scores, gave Wolfe Tones the opportunity to remain in touch.**

Staunton also dominated the scoring stakes in the final on an Arctic evening in Páirc Tailteann. The black and ambers had the lion's share of possession throughout but wayward shooting, thirteen wides to complement thirteen scores, gave Wolfe Tones the opportunity to remain in touch. Mark Caldwell set up both goals for Staunton and Cathal O Dwyer also contributed handsomely to the victory with four points. Staunton's first goal, just after half time, seemed the death-knell for the Tones but they then reeled off five unanswered points to draw level. Dunshaughlin had greater reserves of talent and skill, however, and Staunton's second goal provided the foundation on which to build a winning total of 2-11 to 1-10.

Cathal O Dwyer captained the side, a victory he dedicated to Paddy Doohan, who died from illness in 2006 and was a contemporary of many of the players with St. Martins. Don McLoughlin, Tommy Clusker, Tom Finn and Simon Farrell guided the following team to success:

Seán Doyle

Ciarán Clusker   Tommy Johnson

Alan McLoughlin   Michael Ahern   Fearghal Delaney

Cillian Finn   Ciarán Farrelly (0-1)

Niall Dundon   David Devereux (0-1)   Mark Caldwell (0-1)

Conor Staunton (2-3)   Cathal O Dwyer, Capt. (0-4)

Subs: Dara Devereux (0-1) for Dundon, Tadhg Ó Dúshláine, Shane Kelly, Cathal Moore, Cillian Dennehy, David O Rourke, Duncan Geraghty.

A Long Way from the Summit

> David Crimmins earned a penalty and at least 6.0 for artistic impression with his dive

In 2005 the senior championship featured an eight team group and as usual in such circumstances form fluctuated wildly. Charlie Redmond was team manager with Eamonn Dunne and Don McLoughlin as his selectors. A reasonable start with a seven-point victory over Kilmainhamwood in the first round and a draw with St. Patricks was offset by losses to Skryne and Wolfe Tones. The *Chronicle* reported that against Kilmainhamwood David Crimmins earned a penalty and at least 6.0 for artistic impression with his dive. With just three points from four games and ties against Seneschalstown and Walterstown to come prospects of qualification seemed slim and further bouts of artistic impression might be required!

Then, in the best performance of the year the black and ambers held Seneschalstown scoreless until almost the end of the third quarter. The team was fired up and focused. Niall Kelly and Cillian Finn were in complete command at midfield. Seventeen year old Finn was making only his second senior appearance

Dunshaughlin, Under 21 A Special Champions, 2007

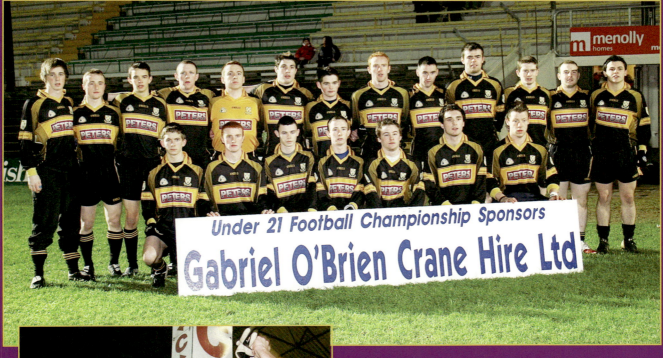

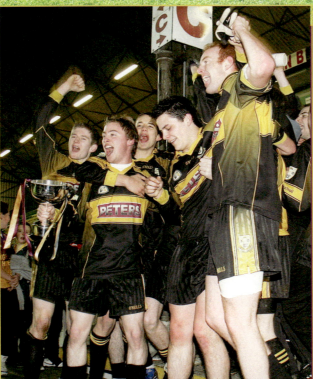

Front: Cillian Dennehy, Dara Devereux, David O Rourke, Fearghal Delaney, Cathal O Dwyer, Tommy Johnson, Michael Ahern.
Back: Duncan Geraghty, Ciarán Clusker, Tadhg Ó Dushláine, Niall Dundon, Seán Doyle, Shane Kelly, Conor Staunton, David Devereux, Alan McLoughlin, Cillian Finn, Ciarán Farrelly, Cathal Moore, Mark Caldwell.
Photo: Declan Lynch.

Cathal O Dwyer and team mates celebrate with Under 21 Trophy, 2007
Celebrations begin after the Under 21 presentation. Pictured are Ciarán Farrelly, Cathal O Dwyer with trophy, Tadgh Ó Dushláine, Mark Caldwell and David Devereux.
Photo: Declan Lynch.

BLACK & AMBER

Presentation to Under 21 Selectors 2007
Tom Finn, Mairéad Delaney, Secretary, Don McLoughlin, Simon Farrell, Tommy Clusker and Jim Smith, Chairman.

and went on to man the midfield slot with Meath as they captured the Leinster minor title in 2006. Denis Kealy returned to centre back after injury and the entire forward line was functioning smoothly, combining incisive running with accurate shooting. Ray Maloney top scored with 2-1, the first after superb play by Finn and a final pass from David Crimmins, the second created by a long ball from Niall Kelly. Seneschalstown had no answer as Dunshaughlin powered to a 2-14 to 0-3 victory.

Another smooth performance against Walterstown, who had Eamonn Barry in charge, suggested that the team was running into form at the right time. The highlights were goals in each half and a flurry of four late points to close out the game. The first of the goals was a simple tap-in for David Crimmins after intelligent approach play by Conor Staunton, the second, a penalty for a foul on Crimmins, dispatched to the net by full-back Kenny McTigue. Cathal O Dwyer accounted for two of the closing points, Ray Maloney and Denis Kealy claimed the others.

Those two wins turned out to be vital as defeat in the final round against Simonstown Gaels left Dunshaughlin, Seneschalstown and Walterstown equal on points. Dunshaughlin advanced by virtue of victories against them both in previous rounds and so for the seventh consecutive year were into the knock-out stages.

The side could not replicate the quarter-final victories of the previous two years. Instead it was Trim that advanced by 2-11 to 0-10 after extra time. The substantial gap between the sides at the end didn't reflect the course of the game. The losers held the lead throughout the first half but wayward shooting in the third quarter and some superb stops by Brendan Murphy prevented them from staying ahead. Trim were more economical, scored a goal late on and Niall Kelly had to produce one of his wonder points to send the game into extra time. Kelly pointed again in the first period of extra time but a Paul Gilsenan goal was the game changer and Trim controlled the closing minutes.

Niall Kelly musing on the defeat noted that,

'We thought we were peaking at the right time going into the quarter-final ... but we missed chances in the second half and that didn't help our cause. We seemed to run out of steam in extra-time and our squad just isn't as strong as before. Four of the Kealys aren't there, Trevor Dowd was in Australia, and Mick McHale was struggling with injury all year. We haven't got the strength in depth that we used to have and that was reflected in our form in the league.'

His comment about the league reflected the team's struggle to stay in the premier division. The regular absence of Kelly and David Crimmins on county duty weakened the squad and its status in the top division, a status jealously guarded since 1992, was only assured when Skryne beat Blackhall to send the latter, instead of the black and ambers, into Division 2.

Another Year: Still Slip Sliding Away

In preparation for 2006 the managerial merry-go-round continued. Dudley Farrell, who had successfully coached Meath junior teams took over from Redmond, and TP Toolan and Stephen Claire joined him as selectors. Both were links to the 2000-03 sides, Toolan as selector and Claire as player. It turned out to be the least successful year of the decade as the side won none of its championship encounters and thereby failed to make the knock-out stage.

Yet, apart from a comprehensive defeat at the hands of St. Patricks all other games were close run affairs. Three ended in defeat, all by a single point and the rest, against Kilmainhamwood, Duleek, Summerhill and Blackhall Gaels ended level. Those points were just sufficient to steer the team clear of a play-off for senior survival. In contrast to the previous year the team had no difficulty retaining its league status as five victories and two draws from eleven games earned a fourth place finish.

Fearghal Gogan
Fearghal in championship action against Navan O Mahonys.

Success in the Green and Gold

Caoimhín King
All Star nominee in 2007, in action for Meath.

On right: Tommy Johnson, Meath captain in Leinster Minor championship victory in 2008.

CHAPTER 20: NEW CENTURY, NEW CHALLENGES

Despite the lack of success in the black and amber jerseys in 2006 a number of clubmen distinguished themselves in the green and gold of Meath. The Royal County juniors captured the Leinster title recording victories over Kilkenny, Kildare and Louth with Richie Kealy and Trevor Dowd featuring throughout. Both scored two points in the semi-final victory against Kildare while Trevor tapped in a late goal to ensure victory in the provincial final against Louth. Trevor was winning his first Leinster medal repeating his father's achievement in 1964 while Richie was collecting his third, a decade after his first.

Cillian Finn was an ever present at midfield as the Meath minors defeated Kildare and Laois before winning the Leinster title with a final victory over Offaly. He made a number of impressive catches in the final and played a significant role in containing the Faithful County's attack by dropping back to assist his defence. David McMahon and John Coleman from St. Martins were also members of the winning panel. Two years later Tommy Johnson captained the Royals and anchored the defence from centre back as they registered another Leinster final victory against Offaly.

Presentation to Cathal O Dwyer to mark his part in St. Patrick's Classical School's All-Ireland Colleges' Hogan Cup victory in 2004. Jim Smith on left, Paddy O Dwyer on right.

Caoimhín King went a few steps further. He was Meath's Under 21 captain in 2006 and was also selected to represent Leinster in the Inter Provincial competition, lining out in the semi-final and final victories against Ulster and Connaught. With victory over the latter in Boston, 2-14 to 2-11, Caoimhín became the first clubman to win a Railway Cup medal. His performance in the Meath back line as the Royals reached the 2007 All-Ireland semi-final was recognized with an All Star nomination and he played in every game of the National League the same year as Meath claimed the Division 2 title.

Midway through the first decade of the new century the vista in the rear view mirror looked much more alluring than the landscape ahead. That vista however, was receding further into the past with each passing year and becoming part of the folk memory. Results from 2003 to 2006 suggested that Dunshaughlin's impetus was downhill with the latter year marking the first time the team had missed out on the knock-out stages since 1998. There were some signposts to indicate that the future would be better, the Under 21 victories in 2004 and 2007 and the continuing success of St. Martins being the most positive. The closing years of the decade would decide if the new generation would produce performances to merit comparison with those in the rear view mirror.

BLACK & AMBER

From Black and Red to Black and Amber: Underage Football 2009-14

January 2009 was both a celebration and a requiem as the red and black jerseys and banners were retired.

On Saturday, 7th October 2006 a full house attended St. Martins' Fiftieth Anniversary Dinner in the Ashbourne House Hotel. The sole surviving founder member, Ciarán Murray, made a brief appearance and the achievements of the club surely surpassed his and the other founders' expectations. St. Martins had won all the major football titles on offer, many of the hurling awards and seemed set for a second half century even more successful than the first. However, monumental change was in the offing, though few realized it at the time.

By 2006 suggestions of a change in the status of St. Martins were in the air. At the Dunshaughlin AGM the Chairman, Jim Smith, indicated that the senior club's committee intended to set up a juvenile section. In response, during 2007, St. Martins explored the possibility of the two adult clubs amalgamating under the name of St. Martins, thereby having one club in the parish. This was not

Ticket to 50th Anniversary Dinner Dance of St. Martins, 2006

Note: All team line-outs or panels, where known, referred to in this chapter who appeared in county finals are listed in Appendix 8. Some are incorporated into the text or contained with the team photographs in this chapter in addition to being included in the Appendix.

> From 2009 under age football teams lined out in the black and amber of Dunshaughlin while hurlers and camogie players sported the red and white of Drumree.

acceptable to Dunshaughlin, as the club did not wish to lose its identity and had expansive development plans, both for facilities and teams. In November 2007, following a St. Martins' Information Night attended by 183 parents the club requested both adult clubs to elect a sub-committee to discuss amalgamation. Dunshaughlin again voted against.

A further complication arose when Croke Park, in response to requests for clarification from Dunshaughlin, declared that juvenile clubs such as St. Martins were sub committees of the adult clubs. The establishment of a juvenile section for Dunshaughlin was temporarily withdrawn and in 2008 St. Martins continued as normal. However, by the end of 2008 Dunshaughlin revived the proposal of a juvenile football section in the club and proposed that Drumree cater for juvenile hurling. Drumree agreed to this approach and thus, by November 2008 St. Martins had no choice but to bow to the inevitable.

In January 2009 an emotional presentation of club jerseys and medals took place in Dunshaughlin Community Centre. Nine of the club's twenty-six teams collected silverware and players were presented with club jerseys. Framed St. Martins' red and black jerseys were presented to former Chairpersons and Presidents. Chairperson Linda Christie declared,

'The jerseys that were given out at the final presentation will serve as life long reminders not only of the honour the recipients had in representing St. Martins with such distinction and of the friendships they made in doing so, but also of the tremendous loyalty and pride of the local community in a club whose contribution to local GAA history has been written in gold and will never be forgotten.'

From 2009 under age football teams lined out in the black and amber of Dunshaughlin while hurlers and camogie players sported the red and white of Drumree.

Many opposed the new arrangements, particularly those involved with St. Martins, but the majority viewed it as the way forward. St. Martins had established a strong tradition and built a reputation as one of the most successful and best organized underage clubs in Meath. In the nineties and early 2000s the club hauled in trophies like a trawler netting fish. In football the haul included Under 12 titles in 2002 and 2004, Under 14 championships in 2001, 2005 and 2006, Féile champions in 2001 followed by three in a row Féile wins, 2004-06, Under 16 titles in 2002 and 2003 and Minor in 1987 and 2002. The hurlers also had their days in the sun with four Under 14 B titles between 1992 and 2001 and Minor B championships in 1997, 2001 and 2003.

The club was the starting point for the hugely successful careers of All-Ireland senior medalists such as Noel Curran, Jimmy Walsh, Evan Kelly, Richie Kealy, John Cullinane and of many others who won Leinster and All-Ireland honours at minor,

Under-21 and junior level. Above all it provided players, mentors and officials with years of enjoyment and fulfilment. January 2009 was both a celebration and a requiem as the red and black jerseys and banners were retired.

For Dunshaughlin the logic of change was overwhelming. It would create continuity from nursery to senior football, players would wear the same jersey as juvenile and adult, and, it would involve parents in the club from the beginning. In the glory days of 2000 to 2002 young players could support their heroes but when lining out themselves couldn't wear the black and amber. This was a source of bemusement and incomprehension to many newcomers to the area not versed in the complex world of local club history or the importance of club colours.

> In an effort to keep everyone on board the GAA has fallen into the mentality of Dodo in *Alice's Adventures in Wonderland* who declared '*Everybody has won, and all must have prizes.*'

Underage in Black and Amber, 2009-14

There has been a revolution in underage football since the re-formation of St. Martins in 1983.

The once ultra competitive championships and leagues from Under 12 to minor have been replaced by an emphasis on participation, coaching and development, with serious competition from Under 13 only. Many of the Under 10, 11 and 12 contests consist of two games played between two competing clubs with the combined score determining the winner, and goals and points having equal value. The Under 12s play semi-competitively per GAA directives and lower grades down to Under 8 participate in the blitzes and nursery programmes. During the club's senior championship games in recent years their underage counterparts played mini-games at half time in Páirc Tailteann. By 2011 Dunshaughlin had in the region of 250 registered underage players and fielded eight competitive teams from Under 13 up to minor. Team managers and coaches are now obliged to obtain coaching qualifications and Garda clearance is compulsory.

The plethora of Spring, Summer and Autumn leagues, championships, shields and blitzes suggest that in an effort to keep everyone on board the GAA has fallen into the mentality of Dodo in *Alice's Adventures in Wonderland* who declared '*Everybody has won, and all must have prizes.*' It would be difficult to document the outcomes of all the competitions from Under 13 up at each age group; if one did, it would try the readers' and writers' patience, so the exceptional performances are acknowledged here with all final appearances and teams, where known, recorded in the appendices.

BLACK & AMBER

Double Under 14 Success 2009 and 2010

Top: Conor Jennings, captain David Dunne, Darren Lawless and Ben Conlon celebrate the Under 14 Reserve Football League victory in 2010.
Above: Ben Duggan, team captain, accepts the Under 14 trophy from Michael McMahon of the Meath Juvenile Board following Dunshaughlin's victory in the 2009 Under 14 League final.
Photo: Declan Lynch

Under 14s Now Appearing in Black and Amber

When the 2009 season commenced St. Martins was no more. The first official under-age game in the Dunshaughlin name and colours was an Under 14 league outing on Saturday 7th March when the young black and ambers annihilated Summerhill by 4-10 to 0-5. Club President, Patsy McLoughlin, threw in the ball to mark the occasion. Lorcán Byrne registered the first score while Ben Duggan captained the side, the first under age team to wear black and amber since the formation of St. Martins in 1983.

The impressive start continued in subsequent games including the final where another scoring spree disposed of St. Colmcilles by 3-17 to 0-4 with Ben Duggan in inspirational form. Frank Gallogly, Robbie Byrne, Jimmy Beattie and Paul McEvoy were the side's mentors while Shane Gallogly, Seán Fitzpatrick and Ben Duggan lined out with the Meath Under 14s during the year.

The victorious line out was Jack O Sullivan; Josh Wall, Seán Fitzpatrick, Gareth Rooney; Oisín Foley, Steven Kinsella, David Reilly (0-1); Ben Duggan, Capt. (0-6), Diarmuid Christie (0-1); Lorcán Byrne, Shane Gallogly (0-3), Stephen Duffy (1-2); David Beattie (0-2), David Moore (2-1), Stephen Farrell (0-1). Subs: Tom Sharp for Farrell, Ronan Geraghty for Duffy, Dan Ormsby for Christie, Craig Cullen for O Sullivan, Conor McEvoy, David Dunne, Martin Nevin.

The club also fielded an Under 14 Reserve team in 2009 and it repeated the success with a four-goal victory over Navan O Mahonys in the replayed final. The honour of accepting the trophy fell to David Dunne, the captain of the reserves.

Between 2010 and 2012 the Under 14 teams performed commendably. In 2010 there was victory for the first team in the Division 2 league final against Seneschalstown by 4-15 to 3-7 and for the reserves in the Division 9 league, the latter defeating Kilbride by 2-6 to 1-7. A year later the first team fell at Division 2 semi-final stage while the reserves went all the way to the final before succumbing to Summerhill.

Good progress continued in 2012. The premier team, lost the Spring League Division 1 final by two points to Dunboyne and later appeared in the Division 1 Shield Final, but Wolfe Tones got the upper hand in extra time. Neil Byrne bagged a hat trick of goals that helped Dunshaughlin to a second half advantage but the Tones drew level with a late point and streaked ahead in extra time to win by 2-21 to 5-7.

A glut of goals was also the salient feature of the Under 14 Summer League Division 2 Final. Between them Dunshaughlin and Summerhill netted a dozen times before Paddy Maher's side emerged victorious by 5-17 to 7-5. Neil Byrne and David Fildes grabbed a brace of goals each but despite their goal advantage

Dunshaughlin, Under 14 Division 1B Winners, 2009

The Dunshaughlin side that captured the Under 14 title in 2009 with a final victory against St. Colmcilles.
Front: Craig Cullen, Lorcán Byrne, Diarmuid Christie, Josh Wall, Conor McEvoy, Ronan Geraghty, David Beattie, Shane Gallogly, Stephen Duffy.
Back: Dan Ormsby, David Moore, Seán Fitzpatrick, Steven Kinsella, Jack O Sullivan, Ben Duggan, Capt., Oisín Foley, Tom Sharp, Gareth Rooney, David Reilly, Stephen Farrell. *Photo: Declan Lynch.*

Dunshaughlin, Under 14 Reserve Football League Winners, 2009

Front: Gavin Maher, Tommy Kinsella, Lorcán Casey, Sam Lavery, Mark Galvin, Ronan Smith, Paddy Maher, Adam Kealy, Conor Huijsdens, Daniel Quinn, Martin Nevin.
Back: Tommy Maher, Michael Nevin, Cormac Fitzpatrick, James Swan, Conor McEvoy, Liam Carey, Conor Jennings, Luke Ennis, Killian Gavin, David Dunne, Aaron Kealy, Kevin Kealy. *Photo: Declan Lynch.*

Dunshaughlin, Under 14 Division 2 Winners, 2010

The Dunshaughlin side that captured the Under 14 title in 2010 with a final victory against Seneschalstown by 4-15 to 3-7.
Front: Mark Galvin, Conor Huijsdens, Ronan Smith, Cillian Duffy, Niall Byrne, Martin Nevin, Daniel Quinn, Mark Donnelly, Conor McEvoy, Tommy Kinsella, Cormac Fitzpatrick.
Back: Michael Nevin, Manager, David Dunne, Jack O Sullivan, Gavin Maher, Liam Carey, Jack Kelly, Dan Ormsby, Ronan Geraghty, Josh Wall, William McCarthy, Stephen Duffy, Capt., Stephen Farrell, James Swan, Conor Jennings, Aaron Kealy, Andy Quinn, Coach.

Dunshaughlin, Under 14 Reserve Football League Division 9 Winners, 2010

This panel defeated Kilbride in the Reserve League Final, 2-6 to 1-7.
Front: Darragh Quinn, Cillian Hart, Lorcán Casey, Evan Ryan, David Dunne, Capt., Darren Lawless, Sam Lavery, Curtis Rattigan, Martin Keane.
Back: Michael Regan, Tom Boyhan, Mark Phelan, Conor Jennings, Martin Nevin, Aaron Kealy, Aaron Keane, Mark Galvin, Stephen Ennis, Ben Conlon, Cormac Fitzpatrick. *Photo: Declan Lynch.*

CHAPTER 21   FROM BLACK AND RED TO BLACK AND AMBER

Dunshaughlin, Under 14 Division 1 Shield Finalists, 2012

This team lost the Shield final to Wolfe Tones after extra time in Páirc Tailteann. Front: Cian Maher, Dylan O Brien, Cormac Byrne, Tom Dalton, Neil Byrne, Conor Keena, Darren Beattie, Paddy Maher. Back: Kevin Kealy, Anthony Fildes, Seán O Neill, Dylan Dunne, Sam Lavery, Adam McDermott, Sam Butler, Robert Holohan, Jack Hetherington, Adam Kealy, Stephen Walker, Frank Gallogly.
Photo: Declan Lynch.

Summerhill couldn't counter the black and ambers' points tally.

Later in the year Dunshaughlin secured the Under 15 Autumn Division 2 League title beating a spirited St Vincents-Curraha side in an exciting final by a solitary point. It required a comeback of Lazarus proportions as the black and ambers faced a six-point deficit at the start of the second half. It took the team practically half an hour to claw back to parity and then in the throes of additional time Sam Butler conjured up a winning point.

Best for Dunshaughlin were keeper Adam McDermott, full back Conor Keena, Paddy Maher at wing-back and team captain Adam Kealy at midfield. The attacking stars were Luke Slater, Neil Byrne and Cian Gallogly while substitute Jack Hetherington made a significant contribution.

Frank Gallogly managed the team that lined out as follows: Adam McDermott; Tom Dalton, Conor Keena, Dylan O Brien; Paddy Maher, Liam Donovan, Stephen Walker; Sam Butler Adam Kealy, Capt.; Seán O Neill, Luke Slater, Darren Beattie; Cian Gallogly, Neil Byrne, Conor Oliver. Subs: Jack Hetherington for Donovan, Kevin Doyle for O Brien, Andrew Leneghan, Shane Claire, Daniel Fildes, Ronan McMahon, Pádraig Clinton, Adam Summerville, Anthony Fildes, Dylan Dunne,

Dunshaughlin, Meath Féile Winners, 2014

Front: Eoin O Connor, Matthew Moyles, Ódhran O Riordan, Kevin Bawle, Harry Dunne, David Fildes, Luke Mitchell, Cathal McCormack.
Back: Thomas Reilly, Michael McHugh, Evan Butler, Paul Briody, Bill Jennings, Aaron Lawlor, Fionn Cummins, Cathal Sheehan, Niall Hurley, Mathew Costello, Wesley Goodwin.

Turlough Malone.

The highlight of recent years at Under 14 level was qualification for the All-Ireland Féile in 2014. Under the banner of St. Martins the club had established a reputation as Féile specialists in the first decade the new century, winning county titles in 2001 and then recording a famous three in a row between 2004 and 2006.

The omens were not favourable when Ratoath, the clear favourites for the title, chalked up an eighteen point victory against the black and ambers in the early rounds. The semi-final meeting of the same sides had the appearances of a reprise, as Ratoath's half time advantage of six points boosted their sense of superiority. Half time predictions were blown away on the restart as the Dunshaughlin youngsters combined skill and spirit in equal measure to first whittle away the lead and then, amid a welter of goals, emerge winners by a single point 4-7 to 4-6.

Arch rivals Dunboyne provided the opposition in the final but in contrast to the semi, Dunshaughlin took an early lead via goals from Mathew Costello and Cathal McCormack and then held on in a tense finish to win by 3-8 to 3-4. It earned the club the Spring League title but more importantly the right to represent Meath in Féile 2014.

Dunshaughlin was placed in Division 2 in a section containing host club Oran of Roscommon as well as Portlaoise and a second Roscommon club, Clann

CHAPTER 21   FROM BLACK AND RED TO BLACK AND AMBER

na nGael. A diplomatic draw against the hosts and a quarter-final victory over Mayo's Ballaghaderreen propelled the boys into the Shield semi-finals held in the Connaught Council's GAA Centre outside Ballyhaunis.

The black and ambers edged out Annaghdown of Galway in the semi-final to set up a repeat encounter with Clann na nGael for the title. Displaying outstanding teamwork and herculean defending Dunshaughlin built up an early three-point lead that stretched to five entering the closing stages. The lead, however, had been hard won and at a high cost in terms of energy in the blistering summer sun. The Gaels slowly gained a stranglehold on the game and their final effort in injury time ensured parity.

The momentum was now with the westerners and despite finishing the first half of extra time level, Dunshaughlin's reserves had run dry and the final score of 3-7 to 1-6 disguised the drama and closeness of an enthralling contest. David McCormack managed the side with Aidan McHugh, Paul Nestor and Eamonn Moyles as mentors. The following team lined out in the final

Aaron Lawlor; Cathal Sheehan, Paul Briody, Ódhran O Riordan; Cathal McCormack, Eoin O Connor, David Fildes; Michael McHugh (1-0), Niall Hurley (0-1); Luke Mitchell, Wesley Goodwin, Matthew Moyles (0-1); Fionn Cummins (0-1), Mathew Costello (0-3), Harry Dunne. Subs: Kevin Bawle, Evan Butler, Bill Jennings, Thomas O Reilly. Others who played in the earlier stages included Alastar Philip, Pádraig Dalton, Liam Reilly, Alan O Connor, Oisín Caldwell and Seán Ennis.

Under 12s and 13s

2010 was the year of near misses in finals and semi-finals for the Under 12s and 13s. The Under 12 premier team finished as runners-up to Trim while the reserves lost out to Ratoath at semi-final stage in Division 5. The Under 13s lost a Shield semi-final to Skryne and the reserves went down at the same stage to North Meath Gaels.

2011 ushered in a remarkable four years at Under 12 level. Summer League titles in 2011 and 2012 were followed up with Spring League honours in the following two years. Two of the victories were recorded against neighbouring rivals Ratoath while the black and ambers accounted for Summerhill and St. Colmcilles in 2011 and 2013 respectively. Such a protracted level of consistent success is unusual, as Under 12 teams have a huge throughput of players from year to year as participants move on to the next level. No player featured in more than two successes and a large number completed this elusive double.

The first of the four titles came in 2011 when the young black and ambers

Under 14 Féile Success.
Pictured above at top with the trophy after victory against Dunboyne in the Meath Féile final 2014 are, joint captains Eoin O Connor and Niall Hurley. Mathew Costello celebrates his goal in the final against Dunboyne as Fionn Cummins gets ready to join in. Note jersey change due to colour clash with Dunboyne. Photos: Declan Lynch.

447

Dunshaughlin, Under 12 Winners, 2014

Celebrations after victory against Ratoath in the 2014 Under 12 decider.
Front: James Traynor, Fursey Blake, Liam O Connor, Adam Territt, partly hidden, Seán Walsh, Conor Gray, Mark O Brien below Conor and partly obscured by hand, John McDonagh partly hidden, Aaron Murphy, Josh Masterson, only top of head visible, Aidan Fraher, Cian Edwards.
Back: Seán O Connor, Cillian McCool, Jake Martin- face visible, Robert Walker, Colm Keane, with hand reaching to cup, Jack Brady, Joseph Dunne looking downwards, Andrew Quinn, Jared Rushe, Harry Magee.
Back right: Cian McLaughlin, Darragh Byrne, Jack Kehoe with black body armour on hand. *Photo: Declan Lynch.*

Presentation to Under 12 Captains, 2012, Ódhran O Riordan and Kevin Bawle.
Front: Brian Clinton, Jack Considine, Ódhran O Riordan, Ciarán Flynn, Secretary Juvenile Board, Harry Dunne, face only, Kevin Bawle, Seán O Connor, face only, Cian Hegarty, Ethan Mahasé.
Back: Mathew Costello, Paddy Dalton, partly hidden, Bill Jennings, Fionn Cummins with hand in air, Paul Murphy. Photo: Declan Lynch.

demolished Summerhill, finishing a monstrous aggregate of forty-two points in front of their rivals. The club's second team replicated the success with victory over the Hill in the Reserve final. The following year's title bout was a much closer affair with victory over Ratoath in a thriller played in Skryne. When the calculations were completed Dunshaughlin had recorded victory by the minimum margin, 29 points to 28. Once again the reserves matched their comrades' achievement with a five-point victory over Donaghmore-Ashbourne.

The titles arrived earlier in the following two years with success in the Spring instead of the Summer League. In 2013 the young black and ambers ousted the sky blues from St. Colmcilles on a 34-18 scoreline with Ódhran O Riordan captaining one team and Kevin Bawle leading the other as both side outscored their rivals.

The fourth consecutive success followed with a 31-22 margin against Ratoath in 2014. This team also participated in the prestigious, long running Newry Mitchell's Tournament where almost fifty clubs from nineteen counties vied for honours. Dunshaughlin made it through to the final where Lavey from Derry were too strong. A well deserved consolation prize arrived when Andrew Quinn was nominated as one of the Players of the Tournament, a fitting reward for a series of all-action, skillful and determined displays.

The Seamus Reilly tournament has also taken its place in the annual calendar in recent years. It commemorates a man who was part of a Carnaross side that thwarted Dunshaughlin's dreams of an intermediate title in 1993 but who, over a decade later, would make a huge contribution to under age football in the parish. Seamus gave sterling service in coaching and mentoring Dunshaughlin under age teams, particularly the successful Community Games sides, before his untimely death in 2011. Since then the club has hosted a tournament in his honour with Carnaross, St. Sylvesters and Dunshaughlin participating- all clubs with whom Seamus had deep and abiding links. St. Sylvesters have taken the honours in two of the finals played to date with Dunshaughlin recording a victory in 2013.

Seamus Reilly
One of the stars in Carnaross' victory over Dunshaughlin in the intermediate semi-final of 1993 who later settled in Dunshaughlin with his wife Ger and children Thomas and Petra. He successfully coached the Under 10 Community Games' team to win a Meath title in 2009. His death in 2011 robbed his family and the club of an inspirational father and coach.

Under 16s and 17s

Whether in the black and red of St. Martins or the black and amber of Dunshaughlin teams from the parish always experienced difficulty in winning Under 16 or Under 17 titles. In the quarter century under the St. Martins' banner there were only two Under 16 championship titles, in 2003 and 2008, and one Under 17 league in 2005.

The change of jerseys from 2009 made little difference and only one title was recorded between 2009 and 2014, the Under 17 Division 3 league victory in 2011.

The side lived precariously before defeating North Meath Gaels by 2-8 to 0-10

Dunshaughlin, Under 17 Division 3, Football League Winners, 2011

Front: Liam Carey, David Dunne, Ronan Geraghty, Kevin Bannon, Niall Byrne, Gavin Malone, Oisín Foley, Diarmuid Christie, Josh Wall, Adam McTigue.
Back: Paul Mooney, Steven Kinsella, David Reilly, Danny McTigue, Dan Ormsby, Alan McEntee, Jack O Sullivan, Glen Fitzpatrick, David Doherty, Gareth Rooney, Shane Gallogly, Patrick Darby.

Presentation to Dunshaughlin Under 17 Panel Winners Division 3 Football League, 2011

Front: Adam McTigue, Kevin Bannon, David Doherty, Capt., Diarmuid Christie, Niall Byrne.
Back: Steven Kinsella, David Reilly, Gavin Malone, Glen Fitzpatrick, Alan McEntee, Liam Carey, Josh Wall, Patrick Darby, Gareth Rooney.

in the semi-final with two late goals giving Dunshaughlin victory despite trailing for lengthy periods. The final against Clanna Gael was an equally tense and tight encounter. A good start brought a three-point advantage but lax defending that resulted in the concession of a goal followed by some cheap points left the Gaels in the driving seat with a three point cushion by half time.

When midfielder Glen Fitzpatrick was red-carded early in the second half prospects looked even grimmer but the team turned adversity to its advantage with a stirring revival. The inspirational Steven Kinsella drove the side forward at every opportunity and slowly the lead was whittled back. Points from Patrick Darby and Alan McEntee were followed by the decisive score, a soccer style goal from Oisín Foley. With two points between the sides Jack O Sullivan had to make a great save to retain the advantage and before the end Paddy Darby ensured victory with a late point and a winning scoreline of 1-9 to 1-6. Simon Farrell, Francis Darby and Noel McTigue were the selectors on the following side, captained by David Doherty:

Jack O Sullivan; Josh Wall, David Doherty, Capt., Gareth Rooney; Dan Ormsby, Steven Kinsella, Oisín Foley (1-0); David Reilly, Glen Fitzpatrick; Gavin Malone, Paddy Darby (0-6), Liam Carey (0-1); Kevin Bannon (0-1), Alan McEntee (0-1), Diarmuid Christie. Subs: Ronan Geraghty for Christie, Niall Byrne, Paul Mooney, Shane Gallogly, Danny McTigue, Adam McTigue, David Dunne.

The 2014 Under 17s had to struggle to qualify for the knock-out stages and when they faced Skryne in the semi-final few gave them a realistic chance in light of a comprehensive defeat to the same opposition earlier. Yet, despite playing on their opponents' home turf, the Dunshaughlin youths dredged up an outstanding performance to overturn the earlier result but, once again, final day brought disappointment as Dunboyne took the honours after a great start.

There were some positives in the performance of the same side in the Under 17 blitz in Dunganny. Dunshaughlin had developed an affinity with the tournament, having a win and a loss in the previous two finals. Kevin Kealy managed a panel that remained unbeaten throughout, compiling victories over St. Cuthberts, St. Patricks, Summerhill, Jenkinstown Gaels and St. Patricks again in the final. The panel consisted of Daniel Quinn, Capt., Cillian Hart, Tommy Kinsella, Aaron Keane, Conor Huijsdens, Seamus Doyle, Adam Kealy, Stephen Walker, Cillian Duffy, Conor Jennings and Conor Mooney.

The Under 16s had no outright success in this period, but, like their predecessors in St. Martins had plenty of near misses. The 2009 crop, who, in younger age groups made little impact, surprised many, by progressing to the decider. It took extra time, deep reservoirs of determination and a late goal from Shane Gallogly, his side's sixth, to dispatch Clanna Gael in the semi. A gallant effort in the final

Action from Under 16 Reserve Final, 2014

Top: Cormac Byrne in possession.
Above: Seán Curtin prepares to pass to a team mate.
Photos: Declan Lynch.

BLACK & AMBER

Dunshaughlin, Under 16 Division 7, Football League Finalists, 2014

Front: Mark Connolly, Ronan McMahon, Adam Summerville, Cormac Byrne, Eric Casserley, Ciarán Quinn, Pádraig Clinton. Back: Andrew Leneghan, Seán Curtin, Shane Claire, Daniel Fildes, Ferdia Foley, Jack Caldwell, Lorcan O Reilly, Anthony Fildes, Robert McConnell, Turlough Malone.

day showdown with a strong Moynalvey team ended in defeat by 3-7 to 0-8. The die was cast by half time as wind assisted Moynalvey had harvested a twelve point advantage. The black and ambers put in a better final half hour and outscored their opponents but shading the scoreline was insufficient to overhaul the deficit.

In other years narrow defeats were the order of the day. The 2012 reserves played in an action packed, enthralling extra time final against Dunboyne but they finished two points in arrears while their premier counterparts reached the semi-final only to fall short of Summerhill by a similar margin. 2013 brought another close encounter and a similar outcome. Now it was St. Vincents-Curraha who administered the heartbreak with a 4-10 to 3-11 victory in the Autumn League.

Having clawed their way to the Autumn Under 15 league title in 2013, as outlined earlier, the reward was a place in Division 1 of the Under 16 league in

2014. This was a bridge too far and the side could make no impact. On the bright side the club was able to field a reserve team featuring a number of players who had dropped out at the younger age groups but were cajoled back to the fold. Playing in Division 7 the team surprised all by reaching the final but was no match for Nobber's first XV. Nevertheless, the ability to field two teams was a significant achievement and gives a solid basis for a future minor team.

Community Games, Under 10s

The most successful of all the groups were the Under 10s who participated in the Community Games. Four different sides came out on top in Meath, the 2008 crew, still fielding under the St. Martins' banner, covered in Chapter 16, the 2009 bunch who wore black and amber and the 2010 squad who made it a hat trick of victories for the parish. In 2012 the club's representatives again emerged as Meath's best and went on to perform outstandingly well at provincial level. The Community Games competition retains the competitive edge of yore and is all the more dramatic for that.

The 2009 side, with Séamus Reilly as coach, emerged as Meath champions but Killoe from Longford halted their progress in the Leinster quarter-final. The 2010 panel disposed of Kilbride, Dunboyne, Cushenstown and Ashbourne, conceded only one goal in total and further embellished its record in the final, holding a physically imposing Ratoath scoreless while putting 2-2 on the board themselves. The Leinster quarter-final once again featured Killoe who took advantage of a strong wind to build up a nine point lead and despite a spirited comeback the Longford boys inflicted a second defeat, this time by four points.

The 2012 crew consisted of a panel of twenty that was unbeaten in the group stages, eliminated Kilbride in the semi and edged out Dunboyne in the final. Like Dunshaughlin in Meath, Killoe have had a stranglehold on the competition in Longford and the clubs met for the third time when Dunshaughlin on home soil gave a commanding performance to become the best in North Leinster and qualify for the Leinster finals in Carlow.

There the young Dunshaughlin stars established an early lead against Maynooth that they would not relinquish and thus made club history by reaching the Leinster final. Early on in the decider it seemed they would take care of Ballyroan-Abbeyleix also, but the stronger, more physical Laois boys prevailed in the end by 3-4 to 2-2. Kieran O Riordan, Ultan Blake and Kieran Rushe managed the following panel to the verge of Leinster honours: Joseph Dunne, Cian Edwards, Colm Keane, Fursey Blake, Conor Gray, John McDonagh, Seán McConnell, Ruairi Kinsella, Tommy Toal, Jared Rushe, Jack O Riordan, Aidan Fraher, Seán Walsh, Charlie

O Connor, Evan Lawlor, Eoin Butler, Aaron Murphy, James Traynor, Cillian McCool and Cian McLaughlin.

Competitive football is not the only attraction on offer at the club. Starting at Under 8 level, coaching, challenge games, Go Game blitzes, local tournaments and exhibition games at half time during senior championship games provide players with a variety of outlets and arenas to begin developing their skills. The club organizes free Easter Camps for children in the 7 to 12 age groups while Meath Coaching and Games usually hold at least one Summer Cúl Camp.

One of the most successful initiatives has been the Street Leagues with over twenty areas from the parish represented. Readers who have read earlier chapters will recall that this scheme has echoes of the successful street leagues from the 1950s. It is now a major community event with almost 200 children participating. In its initial year the participating teams and their managers were: Crannóg/Lagore: Dave Edwards; Drumree Rangers: Derek Gray; The Knocks: Brendan Connolly and Seán O Neill; Greenane: Shirley O Connor; Lagore: Amanda Harrington and Brian O Brien; Maeldúin Rovers: Kieran O Riordan; Ardlea: Benny Byrne; Dublin Road: Alan O Dwyer; Seachnaill Place-Hillview: Brendan Dunne and Heidi Carty; Drumree Gaels: Dominic Mc Donagh; Drumree Harps: Alan Boyle and Seamus Briody; Supple Slayers: Larry O Connor and Shane Byrne; Culmullen: Hugo Lynch; Maeldúin United : Ronan Dalton; Drumree Road: Eamonn Moyles and Fran Darby and Pelletstown: Roy Sheridan.

The competition is run off over a week in conjunction with the Harvest Festival and final night is the highlight, with partisan and neutral supporters thronging the GAA grounds and creating a unique atmosphere. In 2013 Maeldúin Rovers defeated The Knocks in the Cup final while Culmullen got the better of Ardlea in the Shield. Greenane came out on top in the 2014 event, ousting Lagore Rangers.

Another Delaney Cup Victory

The Delaney Cup for the winners of the Minor Football Championship is, alongside the Keegan Cup, one of the most prized pieces of silverware in Meath GAA. Dunshaughlin in 1947, and in 1972 with the assistance of Kilcloon, had fallen at the final hurdle before St. Martins in alliance with Ratoath brought home the iconic trophy for the first time in 1987. Two years later the same combination missed out after a final, a re-fixture and a replay while a fine St. Martins' side, hampered by injuries, fell short in 2005. One Delaney Cup was a poor return and served to emphasize the competitive nature of the minor championship.

The Dunshaughlin minors of 2009 had a top class pedigree. As outlined in Chapter 16 St. Martins had represented the Royal County in the All-Ireland Féile competitions for three consecutive years, 2004 to 2006. Though many of the 2004 side were too old for minor grade in 2009, six of that side were eligible, Stephen Clusker, Barry Jordan, Conor Devereux, Eoin Hagarty, Eamon Bowe and Niall Murphy while thirteen of the side that captured the Under 14 championship in 2005 were part of the 2009 minors. There was almost a zero fall out rate, a record that speaks volumes for the commitment of the players and mentors and the level of organization in St. Martins.

For the first time in many years the minor championship was on a straight knock-out basis with a league later in the year to ensure regular football at this grade. The straight knock-out format didn't allow any room for error and Dunshaughlin lived dangerously on more than one occasion.

At half time in the first round the outlook was as bleak as the weather. Neighbours Ratoath held a six-point lead and Dunshaughlin needed to draw on the resilience, team spirit and the scoring know-how the players had so often displayed in the St. Martins' colours. Points from Conor Devereux, Emmet Staunton and Eamon Bowe and an Alan O Brien goal injected sufficient momentum to carry the team over the line with a two-point winning margin.

The win entitled the side to a semi-final ticket against Simonstown Gaels. Once again the team's powers of recovery were put to the test. Having played against the stiff breeze, they approached half-time on level terms but the Navan side plundered three quick-fire goals - one late in the first half and two more, early in the second half. This opened up a yawning nine-point gap that seemed unbridgeable. All out attack put Simonstown under severe pressure but also left huge gaps in Dunshaughlin's defence. Simonstown, having developed a taste for goals and believing more were there for the taking, spurned insurance points but found keeper Stephen Clusker in unbeatable form with a string of audacious saves.

At the other end Dunshaughlin were more economical. Alan O Brien switched to the edge of the square and orchestrated several good moves. Points were slotted when available, Niall Murphy netted and Fergus Toolan added a second with ten minutes remaining. The momentum was now with the black and ambers. Joe O Brien and Niall Murphy pointed in the closing stages to outscore Simonstown by 2-6 to 0-1 in the final twenty minutes for a stunning 2-11 to 3-6 victory.

After living so dangerously Dunshaughlin entered the final as underdogs against a Donaghmore-Ashbourne side seeking a rare fourth consecutive title in the grade. The consensus proved a false one. The holders were dispatched with a dazzling display of attacking football by a fleet-footed Dunshaughlin side, full of verve and self-belief.

They went to the dressing room with a single point lead that camouflaged their dominance of possession but there was no masking the difference between

> The holders were dispatched with a dazzling display of attacking football by a fleet-footed Dunshaughlin side, full of verve and self-belief. They went to the dressing room with a single point lead that camouflaged their dominance of possession but there was no masking the difference between the sides in the second period.

the sides in the second period. Four of the six forwards got on the score sheet and the winners notched 1-7 to the holders' two points. The goal came in the final quarter after Conor Devereux, Michael McCarthy and Eamon Bowe combined and the latter's shot rebounded off the upright into the waiting hands of Alan O Brien who fired high into the net.

Joe O Brien and Devereux won plenty of possession around midfield, with the hard-working Devereux a very effective link between midfield and attack. O Brien sent Dunshaughlin on their way with two early points from long range frees and he later converted a third. Eamon Bowe was a busy presence around the middle third and despite regularly foraging back in defence for possession he also filleted the Donaghmore defence for three points. Niall Murphy finished with a similar total after an imposing display at full-forward. After his heroics in the semi-final Stephen Clusker welcomed a quieter outing and the rest of the defence was quick to snuff out any threat from Donaghmore-Ashbourne.

While there were some fine individual performances throughout their campaign, team manager TP Toolan was anxious to stress that the key was collective effort.

'Seán Joyce had a wonderful game against both Ratoath and Simonstown. Alastar Doyle was very good in the final. Alan OBrien scored important goals versus Ratoath and again against Donaghmore-Ashbourne in the final. Niall Murphy and my own lad Fergus were also very good at certain stages, but I think it's fair to say that it was a real team effort that won it for us in the end. In every game we played, there were players in every line of the field who were capable of doing something that lifted the whole team and turned things around.'

TP had the assistance of Stephen Claire as coach and trainer, Donnchadh Geraghty and John O Brien as selectors and Eoin Hagarty captained the following side that brought the Delaney Cup to the parish for the second time, but for the first time without the assistance of players from another club:

	Stephen Clusker	
Seán Joyce	Alastar Doyle	Barry Jordan
Fergus Toolan	Conor O Brien	Neil Ridgeway
Joe O Brien (0-3)		Conor Devereux (0-2)
Eoin Hagarty, Capt.	Eamon Bowe (0-3)	Emmet Staunton (0-2)
Alan O Brien (1-1)	Niall Murphy (0-3)	Michael McCarthy

Subs: Daniel Geraghty for McCarthy, Keith Doherty for Jordan, Henry Komolafe for Bowe, Niall Clusker for Alan O Brien, Brian Woods, Gavin Malone, Conor Smith, Aidan Boswell.

Coach Stephen Claire keeps a watchful eye on proceedings during the 2009 minor final. Stephen was a member of the first St. Martins' side to capture the Delaney Cup in 1987.

Delaney Cup Triumph

Minor Championship Winners, 2009. It's Ours!
Winning captain Eoin Hagarty hoists the Delaney Cup after the 2009 minor final, supported by Michael McCarthy on left and Niall Murphy and a partly hidden Henry Komolafe on right of photograph. Photo: Declan Lynch.

The Minor League, intended to give regular games to players eliminated early in the championship dragged on through the summer until St. Martins met Ratoath in the final in October.

Ratoath gained a measure of revenge for their championship defeat with a 2-14 to 2-9 victory. The crucial period was just before half time when the winners hit six unanswered points and also bagged a goal, and though Dunshaughlin reduced the lead to three points late in the game they couldn't overhaul the arrears. Despite the defeat, Dunshaughlin Chairman Jim Smith had some cause for satisfaction as his son Andrew lined out in goals for Ratoath!

The team then took part in the Leinster Minor Club League hosted by Éire Óg, Carlow, extending their outings at training and games to over eighty. The side eliminated Carlow representatives, Palatine, in the first round before going down to Dublin champions Na Fianna in the semi-final.

Part of the reason for the delay in completing the Meath league was the progress of the Meath Minors to the Leinster semi-final. Conor Devereux was a regular at wing forward while Alastar Doyle was introduced in the quarter-final against Westmeath. Stephen Clusker was the reserve keeper for the team. The following year Fergus Toolan was named team captain and he, Conor and Alastar all started in Meath's two games.

Niall Murphy has a secure grip on possession in the 2009 minor final v. Donaghmore-Ashbourne. Photo: Declan Lynch.

Before and After: Minor Football Championship Final 2009

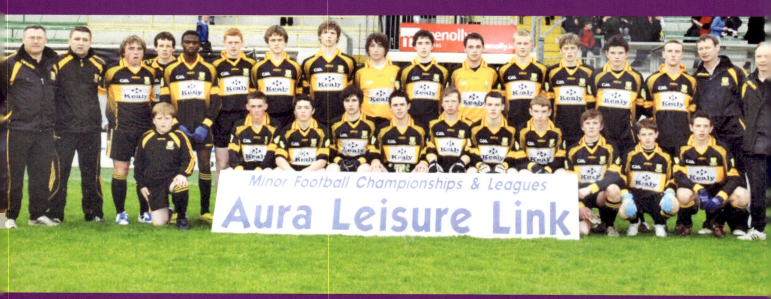

Front: Shane Claire, Seán Joyce, Eamon Bowe, Emmet Staunton, Eoin Hagarty, Alan O Brien, Niall Murphy, Alastar Doyle, Brian Woods, Gavin Malone, Barry Jordan.
Back: TP Toolan, Stephen Claire, Niall Clusker, Conor Smith, Henry Komolafe, Michael McCarthy, Fergus Toolan, Joe O Brien, Aidan Boswell, Conor O Brien, Stephen Clusker, Neil Ridgway, Daniel Geraghty, Keith Doherty, Conor Devereux, Donnchadh Geraghty, John O Brien.
Photo: Declan Lynch.

On ground at front: Niall Murphy and Stephen Claire.
Front Row: Aaron Kealy, Adam Kealy, Tom Sharp, Shane Claire, Daniel Geraghty-slightly behind, Eamon Bowe, Eoin Hagarty, Henry Komolafe, Seán Joyce-partly hidden by hand, Alastar Doyle, Alan O Brien.
Back: Ronan Smith, Stephen Duffy, Shane Gallogly, Conor Smith, Ronan Geraghty, Brian Woods, Michael McCarthy-almost hidden, Fergus Toolan, Emmet Staunton, Joe O Brien, Stephen Clusker, Keith Doherty, Conor O Brien, Neil Ridgeway, Barry Jordan, James Rattigan, Aidan Boswell, Niall Clusker, TP Toolan.
Photo: Declan Lynch.

CHAPTER 21   FROM BLACK AND RED TO BLACK AND AMBER

The promise of 2009 was not maintained in subsequent years. In fact, the opposite was the case as numbers in the age group and commitment from players declined in tandem. The 2011 side performed poorly in the minor league, having only fifteen players in the final game. Turnouts and results improved for the Division 2 championship, with a win, a loss and a walkover being sufficient to earn a semi-final place. A strong Trim side had the better of that encounter by 2-12 to 1-6 with a late penalty goal adding an undeserved one-sided tinge to the score. It took a huge effort by the management team of Simon Farrell, Francis Darby and Noel McTigue to keep the show on the road and they and the committed players got a deserved reward when the Under 17s took the league title as outlined earlier.

2012 was a poor year with the minors recording just a single victory between league and championship but fortunes can change quickly at underage level. The 2013 crop under the stewardship of Frank Gallogly, TP Toolan and Pat Gargan built up a momentum in Division 2 of the league that took them all the way to final victory over Summerhill, 1-12 to 1-8. The performances earned the black and amber boys a place in the championship proper where they shocked eventual winners Navan O Mahonys in the first round, and, despite a single point reverse to Donaghmore-Ashbourne went on to eliminate St. Vincents-Curraha in the quarter-final. Dunboyne however, guillotined further progress, deservedly winning the semi in Dunsany.

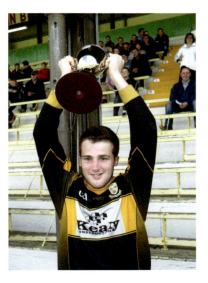

Shane Gallogly raises the Minor Football League, Division 2 trophy following victory over Summerhill in 2013. Photo: Declan Lynch.

The league title was hard earned as Dunshaughlin trailed at the break, overturned the deficit when David Beattie coolly slotted a penalty early in the second half, lost it again when Summerhill rallied but finally claimed the honours with four unanswered points in the closing ten minutes. Superior fire power and fitness won it for the black and ambers with seven players contributing to the scoreboard, Stephen Duffy leading the way garnering six points. Frank Gallogly noted that the team had been 'in and around the winners' enclosure without actually getting there' since Under 8 level and placed victory in the context of the club's future, remarking, 'Our senior team can benefit from what happened out there today, that's important.' This was the successful line out:

Jack O Sullivan

Josh Wall   Ronan Geraghty   Diarmuid Christie

Oisín Foley   Dan Ormsby   Niall Byrne

Ben Duggan (0-1)   David Reilly (0-1)

David Beattie (1-0)   Stephen Duffy (0-6)   Daniel Quinn (0-1)

Shane Gallogly, Capt. (0-2)   Liam Carey (0-1)   Tommy Kinsella

Subs: Conor Jennings for Kinsella, Séamus Doyle for Quinn, Cian Gallogly, Mark Phelan, Adam McDermott, Martin Nevin, Stephen Farrell, Gareth Rooney, Cillian Hart. Team management: Frank Gallogly and TP Toolan.

BLACK & AMBER

Dunshaughlin, Minor Football League, Division 2, Winners 2013

Front: Mark Phelan, David Reilly, Cillian Hart, Liam Carey, Conor Jennings, Shane Gallogly, Ronan Geraghty, Niall Byrne, Diarmuid Christie, Seamus Doyle, David Beattie.
Back: TP Toolan, Cian Gallogly, Gareth Rooney, Oisín Foley, Daniel Quinn, Josh Wall, Jack O Sullivan, Adam McDermott, Dan Ormsby, Ben Duggan, Stephen Duffy, Tommy Kinsella, Martin Nevin, Stephen Farrell, Frank Gallogly, Pat Gargan.
Photo: Declan Lynch.

In contrast to the difficulty of fielding one team in 2012, two years later the club entered two teams for the first time. Both made it through to their respective semi-finals, the first team bowing out to Summerhill and the reserves coming up a point shy of Blackwater Gaels. The championship proved more challenging and an unlucky defeat to St. Colmcilles put paid to the prospect of a re-aquaintance with the Delaney Cup.

Winning the minor title in 2009 seemed a positive omen for further success but it was a short road from the highs of 2009 to the depths of failure three years later, particularly as neighbouring clubs with similar population profiles, Ratoath, Donaghmore-Ashbourne and Dunboyne, have dominated the sector since 2006. Better performances in recent years give hope that there is sufficient talent in the pipeline to compete at the highest level. In the long run though, it is not leagues or championships won that will be important. Instead, the ultimate barometer of success will be the ability of the club to nurture young talent, develop and improve it incrementally and provide players able to establish themselves on the club's adult teams. Six of the successful 2009 side and four from the 2012 crew are regulars on the current senior panel. Identifying, harnessing and developing such emerging talent at minor level is the immediate challenge for the club.

GAA 125 Celebrations 2009

Dunshaughlin players and mentors gather outside the church in 2009, prior to marching to the GAA grounds to mark the 125th anniversary of the founding of the GAA.

Highs and Lows in Recent Years, 2007-2014

Half a decade after the three in a row the team was in transition. Still backboned by players from the successful era, new young replacements were slow to arrive on the scene.

The Seniors and a Managerial Merry Go Round

The performance of the senior team in 2006 had been the worst since the end of the three in a row. The side had failed to win any championship game but a sequence of four draws saved the club from the ignominy of a relegation battle. After one manager in 1999-2004, there were four in the next three years and the managerial merry-go-round was about to take a few more spins. Dudley Farrell departed at the end of 2006 to be replaced by Leo Turley, a former Laois star, remembered in Meath for his battles with Mick Lyons. He had masterminded Blackhall Gaels' first senior title in 2003 and his selectors would be Andy Quinn and Martin Summerville.

Performances stabilized and results improved, especially in the group stages but inconsistency remained a dominant feature. As was the case in previous years positive results were often the harbinger of nightmare performances while poor displays frequently heralded improved exhibitions. Thus, in 2007 an opening victory over a Duleek side managed by Eamonn Barry was followed by defeat to Simonstown and shades of 2001 when John Lunney raced in for early goals. Victory in the next three games dissipated the disappointment, propelled the side to

> Performances stabilized and results improved, especially in the group stages but inconsistency remained a dominant feature.

> Despite reaching the quarter-final and retaining Division 1 league status the club ushered in 2008 with a new coach and a different set of selectors.

the top of the table, and set up a quarter-final meeting with the other Navan side, O Mahonys. They had similar medicine in store for the black and ambers as their fellow townsmen, and Dunshaughlin went down to a heavy defeat, 1-14 to 1-6.

The quarter-final had started encouragingly as Dunshaughlin raced into an early seven points lead. Niall Kelly was central to the early dominance with two points from lengthy frees and a successful '45'. Conor Staunton chipped in to raise another white flag before Martin Reilly caused confusion in the O Mahonys' rearguard and scrambled the ball to the net. However, the townsmen gradually imposed themselves around the middle and with a plentiful supply of possession evened the scores before the interval. Dunshaughlin could only manage two pointed frees in the final forty minutes of the game, from Kelly and Cathal O Dwyer, while O Mahonys moved into overdrive.

League form was a similar curate's egg of five wins matched by five defeats while in the Feis Cup the team recorded good wins against senior sides Wolfe Tones and Trim before falling disappointingly to intermediate club Syddan.

Despite reaching the quarter-final and retaining Division 1 league status the club ushered in 2008 with a new coach and a different set of selectors. Leo Turley departed unexpectedly to take up a coaching position nearer home. One ex-Blackhall Gaels' coach replaced another, as Gordon Ward took over the reins and appointed Simon Farrell and Martin Summerville as his selectors. The appointments brought an element of continuity as Summerville had worked with Turley in 2006 while Farrell was part of the management team with the successful 2007 Under 21 side and was ideally placed to oversee their transition to senior level. He believed that there was a sufficient combination of young talent alongside the experienced players to mount a realistic assault on the championship.

The draw was relatively favourable with newly amalgamated Duleek-Bellewstown, intermediate champions Donaghmore-Ashbourne, Trim and Kilmainhamwood on the agenda.

Duleek-Belewstown and Donaghmore-Ashbourne both proved tenacious before going down by a brace and a single point respectively. In the latter, David Crimmins confidently scored Dunshaughlin's only goal, described by the *Chronicle* as one of the best likely to be seen. The move began deep in defence. Denis Kealy, Conor Staunton and Martin Reilly were all involved in creating the opening for Crimmins, who skilfully side-stepped his marker before curling the ball high into the net. An easy victory against Kilmainhamwood was followed by a hard fought one against Trim and Dunshaughlin progressed to the knock-out stages with a flattering one hundred per cent record.

The form that had carried them through the qualifying games deserted Dunshaughlin in the quarter-final. The black and ambers with an ex-Blackhall manager faced Blackhall with an ex-Dunshaughlin manager, Eamonn Barry, at the helm. Dunshaughlin were below par on the day, conceded far too many frees- Tadhg Brosnan converted eight of them- and failed to score in the final seventeen minutes. This was a recipe for defeat and Blackhall inflicted it, by 1-13 to 0-7.

A week after the championship loss both sides met in a Feis Cup quarter-final and Dunshaughlin reversed the earlier result scoring sixteen points to Blackhall's 1-7. It was scant consolation for championship elimination and no consolation at all when Seneschalstown had the upper hand in the semi-final after extra time. The team performed well in the league with six wins and a draw to finish in the upper echelons of the table. On balance it was a year of progress but after two successive comprehensive quarter-final defeats it was time to reassess form and progress.

Rebuilding, 2009-10

Half a decade after the three in a row the team was in transition. Still backboned by players from the successful era, new young replacements were slow to arrive on the scene. The successful 2002 minors contributed Caoimhín King, Michael Ahern and Cathal O Dwyer while Conor Staunton, Cillian Finn and David Devereux graduated from the victorious Under 16 champions of 2003. However, they were still relatively young and were being asked to step into the large, intimidating boots of players like Graham Dowd, Dermot and Aiden Kealy, Michael McHale and Fearghal Gogan. Anthony and Tommy Johnson were valuable acquisitions to the team and Tommy captained the Meath minors to Leinster success from the centre-back position in 2008. Sensibly, team manager Gordon Ward and his two selectors were retained for the following year.

Despite this, the 2009 campaign continued in the same unpredictable pattern. A first round defeat was followed by a clear-cut eight points victory over 2006 intermediate champions Rathkenny and a single point victory against Trim. Dunshaughlin had to wait for two months before the next championship game and were sluggish and off the pace against a lively Wolfe Tones outfit who recorded a 2-12 to 0-11 victory. Two wins from four wasn't championship form but it was enough to earn a pass to the preliminary quarter-finals against old rivals Blackhall Gaels.

Since 2000 both sides often suffered defeats against the other, only to recover and overturn the outcome in the following championship encounter. It happened in 2002 when Dunshaughlin won the refixture after losing the original clash featuring the illegal Anthony Moyles. It happened in 2003 when Blackhall overturned that result in the semi-final but couldn't repeat it in 2004 when Dunshaughlin had

> After five years, 1999-2003, with one manager, Eamonn Barry, and two selectors Brendan Kealy and TP Toolan, the club had expended six managers and thirteen selectors in as many years.

revenge in the quarter-final. The sides avoided each other in 2005, and in 2006 their encounter ended all square. The pattern resumed with Dunshaughlin winning in 2007 and Blackhall having revenge in 2008.

On that basis Dunshaughlin were due a victory in 2009. True to form the black and ambers advanced. Blackhall missed the same penalty twice, the first superbly saved by Ronan Gogan and the retake sent wide by Alan Nestor, but still led early in the second half. However, the Kilcloon parish side failed to register a single score after the interval while Dunshaughlin shot a goal and supplemented it with eight points.

The following week Dunshaughlin's progress came to a shuddering halt. Opponents Navan O Mahonys were in difficulty early on, rallied to draw level, but fell behind again to a goal. Cathal O Dwyer created an opening, centred to Niall Kelly who had his shot parried but it fell into the path of Conor Staunton who rifled to the roof of the net. The loss of Anthony Johnson before half time and of Niall Kelly after the break, both to injury, weakened Dunshaughlin's resistance and O Mahonys coasted to a 2-12 to 2-6 victory.

Results in the league suggested that the side was on an upward graph. Six victories, three draws and only two defeats put the side within touching distance of a place in the final. The minor championship victory earlier in the year, detailed in the previous chapter, gave further promise of a return to the glory days while the senior B team playing in Division 1 reached their final also.

However, results were always viewed through the prism of the successful years and falling short of those standards generally prompted calls for change. After two years Gordon Ward's reign as manager was terminated and the search was on for a replacement. After five years, 1999 to 2003, with one manager, Eamonn Barry, and two selectors Brendan Kealy and TP Toolan, the club had expended six managers and thirteen selectors in as many years. It had ominous echoes of the intermediate period of the 1990s where managerial and selectorial changes were rife. A modicum of continuity and stability was on the prescription.

Cavan native Gary Farrelly, formerly with Denn in the Breffni County, took over the coaching role and had Michael McHale and Richie Kealy as selectors. Both stepped down later in the year, as they became candidates for a starting place or a substitute's role with Pat Maloney and TP Toolan replacing them. The same two selectors remained on to assist Gary in 2011 and 2012. On the surface the first year, 2010, was an unsuccessful one with just one championship victory and four losses and the resultant failure to advance to the knock-out stages for only the second time in a dozen years. A closer examination of the results suggests otherwise. Three of the losses were by a single point and the team management introduced a number of new players from the successful 2009 minor team. Luckily, the team avoided a relegation battle as victory over St. Ultans doomed the latter to bottom spot.

The side that lined out in the 2010 opener against Walterstown featured just four players from the 2000-2002 era, Ronan Gogan, Ray Maloney, Martin Reilly and David Crimmins, although Denis Kealy and Kenny McTigue appeared as substitutes while Niall Kelly was absent after incurring a broken nose in the club's fundraising boxing tournament against Blackhall. Two players made their championship debuts, Eoin Hagarty and Niall Murphy, both members of the successful 2009 minor side. Later in the year Tadhg Ó Dúshláine made his first senior appearance while Conor Devereux was in his second season at senior level. The following year two more former minors were introduced, Fergus Toolan and Alastar Doyle. The management was gradually blending experience and youth in the hope of concocting a winning formula.

The massive economic recession of the period had a negative effect on the club as was the case with numerous GAA units throughout the country. On the positive side Kevin Ward returned to action after a sojourn in Japan but it was counterbalanced by departures. Both Cillian Finn, a regular at midfield with the Meath minors in 2006, and David Tonge from the 2000-2002 team had emigrated to Canada. Stephen Ward had last played in 2006, prior to leaving for Australia, while in 2011 Ciarán Farrelly, Conor Staunton and Mark Caldwell also left for Canada due to the levels of unemployment at home.

> "The massive economic recession of the period had a negative effect on the club as was the case with numerous GAA units throughout the country.

2011: Real Contenders

A good start always gives confidence for the battles ahead and Dunshaughlin began brightly in Championship 2011 with two victories, over Seneschalstown and newly promoted intermediate champions Nobber. A fourth round win against Rathkenny garnered another two points. Trevor Dowd was back and his contribution from play and frees was crucial in the victories. Cathal O Dwyer was also rediscovering his best form and had 1-3 from the two opening games.

However, two defeats during the campaign resurrected all the doubts about the black and ambers. In the third round Donaghmore-Ashbourne, beaten in their first two outings, easily disposed of Dunshaughlin's insipid challenge in May. In August Navan O Mahonys showed title-winning form in first overhauling Dunshaughlin's early lead and then annihilating them with a devastating display of power-packed football. The final score of 3-14 to 0-8 was a true indication of the gulf between the sides and while both progressed to the quarter-finals O Mahonys prospects looked as bright as Dunshaughlin's appeared bleak.

The glorious unpredictability of sport rendered that prediction redundant

BLACK & AMBER

Dunshaughlin in black & amber before the 2011 Senior County Final.

within a fortnight. First, Summerhill shocked O Mahonys and sent the red-hot favourites tumbling out of the championship. Then Dunshaughlin defeated the other Navan side, Simonstown Gaels, after the game spilled into extra time. It was a game high on drama, if low on quality. It featured two missed penalties, a late goal to force extra time and an even later point to provide the winner. Trevor Dowd's spot-kick struck the woodwork and went wide and the Gaels' Éanna Harrington repeated the feat soon after without calling on the assistance of the upright. Dunshaughlin led by three points as the clock ticked beyond sixty minutes but Shane Carr snatched a last-gasp goal after a move that opened up the defence.

In extra time Shane O Rourke almost single-handedly set up Simonstown for victory. They went three clear before Dunshaughlin responded and in the closing stages Ray Maloney restored parity and all were resigned to a replay. But the drama wasn't over. Seconds from the end of extra time, substitute Niall Kelly picked out wing back Fergus Toolan in acres of space. Toolan settled himself, took aim and arrowed his shot straight between the posts to spark wild celebrations as the final whistle sounded on the kick out.

Very few gave the black and ambers much chance in the semi-final against Donaghmore-Ashbourne in light of the earlier result between the sides. Dunshaughlin made poor use of first half wind advantage to trail by a point and when they fell a further two points in arrears at the start of the second half the pundits seemed justified. However, Donaghmore-Ashbourne failed to score for another twenty minutes as Dunshaughlin went on the rampage. John Crimmins and Ray Maloney began to dictate terms at midfield and a Niall Murphy goal after Cathal O Dwyer's incisive run along the endline ignited the recovery. Trevor Dowd reeled off three superb points and Conor Devereux added another to put the black and ambers in view of a final appearance. The Dons rallied, reduced the lead to a point in addition to wasting a number of good opportunities, but they couldn't conjure up an equalizer and the electronic scoreboard announced Dunshaughlin as the winners by 1-9 to 1-8. It was to be the first final appearance since 2002.

CHAPTER 22: HIGHS AND LOWS IN RECENT YEARS, 2007-2014

Back in a Senior Final Again

Summerhill, who had followed up their shock victory over O Mahonys with another good win against Wolfe Tones, awaited in the final and the Hill were red hot favourites. It turned out to be a tense, exciting struggle on a dark, gloomy afternoon in front of the smallest final attendance in years. Those who stayed away missed an exciting contest illuminated by outstanding performances by Caoimhín King and Cathal O Dwyer with Brian Ennis giving a flawless display of place kicking for Summerhill.

The Hill had the look of champions in the early stages as Dunshaughlin suffered stage fright. The blue and gold seized a three-point advantage but the tide slowly started to turn as the Dunshaughlin defence gained control and frustrated Summerhill's direct approach. Kenny McTigue gave dangerman Stephen Kennedy few opportunities in a display that recalled his imperious days at full back.

Driven on by a supreme display from Caoimhín King, Dunshaughlin seized the initiative and established a minimum lead at the break. Early in the second half came a crucial moment. Brian Ennis had a goal chance but Ronan Gogan's airborne acrobatics kept his net intact and Caoimhín King materialized to divert the rebound over the endline.

The topsy-turvy trend continued. Cathal O Dwyer tormented his opponent with his third point but Ennis pointed after King overcarried. Summerhill's Gillespie shot over from fifty metres and Ennis thrilled the blue and gold clad followers in the stand with the lead point. But Dunshaughlin were resilient. Devereux tied the scores and with three minutes remaining O Dwyer was again fouled and Trevor Dowd converted to put Dunshaughlin one up. A late free after Richie Kealy was adjudged to have picked the ball off the ground was moved closer to the target after dissent from several defenders and Brian Ennis calmly slotted the equalizer. Prior to that Dunshaughlin had wasted two good opportunities but could have lost when a Summerhill defender screwed his late chance of glory wide.

The consensus was that Dunshaughlin had missed the boat. A point up and with plenty of possession they could have held on but tired limbs and lapses of concentration allowed Summerhill back into the game.

The replay was just as dramatic and it took extra time to separate the sides. Close to the end of normal time Dunshaughlin held a single point advantage when Niall Murphy took aim from thirty metres in front of goal. A last ditch tackle resulted in the ball drifting wide and the referee waved away Dunshaughlin's

Supporting the Black and Amber
Éabha Byrne displays her support for the black and amber and her uncle Cathal at the 2011 Senior final against Summerhill. Her mother Nessa is in the bottom left of the picture and Vincent Lane is to the left of the placard. Her grand mother Rita is on the extreme right.
Photo: Pat Murphy, Sportsfile

Senior Final and Replay v Summerhill, 2011

Above:
Kenny McTigue races out to gain possession as Conor Devereux awaits the outcome.

Opposite Page: Pictured clockwise from top left:
Trevor Dowd steadies and shoots.

Tommy Johnson in possession with brother Anthony holding a watching brief.

Dunshaughlin manager Gary Farrelly gives directions with co-selectors
Pat Maloney and TP Toolan in the background.

Caoimhín King with time and space to plan the next move.

Denis Kealy emerges with the ball as Alastar Doyle and Caoimhín King provide support.

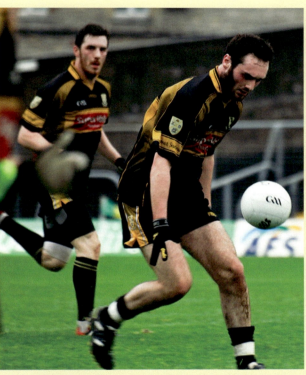

Dunshaughlin, Senior Football Championship Finalists, 2011

The Dunshaughlin team that started the drawn final against Summerhill.
Front: Cathal O Dwyer, Niall Murphy, Ray Maloney, Capt., Conor Devereux, Tommy Johnson, Trevor Dowd.
Back: Caoimhín King, Fergus Toolan, Alastar Doyle, John Crimmins, Ronan Gogan, Kenny McTigue, Anthony Johnson, Michael Ahern, Denis Kealy.
Photo: Pat Murphy, Sportsfile

legitimate appeals for a free. A point then would probably have sealed the issue. Instead Summerhill attacked with renewed hope and spirit and when Conor Gillespie was fouled Summerhill converted the resultant free. The Hill had a late 45 to win the game but opted to go short and the move broke down.

Once again Dunshaughlin had been thwarted at the death when they were unable to retain a narrow lead in the closing stages. Only one goal was scored in the one hundred and forty minutes. It came at the end of the first quarter when Niall Murphy embarked on a defence splitting run, found Tommy Johnson unmarked and the Dunshaughlin corner forward powered low to the left corner.

After coming so close in normal time Dunshaughlin played the first period of extra time against the wind in a shell-shocked state as Summerhill grabbed four vital points. After the change-over Eoin Hagarty slotted an early point and Cathal O Dwyer hit another but there was to be no fairy tale ending. Only a magical 'save of the year' by Ronan Gogan denied Summerhill a goal and in the closing moments Cathal O Dwyer went close to snatching the winning goal, but Summerhill put their name on the cup, winning by 0-14 to 1-9.

Summerhill punished Dunshaughlin for a lethargic finish to normal time and a pedestrian beginning to extra time. They learned from the first outing and reduced the influence of Cathal O Dwyer and Trevor Dowd in the replay. They also had a man of the match display from Adrian Kenny. Confined to a single point in the initial outing he was in top gear the second day, teasing and tormenting the Dunshaughlin defence with his runs from deep and tallying six points.

For Dunshaughlin Kenny McTigue again kept Kennedy scoreless as he never let his man out of his sights. Caoimhín King produced another top class performance and Anthony Johnson regularly turned defence into attack until injury forced him out of the action late on. Michael Ahern gave assured displays in both games while Conor Devereux produced two typical all-action performances. Tommy Johnson spent most of his time assisting the midfield and took his goal superbly. Ray Maloney and John Crimmins shared the honours at midfield over the two games, with the latter making many outstanding catches while the former used possession well to link with his forwards and scored a fine point in the second game.

The team representing the black and ambers in the replay read:

Ronan Gogan; Alastar Doyle, Kenny McTigue, Michael Ahern; Anthony Johnson, Caoimhín King, Denis Kealy; John Crimmins (0-1), Ray Maloney, Capt. (0-1); Fergus Toolan (0-1), Trevor Dowd (0-3), Conor Devereux; Tommy Johnson (1-1), Niall Murphy, Cathal O Dwyer (0-1). Subs: Niall Kelly for Tommy Johnson, Tadhg Ó Dúshláine for Dowd. Extra time: Eoin Hagarty (0-1) for Toolan, Richie Kealy for Anthony Johnson, Kevin Ward for King, Stephen Clusker, Martin Reilly, Paddy McHale, Fearghal Delaney.

Silverware for Ray
County Board Secretary Cyril Creavin hands over the Feis Cup to Dunshaughlin captain, Ray Maloney.

John Crimmins Soars High
John Crimmins fielding in the 2011 Feis Cup Final v Blackhall Gaels.

Flourishing in the Feis Cup

Dunshaughlin didn't end the year empty handed.

During the summer the team made steady, if unspectacular, progress in the Feis Cup with early round victories against Na Fianna and Oldcastle. Intermediate side Longwood were unfamiliar quarter-final opponents in July and Dunshaughlin had to dig deep as the woodwork denied Longwood a goal in injury time. Cathal O Dwyer's 1-3 was crucial in a 1-11 to 1-10 victory. In the following months the championship took precedence and no further games were played until late October.

The by now, all too familiar sight of Summerhill's blue and gold greeted Dunshaughlin in the semi-final but there was a small measure of consolation in booking a final place against Blackhall Gaels. Trevor Dowd made a major contribution with six points and Dunshaughlin confirmed their victory with a terrific second half goal. Cathal O Dwyer delivered a beautiful pass to Trevor Dowd who laid the ball off to the in rushing Tadhg Ó Dúshláine. Noticing Anthony Johnson free on the overlap, he flicked a pass inside and Johnson slotted it home.

The final was a tale of two halves.

One In, All In, for the Feis Cup

Dunshaughlin players celebrate the 2011 Feis Cup victory over Blackhall Gaels in Páirc Tailteann.
Front: Conor Devereux, Ray Maloney, Capt., Tadhg Ó Dúshláine, Fergus Toolan, Niall Murphy, Cathal O Dwyer.
Middle Row: Niall Kelly, Pat Maloney, Selector, Paddy McHale, Fearghal Delaney, James Rattigan, Martin Reilly, Kevin Ward, Fearghal Gogan.
Back: Kenny McTigue, partly hidden, John Crimmins, Caoimhín King, Denis Kealy, Trevor Dowd partly hidden, Ronan Gogan, in green, Stephen Clusker, Alastar Doyle with arms raised, Daniel Geraghty, Anthony Johnson.
Photo: Declan Lynch

A Highly Respectable Bunch, on right
The Feis Cup winning panel at the medal presentation in The Station House Hotel, Kilmessan.
Front: Richie Kealy, Trevor Dowd, Ray Maloney, Michael Johnson.
Second Row: Emmet Staunton, Fergus Toolan, Denis Kealy, Conor Devereux, Cathal O Dwyer, Kevin Ward, Martin Reilly, James Rattigan, Daniel Geraghty, Alastar Doyle.
Back: Pat Maloney, Selector, Gary Farrelly, Manager, Grace O Malley, Physio, TP Toolan, Selector, Niall Murphy, Caoimhín King, Fearghal Gogan, John Crimmins, Mark Devanney, Ronan Gogan, James Horgan, Paddy McHale, Kenny McTigue, Stephen Clusker, Tadhg Ó Dúshláine, Anthony Johnson, Tommy Johnson almost fully hidden.

The Young Guns
The younger members of the team with the Feis Cup, Stephen Clusker, Alastar Doyle, Emmet Staunton, Fergus Toolan, Conor Devereux, James Horgan, Niall Murphy, Tommy Johnson.

BLACK & AMBER

In a woeful, wasteful first period Dunshaughlin landed four points and twice as many wides while Blackhall tallied 1-5. An early Trevor Dowd point set the tone for an improved second half display and captain Ray Maloney added another as Dunshaughlin upped the tempo. Despite the improvement, the eventual winners couldn't eradicate their wayward shooting and doubled their wides tally before the end. This left the outcome uncertain until the closing stages when Cathal O Dwyer netted and Dunshaughlin finished with a late flourish as Conor Devereux pointed from play and Niall Kelly recalled his numerous trademark points of yore with a gargantuan effort from a fifty metre free near the stand.

The Feis Cup is the oldest trophy in the county and is now the only straight knock-out competition at senior level. It has always been regarded as the second most important senior competition, although the Mooney Cup for Division 1 of the league is now of at least equal importance. For Dunshaughlin it couldn't compensate for the absence of the Keegan Cup but it was the symbol of a successful season directed by Gary Farrelly, Pat Maloney and TP Toolan. Ray Maloney had the honour of accepting the cup and the following team brought it to Dunshaughlin for only the second time in the club's history:

Ronan Gogan

Alastar Doyle   Kenny McTigue   Denis Kealy

Anthony Johnson   Caoimhín King   Tommy Johnson

John Crimmins (0-1)   Ray Maloney, Capt. (0-2)

Fergus Toolan (0-1)   Trevor Dowd (0-3)   Conor Devereux (0-1)

Tadhg Ó Dúshláine (0-1)   Niall Murphy   Cathal O Dwyer (1-0)

Subs: Kevin Ward for Anthony Johnson, Niall Kelly (0-1) for Ó Dúshláine, Fearghal Delaney for Ward, Eoin Hagarty for Tommy Johnson, Paddy McHale for Devereux, Stephen Clusker, Richie Kealy, Martin Reilly, Fearghal Gogan, Mark Devanney, James Rattigan, Emmet Staunton, Daniel Geraghty, James Horgan, Michael Johnson, Michael Ahern, Duncan Geraghty.

Where do we go Now?

The achievements of 2011 seemed to provide a strong foundation for further improvement in subsequent years.

It was not to be.

Performances and results regressed and in 2012 the team had its worst year in the senior championship since promotion in 1997. Four losses and a solitary draw placed the team in the basement of the group and were it not for a change of policy at County

> **"** The inevitable occurred when the club was forced into a three-team relegation dog fight.

CHAPTER 22: HIGHS AND LOWS IN RECENT YEARS, 2007-2014

Dunshaughlin, Senior Football Panel, 2013

Front: Liam Ormsby, Alastar Doyle, Cathal O Dwyer, Trevor Dowd, Tadhg Ó Dúshláine, Martin Reilly, Tommy Johnson, Fearghal Delaney, Niall Murphy. Back: Caoimhín King, Fergus Toolan, Niall Kelly, Stephen Ward, Paddy McHale, John Crimmins, Ray Maloney, Ronan Gogan, Stephen Clusker, Michael Ahern, Mark Devanney, Conor Devereux, David McMahon, Kenny McTigue.
Photo: Declan Lynch.

Board level the side would have faced into a battle to avoid relegation. League performances were more encouraging, but only marginally so, with three victories and two draws from eleven games.

The managerial carousal cranked into action once again. Gary Farrelly stepped down with Paddy Christie taking over but the downward spiral of the previous year continued and the inevitable occurred when the club was forced into a three-team relegation dog fight. Christie had departed by then and Michael McHale oversaw operations as Dunshaughlin stuttered to a narrow victory over Nobber and then stumbled to an equally narrow defeat to Oldcastle. This less than convincing form was, however, sufficient to retain senior championship status for 2014 and instead Nobber dropped a grade.

The struggle for survival continued in 2014. Kit Henry was the new man in charge assisted by Martin Reilly and Simon Farrell. A first round defeat to intermediate champions Gaeil Colmcille set the tone for a poor championship season and the first victory wasn't registered until the fourth round in August. That result would not be sufficient on its own to salvage the season and when the black and ambers trailed Simonstown by 2-11 to 0-8 in the last round as the final ten minutes beckoned another relegation dogfight loomed.

Eoin Hagarty ignited a flicker of hope when he rifled a dipping, swerving ball to the Gaels' net from distance and Fergus Toolan added fuel to the flame by crowning a darting run with a long range point. Despite the flickering embers of hope it seemed Dunshaughlin would have neither the oxygen nor the time to fan the flames into a full blown revival as Simonstown countered with two points.

Enter stage left substitute Shane Gallogly who conjured another goal with a venomous shot. Deficit down to four. Then another substitute Niall Byrne expertly placed Caoimhín King who waltzed through the despairing defence before slotting home. Down to a solitary point but with all watches and mobiles indicating we were deep in injury time it seemed the fightback would fall agonizingly short.

As all waited for the shrill final whistle Dunshaughlin compiled a necklace of passes that ended with Shane Gallogly shooting calmly but firmly over the bar. The comeback of Lazarus proportions gave Dunshaughlin a point but more importantly it edged them above Walterstown in the table on score difference leaving the Blacks to fight the relegation battle instead.

If the championship started badly and finished well league form followed the opposite template. Dunshaughlin played eight rounds before tasting defeat but a couple of stumbling performances in the closing rounds denied them a final place as they finished in third position. The discrepancy between league and championship form was easy to identify but difficult to explain. In part it was due to the fact that Dunshaughlin had no player on the county senior panel so usually fielded close to full strength for league games whereas many opponents were handicapped by the absence of their county men. In the championship all clubs had their county players available so Dunshaughlin faced more formidable opposition, but in addition they seemed to lack the sharpness, grit and determination that championship day demands.

Maintaining their championship status for the fifteenth consecutive year and their league position for the twenty-second year in a row- the longest of all current Division 1 teams bar Summerhill, could be deemed a profitable year's work. Finally, the team's critical condition had stabilized and results in the early part of 2015 backed up that diagnosis, as the team has recorded two championship victories from three and an unbeaten ten game run in the league at the time of writing.

However, a more thorough analysis of performances since 2011 suggests there is some cause for concern.

The loss of players to emigration was a consistent problem during the economic recession but even more worrying was the failure to convert the St. Martins' successes of 2000-2008 into similar adult performances. The impressive minor championship winning side of 2009 was expected to make an impact on the Under 21 competition three years later. When the time came only eight of the minor winning team played on the side that crumbled against Dunboyne in the first round. The previous year in the thirteen a side competition the Under 21 team looked strong enough on paper to compete in the championship proper but that turned out to be a misleading view as the side was no match for Kilmainham-Drumbaragh in the semi-final. The North Meath combination struck four goals, two in each half, as the black and ambers were a poor second on a final scoreline of 4-7 to 0-7.

Recent Under 21 results have been both disappointing and worrying. Seven players who had played in the 2011 senior final lined out against Drumbaragh-Kilmainham but made little impact against the combined junior clubs. Since then the Under 21s have made no progress in the championship with early exits to St. Patricks and Nobber-

CHAPTER 22: HIGHS AND LOWS IN RECENT YEARS, 2007-2014

albeit with a very young team- in the most recent seasons. This inability to transfer successful under-age form to adult level should be a source of concern to the club.

The outstanding form displayed by the St. Martins' group of 2001-05 between Under 14 and minor level has brought scant results for Dunshaughlin at adult level. The team recorded Féile and Under 14 wins in 2001. Then in the Under 16 and Minor Championship finals of 2003 and 2005 St. Martins played Summerhill, winning the former and losing the latter. This uber-successful group contributed just one player to the 2011 senior finalists, Michael Ahern. Five players from the 2001 panel had emigrated, all to Canada, Alan McLoughlin the Under 14 captain of 2001, Ciarán Farrelly, Conor Staunton, Cillian Finn and Mark Caldwell. Seven of the team were from the Drumree side of the parish and a number of those continue to play hurling there but none play football. Two of those emigrated also. One of the best players from the group, David Devereux, has played only occasionally for the club in recent years, a situation replicated by half a dozen others.

Summerhill had a vastly superior conversion rate. Five who featured in the 2005 minor victory against St. Martins made it to the senior team in 2011 and another four were among the substitutes.

The outturn from the outstanding treble Féile winners 2004-06 is no better. Those sides were supreme in Meath and competitive at national level. The 2004 panel lost the All-Ireland semi-final by a solitary point to Corofin, a club that has gone on to capture Galway senior championships in 2011, 2013 and 2014, adding Connacht and All-Ireland victories in 2014. The 2005 St. Martins' side went out to Austin Stacks who were Kerry and Munster champions in 2014 while the 2006 side lost out to St. Endas of Omagh, Tyrone senior champions in 2014.

Thus a decade after the Féile successes the three clubs that eliminated St. Martins have five county, two provincial and one All-Ireland between them. Dunshaughlin has only one senior final appearance in that period. Worse still, out of the sixty-three players who made up the 2004-06 panels only four are regulars on the current senior team.

The outcome from the successful 2009 and 2013 minor teams seems more promising. Four of the 2009 minor side started the 2011 senior final while two more made the substitutes' bench. The successful minor team of 2013, mentored by Frank Gallogly, TP Toolan and Pat Gargan, has produced three current senior regulars, Dan Ormsby, Ben Duggan and Shane Gallogly and three substitutes.

Players from the 2009 and 2013 minor teams are crucial to senior success in the years ahead. It is critically important for the club to support team mentors and monitor under age performance and participation rates especially at minor level if the club is to successfully retain its hard won senior status in future years.

Achoimre

Achoimre

1886 -1900

Bunaíodh cumann CLG Dhomhnach Seachnaill go déanach sa bhliain 1886, agus d'úsáid siad na dathanna dubh agus ómra de chuid an úinéara agus an traenálaí áitiúil capaill rása, Stiofáin Ó Ceallaigh, dílseánach de chuid The Fingall Arms. Tugadh Cumann CLG Naomh Seachnall ar an gcumann.

I gcoinne an Rois a bhí an chéad chluiche a d'imríodh sa pháirc bhaile in Eanáir 1887 ar bhóthar Bhaile Átha Cliath i bpáirc a bhí faoi úinéireacht Pádraig Ó Dúshláine.

D'eagraigh an cumann Lá Spóirt gach bliain a mheall sluaite móra ón gceantar máguaird agus ó Bhaile Átha Cliath. Do thaistil go leor daoine ar traein go dtí Droim Rí.

Mar gheall ar an tionchar a d'imir Bráithreachas Phoblacht na hÉireann agus gur chuir Easpag na Mí ina aghaidh, d'imigh an CLG i gcontae na Mí i léig ag deireadh na tréimhse deich mbliana sin. Ní raibh ach ceithre chumann déag sa Mhí faoin mbliain 1891, Domhnach Seachnaill ina measc. Bhí thart ar dhaichead comhalta sa chumann faoin tráth sin, agus bhí Críostóir O Tallúin mar chaptaen, Pádraig Briain mar Uachtarán, Pádraig Mac an Rí mar Rúnaí agus Labhrás Ó Chainnín mar Chisteoir. Níos déanaí an bhliain sin, d'imigh an cumann i léig agus d'imir roinnt dá chomhaltaí le Baile an Bhairínigh ar feadh tamaill, go dtí gur thit an tóin as an gcumann sin chomh maith.

Thit athbheochan amach i lár na 1890í agus d'imir Domhnach Seachnaill i gcoinne a gcomharsan, an Scrín, in 1894 agus ghlac siad páirt sa chraobhchomórtas in 1895. Bhí foireann i nDroim Rí, chomh maith, in 1891 ach ní raibh foirne Dhomhnach Seachnaill agus Dhroim Rí ann a thuilleadh ag deireadh an chéid.

1900-1920

Níor éirigh le Domhnach Seachnaill Baile an Chaisleáin a bhualadh i gcluiche leathcheannais an chontae i 1902, agus i 1904 chas Naomh Seachnall agus Cumann Uí Mhathúna, an Uaimh ar a chéile trí huaire. Baineadh comhscór amach sa chéad dá chluiche agus cuireadh deireadh luath leis an tríú cluiche nuair a dhiúltaigh imreoir de chuid Chumann Uí Mhathúna an pháirc a fhágáil nuair a cuireadh den pháirc é. Bronnadh an bua ar Dhomhnach Seachnaill. D'éirigh le Baile an Chaisleáin, an fhoireann ab'fhearr sa Mhí ag an tráth sin, an ceann is fearr a fháil ar Dhomhnach Seachnaill sa chéad bhabhta ina dhiaidh sin.

I 1901, bhunaigh Peadar Ó Muirí brainse de chuid Chonradh na Gaeilge i nDomhnach Seachnaill, an chéad bhrainse dá shamhail sa Mhí. Bhunaigh an Conradh cumann iománaíochta, ar ar tugadh Na Fir le Chéile agus mhair sé ar feadh roinnt blianta.

I 1910 agus i 1911, bhuaigh Domhnach Seachnaill an craobhchomórtas sinsearach iománaíochta don chéad uair nuair a bhí an bua acu i gcoinne Dhún Búinne, le scór deiridh 2-7 i gcoinne 1-3 sa chéad chraobhchomórtas agus nuair a bhain siad an bua amach ar Mhaigh Dearmhaí le scór deiridh 8-1 i gcoinne 3-0 sa dara craobhchomórtas. Bhí thiar ar an gcumann ar feadh tréimhse, áfach, sular bhain siad cluiche ceannais 1916 amach, babhta ina raibh an bua ag Baile Átha Troim.

I 1916, fuair Séamus Mac an tSionnaigh mac sé mbliana déag d'aois le Pádraig Mac an tSionnaigh bás nuair a scaoileadh é i bhFaiche Stiabhna fad a bhí sé ag troid le hArm Cathartha na hÉireann. Bhí Pat Fox ina chaptaen ar Bhaile an Bhairínigh agus ar Dhroim Rí sna 1890í ach bhI sé ina chónaí I mBaile Átha Cliath ó 1913 amach.

Ghlac an bheirt fhear ba mhó a d'imir tionchar, Pádraig de Blacam agus Peadar Ó Cionnaith, páirt i gCogadh na Saoirse agus cuireadh chun príosúin iad ar feadh tréimhse. Ní raibh an cumann an-ghníomhach mar thoradh air sin go déanach sa tréimhse 1919-1921. D'imir roinnt comhaltaí le Reds Bhaile Pheiléid (Pelletstown Reds) a raibh foireann láidir iománaíochta agus peile acu ar feadh roinnt blianta.

1920 -1945

I 1923, d'éirigh le Pádraig de Blacam Domhnach Seachnaill a thabhairt ar ais san iomaíocht agus lean an cumann orthu le craobhchomórtas sóisearach iománaíochta na Mí a bhuachan in ainneoin gur chuir Cill an Chairn ina choinne sin. Lean feabhas ag teacht ar an gcumann agus bhí roinnt imreoirí óga acu agus bhuaigh siad an craobhchomórtas sinsearach i 1925 nuair a bhí bua 4-5 i gcoinne 2-3 acu in aghaidh Bhaile Átha Buí.

Bhí cáil ar iománaithe Dhomhnach Seachnaill, agus ar de Blacam go háirithe, a bheith crua, agus nuair a chuala bean tí amháin go raibh siad ag teacht i ngar agus iad ag triail ar chluiche san Uaimh, scread sí 'Coimeád na lachain istigh a Maggie, seo chugainn scabhtéirí Dhomhnach Seachnaill!'

Faoi thráth déanach sna 1920í, níor dheachaigh an fhoireann iománaíochta san iomaíocht a thuilleadh sa ghrád sinsearach agus faoi 1930, bhí go leor de na himreoirí ab'fhearr tar éis aistriú go cumainn eile. Roimhe sin, bhuaigh beirt fhear de chuid Dhomhnach Seachnaill, Mick Clusker agus Christy Doran, boinn iománaíochta sóisearaí Uile-Éireann nuair a bhí an bua ag an Mí ar Ghaillimh i gcluiche ceannais 1927.

Bhí an-tóir ar liathróid láimhe sa chontae ag an tráth seo agus bailíodh airgead chun cúirt liathróid láimhe a thógáil i rith na 1920í. Tógadh í in aice Stáisiún na nGardaí agus d'osclaíodh í i 1930.

Sna 1930í, bhí ní ba mhó daoine ag imirt peile ná a bhí ag imirt iománaíochta sa cheantar agus bhain Domhnach Seachnaill an cluiche ceannais amach i 1936 tar éis dóibh agóid sheafóideach a bhuachan in aghaidh Mhaigh Dearmhaí. Mhaígh an cumann go raibh fear darbh ainm Hugh Byrd ar liosta na foirne ach bhí fear darb ainm Hubert Byrd ar an liosta cláraithe oifigiúil. Líomhnaigh Domhnach Seachnaill gurbh ainmneacha éagsúla Hugh agus Hubert agus go raibh liosta na foirne mícheart. Níor éirigh leis an gcumann an bua a fháil ar Bhaile Senchail ar deireadh, agus a dhiabhal tairbhe an bua ar an agóid ar deireadh thiar.

Bhí foireann mhaith peile ann i gCúil Mhaoilín chomh maith sna 1930í agus d'imir siad i dhá chluiche leathcheannais chontae i 1934 agus 1941.

1945 -1960

I ndiaidh an Chogaidh Dhomhanda, bhí na cluichí á n-imirt ní ba rialta. Ní raibh an bua ag Domhnach Seachnaill i gcluiche ceannais mionúr an chontae i 1947 ach bhuaigh siad chéad teideal craobhchomórtais an chumainn i 1950 sa pheil, an chróin shóisearach. Bhí Caoimhín Melia ina chaptaen ar an bhfoireann a bhain bua 2-7 i gcoinne 1-1 amach ar Charn na Ros.

Go luath sna 1950í, b'iomaí comhrac dlúth a bhí ag an bhfoireann leis an Scrín, ach níor bhain siad cluiche ceannais sinsearach amach riamh. D'éirigh leo cluiche ceannais idirmheánach a bhaint amach i 1956 ach ba é Cumann Uí Mhathúna a bhain bua 3-6 i gcoinne 0-5 amach i ndiaidh athimirt an chluiche. Bhí foireann an-láidir de sheachtar imreoirí an taobh ag an cumann i rith na tréimhse seo agus bhuaigh siad go leor comórtais áitiúla.

I 1957, d'fhill go leor imreoirí ar Dhroim Rí agus bhí foireann an-rathúil acu go déanach sna 1950í agus sna 1960í. Bhuaigh Droim Rí an cluiche ceannais sóisearach i 1959 agus bhuaigh siad an teideal idirmheánach i 1961.

Idir an dá linn, d'aistrigh Domhnach Seachnaill anuas chuig an grád sóisearach agus bhuaigh siad an craobhchomórtas sóisearach i 1958. Tharla athbheochan ghearrthréimhseach nuair a rinne Seán MacMánais athbheochan ar thraidisiún na hiománaíochta agus bhuaigh an cumann teideal sóisearach i 1957 ach níor mhair an fhoireann iománaíochta isteach sna 1960í.

D'éirigh le Droim Rí agus Domhnach Seachnaill faichí imeartha a fháil i rith na tréimhse seo, agus tá an dá fhaiche sin fós á úsáid sa lá atá inniu ann.

Bhunaigh Ciarán Murray agus daoine eile cumann sna 1950í, chomh maith, d'imreoirí óga, ar ar tugadh Naomh Máirtín agus bhuaigh siad trí theideal peile faoi 14 bliana d'aois i ndiaidh a chéile idir 1957 agus 1959.

1960 -1980

Ba thréimhse an-rathúil í seo do chumann Dhomhnach Seachnaill. Bhuaigh an fhoireann an teideal sóisearach i 1977 agus deich mbliana ina dhiaidh sin, i ndiaidh go leor crá croí, rinneadh na curaidh idirmheánacha díobh. Bhí Dáibhí Ó Duibhir ina chaptaen ar an bhfoireann shóisearach nuair a chuir siad cluiche ar an Scrín, 5-3 i gcoinne 0-4, agus ba é Pádraig Ó Seoinín an captaen nuair a bhain siad bua 0-13 i gcoinne 0-6 amach in aghaidh na hOibre i 1977.

Ba dhúshlán ró-mhór é an craobhchomórtas sinsearach agus i 1983, bhí ar Dhomhnach Seachnaill filleadh ar an ngrád idirmheánach.

Sa tréimhse chéanna, bhuaigh Droim Rí an teideal idirmheánach i 1969, mar bharr ar an teideal a bhuadh i 1961.

Bhuaigh an Mhí craobhchomórtas sinsearach Uile Éireann i 1967 agus bhí Noel Curran ó Dhomhnach Seachnaill i lár na himeartha mar lántosaí don Chontae Ríoga.

Forbraíodh na faichí imeartha i rith na tréimhse seo chomh maith agus d'osclaíodh an limistéar nua imeartha agus an clubtheach nua i 1967.

1981-1998

Rinne an cumann ceiliúradh ar Chéad Bhliain an CLG trí stair an chumainn, Black and Amber, a fhoilsiú i 1984.

Ba í an fhorbairt ba thábhachtaí sna 1980í ná athbheochan chumann faoi aois, Naomh Máirtín, i 1983 chun freastal ar pheil sa pharóiste iomlán. I 1987, ghlac Naomh Máirtín chomh maith leis an dualgas chun freastal ar an iománaíocht faoi aois. Ba é Bhal Ó Dubhda an chéad chathaoirleach agus ba í Lena Ní Dhúill an rúnaí.

I measc na n-éachtaí ba mhó a bhain an cumann amach bhí an Craobhchomórtas Peile Mionúr a bhuachan le cabhair ó Ráth Tó i 1987 chun bua 0-4 i gcoinne 0-3 a fháil ar Bhaile Shláine sa chluiche ceannais. Bhuaigh an cumann an sraithchomórtas agus an craobhchomórtas peile faoi 14 bliana d'aois i 1999. Bhí an rath ar na hiománaithe ina gcéad bhliain, agus bhuaigh siad cluiche ceannais B faoi 11 bliana, mar aon le teidil eile, ina measc, teideal na hiománaíochta mionúr i 1997, nuair a bhí an bua ag Naomh Máirtín ar Ráth Moliain sa chluiche ceannais, 4-8 i gcoinne 3-1.

Bhuaigh an cumann cúpla teideal Sóisearach sna 1990í, Roinn Shóisearach 3 i 1991 trí bhua 1-8 i gcoinne 0-4 a bhaint amach ar Naomh Mícheál sa chluiche ceannais i ndiaidh athimeartha. Bhuaigh an cumann craobhchomórtas Sóisearach B ceithre bhliana ina dhiaidh sin tríd an gceann is fearr a fháil ar Shodan, 1-9 i gcoinne 1-6.

D'imir na foirne idirmheánacha i sé chluiche leathcheannais, athimirt san áireamh, sna 1990í sular bhain siad an cluiche ceannais amach ar deireadh thiar i 1997 i gcoinne Dhamhliag. Bua ollmhór 3-14 i gcoinne 1-6 ag Domhnach Seachnaill a bhí ann ar deireadh. I rith na tréimhse seo, rinne an fhoireann dul chun cinn réidh i Sraithchomórtas Peile an Chontae, agus lean siad ar aghaidh ó Roinn 3 go dtí Roinn 1 idir 1988 agus 1992. Tá an fhoireann fós sa phríomhroinn ó shin i leith.

Rinneadh athbheochan ar an iománaíocht sa chumann i 1982 agus ba é Gearóid Ó Flannagáin an duine is mó ba chúis leis seo. Bhuaigh Domhnach Seachnaill teideal sóisearach iománaíochta i 1982 agus teidil idirmheánacha i 1983 agus 1987. Ní raibh an ghrian leo i gcluichí ceannais idirmheánacha 1985 agus 1986 ach ní raibh siad riamh láidir a dhóthain le bheith ag imirt ar leibhéal sinsearach. Faoi dheireadh na tréimhse deich mbliana, bhí deacrachtaí ag an gcumann le foireann iománaíochta a chur le chéile agus uaidh sin ar aghaidh, ghlac Droim Rí ceannas ar iománaíocht daoine fásta sa pharóiste.

I 1995, bhunaigh Oilibhéar Bowe agus daoine eile Royal Gaels agus é mar chuspóir acu peil na mban a chur chun cinn sa pharóiste. I dtosach báire, dhírigh an fhoireann ar imreoirí faoi aois agus bhain siad an cluiche ceannais faoi 14 bliana amach go tapa, ach mar gheall ar agóid, níor éirigh leo imirt sa chluiche ceannais. Lean na Gaeil leo agus bhí an rath geal orthu sa chéad deich mbliana den chéad nua.

D'éirigh go han-mhaith le Droim Rí sa tréimhse deich mbliana ag deireadh an chéid. I ndiaidh dóibh aistriú anuas go gráid ní b'ísle sna 1980í, thug siad leo an teideal sóisearach peile i 1998 nuair a bhain siad bua 1-11 i gcoinne 2-5 amach ar Naomh Muire agus lean siad ar aghaidh, ina dhiaidh sin, chun cluiche ceannais shraithchomórtas Laighean a bhuachan, nuair a d'éirigh leo an ceann is fearr a fháil ar Bhaile Átha na Róine (Contae Laoise) i nDomhnach Seachnaill, 2-12 i gcoinne 1-10. Ba é Eimhín Ó Ceallaigh laoch imeartha Dhroim Rí, agus bhuaigh sé boinn shinsearacha Uile Éireann i 1996 agus 1999 agus rinneadh Sárimreoir Peile na Bliana de in 2002. I ndiaidh ceannas a ghlacadh ar an iománaíocht ó chumann Dhomhnach Seachnaill, d'éirigh go geal le Droim Rí leis an gcamán agus leis an sliotar, agus bhuaigh siad craobhchomórtais roinn shóisearach 2 i 1993 agus i 1996 mar aon le craobhchomórtas sóisearach i 1998.

1999 - 2014

Ba í an tréimhse idir 2000 agus 2014 ba rathúla i stair Dhomhnach Seachnaill. Go gairid i ndiaidh bheith curtha ar aghaidh chuig an gcéim shinsearach, bhain an fhoireann cluiche ceannais 1999 amach, ach bhí an Scrín ró-láidir dóibh.

Ach i ngach ceann de na trí bliana ina dhiaidh sin, bhuaigh an fhoireann an craobhchomórtas. Bhuaigh siad in 2000, 1-19 i gcoinne 2-6 ar Choill Chille Mhaighneann, agus fuair siad an ceann b'fhearr ar an Scrín in 2001, 0-11 i gcoinne 1-5, agus bhí bua caol acu ar Bhaile Átha Troim in 2002, 1-11 i gcoinne 2-6. Ba iad Diarmuid Ó Cadhla, Ciarán Ó Broin agus Cionnaith Mac Taidhg, faoi seach, na captaein rathúla. Ba é cóitseálaí rathúil na foirne Éamonn Barry agus ba iad a roghnóirí TP Ó Tuathalláin agus Breandán Ó Cadhla.

Mar gheall ar an mbua a bhí acu sa Mhí, bhí eachtra bhliantúil ann i gcraobhchomórtas Laighean. I gcaitheamh trí bliana, d'imir Domhnach Seachnaill dhá chluiche dhéag i Laighin, agus thug siad faoi Ráth Naoi (Cill Mhantáin) in ocht gcinn díobh. Ar deireadh, in 2002, bhain an cumann teideal Laighean amach nuair a bhain siad an bua amach ar Raonaithe Máiteoige (an Lú) sa chluiche ceannais i bPáirc Tailteann. Bhí bua gan stró 0-13 i gcoinne 0-7 ag an bhfoireann dhubh agus ómra agus bhí sé d'onóir ag Cionnaith Mac Taidhg an corn a ardú. Cuireadh deireadh leis an odáise i bhFeabhra 2003 nuair a bhain imreoirí Chrois Mhaoilíona bua 3-10 i gcoinne 1-12 amach i bPáirc de hÍde, Ros Comáin.

In 2002, bhí an rath geal ar an gcumann dhá bhabhta eile nuair a bhuaigh siad teideal Shraithchomórtas Roinn 1 agus Corn na Feise. Rinne siad gach ceann de na coirn a bhí ar fáil a bhuachan sa bhliain stairiúil sin.

Bhain Domhnach Seachnaill an cluiche ceannais sinsearach amach in 2011 arís eile ach chríochnaigh siad sa dara háit i ndiaidh Dhroim Samhraidh tar éis athimeartha. Ba ábhar sóláis do na himreoirí é Corn na Feise a bhuachan ach don dara huair, nuair a bhain siad bua dícheallach le stró amach i gcoinne Ghaeil Bhláth Gall i gcomhrac dlúth inar bhain Domhnach Seachnaill bua caol 1-10 i gcoinne 1-6 amach. Rinne Réamonn Ó Maoldomhnaigh an fhoireann a thabhairt chun bua.

Bhí an bua ag an gcumann ar leibhéal faoi 21 bliain trí huaire sa chéad tréimhse deich mbliana san aonú haois is fiche. In 2000, bhí Donncha Ó Cadhla mar chaptaen ar an bhfoireann a bhain an bua amach in aghaidh Bhaile Íomhair. In 2004, thug Réamonn Ó Maoldomhnaigh a chomhimreoirí leis chun an bua a fháil ar na Fianna agus bhain foireann Chathail Uí Dhuibhir bua 2-11 i gcoinne 1-10 amach ar Bhulf Tón i 2007.

In 2012, bhuaigh an cumann teideal Sóisearach B nuair a bhuail siad Naomh Muire, 0-12 i gcoinne 0-9, agus ba é Seán Sheosaimh Mac Domhnaill captaen na foirne.

I rith na tréimhse deich mbliana, bhuaigh an cumann dhá theideal sraithchomórtais sna gráid ísle: sraithchomórtas B, Roinn 5 in 2003, sraithchomórtas B Roinn 2 in 2008. Bhí Deasún Ó Catháin agus Graham Ó Dubhda mar chaptaein ar na foirne buaiteacha.

Rinneadh an chéad fhear den chumann de Shoireal Ó Craobháin chun post Rúnaí an Bhoird Chontae a bheith aige, agus bhí an post sin aige ó 2008 go 2012. Ar pháirc na himeartha, bhuaigh Risteard Ó Cadhla bonn sinsearach Uile Éireann leis an Mí i 1999 agus d'ainmníodh Caoimhín Mac an Rí do ghradam Imreoir Peile na Bliana in 2007.

Lean Naomh Máirtín orthu ag imirt go dtí 2008 agus uaidh sin ar aghaidh, imríodh an pheil faoi aois go léir i ndathanna agus faoi ainm Dhomhnach Seachnaill. D'fhreastail Droim Rí ar gach foireann iománaíochta agus camógaíochta do dhaoine fásta agus faoi aois sa pharóiste.

Bhí an rath geal ar Naomh Máirtín roinnt uaireanta sular cuireadh deireadh leo. D'imir an cumann ar son na Mí ag Féile na nGael ceithre huaire in 2001 agus ina dhiaidh sin ar feadh trí bliana i ndiaidh a chéile idir 2004 agus 2006. Bhain foireann 2004 cluiche leathcheannais Uile Éireann amach agus chaill siad i gcoinne Chora Finne (Contae na Gaillimhe).

Cháiligh an fhoireann faoi 14 bliana chun imirt ar son na Mí in imeacht na Féile faoi 14 bliana in 2014 tríd an bua a fháil ar Dhún Búinne i gcluiche ceannais an chontae. Bhain siad Sciath Roinn 2 Uile Éireann amach ach chaill siad i gcoinne Chlann na Gael (Ros Comáin) sa chluiche ceannais i ndiaidh am breise.

Bhuaigh an cumann a chéad teideal faoi 16 bliana in 2003, agus ceann eile in 2008 agus bhuaigh siad na craobhchomórtais faoi 14 bliana in 2001, 2005 agus 2006.

Bhí cúpla bua suntasach ag na hiománaithe a chaith an geansaí dearg agus bán chomh maith. Bhuaigh an fhoireann faoi 14 bliana craobhchomórtas B in 2000 agus teideal na Féile an bhliain dar gcionn. Bhí an bua ag an gcumann chomh maith sa chraobhchomórtas mionúr, grád B, in 2001 agus in 2003.

Lean peileadóirí mionúir Dhomhnach Seachnaill orthu agus an geansaí dubh agus ómra á chaitheamh acu leis an mbua a bhaint amach i gcraobhchomórtas 2009. Ba é seo an chéad uair a bhuaigh an cumann Corn Delany gan bheith ag imirt i gcomhar le cumann eile. Bhí Eoin Ó Hágartaigh ina chaptaen ar imreoirí an chumainn agus bhain siad bua mór 1-14 i gcoinne 1-5 amach ar Dhomhnach Mór-Cill Deagláin. Trí bliana ina dhiaidh sin, bhí Séan Ó Gallóglaigh ina chaptaen nuair a bhain na mionúir teideal an tsraithchomórtais mhionúr amach tríd an mbua a fháil ar Dhroim Samhraidh, 1-12 i gcoinne 1-8.

Bhí fíor-rath ar na Gaeil Ríoga, atá ag imirt ó 1993 ar aghaidh, le blianta beaga anuas. Bhuaigh an fhoireann daoine fásta craobhchomórtas sóisearach B agus sraithchomórtas Roinn 2 in 2002. Ansin, in 2007, bhain siad an rath ba mhó amach a bhí orthu riamh nuair a bhuaigh siad an craobhchomórtas idirmheánach in aghaidh na bhFianna agus sraithchomórtas Roinn 2 i gcoinne Dhroim Samhraidh. Ba í Gemma Ní Fhlannagáin captaen na foirne.

Bhuaigh an cumann liosta fada teidil faoi aois, faoi 14 bliana in 2003, 2010 agus 2013, faoi 16 bliana in 2003, 2006 agus 2013 agus faoi 19 mbliana in 2009, i measc cinn eile. Go luath in 2015, cháiligh an cumann chun imirt ar son na Mí i gcluichí ceannais Fhéile na nGael i Loch Garman agus bhuaigh siad Dún Búinne.

Rinneadh na Gaeil Ríoga a chuimsiú le déanaí i struchtúr chumann Dhomhnach Seachnaill faoi bheartas Cumann Amháin an CLG ach tá a n-ainm á choimeád acu go fóill.

Bhí an-chuid gníomhaíocht forbartha ar siúl sa tréimhse idir 1998 agus 2014. Forbraíodh faiche nua imeartha agus tógadh faiche uile-aimsire. Tá an chéad chéim eile den fhorbairt ar siúl anois agus tá clubtheach athchóirithe agus sínte le bheith curtha i gcrích in 2015.

Níor éirigh le cumann Dhroim Rí an teideal sóisearach a bhuaigh siad i 1998 a shárú agus ar deireadh thiar, rinne siad an cinneadh chun díriú ar an iománaíocht ar leibhéal faoi aois agus ar leibhéal daoine fásta. D'éirigh go geal leo agus bhuaigh an cumann teidil iománaíochta idirmheánacha in 2003 agus in 2010 agus bhí an bua ag an bhfoireann faoi 21 bliain in 2012 agus in 2013. Chomh maith leis sin, d'éirigh leis an bhfoireann mionúr in 2012 agus in 2013, agus d'imir siad i gcomhar le Gaeil Bhláth Gall agus d'éirigh leo bua a bhaint amach sa chraobhchomórtas agus bua Scéithe a bhaint amach.

Appendices

Appendix 1
Biographical Details of Dunshaughlin GAA Club Players, 1887-1950s

This Appendix gives short details of all those mentioned in the main text from Chapters 1 to 5, generally those who were involved with the clubs until the 1950s.

Jimmy Allen
He played in the 1943 junior Semi-Final against Castletown when he lived at Soldier Hill on the Navan Road.

Thomas Armstrong
A porter in Dunshaughlin Workhouse, he played in the first home game against Ross in 1887, and scored the only goal.

P Bird
He played for Dunshaughlin in the senior football semi-final of 1902 but we were unable to establish his identity.

John, Jimmy, Michael and Paddy Blake:
The Blake brothers were originally from the Red Bog area. John was captain of the football team in 1909, but seldom hurled. Jimmy's lorry was often the sole means of transport for the players in the 1920s. Michael was a hurler in the main and usually played in defence. Paddy was better known as 'The Butcher' and was the heart and soul of the club for over 60 years until his death in 1983. Michael was said to be even tougher than Paddy; when a score was badly needed he would go ahead of Paddy and clear the way to goal! Their careers are covered more fully in the main text. Paddy was father of Arnold and Pádraig who played in the 1950s and 1960s and grandfather of Garbhán, Caoimhín and Fionnán who played in the 1980s and 1990s.

Hugh Boyne
Hugh was from Batterstown and played in the 1947 minor football final with Dunshaughlin.

Paddy 'Butson' Brady and Peter Brady
They were from Curraha, and both played with Dunshaughlin in the 1940s. Paddy later played with Skryne.

Jimmy 'Cuttler' Brien
Jimmy played minor hurling in 1940 and adult football in the 1940s. He lived on Main Street, near Family Fashions.

Michael Bruton
Michael was from Culmullen, a tough hurler and a very good runner. After Dunshaughlin broke up c. 1919 he assisted the Pelletstown Reds.

Billy and Larry Byrne
Billy and Larry were from Culmullen and both usually played side by side in the half back line. Billy was also an able cross-country runner, coming third in the All-Ireland cross country of 1947. After joining Drumree both had lengthy careers in the red and white. Thanks to both for help with the 1950s for the original Black and Amber.

Joe 'Little Sport' Byrne
Joe was not related to Billy or Larry and was the regular Dunshaughlin goalkeeper until 1957 when he became the Drumree 'man in the gap'. He was a fine keeper and a humorous character on and off the field.

Laurence F Canning
A founder member of the club, he was its Vice-President and Treasurer a number of times. He doesn't appear to have played himself, being in his mid-thirties when the club was founded. He was a master-baker, working where

Tara News is at present and employed a number of men. Matty Canning, his son, was very helpful with information when we were researching the original Black and Amber.

Mickey Senior, Mick 'The Barrett' and Billy 'Slug' Carberry

Mickey Senior played some football but was better known as a strong forceful hurler and won senior hurling championship medals in 1909 and 1910. He later became Secretary of the club and he was father of Mick 'The Barrett' Carberry and Billy 'Slug' Carberry. 'The Barrett' played hurling and football in the 1930s and 40s and his son Joe also played senior and intermediate football for Dunshaughlin in the 1980s. Billy played minor football for Meath in 1942. A strong, fearless dual player, he won junior medals in football in 1950 and hurling in 1957. Billy provided valuable information and memories from the late 1930s and 1940s for the original Black and Amber.

Christy 'Randall' Carey

Christy was father of Liam who was Treasurer of the club in the 1980s and grandfather of Christopher, a member of the senior panel in 2000-2002.

Jack Carty

Jack was originally from Nobber and captained the hurlers in 1909 and 1911 and probably in 1910. He played in goals and lived in Drumree on the Dunshaughlin side of the bridge over the River Skane.

Bernard and Leo Carolan

One of the men who guided the club through its early years as Secretary, Bernard ran a bicycle shop almost opposite where *Peters'*-formerly *Murray's*- public house is at present. He was also the chief organizer of the annual sports and an inveterate letter writer to the *Drogheda Independent*. In later years he became deeply involved in nationalist politics, was Secretary of the South Meath Branch of the United Irish League and agitated constantly for better housing for the rural labourer. One of his sons, Leo, played during the hurling championship winning campaign of 1925.

Jack Clarke and Michael 'Jacob' Clarke

Jack worked in PJ Murray's as a shop assistant, played on the great Dunshaughlin hurling team of 1908-12 and also represented the club at County Board meetings. Michael was a brother, and was known as Jacob, because he was as tall as Jacob's ladder. He lived in Red Bog and was a farm worker.

Mick and Thomas Clusker

Mick was a top class full back and an excellent handballer. He had an extraordinary career with the club, playing first c. 1910 and lining out for thirty years. He won an All-Ireland Junior Hurling Championship medal with Meath in 1927 and he also played with Erin's Own and the Faughs in Dublin for a period. He worked as a baker's driver. Thomas Clusker was Mick's brother and was better known as Toddy. He also had a lengthy hurling career and like his brother played with Dunboyne on occasion. Seán Clusker, Vincent 'Skipper' Clusker and Tommy Clusker were sons of Toddy and nephews of Mick. Vincent was a good football goalkeeper who lined out with the Meath minors in 1942. Seán was more noted as a hurler with Oberstown while Tommy was a useful athlete and also played junior football for the club in the 1940s. Tommy's son, also Tommy, was very involved with St. Martins in the 1990s and 2000s while another son Harry also assisted with underage teams. Harry's son Stephen and Tommy's sons Ciarán and Niall all played for the club.

Jack Collier

Jack played with Dunshaughlin in the 1910 senior hurling final but did most of his hurling with Kilmessan. A farmer, he lived near Dunsany and was a founder member of Kilmessan Hurling Club. He was a grandfather of Conal Collier, currently a journalist with the *Meath Chronicle*.

Colm Condon

Colm, a native of Ashbourne, played with the club in the late 1940s and later became Ireland's Attorney General, 1965-73.

James J. Connolly

He was the clerk of Dunshaughlin Petty Sessions Court and may have been the first Secretary of the GAA club. He certainly acted as Secretary for the 1887 Sports. He didn't play football but often refereed games.

Barney Cooney

Barney's father was a guard in Dunshaughlin and Barney lived here from his youth. A clean, sporting defender he was corner back on Dunshaughlin's first junior football championship winning team of 1950 and full forward in the intermediate final of 1956 but emigrated to the USA at the end of that decade.

William Corry and John Corry

They played with the Dunshaughlin team in the 1909 junior football league but we could not establish their identities.

Paddy Cosgrave

A good defender in the early 1940s, he lived in Batterstown.

Jerry and Patsy Crosby

Both played for a short period in the 1930s. Jerry later lived in Dublin and Patsy in Culmullen. Both are uncles of Paul Hetherington, the Downs, who has won a number of national sprint titles.

Charles Curley

Charles played with Dunshaughlin in the 1916 senior hurling final but was from Dunboyne, with whom he also played. He also lined out for the Pelletstown Reds.

Matt Daly

Matt was a Westmeath native and he worked in the Parochial House from the 1950s. Matt had an abiding interest in hurling and was one of the chief men behind the hurling revival in 1957. He was a most efficient Secretary for a number of years, won the club's Hall of Fame in 2002 and lives in Finglas at present.

Willie Daly

Willie won senior hurling championship medals in 1909 and 1910 and later became Chairman of the club. A good handballer he was related to the present day Dalys of Clonross and Lagore.

Kevin Darby

Kevin played minor football in 1940. He was a nephew of Paddy Kenny and an uncle of Francis Darby, who played intermediate football with Dunshaughlin in the 1990s. Kevin's brothers Fintan and Dermot were good cross country runners in the 1940s.

Matty Davis

A native of Curraha, he played hurling and football for the club for a number of years in the 1930s.

Bill Delaney

Bill was from Kiltale and was centre-back in the minor football final of 1947. He played senior with the club in the early 1950s.

Patrick Delany and Family

Patrick was a Poor Law Guardian, an elected member of the board that supervised the workhouse. He owned a substantial farm beside the present Roman Catholic Church and gave one of his fields to the club for its early games. The Delanys have a long association with the GAA in Dunshaughlin, both as players and as the ever-obliging providers of fields on which games were played. His son

Thomas Delany was a tremendous athlete in the 1880s, played in the club's first home games in 1887 and lived until 1957.

Patrick's grandson Kevin Delany was a strong powerful defender during the 1930s. He later played full forward and won a senior football championship with Donaghmore in 1942. He retired in his prime and turned his talents to athletics.

Kevin was father of Michael Delany who won an Under 14 championship with St. Martins in 1959 and grandfather of Niall and Shane Kelly, members of Dunshaughlin's three in a row team of 2000-02. Kevin was a tremendous help to us on the 1920s and 1930s and especially in positioning the 1925 winning hurling team for the original Black and Amber. Maurice Delany was another grandson of Patrick and son of Thomas. He was a good forty-yards man who was adept at distributing the ball and opening up play by using the wing men. As a player and official he was a great man to rally a team. He was Chairman of the club for a period and one of those responsible for the purchase of the present playing field. His son Thomas played for the club in the 1980s, won a Meath handball championship and was Secretary of both the football and handball clubs for short periods. Maurice's granddaughter Laura Murray is an outstanding footballer with Royal Gaels who has played for Meath at all levels. Patrick's great great grandson James Kelliher played on the St. Martins' Féile winning team of 2004.

Thanks to Maurice for his memories of the appeals to Leinster Council in 1950 for the first edition of Black and Amber.

Fr. John, Fr. Pat, Fr. Willie, Christy, Colm, Dessie and Tom Delany were brothers of Kevin and Maurice and most of them played for the club at various times.

The Dorans

William Doran was a prominent athlete in the early years of the football club and was an agricultural labourer cum timberman by trade. His son Christy 'The Toes' Doran was a top-class hurler but equally good as a footballer. He captained the Meath senior football team in the late 1920s when he played his club football with Donaghmore as Dunshaughlin had no football team. Like Mick Clusker he won an All-Ireland junior hurling medal in 1927.

Dick 'The Goo' Doran was Christy's brother. Jimmy 'Cheeser' Doran and Peter Doran were brothers of 'The Toes.' The 'Cheeser' was a sweet hurler and won a senior hurling championship in 1925 while Peter was a useful footballer. Bill 'The Geordie' Doran was a son of 'The Toes' Doran. He was a good fielder of the ball and a very intelligent user of it. In the 1950 divisional play-off against Dunboyne Paddy Duffy said to Geordie as the teams took to the field, 'I'll bet you half a whiskey you don't score a goal on Rusk'- then Meath's goalkeeper. The Geordie did score in the first half and at the interval Paddy produced a baby Power but Tommy Gogan intervened. Duffy then said 'Doubles or quits for the second half.' At the end Geordie collected two baby Powers!

Christy, Johnny, Paddy and Tommy Dowd

The Dowds played for the club in the 1930s and 1940s. Paddy played in the 1947 junior semi-final while Christy was better known as a hurler. They were brothers of Tommy Dowd, father of Val and Ger, stalwarts of the club in the 1960-2000 period, whose contributions to the club are related in the main text. Val's sons Clive, Graham and Trevor made outstanding contributions to the club in the 1990s and 2000s while Ger's sons played with Donaghmore-Ashbourne.

Joe Downes

He played on the Dunshaughlin football team against Castletown in 1904. From Bogganstown, he ran a shop there. He was father of Tommy Downes, one of the founders of St. Martins, and Benny and Noel who played in the 1940s. Benny's son Emmett played with St. Martins in the 1980s.

Paddy 'The Rah' and Thomas 'The Connor' Doyle

Both lined out for Dunshaughlin when Drumree was dormant in the 1930s. 'The Rah' was the backbone of the Drumree club for half a century and was father of Brendan, Packie and Seán and grandfather of numerous Doyles. His daughter Kathleen married Michael 'Curate' Walsh and they, with their sons Aidan, Martin and Michael, were also stalwarts of the GAA in the parish. Another daughter Lena was the first Secretary of the reformed St. Martins in 1983.

Drumree Cricket Club

Most of the players listed in Chapter 2 as lining out for Drumree Cricket Club were natives of Knockmark. James Fox was a tailor, his brother Michael was a railway worker. Patrick Marley, John Rooney, John Clarke, and Thomas Geraghty were agricultural labourers. Thomas Johnson was a farmer while John Lynch was a railway signalman. Patrick Muldoon was from Killeen, John Hughes from Kiltale, both agricultural labourers.

J Duffy

He played in the early years of the club and cannot be positively identified but may be John Duffy, father of Senator Michael Duffy.

Michael Duffy

Known as 'The Hank' he was a Senator from 1922 to 1936. He worked for Meath County Council before that and became a member of the National Executive of the Transport Union. He was the guiding light of Dunshaughlin's hurlers as club Secretary in 1907-11 and was captain in 1917. His career is covered more fully in the main text. Paddy 'Gabby Ann' Duffy was his brother and represented the club as a player and official for many years and was Secretary from 1913 to 1915.

Pat Dwan

Pat played in the late 1930s and 1940s. After Dunshaughlin lapsed he played hurling for Oberstown and lined out at midfield in their senior final defeats to Trim in 1942 and Kilmessan in 1945, returning to captain the Dunshaughlin hurlers in 1949. He worked in Gogans.

Noel and Bill Eiffe

They were brothers from Ratoath who played for the club for a few years in the mid 1950s.

Finian Englishby

Finian saw service with a number of clubs in Ireland and England, winning a junior football championship with Dunshaughlin in 1958 and was later Chairman of Meath Hurling Board. He married Mary Foley, a step sister of Christy, Benny, Podger and Joe Foley. Finian was always at hand when help was needed by the club, especially an extra player! Thanks to Finian for information and photographs for the first edition of Black and Amber and for sourcing and presenting Peter Lee's hurling championship medals from 1909 and 1910 to the club.

John Ennis

John was from the Bush and was full back on the minor team of 1947 but played his adult football with Batterstown. He won senior hurling championships with St. Patricks, a combination of Kilmessan, Kiltale and Batterstown, was Meath Referee of the Year in 1974 and refereed from the mid 1950s until 1978. He was a noted cross country athlete, finishing seventh in the senior All-Ireland cross country championship in 1948, helping Meath to second place. His sons Georgie and Mervyn won junior championship medals with Dunshaughlin in 1994 with Georgie captaining the side.

P Everard

He played in Dunshaughlin's first home game in 1887 and may have been Pat Everard who lived where *The Village Restaurant* is now.

Andy, Jim and Tom 'The Butcher' Everard and Tom Everard, Raynestown

Andy, Jim and Tom were natives of Rackenstown and regulars on the revived Dunshaughlin hurling team of the 1930s. They were uncles of Tom Everard from Raynestown. Tom won Junior hurling and football championships and was Secretary and Treasurer of the club in the late fifties. He is currently one of the club's Presidents and was awarded the Hall of Fame in 2003.

John Finnegan

He was Secretary of the GAA Club 1888-1889. Either James J Connolly or Finnegan was the first Secretary of the club. It is not known where he lived, but he left the club in 1890 due to some dispute and became Secretary of Tara Athletic Club.

Charlie Flood

He played hurling for Dunshaughlin in the second decade of the twentieth century and was from Curraha.

The Foleys

Christy Foley, Senior and Junior were both blacksmiths, but Christy senior seems to have been involved in the hurling club only indirectly through the Gaelic League in the 1900s. Christy junior played hurling and football and represented Meath in 1910. He later settled in Ratoath. Of the trio of brothers who played, - he was regarded as the best. The Foleys have had an unbroken association with G.A.A in the village from the beginning of the century to the present.

Henry Foley played little hurling as his health was always poor and he died young.

Patrick 'The Gah' Foley, was also a blacksmith and had his forge at the entrance to Christy's present workshop. Associated with the G.A.A. all his life, he can be seen in the photographs of the Dunshaughlin teams of 1910 and 1957. On occasion he drove Foley's car, which was used to bring Geoff Gilpin's -of the Glebe- staff to mass. One St. Peter and St. Paul's Day as 'The Gah' arrived, Gilpin said "I say Foley, what holiday is this?" "St. Peter's and St. Paul's" answered 'The Gah', to which Gilpin replied 'It's a good f-----g thing the two of them died on the one day.' 'The Gah' was father of Benny, Christy, Joe, Paudger and Seamus Foley.

Benny Foley played for the club for over fifteen years and was a trustee of the football field until his untimely death in 1973. A witty character on and off the field he was a determined footballer and hurler. A noted boxer in his youth, he was twice runner-up for the Irish junior bantamweight title, while he later became a fine amateur actor with the local drama group. He was father of Niall, also a noted athlete, who won a minor football championship in 1987 and captained the Reserve League winning side of 1989.

Christy Foley played very little football but as Chairman of the Carnival Committee for a number of years he was instrumental in helping to finance the club and its playing field. He was a top class boxer winning an Irish National Senior title and also boxed for Ireland. His son Allen captained the St. Martins-Ratoath side to minor championship success in 1987 and won a junior championship, Division 3, in 1991.

Joe Foley was an all-round sportsman, boxer, footballer and hurler. He emigrated to the USA in the late 1950s where he was ordained a priest and spent many years ministering in Liberia and Florida prior to retirement.

Seamus Foley was a stepbrother of Benny, Christy and Joe. Seamus could out-fetch bigger opponents at midfield, was deadly from placed balls and also played in goals in both football and hurling. He was Secretary of the Carnival Committee for many years and he and Christy were the men most responsible for its phenomenal success. He was instrumental in formulating a motion that eventually became a GAA rule that the goalkeeper should wear a distinctive jersey. Also, like all the Foleys, he was no mean performer in the ring.

PJ Fox

PJ Fox was captain of the Drumree team formed on the break-up of the Dunshaughlin and Warrenstown teams in 1891. He owned the *Spencer Arms* in Drumree, now Gilsenan's, and was a staunch supporter of Parnell. He moved to Dublin about 1912 and his sixteen year old son James, who joined Fianna Éireann and the Irish Citizens' Army, was shot dead early on Tuesday morning, 25th of April at St. Stephen's Green during the Easter Rising. Both are buried in Knockmark.

Jimmy Geraghty

Jimmy played for the club in the late 1930s and again in 1951 when he had the misfortune to break a leg in the Ratoath tournament. He was also a fine handballer and lived in Drumree. The family owned the Post Office in Drumree.

Larry 'Sonny' Geraghty

Sonny was a Dunshaughlin minor in 1933 and later played with Donaghmore and was a substitute on the county team. He lived in the Bush but was originally from Cultrommer.

Joe Gibney

Joe was from the Flathouse and played in the 1943 junior Semi-Final. He was father of Ratoath player Stan Gibney who won a Leinster Junior medal with Meath in 1986.

Michael Gilmore

His brother Dan was District Court Clerk in Dunshaughlin but Michael took up a post in Belfast in 1909 and later worked in Dublin. He was deeply involved with the Gaelic League at the beginning of the twentieth century and played some hurling with the club's Na Fir le Céile team. With Michael Duffy he was chosen as a representative of the club to carry the coffin of Fr. Eoghan O Growney, a founder of the Gaelic League, in 1903.

John, Nicky, Paddy and Tommy Gogan

The four brothers played for Dunshaughlin in the 1920s and 30s. Nicky won a senior hurling championship in 1925, was a member of the Meath All-Ireland junior hurling panel of 1927 in the early rounds and was father of Oliver Gogan and grandfather of current players, Fearghal and Ronan. Nicky and John and Paddy were later sterling footballing half backs while John also hurled. Tommy played very little for the club but was Treasurer for a lengthy period and was also elected Chairman. He was a dab hand at fund raising, especially Three Fifteens and a Sweep when money was hard come by.

He died very young and his wife Sheila, a daughter of Peadar Murray, and his son Anthony ran Gogan's public house for many years. They were great supporters and financial backers of the GAA, especially underage teams and the hurling club in the 1980s.

James Griffin

He was Secretary and Treasurer of the Drumree team in 1891 and may have lived in Colvinstown.

Patrick Hand

Patrick was from Derrockstown and worked as a herd. He was a great runner and played some football in the Dunshaughlin colours in the 1900s.

Francis Hobson

He was President (Chairman) of the Drumree team formed in 1891. He may have worked as a Railway Signalman in Drumree while living in Dublin.

Paddy Huggard

In his own words Paddy played 'a game or two' of minor hurling in the club. He was a huge help in compiling the original Black and Amber due to his very clear memory of the 1920s and 1930s. He lived in one of the cottages across from St. Patrick's Hall when we spoke to him in 1984.

Jack and Peter Johnson

The Johnsons were brothers from Scalestown in Skryne. They may have worked with Colonel Stourton of Corbalton Hall. Both played with Greenpark Hurling Club in 1907 when Dunshaughlin fielded no teams. Jack's son Kevin Johnson captained the Dunshaughlin junior football team in the 1943 Semi-Final after transferring from Skryne, but spent only a year with the club. He was a regular Meath senior prior to this when playing with Skryne and returned to them to win senior championships in 1945 and 1947. He also won an All-Ireland junior football medal in 1947. Jack's great-grandchildren Michael, Anthony and Tommy Johnson are current Dunshaughlin players.

Dessie Johnson

He was known as Little Dessie and lives in Killeen at present. He won a junior hurling championship with Dunshaughlin in 1957 and Junior Football medals in 1958.

Theo Joyce

Theo was a Galway native who played for the club for a year or two. He won an All-Ireland Hogan Cup medal with St. Jarlath's, Tuam in 1958 and later emigrated to the USA.

Joe Kelly

Joe, from Batterstown, was full forward on the senior hurling winning team of 1925.

Gerry Kenny

Also known as James, father of Con and grandfather of Dominic Moran who played with the club in the 1970s. He won a senior hurling championship medal in 1925.

Paddy Kenny

Along with Paddy Blake one of the greatest servants of the club during its long history. In his youth he was a fine hurler and a top-class handballer, winning senior hurling championship medals with Dunshaughlin in 1925 and Erin's Own of Kells in 1930. As Chairman and also as acting Secretary, he ran the club almost single-handedly for 20 years. As the club's County Board representative he cycled to and from Navan in all kinds of weather. He was a brother of 'Little Dan' and father of Ernest Kenny. Ernest's best footballing days were spent with Skryne with whom he won a senior championship in 1954, yet he won one Junior hurling and two Junior football championships with Dunshaughlin. He made the right half forward position his own, was deadly accurate from play or frees and was a tremendous man to carry a ball.

Peter Kenny

Known as 'Big Peter', he won senior hurling championship medals in 1909 and 1910. He was father of Patsy, Petey, Seán, Tom and Mickey. Mickey Kenny won several county championship medals as a sprinter and long jumper and his involvement in athletics curtailed his GAA activities somewhat. Nevertheless, he won a junior football championship medal with the club in 1950 and later served as Chairman and Treasurer. Mickey was a tremendous help in compiling the original Black and Amber due to his detailed knowledge of Dunshaughlin history.

Dan Killeen

Killeen was not a native of Dunshaughlin, but played for the club in the 1904 championship game against Castletown. He played previously with Drogheda Independents and that may have been the reason for the criticism of him in the report of the Castletown game.

Patrick King

He was Secretary of the club in the 1890s before it disbanded. He was a tailor in the village living where Pat Murphy's entrance gates are at present.

Stephen Kelly

A racehorse owner, his black and amber racing colours were adopted by the club as its colours also. He owned the

Fingall Arms, currently owned by Pádraig Sherry of Sherry Property Advisers. He died relatively young in 1898.

Mickey Keogan

Mickey was a butcher where Liam Keane's Solicitors' practice is now and lived in the Slane-Rathkenny area later. Donal Keogan current Meath senior team captain is his grandson.

Kevin Lee

Kevin lived with his aunt Nan Reilly in a house opposite the Community College entrance, now belonging to Maura O Dwyer. He was a good cross-country runner during the 1940s.

Mick Lee

Mick, a native of Ashbourne was nicknamed 'The Waggler' Lee and played minor hurling in 1940. He had a brother nicknamed 'The Hammers' Lee.

Peter Lee

Peter worked as a herd in Rathbeggan for Wilkinsons and lived in the lodge. He won senior hurling championship medals with Dunshaughlin in 1909 and 1910 and with Dunboyne in 1912.

Mal Loughran

Mal, a nephew of the famous Joe Loughran, was from Kilmessan. He played with Dunshaughlin in the late 1950s winning a junior football medal in 1958 before transferring back to Kilmessan in 1963.

Paddy and Ben Lynam

As a player Paddy was equally at home in defence or attack in both codes. He was a selector for many years, including 1950 and 1977 when the club took its first ever junior and intermediate football titles respectively. On one occasion when gathering goalposts for a seven-a-side tournament Paddy's horse and cart sank in the soft ground whereupon Paddy exclaimed, 'I wonder would Pádraig Ó Caoimh do this for the GAA?' Ó Caoimh was then Secretary General of the GAA. Paddy was a mine of information on the 1930s and 1940s when we were compiling the original Black and Amber and he was the club's first Hall of Fame winner in 1995. Ben Lynam was a brother of Paddy and was a talented midfielder in the 1930s and played in goals in the 1950 junior football final. His lorry was often used to transport players and he followed Paddy in winning the Hall of Fame in 1996. Their brothers Peadar and Tossie also played for the club, Peadar retiring early due to injury while Tossie, a fine sprinter, emigrated to England after a number of years with the club.

Jack Lynch

He played in the 1909 Junior Football League final v. Navan Harps and joined Skyrne the following year. Father of Mickey who played senior championship football with Skyrne in the 1960s and 70s.

Jim 'Fish' Lynch, Owen Lynch and Paddy Lynch

The family came from Co. Louth originally and played for the club in the early years of the twentieth century. Jim worked as a gardener in the Workhouse and was a great grandfather of Ciarán Byrne, Dunshaughlin's intermediate and senior winning captain of 1997 and 2001. Jim's brother Owen worked with Meath County Council and Paddy worked on Christy Tallon's farm before emigrating to the USA.

Johnny Lynch

He was regarded as an expert keeper by those who remembered him as a player in his heyday when he won a senior hurling championship in 1925. He was an uncle of Andy who played during the 1960s and of Brendan who was Lord Mayor of Dunshaughlin in the 1980s.

Johnny Lynch

Johnny was a son of Joe 'Fiddler' Lynch. He was a substitute in the 1950 junior football final and later lived in England.

T. Lynch
He played in the first home game but it is not known who he was.

Thomas Lynch
Thomas was a native of Limerick, and was Principal of Dunshaughlin Boys National School from c. 1926-31. He represented the club at County Board and probably acted as Secretary during this period. He was also an officer of the Handball Club. In 1932 he returned to his native Limerick as Principal Teacher in Grange NS near Bruff.

Tony Lynch
He played minor hurling for the club and was a committee member during the 1950s. He worked in Gogans and is a grand uncle of current players Alastar and Seán Doyle.

Eddie and Paddy Lyons
Their father, Martin, was a Garda in the village and both were reared here. Eddie won an All-Ireland junior football medal with Dublin in 1948 and was a strong midfielder. He also served the club as Secretary. He was a teacher in Ratoath, Kildare and later in Kilmuckridge in Wexford. His brother Paddy was a good half-back and later served as a Sergeant near Mallow, Co. Cork.

Ikey Madden
Ikey was from Drumree and played in Meath's 1927 All-Ireland junior hurling triumph. He had a few years with Dunshaughlin but played his best hurling with Kilmessan.

B McAuley
He played for the club in the early years of the twentieth century and may have been one of the McAuleys of Rathbeggan.

Big Jack Mahon
Jack lived on the Navan Road and played for a few years with Dunshaughlin, including the 1943 junior Semi-Final.

The Mahons
They lived in Clonross or Pelletstown. Jim was father of Ann who married Tony Rattigan and of Stephen and Andy 'The Cap' Mahon, who played on the St Martins' teams of 1957 and 1959 respectively. Joe was father of John Mahon, minor goalkeeper in 1947 and Rory who played junior in the late 1940s. Other brothers of Jim were Pat, Mick and Christy.

Patrick Mahon
He played for the club in the early years of the twentieth century and was either a farm hand with Dowdall's of Pelletstown or may have worked in PJ Murray's.

Hughie McCarthy
Hughie was a non-player but one of Dunshaughlin's most loyal supporters. He was a dedicated committee man and served as a selector for a number of years. The McCarthy family, and especially his wife Josie, looked after the jerseys for well over a decade and ensured that club teams always lined out spick and span.

His son Dinny was similarly involved with the club and looked after the team kit for the hurlers during the 1980s while he was a valued member of the committee until his untimely death in 2012. Dinny's son Hughie played football and hurling with St. Martins and Dunshaughlin, captaining the junior team that won the inaugural McCarthy-Duffy trophy. He is currently a mentor with Royal Gaels.

Other sons are Christy who won an Under 14 championship with St. Martins in 1957 and won county handball titles in the 1980s. Michael played junior with the club in the 1950s before joining the army. Michael's son Niall played with and was Chairman of St. Martins in 2006. Another son Tommy was also a noted handballer.

PJ McCluskey
PJ was from Dunsany, played with the minors in 1947 and later emigrated to England.

Percy McGuinness

He was from Curraha and played at midfield in the 1947 minor football final but played his senior football with Skryne, winning a senior championship in 1954.

Patsy McLoughlin

Few people in any club could hope to equal Patsy's contribution to the GAA. His career with the club began in 1946 and during his playing career he made the No. 2 jersey his own where he was the essence of reliability. He was also a good cross-country runner. He captained the club in 1954 and served as Chairman or Vice-Chairman in each of the four decades from the 1950s. He served as Chairman of the Meath Juvenile Board for four years, 1969-72 and Deputy Vice Chairman of the County Board in 1979. He was one of the foremost referees in the county in the 1950s and 1960s when he refereed a number of Leinster championship games. He has been Club President for many years, was winner of the club's Hall of Fame award in 1999, the Meath County Board Hall of Fame in 2003, -the only Dunshaughlin man accorded the accolade,- and had the honour of throwing in the ball for the senior county final in 2000.

Seán McManus

A native of Trim, Seán worked in Gogan's and later became involved in the promotion of football and hurling in Dunboyne, with his son Enda captaining the Meath All-Ireland winning minor team of 1990. He was the prime mover in the hurling revival in Dunshaughlin in 1957.

J Marmion

J Marmion played for the club in the early years of the twentieth century. He was most probably John Marmion from Bogganstown, Culmullen, who was later Secretary of GAA clubs in Bogganstown, Culmullen and Drumree. It is also possible that he was a Marmion from Curraha.

Patrick Martin

He worked as a cobbler near the entrance to the present Gables Shopping Centre, a business Paddy 'Or Or' Tugwell later took over. Patrick acted as Treasurer of the club in 1910-11. His brother Michael was also involved with the club.

Patrick and Thomas McClorey

Both originally lived in Gallows Hill, near the Arch Bar, and were nephews of Toddy and Mick Clusker. Both won senior hurling championship medals in 1925 and Tommy played in the early rounds of Meath's junior championship run in 1927. Paddy was an opportunist corner forward who specialized in goal scoring. Thomas, along with Paddy Kenny, represented Dunshaughlin at the inaugural meeting of the GAA inspired Irish Amateur Handball Association in 1924.

William McDermott

He won senior hurling championship medals with Dunshaughlin in 1909 and 1910. He was father of one of Meath's most illustrious GAA men, Peter McDermott, 'The Man in the Cap'.

Kevin Melia

Kevin played for over twenty years with the club, winning junior championship medals in 1950 and 1958 and a junior hurling medal in 1957. He had the honour of being the first man to captain a Dunshaughlin championship winning team in football and later served as a selector. He was deadly accurate from the wing or corner forward positions. His brother Tommy 'The Bonnet' Melia played a little for Dunshaughlin before emigrating to England. Kevin's son Derek won a minor football championship medal in 1987 and an intermediate in 1997.

John 'Dropper' Mooney

He played for the club in the early years of the twentieth century and seems to have got his nickname from his dropkick. He lived in Grangend near where Christy Foley's house is now.

Donald Moore

He was from Ratoath and played some minor hurling with the club. He married Rosie Lynam, a sister of Paddy and Ben Lynam.

Nicky Moran

Played hurling with Dunshaughlin in the 1912-17 period but lined out more often with Dunboyne.

Paudge 'Poker' Morgan and Willy 'Honey' Morgan

Paudge was a fantastic fielder of the ball and during the 1950s Paudge along with Peter Tugwell had few equals as half-backs. Many reckoned them to be the best to represent Dunshaughlin in the 1940-80 period. He won a junior football championship in 1950. Willy was a brother of Paudge and father of Leonard and Raymond.

Aidan, Billy, Fergus and Michael Morrin

The Morrins were farmers from Johnstown beside the town. Aidan was a tall, commanding figure at midfield and full forward during the 1950s. He was a dedicated footballer and a great loss to the club after his suspension by Leinster Council following the 1950 Semi-Final. His brother Fergus won a Kildare championship with the Army Cadet team in 1956 and played with Dunshaughlin for a period. Another brother Michael captained the 1958 junior football winning team. Not a stylist but a strong, determined footballer wherever he lined out. Billy played same football before emigrating to England.

Hugh Mullally

Mullally was from Dunboyne and joined Dunshaughlin after a split in the Dunboyne club. He was a building contractor.

P Mullen

He played in the first home game but it is not known who he was.

Richard Murphy

Richard was probably from the Grange, and acted as Treasurer of the club in the early 1920s.

F Murray

F Murray is recorded as having played for the club in the early years of the twentieth century but we have been unable to trace any such person. The name may have been a misprint in the newspapers.

Peadar J Murray

It is difficult to do justice to Peadar's career. A native of Garristown, he came to Dunshaughlin in 1896 to establish the public house that remained in the Murray family for over a century and is now known as *Peter's*. He was a close friend of Sean T Ó Ceallaigh, the future President of Ireland, and of Patrick Archer, the man who wrote the 1798 poem, *Paud O Donoghue*.

Peadar was the chief architect of the setting up of the Gaelic League in Dunshaughlin- the first branch in Co. Meath- and was also involved in the formation of the first hurling club in Dunshaughlin. He also played a little football and acted as Secretary to the short-lived Hurling League in 1905.

His most lasting contribution is as a photographer. His collection of prints and glass plate negatives contain a social history of the village at the beginning of the twentieth century. We are deeply indebted to him and his son Brendan, for without Peadar's photographic genius the early chapters of this book would have been very bare. Ciarán Murray was a son of Peadar and his career is covered in the main text. He played senior football with Meath, was Principal of Culmullen NS for many years and the inspiration behind the St. Martins' Under 14 team in the late 1950s. He was a tremendous source of information and photographs for the original Black and Amber. Seachnall Murray was another son of Peadar Murray. He was Secretary of the club in 1949 and a good hurler and footballer before joining the civil service in Dublin.

Fr. Aidan Murray was a promising footballer but his priestly studies curtailed his playing career. Nevertheless, he played senior football in 1951, always assisted the club when home on holidays and was chosen to celebrate the mass in Dunshaughlin marking the centenary of the GAA on Centenary Sunday in July 1984.

Christy Newman

He was the netminder in the 1930s and was from Batterstown.

Tom Nugent

Tom was a native of Oldcastle who worked in McMahons, now Lawless' Hardware and played for the club in the mid 1950s.

Dickie, Larry and Patsy O Brien

The three O Briens from Drumree had distinguished careers with Dunshaughlin and Drumree. Dickie played in the full-back and full forward lines and won a Junior hurling championship with the club in 1957. In later years he devoted a great deal of time to juvenile football proving to be a shrewd selector on the sideline. Dickie was of great assistance with information on the 1950s and the juveniles in the 1970s for the original Black and Amber. Larry was one of the most stylish and effective footballers to ever represent the club. A true sportsman, he won a junior All-Ireland medal in 1952 and was a member of the Meath All-Ireland senior panel in 1954. He won an All-Ireland juvenile boxing championship also. Patsy played with the club in the mid 1950s and was particularly effective in seven-a-side competitions. All won junior and intermediate football championships with Drumree in 1959 and 1961 respectively.

Fr. Eamonn O Brien

Fr. Eamonn was an Offaly man who was Chairman of the club for each of the years he was curate in the parish. Under his Chairmanship the club won two junior football championships, 1958 and 1967, and officially opened the playing field. Fr. O Brien was a shrewd Chairman, whose advice was always valued and all who came into contact with him speak highly of his commitment, leadership and impartiality.

Dan O Connell

He was the Garda Sergeant in the village and one of the men responsible for setting up the Boxing Club in the 1940s. He trained the footballers for the 1943 junior Semi-Final. He was a native of Cork.

Patrick and James O Brien

Patrick was one of the founder members of the GAA club, beginning a great tradition as his grandson Pat was Chairman of the club in the GAA's Centenary Year, 1984 and won an intermediate football championship in 1977. Another grandson Michael was a regular on the club's intermediate team of the 1980s and won junior championship medals in 1991 and 1994 while Michael's son Joe won a minor championship with the club in 2009. Patrick was a publican in what is now the *Arch Bar* and was President- equivalent to the modern Chairman- of the Club for almost ten years.

James O Brien was a brother of Patrick. He captained the team against Castletown in 1904 and represented the club at County Board meetings in the early years of the twentieth century.

Seán and Tom O Brien

Tom was a commanding midfielder on the 1947 minor team and won an All-Ireland senior championship as a Skryne clubman and a Meath senior championship in 1954. He also holds an All-Ireland junior medal from 1952. He rejoined Dunshaughlin in the early 1960s. Seán won a junior championship with the club in 1950 and then joined the great Skryne side of the 1950s, winning a senior championship in 1954. He holds an All-Ireland junior medal from 1952 and rejoined Dunshaughlin in the 1960s when he still had a lot to offer. Seán and Tom were brothers and their sister Geraldine married John Maher whose son Derek won Leinster Under 21 and Junior titles with Meath in 1990 and 1991 and minor and intermediate championships with St. Martins-Ratoath and Dunshaughlin in 1987 and 1997 respectively.

Eamonn O Donoghue

Eamonn played most of his football with Drumree but assisted Dunshaughlin for a term in the mid 1950s and hurled with the 1957 team.

Davy, John and Tommy O Dwyer

The O Dwyer family has made an immense contribution to the growth of the GAA club in the village. Davy captained the 1967 junior winning side and he filled a variety of defensive positions, including goalkeeper, with distinction. He was also club Treasurer and mentor on many occasions prior to his sudden, early death in 1995.

Tommy O Dwyer was a regular at left half back for many years and undertook the onerous post of Treasurer for twenty-four years, beginning as a teenager. During his reign the club managed to pay for the development of the playing field and clubhouse. He married Margaret Foley, a step sister of Christy Foley. and their son Pearse played with the club during the 1980s and 1990s.

John O Dwyer won two junior championship medals, in 1958 and 1967. He was also a capable hurler and holds a junior hurling championship medal although he missed the 1957 final due to injury. His son Ciarán won a junior championship in 1991.

Con and Paddy O Dwyer hold junior and intermediate medals from 1967 and 1977 and their careers are covered in detail in the main text.

Michael O Dwyer captained the club in the 1975 intermediate final but moved to Dublin prior to the 1977 victory.

Many thanks to all the O Dwyers for the help with the original and the revised Black and Amber.

Jim O Neill

Jim was from Kilmessan and won a junior hurling championship with Dunshaughlin in 1957.

Rev. J O Neill, P.P.

He was Parish Priest of Dunshaughlin from 1886 until his death in 1901. He was patron of the annual sports for a number of years and it is possible he held a similar role in the GAA. He provided refreshments for all after the game against William O Briens of Clonee in 1888 and was also involved in the formation of the Gaelic League in Dunshaughlin later.

Mick O Neill

He was a consistent hurler and footballer during the 1930s playing in the 1936 junior football final and was a nephew of Paddy Blake.

Larry O Rourke

Larry was Club Chairman in 1953. He was a non-player but a good committee man in the 1950s, involved in the financing of the playing field.

Br. Tom O Sullivan

Tom was a religious brother in Warrenstown College, originally from Co. Kerry. He played a few intermediate championship games with the club in 1956.

Alfie and Thomas O Toole

Both played for the club in the 1930s and were from Curraha originally. Alfie later lived in the Bush.

Mickey 'Weasel' Parr

Mickey lived in Leshemstown and later in Dublin. He was a stylish footballer likely to pop up anywhere and take a score. After Dunshaughlin lapsed he played hurling for Oberstown and lined out at midfield in their senior hurling final defeat to Trim in 1942.

John Rafferty

He was the captain of the 1909 football team but we are unsure of his identity.

Billie, Joe and Tony Rattigan

Billie's spell with Dunshaughlin is covered fully in the main text. He won an All-Ireland senior medal with Meath in 1954 and was the club's chief scorer during the 1950s. Tony was a hard, fearless, tackler in defence or midfield and a superb kicker of a dead ball, a skill he learned from Ned Teeling. Tony was also a very good hurler. He was very involved with the juveniles after retiring and his son Jim won a Leinster medal with Meath Under 21s in 1985. Joe was a proud Drumree man, ran the club single handed for long spells and could always be relied on for a humorous quip to extricate the club from trouble. Among the best remembered is his explanation to the County Chairman for Drumree's failure on one occasion to field a team. The reason, he declared, was that as it was Mother's Day and the players were treating their mothers to meals!

Leo Reaper

Leo lived near Killeen Castle, was a good cross-country runner and member of the Boxing Club.

Jack, Tommy and Tom 'Stalk' Reilly

Tom 'Stalk' Reilly played in the club's first home game in 1887 and lived where O Dwyer's is now, opposite the entrance to the Community College. Jack Reilly, Tom's son played for the club in the late 1930s. Tommy Reilly, a grandson of Tom played minor hurling in 1940, and later lived in Ashbourne. Frank Reilly another grandson was a dedicated committee man, always on hand to collect gates, do 'line' and organize dances in Trim while a third grandson Noel, played with Drumree. He lived opposite the current Meath County Council offices on the Drumree Road.

Matty Russell

Matty played most of his football with Culmullen-Drumree but was a Dunshaughlin selector and committee member during the 1950s. He was one of the mainstays of the Boxing Club and was a step-brother of Dickie, Larry and Patsy O Brien.

Alex Ryan

He was a Garda who brought some of his native Tipperary craft and style to the club in the 1920s.

Mattie 'The Doctor' Ryan, John, Kevin and Matt 'Mutt' Ryan

Mattie lived in the Bush. He won a senior hurling championship in 1925 but a broken leg sustained in the Broadford, Co. Kildare Tournament ended his career. He was father of Matt who played in goals in 1958 and Kevin who was a substitute on the 1950 junior winning team and Johnny now resident in Ratoath who also played with the club for a spell. Their sister Kathleen married Billie Rattigan.

Con Sheridan

From Tullaghmedan, near *The Warrenstown Arms* public house he was involved in many nationalist organizations apart from the GAA. He was President of the Culmullen Clarence Mangan '98 Club to commemorate the 1798 Rising and later of the Back to the Land movement, which agitated for large farms to be divided among local labourers.

John Sherry

John was from Kilbrew and played at centre field in the 1936 junior final against Seneschalstown. He was related to the Dorans. He was also related to Pádraig Sherry of Sherry Property Advisers who sponsored Dunshaughlin during the three in a row era, 2000-02.

C Skully
He played for the club in the 1880s but we have not been able to trace any information on him.

Brian, Kevin and Dessie Smith
Brian holds two All-Ireland senior football and a junior hurling medal with Meath and was later Chairman of the County Board and Secretary of the Hurling Board. He played minor hurling with Dunshaughlin in 1940. Kevin and Dessie both played on the 1947 Dunshaughlin minor final team. They were from Batterstown.

Christy and Ned Smyth
Christy was a native of Culmullen and won a junior hurling championship with Dunshaughlin in 1908. Ned was a stepbrother of Christy, and also won a junior championship in 1908. In the early years of the Dunshaughlin Hurling Club he marked Sean T. O Ceallaigh- the President of Ireland 1945-59- in a hurling match played during an Aeridheacht in the village.

Christy Snow
Christy was a native of Oldcastle and when he lined out for the club he was the Irish Land Commission overseer for the area.

Paddy Swan
Paddy played for the club in the early years of the twentieth century. He lived in Smithstown and worked as a shepherd for Chaytors. An uncle of Joe Plunkett and grandfather of Noel Farrell of Batterstown.

Richard Swan
He took part in a number of the Sports organized by the GAA in the 1880s and may have owned what is now *Peters'* public house before PJ Murray opened his shop there in 1896.

Christy Tallon
Christy was the first captain of the club and also acted as Treasurer. He lived at the junction where Grangend meets the Lagore Road, now the site of an apartment block. He was a farmer and gave 'The Lawn' at the back of where Madden's Stores is at present to the Gaelic League for Aeridheachts (Open air cultural festivals). He died in 1920. When we were writing the original Black and Amber his daughter Mary was still alive and resident in the original house. She died in 1988, aged 93.

John and Ned Teeling
John played for the club in the early years of the twentieth century. The family was known as Teelings of the Mill from the mill in Clowanstown, near Fingall Castle. John worked as a herd for Lord Fingall. His son Ned Teeling joined Dunshaughlin in the late 1940s when the Killeen team broke up and he captained the club in the 1950s. He was noted for his ability to drive a 'dead ball' a phenomenal distance and for the fact that he usually lined out in trousers. He played for the Meath juniors during his career and later lived in Tipperary.

Matt O Toole and Pat "Toddler" Toole
Pat O Tioole was a member of the senior hurling championship winning side of 1909 and 1910. He was an uncle of Matt O Toole, Greenpark who captained Meath's National Football League winning team of 1946. Matt O Toole was from Greenpark, Skryne. He played minor football with Dunshaughlin and later became Meath's full back and centre fielder while a Skryne clubman. Matt was most helpful in identifying past players from photographs for the original Black and Amber.

John 'Fowler' Tugwell, Paddy 'Or Or' Tugwell and Peter Tugwell

The Tugwells originally came to Dunshaughlin c. 1888 with Count Stolberg, who sourced horses for the British Army. Paddy 'Or Or' Tugwell was the local cobbler and his workshop was at the entrance to Knocks' Lane, now the entrance to the *Gables Shopping Centre* and *SuperValu*. He was a great local character who won a senior hurling championship in 1925 and was a selector on the 1950 junior football championship winning team.

John 'Fowler' Tugwell got his nickname from the famous Clare hurler, Fowler McInerney. He was a strong forceful defender who also played in 1925. He lived in the village in 1984 and was very informative on the 1920s and 1930s when we were researching the original Black and Amber. Peter Tugwell was a nephew of 'Or Or' and 'Fowler' and was a superb fielder of the ball. A stylish footballer, along with Paudge Morgan he was regarded as one of the best half backs to wear the black and amber jersey. Peter enjoyed his pint and the story is told that returning home one night he tumbled from his bicycle into an open ditch. Looking up and seeing the full moon he declared, 'F--- you, you're full only once a month, I'm full every night!' Harry Tugwell hurled with club for a time and worked in Harty's, now Lawless. Arthur Tugwell ran a sweet shop along with his sister Florrie Featherstone, but didn't play hurling.

Matty Wallace

Matty played a little hurling for the club in his youth and was always a loyal supporter of the club. He lived in Clonross and when writing the original Black and Amber we were hugely indebted to Matty's remarkable memory of events as far back as the 1920s and his assistance in identifying players in photographs.

Mickey Walls

He played for the club in the early years of the twentieth century and was related to Big Peter Kenny through marriage.

James 'Mebble' Ward and Paddy Ward

James played for the club in the early years of the twentieth century and was a brother of Paddy who became a County Councillor. Both lived in Grangend. Paddy gives his name to Paddy Ward's well located on the Ratoath road.

Reunion of Dunshaughlin's 1967 Junior Football Championship Winning Team

Front: Con O Dwyer, Hughie Carty, Pat O Hare, Paddy O Dwyer, John O Dwyer, Davy O Dwyer, Seamus Foley, Tommy Carty, Seán Moran.
Back: Mossie Caffrey, Tommy O Dwyer, Pádraig Blake, Noel Curran, Val Dowd, John Casey, Andy Lynch, Brian O Sullivan.

Happy after Leinster Final Victory

Declan O Dwyer on the receiving end from Ronan Gogan, Damian Burke, David and John Crimmins and Caoimhín King.

Pat Maloney, Ray Maloney, Michael McHale and David Tonge.

Appendix 2
Where We Sported and Played

Readers who have come this far will recall that the first game played by Dunshaughlin took place in a field loaned by Pat Delany. The field was probably the Eight Acres on the Dublin Road. Later the Cowbyre off Rathill Lane was regularly used, but, for seventy years the club had no permanent home and had to rely on the generosity and co-operation of the Delanys and Murphys.

For many years from the 1920s to the mid-1940s games were played in what was known as the Lagore Road Hurling Field belonging to William Murphy. Teams togged out in a galvanized shed normally used to house sheep and the club would whitewash it before important games. During matches the sheep were herded into a small triangular field nearby. The loss of the field when it was ploughed under the compulsory tillage laws during the war years was probably partly responsible for the club going out of existence at that time. Without a permanent ground and a regular quota of games the club was in severe financial straits. The Session House and the Woodmeadow at the back of the courthouse were used for a period also. The Skryne-Dunshaughlin senior championship game of 1953 was played in the Woodmeadow but the ground was uneven and the remains of ridges were still visible. A few games were also played in one of John Morrin's fields in the mid-40s. During the thirties some practice took place in Goose Park, beside present day Greenane, which was reached by going in through Gogan's Yard.

Many of these fields, especially the Lagore Hurling Field, the Eight Acres and the Cowbyre, were good level fields-although the hurling field was small- and county finals have been played in Dunshaughlin. The 1925 football final in which Navan Gaels defeated Donaghmore was held in the Lagore Road Hurling Field and the *Chronicle* described the field as an excellent one and splendidly kept.

In 1952 the Irish Land Commission took over the land where the Community College, GAA grounds and College Park are now. Part of the area was known as Morgan's Twenty Acres and another part as the Sally Ground. The GAA club was aware of the possibility of getting part of the land but there was a general lackadaisical attitude by many club members towards the issue.

Paddy Blake, in particular, was determined that the club should have a ground of its own and were it not for his determination the club might never have purchased the land. Paddy had been asked for a definite 'yes' or 'no' answer by the Land Commission and after consultations involving Blake, Larry O Rourke and Maurice Delany, among others, it was decided to go ahead.

The six and a half acres taken by the club cost £650 and the sale was finally signed and sealed on 2nd January 1956. The agreement noted that the trustees of the ground 'shall use it as a sportsfield, park or pleasure grounds for sports and games under the rules of the Gaelic Athletic Association.' Meath GAA County Board paid the Irish Land Commission but Dunshaughlin had to repay the money over a number of years. In effect the club, like all others, received an interest-free loan from the County Board. Jack Fitzgerald of Kilcloon was very helpful to the club, getting a grant of £100 from the Leinster Council, which was immediately paid to the County Board as part payment of the loan.

In the first year the ground was set for meadow, and for two years it was set for tillage to the father of Pat O Neill, Dublin's star halfback of the 1970s and All-Ireland winning manager in 1995. O Neill filled in an open ditch but the biggest problem with the grounds was a nine-foot drop from the entrance to the far end. Many wanted to fence in the field and play on it regularly but Seamus Foley was adamant that the field should be leveled as a first priority. This was eventually agreed to and over a number of years it was filled in.

The club was lucky that the right men were in the right place to help out. Larry O Rourke was a clerical officer and Paddy Kenny an overseer with the County Council. Between them they organized the dumping of loads of clay in the field, much of it coming from the road-widening scheme near Rathill Lane. Leveling the pitch in 1964 cost £1,500 and drainage another £490. The drainage system, so effective to the present day, would have cost even more but Tom Everard of the Bush drew up the plans and supervised the work on a voluntary basis.

Finally, in 1966 Larry, Joe and Pat Smith of Lagore and John O Sullivan- better known as *Wee Four*- erected paling around the pitch. Paddy Blake was insistent that the paling should not enclose the pitch in a rectangular fashion but that both sideline palings should form a wide V shape. This would enclose to the field in a hexagonal fashion, giving everybody a uninterrupted view of the action on the field. This idea, though it seems a good one, was not agreed to and the enclosure was erected as it is today.

The clubhouse was also erected in the mid-1960s. The foundations were poured using voluntary labour while John Donnelly erected the building. John Holland organized the planting of trees around the field. These were removed in 2012 as part of the extension to the Community College.

The money to finance the developments in the 1950s and 1960s came in the main from the Carnival. The Carnival commenced under the auspices of the Parish Council but in the early 1950s the GAA club took it over. By the 1960s it was recognized throughout North East Leinster as the premier dance venue in the area. The carnival was an example of superb organization under the general direction and control of Chairman Christy Foley, with Seamus Foley as Secretary

BLACK & AMBER

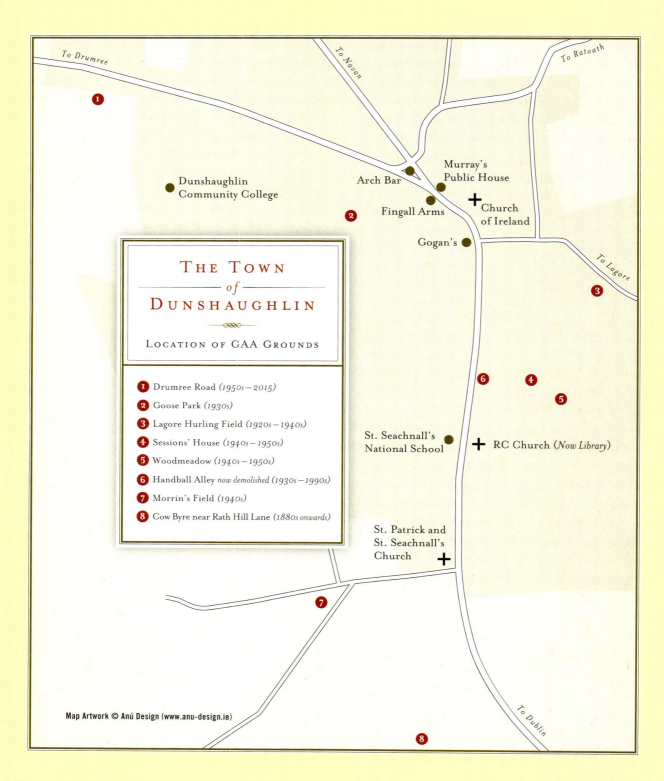

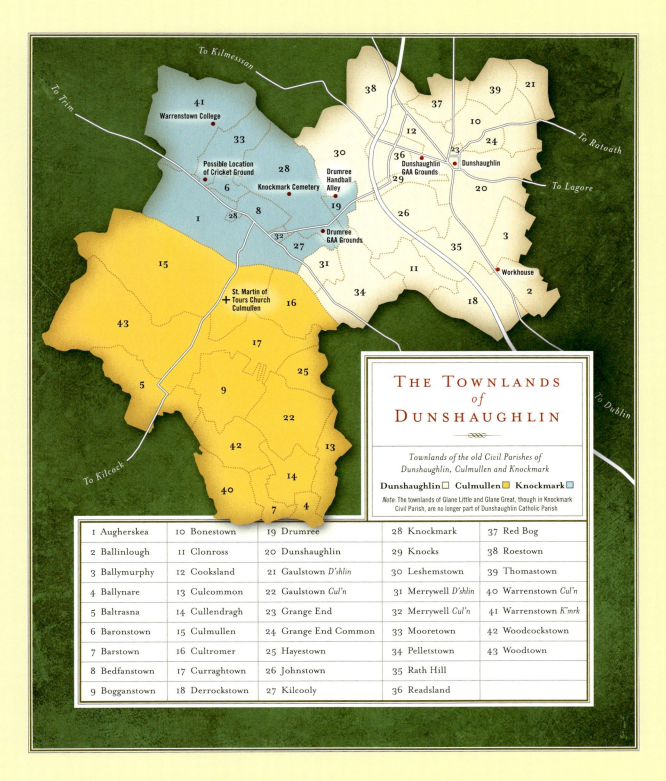

Members of Dunshaughlin Pitch and Putt Club Committee and GAA Club at the 1979 Dinner Dance.
Front: Tommy O Dwyer, Maura O Dwyer, Brona McCarthy, Joe McDonnell.
Middle: N. McCormack, Pitch and Putt Union of Ireland (PPUI), Betty Carey, Liam Carey, Tony Duffy, Chair, Meath County Board, PPUI, Frank Lynch.
Back: John O Dwyer, Michael McCarthy, Vincent Lane, Patsy McLoughlin, Ollie O Neill, Bernie Lane, Pat Naughton, Tom Everard.

ensuring that everything was all right on the night. He, and later secretaries, never booked a band without first going to see them in action.

A Ladies' Committee provided refreshments for patrons. The refreshments were run on a non-profit-making basis, the aim being to provide good meals at cost price to ensure the patrons fully enjoyed their night out and would return. The committee did trojan work to ensure that the high reputation of the carnival was maintained. Annual outings to such exotic resorts as Bray, Newcastle, Co. Down or Tramore were often organized to reward the Carnival and Ladies' Committees for their work.

When the GAA began to run the Carnival it was decided to play a seven-a-side football tournament also. Half the combined proceeds of the seven-a-side and the Carnival was given to parochial funds, part of which was used to extend the National School and maintain St. Patrick's Hall. The seven-a-side attracted large crowds as thirty-two of the best teams in Meath and surrounding counties entered it. One incident from it remains in the memory of witnesses.

The 1960 final between Skryne and Ratoath ended in a draw but Skryne wouldn't accept a local referee for the replay. Chris Delaney, a Garda in Athboy, was prevailed upon to take charge of the game but with about three minutes to go Delaney blew the final whistle with Ratoath four points behind. The crowd then came onto the field and for some reason the referee took to his heels and ran out the gate, probably under the impression that the Ratoath followers were after his blood. WJ Madden, a spectator at the game, held the gate closed after Delaney had gone through, thereby temporarily holding up the pursuing party until Delaney

> Minutes of the Inaugural Meeting of Dunshaughlin Pitch & Putt Club.
>
> A General meeting was held in St. Patrick's Hall on Monday, 12th Dec. 1971 to form a Committee to Run the proposed Dunshaughlin Pitch & Putt Club. There was an attendance of 28 interested parties. With Mr Val Dowd as acting Chairman, Mr Con Dwyer read an Agreement made between Mr Maurice Delaney and the trustees appointed by the Dunshaughlin G.A.A. Club with regard to the leasing of a suitable piece of ground for the purpose of laying down a Pitch & Putt Course. After some discussion it was generally felt that the terms of the agreement were satisfactory.
>
> Mr Dwyer then read a document which stated clearly the involvement of the Dunshaughlin G.A.A had in the formation and financing of the proposed Pitch & Putt Club. It indicated that, while the elected committee of the P.&P. Club would be an autonomous body in the running of the ordinary affairs of the P.&P. Club — the trustees appointed by the G.A.A. Club would be regarded as the ultimate controlling body, particularly in matters relating to the lease, provision of the initial financial outlay and generally safeguarding the substantial interest of the G.A.A. Club in the venture.

Minutes from the first meeting of Dunshaughlin Pitch and Putt Club in December 1971 stressing the role of the football club in forming and financing the new facility.

THE MEATH TEAM

S. McCormack

P. Collier   O. Geraghty   P. Darby

M. White   B. Cunningham   P. Reynolds

P. Wilson   M. Kerrigan

T. Brennan   E. Giles   M. Mellett

P. Bruton   N. Curran   O. Shanley

Subs.:

P. Cromwell, J. Quinn, P. Black, T. Browne, P. Rooney, P. Mulvany, J. Casey, T. Murray

---

MICHAEL KENNY

VICTUALLER

DUNSHAUGHLIN and OBERSTOWN

VEGETABLES, FISH and GROCER

'Phone: DUNSHAUGHLIN 24 and 68

Meath Team for Official Pitch Opening, 1967
The Meath team chosen to play Kildare in a challenge game to mark the official opening of Dunshaughlin GAA Grounds in 1967 taken from the programme produced to mark the event. Dunshaughlin's John Casey is listed among the substitutes while Mickey Kenny advertises his butcher shops in Dunshaughlin and Oberstown. Note the old telephone numbers.

had put some distance between them and himself.

He raced up the street and into Toghers- where Karl Cosgrove's Veterinary Clinic is now- with his chasers in hot pursuit. He burst in past Mrs. Togher and when a group of Dunshaughlin officials came to the house he was afraid to let them in. Eventually, they were admitted by the back door and when the furore died down Chris was taken away to safety.

With the help of money from the Carnival and the seven-a-side the developments on the ground were paid for when the park was officially opened on 7th May 1967. Seán Ó Siocháin, General Secretary of the GAA, performed the opening ceremony and Fr. Eamonn O Brien blessed the facilities. Meath easily defeated Kildare in a challenge game to mark the opening and Dunshaughlin clubmen, Noel Curran at full forward, and John Casey a substitute, both scored three points.

Since then the field and the clubhouse have been in regular use. It is the most visible proof of the existence of the GAA club in the village, and its greatest asset. The park has never been officially named but it is a fitting monument to those who bought and developed it, as it has a surface second to none in the county. In later years a scoreboard and dugout for teams were erected.

The Carnival continued until 1979 and for many years provided a ready-made source of finance. The GAA club was responsible for setting up the Pitch and Putt Club in 1971. The idea of establishing such a club was raised at the AGM of Dunshaughlin GAA and Val Dowd and Tom Everard made inquiries about the availability of the site. Finally the present ground was leased from Kevin Delany. The GAA club paid the first year's rental and organized the laying down of greens involving a total outlay in the region of £1,100 - £1,200. A separate Pitch and Putt committee was later formed to run the club, with Tom Everard as the first Chairman. Thus another invaluable leisure amenity was provided for the people of the village.

By 1979 however the Carnival was losing money as ballroom and carnival dancing was no longer as popular as it had been. The net loss in 1979 was £735 so the scheme was abandoned.

In the mid 1980s consideration was given to building a large facility for community use and a series of discussions were held with the local Community Council on the possibility of a joint venture. These ideas however, never came to fruition and in 1987 the club decided it was time to renovate and improve the existing facilities. The project was initially discussed under Seán Walsh's chairmanship and then pursued with great determination by his successor, Pat Farrell.

At this time Dunshaughlin Pitch and Putt Club was trying to finance the outright purchase of its grounds and a Joint GAA/Pitch and Putt Committee was established to raise funds. Jimmy Mullaney chaired it with Jim Gilligan

A Working Club

Scrap Collection
Dinny in the Driving Seat.
Club Chairman Jim Smith and Dinny McCarthy enjoy a break during the Scrap Metal Fundraiser in 2011.

Top left: Liam Carey, Treasurer 1983-85 and long time dedicated gateman.
Above: Pat Maloney and Christy Purcell, the club's volunteer groundsmen, carry out running repairs on the pitch.
Left: Shaun McTigue, Club Chairman 1989-94 and Vice Chairman 1996-97. The clubhouse was renovated and expanded during his term and junior titles were won in 1991 and 1994.

as Secretary, Frank O Regan as Treasurer and a committee of Liam Carey, Val Dowd, Margaret Kenny, John O Dwyer and Paddy Ward. A draw running from October 1987 to March 1988 raised over £27,000, which the two clubs shared.

The existing clubhouse roof was removed and an extension added to the rear to accommodate four dressing rooms, showers, toilets, a meeting room and kitchenette. Numerous club members put in a great deal of voluntary work on the building but Stephen Burke did the lion's share, ably assisted by Jimmy Mullaney, who worked under the Social Employment Scheme, but who put in many voluntary hours also. All the funds were raised in the local community and The National Lottery provided no financial assistance for the upgrade but did award a grant of £3,000 in 1990 to fund additional work. The project was brought to fruition and opened under the chairmanship of Shaun McTigue while Davy O Dwyer was Treasurer throughout.

Fintan Ginnitty, Chairman of Meath County Board, performed the official opening in June 1989 and Roscommon played Meath, then All-Ireland champions, in a challenge game. Trevor Kane had the honour of captaining the Royals on the day and Meath were convincing 2-15 to 1-10 winners.

With the growth in population in the last three to four decades, demands on the facilities snowballed. Dunshaughlin GFC, Dunshaughlin Hurling Club, St. Martins and Royal Gaels Ladies GFC all had to be catered for and additional playing facilities became a priority. Both Dunshaughlin Community College and Drumree GAA club helped by making their grounds available when required but this was not a long-term solution. The idea of moving the club to entirely new facilities in Bonestown was pursued but the club abandoned the idea when it became clear that Meath County Council would not grant planning permission for housing on the existing grounds. Without such permission the sale of the grounds would not realize the funds needed to buy and build in Bonestown.

Prior to, and subsequent to this, the club lobbied Meath County Council to rezone lands belonging to Evan Newell and Mickey Kenny, adjacent to the GAA field, as community facilities. The club would receive this land when planning permission was granted for housing on the surrounding land. With the downturn in the economy this was a protracted process and the lands, amounting to almost five acres, were eventually handed over in 2009. Three club chairmen, Neil Halpin, Paddy O Dwyer and Jim Smith, pursued the project for over a decade with assistance from property adviser and committee member Pádraig Sherry and at various stages Pádraig Blake, Neil Halpin, Fergus O Rourke and John Maher. Valuable advice and assistance was also provided by local councillors Brian Fitzgerald and Ollie Brooks.

Once the grounds were handed over to the club development plans were activated. A Development sub-committee involving club Treasurer Tom Finn, Michael McHale,

Martin Reilly and Donnacha Lloyd oversaw the scheme and worked with County Board Development Officer Mairéad Delaney and Leinster Council delegate Paddy O Dwyer to secure GAA funding.

The development consisted of a second sand based pitch and an Astro Turf all-weather facility with John Clince installing both, while Kealy Construction erected modern floodlighting. To date the venture has cost in the region of half a million euro. The bulk of it is financed by a bank loan with annual repayments in the region of €28,000. Raising this level of finance annually has entailed ongoing fundraising such as the Club Lotto, Race Nights and Golf Classics with numerous innovative ventures such as a Sportsperson's Gala Banquet in 2008, a White Collar Boxing Tournament in 2010, Scrap Metal Collection in 2011 and Strictly Come Dancing shows in 2012-14. In September 2011 incoming GAA Uachtarán Liam O Neill officially opened the astro turf pitch while the new sand based pitch was first utilised in July 2012 for an Under 10 game against Castleknock, with Fr. Joe Clavin PP blessing the pitch and Patsy McLoughlin throwing in the ball. Later in the year the floodlights were officially inaugurated during the Seamus Reilly Memorial Tournament.

The grounds have always been maintained in immaculate condition. For two decades the playing field was the pride and joy of Stephen Burke. Whether on the Community Employment Scheme or on an entirely voluntary basis he spent hours each day mowing and marking it for games at every level and received recognition for his work when Meath County Board declared it the Club Grounds of the Year in 1988 and 1990 while in the former year Stephen himself became All-Ireland Clubman of the Year.

Since Stephen's untimely death in 2002 Pat Maloney and Christy Purcell have taken over his role. Both men give countless voluntary hours to the maintenance and upkeep of the clubhouse and field. In summer time Pat mows the grass at least three times weekly and as the number of games shows no sign of decreasing Christy is in constant demand, marking and flagging the field and ensuring dressing rooms are available for teams. Both men were worthy winners of Community Awards in 2011 for their voluntary work with the club. Other improvements to the grounds during the past twenty years includes verti-drainage in 1996 with the assistance of John Maher and sanding at least every second year.

BLACK & AMBER

Neil O Dwyer
Neil was Secretary 2010-11 and is now Chairman of Dunshaughlin GAA. He is currently overseeing the Clubhouse renovation and extension.

Another man who has been synonymous with the grounds is gateman Liam Carey. For over three decades he has manned the gate on match days collecting the entrance fee from patrons. Those who take offence and complain, -and there are many-, at having to fork out for their hour's entertainment always discover they have met their match in banter and repartee and the toll is invariably paid.

Renovation and extension to the clubhouse is underway as we write. The design has undergone many alterations since first mooted. A committee under the chairmanship of Adrienne Bowen developed state of the art plans involving the demolition of the existing pavilion and its replacement with a modern glass fronted facility. Although Meath County Council granted permission for the structure the death of The Celtic Tiger forced the club to scale back its ambitions and a modified plan incorporating an extension to, and renovation of, the current clubhouse is now proceeding.

Part of the funding comes from a 2012 allocation of €145,000 under the Sports Capital Programme. The funding was both an opportunity and a threat, because, for the club to avail of the grant, it needed to raise matching funding of its own. Thus, the executive faced the challenging conundrum of going into further, maybe unsustainable debt, by availing of the opportunity or turning down an offer that will not be repeated and condemning the club to second class facilities long into the future. Either way the club's decision would have long-term implications.

The club has chosen the more challenging path of daring to proceed. An appeal for individual and corporate €1,000 donations has accumulated almost €70,000 to date so a positive start has been made. The future, however, is likely to bring as many challenges off the playing field as on it.

Official Opening of Astro Turf Facility
Jim Smith, club Chairman, left, and Patsy McLoughlin, club President, right, assist GAA President Liam O Neill in cutting the ribbon to mark the opening of the astro turf pitch in September 2011.

Ground Development

Dunshaughlin GAA Grounds, Drumree Road.
Top picture shows the new grounds under development.

Picture on left shows the Astro-Turf facility and the new playing field complete, prior to the erection of goalposts.

Picture below shows the new clubhouse under construction, April 2015, with Dunshaughlin Community College, officially opened in November 2014, at the bottom right of the picture.

Photos courtesy of Aidan Murphy.

Appendix 3
Part 1: The GAA in Drumree, 1887-1956

Earliest Teams

The earliest reference we can discover to GAA teams in Drumree dates to 1887, when, on 6th February, Warrenstown played Dunshaughlin on home ground. There was however, another club in the area, Merrywell St. Martins, and the following Sunday the Martins made the short journey to Dunshaughlin and inflicted a first home defeat on St. Seachnalls. The only player named in contemporary reports was M. Rourke of Merrywell. A few weeks later Dunshaughlin defeated Warrenstown in a return game with Fox, Sullivan, Lynch and Johnston playing well for Warrenstown. Fox was undoubtedly PJ Fox, then the proprietor of the *Spencer Arms*, now Gilsenan's public house, and he was later captain of a reformed Drumree Club in the 1890s. His young son James was shot dead in the Easter Rising of 1916 and more details are to be found in the main text.

Merrywell was included in the first Meath championships of 1887, -whereas Dunshaughlin was not-, but the Drumree side seems to have lost out to Kilmessan in the first round. Dowdstown emerged as Meath champions and went on to play in the first All-Ireland final, losing to Limerick Commercials. Merrywell also competed in the Dunshaughlin tournament of 1888 and this caused controversy as outlined in Chapter 1. We could trace only one other game the Saints played in 1888, a defeat to Ratoath Shillelaghs.

It appears that the team wasn't included in the official 1889 championship draw but participated nevertheless, going out to Owen Roes, Moynalty, after a replay, with St. Martins complaining that five of their men were harshly disqualified by the referee. It seems likely they were sent off and Owen Roes scored two goals late in the game. Like many clubs, Merrywell St. Martins faded from the scene after the Irish Republican Brotherhood gained control of the GAA in the late 1880s and the clergy condemned the organization.

There is no reference to Warrenstown in the 1888-89 era but along with Dunshaughlin the club appears among the fourteen Meath clubs listed by the Crime Branch of the Royal Irish Constabulary in 1891, see Chapter 1. The officers were, Patrick Fox the captain, Michael Kenny, Secretary and James Cluskey the Treasurer. The club had about forty-five members. Later in the year the Dunshaughlin club collapsed and Patrick O Brien, the former Dunshaughlin President, played at least one game for Warrenstown, but it too was soon defunct.

The following Warrenstown team played Sextons from Dublin in April 1891 and

PJ Fox, Drumree, captain of Warrenstown FC in 1891 and Drumree in 1892. He was also involved in boxing, cricket, athletics and was a staunch supporter of Parnell. He ran the *Spencer Arms*, now Gilsenan's, and his young son James died while fighting with the Irish Citizens' Army in 1916. The photograph is from the 1920s.

is the earliest known full line out from the parish. The report gives Christian name initials only and the additional details included below are based on our research: Patrick Fox, Capt., Patrick Brien (Dunshaughlin), T Kiernan, J Kiernan, John Mooney and Joe Mooney (Augherskea), Patrick Muldoon (Mooretown, Killeen), James Rourke (Augherskea), Michael Rooney (Knockmark), P Gannon, Thomas Johnson (Knockmark), Denis Kenny (Tullaghmedan), William Doran, G Lamb, John Lynch (Knockmark), F Dunne, John Clarke (Knockmark), G Reilly, R Bonas, J Lynch.

Drumree and Culmullen Clubs

Then in November 1891 a new club appeared on the scene. Known as Drumree Gaelic Athletic Club it was formed '*out of the remains of the Dunshaughlin and Warrenstown clubs, a club that would include the best men from each, and whose headquarters would be at Drumree, a very central position.*' The project was '*enthusiastically taken up by all sides*' and the club '*was formed on the spot.*' The officers were as follows: President: Francis Hobson, Vice President: Michael Rooney, captain: Patrick Fox, sub-captain: Michael Brien, Secretary and Treasurer: James Griffin and Assistant Secretary: J Lynch. The promoters believed that '*the above names should be a guarantee that the club will be a working one.*'

One of the first games was against The Hatchet, a club described as '*in a comatose state since since last February,*' with Drumree winning '*by a narrow shave*' and the best players were Dan Lynch, Pat O Brien, Denis Kenny, William Doran and Christy Tallon, the former Dunshaughlin captain. McCann, Woods, Maguire and Malone were described as the pick of the Hatchet. A return game followed and it ended in a draw. Doran '*excelled*' and was ably assisted by Anthony Bannon (Augherskea) and Joe Cusack (possibly Corballis) while Tom Johnson '*eclipsed himself by his long kicks.*' Horan, McCann and Farrelly were mentioned for The Hatchet with the latter '*the most active man on the field. He was literally ubiquitous.*'

Controversy arose in early 1892 when Drumree claimed to have played, but lost, to Kilmessan after walking six or seven miles through snow to the ground. Kilmessan claimed no game took place and Patrick Fox responded that some of his men were attending devotions at 3.30 in the chapel and asked captain Coady of Kilmessan to wait ten minutes but Coady refused and left the field. Drumree then offered to play 17 against 21 and were again refused. Fox later suggested playing the game on any ground bar Drumree or Kilmessan with Grange or Ballina preferred. There was no further mention of the controversy, nor of Drumree, although The Hatchet, sometimes referred to as St. Patricks, continued to feature and were included in a tournament organized by Dunshaughlin in 1897.

It seems likely that Drumree went out of existence sometime in 1892 and although there was a GAA revival in Meath in the mid 1890s Drumree didn't reappear. Dunshaughlin affiliated for the 1895 championship and the athletic sports continued annually during the decade.

In fact, at this period there is much more reference to Drumree playing cricket and many of the men who played football earlier lined out for the cricket team, including PJ Fox, James and Michael Fox, the Mooneys, Thomas Johnson, Patrick Muldoon, John Clarke and Thomas Geraghty. By 1900 The Hatchet, Batterstown and Warrenstown also had cricket clubs. Some reports on those games are included in Chapter 1. Drumree continued to field a cricket team until 1904 at least and held an annual reunion ball that year in Mr. Johnston's premises, possibly in Knockmark. Cricket was played in later years, and possibly at this period also, in a field opposite the Warrenstown Arms.

In 1898 numerous tournaments were held to commemorate the centenary of the 1798 Rebellion but there is no record of one in Dunshaughlin or Drumree. There was however a Culmullen '98 Club, known as The Clarence Mangan Club and it was probably a political, rather than a sporting, organization. A large number of people from the area travelled to St. Stephen's Green for the laying of the foundation stone of a Wolfe Tone Memorial in August 1798 including the President Con Sheridan, Denis Kenny the Secretary, and Charles Blunt the banner bearer. Kenny was a member of the Warrenstown team seven years earlier while Sheridan, from Tullaghmedan, was very active in political and GAA affairs for at least two decades. Laurence Canning, previously involved with the GAA in Dunshaughlin, was also in attendance.

Three years later in 1901 a tournament in aid of funds to decorate Culmullen Church took place with games in John O Reilly's field at Kilcooley, Drumree. Among local teams taking part were Dunshaughlin, Culmullen, Warrenstown and Killeen. It is possible that teams were formed specifically to take part in the tournament but it is also within the bounds of possibility that a GAA club developed from the Clarence Mangan '98 Club, especially as the team was called Culmullen, a name not used previously. Crom a-Boos of Maynooth defeated Bective in the final. The Culmullen Secretary was Thomas Geraghty of Knockmark.

Culmullen also played in a similar tournament the following year to raise funds for a new Parochial House in Dunshaughlin, a tournament won by the black and ambers, but, according to reports, *'from a financial point of view . . . it cannot be written down as anything in the nature of a success.'* The team continued to exist in 1904 and 1905 with J[ohn], Marmion as the Secretary, but the only mention of a game is a defeat by Galtrim by 0-2 to 0-0, which the press described as *'a disgraceful game.'*

Hurling in Warrenstown and Football in Bogganstown

Meanwhile, following the formation of Meath's first Gaelic League branch in Dunshaughlin, a branch was established in Warrenstown also. In early 1905 plans were afoot to form a hurling club and the *Drogheda Independent* hoped to see hurling taking the place of cricket and other English games. Mr. Kenny, probably Denis Kenny, and Thomas Geraghty, previously referred to in connection with the Culmullen football team and the Drumree cricket team, represented the club at the County Convention. Geraghty stated that Warrenstown had four or five players who assisted Dunshaughlin the previous year and the new club drew Longwood in the championship. It appears Warrenstown lost the game and a subsequent objection but details could not be traced of either. Michael Duffy of Dunshaughlin was one of the players as he was selected on the Meath team to play Queen's County (Laois) in September 1905. Warrenstown had even less success in the 1906 championship, losing to Killyon 5-4 to 0-1.

The club seems not to have survived much longer. Dunshaughlin reorganized itself in 1907 with Michael Duffy as the prime mover and hurling and football teams took to the field. This may have dealt a death blow to Warrenstown for there is no further reference to them. The Hatchet Club was also active in 1906-09 but there is less clarity about Culmullen. A Sports' Day under GAA rules took place in Drumree on 15th August 1908 and the Culmullen club may have organized it.

In 1909 Dunshaughlin played The Hatchet FC, then referred to as the Hatchet O Connell FC, in a game at Dunboyne and it 'finished in a free fight' according to Seaghan Mac na Midhe, the President of the County Board. 'All through the game,' he claimed, 'as much of it as was played, there was grumbling and discontent. No one knew the rules only the Hatchet Club, and the referee was partial.' A Mr T. Colgan, probably from Barstown, Culmullen, responded on behalf of the Hatchet, that other matches were much worse and, he asserted, Navan as the head fountain bore responsibility. The following year at the adjourned County Convention the Hatchet club was suspended for the season, probably arising from the above game.

The Hatchet appears not to have played again but by 1914 a team from Bogganstown had affiliated and this team probably catered for many of the ex-Hatchet players. The newcomers played in what was called the Middle League. In 1912 the Junior League had been confined to players under 20 year of age. J Marmion is recorded as the Secretary of Bogganstown, probably the man who was the Culmullen Secretary in 1904-05, but there was also a Culmullen team in existence at this time. When Kilcloon defeated Bogganstown by 2-3 to 1-1 in the

Middle League a report described both teams as being '*a short while in existence.*' Daly, Flynn, Blount and McCabe were listed as playing well for Bogganstown.

Bogganstown didn't survive very long. All teams in the county were affected by the formation of Volunteers and Sundays were devoted to drilling, marches and rifle practice. Sometime in 1915 a football team was established in Drumree based on those who were members of the Volunteers. In June the team played a friendly against Curraha as part of the Ratoath Aeridheacht prior to a Dunshaughlin senior hurling championship game and the *Drogheda Independent* reported that '*with more practice Drumree should give a good account of themselves anywhere.*' The team also entered the league and there are indications that the club fielded a hurling team later in the year. Who should turn up as Secretary, but the redoubtable J Marmion once again! It is difficult to judge how successful the team was, but it recorded a victory over Trim and a loss to Enfield while, for the Rathmolyon game neither team turned up.

The Pelletstown Reds

Like Bogganstown the Drumree club's life span was short. There is no mention of a club in the area in 1916 or 1917 but in 1918 a club that would have a longer-term impact was established. This was Pelletstown, later to be known as The Pelletstown Reds. Initially it was a hurling club with Michael Rattigan, father of Billie, as captain, James J Wildridge as Treasurer and John Mooney as Secretary. Wildridge was very involved in a number of nationalist organizations and was interned during the War of Independence. He sometimes went under the name of Charlie Hawkins, and generally dressed and behaved as a man of some importance, wearing gloves and carrying an attaché case on his travels. He was noted for exclaiming, 'By the Lord Chief Justice!' when he wished to make a point.

The club used a field belonging to Hugh Geraghty of Merrywell for its games. Wildridge and John O Donnell, a native of Limerick who worked as a chauffeur for Leonards, represented the club at County Convention in 1919 and the former proposed that a camogie league be considered. This was agreed but it seems to have progressed no further than consideration.

Pelletstown participated in the 1919 Hurling championship by entering senior and junior teams, as did Dunshaughlin, an incredible achievement for a sparsely populated parish but of course many of the players came from outside the immediate area. Games were played regularly on the Pelletstown grounds but the press carried very few results or reports of games. The club was suspended for a short while in 1920 for holding an illegal sports' meeting but was reinstated within a month. The suspension was probably due to not holding the sports under the auspices of the GAA.

In 1921 Michael Bruton and Michael Rattigan represented Pelletstown at the adjourned convention and the club had a junior and a senior team. As with Dunshaughlin during this era players transferred regularly from one club to another and this often led to confrontations at subsequent games. In 1921 Joseph Kelly, Charles Curry, John Reilly, John Lynch and John Smith transferred from Pelletstown to Dunboyne. Later in the year the two clubs met in the championship and James Mahon of Pelletstown and Dunboyne's William Rafferty were dismissed. The referee also cautioned Charles Curry for interfering with the umpire whereupon Curry threw down his hurley, assumed a fighting attitude and said he didn't care a damn about any referee or County Committee!

Pelletstown clearly had a formidable team as they defeated Athboy by 2-3 to 1-1 but other results are not known.

When JJ Wildridge was released from Kilmainham Gaol in December 1921 he resumed his involvement in the club and Pelletstown entered teams in the junior football and senior hurling competitions. The Middle League was no longer in existence, with the junior league once again catering for non-senior clubs. The footballers were placed in a division with Curraha, Oberstown, Kilcloon, Dunshaughlin and Dunsany and the outcome was a divisional final in which Pelletstown defeated Dunshaughlin. Among those mentioned as playing well were Michael Rattigan, Jim Wildridge, the Daly brothers, Madden, Connolly, Burke, Englishby and Mahon. The team reached the semi-final where Navan Harps emerged as victors by 2-4 to 0-1 with a suggestion that the losers indulged in rough tactics. It is not clear how the hurlers fared.

Pelletstown footballers repeated their progress in 1923. The team overturned an early loss to Kilcloon by defeating them a few weeks later and also got the better of Ballinabrackey by 2-2 to 0-0 to qualify for a semi-final. Pelletstown easily accounted for Dulane on a 4-3 to 0-3 scoreline but Dulane took the issue to the boardroom with a three-pronged objection. Firstly Michael Madden had played cricket and wasn't reinstated; secondly Patrick Dunne, a member of Kilcloon, played against Dulane and thirdly Peter Lee, who played, wasn't registered. The first part was ruled out, the second was upheld and the third part withdrawn. Pelletstown appealed to Leinster Council and lost there also. Navan Harps eventually defeated Dulane to win the championship. Pelletstown challenged the Harps to a game to decide who, in their view, were the real champions, but the Navan side had a clear-cut 2-8 to 1-1 victory against what was described as a Pelletstown selection.

Around this time cricket was once again popular in Meath and James McCormack and J Allen of Warrenstown represented the Drumree club at meetings. Interestingly J McCormack was among those released from the Rath internment camp in 1921, as was Dunshaughlin hurler Paddy Blake. Later, Thomas Geraghty, who was previously Secretary of Drumree GAA club, acted as Secretary of Warrenstown Cricket Club and Ikey Madden *'the well known hurler'* scored twenty runs while taking a number of wickets- clearly an all round sportsman.

The deeds of the Reds are celebrated in a poem from the time. No one seems to have the definitive version and the following is a reconstruction based on various sources:

The Pelletstown Reds

If you want to see football around County Meath
Just come to Pelletstown for the art and the speed
You know where Drumree is, and from there it's one mile,
To see Pelletstown Reds it would be well worth your while.

With Smith in the goals, he would stand any test
And the man that grabs Madden, it's to him woe betide.
Rattigan is there as if he fell from the moon
If a row shall arise it will settle damn soon.

There's the two brothers Burke, the small man with the knack
When Angie is pressed he will pass out to Jack.
When danger is nigh from a fifty yards free
You could always rely on our Owen Englishby.

There's the two brothers Daly, the cement wall is Son,
The other is Seamus, the lad that could run.
O Donnell and Madden comprised the big four
For every team knows them who met them before.

The pride of the team are Connolly and Downes
With Hawkins in the saddle they have nothing to dread
They cancelled the crookie* for football instead.

* Some hold that crookie may mean hurling but it is also possible it refers to cricket.

APPENDICES

Culmullen Team 1934

It seems that the episode with Dulane dispirited club members for no team played in the 1924 championship and the club wrote to the County Committee withdrawing the team on the grounds that some had transferred and others refused to play. Yet, following that, the newspapers carried notice of a fixture between Pelletstown and Navan Harps. If it ever took place it was probably one of the few games the club played and the following year a number of Pelletstown men transferred to Kilcloon. The club's original captain Michael Rattigan and James and Gerald Daly then played for Kilmessan, for, when they applied to transfer back to play in their own parish with Dunshaughlin the Kilmessan delegate Mr. Collier stated they had been playing with Kilmessan 'for the last five years ever since Pelletstown broke up.' Five years is probably an exaggeration but it confirms that Pelletstown went out of existence by 1924.

There was an effort to revive the club in 1929 when Michael Rattigan and Matty Wallace represented Pelletstown at a county committee meeting. There is also a reference to Drumree FC and there is some confusion as to the correct

This picture may have been taken at a training session rather than a game, as one of the players, Jimmy Courtney, front row with the leather football, is wearing Dunshaughlin's black and amber vertical bars. Courtney and many of the others pictured lined out with Dunshaughlin at various times.
Front: 'Kit' Gannon, T Geraghty, N Brady, Jimmy Courtney, Thomas Doyle, Christy Lynch.
Back: Patrick 'Rah' Doyle, James Daly, Ciarán Murray, Paddy Gogan, M Lambe, Ned Teeling, S Daly. At rear: Jack Lambe, John Gogan, top right.

Culmullen Team 1943

Front: Dessie Englishby, Matt Russell, Billy Byrne, Ted Blount, Billy 'Pole' Kelly.
Middle: Jimmy Geraghty, Christy Lynch.
Back: Con Madden (Selector), Felix McHugh, Kit Gannon, Paddy Murray, Pat Gannon, at rear with cap, Jack Blount, Peter Blount, Jack Halford, Tom Malone, with cap, Benny Downes, Paddy Courtney, John Cullen.

name of the club at this time. The footballers entered the junior championship but the club had to withdraw from the junior hurling competition, as it was unable to field a team. By the following year, 1930, the team was definitely known as Drumree and its year ended in defeat to Martry in the junior quarter-final, 2-5 to 0-8. The star of the team was Michael Pender who hit six points from frees and was described as '*a player who must be watched and cultivated.*' Drumree affiliated in 1931 also but not, it seems, in 1933 or 1934.

Handball was strong in Drumree and Dunshaughlin in the 1930s, as can be seen in Appendix 4.

Culmullen 1934-1941

Between 1934 and 1941 the club played junior football under the name of Culmullen and reached two county semi-finals at the start and end of the period. In 1934 the club participated in a division that also included Kiltale, Flathouse, College Park, Kilcloon, Salesian College and Killeen. It is known that wins were recorded against Kiltale 2-4 to 0-2, and Flathouse by 3-7 to 1-0 but they must have won others also, for, in 1934 Culmullen met Oldcastle in the junior semi-final.

The outcome was a narrow victory for the north Meath men, 1-2 to 0-4. Culmullen led 0-4 to 0-2 a few minutes from the end when Oldcastle broke through for a goal and despite two late frees and a '50' Culmullen failed to grab an equalizer. Players mentioned in the report were Ciarán Murray, Paddy Gogan, John Gogan, Doyle, probably Thomas, in goals, Christy 'Dill' Lynch, Madden, Brady, Daly and Ward. Culmullen objected on grounds similar to Dunshaughlin's objection to Longwood the following year, see Chapter 4, on the Irish version of an Oldcastle player's name, but it was not upheld.

The following year Culmullen moved up to the intermediate grade but lost a number of players on transfer to Dunshaughlin, who once again had a football team. Peter Doran, John and Patrick Gogan, Michael Keogan and Patrick Kelly of Batterstown all signed for the black and ambers and Culmullen made no impact on the championship. The club returned to, and remained in, the junior grade over the next few years without reaching the final stages. A 1937 game against Dunshaughlin, a 3-4 to 0-6 win for Culmullen, is interesting as it provides almost a full line out of fourteen players as follows: Ned Hynes, Mick Pender, Jack Lambe, Jimmy Courtney, Christy Lynch, James Daly, Joseph Smith, Patrick Doyle, L Geraghty, Thomas Doyle, William Shaw, [he owned the Warrenstown Arms and was father of John Shaw of Summerhill], J Madden, W Brady, Christy 'Toes' Doran. For some reason the two Doyles transferred to and played with Dunshaughlin in 1938.

In the early forties the club also fielded a minor football team. Interestingly, the points were shared with neighbours Salesian College in 1941 but Culmullen had to forfeit them for being twenty minutes late, a harsh decision given that many games failed to commence at the appointed time. The adult team had more success, reaching another semi-final but falling once more to north Meath opposition, Carnaross, by 2-7 to 0-7. The Culmullen team on that occasion was Thomas 'Connor' Doyle; Patrick 'Rah' Doyle, Joe Loughran, Jimmy Geraghty; Mickey Lambe, Willie Bashford, Kevin Reilly; Rory Mahon, Willie Carberry; Paddy Lynam, Kevin Clarke, Eugene Mohan; Jack Blount, Mattie Russell, Paddy 'Beezer' Courtney.

The Culmullen team is believed to have worn red and green jerseys and played their games in what was known as the Night Field. It was between the present Drumree GAA field and the new roundabout and was so called because it was used by farmers to hold cattle overnight prior to taking them to the Dublin Cattle Market.

St. Martins, 1942-1945

There was a surprising development at the start of 1942 when the county board received applications for registration from Culmullen and from Drumree. It is not known why this happened, or, if there were any prior discussions on the wisdom of two teams in such a small area. At any rate, common sense prevailed when Seán Newman, the Vice Chairman of the County Board, got agreement that just one club be registered and it would use the name of the patron saint of the parish. Thus, from 1942 the club was known as St. Martins, games were played in Drumree and the club was placed in the intermediate championship for its first year but was graded junior thereafter.

For a couple of the years St. Martins fielded a minor team and at one stage the Chairman, Secretary and captain were suspended for twelve months due to playing two unregistered players, John Finlay and George Downes. In addition the latter was overage. As outlined in Chapter 6, incidents such as this were rife in minor football in the county.

The St. Martins experiment didn't last long and its demise may have been due to the suspension of the Chairman and Secretary, but there is no evidence to support or disprove this theory.

APPENDICES

Drumree, 1946-1952

In 1946 and 1947 a hurling team called Drumree took part in the junior hurling championship but it seems no football team was entered. The hurlers suffered a couple of heavy defeats and in 1947 against Oberstown only eleven players were available, as according to Patrick 'The Rah' Doyle, the car engaged to transport the players did not turn up.

The following year, 1948, was an important one. A number of players transferred back from Dunshaughlin, including Rory McGuinness, Bernard Downes, Noel Downes and Patrick Doyle while Larry Geraghty transferred from Donaghmore. The reason is outlined in the following report from *The Meath Chronicle* in March headed *'The New Drumree Team.'*

At Warrenstown College Grounds on Sunday, the large crowd was delighted to see the new Drumree junior football team turn out in their new set of red jerseys, with red and white stockings, ready to jump onto the pitch the minute the Dunshaughlin-Batterstown match was finished. This young team is a credit to the committee, which turned them out so well and with L Geraghty (Sonny), late of Donaghmore and Meath county team, as skipper, we can visualize big things ahead. This was the first time they played together.

The revived club played in a division of the junior championship that contained Dunshaughlin, Kilmessan, Batterstown, Skryne and Dunboyne and also organized a Medal Tournament. Dunshaughlin won the Tournament and the Drumree Chairman presented the medals at a ceilí during the Drumree Carnival.

The officers of the new club were Chairman: Eugene Gilsenan, Vice Chairman: Thomas Farnan, Secretary: Eugene Englishby, Treasurer: Eugene Gilsenan. County Board delegates were Patrick Doyle and William Byrne while others on the committee were James Daly, Michael Madden, Laurence Geraghty, John Cullen, William 'The 'Pole' Kelly, Des Englishby, Dónal Donoghue and Ned Hynes.

Despite the initial high hopes the first year brought no success. Indeed the club had to concede a walkover and play a friendly instead against Dunshaughlin but the second year brought significant improvement and progress. At the time the junior championship was organized on a regional basis with the Tara District GAA Board responsible for completing the competition. Drumree emerged from a group consisting of Kilbride, Kilmessan, Batterstown, Drumree, Dunshaughlin, Dunboyne, and Skryne despite a single point loss to Dunshaughlin. However, a Drumree objection to Eddie Lyons, who played with Dunshaughlin, having earlier played with Erin's Hopes, was upheld and the reds qualified for a semi-final tilt with Rathkenny.

BLACK & AMBER

Billie Rattigan
Outstanding Drumree player of the 1950s and 1960s.

This time Drumree got the better of a north Meath side. Ten minutes from time Drumree held a 2-6 to no score lead but Rathkenny goaled twice in the closing stages without ever threatening to win. Unusually, all four goals came from frees. The Drumree team read: Thomas Kane; Bill Delany, Larry Geraghty, Paddy Kelly; R O Connor, Br. Tom O Sullivan, P Lynch; Billy Byrne, Jack O Connor; Jimmy Flynn, John Bashford, Jimmy Geraghty; Larry Dunphy, J Doherty, Noel Downes.

The final at Trim in December against Navan O Mahonys was played in the *'foulest of foul weather'* on a pitch that resembled a mud bath but, reported the local press, *'the encounter gave birth to one of the best junior finals for a number of years.'* The mud splashed contestants produced fast, exciting and at times brilliant football but the Drumree forward line failed to take full advantage of its chances and *'had all the bad luck that was going.'* O Mahonys goaled from a penalty while Drumree had a 'goal' disallowed and claimed another was over the line before it was cleared. After leading by 1-3 to 0-2 at the interval Drumree wilted in the second half as O Mahonys forged a narrow 2-3 to 1-4 victory. Bashford, Sullivan, Lynch, Delany, Geraghty, Dunphy were described as *'always prominent.'*

There is no consensus on how long the club remained in existence, but it seems to have lapsed about 1952. In 1950 John Bashford transferred to Syddan but in 1951 and 1952 Drumree entered teams in juvenile and Under 16 competitions. The story of underage football in the parish is covered in detail in Chapter 6. However, Dunshaughlin had won the Junior Championship in 1950, and in the early fifties were real contenders at senior level. A number of young talented Drumree players like Larry, Dickie and Patsy O Brien, Billie and Tony Rattigan, Billy and Larry Byrne, joined Dunshaughlin, with Larry becoming vice captain in 1952 while Drumree stalwart Patrick 'The Rah' Doyle was Dunshaughlin's delegate to the county board that year also.

Although Drumree did not take part in the championship during the early fifties, the club may not have folded entirely. Billie Rattigan recalls that Peter Rattigan, Eamonn Donoghue, Oliver Walsh and Seamus Troy promoted a Drumree team and went around the houses in the area collecting for a set of red and white jerseys.

The tradition was dormant.

Not dead.

Drumree, Junior Camogie Champions, 2011

Front: Adi Pritchard, Leanne McMorrow, Maeve Scanlon, Jessica Wall, Louise Griffin, Cliona Murphy, Sarah Keane, Emma Doyle, Emer O Reilly, Cliona Ní Dhúshláine.

Back: Vincent Brennan, Selector, Áine Brennan, Gemma Flanagan, Sinéad Ennis, Ciara Kennedy, Annemarie Rattigan, Rosie Hand, Lisa Donnelly, Trish Monks, Maureen Doyle, Selector, Kim Slater, Noeleen Greevy, Brenda Greevey, Niamh Kelliher, Emma Kennedy, GT Troy, Manager.

Drumree Captain Clíona Murphy accepts the Junior Championship Cup from Terry Tormay, Meath Camogie Board, following the 2011 Final.

Pictured at a presentation in 1999 to members of Drumree's victorious Junior Championship winning team of 1959 were Billie Rattigan, Pat 'Red' Collier, Meath All Ireland senior winner 1967, Tony Rattigan, Patsy O Brien and Liam Smith.

Appendix 3

Part 2: The GAA in Drumree 1957-2014

After a number of successful years with Dunshaughlin many of the players from the Culmullen end of the parish transferred back to Drumree in 1957. One of the reasons given was the danger of losing the pitch in Drumree if there was no affiliated team using it. The land had belonged to Frank Dignam, originally from Roscommon. He also had land in Creemore, and bought and sold cattle for a living. After his body was discovered in a ditch near Neary's, -possibly hit by a car-, the Land Commission took over the land and eventually divided it between Jack Geraghty and Drumree GAA.

Billie Rattigan recalls that when the players returned from Dunshaughlin there was some discussion on the name of the club. The options were Culmullen or Drumree, and the latter was chosen, probably because of the pitch's location in Drumree.

There followed the most successful era in Drumree's history. The team reached a divisional final in 1957 but Kiltale came out on top. Dunshaughlin also took part in the junior championship at this time, winning the B title and the championship proper in 1958 but 1959 was Drumree's year. Playing in the A championship they had a narrow semi-final victory against Millbrook, 0-4 to 0-2. Close calls continued in the final against St. Patricks. It took three games to produce a winner. In the first game both sides scored 1-8, the next day Drumree repeated their score but the Saints matched it with 2-5 and in the third game Drumree took the honours by 1-4 to 0-5. At the time the A winners played the B winners, and generally beat them, and Drumree had no trouble disposing of Longwood 1-10 to 0-5.

The team that defeated St Patrick's read as follows, Tony Walsh; Billy Byrne, Jimmy Murray, Tommy Troy; Patsy O Brien, Larry O Brien, Larry Byrne; PJ Rowley, Tony Rattigan; Jimmy Walsh (0-1), Billie Rattigan (0-2), Packie Doyle (1-0); Michael Flaherty, Dickie O Brien (0-1), Patsy O Sullivan, Capt. Sub: Michael Walsh for P Sullivan, Seán Doyle, Tommy Clerkin, Bertie O Malley, Jimmy O Rourke.

Intermediate Double

The title resulted in automatic promotion to the intermediate grade, where Dunshaughlin was also operating. The clubs went within one game of meeting in a county final in 1961 when both reached the semi-final, on opposite sides of the draw. Drumree navigated their way to the decider but Dunshaughlin foundered against Slane, losing 3-8 to 1-6, thus extinguishing the mouth-watering prospect of a parochial final in Navan.

Instead Drumree had the task of upholding the honour of the parish and this

Drumree, Intermediate Football Champions, 1969

Front: Neil O Riordan, Johnny Lynch, Larry O Brien, Thomas Carty, Oliver Walsh, Jimmy Walsh, Michael Walsh, Michael Geraghty, Jimmy O Rourke, Tony Rattigan.
Back: Tommy Troy, Tom Murray, John Murphy, Seán Doyle, Tony Walsh, Andy Mahon, Ray Carty, Paddy Burke, Pat Muldowney, Billie Rattigan, Joe Rattigan.

they did in some style, overcoming the Boynesiders by 2-7 to 1-3. The following team lined out on final day:

Tony Walsh; Seán Doyle, Tony Rattigan, Tom Murray; Patsy O Brien, Larry O Brien, Larry Byrne; Tommy Troy, Jack Kane (0-1); Jimmy Walsh (1-0), Patsy O Sullivan, Billie Rattigan (0-2), Capt.; Packie Doyle (1-0), Billy Byrne (0-2), Jimmy Rourke (0-2). Subs: Mickey Regan, Mick Kane, Dickie O Brien, Paddy Burke, Michael Walsh, Bertie O Malley.

Whereas Dunshaughlin failed to build on their success in reaching the semi-final, -a few years later they were junior once again-, Drumree was on an upward curve for almost a decade. The team reached the Feis Cup final in 1962 but lost to St. Vincents and fell in the senior championship semi-final of 1964 to one of the strongest teams in the 1960s, Kells, by 3-11 to 1-8. Jimmy Walsh captained the Meath junior team to All-Ireland victory in 1962, scoring four points in the Leinster final victory against Wexford and the following year he was part of the senior team that defeated Dublin in the Leinster senior final and eventually won an All-Ireland senior medal in 1967.

Though Drumree reached the senior semi-final of 1964 some of the more senior men were now in their twilight years and in 1967 the club reverted to intermediate status. It was still a powerful combination at this level and in 1969 added another intermediate title to its honours. En route to Páirc Tailteann the reds defeated Dunshaughlin by six points and eliminated Martry by a similar margin in the semi-final, 1-7 to 0-4.

The final was a tighter affair and as had happened so often in the past Drumree met north Meath opposition when they faced Castletown in Páirc Tailteann in early October. The Hoops held a three-point advantage with four minutes remaining when Castletown's Paddy Smith struck a goal. The sudden reverse stunned Drumree into a rapid response. Jimmy Walsh missed a point chance before he won a centre from Tommy Troy and drove the ball to the net. It was enough to shield Drumree against a Castletown raid that yielded a point and the club had its second intermediate title on a scoreline of 2-6 to 1-7.

Drumree's strength was in attack. Larry O Brien commanded the 'forty' before moving to full forward and Castletown had to switch their goalkeeper Peter Price outfield in an attempt to curtail his influence. Jimmy Walsh's scores were the difference between the sides and others to shine were Neil O Riordan, Andy Mahon, Tommy Troy, Jimmy O Rourke and Ray Carty when introduced as a substitute. Tony Rattigan grabbed the first goal as early as the third minute. O Brien and Walsh initiated the move and when Rattigan grabbed the ball he swiveled before hammering it to the net. The victorious team read, Tony Walsh; Michael Geraghty (Kiltale), Johnny Lynch, Seán Doyle; Andy Mahon, Neil O Riordan, Michael Walsh; Tommy Troy, Tommy Murray; Jimmy O Rourke (0-2), Larry O Brien, Jimmy Walsh (1-3); Tony Rattigan (1-0), Paddy Burke, Oliver Walsh (0-1). Subs: Billie Rattigan for Murray, Ray Carty for Geraghty, Thomas Carty, John Murphy, Pat Muldowney, Joe Rattigan.

Later in the month Tommy Troy and Jimmy Walsh added a senior hurling championship medal to their haul when assisting Kilmessan to a 2-12 to 0-10 victory against Ratoath. A number of the team also played hurling at the highest level. The year after the intermediate triumph Tommy Troy collected Leinster and All-Ireland junior hurling championship medals when Meath overcame Wicklow in the provincial final and Herefordshire, after a replay, in the All-Ireland decider and in 1972 Neil O Riordan was a wing back on the team that defeated Kildare in the Leinster final.

Like Dunshaughlin almost a decade later, the intermediate victory was the swan song of a team that had prospered for a decade but was now in need of a transfusion of fresh blood. The demands of the senior grade once again proved too great, and from 1973 both Dunshaughlin and Drumree soldiered in the intermediate championship. In comparison to a decade earlier Dunshaughlin was on the rise while the Drumree graph was headed downwards. The black and ambers went on to contest the semi-final in 1973 and the quarter-final in 1974. Then in 1975 many of the Drumree players transferred to their neighbours. When Dunshaughlin eventually captured a first intermediate title in 1977 the winning side sported three of the Drumree team that captured the same trophy eight years earlier, Michael and Jimmy Walsh and Neil O Riordan.

Drumree, East Meath Football League Winners, 1985

Front: Jim Rattigan, Patrick O Brien, Michael Jones, Martin Smith, Dónal Carroll, Val McMahon, Michael Boyle, Gerry Wall, Tom Donoghue, Gerry Boyle.
Back: Paul Rattigan, David O Brien, Joe Doran, Dónal Wall, Martin Wall, Ray Byrne, Macartan McGroder, Anthony Wall, Seán Walsh, Jimmy O Rourke, Ben Fitzpatrick.

Drumree, Meath Junior Champions, 1998

Front: Gavin Kilbane, Christopher Doyle, Mark Rattigan, Declan Troy, Shane Mahon, James Walsh, Aaron Fitzpatrick, Capt., Darren Rattigan- Mascot, Roy Sheridan, Jim Rattigan, Dermot Doyle, Damien Fitzpatrick, Aidan Walsh.
Back: Jim Hayes, David Troy, Pauric Shanley, Gary Donoghue, Garreth Kelly, Bobby Geraghty, John Boyle, Gerard Troy, Patrick Doyle, Evan Kelly, Paul Gaughan, John Cullinane, Seán Walsh.

BLACK & AMBER

A Steep Decline and a Steady Recovery, 1975-1998

It was a decade before Drumree recovered sufficiently to challenge for titles again. The team dropped precipitously down the grades to Junior Division 3 before the recovery began. It started with victory in the East Meath League final of 1985 against St. Vincents and defeat in the 1986 Junior Division 3 final to Robinstown but the reds finally garnered a championship in 1988 with victory against Kilmainham by 2-6 to 1-4. An early Shane Mahon goal provided the foundation for victory, for, although Kilmainham equalized shortly afterwards, Drumree built on the good start to lead at half time by double scores 2-2 to 1-1. Drumree dominated the second half but met a resilient opposing defence that confined the reds' attack to four points. It was more than enough for a convincing 2-6 to 1-4 victory with Michael Boyle and Seán Walsh superb in defence and David O Brien and Shane Mahon tormenting the Kilmainham backs, while scoring 2-3 between them.

The victorious side had many experienced performers but of more importance was the array of young players, many still substitutes, who would backbone the team in years to come. The re-establishment of St. Martins in 1983 was already reaping dividends as players like Larry McMahon, Shane Mahon, Paul Molloy made the starting fifteen and John and Alan Boyle, Liam Holton, Trevor Doyle and Declan Troy were among the substitutes. The winning side was Dónal Carroll; Gerry Boyle, Michael Boyle, Ben Fitzpatrick; Jim Rattigan (0-1), Seán Walsh, Paul Molloy; Tony Gleeson, Larry McMahon; Shane Mahon (1-1), David O Brien (1-2), Paul Rattigan (0-1) Capt; Michael Jones (0-1), Martin Wall, Jimmy Walsh. Subs: Dónal Treacy for Molloy, Dónal Wall, Martin Smith, John Boyle, Charlie O Brien, Alan Boyle, Macartan McGroder, Jimmy O Rourke, Martin Lynch, Philip Byrne, Liam Holton, Michael Rattigan, Trevor Doyle and Declan Troy. Note: Jim Rattigan became acting captain and accepted the trophy as Paul Rattigan was sent off during the game.

The younger players gradually populated the team, and, even if outright success proved elusive in the 1990s the club was always in contention for the junior crown. Another priority was to escape from the basement of the All County Football League to ensure a higher standard of opposition that would benefit the club in the long term. In 1990 the team went close in both league and championship, losing a play-off in the former and a championship semi-final against Simonstown Gaels. The following year Drumree went a step further, reaching the final against Carnaross. But like Dunshaughlin they would discover that the path to the title is a rocky one with many twists and turns.

Carnaross recorded a convincing victory in 1990, 1-14 to 0-5, but they were an

Jim Rattigan, Drumree's acting captain, accepts the 1988 Division 3 Championship Cup from Tommy Collins, Vice Chairman, Meath County Board.

All Star Evan
Evan Kelly accepts his 2001 All Star award from Taoiseach Bertie Ahern.

exceptionally strong junior team who would shatter Dunshaughlin's intermediate hopes three years later and reach senior status. Meath star PJ Gillic was central to their advance but Drumree also fielded a young man who would go on to become the club's best ever player.

Evan Kelly wasn't selected on the Meath minor panel in 1991, but he made the Under 21 team beaten by Laois in the Leinster final replay in 1994. His performances impressed Seán Boylan who called him onto the senior panel and he made his National League debut against Derry and his first championship outing was against his mother Mary's native county, Offaly, in 1995. A year later he collected his first Leinster senior medal as Meath beat Dublin by two points and an All-Ireland after the Royals defeated Mayo in a replay.

That was just the beginning of a star-studded career. He captured another Celtic cross in 1999 as Meath overcame Cork, but missed a third when Galway proved too strong in 2001. Compensation came in the form of a coveted All Star award at right half forward, the only one to come to the parish. He played for Ireland in the Compromise Rules Series against Australia in 2002 and won a brace of Railway Cup medals with Leinster in 2001 and 2002. In an inter-county career that spanned a decade he made sixty-three National League appearances and played in thirty-six championship games. Evan was immensely strong, determined, dedicated and versatile. He played in all forward positions for Meath as well as making some appearances in the half back line. In five championship starts in his first year he hit 3-7 and followed it with ten points the following year.

He was Drumree's trump card for many years but the team was not a one-man show. John Cullinane joined Evan on the inter county scene from 2001, winning a Leinster medal against Dublin and entering the fray in the All-Ireland decider. The Doyles, Troys, Aaron Fitzpatrick and Jim Rattigan were others who turned Drumree from a lowly junior Division 3 side to a contender for junior and later intermediate honours.

Expectations of another county final appearance were crushed with monotonous regularity. It was 1998 before the club made the return trip on championship final day. But the intervening years were not completely barren, as the club climbed out of Division 5 of the league in 1993 beating Kilmainham in the final, and in 1995 went a step further after beating St. Ultans 1-11 to 0-7 in the Division 4 final.

1998 will always be recalled as the most successful in the club's history. The team defeated St. Vincents, Simonstown Gaels, Wolfe Tones, and drew with Dunsany to qualify for a semi-final against Moylagh. Drumree defeated the north Meath side by 1-9 to 1-4 but the sending off of Mick Collins deprived the team of one of its regular midfielders for the final.

Opponents St. Marys had been strong intermediate contenders for a number of years and were intent on regaining that status. Former Dublin star Stephen Wade coached the Drumree side with Pat Kelly and Joe Kelliher as his selectors and the troika decided on minimal disruption for the final, drafting in Bobby Geraghty as a direct replacement for the absent Collins. Early on the omens were poor. Despite wind advantage Drumree found themselves 1-2 to 0-3 in arrears after fifteen minutes and then conceded another goal. Just before the break Evan Kelly renewed the reds' optimism with a goal that left them just two points in arrears.

An early second half point increased the deficit but St. Marys failed to score again as Drumree dominated to the finish. Kelly won two frees, then hit a superb point to draw the sides level. Kelly again, Bobby Geraghty and Jim Rattigan then turned a three-point deficit into a three-point advantage and it finished 1-11 to 2-5 for the Drumree men. Paddy Doyle excelled at fullback, Declan Troy and Aaron Fitzpatrick were outstanding and Evan Kelly was man of the match with 1-3. The team represented the continuity and tradition of Drumree football. Five men who had played in the previous junior victory in 1959, Seán Doyle, Tommy Troy, Jimmy Walsh, Tony Rattigan and Michael Walsh, all had sons on the panel.

The winning team was John Boyle; Dermot Doyle, Patrick Doyle, Aaron Fitzpatrick, Capt.; Gerard Troy, Declan Troy (0-1), Roy Sheridan; John Cullinane, Bobby Geraghty (0-1); James Walsh, Jim Rattigan (0-2), Paul Gaughan (0-1); Jim Hayes (0-3), Evan Kelly (1-3), Shane Mahon. Subs: Damien Fitzpatrick, David Troy, Pauric Shanley, Gary Donoghue, Garreth Kelly, Seán Walsh, Gavin Kilbane, Christopher Doyle, Mark Rattigan, Aidan Walsh.

The victory gave the club a unique opportunity, participation in the Leinster Junior Club Tournament. The competition was originally designed as a forum in which to test some experimental rules, mainly one solo, one hop and clean pick-up off the ground. Drumree won the group stage with victories over John Mitchells of Louth and St. Peregrines, the Dublin representatives coached by Eamonn Barry. They followed this with an easy semi-final victory over Offaly's Ballinamere by 2-14 to 1-5.

The final in Dunshaughlin pitted Drumree against Ballyroan of Laois. Although it was the Laois club's second team, it was a quality side with eight having played in the Leinster senior club final in 1992 against Éire Óg of Carlow. The game was played in terrible conditions as heavy rain and strong winds made good football difficult. Despite this, an exciting contest ensued. Ballyroan held the initiative in the early stages, building a 0-3 to 0-1 lead, but as John Cullinane began to control midfield, Drumree struck eight points without reply before the Laois men reduced the lead to 0-10 to 0-6 at the interval.

They maintained that form into the second half as two points either side of a goal put them a single point ahead. Then, two Drumree goals from Evan Kelly in the final quarter proved decisive. For the first, James Walsh set him up and soon after Jim Rattigan created the second with Kelly finishing clinically on both occasions. Drumree tasted Leinster success on a final score of 2-12 to 1-10 and the winning team read: John Boyle; Dermot Doyle, Mick Collins, Aaron Fitzpatrick Capt.; Gerard Troy, Declan Troy, Roy Sheridan; John Cullinane (0-1), Bobby Geraghty (0-1); Shane Mahon (0-2), Jim Rattigan (0-1), Paul Gaughan (0-1); Jimmy Walsh (0-1), Evan Kelly (2-2), Jim Hayes (0-2). Subs: David Troy and Patrick Doyle (0-1).

Two years later, Millennium Year, Drumree surprised many by reaching the intermediate semi-final but lost to eventual champions St. Patricks. However, in the medium to long term the side would not sustain performances at that level. By then the club had built a reputation as a dual club and its hurling achievements at first matched and then surpassed its football triumphs.

Hurling

When the Dunshaughlin hurling revival foundered in 1991, see Chapter 9, Drumree grabbed the baton and continued where their neighbours had left off.

The club entered a team in Junior Division 2 and after two final defeats, to Kilmessan in 1991 and Athboy in 1992 made it third time lucky in 1993 after surging through the preliminary stages undefeated. That team had a deep reservoir of experience in Jimmy Walsh, Patsy Curley, Tommy Troy and Pat Kenny but relied in the main on youth.

Final opponents Boardsmill held Drumree to a draw in the early rounds but the Drums triumphed in the ultimate encounter. Against the wind in the first half Drumree limited the 'Mill to 1-2 while scoring 0-4, but the task was no easier with wind assistance until David Troy combined with Aaron Fitzpatrick who netted midway through the second half. A Tommy Troy goal finally settled the outcome ten minutes from time on a score of 2-7 to 1-4. Patsy Curley, who had done so much to establish underage hurling in St. Martins, coached the team and his selectors were Michael Boyle, Seán Doyle and Willie Shanley. The team lined out as follows:

Patsy Curley; Mark Rattigan, David Farrell, Trevor Doyle; Liam Holton, Willie Shanley, Paul Rattigan; Paddy Doyle (0-2), Michael Boyle; Aaron Fitzpatrick (1-2), Paul O Rourke, David Troy (0-3); Dermot Doyle, John Considine, Jimmy Walsh Snr. Subs: Tommy Troy (1-0) for Considine, Pat Kenny for M Rattigan, James Walsh, Jnr., Thomas Walsh, Adrian Faherty, Derek Doyle, Hugh McCabe, Wayne Cottrell, Charlie Leonard.

Drumree captured the trophy for a second time three years later, although the final and replay were not played until early 1997. An injury time point from captain Dermot Doyle enabled Drumree match Ratoath's 1-6 in the initial meeting but the replay was much easier as they cruised to a 2-5 to 0-3 victory. The winning team, which Peter Mooney trained, was Willie Shanley; Gerard Clarke, Charlie Leonard, Rory O Sullivan; Paul Doyle (0-1), Declan Troy, Pádraig Shanley; Dermot Doyle, Capt., Paul O Rourke; Paul Gaughan, David Troy (1-1), David Crimmins (0-3); Seán Curley (1-0), Patrick Boyle, Ronan Curley. Subs: Gary Donoghue for R Curley, Gerard Troy for S Curley.

Later in the year the club reached the Junior A hurling final but had to give way to Killyon. However, as was the case in the early years of the decade the team returned the following year to meet Trim in the final after rattling Kiltale's net seven times in the semi. It took a replay to separate the sides.

Trim had a number of first half goal opportunities but Willie Shanley proved equal to the task with two superb stops. Meanwhile Drumree were more clinical in turning opportunities into scores and held a goal lead at the interval. Gary Donoghue added another point soon after play resumed but Trim then dominated with two points followed by a goal for a one-point lead.

It turned out to be the town side's last score and Declan Troy took advantage of two placed balls to edge Drumree into the winners' enclosure on a 1-6 to 1-5 scoreline. First he pointed a '65' and then after a melee and the dismissal of a player from each side he calmly slotted the winning point from the resultant free. The victory was noteworthy for the fact that the team consisted almost entirely of a new generation of players. The men who had backboned Dunshaughlin during the 80s had been replaced with young hurlers who had come through St. Martins and this provided a solid foundation for future success.

Drumree's winning team read: Willie Shanley; Gerard Clarke, Trevor Doyle, Paul O Rourke; Paul Doyle, Declan Troy (0-2), Pauric Shanley; Dermot Doyle, David Crimmins; Paul Gaughan, Gerard Troy (1-1), Gary Donoghue (0-1); Seán Curley (0-1), David Troy, Capt. (0-1), Shane Kennedy. Subs: George Troy for Kennedy, Kennedy for Curley.

This result made 1998 the most successful and significant in the club's history with the Meath and Leinster Junior Football titles to accompany the hurling silverware.

The emerging talent went on to capture the Under 21 Special Hurling title in 1999 by defeating Kildalkey by 3-5 to 2-2, with goals from Seán Curley, David Crimmins and Pauric Shanley. The following team brought home the honours: John Gilsenan; Paul Doyle, Gerard Clarke, Capt.; Kevin Burke, David Crimmins (1-2) Brian Kenny; Christopher Doyle, Alan Kenny; Pauric Shanley (1-0), Gary Donoghue, George Troy; Seán Curley (1-3), Shane Kennedy. Sub Paddy Boyle.

Drumree Panel, Intermediate Hurling Champions 2010

Front: Daire Flanagan, Paul Walsh, Paul Kiernan, Fearghal Delaney, Stephen McGroder, Brian Coughlan, Ronan Curley, Evan Curley, John Gilsenan, Capt., Leah Doyle, Christopher Doyle, Seán Doyle, Brendan Walsh, David Wallace, Robert Lyons, James Reilly, Pete Rattigan.
Back: Liam Shanley, Mark Devanney, Caoimhín King, Paul Hendrick, David Crimmins, John Crimmins, Andrew Kiernan, Shane Troy, Keith Rooney, Martin Kelly, Robert Connolly, Ciarán Kenny, Brian Kenny, Bill Reilly, Conal O Sullivan, Stephen Doyle, Dermot Doyle, James Gaughan, GT Troy, David Donoghue.

Olé, Olé, Olé, Drumree celebrate victory in the Intermediate Hurling Final, 2010

On ground at front: Shane Troy.
Front: Paul Kiernan, Caoimhín King, Stephen Doyle, Keith Rooney, Andrew Kiernan, behind Rooney, Seán Doyle, mascot, Fearghal Delaney, Paul Walsh, James Reilly, Peter Rattigan.
Second Row: Dermot Doyle, Johnny Gilsenan, Capt., David Moore, Brian Coughlan, Liam Shanley.
Third Row: Martin Kelly, GT Troy, John Crimmins, Daire Flanagan, partly covered by John Crimmins' hand, Robert Lyons, Robert Connolly, Paul Hendrick, Ronan Curley, James Gaughan.
At Rear: Brian Kenny, partly obscured, Conal O Sullivan, Bill Reilly, Stephen McGroder, Ciarán Kenny, partly obscured, Mark Devanney, David Crimmins, David Wallace, David Donoghue.

BLACK & AMBER

A Family Affair
Top: Mairéad Delaney presents the trophy to her son Fearghal following Drumree's victory in the Division 2 Hurling League Final 2015. On right is sponsor CJ Murtagh.
Bottom: Conal O Sullivan, Joint Captain Drumree Under 21 Hurling Champions 2012 with his parents, Dónal and Margaret.

Football Again, 1999-2010

Following the junior football title win in 1998 Drumree seemed destined to make an impact on the intermediate grade when they reached the semi-final in only their second year in the grade. St. Patricks, who went on to win the title, proved too strong, winning by 0-15 to 1-8 but it suggested that Drumree would be a match for the best. It proved to be a false dawn. Performances went downhill gradually with the team teetering on the brink of a return to junior for a number of years before finally toppling. Defeat in all the group games, followed by a relegation play-off defeat to Slane by 1-10 to 2-1 in late 2005, consigned the reds to junior grade from 2006.

A rapid return might have been predicted but with many of the 1998 team no longer playing the team found the lower grade too demanding also. The club's talismen, Evan Kelly and John Cullinane had moved from the area and joined Simonstown Gaels and Longwood respectively. In 2006 the side recorded two draws in the championship and reached the Division 5 All County League final only to go under to Curraha by 0-7 to 0-4. Two championship victories in 2008 seemed to suggest a degree of stability but after heavy defeats to Skryne and Kilbride in 2009 the side withdrew from the championship and faced into the Junior B grade in 2010. Even then the side struggled, recording but one victory and a walkover in the championship while losing five games. It was to be the club's final year in the football championship.

By now huge changes had taken place in the underage structure in the parish, outlined in Chapter 20. St. Martins was no more and Drumree and Dunshaughlin had agreed that the former would cater for underage hurling, the latter for underage football. There was a proviso that when footballers graduated to adult level they could play for either Drumree or Dunshaughlin but given the level at which Drumree was playing the club was never likely to attract the better footballers in the parish.

In 2008 a motion to dissolve Drumree football club was successfully proposed at the AGM. This was due mainly to changes in GAA rules that would have prevented dual players like David Crimmins and Caoimhín King continuing to play football with Dunshaughlin while hurling with Drumree when the latter had both hurling and football affiliations. However, after a number of club members signed a letter strongly opposing the decision an extraordinary general meeting was held to consider the issue. The move to dissolve the club was overturned when Meath County Board assured delegates that the rule would not apply in 2009 and thus the traditional red and white hoops continued to feature in the football championships. Nevertheless, the writing was on the wall for the football team with the changes in St. Martins

Drumree, U13 Hurling Division 2 Runners-Up, 2009

Front: Mark Phelan, Lorcán Casey, David Dunne, Senan Ó Muirí, Martin Keane, Andrew Doolan, James Logan, Aidan McMahon, Jack Leonard, Mark Galvin. Back: Stephen Farrell, Josh Wall, Alan Reilly, Liam Carey, Darragh Walsh, Darren Lawless, Dan Ormsby, Stephen Ennis, Stephen Duffy, William McCarthy, Darragh Nolan.

and Drumree's rapid decline on the football field. The club's final championship outing in football was, ironically, against Dunshaughlin in 2011 and since then the club has concentrated on hurling and camogie.

It was an abrupt end to well over a century of football. Like Dunshaughlin, the Drumree club had its ups and downs, especially in the early years, with a variety of names, periods of triumph and times of despair. Since the 1950s the club has always been among the honours with junior titles in 1959 and 1998, two intermediate championships in the sixties, 1961 and 1969, and a victory in the Leinster junior competition in 1998. Many of its players represented the Royal County, none with more glory and honour than Evan Kelly, Larry O Brien, Billie Rattigan and Jimmy Walsh.

Hurling, 1999-2014

Hurling continued to prosper as the fortunes of the footballers waned. After annexing the 1998 junior title the hurlers made a determined bid for glory at intermediate level. A losing final appearance to Boardsmill in 2000 was followed by two frustrating years but finally in 2003 the team took the title.

The final saw Drumree produce an outstanding display in rain-swept Páirc Tailteann as they overwhelmed Clann na Gael. The loss of David Troy prior to the final due to illness didn't hinder the reds for whom Dermot Doyle goaled early in the game. Paul Gaughan added a second to build a 2-4 to 0-4 interval advantage. Another two goals in the second half, both from substitutes, David Crimmins and David Troy, ended the Athboy men's hopes of a rapid return to the senior ranks. The game concluded in a comprehensive thirteen-point victory, 4-7 to 0-6.

Drumree, Runners-Up Under 16 B Hurling, 2011

Front: Darragh Nolan, Lorcán Casey, Liam Carey, David Dunne, Edward Murphy, Jack Leonard, Martin Keane, Diarmuid Christie.
Back: Conor Gavin, Darren Lawless, Killian Gavin, Shane Gallogly, David Moore, David Reilly, Josh Wall, Gareth Rooney, Daniel McTigue, Alan Reilly, Vincent Brennan, Frank Bawle.

Drumree, Winners Under 12 B Hurling Shield Final, 2011

The panel below defeated Rathmolyon in the final to take the title.
Front: Kevin Bawle, Pádraig Clinton, Alastair Philip, Liam Hanley, Luke Mitchell, David Fildes, Matthew Moyles, Daniel Fildes.
Back: Conor Gavin, Jamie Rattigan, Andrew Baggott, Ross McQuillan, Mathew Costello, Kevagh Slater, Andrew Leneghan, Conor Jones, Aaron Lawlor, Ava Foley, Niall Gavin, Niall Hurley, Frank Bawle, Willie Hanley.

Drumree, Minor Hurling Shield Winners, 2013

Front: Edward Murphy, Fergus Ryan, Diarmuid Christie, David Reilly, Killian Gavin, Hugh Smith.
Back: Darragh Walsh, Josh Wall, Liam Carey, Niall Kelly, Darren Lawless, Paul Kelly, Gareth Rooney, Alan Reilly, Pádraig Keane, Andy Doolan. Missing from picture: Shane Gallogly.

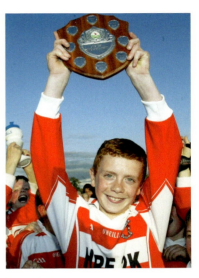

Ross McQuillan
Drumree captain, Ross McQuillan, hoists the Shield aloft after victory in the 2011 Under 12 final.

Michael Wallace, who had been instrumental in the rise of hurling in St. Martins, coached the side with assistance from John Davis and fellow selectors Peter Mooney and Patrick Doyle. The victorious Drumree side was: David Farrell (Capt.); Kevin Burke, Gerard Troy, John Gilsenan; Brian Kenny, Ronan Curley, Christopher Doyle; Caoimhín King, John Crimmins; David Wallace (0-1), Seamus Wallace (0-5), Dermot Doyle (1-1); Brendan Walsh, Paul Gaughan (1-0), Seán White. Subs: David Crimmins (1-0) for Curley, Curley for Walsh, David Troy (1-0) for White, Séamus Smith for Dermot Doyle, Gary Donoghue, Gerard Clarke, Brian Walsh, Brian Coughlan, Ronan Gilsenan, Ciarán Kenny.

Drumree was now hurling in the senior championship following a first ever intermediate title, but the team would find the going tough. The target was retention of senior status and this they achieved until 2008 when losing a relegation play-off to Killyon by 2-11 to 2-9, to drop down a grade. The year brought one positive achievement with David Crimmins' selection on the Leinster hurling panel that claimed inter provincial honours at Munster's expense.

If not good enough for the senior grade, Drumree soon proved that they were more than capable of performing among the best at intermediate level. In 2010 they were back again on final day. An impressive victory over Blackhall Gaels in the semi-final by 1-14 to 1-7 set up a meeting with Boardsmill who had a comprehensive win when the two sides met in the first round. The 'Mill were strong favourites to take the title but Drumree, coached by former Meath star Mickey Cole, with David Farrell and Stephen McMorrow as selectors, were not ready to concede to the pundits' expectations. Ironically, Boardsmill were coached by one of Drumree's outstanding former hurlers David Troy.

This time the outcome was in doubt up to the final whistle. Boardsmill seemed the likely winners at half time as they held a 2-3 to 0-8 lead. Though Stephen Doyle had hit six points and Brian Coughlan and John Crimmins also raised the white flag it was the 'Mill's ability to score goals that gave them the advantage. Drumree introduced three half-time substitutes but they could make no impact against the wind. Not that Boardsmill were using the elements to their advantage for it took them seventeen minutes to double their lead. Drumree remained in contention with Doyle knocking over two more points from frees but Boardsmill responded with a brace of their own that seemed to guarantee them the Tommy Kane Cup.

Then, deep into added time Shane Troy forcefully drove a 20m free into the goalmouth in search of a goal. It was blocked out, but only as far as one of the substitutes, David Crimmins, who reacted immediately, pulled and steered it to the net past a forest of sticks and legs for a single point lead. Six additional minutes had already been played but there was still time for a Mill riposte. A free from the half way line had the distance but not the accuracy as the ball drifted wide of the posts and Drumree had a second intermediate title in less than a decade on a 1-10 to 2-6 scoreline.

The winning team read: Ronan Curley; Ciarán Kenny, Shane Troy, Stephen McGroder; Paul Walsh, Caoimhín King, Johnny Gilsenan, Capt.; Brendan Walsh, Brian Coughlan (0-1); Stephen Doyle (0-8), John Crimmins (0-1), David Wallace; Fearghal Delaney, Christopher Doyle, Liam Shanley. Subs: David Crimmins (1-0) for C Doyle, James Reilly for Delaney, Keith Rooney for Shanley, Daire Flanagan, Paul Kiernan, Robert Lyons, Peter Rattigan, Mark Devanney, Paul Hendrick, Andrew Kiernan, Martin Kelly, Robert Connolly, Brian Kenny, Bill Reilly, Conal O Sullivan, Dermot Doyle, James Gaughan, GT Troy, David Donoghue.

The club added to its list of honours by capturing the Division 2 Hurling League title in 2010 also with victory over Kiltale by 2-6 to 1-6. However, the premier side's hopes of a fruitful Leinster campaign came unstuck when Delvin proved too strong, defeating Drumree by 1-10 to 0-9.

Drumree retained their senior status the following year but ominously failed to record a victory in the 2012 championship. Nevertheless, they avoided the drop for 2013 as Gaeil Colmcille failed to fulfil their relegation refixture with the Drumree men. This merely postponed the inevitable and in 2013 Boardsmill overcame the reds in the relegation play-off.

Back in the lower grade the red and whites were as competitive as ever reaching the 2014 semi-final after a flawless undefeated run through the group stages. A delay in playing the semi didn't help and Kilskrye emerged triumphant leaving Drumree envious bystanders for the final between two sides they had mastered in the group stages.

Results in the 1999-2014 period continued the pattern experienced by Dunshaughlin in the 1980s when teams were always competitive at intermediate level but invariably found the senior grade a bridge too far.

Nevertheless, hope springs eternal and if the club can nurture the players who, in conjunction with Blackhall Gaels, won the Under 21 B championship in 2012 and the A title in 2013, then another tilt at senior status may not be long delayed.

It took two games to separate the protagonists in the 2012 Under 21 final. The first meeting went to extra time after both sides dominated for periods and in the closing minutes Dunderry snatched a late equalizer. A vastly superior Drumree bossed the replay, two days before Christmas, from start to finish, with two goals from James Reilly giving them a comfortable 2-11 to 1-7 victory. The winning team, selected by Daire Flanagan, Christy Mangan, Dermot Doyle, and Ronan Curley, lined out as follows: Paul Kelly; Gavin Byrne, Conor Delany, Co-Capt; Gareth Rooney, Shane Whitty (0-2), Conal O Sullivan, Co-Capt; Stephen Morris, James Rattigan (0-3); Stephen Doyle, Keith Rooney, Colm Whitty (0-2); Niall Mangan, James Reilly (2-0). Subs: David Reilly for Doyle, Niall Kelly for O Sullivan, Brendan O Malley for Mangan, Andrew Kiernan for Byrne.

The 2013 final was an embarrassing farce as final opponents Kiltale declined to field due to the inclusion of two of their players on Summerhill's Leinster club football semi-final panel. Reaching the final of this grade was an achievement in itself and it featured impressive quarter and semi-final victories over the traditional hurling strongholds of Kildalkey and Killyon.

Success on the field has been matched by progress off it. The Community Centre was built in 1988, a juvenile pitch purchased in 2007 and additional facilities were added in 2010 with the establishment of an astro turf training pitch, the erection of a hurling wall and a revised layout for the main pitch.

Hope for the Future

The Drumree club took over responsibility for underage hurling from St. Martins from the beginning of 2009 and has recorded significant successes in recent years. The official launch took place on 21st February in the presence of legendary GAA commentator Micheal Ó Muircheartaigh, Kilkenny's honour laden manager Brian Cody and Liz Howard President of the Camogie Association.

In its first year the club's Under 13s and Under 14s reached finals with the latter grabbing a title when they won the Division 2 championship. It took a titanic struggle at Dunganny to overcome Clann na nGael by 5-8 to 5-7. In a reversal of St. Martins' experience against Kilmessan in 2006, Drumree trailed by seven points in the closing stages. As the game moved into injury time there still remained a gap of two points to be bridged. Then, when it seemed almost too late, Killian Gavin connected with a free from out the field to coolly slot the ball to the net for a point lead and victory. The selectors with the successful squad were Frank Bawle, Eamonn Dunne, Conor Gavin and Martin Wall and the successful side lined out as follows:

Lorcán Casey; Darren Lawless, Diarmuid Christie; David Dunne, Gareth Rooney Capt., Darragh Nolan; Shane Gallogly, David Reilly 0-1; Josh Wall 1-3, Dan Ormsby 0-1, Killian Gavin 1-0; Liam Carey 1-3; David Moore 2-0. Subs: Alan Reilly for Casey, Darragh Walsh for Nolan, Stephen Farrell for Christie, Kevin Madden, Eddie Murphy, James Logan, Aidan McMahon, Andrew Doolan, Senan Ó Muirí.

Two years later many of the same players were on the receiving end of a similar experience in the Under 16 B final. Drumree exploited first half wind assistance to build up a seven-point lead but Rathmolyon gnawed away at the lead during a tense second half equalizing shortly before the final whistle. Drumree again established a lead in extra time but in the final period Rathmolyon leveled and then crept into a two-point lead to emerge with the honours on a 3-16 to 3-14 scoreline. Lorcan Casey, David Reilly, Josh Wall, Shane Gallogly and David Moore, with a massive 1-7, were outstanding for Drumree.

The younger age groups maintained the winning feeling with the Under 12s beating Rathmolyon in the 2011 B Shield final, while a year later the Under 13s again claimed a title when winning the Shield final against Ratoath. The game ended in a welter of excitement as Drumree's lead of a point was twice overtaken with late Ratoath goals and regained on each occasion by similar scores at the other end. Niall Gavin and Paddy Conway snatched the vital late goals in the 3-9 to 2-10 victory. Conor Gavin, Edward O Riordan, Frank Bawle and Willie Hanley managed the following panel: Conor Jones, Conor Moyles, Jamie Rattigan, Liam Hanley, Niall Hurley, Ross McQuillan, Daniel Byrne, Paul Briody, Mathew Costello, David Fildes, Paddy Conway, Kevin Bawle, Pádraig Clinton, Andrew Leneghan, Niall Gavin, Ódhran O Riordan, Jonathan Pearle, Luke Mitchell, Josh Kallides.

The good form continued in 2013 when the Under 12s captured the B title and the Under 13s lost the Division 1 Shield Final. The younger team took the title after a replay, eventually outscoring Kildalkey by 4-11 to 3-7. Ed O Riordan, Martin Wall and John Fraher managed the team.

Minor Successes

2012 brought success at minor level when Drumree with Blackhall assistance took the B title. Drumree had finished as runners-up to Dunderry in the minor league the previous year but this time, after some close calls, they made no mistake. It took a semi-final replay to eliminate Kilmessan and extra time to capture the title against Rathmolyon-Na Fianna. David Reilly's early second-half goal wasn't enough to ensure victory in ordinary time and Shane Whitty had to snatch two late points to force extra time. The scoring form continued after the restart and the team went on to record a three-point victory, 1-16 to 1-13. The winning combination read, Paul Kelly, Darren Lawless, Paddy Smith, Diarmuid Christie, Gareth Rooney, Niall Kelly, Shane Whitty (0-10), David Reilly (1-3), Philip Carey, Seán Gavin, Josh Wall (0-2), Shane McGuinness, Liam Carey (0-1). Subs: Killian Gavin for McGuinness, Hugh Smith for Carey, Shane Gallogly for Sean Gavin, Colin Farrell, Darragh Walsh, Fergus Ryan, Pádraig Keane.

In 2013 the club participated in Division 1, reaching the Shield final where neighbours Ratoath were steamrolled into submission by 1-15 to 1-6. Victory for the Drumree/Blackhall combination was rarely in doubt as David Reilly gave an imposing display ably assisted by Niall Kelly, Diarmuid Christie, Liam Carey and Darragh Walsh. The winning combination read: Paul Kelly; Darren Lawless, Diarmuid Christie Capt., Killian Gavin; Fergus Ryan, Gareth Rooney, Alan Reilly; Josh Wall, Niall Kelly; Liam Carey, David Reilly, Darragh Walsh; Eddie Murphy, Hugh Smith, Andrew Doolan.

These results, and the fact that three Drumree players, David Reilly, Josh Wall and Gareth Rooney, made the Meath panel that lost out to Kerry in the All-Ireland Minor B final are positive pointers for the future. They indicate that there is enough talent emerging from the underage ranks to ensure that the parish continues to maintain a vibrant hurling presence at under age and adult level.

Three decades have now elapsed since the revival of the Dunshaughlin hurling club in 1982, and that represents the longest uninterrupted period of hurling in the parish since the formation of the GAA.

Appendix 4
Handball

GAA Handball Convention, 1931
Group pictured at the GAA Handball Convention in Navan on 8th February 1931 includes at the rear, 2nd from left, Paddy Kenny and 7th from left Thomas McClorey, both Dunshaughlin.

Handball was included in the G.A.A. Charter of 1884 as one of the sports to be promoted by the new Association but it did not become a priority for the GAA until the 1920s. Some of the games in the early years involved substantial side bets, particularly between champions of Ireland and the USA and in 1912 a meeting was convened that set up the Irish Handball Association 'to control amateur and professional handball.' It seems not to have had much impact.

Handball must have been flourishing in the Dunshaughlin-Drumree area in the early years of the twentieth century. *The Meath Chronicle* records a number of handball tournaments in Drumree in 1913 with sets of medals for the victors. Bill Doran, father of Christy 'Toes' Doran, and Willie Daly, who won senior hurling medals with Dunshaughlin in 1909 and 1910, defeated Jack Carty of Drumree and Michael Duffy. In the junior final N Smith and J Duffy beat P Kenny and P O Brien. Kenny may have been Peter from Roestown, Mickey's father, while there were a number of P O Briens in the area at the time, including a Patrick in Roestown, another in Readsland and a third, from Cork, who was a boarder in Gogans. Reference has been made in Chapter 4 to Paddy Kenny winning a handball tournament while in Kilmainham Gaol in 1921.

In the 1920s and 1930s there were two separate organizations claiming to speak for handball. The older was the Irish Amateur Handball Union (IAHU) and Dr. PJ Cusack of Nobber was its Treasurer initially and later its President. The

Leinster Council of the GAA eventually set up a provincial handball council in May 1923 and the following year a national organization was formed, the Irish Amateur Handball Association (IAHA). John Lawlor was its first President, with a Vice-President from each province. Two Dunshaughlin men, Thomas McClorey and Paddy Kenny represented Meath at the founding meeting. The organizations disagreed on a number of issues with the Irish Amateur Handball Union (IAHU), having a less restrictive attitude to foreign games than the GAA inspired IAHA.

Dr Cusack frequently berated the GAA for its lack of support for handball. In a letter to *The Irish Independent* in December 1923 he asserted that

'Since the foundation of the GAA forty years ago I find nothing to show that the Association did anything to encourage handball. The handball history of those years is one of sordid professionalism. One leading player challenged another for a stake of anything from £10 to £100. The loser was invariably dissatisfied, unpleasant incidents frequently arose, and an acrimonious and unsportsmanlike press controversy ensued.'

The IAHU was strong in north Meath. In 1924 Nobber, Kilmainhamwood, Crossakiel, Drumconrath, Tankardstown, Edengora, Kells and Oldcastle were affiliated to the organization. Cusack, as President of the IAHU, met General Eoin O Duffy, then President of the IAHA, in 1924, aiming to resolve the conflict between the organizations. O Duffy promised to do what he could to have the rule on the playing of 'foreign games' altered but no change occurred. The IAHU remained in existence until 1936 and the period 1927-36 was a time of great enthusiasm for the game as both organizations promoted it with numerous tournaments throughout the country.

Prior to the meeting to establish the GAA-inspired IAHA a Meath Handball Board was set up in early 1923 and Cusack was its President. It seems likely therefore, that it was affiliated to the IAHU. An opinion piece in *The Meath Chronicle* in 1924 stated that, *'As far as Meath is concerned the handball Union appears to have the greatest appeal, the GAA gaining but little support.'* The 1923 finals were played in Drumree and JJ Wildridge was one of the leading lights in the club.

The formation of a handball club in Dunshaughlin in 1924 is probably linked to the establishment of the IAHA. The officers of the Dunshaughlin club in 1924 were President: Senator Michael Duffy, Vice-President: Mickey Carberry, Treasurer: T. Gleason, possibly from Co. Tipperary, Secretary: Paddy 'Racker' Kenny. As recorded in Chapter 4, the GAA club's fundraising tournament of 1923-24 provided some of the funds to erect a handball alley on the Dublin side of the Garda Barracks. This was an open three-sided structure, with the back wall against the gable end of the barracks and two tapering wing walls, level with the

Drumree Handball Alley
The now derelict Drumree alley pictured in 2013.

wall plate of the barracks at their highest point.

PJ Mulvany, a Farmers' Party TD from 1923 to 1927, who owned what is now Kealy's farm in Ballinlough on the Dublin Road and also auctioned cattle at the rear of Maddens, presided at the official opening of the alley on Sunday 3rd August 1930. Other speakers included JT Skelly, the County Handball Secretary and Seán O Hanlon, the Chairman of the International Handball Association. A game involving Meath and Dublin teams followed. Press reports described the alley as one of the best three walled alleys in the country, built with the co-operation of members of the Dunshaughlin club and the Garda Síochána.

Garda involvement in handball was a common feature at the time. General Eoin O Duffy, who was Commissioner of the Garda Síochána between 1922 and 1933, encouraged athletes to join the Gardaí and had handball courts erected near Garda stations throughout the country. Even prior to independence handball was popular among the police, one reason being that, while the GAA could refuse to admit police to the organization, it couldn't prevent them playing on their own property.

The week after the official opening there was a tournament with gold medals for a boys' under 17 competition, while later in the month Edward Fitzgerald and Willie Gilsenan, of Drumree, qualified to meet Kells in a county final after defeating Paddy Kenny and Mick Clusker. *The Drogheda Independent* described Clusker as one of Meath's oldest handballers, whose '*hard hitting was a treat to see, and his good killing created rounds of applause.*'

Kells emerged victorious after two hours of play, four games to three, but Drumree had thirty-one aces more on the incredible scoreline of 21-19, 5-21, 21-17, 2-21, 6-21, 21-15, 21-14. Fitzgerald then faced Paddy Bell of Kells in the junior softball finals but had to retire when 2-1 down due to the exertions of the two games. Bell magnanimously agreed to a refixture starting from scratch but the outcome is not recorded. Bell was a top handball player, winning All-Ireland double titles for Meath with Joe Doyle as his partner, in 1932, 1933 and 1935.

Handball was popular in Drumree at this time also. In 1932 a meeting convened in Drumree attempted to set up a South Meath Handball Board. The Secretary of the Central Handball Council, Seán O Hanlon, attended and Thomas Geraghty of Drumree presided. JP Cullen and JJ Wildridge represented Drumree with Paddy Kenny and Paddy Duffy in attendance on behalf of Dunshaughlin. The suggestion of a board in the south of the county implies that clubs there believed that the existing structures favoured teams from the north of the county. The Drumree meeting was informed that there were six clubs in south Meath but no

Dunshaughlin Handball Alley, 1960s
Raymond Morgan and John Casey in action at one of the Sunday morning games.
Pictures courtesy of the Morgan family.

competitions apart from those for two sets of medals presented by Fr. Patrick Murphy, the local PP.

During the 1930s handball had a high profile nationally and this was equally true in Meath. However, with the outbreak of war in 1939 the game seems to have declined and to have taken a back seat to football and hurling in the parish. The handball alley in Dunshaughlin still stood so the game was not entirely moribund. Locals recall the then Garda Sergeant, Dan O Connell, locking the alley at one stage during the 1950s. One day Fr. Ulick F. Kyne, the Catholic curate, was driving past when he saw some young lads loitering outside the alley and said, 'It's a shame for ye to be standing around outside instead of being inside playing handball.' When they explained that the alley was locked he sent Benny Foley away for a hammer to force the lock and another lad into the barracks to complain. The Sergeant appeared and unlocked the gate with Fr. Kyne's instructions ringing in his ears, 'As long as I'm here you're never to lock it again!'

There was a mini revival of the game in the 1950s. A Meath Handball Board was established in 1957 and Dunshaughlin's most notable exponent of the game was Seán Kenny who won the Meath senior singles title in that year. The club's own finals in 1957 resulted in Jimmy Geraghty and Larry O Brien beating Seán Kenny and Ben Lynam in the seniors and Christy Foley and J Murphy beating Matt Daly and Tommy Nugent in the junior event. Newspaper reports indicate that the first inter-club handball games *'for many years'* were played in the alley on Sunday 24th March 1957. The officers of the club were Honorary President: Rev. Ulick F. Kyne, Chairman: Mickey Carberry, Vice Chairman: Patsy McLoughlin,

Dunshaughlin Handball League Draws, 1974

```
Dunshaughlin Handball                    League '74.

   Division 1              Division 11.                  Division 111

J. Casey   and L. Carey   C. Donnelly and P.J. Rourke    P. Carthy   and  D. Dwyer
S. Kenny    "  D. Kenny   J. Browne    "  J. Carberry    J. Murphy   and  S. Gillic
S. Burke    "  S. Lynch   C. Dwyer     "  P. Devanney    J. Sullivan  "   S. Mangan
P. Burke    "  P. Kenny   P. Dwyer     "  C. Coady       G. Dowd      "   M. Mangan
S. Burke    "  D. McLoughlin  C. Mc Carthy "  B. O'Mahoney  F. Durcan    "   T. Carty
T. Mc Carthy and L. Morgan   R. Morgan    "  J. Walsh      J. Lynch     "   M. Delaney
T. Walshe and Sgt. Mc Gee.   B. Johnson   "  P. O'Brien    P. Blake     "   John Dwyer
P. Delaney and V. Dowd.      N. Mangan    "  P. Kenny      B. Murphy    "   M. Dwyer

      Commencing:  17th February, 1974.

Each team has to play seven games of 20 minutes each game and will be required to play every second
Sunday.   Team not turning up for game loses points.    Winners will be decided on the overall
score of the whole league.

      Fee:  10p per game.
      Annual Subs:  £1 due before 1st of April, 1974.
```

Secretary: Matt Daly and Treasurer: Benny Foley. The committee comprised Seán Kenny, Ernest Kenny, Pat Delany and Walter Smyth.

There is occasional reference to handball during the 1960s, for example in 1963 Seán Kenny again won the Meath senior singles title beating Francis McGovern of Kells.

In the 1970s the club had its most successful period ever. That revival started with lads playing informally, usually on Sunday mornings. Among those involved were Christy McCarthy, Tommy Stoney, Pat Delany, Tommy McCarthy and Tommy Walsh who was a member of the Garda Band and the Graduates Showband. Brendan McEntaggart, senior, donated money to help re-establish the club.

The person most associated with the revival was Stephen Burke. A native of Tourmakeady, Co. Mayo, his family moved to Curraghtown in the late 1950s and while he was a useful player himself his chief contribution was in the area of nurturing young talent in conjunction with Seán Kenny. No records remain of the founding officers but among those who served the club were John O Sullivan, Mick O Brien, Tommy McCarthy, John Murphy and Jim Smith as Chairmen, John Murphy as Deputy Vice Chairman, Thomas Delany, Mick O Brien, Christy McCarthy and Brendan Murphy as Secretary while Leonard Morgan, John O Sullivan and Brendan Murphy were among those who acted as Treasurer. Seán Kenny, 1972-73 and John O Sullivan, 1984, were also Chairmen of the County Hand Ball Board. Stephen Burke was for many years the face of Meath handball, initially as Treasurer, 1976-80, and especially as Secretary and Public Relations Officer from 1980 until 1985. He also served on the National Development Committee and refereed the All-Ireland senior singles and senior doubles finals in 1979. On his resignation as Secretary in 1985 he received a standing ovation from the Handball Convention and was elected a President of the Board in recognition of his contribution to the organization.

All who knew Stephen Burke attest to his prowess as an organizer. He drove players to tournaments in all corners of the country, visited houses and farmyards during the week to inform players of events and booked the courts in Croke Park and Gormanston for practice games. He did some coaching, but his main focus was to ensure that conditions were right for players to develop and improve. As noted earlier the Dunshaughlin alley was initially a three-sided structure whereas many of the alleys were four sided or box alleys. Without the four walls the ball could shoot out the rear of the court and players spent as much time chasing it as they did playing.

Stephen was working in the alley one day, when local curate Fr. Cassidy came in. 'What's going on?' enquired the curate to which Stephen replied,

'We're looking to put a back wall on it.'

'And what are you waiting for?' asked Fr. Cassidy.

'The only thing that's holding us up is the cost of blocks,' said Stephen. 'I'd lay them and plaster it myself.'

Fr. Cassidy retorted, 'Go and order the blocks now, and worry about paying for them later. Possession is nine points of the law.'

The blocks were ordered and the money to pay for them came in and soon the alley had its extra wall. It also contained a viewing platform. Brendan O Mahony, a Dublin solicitor and President of the club, funded a net, while Christy McCarthy provided cleats to attach the net to the walls. With the additional facilities handball got more serious and tournaments could be played. Sunday competitions were very popular, starting around midday and continuing until evening. Locals recall it as 'black with people,' with large numbers of participants and spectators. Games were generally doubles. Players were grouped into two sets, an A and a B group, with a random draw to pair an A player and a B player to make a doubles team to play another A and B combination. Players competed for various trophies including the Benny Foley Memorial Cup, and *The Top House* Trophy sponsored by Murt Leonard initially, and later Bertie Donnelly. *The Top House* is now *An Síbín*.

All-Ireland Champions

All-Ireland Colleges Under 17 Champions 1981, Michael McGovern, Kells, and Jim Smith.

More formal leagues with teams placed in Divisions were also organized. A 1974 league consisted of three divisions with forty-eight players in total. Each doubles pairing had seven games over a number of Sundays with games of twenty minutes duration and the fee was 10 pence [13c] per game.

This was the prelude to a period of extraordinary success for the club. At adult and juvenile level club members regularly won county, provincial and national titles. The following gives a sample of the achievements.

The most successful handballer from the club was Egin Jensen. The son of Maura Murphy and Hans Jensen, he was born in Dublin but moved to Dunshaughlin when he was ten. He went on to capture titles at all grades, including All Irelands in the Under 15 singles in 1980; Under 18 Colleges' title and an Under 17 Colleges' doubles title, partnered by Ronan Morris, both with Trim CBS in 1982; Minor softball doubles with Christy McGovern of Kells in 1981 and Minor hardball doubles with Ronan Morris in 1982; Under 21 Softball Singles in 1985 and 1986. He also represented Ireland in the Under 23 World championships in Canada in 1986. In 1987 he won the All-Ireland Junior title. The victory was unusual as it took two days to decide. The game had to be stopped due to condensation on the Croke Park court with the players tied on one set each, and in the final set a fortnight later Jensen edged out Billy McCarthy of Tipperary 21-19. When the Dunshaughlin club became defunct Jensen continued to play and still competes competitively in Dublin. In partnership with Eoin Kennedy he won three consecutive All-Ireland doubles in 2005-07 and 2009-11 and took the Silver Masters A singles and doubles titles at the world championships in Dublin in 2012.

Paul O Rourke, who has club championship medals in football and hurling also, won a number of Leinster and All-Ireland doubles titles, invariably in partnership with David Gough, a Navan native but a member of Dunshaughlin Handball Club. He won Leinster and All-Ireland championships in the following grades- doubles: Under 13 in 1982, Under 14 in 1983, Under 16 in 1985 and Minor 40 x 20 in 1987 against Limerick. He was also runner up in the All-Ireland 60 x 30 doubles, both hardball and softball in 1987. Later in the same year, 1987, Paul displayed his incredible versatility, winning a minor football championship with St. Martins-Ratoath and an intermediate hurling championship with Dunshaughlin, the former as a forward and the latter as a back.

In 1981 he and David Gough took the Under 12 Leinster 40 x 20 doubles title but the championship didn't continue to All-Ireland level while he was also a member of the Dunshaughlin Community Games team that won the Leinster Under 15 title and the runners-up spot at All-Ireland level. His team mates were David Gough, Gary Daly, Vincent Moore, Stephen Harkin and Aidan Devanney.

Membership List 1981
Some of the membership of Dunshaughlin Handball club as recorded in 1981.

Certificate presented by Meath Handball Board to Seán Joyce to mark his part in Dunshaughlin Handball Club's All-Ireland Junior title in 1987.

BLACK & AMBER

All-Ireland Handball medal won by Dunshaughlin. The inscription on the rear of the medal reads Novice Inter Club 1982.

All-Ireland Handball medal won by Dunshaughlin. The inscription on the rear of the medal reads Comortas Idir Chlub J, 40x20 1987.

Jim Smith, Chairman of Dunshaughlin GAA Club from 2005-13 became the first player from Dunshaughlin to win an All-Ireland title when he partnered Michael McGovern of Kells to the All-Ireland Under 16 Colleges' title in 1977, defeating Sligo in the final, 13-15, 15-0, 15-7. The same pair repeated the achievement with the Minor Doubles in 1979, beating Mayo in the final 21-11, 21-8.

The 1980s was the most successful period ever for the club as members took numerous county titles and were also successful at provincial and national level. The absence of detailed records precludes a comprehensive listing of titles but Dunshaughlin won thirteen of the twenty-six Meath titles in 1982 while the list for 1985 gives a flavour of the level of success achieved by the club. All-Ireland 40 x 20 titles were captured by Egin Jensen in the Under 21 singles, and Paul O Rourke and David Gough in the Under 16 doubles. Jensen took a Leinster singles title, and a doubles crown at Under 21 level, partnered by Ronan Morris. The club took six titles at county level, Senior B Doubles, Christy McCarthy and John Casey; Masters Doubles, Christy McCarthy and Seamus Magee; Intermediate Doubles, Egin Jensen and Michael O Brien; Junior Singles, Ronan Morris; Minor Doubles, Brendan O Rourke and David Gough; Intermediate 60 x 30 Singles, Egin Jensen.

Success at individual events was embellished by outstanding performances in All-Ireland team events. After a Leinster final defeat to Ballymore-Eustace in 1981 the club went on to capture the All-Ireland Novice competition the following year. The arrival of Pat 'Yank' Murphy was a huge boost to the club. He was a native of Cork who had spent some time in Boston before settling in Rathbeggan. He brought American self-belief and did some coaching also. Murphy always led off in the singles and remained unbeaten throughout the competition. He was followed by the outstanding doubles partnership of the left-handed Johnny Burke and right-handed Eamonn Donovan who complemented each other perfectly. Seán Joyce had the onerous task of anchoring the team in the final singles. The team had a convincing semi-final win against Capwell from Cork 122 to 115 and finished up easy winners in the final against Mayo opposition Newport, by 136 to 113.

Five years later the club stepped up a level, winning the All-Ireland Junior Club 40 x 20 championship. The team defeated Kells in the Leinster semi-final and then O Loughlins of Kilkenny in the final before overcoming Gael Uladh in the All-Ireland semi at Warrenstown, 126-98. Fermoy provided formidable opposition in a thrilling All-Ireland decider. Hero Egin Jensen went into the final singles match needing to wipe out a twenty-six point deficit. An incredible display culminated in a 21-7, 21-7 win to give Dunshaughlin a narrow 110-107 victory. Ronan Morris, David Gough and Seán Joyce were the other team members with Ollie Gough as reserve. Two All-Ireland team titles in half a decade was a tremendous achievement for a club so recently established.

The club was ahead of its time in catering for girls with a team taking part in the Community Games Under 15 event in 1983 consisting of Eilish O Sullivan, Rachel Delany, Mary O Sullivan and Louise O Rourke.

The extension to the alley was demolished in 1984 but it continued in use in subsequent years with £1,075 expended on sandblasting the facility in late 1985. The club later transferred much of its activity to Warrenstown as the condition of the Dunshaughlin site deteriorated, and, as it was outdoors it could not be used for much of the winter. In its heyday the club was extremely successful as the number of titles won attests. Its annual dinner dances were held mainly in the *County Club* and attracted up to two hundred patrons. The club rarely had less than forty paid-up members, often many more, a figure the football club struggled to achieve.

However, when decline set in, it was rapid. In the late 1980s Stephen Burke transferred much of his energies into the football club and umpiring at games for Paddy O Dwyer and Jim Smith. Many of the adult players retired and when the successful underage players like Paul O Rourke, Egin Jensen and Ronan Morris moved on there was no one to coach the next generation. Over time the condition of the alley deteriorated and it was eventually demolished and when the refurbished Garda Barracks was reopened in 2001 there was no alley attached.

The listing that follows is not comprehensive, as poor record keeping and uncertain memories prevented this. Newspaper coverage was intermittent and when details were carried it was often unclear if results were those of finals or earlier round games. Most of those listed below have been established with a reasonable degree of certainty. Where the year is uncertain n.d., meaning not dated, indicates this. There are, without doubt, many omissions but the details given provide, at least, a baseline for future research.

Summary of Handball Honours Won

All-Ireland and Provincial Honours

Paul O Rourke and David Gough

Leinster U-12 Doubles, 1981; All-Ireland and Leinster U-13 Doubles, 1982; All-Ireland and Leinster U-14 Doubles 1983; All-Ireland and Leinster Under 16 Doubles 1985; All-Ireland and Leinster Minor Doubles 40 x 20, 1987; Leinster 60 x 30 Minor Doubles 1987.

Egin Jensen

All-Ireland and Leinster U-15 Singles 1980. All-Ireland and Leinster Colleges Singles, representing Trim CBS, 1982. All-Ireland and Leinster U-21 Singles, 1985, 1986 1987. All-Ireland and Leinster Junior softball, 1987, the first Meath player to win this title. All-Ireland and Leinster Junior 40 x 20 Singles, 1989. All-Ireland Inter Varsity team championship with UCD 1989. Egin later joined the Kells Club and won All-Ireland doubles titles when partnered with Tom Sheridan in the 1990s. He later settled in Dublin and combined with Eoin Kennedy in 2005 to win the All-Ireland in both 40 x 20 and 60 x 30 events. The pair went on to win further All-Ireland softball titles in 2006, 2007, 2009, 2010 and 2011 alongside numerous Dublin titles. He also won Silver Masters A singles and doubles, 2012.

Egin Jensen and Ronan Morris

All-Ireland and Leinster Colleges U-17 Doubles, representing Trim CBS, 1981; All-Ireland and Leinster Minor Hardball Doubles, 1982, 1983; Leinster U-21 Doubles 1985; U-21 Doubles, 1986.

Egin Jensen and Christy McGovern (Kells)

All-Ireland and Leinster Minor SB Doubles, 1981.

David Gough, see above with Paul O Rourke

Also: All-Ireland and Leinster U-21 60 x 30 Doubles with Declan McDonnell, Kells, 1988; All-Ireland and Leinster U-21 Singles, 1989; All-Ireland and Leinster U-21 Doubles with Joe Lynch, Kells, 1989; All-Ireland and Leinster U-21 60 x 30 Doubles with Joe Lynch, Kells, 1989.

Pat 'Yank' Murphy

Leinster Masters' Singles 1983.

Jim Smith and Michael McGovern (Kells)

All-Ireland and Leinster U-16 Doubles 1977. This was the first ever All-Ireland title won by a member of Dunshaughlin Handball Club. All-Ireland and Leinster Minor Hardball Doubles 1979.

Team Winners
Leinster Juvenile League, 1977

Michael O Brien and Niall McCarthy were part of the winning Meath team.

Leinster Juvenile League, 1980

Niall McCarthy, Egin Jensen and Shane Holland were part of the winning Meath team.

All-Ireland and Leinster Novice Inter-Club Winners, 1982

Team: Pat Murphy (Singles), Eamonn Donovan and Johnny Burke (Doubles), Seán Joyce (Singles), Ollie Gough (Reserve). The team beat Capwell from Cork 122 to 115 in the semi-final and Newport from Mayo in the final by 136 to 113.

All-Ireland and Leinster Junior Inter-Club 40 x 20, Winners, 1987

Team: Seán Joyce, Ronan Morris, David Gough, Egin Jensen, Ollie Gough. The team beat Gael Uladh 126-98 in the semi-final and Fermoy in the final, 110-107.

Leinster Community Games U-15 Winners and All-Ireland Runners Up, 1983

Team: Paul O Rourke, Gary Daly, David Gough, Vincent Moore, Stephen Harkin, Aidan Devanney, Trevor Conroy.

County Championship Winners

Singles

Senior Singles: Seán Kenny 1957, 1963; Egin Jensen 1989.
Senior B, first held in 1985: Thomas Delany, 1987.
Intermediate Singles: Thomas Delany, 1982; Matt McEntaggart 1983; Egin Jensen, 60 x 30, 1985; Thomas McCarthy, n.d. Gerry Flanagan, n.d.
Junior Singles: Johnny Burke, 60 x 30, 1981; Dónal Wall, 1983; Matt McEntaggart, 40 x 20, 1983; Ronan Morris, 1985; Thomas McCarthy, n.d.
Novice Singles: Johnny Burke 1981; Paul Devanney, 60 x 30, 1981; Matt McEntaggart 1982.
Masters Singles: Pat Murphy, 1983; Ollie Gough 1987; John Casey, 1990, 1991.
Minor Singles: Egin Jensen 1982; David Gough, 1987.

Doubles

Senior Doubles: Seán Joyce and John 'Boy' Molloy (Kells) 1981.
Senior B Doubles: John Casey and Christy McCarthy, 1985; Egin Jensen and David Gough 1989.
Intermediate Doubles: John Casey and Paddy Burke, 1976; Johnny Burke and Eamonn Donovan, 1982; Oliver Gough and Jim Smith, hardball, 1982; Egin Jensen and Michael O Brien, 1985; Christy McCarthy and Thomas Delany n.d.
Junior Doubles: Thomas Delany and Christy McCarthy 1981; Michael O Brien and Matt McEntaggart 1982; Brendan O Rourke and John Murphy, 1987.

Masters Doubles

Séamus Magee and Seán Kenny, 1977; Oliver Gough and Christy McCarthy, n.d.; Seamus Magee and Christy McCarthy, 1985; John Casey and Christy McCarthy, 1987, 1989.

Minor Doubles

Don McLoughlin and Paddy Kenny, 1971; Egin Jensen and Niall McCarthy, 1981; Egin Jensen and Brendan O Rourke, 60 x 30, 1981; Ronan Morris and Brendan O Rourke, 1982; Ronan Morris and Seán O Connor, hardball, 1982; Egin Jensen and Ronan Morris, 1983; David Gough and Brendan O Rourke, 1985; Paul O Rourke and David Gough 1986; Paul O Rourke and Derek Jones, 1987.

Novice Doubles

Stephen Burke and Oliver Gough, 1975; Eamonn Donovan and Dónal Wall 1981; Matt McEntaggart, no record of partner, 1980; Eamonn Donovan and Thomas Delany, 60 x 30, 1981; John Murphy and John O Brien, 1983; Thomas Byrne and Noel Devanney, 1988; Christy McCarthy and John Murphy, n.d.; Christy McCarthy and Stephen Burke, 60 x30, n.d.

Clubmen as County Officers

County Chairman:	Seán Kenny 1972-73
	John Sullivan 1984
Vice Chairman:	Con Kenny 1968
Secretary and PRO:	Stephen Burke 1976-80
Treasurer:	Stephen Burke 1976-80
Nat. Dev.Comm:	Stephen Burke 1982-85

Dunshaughlin Handball Club Officers, 1988

The last recorded set of officers of the Handball Club dates to the AGM of 29th April 1988 and they were as follows:

Chairman:	Tommy McCarthy
Vice Chairman:	John Murphy
Secretary:	Christy McCarthy and Michael O Brien
Treasurer:	Brendan Murphy
Committee:	Officers plus Seán Joyce and John Casey

Appendix 5
Camogie

Meath has a long camogie tradition and the first recorded game of camogie in Ireland was played in Navan on July 17th 1904. The contest featured two Dublin teams, Keatings and Cuchullains. Both clubs had their origin in the Gaelic League branches of the same names and Keatings drew up the first set of rules for camogie in 1903. The Navan Branch of the Gaelic League organized the game and it ended in a one goal to no score victory for Keatings. However, the sport didn't expand very much, either in Meath or Dublin, in the years that followed.

Efforts were made to reestablish a national camogie association in 1911 and Elizabeth, Countess of Fingall, of Killeen Castle outside Dunshaughlin, acted as President. Her role was nominal only, but it gave the association recognition and status. Teams were established in Dunsany and Kilmessan and Lady Fingall assigned a playing pitch on her land and paid for two dozen hurleys and two balls. A Meath side, selected from the Killeen and Dunboyne teams took part in what were described as championships in 1915 in Jones' Road, now Croke Park. Admission was 4 old pence and a special train from Navan calling at Drumree, was laid on to ferry supporters to the contests. Meath played Dublin North with Louth meeting Dublin South. Meath lost out on a scoreline of 1-2 to 0-1 but no team details are available.

In the early 1920s Pelletstown's delegate to the Meath GAA Board, JJ Wildridge, proposed the establishment of a camogie league on at least two occasions and his ideas had some impact, as in September 1923 the camogie clubs set up a county camogie committee. South Meath, and in particular Kilmessan, seems to have been at the heart of the revival. Both Dunshaughlin and Culmullen fielded teams and competed in the leagues for a time, while there were also teams in Greenpark, Rathfeigh, Dunsany, Kilcarty and Oberstown. By the end of the decade the organization appears to have flagged and a revival in the early 1930s was initially north Meath based, with regular meetings in Crossakiel.

By the mid 1930s there were numerous clubs in the county, among them Trim, Kentstown, Clonee, Athboy, Martry, Moynalty, Navan, Dunderry, Bellaney, Oristown, Seymourstown, Boyerstown, Maperath, Dulane, Kilallon and Knocklough. In 1934 Dunshaughlin was placed in a division with Dunboyne, Ratoath, Donaghmore, Ashbourne, Kilcloon and Curraha and a report on a 1933 game against Colvinstown lists Mary Kenny, Elsie Clusker, Bridie Kenny and Sarah Tuite, with Rita Darby in goals, on the Dunshaughlin team. A writer in the *Meath Chronicle* at this time offered the view that there were more camogie

Culmullen Camogie Team, 1945

Front: Kathleen Sullivan, Nancy Byrne, Patty Blount, Maisie Bannon, Tiny Smyth, Rosie Byrne, Úna Englishby.
Back Rows, Ladies only: May Blount, Maeve Crosbie, Eithne Crosbie, Clair Bannon, Mollie Malone, Peg Cummins, Bridie Durnin.
Back Rows, Men only: Bill Leonard, Bill Malone, Willie O Neill, Tom Malone, Patsy Mooney, Patsy Crosbie.

Plaque unveiled outside Páirc Tailteann on 17th July 2004 to mark the 100th anniversary of Ireland's first ever camogie match. The game between Dublin clubs Keatings and Cúchulainns was played in Navan on 17th July 1904.

Dunshaughlin Vocational School Camogie Team, 1942

Front: Seán O Brien, Maura Faherty, Ciarán Leahy, Principal of the school.
Middle: May Reilly, Claire Bannon, __ O Byrne, Patty Blount, Tiny Smith, Betty Hughes, Dina Downes, Maureen Manning.
Back: Bernadette O Connell, Carmel O Connell, , Not identified, Maureen Carberry, Vera Clusker, Elsie Clusker, Mairéad O Brien, Maggie Crocock, Mary Rourke, Ita Fleming.
Man in hat at rear: Ciarán O Connell, former Principal of the school.

Meath Camogie Team 1951, with three players from Dunshaughlin who played with other clubs as there was no camogie club in Dunshaughlin at the time, Bernadette Kenny, Patricia Kenny and Ger O Brien. The Condons were sisters of Colm Condon who played for Dunshaughlin, had a central role in Dunshaughlin's appearance at Leinster Council prior to the 1950 Junior final, see Chapter 5, and was Irish Attorney General 1965-73.
Front: Connie McDonnell, Delia Murphy, Ger O Brien.
Middle: Bernadette Condon, Ettie Kearns, Aileen Kearns, Agnes Murphy, Maureen Kearns.
Back: Bernadette Kenny, Úna Murphy, Maureen McMahon, Patricia Kenny, Máire Durnin, Mir Condon, Dell Condon.

clubs than hurling clubs in Meath.

Press reports on games were uncommon, but, in 1934 Dunshaughlin defeated Dunboyne by 3-0 to 2-0 in what was described as a *'strenuous game.'* Dunshaughlin's best were Misses Kenny, Julia Brennan and Sheila Murray. Kentstown, one of the strongest teams at the time, defeated Dunshaughlin by three goals to two with the losers showing *'the cailíní of that district could handle a camán as well as the menfolk.'* Their mentors were two men with long experience of Dunshaughlin hurling, Mick Clusker and Paddy Kenny. It is not clear how long the team lasted but many camogie sides tended to fold once some of their members married and this may have happened in Dunshaughlin's case.

The next reference to camogie in the parish is in the mid forties when the club was known as St. Patrick's Camogie Club. Prior to that a Dunshaughlin Feis was held in 1943 and 1944 and Dunshaughlin played Ashbourne in a camogie tournament, losing on both occasions. The officers in 1947 were, President: Miss Maureen Carberry, Secretary and Treasurer: Miss Mary Rourke, Captain: Mrs Rosie Moore. The club probably benefitted from the work done in the Vocational School where teachers like Maura Faherty and Ciarán Leahy promoted the sport. In 1942, school teams had wins against Athboy and Navan, the latter by five goals to three with the *Meath Chronicle* reporting that Miss Faherty's side showed careful training and deserved their victory.

In 1945 a St. Patrick's side defeated Dowdstown in the final of a medal tournament in the Vocational School's sportsfield, by 7-0 to 5-0. The field was located on the Dublin side of Dunshaughlin Workhouse. Mentioned as prominent were Mrs. Ben Lynam, Rosie Lynam (Mrs Moore), Nancy O Brien and Doreen Darby (Mrs. Ned Young). The club appears not to have survived into the 1950s- many of those involved played for Ratoath instead. Gertrude O Brien went on to play for Meath and Leinster though just a young teenager.

There was a Culmullen team during the 1940s, but it seems its activities were confined to sports' days and challenge games. An encounter between the Culmullen and Dunshaughlin ladies at a Kilcock sports' day concluded with clashes between the players and widespread brawling. At a challenge between the sides shortly after in Duffy's field hostilities continued, with verbal retorts and physical challenges the order of the day.

Tradition locally states that among those who played in the 1940s and 1950s, married name in brackets, -some mentioned previously-, were Gertrude O Brien (Mrs. Maher, The Bush), May Brien (Mrs. Hoey), Nuala O Brien (Mrs. Owens), Pauline Brien, Carmel Clarke (Mrs. Mitten), Angela Clusker (Mrs. Johnny McLoughlin), Vera Clusker (Mrs. Paddy Dillon), Eithne Crosby (Mrs. Tommy Hetherington), Maeve Crosby (Mrs. Jack Lambe), Bernadette Darby, Cecilia Darby

(Mrs. O Grady), Rita Darby (Mrs. Paddy Lynam), Esther Dowd (Mrs. Pat Farrell), Patsy Flynn (Mrs. Vincent Teeling), Kathy Gogan (Mrs. Willie Madden), Betty Hughes, (Mrs Peter O Brien), Bernadette Kenny (Mrs Brendan O Farrell), Bree Kenny (Mrs. Joe Curry), Fionnuala Kenny, Kathy Kenny (Mrs. Healy), Patricia Kenny (Mrs. Micheal O Brien), Sheila Kenny, Cecilia Lee, Maura Mangan, Nancy Mangan (Mrs. Michael Glennon), Nuala Mangan (Mrs. Paddy Wall, Navan), Kathy McClorey (Mrs. Packie Dixon), Imelda McEntaggart (Mrs. Tony McNally), Kathleen McLoughlin (Mrs. Jack McDonnell), Phil McLoughlin (Mrs. Ronan Cook), Rosie Parr, May Reilly, Nancy Sullivan (Mrs. Martin Lynskey), Kathleen Toole. The trainers in the 1940s were Harry Tugwell and Tom Kenny while practice and games were held in Paddy Duffy's field beside the Workhouse, Jimmy Tallon's field and Goose Park, at the rear of Sherry Property Advisers facing Greenane.

Meath reached the Leinster final in 1951 after a convincing victory over Laois in the semi-final. However, the Royal ladies were no match for an outstanding Dublin team that featured Kathleen Mills, who went on to win a record fifteen senior All-Ireland medals. The Royals suffered a severe setback when losing by

St. Martins, Camogie Team 2008

Front: Charlotte Lord, Áine Lawless, Conor Lawless, Sonia Leonard, Kate Brady, Megan O Reilly, Isabelle Lord, Lara Reynolds.
Back: Treasa Murphy, Orla Bannon, Ava O Brien, Latisha Rattigan, Orlagh Keane, Ciara Galvin, Natasha Rattigan, Evelyn Watté, Caitlin Power-King.

Drumree, Under 16B Camogie Champions, 2013

Front: Rebecca Farrell, Aisling Moyles, Liadan O Riordan, Brona Gavin, Chloe Mahon, Siobhán Whitty, Saoirse Carey, Orlaith Moyles, Éabha Ryan, Aisling Maye.
Back: Sabrina Kelly, Sorcha Casey, Beibhinn O Hora, Ruth Byrne, Niamh Gallogly, Alannah Chalkley, Juliette Wall, Ciara Jones, Hayley Reynolds, Caoimhe Rooney, Áine Maye.

Drumree, Junior Championship Runners Up, 2014.

Front: Maureen Doyle, Juliette Wall, Louise Griffin, Trish Rattigan, Cliodhna O Riordan, Cliona Murphy, Sarah Keane, Jessica Wall, Liadan O Riordan, Ciara Jones, Eimear O Reilly.
Back: Shane Mahon, Lisa Donnelly, Chloe Mahon, Emma Doyle, Annemarie Rattigan, Aide Pritchard, Alannah Chalkley, Marissa Horan, Brona Gavin, Gemma Flanagan, Niamh Gallogly, Conor Gavin, Ed O Riordan.

BLACK & AMBER

Drumree, Under 13 Division 2 Finalists, 2014

Front: Rachel Duke, Aoife Harrington, Shayla Rattigan, Joy Smith, Raina Byrne, Ciara Philip.
Back: Alannah Brennan, Ciara Fitzpatrick, Latisha Rattigan, Ava O Brien, Sonia Leonard, Orla Bannon, Ella Morris, Sinéad Moyles, Muireann Ryan, Emma Flynn, Jesse Pritchard-Egan.

10-1 to 1-1. Dunshaughlin players on the team, though no longer playing in Dunshaughlin, were Bernadette Kenny and Patricia Kenny while Ger O Brien, who later settled in Dunshaughlin after marrying John Maher, was one of the young stars of the team.

Camogie seems to have declined in the county generally in the 1950s and it was the early 1960s before it regained a foothold. In a report on a Leinster league schools' game in 1960 involving Athboy the *Meath Chronicle* claimed, as it praised Athboy's trainer Annette Corrigan for reviving the game in Meath, that '*a few years ago camogie was dead in the Royal County … there was not then one camogie player in the county.*'

A County Board was established circa 1964, with Hilda Cosgrave of Boardsmill as Secretary, and nine teams took part in a league. Dunshaughlin parish was not represented nor is there any evidence of the sport in the 1970s or 1980s in the locality.

Camogie in Recent Years

Before St. Martins faded from the scene in 2009, see Chapter 21, it had established the foundations of a camogie team. Conor and Nuala Gavin, Mairéad Mc Mahon, Maureen Doyle and Maureen Kennedy were instrumental in introducing camogie to St. Martins in 2005.

The club started with Under 10 and 12 panels, later adding an Under 14 team. The latter initially suffered heavy defeats and failed to score, but, persistence and perseverance paid off and in 2008 the team was much more competitive reaching the Under 14B final before losing out to Dunboyne, 3-2 to 1-4. The team line out was as follows: Cliodhna O Riordan; Siobhán Scully, Jessica Wall, Rebecca Sweeney; Ciara Kennedy, Catriona Kennedy, Emma Connolly; Clíona Murphy, Orla Bracken; Rebecca Keane, Louise Griffin, Méabh Gallogly; Hannah McNamee, Emma Kennedy (1-0), Áine Brennan. Subs: Saoirse Conlon for Brennan, Marissa Horan for Catriona Kennedy, Catriona Keane for McNamee.

In 2008 the game was deep rooted enough for St. Martins to win the Under 12 Shield on a scoreline of 3-0 to 2-1. Nuala Gavin and Edward O Riordan took charge of the following panel, Cliodhna O Riordan, Niamh Kennedy, Hannah O Brien, Marissa Horan, Muireann O Hora, Ciara Reynolds, Chloe Byrne, Brona Gavin, Shona Lynch, Niamh Gallogly, Ciara Jones, Sophie Mc Namara, Gráinne Hanley, Hayley Briody, Sarah Sweeney, Kerri Moran, Rebecca Farrell, Alannah Chalkley, Eimear Woods and Megan Pritchard.

A year later, with St. Martins just a nostalgic memory, camogie teams fielded in the red and white of Drumree and the successes continued. The Under 14s captured the shield with a comprehensive 5-2 to 0-1 victory against Killyon and in 2010 the Under 12 side won a closely contested Division 2B final against Dunderry. Both the Under 14s and Under 16s exited at semi-final stage while for the first time ever a minor team represented the club in the championship.

The younger groups maintained their competitiveness in 2011 with the Under 14s easily disposing of Kilmessan in a Semi-Final, 9-2 to 5-1, before giving way to Dunboyne in the final on a 7-4 to 4-0 scoreline. The semi-final panel was Rebecca Farrell, Kerri Moran, Liadan O Riordan, Aisling Moyles, Sorcha Casey, Alannah Chalkley (1-0), Chloe Mahon, Ciara Jones, Siobhán Whitty, Juliette Wall, Kevagh Slater, Brona Gavin, Sadhbh Ó Muirí (4-1), Ruth Byrne, Shona Lynch (3-1), Caoimhe Rooney (1-0), Aisling Maye, Áine Maye, Niamh Gallogly, Emma Bannon, Beibhin O Hora.

Success at under age grades eventually led to a team gingerly stepping out at adult level. Before the end of the decade the club entered an adult side in the junior league and in their first outing went under to Na Fianna by 3-3 to 0-1. That team, the first adult side from the parish in fifty years, lined out as follows: Kim Slater; Jessica Wall, Gemma Flanagan, Catríona Kennedy; Rebecca Keane, Clare Donohue, Carol Hanrahan; Cliona Murphy, Orla Bracken; Sarah Jane Brady, Shiobhra Delaney, Louise Griffin; Leanne McMorrow, Sinéad Ennis, Saoirse Conlon. Subs: Sarah Keane, Rebecca Sweeney, Méabh Gallogly, Laura McDermott, Emma Connolly, Carol Smith. Their first victory arrived in 2010 with a comprehensive 7-8 to 0-2 rout of Donaghmore-Ashbourne, Lisa Donnelly scoring six goals in the process. The team was now competitive and by September had qualified for the county final. Drumree entered the decider as massive underdogs, having previously lost to their opponents, Boardsmill.

They almost pulled off a major shock.

In the first half Drumree put on a superb defensive display and then midway through the second Emma Doyle struck for a goal, and the minimum lead, with fifteen minutes remaining. Boardsmill eventually edged a single point in front but had to withstand intensive Drumree pressure as the reds camped close to goal for the closing ten minutes. The massed attack couldn't breach the Mill's defence who escaped with a narrow 2-4 to 2-3 victory. Drumree's team was: Cliodhna O Riordan; Catríona Kennedy, Aimee McQuillan, Sinéad Ennis; Leanne McMorrow, Gemma Flanagan, Sarah Keane; Róisín Ní Dhúshláine, Cliona Murphy (0-1); Cliona Ni Dhúshláine, Niamh Kelleher, Emma Kennedy; Áine Brennan, Kim Slater (0-1), Emma Doyle (2-1). Subs: Ciara Kennedy for Keane, Lisa Donnelly for Brennan, Aide Pritchard, Eleanor Troy, Saoirse Inge, Ann Marie Rattigan, Rita Weber, Louise Griffin, Patricia Monks, Melissa Leonard, Jessica Wall.

A year later Drumree returned to the final stage and took the club's first adult camogie title with a 2-5 to 1-1 victory over Trim. The girls in red and white were always in control, had a three-point advantage at the break and assured victory with second half goals from Emma Kennedy and Cliona Murphy. A late Trim revival never looked like overturning the lead and Drumree earned the title by a 2-5 to 1-1 margin. GT Troy, Maureen Doyle and Vicncent Brennan comprised the team management.

In 2013 and 2014 the girls once again made their way to the final but in 2013 opponents Dunderry hit them for six, with five of the goals coming before half time. A good second half display couldn't overhaul the early advantage and Dunderry won by 6-5 to 2-7. Drumree lined out as follows: Annmarie Rattigan; Jessica Wall, Rosie Hand, Eimear O Reilly; Muireann O Hora, Alannah Chalkley, Hannah O Brien; Louise Griffin, Áine Brennan; Gemma Flanagan, Cliodhna O Riordan, Cliona Murphy; Emma Kennedy, Cliona Ní Dhúshláine, Patricia Monks.

The following year it took Donaghmore-Ashbourne two games to dispose of

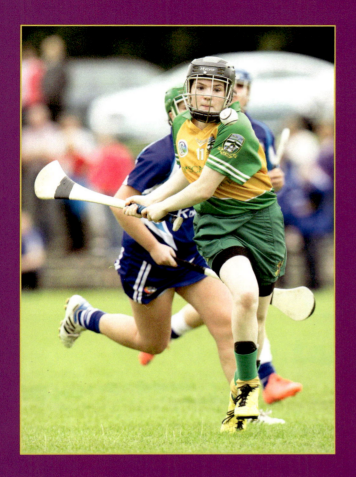

Clockwise from top left:
Niamh Gallogly has eyes for the ball only in the Under 16C All-Ireland final against Laois in 2013.

Cliodhna O Riordan, Meath's captain, accepts the trophy after Meath won the All-Ireland Minor C title in 2014.

Drumree mentors Shane Mahon and Ed O Riordan.

Caoimhe Rooney receives the shield after captaining the Meath Under 16s to victory in the 2015 Leinster Under 16 B Shield final where the Royals beat Carlow 3-11 to 2-4.

Drumree's challenge. The first outing ended in a draw, 1-9 each, but Drumree came out second best in the replay.

Despite those setbacks the younger players have been graduating through the ranks and in 2013 the first Under 16 title arrived, when the red and whites went on a clean sweep in the B competition, beating Killyon, Navan O Mahonys, Donaghmore-Ashbourne and Kildalkey, home and away, in the group stages. The final paired Drumree with Kildalkey for their third encounter. The outcome mirrored the previous results, a comprehensive victory for the red and white to the tune of 6-9 to 1-3.

Niamh Gallogly captained and Ed O Riordan, Shane Mahon and Martin Wall managed the following successful side: Rebecca Farrell; Ruth Byrne, Liadan O Riordan, Aisling Moyles; Hayley Reynolds, Siobhán Whitty, Caoimhe Rooney; Chloe Mahon, Niamh Gallogly, Capt.; Ciara Jones, Alannah Chalkley, Juliette Wall; Sabrina Kelly, Brona Gavin, Orlaith Moyles. Subs: Sorcha Casey, Saoirse Casey, Áine Maye, Aisling Maye, Beibhín O Hora, Éabha Ryan, Kevagh Slater.

Their 2014 counterparts started excellently but just missed out on a semi-final place while the Under 13s went down by a single point in the decider with Kiltale. Despite a lack of success at minor level, Drumree is now one of only four clubs in the county fielding a minor team without having to resort to amalgamation.

County Teams

Club members made a significant impact at county level in 2013. Royal county camogie teams had long been a soft touch but the appointment of John Davis as coach in 2006 brought initial improvement, followed by competitiveness and eventually phenomenal success. John's contribution to the GAA with Dunshaughlin footballers and hurlers and with the Meath hurlers in the 1980s and 1990s has been alluded to earlier in the book.

In a few short years under his command the Meath camogie team went from Division 4 to Division 2 and crowned it with victory in the All-Ireland junior decider in 2012. Victory over Down, in Croke Park brought the county its first All-Ireland title. The following year Davis guided his charges to the All-Ireland Intermediate semi-final but equally importantly teams in lower grades were also successful.

The county's second team captured the 2013 All-Ireland Junior B title with a 2-4 to 1-5 victory over Kerry and Drumree had a substantial fingerprint on the success. GT Troy coached the team with Brian Coughlan as a selector, Louise Griffin started in the forwards with Áine Brennan replacing her late on while Cliodhna O Riordan, and Muireann O Hora were also part of the panel. Sinéad

Beagan, formerly a Royal Gaels' star, but then playing her camogie with Ratoath, notched over half of the winners' total, finishing with 1-3.

On the same day the Under 16s added further silverware to the sideboard with a hard earned All-Ireland C victory against Laois. Once again Drumree had a large representation with Alannah Chalkley at right half back, Niamh Gallogly at centre forward and Liadan O Riordan, Juliette Wall, Chloe Mahon and Ciara Jones among the green and gold substitutes. Siobhán Whitty and Ruth Byrne from Blackhall Gaels, who played their camogie with Drumree, brought the club's representation to eight. The previous day Gallogly had captained the Meath Under 16 ladies' Gaelic football team against Waterford in their unsuccessful bid to win the All-Ireland at that grade. Meath were Leinster Under 16B Shield winners in 2015 when Drumree's Caoimhe Rooney captained the side.

Drumree girls also featured on the successful Royal County squad that captured the 2014 All-Ireland Minor C title beating Armagh by 1-13 to 0-5 with team captain Cliodhna O'Riordan, Alannah Chalkley, Ciara Jones, Marissa Horan, Chloe Mahon, Siobhan Whitty and Juliette Wall all part of the panel. This was Meath's first ever minor title. A step up the grades the following year didn't intimidate the young Royals as they repeated the success at Minor B grade, accounting for Derry by 4-6 to 2-10. Niamh Gallogly notched two first half goals and other Drumree girls to feature included Ciara Jones, Chloe Mahon and Juliette Wall while GT Troy and Ed O Riordan were part of the management team.

As was the case with the revival of hurling in the parish, a long dormant camogie tradition has been successfully revived in the past decade. Despite a struggle at times to field teams at all grades the current wielders of the camán have recorded a level of success at club and county level that their predecessors could only dream of.

Appendix 6
Club Officers, Parish Clubs 1886-2015

Dunshaughlin GAA Club

It was hoped to compile a detailed account of the main office holders in the various clubs from 1886 to the present but as minute books are not available this ambition could not be achieved. However, the information that could be gleaned is presented.

1886-1891

Throughout this period Patrick O Brien was President, a position equivalent to Chairman nowadays, and Laurence F. Canning was Vice President. The first Secretary was either James J Connolly, then Clerk of the Petty Sessions or John Finnegan. Finnegan resigned in mid 1890 and was replaced by Bernard Carolan and William Swan as joint Secretaries. Patrick King may have been Secretary in late 1890 and was then replaced by Bernard Carolan. Christy Tallon was captain throughout this period, and Treasurer from 1886-90 when Laurence Canning took on the job.

1894-1899

The club didn't function in the 1891-94 period. Patrick O Brien was elected as President in 1894 and probably served for a number of years. PJ Mulvany acted as Vice-President for two years at least, 1894-95, with Canning as Treasurer and Bernard Carolan again Secretary. Paddy Ward became Secretary in 1897-98 but nothing is known of the other positions.

1901-1905

During 1899 and 1900 the club was again inactive and from 1902 onwards there were two separate clubs, St. Seachnall's FC and the hurlers, known as Na Fir le Céile (The United Men), a Gaelic League inspired club. Peadar J. Murray was probably an official of the hurling club while James O Brien very likely held one of the major positions in the football club. Jack Clarke, on his own in 1902 and with Paddy Ward from 1903 onwards, acted as Secretary. James O Brien was captain in 1904 but nothing is known of the other officers.

1907-1919

After another lapse in 1905-06 the club was revived in 1907. One club, St. Seachnalls, catered for both footballers and hurlers and Michael Duffy was the driving force behind the revival. He was Secretary from 1907 to 1911, while Patrick Martin was Treasurer in 1910-11. Nothing is known of Presidents or Vice-Presidents. In 1909 the football captain was John Blake while John Carty captained the hurlers. As Carty again led the hurlers in 1911 it is reasonable to assume he was captain in 1910 also. If so, he led Dunshaughlin to two senior titles. The club disappeared in 1912 but was back again the following year with William Daly in the Chair, J. O Brien as Treasurer and Paddy Duffy as Secretary. Little is known of the 1913-21 period but Paddy Duffy was Secretary 1913-15 when Paddy Blake took over for at least one year. Michael Duffy was captain in 1917 but no other information on captains came to light.

1923-1928

No information is available on the Chairman or Vice-Chairman for this period. Mickey Carberry acted as Secretary 1923-24, Paddy Kenny took on the job in 1926 and it is likely, though unproven, that Thomas Lynch, N.T. spent some time in the post. Paddy Blake was captain in 1926 and probably during most of this era; he was certainly in charge of pep talks and practice matches.

1933-1946

The club was again inactive in the 1929-32 period and little information survives from 1933-40. Paddy Kenny was Chairman in 1933 and probably retained the post throughout. Paddy Blake was captain in 1933 while Johnny Gogan captained the 1939 hurlers. There were a variety of Secretaries but Paddy Kenny did both the Chairman's and Secretary's jobs for a time. The club failed to field teams in 1941-42 and 1945 and no information survives from this period other than that Kevin Johnston captained the 1943 team. Paddy Kenny was most likely the Chairman until the late 1940s.

Dunshaughlin GAA Club Officers 1947-2015

	Chairperson	Vice Chairperson	Secretary	Treasurer
1947	Paddy Kenny	Billy Carberry	Paddy Lynam	Tommy Gogan
1948	Tommy Gogan	Paddy Blake	Seachnall Murray	Tommy Gogan
1949	Tommy Gogan	Paddy Blake	Seachnall Murray	Tommy Gogan
1950	Maurice Delany	Paddy Blake	Barney Cooney	Mickey Kenny
1951	Maurice Delany	Paddy Blake	Barney Cooney	Mickey Kenny
1952	Mickey Kenny	Larry O Rourke	Eddie Lyons	Barney Cooney
1953	Larry O Rourke	Mattie Russell	Matt Daly	Dickie O Brien
1954	Patsy McLoughlin	Mattie Russell	Matt Daly	No Record
1955	Patsy McLoughlin	Larry O Rourke	Matt Daly	Matt Daly
1956	Patsy McLoughlin	Paddy Lynam	Tom Everard	Tom Everard
1957	Patsy McLoughlin	Paddy Lynam	Matt Daly	Tom Everard
1958	Fr. Eamonn O Brien	Patsy McLoughlin	Matt Daly	Matt Daly
1959	Fr. Eamonn O Brien	Patsy McLoughlin	Seán McManus / Tom Everard	Tom Everard / Tommy O Dwyer
1960	Fr. Eamonn O Brien	John Holland	John Donnelly	Tommy O Dwyer
1961	Fr. Eamonn O Brien	John Holland	Seamus Flynn	Tommy O Dwyer
1962	Fr. Eamonn O Brien	Patsy McLoughlin	Seamus Flynn	Tommy O Dwyer
1963	Fr. Eamonn O Brien	Patsy McLoughlin	Seamus Flynn	Tommy O Dwyer
1964	Fr. Eamonn O Brien	Patsy McLoughlin	Seamus Flynn	Tommy O Dwyer
1965	Fr. Eamonn O Brien	Patsy McLoughlin	Paddy O Dwyer	Tommy O Dwyer
1966	Fr. Eamonn O Brien	Patsy McLoughlin	Con O Dwyer	Tommy O Dwyer
1967	Fr. Eamonn O Brien	Patsy McLoughlin	Con O Dwyer	Tommy O Dwyer
1968	Fr. Eamonn O Brien	Patsy McLoughlin	Con O Dwyer	Tommy O Dwyer
1969	Fr. Eamonn O Brien	Patsy McLoughlin	Con O Dwyer	Tommy O Dwyer
1970	Seamus Flynn	Patsy McLoughlin	Con O Dwyer	Tommy O Dwyer
1971	Seamus Flynn	Patsy McLoughlin	Con O Dwyer	Tommy O Dwyer
1972	Val Dowd	Tom Everard	Seamus Flynn / John Jennings	Tommy O Dwyer
1973	Patsy McLoughlin	Paddy O Dwyer	Michael O Dwyer	Tommy O Dwyer
1974	Jim Browne	Val Dowd	Michael O Dwyer	Tommy O Dwyer
1975	Val Dowd	No record	Michael O Dwyer	Tommy O Dwyer
1976	Val Dowd	Jimmy Walsh	Paddy O Dwyer	Tommy O Dwyer
1977	Val Dowd	Jimmy Walsh	Pat Jennings	Tommy O Dwyer
1978	Con O Dwyer	Jimmy Walsh	Thos Delany / Johnny McLoughlin	Tommy O Dwyer
1979	Val Dowd	Tom Everard	Seán Mangan	Tommy O Dwyer
1980	Gerry Flanagan	Val Dowd	Mick O Keefe	Tommy O Dwyer
1981	Gerry Flanagan	Val Dowd	Mick O Keefe	Tommy O Dwyer
1982	Gerry Flanagan / Derek Kenny	Seamus Flynn	Paddy O Dwyer	Tommy O Dwyer
1983	Val Dowd / Patsy McLoughlin	Seán Walsh	Gabrielle Kenny / Con O Dwyer	Liam Carey
1984	Pat O Brien	Seán Walsh	Con O Dwyer	Liam Carey

	Chairperson	Vice Chairperson	Secretary	Treasurer
1985	Val Dowd	Seán Walsh	Con O Dwyer	Liam Carey
1986	Val Dowd	Seán Walsh	Jerry O Donoghue	Tom Finn
1987	Seán Walsh / Pat Farrell	Pat Farrell	Tom Finn	David O Dwyer
1988	Pat Farrell	Stephen Burke	Tom Finn	David O Dwyer
1989	Shaun McTigue	Stephen Burke	Pat Farrell / Donnchadh Geraghty	David O Dwyer
1990	Shaun McTigue	Stephen Burke	Jim Gilligan	David O Dwyer
1991	Shaun McTigue	John Maher	Garbhán Blake	Jim Smith
1992	Shaun McTigue	John Maher	Jim Gilligan	Jim Smith
1993	Shaun McTigue	John Maher	Jim Gilligan	Jim Smith
1994	Shaun McTigue	John Maher	Donnchadh Geraghty/Cyril Creavin	Jim Smith
1995	Don Kane	John Maher	Cyril Creavin	Jim Smith
1996	Neil Halpin	Shaun McTigue	Cyril Creavin	Jim Smith
1997	Neil Halpin	Shaun McTigue	Cyril Creavin	Cyril Creavin
1998	Neil Halpin / Paddy O Dwyer	Paddy O Dwyer / Brian O Rourke	Cyril Creavin	Brendan Kealy
1999	Paddy O Dwyer	Jim Smith	Cyril Creavin	Brendan Kealy
2000	Paddy O Dwyer	Neil Halpin	Cyril Creavin	Brendan Kealy / Fergus O Rourke
2001	Paddy O Dwyer	Neil Halpin / Jim Smith	Cyril Creavin	Fergus O Rourke
2002	Paddy O Dwyer	Jim Smith	Cyril Creavin	Oliver Farrell
2003	Paddy O Dwyer	Jim Smith	Cyril Creavin	Oliver Farrell
2004	Paddy O Dwyer	Jim Smith	Cyril Creavin	Oliver Farrell
2005	Paddy O Dwyer	Jim Smith	Cyril Creavin	Pat Herlihy
2006	Jim Smith	Paddy Ward	Mairéad Delaney	Pat Herlihy
2007	Jim Smith	Paddy Ward	Mairéad Delaney	Pat Herlihy
2008	Jim Smith	Paddy Ward	Mairéad Delaney	Pat Herlihy
2009	Jim Smith	Paddy Ward	Mairéad Delaney	Tom Finn
2010	Jim Smith	Donnacha Lloyd	Neil O Dwyer	Tom Finn
2011	Jim Smith	Donnacha Lloyd	Neil O Dwyer	Tom Finn
2012	Jim Smith	Michael McHale	Caroline Malone	Tom Finn
2013	Jim Smith	Shane Kelly	Caroline Malone	Tom Finn & Denis Staunton
2014	Neil O Dwyer	Shane Kelly	Caroline Malone	Tom Finn & Denis Staunton
2015	Neil O Dwyer	Colum Bracken	Caroline Malone	Tom Finn

Dunshaughlin Hurling Club Officers, 1982-1991

	Chairperson	Vice Chairperson	Secretary	Treasurer
1982	Gerry Flanagan	Not appointed	Christy O Sullivan	Christy O Sullivan
1983	Gerry Flanagan	Not appointed	Hugh Doyle	Gerry Keane
1984	Gerry Flanagan	Tadhg Ó Dúshláine	Hugh Doyle	Gerry Keane
1985	Gerry Flanagan	Oliver Brooks	Tadhg Ó Dúshláine	Oliver Brooks
1986	Gerry Flanagan	Oliver Brooks	Denis Neville/Paddy Ward	Brian O Sullivan
1987	Gerry Flanagan	Oliver Brooks	Paddy Ward	James Walsh
1988	Gerry Flanagan/Oliver Brooks	John Davis	Paddy Ward	James Walsh
1989	Oliver Brooks	No Record	Paddy Ward	Mick O Keefe
1990	Oliver Brooks	John O Sullivan	Paddy Ward	Mick O Keefe

St. Martins' GAA Officers, 1983-2008

	Chairperson	Secretary	Treasurer
1983	Val Dowd	Lena Doyle	None appointed
1984	Val Dowd	Tadhg Ó Dúshláine	Joe Rattigan
1985	Val Dowd	Jim Gilligan	Joe Rattigan
1986	Val Dowd	Jim Gilligan	Maura O Dwyer
1987	Val Dowd	Jim Gilligan	Maura O Dwyer
1988	Pat Kelly	Jim Gilligan	Maura O Dwyer
1989	Pat Kelly	Oliver Gogan	Maura O Dwyer
1990	Pat Kelly	Oliver Gogan	Maura O Dwyer
1991	Pat Kelly	Oliver Gogan	Maura O Dwyer
1992	Pat Kelly	Cyril Creavin	Maura O Dwyer
1993	Jimmy Walsh	Cyril Creavin	Maura O Dwyer
1994	Jimmy Walsh	Cyril Creavin	Maura O Dwyer
1995	Jimmy Walsh	Peter Mooney	Gabrielle Kenny
1996	Jimmy Walsh	Peter Mooney	Gabrielle Kenny
1997	Paddy Ward	Mairéad Delaney	Gabrielle Kenny
1998	Paddy Ward	Mairéad Delaney	Gabrielle Kenny
1999	Paddy Ward	Mairéad Delaney	Angela Reilly
2000	Paddy Ward	Mairéad Delaney	Angela Reilly
2001	David Crimmins	Mairéad Delaney	Angela Reilly
2002	David Crimmins	Linda Devereux	Pat Herlihy
2003	David Crimmins	Linda Devereux	Pat Herlihy
2004	Don McLoughlin	Linda Devereux	Conor Gavin
2005	Don McLoughlin	Linda Devereux	Conor Gavin
2006	Niall McCarthy	Dolores Murphy	Conor Gavin
2007	Linda Christie	Rachel Connolly	Caroline Malone
2008	Linda Christie	Carmel Kennedy	Caroline Malone

Dunshaughlin GAA Underage 2009-15

	Chairperson	Secretary
2009	Linda Devereux	Caroline Malone
2010	Linda Devereux	Caroline Malone
2011	Jim Mitchell	Caroline Malone
2012	Jim Mitchell	Ultan Blake Under 8s – 14s; Alan O Dwyer Under 15- Minor
2013	Jim Mitchell / Frank Gallogly	Lyndsey McCormack Under 8s – 14s; Alan O Dwyer Under 15- Minor
2014	Frank Gallogly	Lyndsey McCormack Under 8s – 14s; Alan O Dwyer Under 15- Minor
2015	Frank Gallogly	Lyndsey McCormack Under 8s – 14s; Alan O Dwyer Under 15- Minor

Royal Gaels' GAA Officers, 1995-2015

	Chairperson	Secretary	Treasurer
1995	Catherine McHale & Ead Kealy	Anne Power	Maura O Neill
1996	Catherine McHale & Ead Kealy	Anne Power	Maura O Neill
1997	Catherine McHale & Ead Kealy	Anne Power	Maura O Neill
1998	Catherine McHale & Ead Kealy	Anne Power	Christine Bowe & Nuala Mahon
1999	Catherine McHale	Anne Power	No Record
2000	Catherine McHale	Anne Power	No Record
2001	Catherine McHale	Anne Power	Ead Kealy
2002	Catherine McHale	Anne Power	Ead Kealy
2003	Catherine McHale	Anne Power	Ead Kealy
2004	Catherine McHale	Anne Power	Ead Kealy
2005	Catherine McHale	Mary O Sullivan	Ead Kealy
2006	Catherine McHale	Mary O Regan	Ead Kealy
2007	Ead Kealy	Mary O Regan	Mary O Sullivan
2008	Dan Sullivan	Mary O Regan	Sandra Traynor
2009	Dan Sullivan	Mary O Regan	Sandra Traynor
2010	Veronica Conlon	Mary O Regan	Sandra Traynor
2011	Veronica Conlon	Mary O Regan	Patricia Usher
2012	Colum Bracken	Mary O Regan	Patricia Usher
2013	Colum Bracken	Mary O Regan	Patricia Usher
2014	Colum Bracken	Mary O Regan	Patricia Usher
2015	Colum Bracken	Mary O Regan	Patricia Usher

BLACK & AMBER

Drumree GAA Officers

When the club re-organized in 1948 the full list of officers read as follows:
Chairman: Eugene Gilsenan, Vice Chairman: Thomas Farnan, Secretary: Eugene Englishby, Treasurer: Eugene Gilsenan, County Board Delegates: Patrick 'The Rah' Doyle and William Byrne. Committee: James Daly, Michael Madden, Laurence Geraghty, John Cullen, William Kelly, Des Englishby, Dónal Donoghue, M Hynes.
In 1961 the officers were: Chairman: Dickie O Brien, Vice Chairman: Billy Byrne, Secretary: Patsy O Brien, Treasurer: Liam Smith, who was also Treasurer in 1959. Committee: Tony Rattigan, Tommy Troy, Larry Byrne, Michael Walsh, Senior, Tony Walsh, T Mulligan, Seán Doyle. Captain: Billie Rattigan, Vice Captain: James Walsh. Junior Captain: Tommy Troy, Vice Captain: T Mulligan. The list below has been compiled from memory and is subject to error.

	Chairperson	Secretary	Treasurer
1961	Dickie O Brien	Patsy O Brien	Liam Smith
1962	Dickie O Brien	Patsy O Brien	Liam Smith
1963	Dickie O Brien	Patsy O Brien	Liam Smith
1964	Dickie O Brien	Patsy O Brien	Liam Smith
1965	Dickie O Brien	Patsy O Brien	Liam Smith
1966	Dickie O Brien	Patsy O Brien	Liam Smith
1967	Dickie O Brien	Billie Rattigan	Liam Smith
1968	Dickie O Brien	Joe Rattigan	Liam Smith
1969	Dickie O Brien	Joe Rattigan	Liam Smith
1970	Tony Rattigan	Joe Rattigan	Liam Smith
1971	Tony Rattigan	Neil O Riordan	Liam Smith
1972	Tony Rattigan	Neil O Riordan	Liam Smith
1973	Tony Rattigan	Joe Rattigan	Liam Smith
1974	Tony Rattigan	Jimmy Walsh	Liam Smith
1975	Tony Rattigan	Billie Rattigan	Liam Smith
1976	Tony Rattigan	Joe Rattigan	Liam Smith
1977	Tony Rattigan	Joe Rattigan	Liam Smith
1978	Tony Rattigan	Joe Rattigan	Liam Smith
1979	Tony Rattigan	Joe Rattigan	Liam Smith
1980	Johnny Walsh	Joe Rattigan	Liam Smith
1981	Johnny Walsh	Joe Rattigan	Liam Smith
1982	Eamonn Donoghue	Lena Walsh	Liam Smith
1983	Eamonn Donoghue	Lena Walsh	Sally Donoghue
1984	Pat Kelly	Joe Rattigan	Macartan McGroder
1985	Pat Kelly	Joe Rattigan	Macartan McGroder
1986	Patsy Curley	Joe Rattigan	Macartan McGroder
1987	Patsy Curley	Joe Rattigan	Macartan McGroder

	Chairperson	Secretary	Treasurer
1988	Patsy Curley	Joe Rattigan	Johnny Lynch
1989	Patsy Curley	Joe Rattigan	Johnny Lynch
1990	Patsy Curley	Joe Rattigan	Johnny Lynch
1991	Patsy Curley	Joe Rattigan	Johnny Lynch
1992	Patsy Curley	Joe Rattigan	Johnny Lynch
1993	Seán Walsh	Martin Wall	Johnny Lynch
1994	Seán Walsh	John Boyle	Johnny Lynch
1995	Seán Walsh	John Boyle	Johnny Lynch
1996	Johnny Lynch	Joe Rattigan	Peter Mooney
1997	Johnny Lynch	Joe Rattigan & Seán Doyle	Phil Coffey
1998	Johnny Lynch	Joe Rattigan	Phil Coffey
1999	Johnny Lynch	Joe Rattigan	Phil Coffey
2000	Martin Wall	Seán Walsh	Phil Coffey
2001	Martin Wall	Seán Walsh	Phil Coffey
2002	Martin Wall	Seán Walsh	Phil Coffey
2003	Martin Wall	Seán Walsh	Phil Coffey
2004	Martin Wall	Seán Walsh	Phil Coffey
2005	Martin Wall	Mary McMorrow	Phil Coffey
2006	Neil McCarrick	Mary McMorrow	Phil Coffey
2007	Neil McCarrick	Mary McMorrow	Phil Coffey
2008	Neil McCarrick	Mary McMorrow	Phil Coffey
2009	Neil McCarrick / Eamonn Dunne 1st Juv. Chair	Mary McMorrow / Ettie Philip Juv Secr.	Phil Coffey
2010	Martin Wall / No Juv. Chair	Mary McMorrow / Ettie Philip, Juv. Secr.	Fiona Lawless
2011	Martin Wall / No Juv. Chair	Mary McMorrow / Ettie Philip, Juv. Secr	Fiona Lawless
2012	Martin Wall / Vincent O Hora, Juv Chair	Rosaleen Rooney / Ettie Philip, Juv. Secr.	Fiona Lawless
2013	Martin Ryan / Vincent O Hora, Juv Chair	Rosaleen Rooney/Ettie Philip, Juv. Secr.	Fiona Lawless
2014	Martin Ryan / No Juv Chair	Rosaleen Rooney / Ettie Philip, Juv. Secr.	Fiona Lawless
2015	Martin Ryan / Ettie Philip, Juv Chair	Rosaleen Rooney /Ettie Philip, Juv. Secr.	Fiona Lawless

Dunshaughlin Club Captains, 1949-2015

The captain given is the captain of the most senior team in the club. When both football and hurling teams were fielded the former is indicated by (F), the latter by (H).

Year	Captain	Year	Captain
1949	Ben Lynam (F) Pat Dwan (H)	1983	Pat O Brien (F), Ollie O Neill (H)
1950	Kevin Melia	1984	Tom Finn (F), Jim Condon (H)
1951	Ned Teeling	1985	Pat O Brien (F) Frank Kelly (H)
1952	Benny Foley	1986	Aidan Walsh (F) John Neville (H)
1953	Larry O Brien	1987	Aidan Walsh (F) John Neville (H)
1954	Patsy McLoughlin	1988	No football record / John Davis, Martin Walsh (H)
1955	Larry O Brien	1989	Aidan Walsh
1956	Billy Byrne	1990	Derek Maher
1957	Tom Everard (F), Seán McManus (H)	1991	Pat Kealy
1958	Michael Morrin (F), Seán McManus (H)	1992	Ger Dowd, Colum Bracken
1959	Peter Tugwell (F), Benny Foley (H)	1993	Colum Bracken
1960	Peter Tugwell	1994	Colum Bracken
1961	Seán O Brien	1995	Derek Maher
1962	Seamus Foley	1996	Dermot Kealy
1963	Seamus Foley	1997	Ciarán Byrne
1964	Seamus Foley	1998	Ciarán Byrne
1965	Paddy O Dwyer	1999	Dermot Kealy
1966	Davy O Dwyer	2000	Dermot Kealy
1967	Davy O Dwyer	2001	Ciarán Byrne
1968	Val Dowd	2002	Aiden Kealy, Kenny McTigue
1969	No details	2003	Kenny McTigue
1970	John Casey	2004	Michael McHale
1971	No details	2005	Ronnie Yore
1972	Pat Farrell	2006	Richie Kealy
1973	Mossie Caffrey	2007	Niall Kelly
1974	Michael O Dwyer	2008	Ray Maloney
1975	Michael O Dwyer	2009	Denis Kealy
1976	Neil O Riordan	2010	Anthony Johnson
1977	Pat Jennings	2011	Ray Maloney
1978	Pat O Brien	2012	Ray Maloney
1979	Ger Dowd	2013	Trevor Dowd
1980	Gerry Keane	2014	Ray Maloney
1981	Mick O Keefe	2015	Michael Ahern
1982	Paddy Kenny (F), Jimmy Walsh (H)		

A Galaxy of GAA Greats

Pictured in 2000
Front: Gráinne Gallogly, Cian Gallogly in Sam Maguire Cup.
Seated Centre: Angela and Niamh Gallogly, Patsy McLoughlin, Meath Hall of Fame 2003, Jim Kearney, father of Angela Gallogly, All-Ireland winner with Meath, 1949, Meath Hall of Fame 1989, Mattie Gilsenan, All-Ireland winner with Meath, 1949 and 1954, Meath Hall of Fame 1986, Seán Boylan, Meath Coach/Manager in All-Ireland wins of 1987, 1988, 1996 and 1999, Meath Hall of Fame 1999, Méabh Gallogly.
Standing: Richie Kealy, Meath Footballer of Year 2000, All-Ireland winner with Meath 1999, Trevor Giles, All-Ireland winner with Meath, 1996, 1999, All-Ireland Footballer of the Year 1999, All Star 1996, 1997, 1999, Captain Ireland Compromise Rules 2000, Meath Footballer of Year 1996, 1999, Fr. John Kerrane, PP Dunshaughlin, Leinster minor football winner with Westmeath 1952, Frank Gallogly with Shane Gallogly.

Dunshaughlin GAA Senior Panel, 2015

Front: Niall Byrne, Trevor Dowd, Fergus Toolan, Conor Devereux, Fearghal Delaney, Michael Ahern, Capt., Tadhg Ó Dúshlaine, Shane Gallogly, Cathal O Dwyer.
Back: David McMahon, Caoimhín King, Niall Murphy, David Dunne, Mark Devanney, Dan Ormsby, Ray Maloney, Ben Duggan, Alastar Doyle, Tommy Johnson.

Appendix 7
Dunshaughlin: Results of Championship Semi-Finals, Finals and League Finals

Note: Teams were seventeen a side until 1913. For championship games, semi-final and final, results are given, when available. For league and Feis Cup games, only final results and teams are given. Teams and selectors are listed where available.

1900-1919

1902: Senior Football Championship
Semi-Final: Dunshaughlin 0-3 Castletown 0-3 at Athlumney
Replay: Castletown 1-11 Dunshaughlin 0-1 at Athlumney
James O Brien, Capt., Patrick O Brien (Goals), Jack Clarke, Owen Lynch, Jack Johnson, Paddy Johnson, Paddy Swan, Peadar Murray, Peter Lee, Patrick Hand, Patrick Mahon, Michael 'Jacob' Clarke, B Mc Auley, J Murray, Michael Duffy, Dan Killeen, William Daly.

1908: Junior Hurling Championship
Semi-Final: Dunshaughlin 6-6 Young Irelands, Navan 0-1 at Kilmessan
Final: Dunshaughlin 7-14 Ratoath 3-3 at Dunboyne
Full team details unavailable, but the following played: Michael Duffy, Jack Clarke, Michael Bruton, Jack Johnson, Ned Smith, Christy Smith and Christy Foley.

1909: Senior Hurling Championship
Semi-Final: Dunshaughlin 1-8 Young Irelands, Navan 1-5 at Kilmessan
Final: Dunshaughlin 2-7 Dunboyne 1-3 at Ratoath. Team details unavailable. Players most likely similar to 1910 list below.

1909: Junior Football League
Semi-Final: Dunshaughlin 2-18 Kilbeg 0-2 at Show Grounds, Navan
Final: Navan Harps 3-9 Dunshaughlin 0-6 at Show Grounds, Navan
Semi-Final team: John Rafferty, Jack Johnson, Jack Clarke, Peter Johnson, Pat Toole, John Curry, Peter Lee, Jack Lynch, William McDermott, Michael Duffy, Michael Bruton, Peter Kenny, Michael Carberry, William Corry, Tom Clusker, William Daly, Dick Doran.

1910: Senior Hurling Championship
Semi-Final: Dunshaughlin beat Dunboyne at Ratoath
Final: Dunshaughlin 8-1 Longwood 3-0
Jack Clarke, John Carty, Jack Johnson, Peter Johnson, Pat Toole, Michael Carberry, Michael Duffy, William Daly, William McDermott, Michael Bruton, Peter Lee, Jack Collier, Peter Kenny, Thomas Clusker, Patrick 'The Gah' Foley, Christopher Foley, Michael Clusker.

1910: Leinster Junior Hurling Championship
Meath represented by Dunshaughlin mainly
Semi-Final: Meath 7-1 Kildare 3-0 at Jones' Road
Final: Laois 12-2 Meath 2-1 at Jones' Road
Eleven of the team were from Dunshaughlin, John Carty, Michael Carberry, Pat Toole, William McDermott, Michael Bruton, Michael Duffy, Jack Collier, Thomas Clusker, Michael Clusker, Patrick 'The Gah' Foley, Christy Foley.

1911: Senior Hurling Championship
Semi-Final: Dunshaughlin 4-1 Kilmessan 3-0 at Skryne
Final: Dunboyne 5-3 Dunshaughlin 2-0 at Ratoath
Team v Kilmessan: John Carty, Capt., (Goals), Jack Clarke,

Peter Johnson, Thomas Clusker, Michael Carberry, Pat Toole, Michael Bruton, William McDermott, Peter Lee, C Smith, Michael Duffy, William Daly, Paddy Duffy, Paddy Kenny, Christy Foley, Patrick Foley, Mick Clusker.

1914: Senior Hurling Championship
Semi-Final: Dunboyne 4-2 Dunshaughlin 2-0 at Ratoath
Team details unavailable.

1916: Senior Hurling Championship
Semi-Final: Dunshaughlin 3-5 Ratoath 3-2 at Ashbourne
Final: Trim 7-4 Dunshaughlin 6-4 at Navan, played July 1917.

John Carty, Nicky Moran, Michael Blake, Paddy Blake, Michael Carberry, Michael Duffy, Jack Clarke, Hugh Mullally, Christy Doran, Michael Bruton, Gerry Kenny, Charles Curley, Thomas Clusker, William Daly and Paddy Kenny.

1920-1949

1923: Junior Hurling Championship
Played on a League Basis
Round 1:	Dunshaughlin 3-1 Ceanannus Mór 2-1 at Kilmessan
Round 2:	Dunshaughlin 9-1 Ratoath 1-1 at Pelletstown, Drumree
Round 3:	Dunshaughlin 4-1 Curraha 3-1
Round 4:	Dunshaughlin beat Kilcarne
Round 5:	Dunshaughlin 3-1 Athboy 1-0.

Dunshaughlin became champions after objections. See Chapter 4 for details. Team not available.

1925: Senior Hurling Championship
Played on a League Basis
Round 1:	Dunshaughlin 4-4 Kilmessan 3-2 at Navan
Round 2:	Dunshaughlin 2-0 Trim 1-2 at Trim
Round 3:	Dunshaughlin 4-5 Athboy 1-6 or 2-3 at Navan
Round 4:	Dunshaughlin 5-2 Killyon 3-3 at Navan

Dunshaughlin champions. Games v Ratoath and Ceanannus Mór not played.
Team v Athboy: John Lynch; James Doran, Mick Clusker, Paddy Tugwell; Gerry Kenny, Michael Blake, Paddy Duffy; Paddy Blake, Nicky Gogan; Matt Ryan, Christy Doran, Paddy Kenny; Thomas McClorey, Joe Kelly, Paddy McClorey. Subs: Leo Carolan, John Tugwell, Alex Ryan.

1926: Senior Hurling Championship
Semi-final: Dunshaughlin beat Ratoath
Final: Athboy 5-4 Dunshaughlin 4-4
Team details unavailable.

1933: Senior Hurling Championship
Semi-Final: Kilmessan 8-8 Dunshaughlin 0-0
Team v Dunboyne earlier in the year. Newspaper report contained only fourteen names.

Paddy Kenny, Christy Doran, Paddy Blake, Paddy McClorey, Nicky Gogan, Ciarán Murray, Matty Davis, Thomas Toole, Tom Everard, Jim Everard, Andy Everard, John Gogan, Johnny Lynch, Ikey Madden.

1936: Junior Football Championship
Semi-Final: Longwood 0-6 Dunshaughlin 1-1 at Páirc Tailteann
Dunshaughlin successfully objected to Longwood
Final: Seneschalstown 0-4 Dunshaughlin 0-2 at Páirc Tailteann

Christy Newman; Peter Brady, Mickey Carberry, Thomas Toole; Paddy Gogan, Johnny Gogan, Peter Doran; John Sherry, Ben Lynam; Matty Davis, Paddy Brady, Peter Kenny; Mick O Neill, Mickey Parr, Paddy Lynam.

1943: Junior Football Championship
Semi-Final: Castletown 3-7 Dunshaughlin 0-1 at Páirc Tailteann

Vincent Clusker; Paddy Cosgrave, Billy Carberry, Rory Mahon; Kevin Johnson, Capt., Seán Kenny, Peadar Lynam; Paddy Lynam, Toss Lynam; Mickey Parr, Kevin Melia, Joe Gibney; Jimmy Allen, Jack Mahon, Seán Clusker.

1947: Junior Football Championship
Semi-Final: Moynalty 3-9 Dunshaughlin 2-6 at Páirc Tailteann

Rory Mahon; Paddy Lynam, Ben Lynam, Billy Carberry; Patsy McLoughlin, Paudge Morgan, Seán Kenny; Aidan Morrin, Noel Downes; Toss Lynam, Benny Foley, Jimmy Geraghty; Tommy Clusker, Vincent Clusker, Paddy Dowd. See main text for probable error in this line-out.

1950-1969

1950: Junior Football Championship
Semi-Final: Dunshaughlin 3-5 Martry 2-5 at Páirc Tailteann
Final: Dunshaughlin 2-7 Carnaross 1-1 at Trim, played May 1951

Ben Lynam; Patsy McLoughlin, Ned Teeling, Barney Cooney; Larry O Brien, Paudge Morgan, Peter Tugwell; Eddie Lyons, Seán O Brien; Ernest Kenny, Maurice Delany, Paddy Lyons; Kevin Melia, Capt., Billy Carberry, Benny Foley. Subs: Mickey Kenny for Delany, Johnny Lynch, Kevin Ryan.

1951: Senior Football Championship
Semi-Final: Skryne 1-11 Dunshaughlin 0-6 at Skryne, played April 1952. Team details unavailable.

1952: Senior Football Championship
Semi-Final: Skryne 2-7 Dunshaughlin 1-3 at Warrenstown
Team details unavailable.

1955: Intermediate Football Championship
Semi-Final: Duleek 2-4 Dunshaughlin 0-7 at Skryne
Team not available. Following team played Duleek earlier in the year: Joe Byrne; Patsy O Brien, Patsy McLoughlin, Paschal Smyth; Larry Byrne, Billy Byrne, Tom Everard; Tony Rattigan (0-1), Peter Tugwell; Eamonn Donoghue, Dermot O Keefe, Billie Rattigan (0-4); Larry O Brien, Capt., Dickie O Brien, Kevin Melia (0-1). Sub: Benny Foley (0-1).

1955: Feis Cup
Semi-Final: Ballinlough 3-7 Dunshaughlin 1-7 at Trim. Played May 1956. Team details unavailable.

1956: Intermediate Football Championship
Semi-Final: Dunshaughlin 3-6 Clonard 2-4 at Trim
Final: Dunshaughlin 1-6 Navan O Mahonys 1-6 at Trim
Replay: Navan O Mahonys 3-6 Dunshaughlin 0-5 at Trim

Joe Byrne; Patsy McLoughlin, Billy Byrne, Capt., Dickie O Brien; Patsy O Brien, Brother Tom O Sullivan, Larry Byrne; Tom Nugent, Peter Tugwell; Finian Englishby, Tony Rattigan, Billie Rattigan (0-5); Joe Foley, Benny Foley, Larry O Brien. Subs: Dermot O Keefe for Larry O Brien, Kevin Melia for Billie Rattigan, Barney Cooney.

1957: Junior Hurling B Championship
Played on a League Basis
Final Game: Dunshaughlin 4-6 Kells 0-3 at Kilmessan

The final line-out is the subject of some controversy, but most players and officials agree on the following: Seamus Foley; Matt Daly, Billy Byrne, Dessie Johnson; Dickie O Brien, Benny Foley, Tom Everard; Larry O Brien, Barney Cooney; Tony Rattigan, Seán Mc Manus, Capt., Tommy O Dwyer; Ernest Kenny, Billy Carberry, Kevin Melia. Subs: Bill Murphy, Eamonn O Donoghue, Tommy Troy, Dickie Donnelly. Unable to play: John O Dwyer (inj.), Billie Rattigan (ill).

1958: Junior Football B Championship
Semi-Final: Dunshaughlin 1-7 Dunderry 1-7
Replay: Dunshaughlin 2-8 Dunderry 1-1, Páirc Tailteann
Final: Dunshaughlin 1-6 Rathmolyon 1-2 at Páirc Tailteann

Matt Ryan; Patsy McLoughlin, Jim O Neill, Dessie Johnson; Tom Everard, Peter Tugwell, Tommy O Dwyer; Finian Englishby, Theo Joyce; John O Dwyer (0-1), Benny Foley (1-2), Seamus Foley; Ernest Kenny (0-2), Michael Morrin, Capt., Kevin Melia. Sub: Mal Loughran (0-1) for Michael Morrin.

The County Board later awarded Dunshaughlin the Junior title proper, as Curraha, the winners of the A Division, fielded an illegal player and the team was suspended.

1961: Intermediate Football Championship
Semi-Final: Slane 3-8 Dunshaughlin 1-6 at Páirc Tailteann

Davy O Dwyer; Benny Foley, Tom O Brien (0-1), Dickie Donnelly; Tom Morgan, Tom Everard, Tommy O Dwyer; John O Sullivan, Noel Curran; Seamus Foley (0-3), Finian Englishby, Seán O Brien, Capt.; Val Dowd, Peter Tugwell (1-2), John O Dwyer.

1967: Junior Football A Championship
Semi-Final: Dunshaughlin 1-2 Dunderry 0-4 at Kilmessan
Final: Dunshaughlin 0-8 Athboy 0-5 at Páirc Tailteann

Junior Football Championship Proper
Final: Dunshaughlin 5-3 Skryne 0-4 at Páirc Tailteann

Seamus Foley; Davy O Dwyer, Capt., Mossie Caffrey, Seán Moran; Andy Lynch, Val Dowd, Tommy O Dwyer; John Casey (0-2), Pat O Hare; Paddy O Dwyer, Noel Curran, Con O Dwyer (1-0); John McNally, Pádraig Blake (1-1), Brian O Sullivan (3-0). Subs: Hughie Carty, John O Dwyer, Tom Everard, Brendan Johnson. Selectors: Davy O Dwyer, Seamus Flynn, Benny Foley, Paddy Lynam and Joe Smith.

1970-1989

1973: Intermediate Football Championship
Semi-Final: Bohermeen 1-8 Dunshaughlin 2-4 at Páirc Tailteann

Pat Jennings; Con O Dwyer, Val Dowd, Jody Madden; Pat Farrell, Michael O Dwyer, Mossie Caffrey, Capt.; Michael Walsh (Mayo) (0-1), Pat Murphy; Derek Kenny, Paddy Kenny (1-0), Ger Dowd; Brian Geraghty (1-0), Noel Curran (0-1), Paddy O Dwyer (0-2). Subs: John Casey for Derek Kenny, Seán Mangan for Pat Farrell.

1975: Intermediate Football Championship
Semi-Final: Dunshaughlin 1-7 Castletown 0-7 at Kells
Final: Moylough 2-5 Dunshaughlin 0-9 at Páirc Tailteann

Pat Jennings; Michael Walsh, Val Dowd, Jody Madden; Michael Wead, Neil O Riordan, Michael O Dwyer, Capt.; Pat Mooney, John Jennings; Jimmy Walsh (0-5), Tony Kenny, Ger Dowd; Con O Dwyer (0-1), Noel Curran (0-3), Jimmy O Rourke. Subs: Paddy O Dwyer for Jimmy O Rourke, Pat O Brien for Madden.

1975: Intermediate Football League
Final: Dunshaughlin 2-7 Moylough 0-10 at Páirc Tailteann

Pat Jennings; Pat O Brien, Val Dowd, Jody Madden; Seán Mangan, John Jennings, Michael O Dwyer; Peter Mooney, Michael Wead; Mossie Caffrey, Tony Kenny, Ger Dowd; Con O Dwyer (1-0), Noel Curran (0-3), Paddy O Dwyer (1-4).

1976: Intermediate Football Championship
Semi-Final: Dunshaughlin 0-10 Castletown 2-4 at Kilberry
Replay: Castletown 0-11 Dunshaughlin 0-4 at Páirc Tailteann

Pat Jennings; Jimmy O Rourke, Val Dowd, Michael Walsh; Michael Wead, Pat O Hare, Mossie Caffrey; Tommy Troy, John Jennings; Neil O Riordan, Capt., Ger Dowd (0-1), Pat Mooney; Jimmy Walsh (0-1), Noel Curran (0-2), Paddy O Dwyer. Subs: Michael O Dwyer for Caffrey, Paddy Kenny for Paddy O Dwyer, Con O Dwyer for Tommy Troy, Don

McLoughlin, Seán Mangan, Gerry Keane, Joe McDonnell, Joe Carberry, Tony McConnell, Michael Keane.

1976: Intermediate Football League
Final: Dunshaughlin probably defeated Moynalty

1977: Intermediate Football Championship
Semi-Final: Dunshaughlin 3-6 Donaghmore 0-10 at Trim
Final: Dunshaughlin 0-13 Nobber 0-6 at Páirc Tailteann
Pat Jennings, Capt.; Don McLoughlin, Val Dowd, Michael Walsh; Michael Wead, Pat O Hare, Seán Mangan; Pat O Brien, John Jennings; Ger Dowd (0-1), Neil O Riordan, Jimmy Walsh (0-3); Con O Dwyer (0-1), Noel Curran (0-6), Paddy O Dwyer (0-2). Subs: Pat Farrell, Mossie Caffrey, Gerry Keane, Tony McConnell, Jimmy O Rourke, Tommy Reilly, John Forde.

1977: Intermediate Football League
Final: Dunshaughlin 2-9 Castletown 2-5 at Seneschalstown
Pat Jennings, Capt.; Jimmy O Rourke, Val Dowd, Michael Walsh; Michael Wead, Pat O Hare, Don McLoughlin; Pat O Brien, John Jennings; Jimmy Walsh (0-3), Gerry Keane, Ger Dowd (0-4); Con O Dwyer (1-0), Noel Curran (0-1), Paddy O Dwyer (1-1). Subs: Pat Farrell for Keane.

1980: Junior Football Championship, Division 2
Semi-Final: Walterstown 1-5 Dunshaughlin 0-6 at Kilmessan
John Summerville; Joe McDonnell, Michael O Brien, Michael Walsh; John Kelly, Pat Farrell, Michael Wead; Ollie Brooks (0-1), Pat O Hare; Tommy Kane (0-2), Jimmy O Rourke (0-1), Derek Kenny; Tommy Troy, Fergus O Rourke, Paddy O Dwyer (0-2). Subs: Aidan Walsh for Brooks, Val Dowd for McDonnell, Paddy Kenny for Troy.

1982: Junior Hurling Championship
No semi-final as finalists qualified from a league round robin.
Final: Dunshaughlin 5-4 Killyon 2-4 at Trim
Martin Walsh; Ollie O Neill, Tommy Troy, Hugh Doyle; Gerry Flanagan, John Neville, Gerry Keane; Frank Kelly, Jimmy O Rourke; Gerry Tuohy, Jim Condon (0-1), Tadhg Ó Dúshláine (0-1); Jimmy Walsh, Capt. (1-2), Michael O Brien (1-0), Mick O Keefe (3-0). Subs: Maitias MacDonnacha, Pearse O Dwyer, Tom Keegan, Bernard Jones, Peter Fahy, Aidan Walsh, Christy O Sullivan, John O Sullivan. Pat Kenny didn't play due to illness. Selectors: John Davis, John O Sullivan, Oliver Brooks and Tommy Troy.

1982: Junior Football Championship, Division 2
Semi-Final: Syddan 1-12 Dunshaughlin 1-3 at Kells
Martin Everard; Don McLoughlin, Joe Carberry, Matt McEntaggart; Jimmy O Rourke, Pat Farrell, Seán Mangan; John Kelly, Christy O Sullivan; Michael Wead, Martin Summerville, Derek Kenny; Con O Dwyer, Jimmy Walsh (1-3), Paddy O Dwyer. Subs: Michael Walsh for O Rourke, Neil O Riordan for P O Dwyer, Joe McDonnell for S Mangan.

1983: Intermediate Hurling Championship
No semi-final as finalists qualified from a league round robin.
Final: Dunshaughlin 1-5 Ratoath 0-6 at Trim
Martin Walsh; Ollie O Neill, Capt., Pat Kenny, Tommy Troy; Jimmy O Rourke, Gerry Flanagan, Gerry Keane; Peter Byrne (1-1), Gerry Tuohy; Frank Kelly, Jim Condon (0-1), Mick O Keefe; Jimmy Walsh, Jnr., Mick O Brien, Jimmy Walsh, Snr. (0-3). Subs: Tadhg Ó Dúshláine for Jimmy Walsh, Jnr., Declan Condon for O Keefe, Pearse O Dwyer for Tuohy. Selectors: John Davis, Oliver Brooks, Tommy Troy, John O Sullivan.

1985: East Meath Football League
Final: Ratoath 1-12 Dunshaughlin 2-7 at Donaghmore
Pat Jennings; Matt McEntaggart, Michael O Brien, Michael Wead; Martin Summerville, Dan O Sullivan, Tom Finn; Pat O Brien (0-1), Jimmy O Rourke (0-1); Derek Kenny, Jerry O Donoghue (0-1), Aidan Walsh (1-4); Mick Rawdon (1-0), Joe Carberry, Don McLoughlin.

1985: Intermediate Hurling Championship
No semi-final as finalists qualified from a league round robin.
Final: Athboy 1-8 Dunshaughlin 2-3
Martin Walsh; Tommy Troy, Pat Kenny, Ollie O Neill; Tom Neville, Gerry Flanagan, Jimmy O Rourke, Jr.; John Neville, Tom Finn; Jim Rattigan, Frank Kelly, Capt. (0-1), Nicholas Walsh; Mick O Keefe (0-1), JJ Walsh (1-1), Jimmy Walsh, Snr. Subs: Larry Kirwan (1-0) for Finn, Michael Kennedy for Rattigan.

1986: Intermediate Hurling Championship
No Semi-Final as finalists qualified from a league round robin.
Final: Dunboyne 0-11 Dunshaughlin 1-7
Martin Walsh; Gerry Flanagan, Pat Kenny, Mick O Keefe; Jimmy Walsh Jnr., John Neville, Capt., Larry Kirwan; Jimmy O Rourke (0-1), Denis Burke (0-5); Frank Kelly (1-0), Fintan Delaney, John Davis (0-1); Seán Minihane, Gerry Tuohy, Jimmy Walsh Snr. Subs: Tom Moyler for Tuohy, Jim Rattigan for J Walsh Snr. Selectors: John Davis, Oliver Brooks, John O Sullivan, Tommy Troy.

1987: Intermediate Hurling Championship
No semi-final as finalists qualified from a league round robin.
Final: Dunshaughlin 3-11 Athboy 4-4 at Trim
Ollie O Neill; Larry Kirwan, Pat Kenny, Mick O Keefe; Liam Neville, PJ Townsend, Paul O Rourke; John Neville, Capt., Jim Rattigan (1-0); Martin Walsh, Denis Burke (0-4), John Davis (1-2); Jimmy Walsh (1-4), Jimmy O Rourke (0-1), Gerry Flanagan. Subs: Vinny Moore for Mick O Keefe, Dermot Carey, Frank Kelly, Paul Davis, Declan Brooks, Tommy Troy, Fintan Delaney. Selectors: Oliver Brooks, John Neville, John Davis.

1987: Junior Hurling Championship, Division 2
No semi-final as finalists qualified from a league round robin.
Final: Kildalkey 2-8 Dunshaughlin 3-3 at Trim
Paddy Ward; Gerry Keane, Tommy Troy, Denis Hynes; John Bacon, Seán Walsh, Paul Rattigan; Michael Boyle, Brendan O Rourke; Dermot Carey, Tadhg Ó Dúshláine, Thomas Walsh; Declan Brooks, Mick Farrell, Johnny Leonard. Subs: John O Sullivan, Jimmy O Rourke, Colm Burns, Liam Holton, Declan Cottrell, Jeremy Cottrell, Michael Nixon, William Carey, Paul Davis, Derek Jones, Patrick Stoney, Michael O Brien, Tom Keegan, Tom Condon, David Walsh.

1988: All County League, Division 3
Final: Ballinlough 5-5 Dunshaughlin 1-10 at Walterstown
Derek Melia; Matt McEntaggart, Michael O Brien, Garbhán Blake; Donnchadh Geraghty, Derek Maher, Tom Finn (0-1); Ger Dowd, Pádraig Gallagher; Pat Kealy, Pat O Brien (0-1), Aidan Walsh (0-4); Dermot Kealy (0-3), Pat Flanagan (0-1), Simon Farrell (1-0). Sub: Martin Walsh for Pat Kealy. Selectors: Pat Farrell, Ger Dowd, Michael Walsh.

1988: Under 21 FC
Semi-Final: Dunshaughlin and Seneschalstown drew at Skryne
Replay: Dunshaughlin 2-5 Seneschalstown 1-6 at Walterstown
Final: Gaeil Colmcille 0-9 Dunshaughlin 0-1 at Páirc Tailteann
Derek Melia; David Kane, Derek Maher, Garbhán Blake;

John Davis, Michael Duffy, Capt., Niall Foley; Alan Cummins, Kevin Kealy; Pat Kealy, Stephen Claire, Alan Fahy; Michael Walsh, Simon Farrell (0-1), Dermot Kealy. Subs: Brendan Kealy for Cummins, Colm Naughton for Claire, Paul Hession for Foley. Absent: Brian Duffy, Trevor Kane, both injured, Vincent Moore, suspended. Selectors: Jim Gilligan, Val Dowd, Paddy O Dwyer or Donnchadh Geraghty.

1989: Reserve League.
Final played 1991
Final: Dunshaughlin 1-15 Kilmainhamwood 0-5 at Kilberry
Pearse O Dwyer; David Kane, Donnchadh Geraghty, Niall Foley, Capt.; Ciarán Byrne, Dermot Kealy, Garbhán Blake; Colm Naughton, Alan Cummins (0-1); Pat Kealy (0-2), Francis Darby (0-1), Brendan Kealy (0-2); Pearse Fahy (1-3), Simon Farrell (0-4), Paul O Rourke (0-2). Subs: Aiden Kealy for Byrne, Alan Duffy for Fahy, Martin Summerville for Kane. Selectors: Jim Gilligan, Aidan Walsh.

1990 - 1999

1990: Under 21 FC
Semi-Final: St. Patricks 1-11 Dunshaughlin 1-9 at Rathkenny
Derek Melia; David Kane, Derek Maher, Garbhán Blake; David O Neill, Niall Foley, Pat Kealy, Capt.; Colm Naughton, Dermot Kealy (0-1); Stephen Claire (1-1), Simon Farrell (0-1), Brendan Kealy (0-4); Alan Duffy (0-1), Ciarán Byrne (0-1), Pearse Fahy. Sub: Aiden Kealy for Kane, Alan Fahy for Naughton. Selectors: Val Dowd, Jim Gilligan, Aidan Walsh.

1990: Reserve League
Final played December 1991
Final: Dunshaughlin 3-4 Skryne 1-10 at Páirc Tailteann
Replay: Skryne 2-6 Dunshaughlin 2-5 at Páirc Tailteann
Pearse O Dwyer; Paul O Rourke, Michael O Brien, Aiden Kealy; Ciarán Byrne, Donnchadh Geraghty, Niall Foley; Pat O Brien, Capt., Pat Kealy (0-4); Stephen Claire, Pearse Fahy (1-0), Allen Foley; Alan Duffy, Tiernan O Rourke (1-1), Alan Fahy. Subs: Alan Claire for Alan Fahy, Alan Cummins for Stephen Claire, Martin Summerville, Noel McTigue, David Faughnan, Brian O Rourke, Robbie Keane, Kevin Kealy.

1991: Junior FC, Division 3
Semi-Final: Dunshaughlin 2-6 Carnaross 1-5 at Walterstown
Final: Dunshaughlin 0-11 St. Michaels 2-5 at Páirc Tailteann
Replay: Dunshaughlin 1-8 St. Michaels 0-4 at Páirc Tailteann
Derek Melia; Paul O Rourke, Michael O Brien, Aiden Kealy; Allen Foley, Donnchadh Geraghty, John Considine (0-1); Alan Cummins, Capt., Colm Naughton (0-1); Stephen Claire, Pádraig Gallagher, Alan Fahy (0-1); Alan Duffy (0-4), Val Gannon (1-0), Ciarán O Dwyer. Subs: Alan Claire (0-1) for O Dwyer, Liam O Neill for Gallagher, David O Neill for Foley, Martin Summerville, Brian O Rourke, Joe McDonnell, TP Toolan, Noel McTigue, Martin Walsh, David Faughnan, Robbie Keane. Selectors: Val Dowd, Stephen Burke, Jim Smith.

1991: All County A Football League Division 2
Final: Dunboyne 0-11 Dunshaughlin 0-9 at Páirc Tailteann
Pearse O Dwyer; David Kane, Derek Maher, Garbhán Blake; Ciarán Byrne, Kevin Kealy, Niall Foley; Trevor Kane, Pat O Brien; Simon Farrell (0-3), Francis Darby (0-1), Pat Kealy Capt., (0-1); Aidan Walsh, Pearse Fahy (0-2), Ger Dowd (0-1). Subs: Brendan Kealy (0-1) for Walsh, Alan Duffy for Dowd, Alan Fahy for Darby, Derek Melia, Matt McEntaggart, Tiernan O Rourke, Paul O Rourke, Donnchadh Geraghty, Michael O Brien, Colm Naughton, Dermot Kealy. Selectors: Mick Fennell, John Davis.

1991: Under 21 FC
Semi-Final: St. Patricks 2-10 Dunshaughlin 1-5 at Donore

Derek Melia; David Kane, Aiden Kealy, David O Neill; Ciarán Byrne, Dermot Kealy, Garbhán Blake; Colm Naughton, Stephen Claire (1-1); Ciarán O Dwyer, Pearse Fahy (0-1), Brendan Kealy; Liam O Neill (0-1), Tiernan O Rourke, Alan Fahy. Subs: Alan Claire for Dermot Kealy. Two points unaccounted for.

1992: Intermediate FC
Semi-Final: Dunboyne 1-13 Dunshaughlin 0-5 at Summerhill

Pearse O Dwyer; David Kane, Derek Maher, Paul O Rourke; Ciarán Byrne, Stephen Claire, Pat Kealy; Trevor Kane, Pat O Brien; Alan Claire, Colum Bracken Capt., Francis Darby; Alan Duffy (0-5), Tiernan O Rourke, Pearse Fahy. Subs: Niall Foley for S Claire, Simon Farrell for Foley. Selectors: Mick Fennell, Don Kane, John Davis.

1992: Junior B Championship
Semi-Final: Dunshaughlin 1-10 Seneschalstown 2-5 at Summerhill
Final: Batterstown 2-8 Dunshaughlin 0-10 at Páirc Tailteann

Derek Melia; Matt McEntaggart, Michael O Brien, Noel McTigue; Ciarán O Dwyer, Donnchadh Geraghty, Capt., John Considine; Alan Cummins, Colm Naughton; David O Neill (0-1), Kevin Kealy, Alan Fahy (0-1); Ger Dowd (0-1), Brian O Rourke, Aidan Walsh (0-5). Subs: Diarmuid Leen (0-1) for McTigue, Pádraig Gallagher (0-1) for O Rourke, Michael Keane for O Dwyer, Thomas Walsh, Liam O Neill, TP Toolan, David Faughnan, Martin Summerville, Garbhán Blake, Seamus Magee, Robbie Keane, Ronnie Yore, Ollie McLoughlin. Selectors: Val Dowd, Stephen Burke, Jim Smith.

1992: Division 5 FL
Final: Dunshaughlin 1-7 Gaeil Colmcille 0-10 at Castletown
Replay: Dunshaughlin 0-10 Gaeil Colmcille 1-7 at Páirc Tailteann. Played November 1993.
Replay: Dunshaughlin 1-9 Gaeil Colmcille 2-5 at Rathkenny. Played December 1993.

Derek Melia; Donnchadh Geraghty, Capt., Michael O Brien, David O Neill; Michael Keane, Aiden Kealy, Stephen Claire (0-1); Alan Cummins (0-1), Colm Naughton; Richie Kealy (0-4), Diarmuid Leen, Alan Fahy (0-2); Ger Dowd (1-1), Tiernan O Rourke, Aidan Walsh. Subs: David Faughnan for O Rourke, Brian O Rourke for Walsh, Ronnie Yore for Michael O Brien, Paul O Rourke, Garbhán Blake, Thomas Walsh, Alan Duffy, John Considine. Selectors: Val Dowd, Con O Dwyer, Joe McDonnell.

1993: Intermediate FC
Semi-Final: Dunshaughlin 0-7 Carnaross 1-4 at Páirc Tailteann
Replay: Carnaross 3-15 Dunshaughlin 1-17 after extra time at Páirc Tailteann

Pearse O Dwyer; Dermot Kealy, Derek Maher, Garbhán Blake; Ciarán Byrne, Aiden Kealy, Kevin Kealy; Trevor Kane, Colm Naughton; Aidan Walsh (1-8), Francis Darby, Brendan Kealy (0-2); Alan Duffy (0-5), Pat O Brien (0-1), Ger Dowd (0-1). Subs: Michael O Brien for Darby, Darby for Blake, Blake for M O Brien. Others who played during the year included Colum Bracken, Tiernan O Rourke, David Kane, Diarmuid Leen, Stephen Claire, Richie Kealy, Simon Farrell, Pearse Fahy. Selectors: Don Kane, Paddy O Dwyer. Coach: Anto McCaul.

1993: Under 21 FC
Semi-Final: Moynalvey 2-4 Dunshaughlin 1-6 at Páirc Tailteann

Kenny McTigue; Hugh McCarthy, Ronnie Yore, Brian Murray; David Faughnan, David O Neill, Robbie Keane; Aiden Kealy (0-3), Michael Keane; Clive Dowd, Tiernan O Rourke, Alan Claire (1-0); Brian O Rourke, Brendan Kealy (0-3), Cathal O Connor. Subs: Fionnán Blake for McCarthy, Mick Summerville for O Connor, Denis Kealy for Dowd, Brendan Tuite, Andrew Keane, Caoimhín Blake, Richie Kealy, Ollie McLoughlin.

1994: Intermediate FC
Semi-Final: Kilmainhamwood 0-10 Dunshaughlin 0-7 at Seneschalstown

Derek Melia; David Kane, Aiden Kealy, Garbhán Blake; Ciarán Byrne, Derek Maher, Francis Darby; Colum Bracken, Capt., Kevin Kealy; Simon Farrell (0-2), Dermot Kealy (0-1), Alan Fahy; Richie Kealy (0-2), Brendan Kealy, Aidan Walsh (0-2). Subs: Colm Naughton for Fahy, Ger Dowd for Walsh. Coach: Liam Harnan. Selectors: Paddy O Dwyer, Val Dowd, Pat O Brien.

1994: Junior B Championship
Semi-Final: Dunshaughlin 2-13 St. Patricks 2-6
Final: Dunshaughlin 1-9 Syddan 1-6 at Páirc Tailteann

Kenny McTigue; Matt McEntaggart, Michael O Brien, Brian Murray; Stephen Kelly, Donnchadh Geraghty (1-0), Thomas Walsh; Michael Keane, Alan Cummins; Clive Dowd, Diarmuid Leen, Mervyn Ennis (0-6); Alan Duffy (0-2), Pat O Brien, George Ennis, Capt. (0-1). Subs: David O Neill for Cummins, Niall Foley for P O Brien, Noel McTigue for Leen, Ronnie Yore, Alan O Dwyer, John Considine, David Faughnan, Cathal O Connor, Martin Summerville, Eric Yore, Liam O Neill, Mick Summerville. Derek Melia, Alan Fahy, Colm Naughton promoted to intermediate team so unavailable for junior final. Selectors: Val Dowd, Con O Dwyer, Derek Kenny.

1995: Under 21 A, FC
Semi-Final: Dunshaughlin 3-6 Blackhall Gaels 1-9 at Rathkenny.
Final: Slane 1-9 Dunshaughlin 1-8 at Rathkenny

Fearghal Gogan; Kenny McTigue, David Faughnan; Pádraic O Dwyer, Aiden Kealy, Capt., Robbie Keane (0-1); Richie Kealy (0-1), Michael Keane; Clive Dowd (0-2), Brian O Rourke, Denis Kealy (0-1); Graham Dowd (0-3), David Tonge (1-0). Subs: Alan Claire for Denis Kealy, Mick Summerville for O Rourke, Fionnán Blake, Ulick McDonnell, Andrew Keane, Caoimhín Blake, Shane Kelly, Eric Yore, Neil O Dwyer, Dessie Keane, Raymond Yore, Eamonn O Dwyer.

1996: Intermediate FC
Semi-Final: Dunshaughlin 0-11 Duleek 1-8 at Páirc Tailteann
Replay: Duleek 2-5 Dunshaughlin 0-9 at Páirc Tailteann

Derek Melia; Derek Maher, Brendan Mooney, Kenny McTigue; Ciarán Byrne, Dermot Kealy (0-3), Francis Darby (0-1); Colum Bracken (0-1), Colm Naughton; Kevin Kealy, Aiden Kealy, Denis Kealy (0-1); Simon Farrell (0-1), Richie Kealy (0-2), Tiernan O Rourke. Subs: Brendan Kealy for O Rourke, Alan Duffy, Graham Dowd, Michael Keane, Barry Doyle, Ronnie Yore. Garbhán Blake played in earlier rounds. Team Manager: Paddy O Dwyer, Trainer/Coach: Jim Gilligan, Selector: Mick Fennell.

1996: Under 21 A, FC
Semi-Final and Final played in February 1997
Semi-Final: Dunshaughlin 1-9 St. Ultans 0-8 at Kilberry
Final: Carnaross 1-15 Dunshaughlin 0-9 at Seneschalstown

Eoin Gorman; Fearghal Gogan, Shane Kelly; Pádraic O Dwyer, Kenny McTigue, Denis Kealy; Richie Kealy, Capt., Fionnán Blake; David Tonge (0-2), Graham Dowd (0-4), David Crimmins (0-1); David McCormack, Clive Dowd (0-2). Subs: Paul Hendrick for Blake, Mick Summerville for Clive Dowd, Ulick McDonnell, Paddy McHale, Neil O Dwyer, Dessie Keane, Niall Kelly. Selectors: Jim Gilligan, Paddy O Dwyer, Mick Fennell.

1997: Intermediate FC
Semi-Final: Dunshaughlin 2-13 Blackhall Gaels 1-12 at Páirc Tailteann
Final: Dunshaughlin 3-14 Duleek 1-6 at Páirc Tailteann

Brian O Rourke; Kenny McTigue, Dermot Kealy, Brendan Mooney; Francis Darby, Ciarán Byrne, Capt., Ronnie

Yore; Colum Bracken, Colm Naughton (0-1); Denis Kealy (1-1), Graham Dowd (1-5), David Tonge (0-2); Richie Kealy (0-2), Tiernan O Rourke (1-1), Pádraic O Dwyer (0-2). Subs: Robbie Keane for O Dwyer, Michael Keane for Yore, Kevin Kealy for Denis Kealy, Derek Melia, Clive Dowd, Alan Duffy, David Kane, David O Neill. The following were not listed on the county final programme but had played or were members of the panel during the year: Simon Farrell, injured for the final, Barry Doyle, sent-off in the semi-final, Derek Maher, David Moroney, Paul O Rourke, Declan Rock, Ger Dowd, Michael O Brien and Niall Kelly. Team Manager: Val Dowd, Selectors: Don Kane, Matt McEntaggart, Seamus Magee. Trainer: Philip Phelan, Coach: Colm O Rourke.

1999: Senior Football Championship
Semi-Final: Dunshaughlin 1-8 Dunderry 2-2 at Páirc Tailteann
Final: Skryne 1-12 Dunshaughlin 0-8 at Páirc Tailteann
Brian O Rourke; Fearghal Gogan, Kenny McTigue, Ciarán Byrne; Denis Kealy (0-6), Aiden Kealy, Shane Kelly; Dermot Kealy, Capt., Niall Kelly; David Moroney, Richie Kealy, Stephen Claire; David Crimmins, Tiernan O Rourke (0-1), Graham Dowd (0-1). Subs: Brendan Kealy for Niall Kelly, Ronnie Yore for Shane Kelly, Ronan Gogan, Brendan Kealy, Trevor Dowd, Ciarán O Dwyer, David Tonge, Michael McHale, Kevin Moyles, Kevin Kealy. Selectors: Brendan Kealy, TP Toolan, Trainer/Coach: Eamonn Barry.

1999: All County B Football League, Division 1
Final played February 2000
Final: Dunshaughlin 3-9 Summerhill 0-9 at Gibbstown
Ronan Gogan; John Davis, Ulick McDonnell, Shane Kelly, Capt.; Kevin Moyles, Fearghal Gogan, Garbhán Blake; Simon Farrell, Kevin Kealy; David Crimmins (0-1), Brendan Kealy (0-1), David McNerney (1-0); Paddy McHale (1-1), Michael McHale (0-1), Trevor Dowd (1-5).

Subs: Pádraic O Dwyer for Crimmins, Christopher Carey, Declan Fahy, Niall Foley, Alan O Dwyer, Neil O Dwyer, Brian Murphy, George Ennis. Selectors: Neil Halpin, Fergus O Rourke, Martin Summerville.

2000-2014

2000: Senior Football Championship
Semi-Final: Dunshaughlin 2-11 Trim 0-12 at Páirc Tailteann
Final: Dunshaughlin 1-19 Kilmainhamwood 2-6 at Páirc Tailteann
Ronan Gogan; Fearghal Gogan, Kenny McTigue, Ciarán Byrne; Denis Kealy, Aiden Kealy, Ronnie Yore; Dermot Kealy, Capt., (0-2), Graham Dowd (1-0); Niall Kelly (0-3), Paddy McHale (0-1), Brendan Kealy; Richie Kealy (0-7), David Crimmins (0-1), Trevor Dowd (0-4). Subs: Tommy Sullivan (0-1) for McHale, Kevin Kealy for Trevor Dowd, Garbhán Blake for Fearghal Gogan, Damien Eames, David Tonge, David Moroney, Stephen Claire, Pádraic O Dwyer, Shane Kelly, Kevin Moyles, Tiernan O Rourke, Christopher Carey, Declan Fahy, David McNerney, Ulick McDonnell, Michael McHale.

2000: Leinster Club Championship
Round 1: Dunshaughlin 2-5 Rathnew 0-11 at Páirc Tailteann
Replay: Dunshaughlin 1-11 Rathnew 0-14, after extra time at Aughrim
Second Replay: Dunshaughlin 3-8 Rathnew 1-6 at Páirc Tailteann
Quarter-final: Moorefield 4-7 Dunshaughlin 0-6 at Páirc Tailteann
Ronan Gogan; Fearghal Gogan, Kenny McTigue, Ciarán Byrne; Denis Kealy, Aiden Kealy, Ronnie Yore; Dermot Kealy, Graham Dowd (0-1); David Tonge, Paddy McHale (0-3), Brendan Kealy; David Crimmins, Michael McHale, Trevor Dowd (0-2). Subs: Stephen Claire for Graham Dowd, Kevin Kealy for T Dowd, Tiernan O Rourke for

Tonge, Shane Kelly for M McHale, Tommie O Sullivan for Crimmins.

2000: All County Football League, Division 1
Final: St. Patrick's 0-9 Dunshaughlin 0-8 at Simonstown
Ronan Gogan; Fearghal Gogan (0-1), Kenny McTigue, Garbhán Blake; Denis Kealy, Aiden Kealy, Ronnie Yore; Dermot Kealy, Capt., (0-1), Graham Dowd; Niall Kelly, Paddy McHale, Brendan Kealy (0-1); Richie Kealy (0-1), David Crimmins (0-1), Trevor Dowd (0-3). Subs: David Tonge for Graham Dowd, Kevin Kealy for Kelly, Stephen Claire for Crimmins, Michael McHale for P McHale, Damien Eames, Shane Kelly, Garbhán Blake, Stephen Claire, Pádraic O Dwyer, Christopher Carey, Declan O Dwyer, Declan Fahy, David McNerney, Ulick McDonnell, David Moroney, Kevin Moyles, Tiernan O Rourke, Tommy O Sullivan. Ciarán Byrne missed the final due to his sending off in the SFC final. Selectors for three competitions above: Brendan Kealy, TP Toolan, Trainer/Coach: Eamonn Barry.

2000: Under 21 A, FC
Semi-Final: Dunshaughlin 3-11 St. Ultans 3-7 at Kilberry
Final: Dunshaughlin 3-7 Ballivor 1-9 at Páirc Tailteann
Ronan Gogan; Kevin Moyles, Denis Kealy, Capt.; Christopher Carey, Michael McHale, Paul Hendrick; Niall Kelly, David Tonge; David McNerney, Paddy McHale, Keith Mangan; David Crimmins (3-2), Trevor Dowd (0-5). Subs: John Joe McDonnell for Hendrick, Ray Maloney for Mangan, Declan Fahy for Moyles, David Tormay, Ronan Murphy, Piaras Delany, John McKenna, John Crimmins. Selectors: Graham Dowd, Jim Gilligan, Pat Maloney. Team Manager: Fergus O Rourke.

2001: Senior Football Championship
Semi-Final: Dunshaughlin 2-11 Walterstown 2-7 at Páirc Tailteann
Final: Dunshaughlin 0-11 Skryne 1-5 at Páirc Tailteann
Ronan Gogan; Fearghal Gogan, Kenny McTigue, Ciarán Byrne, Capt.; Ronnie Yore, Aiden Kealy, Denis Kealy; Dermot Kealy, Graham Dowd (0-2); Niall Kelly (0-1), Michael McHale, Martin Reilly (0-7); Richie Kealy (0-1), David Crimmins, Trevor Dowd. Subs: Christopher Carey, David Tonge, Garbhán Blake, Shane Kelly, Tiernan O Rourke, Paddy McHale, Kevin Kealy, Brendan Kealy, Stephen Claire, Keith Mangan, Ray Maloney, Tom O Sullivan, Kevin Moyles, David McNerney, Damien Eames. Selectors: Brendan Kealy, TP Toolan, Trainer/Coach: Eamonn Barry.

2001: Leinster Club Championship
Quarter-final: Dunshaughlin 0-10 Rathnew 0-10 at Aughrim
Replay: Dunshaughlin 0-16 Rathnew 2-10, after extra time at Páirc Tailteann
Second Replay: Rathnew 2-9 Dunshaughlin 1-6 at Aughrim
Ronan Gogan; Ciarán Byrne, Kenny McTigue, Aiden Kealy; Ronnie Yore, Denis Kealy, Fearghal Gogan; Dermot Kealy, Graham Dowd; Niall Kelly (0-1), David Crimmins (0-1), Martin Reilly (0-1); Richie Kealy (0-1), Michael McHale (0-2), Trevor Dowd (1-0). Subs: Brendan Kealy for G Dowd, Christopher Carey, David Tonge, Garbhán Blake, Stephen Claire, Shane Kelly, Brendan Kealy, Kevin Kealy, Keith Mangan, Ray Maloney, David McNerney, Kevin Moyles. Selectors: Brendan Kealy, TP Toolan, Trainer/Coach: Eamonn Barry.

2002: Senior Football Championship
Semi-Final: Dunshaughlin 0-10 Seneschalstown 1-4 at Páirc Tailteann
Final: Dunshaughlin 1-11 Trim 2-6 at Páirc Tailteann
Ronan Gogan; Fearghal Gogan, Kenny McTigue, Capt., Ciarán Byrne; Ronnie Yore, Michael McHale, Denis Kealy (0-1); Niall Kelly (0-1), Dermot Kealy; Brendan Kealy (0-1), Ray Maloney (0-1), Martin Reilly (0-3); Richie Kealy (0-1), David Crimmins (0-3), Trevor Dowd (1-0). Subs: Damian Burke for Dowd, Dowd for Yore, Stephen

Claire for Brendan Kealy, Chris Carey, David Tonge, Kevin Moyles, Kevin Kealy, Shane Kelly, John Crimmins, Declan O Dwyer, Keith Mangan, Caoimhín King, Graham Dowd. Aiden Kealy.

2002: Leinster Club Championship
Quarter-final: Dunshaughlin 1-11 Rathvilly 0-2 at Carlow
Semi-Final: Dunshaughlin 0-12 Rathnew 1-9 at Newbridge
Replay: Dunshaughlin 1-7 Rathnew 0-4 at Newbridge
Final: Dunshaughlin 0-13 Mattock Rangers 0-7 at Páirc Tailteann

Ronan Gogan; Fearghal Gogan, Kenny McTigue, Capt., Denis Kealy; Ronnie Yore, Michael McHale, Richie Kealy (0-2); Niall Kelly (0-3), Dermot Kealy; Martin Reilly (0-2), David Crimmins (0-2), David Tonge (0-2); Brendan Kealy, Ray Maloney (0-1), Trevor Dowd (0-1). Subs: Damian Burke for Ray Maloney, Christopher Carey, Ciarán Byrne, Kevin Moyles, Kevin Kealy, Shane Kelly, John Crimmins, Declan O Dwyer, Keith Mangan, Caoimhín King. Stephen Claire unavailable, overseas on UN duty.

2002: All-Ireland Club Championship
Semi-Final: Crossmolina 3-10 Dunshaughlin 1-12 at Hyde Park, Roscommon.

Ronan Gogan; Fearghal Gogan, Kenny McTigue, Capt., Denis Kealy; Ronnie Yore, Michael McHale, Richie Kealy (0-2); Niall Kelly, Dermot Kealy; Brendan Kealy (1-0), Ray Maloney (0-1), David Tonge; Martin Reilly (0-6), David Crimmins (0-3), Trevor Dowd. Subs: Aiden Kealy for Yore, Ciarán Byrne for Dowd, John Crimmins for Brendan Kealy, Christopher Carey, Kevin Moyles, Caoimhín King, Shane Kelly, Kevin Kealy, Declan O Dwyer, Keith Mangan, Stephen Claire, Graham Dowd.

2002: All County Football League Division 1
Final: Dunshaughlin 4-12 Dunboyne 2-8 at Donaghmore

Ronan Gogan; Denis Kealy, Kenny McTigue, Capt., Ciarán Byrne; Fearghal Gogan, Michael McHale, Richie Kealy; Niall Kelly (0-2), Dermot Kealy (0-1); Brendan Kealy (0-1), David Crimmins (1-1), David Tonge (1-2); Martin Reilly (0-4), Ray Maloney (1-0), Trevor Dowd (1-0). Subs: Damian Burke for Reilly, Declan O Dwyer for B Kealy, Kevin Moyles for F Gogan, Kevin Kealy for Tonge, Keith Mangan (0-1) for Dowd, Christopher Carey, Shane Kelly, John Crimmins, Caoimhín King. Graham Dowd ruled out through injury.

2002: Feis Cup
Final: Dunshaughlin 1-18 Castletown 1-3 at Simonstown

Christopher Carey; Fearghal Gogan, Kenny McTigue, Ciarán Byrne; Ronnie Yore, Capt., Richie Kealy (0-1), Kevin Moyles; Niall Kelly (0-1), Dermot Kealy; Brendan Kealy, Ray Maloney, Martin Reilly (0-7); David Crimmins (1-2), Michael McHale (0-3), Trevor Dowd (0-3). Subs: David Tonge (0-1) for B Kealy, Caoimhín King for Byrne, Shane Kelly for Reilly, Damian Burke for McHale, Kevin Kealy for Dowd, Ronan Gogan, Declan O Dwyer, Keith Mangan, John Crimmins. Graham Dowd and Denis Kealy ruled out through injury. Selectors for all 2002 games above: Brendan Kealy, TP Toolan. Trainer/Coach: Eamonn Barry.

2003: Senior Football Championship
Semi-Final: Blackhall Gaels 3-9 Dunshaughlin 1-12 at Páirc Tailteann

Ronan Gogan; Fearghal Gogan, Kenny McTigue, Capt., Ciarán Byrne; Ronnie Yore, Aiden Kealy, Caoimhín King; Niall Kelly (0-7), John Crimmins; Martin Reilly, Shane Kelly, David Tonge (0-1); David Crimmins (1-0), Ray Maloney, Trevor Dowd (0-4). Subs: Michael McHale for King, Richie Kealy for Shane Kelly, Mick Ryan for Maloney, Brendan Kealy for Tonge, Damian Burke for John Crimmins.

2003: All County Football A League Division 1
Final: Walterstown 3-4 Dunshaughlin 1-9 at Páirc Tailteann

Ronan Gogan; Fearghal Gogan, Kenny McTigue, Capt., Ciarán Byrne; Ronnie Yore, Michael McHale, Caoimhín King; Aiden Kealy (0-1), John Crimmins; Brendan Kealy, David Crimmins (0-1), Martin Reilly (0-2); Richie Kealy, Niall Kelly (1-3), Trevor Dowd (0-2). Subs: Ray Maloney for Richie Kealy, Mick Ryan for Yore, Andy Quinn for Dowd, Damian Burke for John Crimmins, Denis Kealy for McHale.

2003: All County Football B League Division 5
Final: Dunshaughlin 2-14 Carnaross 0-8 at Bective
Shane Byrne; Brian Murphy, Noel McTigue, Neil O Dwyer; Ciarán O Dwyer, Hugo Lynch, Francis Darby; Owen Herlihy, Pearse Fahy; Dessie Keane, Capt., Kevin Ward, JJ McDonnell; David McCormack (1-1), Stephen Ward (0-4), Cathal O Dwyer (1-7). Subs: Pádraic O Dwyer (0-2) for JJ McDonnell, Ciarán Hoary for Keane, Eoin Farrelly for Darby, Jamie Minnock. Team Manager: Hugh McCarthy. Selectors: George Ennis, Ollie Gogan, Lally McCormack.

2004: Senior Football Championship
Semi-Final: Dunshaughlin 0-14 Skryne 1-11 after extra time at Páirc Tailteann
Replay: Skryne 0-15 Dunshaughlin 1-7 at Páirc Tailteann
Ronan Gogan; Fearghal Gogan, Kenny McTigue, Caoimhín King; Ronnie Yore, Denis Kealy, Kevin Ward; Aiden Kealy (0-1), Niall Kelly (0-2); Trevor Dowd (1-1), Ray Maloney, David Tonge; Richie Kealy, David Crimmins, Cathal O Dwyer (0-3). Subs: Martin Reilly for Tonge, Dermot Kealy for Ward, Michael McHale, Capt. for Crimmins.

2004: Under 21 A, FC
Semi-Final: Dunshaughlin 3-13 Skryne 2-6 at Ratoath
Final: Dunshaughlin 0-11 Na Fianna 1-6 at Ratoath
Michael Ahern; Caoimhín King, Ciarán Hoary; Alan McLoughlin, Kevin Ward, Owen Farrelly; Ray Maloney, Capt. (0-2), Owen Herlihy; Ciarán Farrelly, Stephen Ward (0-2), David Devereux (0-3); Cathal O Dwyer (0-3), Conor Staunton (0-1). Subs: Gavin O Regan for Ahern, Cormac Delaney for Farrelly, Shane Kelly for Devereux, Paul Sheehy, Adrian Toolan, Diarmuid Delaney, Jamie Minnock, Brian Murphy. Team Manager: Gabriel King. Selectors: Pat Herlihy, David Crimmins, Sen. Coach: Denis Kealy.

2005: Junior C Football Championship
Semi-Final: St. Colmcilles 2-11 Dunshaughlin 1-9 at Duleek.
Gavin O Regan; Brian Murphy, Hugo Lynch, Pearse Fahy; Alan McLoughlin (0-2), Francis Darby, Cathal Moore; Simon Farrell (1-2), Thomas Walsh (0-2); John McKenna (0-1), Ciarán Hoary, Mick Summerville; Robbie Keane, Noel McTigue, Mark Caldwell (0-2). Subs: Martin Duffy for McTigue, Declan Fahy for Keane, Brendan Killoran for Summerville. Selectors: George Ennis, Pat Herlihy, Mick Summerville.

2006: Under 21 A, FC
Semi-Final: Gaeil Colmcille 2-9 Dunshaughlin 0-14 at Dunganny
Derek Jordan; Anthony Johnson, Ciarán Hoary; Kevin Ward, Michael Ahern, Owen Herlihy (0-1); Cillian Finn, Caoimhín King (0-1); Ciarán Farrelly, David Devereux (0-2), Alan McLoughlin; Conor Staunton (0-1), Cathal O Dwyer (0-9). Subs: Tommy Johnson for McLoughlin, Mark Caldwell for Farrelly. Selectors: Gabriel King, Pat Herlihy, Damian Burke.

2006: Junior B Football Championship
Semi-Final: St. Brigid's 1-16 Dunshaughlin 1-8 at Walterstown
Derek Jordan; Brian Murphy, Ulick McDonnell, Kevin Moyles; Neil O Dwyer, Shane Kelly, Declan O Dwyer; Michael Beagan, Paul Sheehy; Alan McLaughlin, Shane Kelly, Tommy Johnson; David McCormack, Pádraic O Dwyer, Mark Caldwell. Selectors: Noel McTigue, Martin Summerville, Paddy Ward.

2007: Under 21 A, FC
Semi-Final: Dunshaughlin 3-16 Na Fianna 2-15 after extra time at Summerhill
Final: Dunshaughlin 2-11 Wolfe Tones 1-10 at Páirc Tailteann

Seán Doyle; Ciarán Clusker, Tommy Johnson; Alan McLoughlin, Michael Ahern, Fearghal Delaney; Cillian Finn, Ciarán Farrelly (0-1); Niall Dundon, David Devereux (0-1), Mark Caldwell (0-1); Conor Staunton (2-3), Cathal O Dwyer, Capt. (0-4). Subs: Dara Devereux (0-1) for Dundon, Duncan Geraghty, Tadhg Ó Dúshláine, Shane Kelly, Alan McLoughlin, Cathal Moore, Cillian Dennehy, David O Rourke. Team Manager: Don McLoughlin. Coach: Tommy Clusker. Selectors: Simon Farrell, Tom Finn.

2007: All County Football B League Division 4
Final: Rathkenny 0-13 Dunshaughlin 2-6 at Simonstown

Christopher Carey; Ronnie Yore, Martin Duffy, Eoin Farrelly; Ciarán Clusker, Owen Herlihy, Mark Devanney; Simon Farrell, Shane Kelly; Fearghal Delaney, Gerry Keenan, Mick Summerville, Capt.; Niall Dundon (0-1), Pádraic O Dwyer (1-3), Mark Caldwell (0-2). Subs: Tadhg Ó Dúshláine for Summerville, Gerard O Brien (1-0) for Keenan, Cathal Moore for Duffy, Paul Hendrick for Devanney. Team Manager: Lally McCormack. Selectors: Pat Herlihy, Hugo Lynch.

2008: All County Football B League Division 2
Final: Dunshaughlin 0-11 Donaghmore-Ashbourne 0-10 at Ashbourne

Stephen Clusker; Donnacha Lloyd, Tommy Johnson, Fearghal Delaney; Alan McLoughlin, Kevin Moyles, Tadhg Ó Dúshláine; Graham Dowd, Capt., Ciarán Farrelly; Dara Devereux, Trevor Dowd (0-3), Ciarán Hoary; Eamon Bowe, David Devereux (0-1), Michael Johnson (0-1). Subs: Niall Dundon for Dara Devereux, Brian Murphy for Lloyd, Shane Kelly (0-1) for Ó Dúshláine, Mark Devanney for Delaney, Seán Doyle, Eoin Hagarty, Duncan Geraghty, Mark Caldwell, John Coleman, Neil O Dwyer. Five points unaccounted for. Selectors: Simon Farrell, Noel McTigue. Team Manager: Don McLoughlin.

2009: Junior B Football Championship
Semi-Final: Dunshaughlin 3-10 Duleek - Bellewstown 2-13 at Ratoath
Replay: Duleek - Bellewstown 1-9 Dunshaughlin 1-8 at Skryne

Stephen Clusker; Kevin Moyles, Brian Murphy, Fearghal Delaney; Fearghal Gogan, Ronnie Yore, Tadhg Ó Dúshláine; Paddy McHale (0-1), Duncan Geraghty (0-1); Dara Devereux, David Devereux (1-2), Ciarán Clusker; Eamon Bowe (0-2), Eoin Hagarty (0-1), Niall Murphy (0-1). Subs: David McMahon for Delaney, Alan McLoughlin for Dara Devereux, Shane Kelly for Hagarty, Mark Devanney for McMahon. Selectors: Michael McHale, Don McLoughlin, Noel McTigue.

2009: All County Football B League Division 1
Final: Navan O Mahonys 0-11 Dunshaughlin 0-8 at Donore

Stephen Clusker; Kevin Moyles, Capt., Brian Murphy, Fearghal Delaney; Fearghal Gogan, Ronnie Yore, Tadhg Ó Dúshláine; Ray Maloney (0-1), Cillian Finn; Eoin Hagarty (0-1), Paddy McHale (0-1), Conor Devereux (0-2); David Devereux (0-1), John Crimmins (0-1), Niall Murphy (0-1). Subs: Eamon Bowe for Hagarty, David McMahon for N Murphy. Selectors: Don McLoughlin, Michael McHale.

2011: Senior Football Championship
Semi-Final: Dunshaughlin 1-9 Donaghmore-Ashbourne 1-8 at Páirc Tailteann
Final: Dunshaughlin 0-10 Summerhill 0-10 at Páirc Tailteann
Replay: Summerhill 0-14 Dunshaughlin 1-9 after extra time at Páirc Tailteann

Ronan Gogan; Alastar Doyle, Kenny McTigue, Michael Ahern; Anthony Johnson, Caoimhín King, Denis Kealy;

John Crimmins (0-1), Ray Maloney, Capt. (0-1); Fergus Toolan (0-1), Trevor Dowd (0-3), Conor Devereux; Tommy Johnson (1-1), Niall Murphy, Cathal O Dwyer (0-1). Subs: Niall Kelly for Tommy Johnson, Tadhg Ó Dúshláine for Dowd. Extra time: Eoin Hagarty (0-1) for Toolan, Richie Kealy for Anthony Johnson, Kevin Ward for King, Stephen Clusker, Martin Reilly, Paddy McHale, Fearghal Delaney. Selectors: Pat Maloney, TP Toolan. Trainer/Coach: Gary Farrelly.

Scorers in original final: Cathal O Dwyer (0-3), Conor Devereux (0-2), Trevor Dowd (0-2), Denis Kealy, Niall Murphy and Fergus Toolan (0-1 each).

2011: Feis Cup
Final: Dunshaughlin 1-10 Blackhall Gaels 1-6 at Páirc Tailteann

Ronan Gogan; Alastar Doyle, Kenny McTigue, Denis Kealy; Anthony Johnson, Caoimhín King, Tommy Johnson; John Crimmins (0-1), Ray Maloney, Capt., (0-2); Fergus Toolan (0-1), Trevor Dowd (0-3), Conor Devereux (0-1); Tadhg Ó Dúshláine (0-1), Niall Murphy, Cathal O Dwyer (1-0). Subs: Kevin Ward for Anthony Johnson, Niall Kelly (0-1) for Ó Dúshláine, Fearghal Delaney for Ward, Eoin Hagarty for Tommy Johnson, Paddy McHale for Devereux, Stephen Clusker, Richie Kealy, Martin Reilly, Fearghal Gogan, Mark Devanney, James Rattigan, Emmet Staunton, Daniel Geraghty, James Horgan, Michael Johnson, Michael Ahern, Duncan Geraghty. Selectors: Pat Maloney, TP Toolan. Trainer/Coach: Gary Farrelly.

2011: Under 21, A FC
Semi-Final: Drumbaragh-Kilmainham 4-7 Dunshaughlin 0-7 at Simonstown

Stephen Clusker; Seán Joyce, Alastar Doyle; Eoin Hagarty (0-1), Tommy Johnson, Ciarán Clusker (0-1); James Horgan, Fergus Toolan; Tadhg Ó Dúshláine, Capt., Conor Devereux (0-2), Emmet Staunton; Niall Murphy (0-2), James Rattigan (0-1). Subs: Joe O Brien for Horgan, David Doherty for Joyce, Patrick Darby for Rattigan, Cillian Dennehy for Ó Dúshláine. Selectors: Graham Dowd, Simon Farrell, Michael McHale.

2011: All County Football B League Division 1
Final: Donaghmore-Ashbourne 1-10 Dunshaughlin 0-8 at Ashbourne

Stephen Clusker; Kevin Moyles, Kenny McTigue, Mark Devanney; Kevin Ward, Fearghal Delaney, Anthony Johnson (0-1); Paddy McHale, Capt., Eoin Hagarty (0-1); Niall Kelly, Emmet Staunton (0-2), James Horgan; Ciarán Hoary, Martin Reilly (0-2), James Rattigan (0-1). Subs: Richie Kealy (0-1) for Hoary, Alan McLoughlin for Johnson, David McCormack for Rattigan, Daniel Geraghty for Moyles, James Kelliher, Ronan Geraghty, John Coleman, Ciarán Clusker, Cillian Dennehy. Selectors: Graham Dowd, Michael McHale, TP Toolan.

2012: Junior B Football Championship
Semi-Final: Dunshaughlin 1-7 St. Vincents 0-9 at Ashbourne

Final: Dunshaughlin 0-12 St. Marys 0-9 at Páirc Tailteann
Seán Doyle; John Joe McDonnell, Capt., Ulick McDonnell, Kevin Ward; Eoin Farrelly, Niall Kelly (0-2), Mark Devanney; Michael Ahern (0-1), Ciarán Clusker; David Tonge, Stephen Ward (0-3), David McMahon (0-1); Daniel Geraghty, David Crimmins, James Rattigan (0-5). Subs: Emmet Staunton for Clusker, John Coleman for Geraghty, Duncan Geraghty for Tonge, Shane Kelly, Graham Dowd, Cillian Dennehy, Patrick Darby, Liam Ormsby, Stephen Doyle. Selectors: Simon Farrell, Martin Reilly. Manager: Michael McHale.

Dunshaughlin Under Age 2009-2014

Under Age results prior to 2009 are in Appendix 8 under St. Martins. Due to the number of competitions we have recorded the outcome of finals only, apart from the Minor grade where semi-final details are also listed.

2009

Under 10
Meath Community Games champions.
Leinster Quarter-Final: Killoe, Longford 4-4 Dunshaughlin 1-1

Wesley Goodwin; Liam Hanley, Conor Jones, Evan Butler; Matthew Moyles, Paddy Maher, Niall Gavin; Conor Keena, Capt., Niall Hurley; Mark Connolly, Sam Cowan, James Ryan; Seán Ennis, Conor Oliver (1-1), Cathal Sheehan. Subs: Alastair Philip for Sheehan, Gary Power for Ennis, Aaron Lawlor for Cowan, Alan O Connor, Liam O Reilly. Team Management: Stephen Claire, Brendan Connolly, Paul Hetherington.

Under 14, Division 1 B, FL
Final: Dunshaughlin 3-17 St. Colmcilles 0-4 at Ratoath

Jack O Sullivan; Josh Wall, Seán Fitzpatrick, Gareth Rooney; Oisín Foley, Steven Kinsella, David Reilly (0-1); Ben Duggan, Capt. (0-6), Diarmuid Christie (0-1); Lorcán Byrne, Shane Gallogly (0-3), Stephen Duffy (1-2); David Beattie (0-2), David Moore (2-1), Stephen Farrell (0-1). Subs: Tom Sharp for Farrell, Ronan Geraghty for Duffy, Dan Ormsby for Christie, Craig Cullen for O Sullivan, Conor McEvoy, David Dunne, Martin Nevin. Team Management: Frank Gallogly, Robbie Byrne, Jimmy Beattie and Paul McEvoy.

Under 14, Reserve FL
Final Replay: Dunshaughlin 6-6 Navan O Mahonys 2-6

Panel: Gavin Maher, Tommy Kinsella, Lorcán Casey, Sam Lavery, Mark Galvin, Ronan Smith, Paddy Maher, Adam Kealy, Conor Huijsdens, Daniel Quinn, Martin Nevin, Cormac Fitzpatrick, James Swan, Conor McEvoy, Liam Carey, Conor Jennings, Luke Ennis, Cillian Gavin, David Dunne, Capt., Aaron Kealy. Team Management: Kevin Kealy, Tommy Maher, Michael Nevin.

Under 16, Division 1A, FL
Semi-Final: Dunshaughlin 6-8 Clanna Gael 3-13 after extra time at Dunsany
Final: Moynalvey 3-7 Dunshaughlin 0-8 at Páirc Tailteann

Jack O Sullivan; Steven Kinsella, Aidan Boswell, David Doherty; Andrew Kiernan, James Reilly, Keith Rooney; Eoin Hannon, Niall Hannon; Gavin Regan (0-1), Eimhín Kinsella, Sam Duggan; Patrick Darby (0-2), David Baggott (0-5), Gavin Malone. Subs: Gary Flanagan, Glen Fitzpatrick, Paul O Connell, Paul Mooney, Oisín Foley, Shane Gallogly, Ben Duggan, Seán Fitzpatrick, Tom Sharp, Stephen Farrell. Selectors: Macartan McGroder, Neil O Dwyer, Dominic Devereux.

Minor Football Championship
Semi-Final: Dunshaughlin 2-11 Simonstown Gaels 3-6 at Walterstown
Final: Dunshaughlin 1-14 Donaghmore-Ashbourne 1-5 at Páirc Tailteann

Stephen Clusker; Seán Joyce, Alastar Doyle, Barry Jordan; Fergus Toolan, Conor O Brien, Neil Ridgeway; Joe O Brien (0-3), Conor Devereux (0-2); Eoin Hagarty, Capt., Eamon Bowe (0-3), Emmet Staunton (0-2); Alan O Brien (1-1), Niall Murphy (0-3), Michael McCarthy. Subs: Daniel Geraghty for McCarthy, Keith Doherty for Jordan, Henry Komolafe for Bowe, Niall Clusker for Alan O Brien, Brian Woods, Gavin Malone, Conor Smith, Aidan Boswell. Team Manager: TP Toolan. Selectors: Stephen Claire, Donnchadh Geraghty and John O Brien.

Minor Football League

Final: Ratoath 2-14 Dunshaughlin 2-9 at Páirc Tailteann
Stephen Clusker; Seán Joyce, Alastar Doyle, Keith Doherty; Fergus Toolan (0-1), Conor O Brien, Barry Jordan; Eoin Hagarty, Niall Murphy; Emmet Staunton, Eamon Bowe (0-1), James Rattigan (0-1); Alan O Brien (1-0), Conor Devereux (1-6), Daniel Geraghty. Subs: Niall Hannon for Geraghty, Brian Woods for Joyce, Niall Clusker, no record of whom he replaced, Henry Komolafe for Doherty, Gavin Malone for O Brien. Team management as per championship above.

2010

Under 10 Community Games
Meath Final: Dunshaughlin 2-2 Ratoath 0-0
Leinster Qtr Final: Killoe, Longford beat Dunshaughlin
Team Management: Seamus Reilly.

Under 12, Division 2, FL
Final: Trim 4-10 Dunshaughlin 3-5
Panel: Shane Connolly, Cian Gallogly, Roy Horan, Conor Meehan, Seán O Neill, Adam McDermott, Anthony Fildes, Sam Lavery, Adam Kealy, Neil Byrne, Niall Swan, Ben Marsden, Conor Keena, Enda Kennedy, Paddy Maher, Jack Hetherington, Darren Beattie, Dylan O Brien, Eric Casserley. Team Management: Seán O Neill and Frank Gallogly.

Under 14, Division 2, FL
Final: Dunshaughlin 4-15 Seneschalstown 3-7 at Páirc Tailteann
William McCarthy; Ronan Geraghty, Dan Ormsby, David Dunne; Gavin Maher, Josh Wall, Niall Byrne; Jack Kelly, Stephen Duffy, Capt.; Daniel Quinn, Conor Huijsdens, James Swan; Tommy Kinsella, Stephen Farrell, Liam Carey. Subs: Jack O Sullivan for Geraghty, Aaron Kealy for Kinsella, Cillian Duffy for Swan, Martin Nevin for McCarthy, Ronan Smith for Quinn, Conor McEvoy, Cormac Fitzpatrick, Mark Galvin, Mark Donnelly.

Manager: Michael Nevin. Selectors: Andy Quinn, Benny Byrne, Kevin Kealy.

Under 14, Division 9, FL
Final: Dunshaughlin 2-6 Kilbride 1-7 at Páirc Tailteann
Panel: David Dunne, Capt., Darragh Quinn, Cillian Hart, Lorcan Casey, Evan Ryan, Darren Lawless, Sam Lavery, Curtis Rattigan, Martin Keane, Michael Regan, Tom Boyhan, Mark Phelan, Conor Jennings, Martin Nevin, Aaron Kealy, Aaron Keane, Mark Galvin, Stephen Ennis, Ben Conlon, Cormac Fitzpatrick. Team Management: Michael Nevin, Kevin Kealy, Martin Ryan.

2011

Under 12, Summer League, Group C Final
Consisted of aggregate score of two teams
Final: Dunshaughlin's two teams recorded an aggregate victory of 42 points over Summerhill.
Match 1: Niall Hurley, Capt., Oisín Caldwell, Mark Connolly, David Fildes, Eoin O Connor, James Ryan, Paddy Maher, Adam Summerville, Conor Jones, Jack Hetherington, Pádraig Clinton, Aaron Lawlor, Evan Butler. Mentors: Brendan Connolly, Paul Hetherington. Match 2: Neil Byrne, Capt., Rhys Bruce, Michael McHugh, Matthew Moyles, Liam Reilly, Liam Hanley, Josh Kallides, Alan O Connor, Jack Caldwell, Daniel Fildes, Andrew Leneghan, Eric Casserley, Robert O Connell, Conor Keena, Seán Ennis, Sam Cowan, Cathal Sheehan. Mentors: Aidan McHugh, Eamonn Moyles, Gerry Casserley.

Under 13, Division 2, FL
Final: Wolfe Tones 7-7 Dunshaughlin 1-10
Neil Byrne; Tom Dalton, Sam Butler, Conor Keena; Cormac Byrne, Adam McDermott, Mika Mikamibua; Adam Kealy, Capt., Seán O Neill; Sam Lavery, Robert Holohan, Niall Swan; Jack Hetherington, Paddy Maher, Cian Gallogly. Subs: Anthony Fildes, Eric Casserley, Dylan O Brien, Stephen McGrath, Luke Hynes. Selectors: Frank

Gallogly, Kevin Kealy, Ronan Dalton, Seán O Neill.

Under 14, Division 9, Reserve FL
Final: Summerhill 7-15 Dunshaughlin 2-7
Panel: Andrew Leneghan, Neil Byrne, Tom Dalton, Paddy Maher, Darren Beattie, Jack Hetherington, Sam Lavery, Anthony Fildes, Eric Casserley, Cormac Byrne, Ciarán Malone, Enda Kennedy, Cormac Meehan, Sam Butler, Ben Marsden, Adam McDermott, Cian Maher, Roy Horan, Adam Kealy, Seán O Neill, Cian Gallogly, Conor Jones, Dylan O Brien, Conor Keena. Mentors: Seán O Neill, Frank Gallogly and Ronan Dalton.

Under 17, Division 3, FL
Final: Dunshaughlin 1-9 Clanna Gael 1-6 in Seneschalstown
Jack O Sullivan; Josh Wall, David Doherty, Capt., Gareth Rooney; Dan Ormsby, Steven Kinsella, Oisín Foley (1-0); David Reilly, Glen Fitzpatrick; Gavin Malone, Paddy Darby (0-5), Liam Carey (0-1); Kevin Bannon (0-2), Alan McEntee (0-1), Diarmuid Christie. Subs: Ronan Geraghty for Christie, Niall Byrne, Paul Mooney, Shane Gallogly, Danny McTigue, Adam McTigue, David Dunne. Team Management: Simon Farrell, Francis Darby and Noel McTigue.

Minor Football Championship, Div 2
Semi-Final: Trim 2-12 Dunshaughlin 1-6 in Summerhill
Aidan Boswell; David Doherty, Capt., Keith Rooney, Oisín Foley; Eimhín Kinsella, Glen Fitzpatrick, Gavin Malone; James Reilly, Niall Hannon; Gary Flanagan, Alan McEntee, David Baggot (1-2); Shane Gallogly (0-1), Paddy Darby (0-3), Kevin Bannon. Subs: Darragh Smith for Malone, Paul Mooney for Rooney, Liam Carey for Bannon, Daniel McTigue for Flanagan, Adam McTigue for Baggot. Team Management: Simon Farrell, Francis Darby and Noel McTigue.

2012

Under 10 Community Games
Meath Final: Dunshaughlin 4-3 Dunboyne 1-1.
Leinster Quarter-final: Dunshaughlin beat Killoe, Longford
Leinster Semi-Final: Dunshaughlin beat Maynooth
Final: Ballyroan/Abbeyleix beat Dunshaughlin
Panel v Killoe: Colm Keane, Cian Edwards, James Traynor, Seán Walsh, Joseph Dunne, Conor Gray, Capt., Fursey Blake, John McDonagh, Tommy Toal, Jared Rushe, Ruairi Kinsella, Aidan Fraher, Eoin Butler, Aaron Murphy, Cillian McCool, Jack O Riordan, Charlie O Connor, Evan Lawlor, Seán McConnell, Cian McLaughlin. Team Management: Kieran Rushe, Ultan Blake, Kieran O Riordan.

Under 12, Division 1, Summer League
Final: Dunshaughlin 29 Ratoath 28 (Two eleven-a-side matches played simultaneously in Skryne.)
Match 1: Liam Reilly, Capt., Michael McHugh, Mathew Costello, Niall Gavin, Cathal Sheehan, Fionn Cummins, Thomas Reilly, Rhys Bruce, David Fildes, Evan Butler, Paddy Dalton, Ethan Mahasé, Matthew Moyles.
Match 2: Brandon Hand, Capt., James Ryan, Niall Hurley, Paul Briody, Eoin O Connor, Luke Mitchell, Cian Hegarty, Kevin Bawle, Alan O Connor, Darren Murphy, Liam Hanley, Seán Kennedy, Oisín Caldwell.
Unaivalable on final day: Seán Ennis, Josh Kallides, Aaron Lawlor, Cathal McCormack, Bill Jennings. Team management: Paul Costello, Aidan McHugh, Eamonn Moyles.

Under 12, Reserve FL
Final: Dunshaughlin 24 Donaghmore-Ashbourne 19
Match 1: Dillon Cranley, Brian Clinton, Seán Kennedy, Patrick Dalton, Jack Considine, Thomas Reilly, Mathew Costello, Harry Dunne, Gary O Connor, Leo Marsden.
Match 2: Paul Kean, Ódhran O Riordan, Saran O Hora,

Petra Reilly, Luke Mitchell, Cathal McCormack, Darren Murphy, Cormac Curtin, Dean Murphy, Luke McCarthy. Panel members unavailable for final: Bill Jennings, Ethan Mahasé, Kevin Bawle, Seán Doyle, Cian Hegarty, Fionn Cummins, Evan Walsh. Team Management: Paul Murphy, Jim Mitchell, Damien Kennedy, Ronan Dalton, David McCormack.

Under 14, Division 2, Spring League

Final: Dunboyne beat Dunshaughlin in Dunganny by two points.

Adam McDermott; Dylan O Brien, Adam Kealy, Conor Keena; Tom Dalton, Rob Holohan, Mika Mikamibua; Sam Butler, Cormac Byrne; Cian Gallogly, Capt., Seán O Neill, Darren Beattie; Sam Lavery, Paddy Maher, Neil Byrne. Subs: Anthony Fildes, Dylan Dunne, Cian Maher, Stephen Walker, Jack Hetherington, Luke Hynes. Team Management: Kevin Kealy, Seán O Neill, Frank Gallogly.

Under 14, Division 1 Shield

Final: Wolfe Tones 2-21 Dunshaughlin 5-7 in Páirc Tailteann after extra time.

Adam McDermott; Dylan O Brien, Adam Kealy, Conor Keena; Tom Dalton, Rob Holohan (0-1), Jack Hetherington; Sam Butler, Capt. (0-1), Cormac Byrne; Seán O Neill (1-1), Darren Beattie, Paddy Maher (0-3); Sam Lavery (1-1), Neil Byrne (3-0), Dylan Dunne. Subs: Cian Maher, Stephen Walker, Cian Gallogly, Anthony Fildes. Team Management: Kevin Kealy, Seán O Neill, Frank Gallogly.

Under 16, Reserve Spring FL

Final: Dunboyne 3-15 Dunshaughlin 3-13 after extra time Panel: Sam Lavery, Lorcan Casey, Cillian Hart, Tommy Kinsella, Evan Ryan, Ben Conlon, Daniel Quinn, Curtis Rattigan, Aaron Keane, Darragh Quinn, Sam Butler, Seamus Doyle, Tom Boyhan, Mark Galvin, Conor Huijsdens, Martin Keane, Martin Nevin, Mark Phelan.

2013

Under 12, Division 1, Spring League

Final: Dunshaughlin 34 St Colmcilles 18

Match 1: Ethan Mahasé; Ódhran O Riordan, Capt., Saran O Hora; Paddy Dalton, Paul Kean; Luke Mitchell, Mathew Costello; Harry Dunne, Leo Marsden; Bill Jennings, Ruairi Meehan.

Match 2: Gary O Connor; Kevin Bawle, Capt., Seán Kennedy; Cian Hegarty, Cormac Curtin; Fionn Cummins, Cathal McCormack; Jack Considine, Brian Clinton; Darren Murphy, Luke McCarthy. Team management: Ronan Collier, Damien Kennedy, Jim Mitchell, Paul Murphy.

Under 12, Reserve League

Final: Ratoath defeated Dunshaughlin by 2 points in Stamullen.

Luke McCarthy, Conor Gray, Liam O Connor, Darragh Byrne, Adam Territt, James Traynor, Andrew Quinn, Josh Masterson, Shane Kennedy, Mark O Brien, Dean Murphy, Cian McLaughlin, Adam O Donoghue, Aidan Fraher, Seán Walsh, Evan Lawlor, Ciarán McCarrick, Seán O Connor, Robert Walker, Tommy Toal, John McDonagh, Cillian McCool, Harry Magee and Jack Brady. Team management: John Fraher, Ciarán O Connor, Andy Byrne, Seamus Traynor and Liam McLaughlin.

Under 14, Division 2, Spring FL

Final: Trim 4-9 Dunshaughlin 3-8 in Páirc Tailteann.

Panel: Daniel Fildes, Conor Keena, Matthew Moyles, David Fildes, James Sherry, Wesley Goodwin, Eric Casserley, Eoin O Connor, Paddy Maher, Josh Kallides, Paul Kennedy, Paul Briody, Andrew Leneghan, Jack Caldwell, Jack Hetherington, Shane Claire, Cathal Sheehan, Neil Byrne, Niall Hurley, Conor Oliver, Michael McHugh.

Under 14, Division 2, Summer League

Final: Dunshaughlin 5-17 Summerhill 7-5 at Dunsany.

Aaron Lawlor; Pádraig Clinton, Paul Kennedy, Andrew

Leneghan; Mika Mikamibua, Conor Keena, Cathal Sheehan; Paddy Maher, Capt, (1-2), Niall Hurley (0-1); Wesley Goodwin, Conor Oliver (0-5), Matthew Moyles; Shane Claire (0-1), Neil Byrne (2-5), David Fildes (2-1). Subs: Eric Casserley (0-1), Oisín Caldwell, Evan Butler, Eoin O Connor, Adam Summerville, Paul Briody, Daniel Fildes, Alan O Connor, Alastair Philip, Michael McHugh, Josh Kallides, Jack Hetherington, Turlough Ó Maoiléain, Brandon Hand, Liam Reilly, Seán Ennis, Senan Dunne, Jack Caldwell, Andrew Baggott. Team management: Paul Callaghan, Paul Hetherington, Aidan McHugh, Eamonn Moyles, Paul Sheehy.

Under 14, Reserve Shield, Division 1
Final: Dunboyne defeated Dunshaughlin.

Under 15, Division 2, Autumn FL
Final: Dunshaughlin 4-7 St. Vincents-Curraha 3-9 at Kilbride
Adam McDermott; Tom Dalton, Conor Keena, Dylan O Brien; Paddy Maher, Liam Donovan, Stephen Walker; Sam Butler, Adam Kealy, Capt.; Seán O Neill, Luke Slater, Darren Beattie; Cian Gallogly, Neil Byrne, Conor Oliver. Subs: Jack Hetherington for Donovan, Kevin Doyle for O Brien, Jack Caldwell, Andrew Leneghan, Shane Claire, Anthony Fildes, Dylan Dunne, Daniel Fildes, Ronan McMahon, Pádraig Clinton, Adam Summerville, Turlough Malone. Team Management: Frank Gallogly, Paul Hetherington, Paul Keena, Daniel Geraghty, Eoin Farrelly.

Minor Spring League
Semi-Final: Dunshaughlin 1-16 Jenkinstown Gaels 3-4
Final: Dunshaughlin 1-12 Summerhill 1-8 at Páirc Tailteann
Jack O Sullivan; Josh Wall, Ronan Geraghty, Diarmuid Christie; Oisín Foley, Dan Ormsby, Niall Byrne; Ben Duggan (0-1), David Reilly (0-1); David Beattie (1-0), Stephen Duffy (0-6), Daniel Quinn (0-1); Shane Gallogly, Capt. (0-2), Liam Carey (0-1), Tommy Kinsella. Subs: Conor Jennings for Kinsella, Seamus Doyle for Quinn, Mark Phelan, Adam McDermott, Martin Nevin, Stephen Farrell, Gareth Rooney, Cillian Hart, Cian Gallogly inj. Team Manager: Frank Gallogly. Selectors: Pat Gargan, TP Toolan.

Minor Football Championship, Division 1
Semi-Final: Dunboyne 2-8 Dunshaughlin 0-5 at Dunsany
Jack O Sullivan; Josh Wall, Ronan Geraghty, David Dunne; Oisín Foley, Dan Ormsby, Diarmuid Christie; Ben Duggan, David Reilly; David Beattie (0-1), Shane Gallogly, Capt. (0-3), Conor Jennings; Tommy Kinsella, Daniel Quinn, Liam Carey. Subs: Stephen Duffy (0-1) for Kinsella, Niall Byrne for Carey, Steven Kinsella for Duffy. Team Manager: Frank Gallogly. Selectors: Pat Gargan, TP Toolan.

2014

Under 12, Division 1, Spring League
Final: Dunshaughlin 31 Ratoath 22
Panels: Cian McLaughlin, Conor Gray, Jack Kehoe, Robert Walker, Andrew Quinn, Aidan Fraher, Cian Edwards, Colm Keane, Jack Brady, Daragh Byrne, Ciarán McCarrick, Seán O Connor, Joseph Dunne, Josh Masterson, Jared Rushe, Liam O Connor, Mark O Brien, Evan Lawlor, Seán Walsh, Shane Kennedy, James Traynor, Aaron Murphy, Jake Martin, Fursey Blake, Adam Territt, Cillian McCool, John McDonagh. Team Management: Ciarán O Connor, Andy Quinn, Andy Byrne, Seamus Traynor.

Under 14, Division 1, Spring League
Semi-Final: Dunshaughlin 4-7 Ratoath 4-6
Final: Dunshaughlin 3-8 Dunboyne 3-4 at Dunsany
Aaron Lawlor; Ódhran O Riordan, Cathal Sheehan, Evan Butler; Eoin O Connor, Co-Capt., Niall Hurley, Co-Capt., David Fildes; Michael McHugh (0-1), Matthew Moyles (0-1); Mathew Costello (2-1), Paul Briody (0-2), Wes Goodwin; Cathal McCormack (1-1), Fionn Cummins (0-1), Harry Dunne (0-1). Subs: Kevin Bawle for Cathal

Sheehan, Thomas Reilly for Eoin O Connor, Luke Mitchell for Harry Dunne, Paddy Dalton. Manager: David McCormack, Selectors: Aidan McHugh, Paul Nestor and Eamonn Moyles.

Under 14, All-Ireland Féile, Division 2, Shield

Semi-Final: Dunshaughlin 2-3 Annaghdown, Galway 1-3 in Connacht GAA Centre, Bekan.
Final: Clann na nGael, Roscommon 3-7 Dunshaughlin 1-6, after extra time, in Connacht GAA Centre, Bekan.

Aaron Lawlor; Cathal Sheehan, Paul Briody, Ódhran O Riordan; Cathal McCormack, Eoin O Connor, Co-Capt., David Fildes; Michael McHugh (1-0), Niall Hurley, Co-Capt. (0-1); Luke Mitchell, Wesley Goodwin, Matthew Moyles (0-1); Fionn Cummins (0-1), Mathew Costello (0-3), Harry Dunne. Subs: Kevin Bawle, Evan Butler, Bill Jennings, Thomas O Reilly. Team Management as for Spring League final, details above.

Under 16, Division 7, Spring League

Final: Nobber 6-7 Dunshaughlin 0-7 at Rathkenny

Daniel Fildes; Andrew Leneghan, Ronan McMahon; Mark Connolly Ferdia Foley, Seán Curtin; Lorcan O Reilly, Cormac Byrne (0-1); Anthony Fildes (0-2), Shane Claire (0-3), Ciarán Quinn; Jack Caldwell, Eric Casserley (0-1). Subs: Pádraig Clinton, Adam Summerville, Robert McConnell, Turlough Malone. Team Manager: Paul Hetherington.

Under 17, Football League

Final: Dunboyne 3-10 Dunshaughlin 2-6

Adam McDermott; Tom Boyhan, Aaron Keane, Stephen Walker; Conor Huijsdens, Seamus Doyle, Conor Mooney; Tommy Kinsella, Daniel Quinn; Adam Kealy, Cillian Hart, Cillian Duffy; Evan Ryan, Darragh Quinn, Cian Gallogly. Subs: Mark Galvin, Ben Conlon, Liam Donovan, Kevin Doyle, Anthony Fildes, Conor Jennings, Tom Dalton, Martin Keane, Seán O Neill, Sam Butler.

Under 17, Sevens Blitz

Final: Dunshaughlin beat St. Patricks by 4 points in Dunganny

Panel: Daniel Quinn, Capt., Cillian Hart, Tommy Kinsella, Aaron Keane, Conor Huijsdens, Seamus Doyle, Adam Kealy, Stephen Walker, Cillian Duffy, Conor Jennings, Conor Mooney. Team Manager: Kevin Kealy.

Minor Football, Division 5 Spring League

Semi-Final: Blackwater Gaels 1-8 Dunshaughlin 0-10 at Drumbaragh

Martin Nevin; Ronan Smith, Stephen Walker, Ben Conlon; Liam Donovan, Darragh Quinn, Sam Butler; Tom Boyhan, Conor Huijsdens; Seán O Neill, Cillian Duffy, Luke Slater; Cian Gallogly, Aaron Kealy, Evan Ryan. Subs: Seamus Doyle, Adam Kealy, Conor Mooney, Aaron Keane, Kevin Doyle, Anthony Fildes.

Minor Football, Division 1, Spring League

Semi-Final: Summerhill 4-13 Dunshaughlin 1-8 at Summerhill

Adam McDermott; Aaron Keane, Seamus Doyle, Darragh Quinn; Adam Kealy, Dan Ormsby, Conor Mooney; David Dunne, Ronan Geraghty; Daniel Quinn, Stephen Farrell, Tommy Kinsella; Stephen Duffy, Niall Byrne, Liam Carey. Subs: Tom Boyhan, Cillian Duffy.

Dunshaughlin Panel, Meath Senior Champions with Keegan Cup, 2000

Front: Kevin Moyles, Pádraic O Dwyer, Declan Fahy, Trevor Dowd, David McNerney, Paddy O Dwyer, Chairman, Dermot Kealy, Capt., Cyril Creavin, Secretary, Denis Kealy, Ronnie Yore, David Tonge, Brendan Kealy, Selector.
Middle: Tom O Sullivan, Garbhán Blake, Ulick McDonnell, Stephen Claire, Damien Eames, Eamonn Barry, Coach, TP Toolan, Selector, Ronan Gogan, Paddy McHale, Fearghal Gogan, Kenny McTigue.
Back: Tiernan O Rourke, Niall Kelly, Shane Kelly, Michael McHale, Christopher Carey, Graham Dowd, David Crimmins, Ciarán Byrne, Aiden Kealy, Kevin Kealy, Richie Kealy.

Keeping an Eye on the Silverware
The Maloneys, Frances, Ray and Pat with an array of silverware won by Dunshaughlin and St. Martins in 2002 at the club's Dinner Dance in January 2003.

And this is how we won it!
Dunshaughlin Captain Ollie O Neill outlines how Dunshaughlin won the Intermediate Hurling Championship Final in 1983 to Michael O Connor, Chairman, Meath Hurling Board.

Appendix 8
St. Martins: Football and Hurling Results

Results of Under Age Football Championship Semi-Finals and Finals and League Finals

Results from 2009-2014 when the footballers fielded as Dunshaughlin are recorded in Appendix 7. It has not been possible in all instances to list scores, venues, team captains, selectors or substitutes. Where those details are known they are given.

UNDER 10

2008: Community Games
Meath Final: St. Martins defeated Skryne
North Leinster Final: Defeated Shannon Gaels, Longford.
Leinster semi-final: Defeated by Emo, Laois.
Panel: Adam Kealy, Capt., Conor Keena, Cian Gallogly, Pádraig Clinton, Tom Watté, Enda Kennedy, Luke Shannon, Darren Beattie, Dylan O Brien, Cian Lynch, Conor Jones, Conor Oliver, Neil Byrne, Shane Claire, Andrew Leneghan, Paddy Maher, Jack Hetherington, Mark Connolly. Team Management: Kevin Kealy, Seán O Neill, Paul Hetherington.

UNDER 12

1981: Under 12 Championship
Semi-Final: Culmullen 3-5 St. Colmcilles 0-3 at Seneschalstown
Final: Slane 2-12 Culmullen 0-1 at Páirc Tailteann
Allen Foley Capt.; David Kane, Dermot Kealy, Alan Doyle; John Davis, Simon Farrell, Niall Foley; John O Brien (0-1), Brian Duffy; Paul O Rourke, Pat Kealy, Michael Walsh; Vincent Moore, Shane Mahon, Ephrem Caffrey. Subs: Adrian Faherty, Richard Forde, Derek Jones, Derek Melia, Paul Molloy, Philip McCarthy, Alan O Dwyer, Karl Stoney. Selectors: Jim Gilligan, Dickie O Brien, Tony Rattigan.

1983: Under 12 Championship
Semi-Final: Dunboyne 0-10 St. Martins 1-5 at Skryne
Alan Boyle; Colm Naughton, John Bacon, Fergus Summerville; Garbhán Blake, Paul Molloy, Liam O Neill; John Boyle, Capt., Liam Holton; Brendan Kealy, Thomas Walsh, Declan Troy; Trevor Doyle, David Forde, Neil McCarrick. Subs: David Morgan for Walsh, Philip Burke, Martin Lynch, David O Neill, Ciarán O Dwyer, Willie Brennan.

1987: Under 12 Championship
Semi-Final: Seneschalstown 3-6 St. Martins 2-5 at Walterstown
Noel Burke; Aaron Fitzpatrick, Dermot Doyle, Kenny McTigue; Keith Wickham, Paul Baker, David Troy; Richie Kealy, Capt., Brian Murray; Nigel Daly, James Walsh, David Power; Clive Dowd, Caoimhín Blake, Ronan Curley. Subs: Alan Barber for Blake, Anthony Conlon, Michael James O Rourke, Mick Summerville, Fionnán Blake, David Power, Mark Neary. Selectors: Frank Egan, Gerry Flanagan, Jim Gilligan, Oliver Gogan.

1992: Under 12 Championship
Semi-Final: St. Martins defeated Gaeil Colmcille
Final: Simonstown 2-7 St. Martins 1-5 at Páirc Tailteann
Barry Murphy; Brian Kenny, John McKiernan, Christopher Doyle; Conor Power, Vincent Cullinane (0-1), Alan Kenny; David Crimmins, Niall Kelly; Michael McHale, Gary Donoghue (0-1), John McKenna (0-1); Trevor Dowd,

David Tormay (0-2), George Troy (1-0). Subs: John Mulroy, Brian Murphy, Marcus Maloney, Kevin Craven, Robert Kiernan, Conor Mahon, Neil Mooney, Keith Mangan, Philip Doyle. Selectors: Macartan McGroder, Noel Mangan, Cyril Creavin, Joe Mahon.

1992: Under 12 FL, Division 1
Final: St. Martins 3-11 Simonstown Gaels 3-8 at Dunsany
Barry Murphy; John Joe McDonnell, John McKiernan, Christopher Doyle; Alan Kenny, Vincent Cullinane, Conor Power; Gary Donoghue, David Crimmins, Capt, (0-2); Michael McHale (0-2), Niall Kelly (0-1), John McKenna (0-1); George Troy (1-0), David Tormay (1-2), Trevor Dowd (1-3). Subs: Gerard Troy, Kevin Creavin, Robbie Kiernan, Keith Mangan, Brian Murphy, Conor Mahon, Philip Doyle, John Mulroy, Marcus Maloney, Neil Mooney. Selectors: Macartan McGroder, Noel Mangan, Cyril Creavin, Joe Mahon.

1993: Under 12 FL, Division 1
Semi-Final: Navan O Mahonys defeated St. Martins. No details available.

1995: Under 12 FL, Division 2
Final: St. Martins 1-18 Donaghmore 1-9 at Skryne
John Murphy; Seán Hayes, John Crimmins, Caoimhín King; Mark Devanney, Ray Maloney, Capt., Stephen Burke; Colm Finlay, Ciarán Murray (0-9); Seán White, JJ McCarthy (0-4), Stephen Ward (0-2); Liam Shanley, John Brennan (1-1), David O Neill (0-2). Subs: Bryan Duffy, Joe McHale, Seamus Wallace, Alan Kenny, Gavin O Regan, Ronan Gilsenan, Paul Faherty. Selectors: Pat Maloney, Macartan McGroder, Paddy Ward, Cian Murray.

1999: Under 12 FL, Division 1
Semi-Final: St. Martins 1-8 Simonstown Gaels 0-10 at Dunsany
Final: Round Towers 5-14 St. Martins 2-6 at Walterstown
Brian Coughlan; James Gaughan, John Coffey, Stephen McGroder; Alan McLoughlin, Michael Ahern, Ian Hand; Shane Kelly, David Wallace; Ciarán Farrelly, David Devereux (1-2), Adrian Toolan (0-1); Fionán O Kane, Christopher Dixon (0-2), John Coleman. Subs: Patrick Doohan (1-0) for O Kane, Mark Caldwell (0-1) for Toolan, Conor Staunton.

2002: Under 12 FL, Division 1
Final: St. Martins 7-5 Simonstown Gaels 2-11 at Bective
Mark Coffey; Paul Walsh, James Kelliher, Joe Boyhan; Niall Murphy, Dara Devereux, Stephen Clusker (1-0); Colm McLoughlin, Co-Capt., James Horgan (0-1); Eoin Hagarty, Danny Logan (1-0), David Fitzmaurice; Eamon Bowe (1-1), Barry Jordan, Shane Troy (4-3). Subs: Tadhg Ó Dúsláine, Conor Ennis, Bill Reilly, Robert Crosbie, Aaron Redmond. Co-Capt. Ciarán Clusker, was injured for the final. Selectors: Tommy Clusker, Des Boyhan, Paul Logan, Brendan Murphy.

2002: Under 12 Reserve FL
Final: Navan O Mahonys 4-6 St. Martins 0-5 at Bective
Kevin Burke; Luke Briody, Robert Crosbie, Eoin O Farrell; Stephen Doyle, Capt., Tadhg Ó Dúsláine (0-1), Alan O Brien; Aaron Redmond, Conor Devereux (0-1); Lee Duffy (0-3), Conor Ennis, James Rattigan; Daniel Geraghty, Ian Donoghue, Niall Clusker. Subs: Conor O Brien, Conal O Sullivan, Aodhán Woods, Daniel Hayes, James Doolan, Ciarán McMahon, Gavin Byrne, Stephen Pepper.

2004: Under 12 FL, Division 1
Semi-Final: St. Martins defeated St. Cianans
Final: St. Martins 3-9 Ratoath 1-10 at Skryne
Aidan Boswell; Gavin Byrne, Alastar Doyle, Liam Ormsby; Fergus Toolan, Conor O Brien, Ian Donoghue; Conor Devereux, Capt. (0-1), Joe O Brien (0-2); Keith Doherty (0-1), Michael McCarthy (1-2), Alan O Brien (0-1); Frankie Lally, Niall Clusker (2-1), David Baggott (0-1). Subs: Neil Ridgeway for Lally, Keith Donoghue for Baggott, Jeff Flanagan for Doherty, Andrew Kiernan, Gary Flanagan, Oisín de Bhál, Martin John Maguire, Peter Donnelly, Terry McMahon, Stephen McCarthy.

UNDER 13

1983: Community Games Competition:
Semi-Final: Dunshaughlin 0-13 Duleek 2-3 at Duleek
Final: Dunshaughlin 5-13 Kilcloon 3-3 at Summerhill
Leinster Qtr. Final: Newbridge 3-11 Dunshaughlin 1-7 at Newbridge

Line out v. Kilcloon: Stephen Lane; John Bacon, Simon Conlon, Ciarán O Connor; Garbhán Blake, Karl Stoney, Piaras O Connor; Liam Holton, Dermot Kealy, Capt; Morty O Sullivan, John Boyle, Brendan Kealy; Paul Molloy, Thomas Walsh, Declan Troy. Subs: Neil McCarrick for Paul Molloy, Colm Naughton for Ciarán O Connor, Trevor Doyle, David Forde, Liam O Neill. Selectors: Pat Farrell, Jim Gilligan.

1993: U 13 FL Division 1, Féile
Final: St. Cuthberts 3-13 St. Martins 1-7 at Walterstown

Team line out not available. Panel as follows: John Gilsenan, John Joe McDonnell, Kevin Creavin, Jason Clarke, Neil Mooney, Alan Kenny, Gary Donoghue, John McKiernan, Trevor Dowd, Christopher Carey, Peter Smith, Barry O Shea, Marcus Maloney, Michael McHale, Brian Faherty, Vincent Cullinane, Conor O Sullivan, Colm Delaney, David Tormay, Neil Reilly, David Crimmins, Niall Kelly, Gerard Troy.

1998: U-13 Division 2 Football League
Final: Summerhill 3-12 St. Martins 1-2 at Longwood

Shane Kelly; Ronan Gilsenan, Liam Barber; Ciarán Hoary, David McMahon, Kevin Ward; Owen Herlihy, Caoimhín King (0-1); Cathal O Dwyer (1-1), Rory Bowe, Paul Cosgrove; Jamie Minnock, Cormac Delaney. Subs: Ciarán Kenny for Cosgrove, David Murphy for Delaney, John Kieran for Minnock, Robert Lyons, David Devereux, Colin Murphy.

1999: U-13 Division 2 Football League
Final: Donaghmore 1-8 St. Martins 0-5 at Ratoath

Eoin Reilly; Alan McLoughlin, Michael Ahern; David Devereux, David Hall, Ciarán Kenny; Shane Kelly, John O Callaghan; Joseph Coffey, Cathal O Dwyer, Capt., (0-1), Ciarán Farrelly; Cormac Delaney (0-4), Robert Lyons.

2000: U-13 FL Division 1
Féile Final to represent Meath in Tipperary, 2001
Final: St. Martins 4-9 Round Towers 1-5 at Bective

Brian Coughlan; Stephen McGroder, James Gaughan, Patrick Doohan; Alan McLoughlin, David Wallace, John Coleman; Michael Ahern (0-2), Christopher Dixon; Ciarán Farrelly, Shane Kelly (2-1), Conor Staunton (2-1); Cillian Finn, David Devereux, Capt. (0-2), Mark Caldwell (0-3). Subs: John Coffey for Coleman, Shane Toher for Farrelly, Martin Cosgrove for Finn. Selectors: Macartan McGroder, Tim O Kane, Don McLoughlin, Tom Finn.

2001: U-13 FL Division 2
Semi-Final: Skryne defeated St. Martins. No details available.

2002: U-13 FL Division 2
Final: St. Martins 4-4 Drumconrath/Meath Hill 1-7 in Kilberry

Mark Coffey; Fearghal Delaney, Colm McLoughlin; Dara Devereux, Keith Caffrey, Des Dolan; Seán Doyle, Paul Barry, Capt.; Ciarán Clusker (0-1), Duncan Geraghty (0-2), Kieran Murphy; Danny Logan (3-1), Seamus White (1-0). Subs: Shane Troy for White, Niall Dundon for Clusker, Tadhg Ó Dúshláine for Logan, Keith Commons, Cillian Dennehy, Conor Ennis, Dermot McGreal, Thomas Evans, James Kelliher, James Horgan, Robert Kane, Paul Caffrey, Paul Logan, Joe Boyhan, Conor Hagarty. Selectors: Des Boyhan, Tommy Clusker, Donnchadh Geraghty, Don McLoughlin.

2003: U-13 FL Division 1
Féile Final to represent Meath in Tyrone, 2004
Final: St. Martins 3-8 Round Towers 0-5 at Bective

James Kelliher; Conor Devereux, Ciarán Clusker, Cillian Dennehy; David O Rourke, Colm McLoughlin, Stephen

Clusker; Mark Coffey (1-0), Bill Reilly; James Horgan (1-0), Dara Devereux (0-1), Eamon Bowe (0-2); Niall Murphy, Shane Troy (0-3), Danny Logan (1-2). Subs: Joe Boyhan for Troy, Barry Jordan for S Clusker, Tadhg Ó Dúshláine for Murphy, Paul Walsh for Bowe, Eoin Hagarty, David Fitzmaurice, Robert Crosbie, Daniel Geraghty, Conor Ennis, Eoin Sheehy. Selectors: Des Boyhan, Donnchadh Geraghty, Tommy Clusker, Paul Logan, Brendan Murphy and Dolores Murphy.

2004: U-13 FL Division 1

Féile Final to represent Meath in Limerick, 2005
Final: St. Martin's 5-8 Navan O Mahonys 0-8 at Donore
Michael McCarthy; Seán Joyce, Joe O Brien, Shane Connolly; Barry Jordan, Stephen Doyle, Emmet Staunton (1-0); Eoin Hagarty (0-1), Conor Devereux (0-2); Eamon Bowe (1-1), Ian Donoghue, James Rattigan (1-1); Niall Murphy (0-2), Stephen Clusker (1-0), Daniel Geraghty (1-0). Subs: Conor O Brien for Donoghue, Fergus Toolan (0-1) for Geraghty, Alan O Brien for Jordan, Luke Briody for Rattigan, Gavin Byrne, Brian Woods, James Doolan, Cian Christie, Conal O Sullivan, Neil Ridgeway. Selectors: Don McLoughlin, John O Brien, Harry Clusker, Brendan Murphy and Dolores Murphy.

2005: U-13 FL Division 1

Féile Final to represent Meath in Wicklow, 2006
Final: St. Martins 1-10 Ratoath 0-10 at Skryne
Aidan Boswell; Keith Doherty, Alastar Doyle, Fergus Toolan; David Baggott, Joe O Brien, Conor O Brien (0-1); Conor Devereux (1-4), Neil Ridgeway (0-1); Alan O Brien, Ian Donoghue (0-2), Jeff Flanagan; Eimhín Kinsella (0-1), Niall Clusker, Michael McCarthy (0-1). Subs: James Beattie, Frankie Lally, Gavin Byrne, Liam Ormsby. Selectors: Tommy Clusker, John O Brien, Dominic Devereux.

2008: U-13 FL Division 1B, Féile

Final Replay: Seneschalstown 0-10 St. Martins 0-8 aet. At Walterstown

Jack O Sullivan; Oisín Foley, David Reilly, Josh Wall; Lorcan Byrne, Seán Fitzpatrick, Capt., Dan Ormsby; Ben Duggan, Steven Kinsella; Shane Gallogly, David Beattie, Stephen Duffy; Diarmuid Christie, Stephen Farrell, Gareth Rooney. Subs: David Dunne, Conor Jennings, Ronan Geraghty, Conor McEvoy, Liam Carey, Martin Nevin, James Logan. Team Management: Managers: Frank Gallogly, Robbie Byrne, Selectors: James Beattie, Paul McEvoy.

UNDER 14

1953: Under 14 Football League

Semi-Final: Drumree 2-6 Ballivor 1-7
Ballivor awarded the game following an objection.

1957: Under 14 Rural Football Championship

Semi-Final: St. Martins drew with Stamullen at Páirc Tailteann
Replay: St. Martins 2-5 Stamullen 3-1 at Páirc Tailteann
Final: St. Martins 0-7 Ballivor 1-3 at Páirc Tailteann
P.J. O Rourke; David Cantwell, Val Dowd, Arnold Blake; Stephen Mahon, Paddy Burke, Neil O Riordan; Jimmy Walsh, Capt, Christy McCarthy; Joe Rattigan, Noel Curran, Johnny Lynch; Oliver Walsh, Brendan O Shea, Brendan Cantwell. Subs: Thomas Carty, John Murphy.

1958: Under 14 Rural Football Championship

Semi-Final: St. Martins 2-9 Ballivor 1-4, Páirc Tailteann
Final: St. Martins 0-3 Bohermeen 0-2, Páirc Tailteann
P.J. O Rourke; Andy Mahon, Johnny Lynch, Johnny Gilsenan; Thomas Carty, Paddy Burke, Capt., Neil O Riordan; Gerry Kearney, Brendan O Shea; John Murphy, Syl McAuley, David Halford; Oliver Walsh, Leonard Morgan, Brendan Doyle. Subs: Charlie Johnson, Joe Keogh, Ulick McDonnell, Seamus Flynn, Brendan Cantwell.

1959: Under 14 Rural Football Championship

Semi-Final: St. Martins 1-5 Castletown 1-5 at Páirc Tailteann

Replay: St. Martins defeated Castletown by 3 points at Páirc Tailteann
Final: St. Martins 3-4 Kilmainhamwood 0-5 at Páirc Tailteann

Andy Mahon; Pat Faherty, Johnny Lynch, Joe Keogh; John Casey, Neil O Riordan, Pádraig Blake; Paddy Burke, Capt., Syl McAuley; Brian O Sullivan, Brendan O Shea, David Halford; Hugh Carty, Seamus Flynn, Liam Carey. Subs: Michael Delany, Dinny McCarthy, Michael Spillane.

1979: Under 14 FC Division 3
Semi-Final: Culmullen 6-7 United Gaels 3-14
Final: Culmullen 4-10 Enfield 1-6 at Summerhill

Pearse O Dwyer; Kevin Kealy, Thomas Byrne, Gerard McDonnell; Patrick O Brien, Michael Boyle, Val McMahon; Aidan Walsh, Capt., Niall McCarthy; Martin Walsh, Martin McDonnell, Ronan Morris; Shane Holland, John Madden, Seamus Magee. Subs: Michael Duffy, Cathal Gallagher, Vincent O Brien, David Summerville. Selectors: Val Dowd, Jimmy Walsh.

1984: Under 14 FC
Semi-Final: St. Patricks defeated St. Martins.
Selectors: Hugh Daly, Patsy McLoughlin, Pat Kelly.

1987: Under 14 Division 2 FL
Run on league basis
Play-Off Final: St. Martins 1-8 Kilmainhamwood 0-1 at Walterstown

Alan Boyle; Hugh McCarthy, Patrick Doyle, Dermot Doyle; Aiden Kealy, Gary Baker, Robert McCarthy; David O Neill, Capt., Ciarán O Dwyer; Richie Kealy, Evan Kelly, Barry Walsh; David Faughnan, Willie Brennan, Emmett Downes. Subs: David Murray for Patrick Doyle, Tiernan O Rourke, Kenny McTigue, David Troy, Seamus Flynn, Paul Baker, James Walsh, Michael Keane, Ronan O Dwyer, Noel Burke, Brian O Rourke, Jonathon O Connor, Peter Rattigan. Selectors: Hugh Daly, Pat Kelly, Ollie O Neill.

1988: Under 14 Division 2 FL
Final: Slane 1-6 St. Martins 0-7 at Páirc Tailteann

David Troy; Michael Keane, Patrick Doyle, Dermot Doyle; Paul Baker, Aiden Kealy, Robbie McCarthy; Gary Baker, Capt., (0-2), Hugh McCarthy; Richie Kealy (0-1), James Walsh (0-1), Barry Walsh (0-2); Cathal O Connor (0-1), Brian Murray, David Faughnan. Subs: Aaron Fitzpatrick, Kenny McTigue, Mark Rattigan, Noel Burke, Ian McTigue. Colin Foley, Wayne Cottrell. Selectors: Val Dowd, Seán Doyle, Pat Kelly.

1989: Under 14 Division 4 FL
Final: St. Martins 1-7 Walterstown 0-5

Noel Burke; Simon Duffy, Dermot Doyle, Kenny McTigue; David Power, David Troy, Aaron Fitzpatrick; Paul Baker, Brian Murray; Richie Kealy, James Walsh, Capt., Cathal O Connor; Clive Dowd, Darragh Cannon, Mick Summerville. Subs: Michael James O Rourke for Summerville, Keith Wickham, Garreth Kelly, Wayne Cottrell, Ian McTigue. Selectors: Val Dowd, Paul Rattigan, Jimmy Walsh.

1991: Under 14 Football Championship
Semi-Final: St. Martins defeated Trim or O Mahonys
Final: Oldcastle 2-18 St. Martins 0-1 at Páirc Tailteann.

Damien Spillane; Ronan Power, Ulick McDonnell, Paul Doyle; John Cullinane, Fionnán Blake, Shane Kelly; Ronan Keating, Garreth Kelly, Capt,; Denis Kealy, Graham Dowd, Damien Fitzpatrick; Pádraic O Dwyer, Gordon O Rourke (0-1), Derek Doyle. Subs: Dessie Keane for O Dwyer, Fearghal Gogan for Power, Brendan Killoran, Dominic Jones, Niall Kelly, Neil O Dwyer, Colm O Dwyer, Joseph Smith, Pádraig Herlihy, Niall O Connor, Andrew Neary, John Delany. Selectors: Michael Boyle, Paddy O Dwyer, Tony Rattigan and Seán Spillane.

1991: Under 14 Division 2 FL
Final: Yellow Furze 3-12 St. Martins 3-7. Team probably similar to championship side above.

1994: Under 14 Division 1 FL
Semi-Final: St. Cuthberts defeated St. Martins by two points.

1995: Under 14 Football Championship
Semi-Final: Simonstown Gaels 3-12 St. Martins 1-6 Team line out not available but it was probably similar to the line out in the Division 2 FL final below. Scorers: John Joe McDonnell 1-0, Peter Smith 0-2, Trevor Dowd, Christopher Doyle, Brian Walsh, Keith Mangan 0-1 each.

1995: Under 14 Division 2 FL
Final: St. Martins 3-7 Yellow Furze 1-11 at Dunsany Barry Murphy; Martin Duffy, Christopher Carey, Colm Barber; Brian Kenny, Alan Spillane, Philip Doyle; Christopher Doyle, John Joe McDonnell, Capt. (0-1); John Gilsenan (0-1), Trevor Dowd (3-3), David McNerney; Keith Mangan, Peter Smith (0-1), Brian Walsh. Subs: Ray Maloney for P Doyle, Kevin Burke for Walsh, Seán Jordan, Kevin Creavin. Selectors: Noel McNerney, Noel Mangan.

1999: Under 14 Football Championship
Semi-Final: Summerhill 4-13 St. Martins 3-5 at Bective. No team details available.

1999: Under 14 Football League
Final: Summerhill defeated St. Martins. No team details available.

2001: Under 14 Football Championship
Semi-Final: St. Martins 4-14 Summerhill 2-4 at Dunsany
Final: St. Martins 1-8 Round Towers 0-3 at Bective Brian Coughlan; Stephen McGroder, James Gaughan, John Coffey; Alan McLoughlin, Capt., David Wallace, Adrian Toolan; Christopher Dixon, Michael Ahern (0-1); Shane Kelly, Ciarán Farrelly (1-1), Conor Staunton (0-2); Cillian Finn, David Devereux (0-4), Patrick Doohan. Subs: Ian Hand for McGroder, Mark Caldwell for Finn, Fionán O Kane for Staunton, Martin Cosgrove for Coffey, John Coleman for Doohan, Shane Toher, Paul Kiernan, Cathal O Reilly, Keith Byrne. Selectors: Macartan McGroder, Tim O Kane, Don McLoughlin and Tom Finn.

2001: Under 14 Division 1 Football League
Semi-Final: St. Martins 6-9 Summerhill 1-7 at Dunsany
Final: St. Martins 3-18 Simonstown Gaels 1-7 at Bective Brian Coughlan; Ian Hand, James Gaughan, John Coffey; Alan McLoughlin, Capt., David Wallace (0-1), Adrian Toolan (0-1); Christopher Dixon (1-0), Michael Ahern (0-3); Shane Kelly (1-0), Ciarán Farrelly, Conor Staunton (0-3); Cillian Finn (1-0), David Devereux (0-8), Patrick Doohan (0-1). Subs: John Coleman for Hand, Mark Caldwell for Doohan, Stephen McGroder for Gaughan, Fionán O Kane for Finn, Cathal O Reilly (0-1) for Farrelly. Selectors: Macartan McGroder, Tim O Kane, Don McLoughlin and Tom Finn.

2001: Under 14 Football Reserve League
Final: Simonstown Gaels 5-12 St. Martins 4-2 at Bective. No team details available.

2004: Under 14 Football League, Division 1
Semi-Final: St. Cianans 2-8 St. Martins 2-6 at Curraha James Kelliher; Conor Devereux, Ciarán Clusker, Cillian Dennehy; David O Rourke, Colm McLoughlin, Mark Coffey; Bill Reilly, Tadhg Ó Dúshláine; Dara Devereux, David Fitzmaurice, Eamon Bowe; James Horgan, Niall Murphy, Paul Walsh.

2005: Under 14 Football Championship
Semi-Final: St. Martins 3-15 Simonstown Gaels 0-8
Final: St. Martins 4-13 Navan O Mahonys 2-13 at Páirc Tailteann
Michael McCarthy; Seán Joyce, Joe O Brien, Shane Connolly; Conor O Brien, Stephen Doyle (0-1), Barry Jordan (0-1); Eoin Hagarty (0-4), Conor Devereux (0-3); Eamon Bowe (0-1), Emmet Staunton, Capt, (1-0), James Rattigan; Fergus Toolan (1-2), Stephen Clusker (1-0),

Niall Murphy. Subs: Alan O Brien (1-1) for Bowe, Alastar Doyle, Daniel Geraghty, James Doolan, Cian Christie, Brian Woods, Neil Ridgeway, Gavin Byrne, Luke Briody, Conal O Sullivan.

2006: Under 14 Football Championship
Final: St. Martins 2-14 Na Fianna 2-4

Aidan Boswell; Keith Doherty (0-1), Alastar Doyle, Niall Hannon (0-1); David Baggott (0-1), Conor O Brien, Fergus Toolan; Joe O Brien (0-1), Conor Devereux, Capt. (1-2); Eimhin Kinsella, Ian Donoghue (0-1), James Beattie (0-1); Alan O Brien (1-0), Niall Clusker, Michael McCarthy (0-5). Subs: Gavin Byrne (0-1) for O Brien, Liam Ormsby for Beattie, Eoin Hannon for Toolan, Stephen McCarthy for Donoghue, Jeff Flanagan, James Reilly, Neil Ridgeway, Henry Komolafe, Leon Everett, Gary Flanagan, Frankie Lally.

2006: Under 14 Football League
Final: St. Martins 2-24 Round Towers 0-6 at Páirc Tailteann

Aidan Boswell; Keith Doherty, Alastar Doyle, Liam Ormsby; Gavin Byrne, Conor O Brien (1-0), Fergus Toolan (0-1); Joe O Brien (0-1), Conor Devereux, Capt. (0-2); Eimhín Kinsella (0-2), Ian Donoghue (0-2), James Beattie (0-4); Alan O Brien (0-4), Niall Clusker (0-3), Michael McCarthy. Subs: Henry Komolafe (0-1), David Baggott, Niall Hannon, Eoin Hannon, Leon Everett, Stephen McCarthy, Jeff Flanagan, James Reilly, Neil Ridgeway, Gary Flanagan, Frankie Lally. 1-4 unaccounted for.

UNDER 15

2007: Under 15 Football League
Semi-Final: St. Martins defeated Navan O Mahonys
Final: Ratoath 2-6 St. Martins 1-5. No team details available.

UNDER 16

1980: Under-16 Football Championship
Semi-Final: St. Colmcilles 3-10 Dunshaughlin 0-9. No team details available.

1982: Under-16 Football Championship
Semi-Final: Bohermeen defeated Dunshaughlin. No team details available.

1985: Under-16 Football Championship
Semi-Final: Gaeil Colmcille 1-5 St. Martins 0-3, at Páirc Tailteann. Abandoned after 47 minutes.
Refixture: St. Martins 1-3 Gaeil Colmcille 1-3
Replay: St. Martins 1-5 Gaeil Colmcille 1-3
Final: Slane 1-10 St. Martins 0-4 at Seneschalstown

Derek Melia; David Kane, John Davis, Karl Stoney; Shane Mahon, Simon Farrell, Allen Foley; Niall Foley, Dermot Kealy; Michael Walsh (0-3), Brian Duffy, Vinny Moore; Paul O Rourke, Pat Kealy (0-1), Liam O Neill. Subs: Brendan Kealy for Liam O Neill, Liam Holton for O Rourke, Morty O Sullivan, Colm Naughton, John Bacon, Piaras O Connor, John Boyle. Selectors: Val Dowd, Pat Farrell, Jim Gilligan.

1987: Under-16 Football League
Semi-Final: Athboy defeated St. Martins.
No team details available.
Selectors: Patsy Curley, Michael Bacon, Seán Doyle, John Holton.

1996: Under-16 Football Championship
Semi-Final: St. Martins 3-7 Round Towers 2-8
Final: Walterstown 1-7 St. Martins 0-8, Páirc Tailteann

Christopher Carey; John Joe McDonnell, John McKiernan, Michael McHale; Gerard Troy, Niall Kelly (0-1), John McKenna (0-2); David Crimmins (0-1), Gary Donoghue (0-2); Vincent Cullinane, Neil Reilly, Pater Smith (0-2); Alan Kenny, David Tormay, Trevor Dowd. Subs: Damien Minnock, Robert

Harrington, Kieran Crimmins, Lee Watson, Jason Clarke, Brian Kenny, Colm Delany. Selectors: David Crimmins, Pat Reilly, Brendan Tonge. Trainer & Coach: John Boyle.

1997: Under-16 Football Championship
Semi-Final: St. Martins 2-8 Blackhall Gaels 1-6
Final: Navan O Mahonys 0-12 St. Martins 0-7 at Walterstown

Barry Murphy; Martin Duffy, Christopher Carey, Brian Walsh; Seán Jordan, Alan Spillane, Tristan Fahy; John Joe McDonnell (0-1), Brian Kenny (0-1); John Gilsenan, Trevor Dowd (0-1), David McNerney; Christopher Doyle, Peter Smith (0-4), Keith Mangan. Subs: Philip Doyle, Colm Barber, Kevin Burke, Ray Maloney. Selectors: Noel McNerney, Noel Mangan.

2001: Under-16 Football League
Lost Semi-Final.

2002: Under-16 Football League, Division 2
Semi-Final: St. Martins 1-9 Skryne 1-7
Final: St. Martins 2-6 St Colmcilles 1-8 at Duleek

Eoin Reilly; David Hall, Ciarán Kenny, James Gaughan; David Quinn, David Wallace (0-1), Alan McLoughlin; Christopher Dixon, Michael Ahern; Ciarán Farrelly, Conor Staunton (1-3), Cathal O Dwyer (1-2); Brian Coughlan, Dara Devereux, Adrian Toolan. Subs: John O Callaghan for Coughlan, Colm Quinn for Hall, Patrick Doohan for Quinn, Cormac Delaney, Shane Kelly, John Crosbie, Derek Jordan, Stephen McGroder, Colin Murphy, Thomas O Regan. Selector: Macartan McGroder.

2003: Under-16 Football Championship
Semi-Final: St. Martins 1-14 Round Towers 0-4 at Kilberry
Final: St. Martins 1-9 Summerhill 0-9 at Páirc Tailteann

Christopher Dixon; John Coffey, James Gaughan, Bryan McKeown; Alan McLoughlin, David Wallace, Adrian Toolan; Conor Staunton (0-1), Michael Ahern Capt. (0-2); Shane Kelly (0-1), David Devereux (0-2), Ciarán Farrelly (0-1); Cillian Finn (0-2), Brian Coughlan (1-0), John Coleman. Subs: Emmet O Callaghan for Kelly, Mark Caldwell for Coughlan, Kelly for Coleman, Stephen McGroder, Fionán O Kane, Shane Toher, Ian Hand, Stephen Fox. Patrick Doohan was unavailable as he was in St. Finian's College Mullingar. Selectors: Macartan McGroder, Tim O Kane, Don McLoughlin, Tom Finn, TP Toolan.

2006: Under-16 Football Championship
Semi-Final: Donaghmore-Ashbourne defeated St. Martins.

2007: Under-16 Football Championship
Semi-Final: Skryne 4-12 St. Martins 2-16 at Dunsany, after extra time. No team details available.

2008: Under-16 Football Championship
Semi-Final: St. Martins 4-10 Ratoath 2-11
Final: St. Martins 3-11 Round Towers 2-4 at Páirc Tailteann

Aidan Boswell; Keith Doherty, Alastar Doyle, Liam Ormsby; Conor Devereux, Capt. (1-5), Conor O Brien, Neil Ridgeway; Joseph O Brien (0-1), Niall Hannon; Alan O Brien (0-3), Eoin Hannon, James Reilly; Henry Komolafe, Niall Clusker (1-0), Michael McCarthy (1-2). Subs: David Doherty for Joe O Brien, Joe O Brien for Reilly, Robert Connolly for Komolafe, Andrew Kiernan, Gavin Malone, Sam Duggan, Eimhín Kinsella, David Baggott, Fergus Toolan. Selectors: Tommy Clusker, Dominic Devereux, John O Brien and TP Toolan.

UNDER 17

2004: Under 17 Division 1, FL
Final: Round Towers 1-12 St. Martins 1-9 at Páirc Tailteann

Christopher Dixon; Stephen McGroder, Brian Coughlan, Emmet O Callaghan; Alan McLoughlin, David Wallace,

Adrian Toolan; Cillian Finn (1-0), James Gaughan; Shane Kelly, David Devereux (0-4), Ciarán Farrelly (0-2); John Coleman, Conor Staunton (0-3), Mark Caldwell. Subs: Paddy Doohan for O Callaghan, John Coffey for Coleman, Colm McLoughlin, Fionán O Kane, Ciarán Clusker, Cathal Moore, Duncan Geraghty, Dara Devereux. Michael Ahern unable to play due to injury.

2005: Under 17 Division 2, FL
Final: St. Martins 0-8 Walterstown 0-6.
No details available

MINOR

1933: Minor Football Championship
Semi-Final: Erin's Own (Kells) 5-0 Dunshaughlin 2-1

1947: Minor Football Championship
Dunshaughlin qualified as divisional winners.
Final: Dunshaughlin 2-1 Julianstown 1-4 at Duleek.
Played April 1948
Replay: Julianstown 0-9 Dunshaughlin 0-7 at Skryne.
Played May 1948

John Mahon; Michael Morrin, John Ennis, Peter Tugwell; Patsy McLoughlin, Bill Delaney, Hugh Boyne; Percy McGuinness, Tom O Brien; Ernest Kenny, Dessie Smith, PJ McCluskey; Seán O Brien, Kevin Smith, Benny Foley. Sub: Mickey Regan.

1971: Minor Football Championship
Semi-Final: Walterstown 4-12 Dunshaughlin 1-7. No team details available.

1972: Minor Football Championship
Semi-Final: Dunshaughlin 0-8 Parnells 0-3 at Páirc Tailteann
Final: Trim 3-4 Dunshaughlin 0-9 at Páirc Tailteann
Pat Jennings; JJ Whitty, Pat O Brien, Jody Madden; Don McLoughlin, Pat Callinan, Pádraig Gallagher; John Jennings, Tony Johnson; Paddy Kenny, Dessie Fitzgerald, Andy Whitty; Joe McDonnell, PJ Duffy, Ger Dowd. Subs: Tom Nolan for Pat Jennings, Noel Mangan for Gallagher, John Madden for Duffy, Joe Donoghue, Sean Dunne, PJ Kelly, Seán Smyth, Bernie Sneed. Selectors: Val Dowd; John Kelly, Jack Fitzgerald, Kilcloon.

1987: Minor Football Championship
Semi-Final: St. Martins/Ratoath 1-14 St. Cuthberts 2-5 at Walterstown
Final: St Martins/Ratoath 0-5 Slane 0-4 at Walterstown
Derek Melia; Niall Foley, Derek Maher, Terry Rooney; John Davis, Dermot Kealy (0-3), Allen Foley, Capt.; Dermot White, Liam Eiffe; Simon Farrell (0-1), Stephen Claire (0-1), Ciarán Byrne; Paul O Rourke, Larry McMahon, Pat Kealy. Subs: Brian Rooney for McMahon, Brendan Kealy for O Rourke, Michael Walsh, Karl Stoney, Philip Dolan, Pádraig Galvin. The following played in earlier rounds Alan Fahy, Dessie Donnelly, Vincent Moore, David Kane, Philip Dolan, Kevin Moroney. Selectors: Jim Gilligan, Pat Farrell, David O Donoghue, Dermot Rooney.

1988: Minor Football Championship
Semi-Final: Duleek 1-8 Ratoath/St. Martins 0-6 at Walterstown
Derek Melia; Karl Stoney, Liam Eiffe, Capt., Dónal Coyne; Ciarán Byrne, Dermot Kealy, Peter McCabe; Terry Rooney, Stephen Claire; Brendan Kealy, Kevin Moroney (0-3), Alan Fahy (0-2); David Kane, Dessie Donnelly, Barry Donnelly. Subs: Shane Mahon for McCabe, Garbhán Blake, Colm Naughton, David Moroney, Vincent Moore, Shane O Neill, John Dollard, Noel McTigue, Morty O Sullivan. One point unaccounted for. Selectors: Jim Gilligan, Pat Farrell, David O Donoghue, Dermot Rooney.

1989: Minor Football Championship
Semi-Final: St. Martins/Ratoath defeated Gaeil Colmcille at Dunderry.
Final: Duleek 0-6 St. Martins/Ratoath 0-4. at Páirc

Tailteann. Abandoned due to death of Duleek player's father in stand

Refixture: St. Martins/Ratoath 0-9 Duleek 2-3 at Páirc Tailteann

Replay: Duleek 2-6 St. Martins/Ratoath 1-6 at Páirc Tailteann

Robert Ennis; Ciarán Byrne, Garbhán Blake, Capt., Peter McCabe; Liam Holton, Terry Rooney (0-1), Dónal Coyne; Colm Naughton (0-2), Barry Donnelly (0-2); Pearse Fahy, Brendan Kealy, Declan Troy (1-1); Robert McGuinness, Shane O Neill, John Boyle. Subs: Liam O Neill, David Moroney, John Dollard, Ivor Reilly, Martin Lynch, Paul Molloy, Tiernan O Rourke, Alan Boyle, Evan Kelly, Thomas Walsh. Selectors: John Holton, Ollie O Neill (St. Martins) David Donoghue, Dermot Rooney (Ratoath).

1998: Minor Football Championship

Semi-Final: Walterstown 1-15 St. Martins 1-9 at Skryne

Christopher Carey; John Joe McDonnell, Brian Kenny, Kevin Moyles; Damien Minnock, Niall Kelly, John McKenna; Gary Donoghue (0-1), Gerard Troy; John Gilsenan, Christopher Doyle, David McNerney (0-1); Alan Kenny, David Crimmins (0-1), Trevor Dowd (1-6). Sub: Brian Murphy for McKenna. Team Manager: Brendan Kealy, Selectors: David Crimmins, Pat Kenny.

2002: Minor Football Championship, Division 2

Semi-Final: St. Martins 1-10 Dee Rangers 1-10 at Rathkenny

Replay: St. Martins 2-11 Dee Rangers 2-9 at Martry

Final: St. Martins 0-11 Ratoath 2-5 at Skryne

Replay: St. Martins 3-5 Ratoath 2-7 at Donaghmore

James White; Ciarán Hoary, Caoimhín King, David Donoghue; David McMahon, Kevin Ward, Owen Herlihy; John Crimmins, Capt., Michael Ahern; Ronan Gilsenan (0-1), Rory Bowe, Jamie Minnock (1-0); Diarmuid Delaney, David Devereux (0-2), Cathal O Dwyer (1-2). Subs: Gavin O Regan for Delaney, Stephen Caffrey (1-0) for Minnock, Mark West for Donoghue. Selectors: David Crimmins, Snr., Gabriel King, Pat Herlihy.

2005: Minor Football Championship

Semi-Final: St. Martins 3-11 Round Towers 1-14 at Martry.

Final: Summerhill 2-16 St. Martins 2-9 at Páirc Tailteann

Seán Doyle; Bryan McKeown, James Gaughan, Cathal Moore; Alan McLoughlin, David Wallace, Emmet O Callaghan; Cillian Finn, Michael Ahern; Ciarán Farrelly, Shane Kelly (0-1), Conor Staunton, Acting Capt. (1-2); John Coleman, David Devereux (0-6), Mark Caldwell (1-0). Subs: Dara Devereux for Moore, Stephen McGroder for McKeown, Shane Toher for Farrelly, Adrian Toolan, Capt., Brian Coughlan, Paddy Doohan, Fionán O Kane, Fearghal Delaney, Duncan Geraghty, John Coffey, Christopher Dixon. Selectors: Macartan McGroder, TP Toolan, Tom Finn.

2006: Minor Football League

Semi-Final: Duleek defeated St. Martins.

2007: Minor Football League, Division 2

Semi-Final: Walterstown defeated St. Martins at Dunganny.

HURLING

From 1983 to 1986 under age hurling teams fielded as Dunshaughlin. From 1987 until 2008 under age hurling teams fielded as St. Martins and from 2009 to the present teams fielded as Drumree. Results while playing as Drumree are contained in Appendix 9.

Due to extremely poor coverage in the local press, mainly due to inconsistent filing of results by club PROs, semi-final details are omitted, except where known. Information on many of the finals is also scarce and despite the authors' best efforts it was not always possible to unearth the scores or team line outs. Note: Some competitions were thirteen or eleven a side.

UNDER 11

1987: Under 11 B Hurling Championship
Final: St. Martins 5-2 Wolfe Tones 0-0 at Trim
Garreth Kelly; Enda Lynch, Wayne Cottrell, Eoin Coffey; Noel Doyle, Ronan Coffey, Paul Doyle; Ronan Curley, Capt., (1-0), Aaron Fitzpatrick (1-0); Damien Fitzpatrick, Derek Doyle (1-2), Shane Kelly; B. Jones, Adrian Flanagan (1-0), Patrick Burke (1-0). Subs: Ross Geraghty, Derek Davis, Peter Egan, Joseph Smith, Seán Curley, Cathal Smith, Ian Rattigan, Alan McCarthy, Jonathon Farrell. Selectors: Patsy Curley, Gerry Flanagan and Ben Fitzpatrick.

1993: Under 11 B Hurling Championship
Final: Killyon 3-0 St. Martins 2-0 in Kilmessan
Philip Doyle; Seamus Wallace, John Crimmins, Caoimhín King; Keith Mangan, Kevin Burke, Shona Donoghue; Christopher Doyle, Martin Duffy; Liam Shanley (1-0), Ciarán Murray, Stephen Ward; Seán White, David Reid, Brendan Walsh (1-0). Subs: Emma Doyle, David Donoghue.

1994: Under 11 B Hurling Championship
Final: Kilmessan 2-1 St. Martins 1-1 in Dunboyne
Panel: Ronan Gilsenan, Shona Donoghue, Seán Hayes, Caoimhín King, Seamus Wallace, John Crimmins, David Donoghue, Ciarán Murray, Stephen Ward, Seán White, Paul Sheehy, Brendan Walsh, Liam Shanley, Ray Maloney, John Murphy, Mark Devanney, Paul Hand, Diarmuid Delaney, John Reynolds, Cormac Delaney, Emma Doyle, Ciarán Gilsenan, Blake Kelly, John O Callaghan, David Murphy. Selectors: Paul Barry, Willie Shanley, Jimmy Walsh, Jnr.

1995: U 11 B Hurling Championship
Final: St. Martins 3-3 Blackhall Gaels 2-0 at Dunboyne
Ronan Gilsenan; Joseph Coffey, Caoimhín King; Diarmuid Delaney, John Crimmins, Capt., Fergal Moore; Paul Sheehy, David Donoghue; David O Neill, Ciarán Murray (2-2), Paul Cosgrove; Cormac Delaney (1-0), Mark Devanney (0-1). Subs: Emma Doyle for O Neill, John Crosbie for D Delaney.

1996: Under 11 Ground Hurling, Grade 1
Final: St. Martins 2-1 Kilmessan 0-0.
Panel: John O Callaghan, David Quinn, Caroline Duffy, David Wallace, Ronan Gilsenan, Caoimhín King, John Kieran, Cormac Delaney, Fergal Moore, Joseph Coffey, Breda White, Aileen White, Pádraic Smith, Brian Coughlan, Alan Carey, Edel Walsh, Stephen McGroder, Orla Power, Séamus White.
Selectors: Paul Barry, Jimmy Walsh, Jun, Willie Shanley.

1998: U-11 Division 2 Hurling Championship
Final: Rathmolyon defeated St. Martins

2000: U-11 Shield Winners
St. Martins winners
Panel: Duncan Geraghty, Mark Coffey, Seamus White, Bill

Reilly, Shane Troy, Kieran Murphy, Paul Barry, Thomas Evans, Michael McCarthy, Niall Murphy, Paul Walsh, Daniel Geraghty, James Rattigan, Stephen McCarthy, Robert Crosbie.

2003: Under 11C
Final: Killyon defeated St. Martins
Panel: Stephen McCarthy, Cathal Gavin, John McGovern, Kevin Kinsella, Alastar Doyle, Michael Kennedy, Fergus Toolan, Michael McCarthy, David Baggott, Kristina Troy, Charlie Doolan, Shiobhra Delaney, James Reilly, Gavin Byrne, Seán Gavin, Kevin Lynch, Kevin Reynolds, Terry McMahon, Jamie Lawless, Oliver Killoran, Killian Gavin, Steven Kinsella, Mark Briody, Kevin Sweeney. Management team: Conor Gavin, Niall McCarthy & Jim Reynolds.

2003: Under 12 B:
Final: Killyon defeated St. Martins
Panel: Stephen McCarthy, Cathal Gavin, John McGovern, Brian Woods, Niall Murphy, Charlie Doolan, Fergus Toolan, Michael McCarthy, James Rattigan, Stephen Doyle, David Baggott, Paul Keane, Gavin Byrne, Shiobhra Delaney, Kevin Lynch, Kevin Burke, Seán Gavin, Conal O Sullivan. Management team: Conor Gavin, Niall McCarthy.

2008: U-11 C Hurling Championship
Final: Runners Up. No details available

UNDER 13

1992: U-13 B Hurling Championship
Final: St. Martins defeated Killyon
John McKiernan; David Kenny, Philip Salmon, Brian Kenny; Alan Kenny, Gary Donoghue, Jason Clarke; Paddy Boyle, Paul Doyle; Karen Ward, David Crimmins, Pádraig Shanley; Gerard Troy, Seán Curley, Neil Mooney. Subs: George Troy, Simon Maher, Ronan Eagle, Liam Shanley, John Gilsenan, Philip Doyle, Christopher Doyle, Brian Walsh, Kevin Burke, Kevin Kilbane, Cathal Smith, Justin Martin. Selectors: Willie Shanley, Joe Mahon, Paddy Ward.

1993: U-13 B Hurling Championship
Semi-Final: Rathmolyon 2-2 St. Martins 2-1
Philip Doyle; Kevin Burke, Gary Donoghue, Brian Kenny; Alan Kenny, John McKiernan, Christopher Doyle; David Crimmins, Neil Reilly; John Gilsenan, GT Troy, Gerard Troy; Brian Walsh, Jason Clarke, Justin Martin. Sub: Neil Mooney for Martin.

1994: U-13 B Hurling Championship
Final: Gaeil Colmcille 1-1 St Martins 0-3 in Navan
Philip Doyle; John Crimmins, John Joe McDonnell, Kieran Crimmins; Keith Mangan, Brian Kenny, Ciarán Murray; Christopher Doyle, Kevin Burke; John Gilsenan, Martin Duffy, Brendan Walsh; Stephen Ward, Christopher Carey, Liam Shanley. Selectors: David Crimmins, Peter Mooney, Willie Shanley, Paddy Ward.

1996: U-13 B Hurling Championship
Final: Boardsmill defeated St. Martins in Kiltale. No details available.

1998: U-13 B Hurling Championship
Final: St. Martins 2-9 Boardsmill 4-0
Panel with scorers in the final: Fergal Moore, Ciarán Kenny, Ronan Cleary, Paul Cosgrove, Caoimhín King, Joseph Coffey, Ronan Gilsenan (1-5), Rory Bowe, David Wallace (0-2), John Kieran (1-1), Cormac Delaney, John Crosby, Eoin Reilly, David Quinn, Stephen McGroder (0-1), Brian Coughlan, Robert Lyons, Pádraic Smith, John Coffey, Brian McEntee, Gary Woodruffe, Ciarán Hoary. Selectors: Michael Wallace, Jimmy Walsh, Jnr., Manager: Paul Barry.

1999: U-13 Division 2 Hurling Championship
Final: Blackhall Gaels 4-10 St. Martins 2-8
John Coffey; Eoin Reilly, David Quinn; Brian Coughlan, Ciarán Kenny, Joseph Coffey; Cormac Delaney (0-1), David Wallace (0-7); John Crosbie, Robert Lyons, Adrian

Toolan (1-0); Fergal Moore, Shane Kelly. Subs: Stephen McGroder for Crosbie, Brian McEntee (1-0) for Kelly, Ronan Cleary for McGroder.

2000: U-13 B Hurling Championship
Final: Kiltale 4-1 St. Martins 3-2 at Rathmolyon

2006: U-13 B Hurling Championship
Semi-Final: St. Martins 1-8 Dunderry 1-4
Final: Kilmessan 4-3 St. Martins 4-1

Semi Team: David Reilly; Alan Keane, Kristina Troy, Seán Gavin; Eoin Hannon, Keith Rooney, Niall Hannon (1-1); James Reilly (0-3), David Baggott; Stephen McCarthy (0-4), Kevin Sweeney, Oisín de Bhál; Caimin Dunne, Gary Commons. Subs: Ruadhán O Riordan, Darragh Kennedy, Leon Everett, Andrew Kiernan, Oliver Killoran, Killian Gavin, David Moore, Sam Houlihan.

2007: U-13 B Hurling Championship
Semi-Final: Navan O Mahonys defeated St. Martins

UNDER 14

1984: U-14 Féile na Mí, Section C
Semi-Final: Dunshaughlin 4-3 Boardsmill 3-3
Final: Dunshaughlin 5-6 Kildalkey 1-4

Panel: William Carey, Karl Stoney, Paul Davis, Trevor Doyle, Garbhán Blake, Liam O Neill, David O Neill, Vinny Moore, Shane Mahon, Thomas Walsh, Declan Troy, Declan Cottrell, Philip Burke, Trevor Conroy, James Farrell, Hugh McCarthy, David Walsh, Denis Burke and David Farrell.

1985: U-14 B Hurling Championship
Final: Dunshaughlin 6-3 Rathmolyon 3-0 at Trim

David Farrell; Martin Lynch, Liam O Neill, Peter Rattigan; David O Neill, Garbhán Blake, James Farrell; John Bacon, Colm Naughton; Declan Troy (0-1), Capt., Thomas Walsh (1-1), Liam Holton; Declan Cottrell (2-1), Trevor Doyle (1-0), Fergus Summerville (2-0). Subs: Mark Rattigan, Hugh McCarthy, Darragh O Sullivan, Alan Boyle, Mark Cottrell, James Farrell. Selectors: Patsy Curley, Ollie O Neill.

1989: U-14 B Hurling Championship
Final: Dunboyne defeated St. Martins

1992: U-14 B Hurling Championship
Final: St. Martins 0-4 Gaeil Colmcille 0-1 at Kildalkey

Gary Donohoe; Eoin Coffey, Noel Doyle, Mick O Brien; Alan Kenny, Rory O Sullivan, Capt., David Crimmins; Paul Doyle, Gerard Clarke; Pádraig Shanley, Seán Curley, Damien Fitzpatrick (0-2); Jason Clarke (0-1), Brendan Boyle (0-1), Paddy Boyle. Subs: Philip Burke for Curley, George Troy for Burke, Gerard Troy. Selectors: Willie Shanley, Paddy Ward, Joe Mahon.

1992: Feile na nGael, U-14, Division 2
Final: St. Martins 4-2 Kildalkey 1-1

Gary Donoghue; Eoin Coffey, Noel Doyle, Mick O Brien; David Crimmins, Rory O Sullivan, Capt., Patrick Burke; Paul Doyle (1-0), Gerard Clarke; Paddy Boyle, Sean Curley (1-0), Damien Fitzpatrick (0-2); Pádraig Shanley (1-0), Brendan Boyle, Colm O Dwyer (1-0). Subs: Alan Kenny for Boyle, GT Troy for Clarke, Jason Clarke for O Dwyer.

1994: U-14 County Féile
Final: St. Martins 6-5 Rathmolyon 0-3

Gary Donoghue; Kevin Burke, Gerard Troy, Brian Kenny; Alan Kenny, John McKiernan, Christopher Doyle; David Crimmins, Neil Reilly (1-0); John Gilsenan, GT Troy (1-2), Jason Keogh (0-3); Brian Walsh, Christopher Carey (3-0), Neil Mooney (1-0). Other Féile panel members: Stephen Ward, Martin Duffy, John Crimmins, Keith Mangan, Liam Shanley, Philip Doyle, John Joe McDonnell, Kieran Crimmins, Vincent Cullinane, Ciarán Murray and David McNerney.

1994: U-14 Leinster Mini Féile
St. Martins 2-1 Navan O Mahonys 0-3 in Trim

Gary Donoghue; John Joe McDonnell, Gerard Troy, Brian Kenny; Alan Kenny, John McKiernan, Christopher Doyle; Neil Reilly, David Crimmins; John Gilsenan, Kevin Burke, Brian Walsh; Neil Mooney, Jason Clarke, GT Troy.

1994: U-14 B Hurling Championship
Final: St. Martins 1-7 Rathmolyon 1-3 at Boardsmill
Gary Donoghue; John Joe McDonnell, Gerard Troy, Brian Kenny; Kevin Burke, John McKiernan, Capt, Alan Kenny; Neil Reilly, David Crimmins; John Gilsenan, GT Troy, Christopher Doyle; Neil Mooney, Jason Clarke, Christopher Carey. Subs: Brian Walsh for Mooney, Vincent Cullinane for McKiernan.

1994: U-14 Rural Championship
Inaugural Year of event.
Final: St. Martins defeated Rathmolyon at Kilmessan

2000: U-14 B Hurling Championship
Final: St. Martins 2-8 Wolfe Tones 3-1
John Crosby; Eoin Reilly, Brian Coughlan; Robert Lyons, Cormac Delaney, John Coffey; Ciarán Kenny, David Wallace (0-1); Adrian Toolan (0-3), Ronan Cleary, Brian McEntee (1-0); Fergal Moore (1-4), David Quinn. Subs: Adam Kelly for Quinn, Conor Staunton for Kelly.

2000: U-14 Hurling B Féile
Final: St. Martins defeated Boardsmill

2001: U-14 Division 1 Féile
Semi-Final: St. Martins 5-0 Trim 2-4
Final: St. Martins 4-4 Kilmessan 2-2
Panel: John Coffey, David Bracken, Shane Kelly, Adrian Toolan, David Wallace, Capt., Ciarán Farrelly, Seamus White, James Gaughan, Paul Kiernan, Brian Coughlan, Paul Coffey, Emmet O Callaghan, Christopher Dixon, Duncan Geraghty, Fionán O Kane, Timothy O Regan, Shane Troy, Fearghal Delaney, Stephen McGroder, Val Gannon, Martin Cosgrove, Bryan McKeown, Conor Staunton.

UNDER 15

1992: U-15 B Hurling League
Final: Baconstown 4-5 St. Martins 1-1
Gary Donohoe; Eoin Coffey, Garreth Kelly, Mick O Brien; Noel Doyle, Paul Doyle, David Crimmins; Gerard Clarke, Alan Egan; Seán Curley, Derek Doyle (1-0), Damien Fitzpatrick; Joseph Smith, Brendan Boyle (0-1), Alan Eagle. Subs: Alan Kenny for Eagle, Jason Clarke for Kenny, Ian Rattigan for Curley, Pádraig Shanley, Paddy Boyle.

1995: U-15 Hurling League
Final: St. Martins 1-7 Navan O Mahonys 2-4 at Kildalkey
Replay: Navan O Mahonys 6-10 St. Martins 0-4 at Athboy
John Gilsenan; John Joe McDonnell, Gerard Troy, Brian Kenny; Cormac Delaney, John Kieran, Christopher Doyle; David Crimmins (0-3), Vincent Cullinane; Alan Kenny, Jason Clarke (0-1), George Troy; Christopher Carey, Neil Reilly, Gary Donoghue. Subs: Martin Duffy for Doyle, Brian Walsh for Kenny.

UNDER 16

1993: U-16 B Hurling Championship
Semi-Final: St. Martins defeated Baconstown
Final: Boardsmill 2-7 St. Martins 0-1

2006: U-16 B Hurling Championship
Semi-Final: St. Martins 3-6 Na Fianna 1-1
Final: Navan O Mahonys 1-10 St. Martins 0-5 at Dunsany.

2007: U-16 B Hurling Championship
Play-Off: St. Martins defeated Kildalkey
Final: Na Fianna 4-5 St. Martins 2-9 at Dunganny
Panel: James Reilly, James Doolan, Gavin Byrne, James Rattigan, Robert Connolly, Michael Kennedy, Charlie Doolan, Cathal Gavin, Fergus Toolan, Niall Murphy,

Stephen Clusker, Stephen Doyle, Conal O Sullivan, Eoin Hannon, Michael McCarthy, Niall Hannon, Keith Rooney. Selectors: Christopher Doyle, GT Troy.

MINOR

1993: Minor B Hurling Championship
Semi-Final: St. Martins 3-5 Kildalkey 3-4
Final: St. Martins 2-2 Kiltale 0-8
Replay: Kiltale 5-4 St. Martins 2-3 at Kilmessan

Ronan Curley (1-0); Noel Burke, Wayne Cottrell; Mick Summerville, Dermot Doyle (1-0), Roy Sheridan; James Walsh, David Troy (0-3); Paul Doyle, Seamus Smith, Aaron Fitzpatrick; Alan Egan, Derek Doyle. Subs: Noel Doyle for Summerville, Brendan Tuite for Smith, Ronan Coffey for Tuite.

1996: Minor B Hurling Championship
Semi-Final: St. Martins 9-8 Blackhall Gaels 3-8 at Boardsmill
Final: Killyon defeated St. Martins
Team management: David Crimmins, Peter Mooney, Willie Shanley.

1997: Minor B Hurling Championship
Semi-Final: St. Martins 2-11 Killyon 3-5 at Kilmessan
Final: St. Martins 4-8 Rathmolyon 3-1 at Kildalkey

John Gilsenan; Kevin Burke, Gerard Troy; Neil Reilly, Paul Doyle (0-1), Brian Kenny; Pádraig Shanley, Paddy Boyle; GT Troy (2-0), David Crimmins (0-3), Gary Donoghue (1-1); Cathal Smith, Seán Curley, Capt. (1-3). Selectors: Willie Shanley, David Crimmins, Peter Mooney.

1998: Minor A Hurling Championship
Semi-Final: Boardsmill/Kildalkey 2-9 St. Martins 2-4

2000: Minor B Hurling Championship
Played April 2001
Final: Killyon 1-4 St. Martins 0-4 at Longwood

Ronan Gilsenan; Paul Sheehy, Caoimhín King; Kevin Burke, Seán White, David Donohoe; John Crimmins, Christopher Doyle (0-1); Liam Shanley, Seamus Wallace (0-2), Brendan Walsh; Rory Bowe (0-1), Philip Doyle.

2001: Minor B Hurling Championship
Semi-Final: St. Martins defeated Moylagh in Athboy
Final: St. Martins 0-5 Killyon 0-5 at Kiltale
Replay: St. Martins 1-12 Killyon 2-7 at Kilmessan

Cormac Delaney; John Crimmins, Paul Sheehy; Peadar Smith, Caoimhín King, David Donoghue; Seán White (1-1), Brendan Walsh; Ronan Gilsenan, Capt., Seamus Wallace (0-10), Liam Shanley (0-1); John Brennan, David Wallace. Subs: Rory Bowe, John Kieran, Padraig Smith, Eoin Reilly, Brian Coughlan, John Crosbie, Ciarán Gilsenan.

2003: Minor B Hurling Championship
Semi-Final: St. Martins 2-11 Gaeil Colmcille 0-3 at Kilmessan
Final: St. Martins 0-10 Blackhall Gaels 1-6 at Páirc Tailteann

John Crosbie; Eoin Reilly, Caoimhín King (0-1); James Gaughan, Brian Coughlan, Joseph Coffey; Ronan Gilsenan, Capt., Ciarán Kenny; Pádraig Smith, David Wallace (0-6), Cormac Delaney (0-3); Ronan Cleary, Rory Bowe. Subs: Stephen McGroder for P Smith, Christopher Dixon for Cleary, Robert Lyons for McGroder, John O Callaghan, Thomas O Regan, John Coffey. Selectors: Gabriel King, Michael Wallace, Seán Delaney.

APPENDICES

St. Martins, Under 12 Blitz Winners, 1991

Pictured at the presentation to St. Martins after the 1991 Under 12 Blitz are Paddy McHale, Paul Doyle, Captain, Ronan Gogan, Denis Kealy, Paddy Brannigan and Liam Brady Chairman and Secretary respectively, Meath Juvenile Board. In the background in cap is Brendan Tonge.

Winner All Right, 2001
Mairéad Delaney presents the Under 14 trophy to the captain of St. Martins, Alan McLoughlin, following final victory against Round Towers in Bective.

Presentation Night for St. Martins, 1998
Following a successful 1998 St. Martins' selectors, officers and County Board officials are pictured at the club presentation night in January 1999
Front: Gabriel King, Mairéad Delaney, Secretary, Pat Herlihy.
Back: Michael Wallace, Enda Smith, Meath Juvenile Hurling Secretary, John Reilly, Meath Juvenile Hurling Chairman, Paul Barry, Jimmy Walsh, Junior.

Appendix 9
Drumree: Results of Championship and League Finals

Football

1934: Junior Football Championship
Semi-Final: Oldcastle 1-2 Culmullen 0-4 at The Show Grounds, Navan, later Páirc Tailteann
No line out available but the following played: Ciarán Murray, Paddy Gogan, John Gogan, Thomas 'Connor' Doyle, C Lynch. For a few players only their surnames are known, their probable Christian names are given in brackets- [Ikey] Madden, [Mickey] Lambe and Brady, Daly and Ward, no Christian names for the final three.

1941: Junior Football Championship
Semi-Final: Carnaross 2-7 Drumree 0-7 at Páirc Tailteann
Thomas 'Connor' Doyle; Patrick 'Rah' Doyle, Joe Loughran (0-1), Jimmy Geraghty; Mickey Lambe, Willie Bashford (0-2), Kevin Reilly; Rory Mahon (0-1), Willie Carberry; Paddy Lynam, Kevin Clarke (0-3), Eugene Mohan; Jack Blount, Mattie Russell, Paddy 'Beezer' Courtney.

1948: Junior Football Championship
Semi-Final: Drumree 2-6 Rathkenny 2-0
Final: Navan O Mahonys 2-3 Drumree 1-4 at Trim
Semi-Final team: Thomas Kane; Bill Delany, Larry Geraghty, Paddy Kelly; R O Connor, Br. Tom O Sullivan, P Lynch; Billy Byrne, Jack O Connor; Jimmy Flynn, John Bashford, Jimmy Geraghty; Larry Dunphy, J Doherty, Noel Downes.

1959: Junior Football A Championship
Semi-Final: Drumree 0-4 Millbrook 0-2 at Páirc Tailteann
Final: Drumree 1-8 St. Patricks 1-8 at Trim
Replay: Drumree 1-8 St. Patricks 2-5 at Skryne
Second Replay: Drumree 1-4 St. Patricks 0-5 at Skryne

Final Proper: Drumree 1-10 Longwood 0-5 at Trim
Victorious team v St. Patricks was: Tony Walsh; Billy Byrne, Jimmy Murray, Tommy Troy; Patsy O Brien, Larry O Brien, Larry Byrne; PJ Rowley, Tony Rattigan; Jimmy Walsh (0-1), Billie Rattigan (0-2), Packie Doyle (1-0); Michael Flaherty, Dickie O Brien (0-1), Patsy O Sullivan, Capt. Subs: Michael Walsh for P Sullivan, Sean Doyle, Tommy Clerkin, Bertie O Malley, Jimmy O Rourke.
Team for final proper v. Longwood:
Tony Walsh; Tony Rattigan, Seán Doyle, Jimmy Murray; Larry Byrne, Billy Byrne, Patsy O Brien; PJ Rowley, Larry O Brien (0-1); Packie Doyle (0-1), Patsy O Sullivan, Billie Rattigan (0-7); Dickie O Brien (0-1), Michael Flaherty (1-0), J Sullivan.

1961: Intermediate Football Championship
Final: Drumree 2-7 Slane 1-3 at Páirc Tailteann
Tony Walsh; Seán Doyle, Tony Rattigan, Tom Murray; Patsy O Brien, Larry O Brien, Larry Byrne; Tommy Troy, Jack Kane (0-1); Jimmy Walsh (1-0), Patsy O Sullivan, Billie Rattigan Capt. (0-2); Packie Doyle (1-0), Billy Byrne (0-2), Jimmy O Rourke (0-2). Subs: Mickey Regan, Mick Kane, Dickie O Brien, Paddy Burke, Michael Walsh, Bertie O Malley.

1962: Feis Cup Football
Final: St. Vincents 1-10 Drumree 1-5 at Páirc Tailteann
Tony Walsh; Seán Doyle, Tony Rattigan, Paddy Burke; Patsy O Brien, Larry O Brien, Michael Walsh; Jack Kane, Tommy Troy; Jimmy O Rourke (1-0), Billie Rattigan (0-4), Jimmy Walsh (0-1); Patsy O Sullivan, Billy Byrne, Packie Doyle. Sub: Mick Kane for Byrne.

1964: Senior Football Championship
Semi-Final: Colm. Gaels 3-11 Drumree 1-8, Páirc Tailteann

Billy Byrne; Johnny Lynch, Tony Rattigan, Seán Doyle; Larry O Brien, Jack Kane, Michael Walsh; Tommy Troy, Tom O Brien; Brendan Cantwell, Jimmy Walsh (0-5), Jimmy O Rourke (0-1); Neil O Riordan (1-1), Tony Walsh, Billie Rattigan (0-1). Sub: Patsy O Sullivan for Walsh.

1969: Intermediate Football Championship

Semi-Final: Drumree 1-7 Martry 0-4 at Trim
Final: Drumree 2-6 Castletown 1-7 at Páirc Tailteann
Tony Walsh; Michael Geraghty (Kiltale), Johnny Lynch, Seán Doyle; Andy Mahon, Neil O Riordan, Michael Walsh; Tommy Troy, Tommy Murray; Jimmy O Rourke (0-2), Larry O Brien, Jimmy Walsh (1-3); Tony Rattigan (1-0), Paddy Burke, Oliver Walsh (0-1). Subs: Billie Rattigan for Murray, Ray Carty for Geraghty, Thomas Carty, John Murphy, Pat Muldowney, Joe Rattigan.

1986: Junior Football Division 3

Final: Robinstown 2-8 Drumree 0-8 at Seneschalstown
Dónal Carroll; Martin Wall, Michael Boyle, Ben Fitzpatrick; Seán Walsh (0-1), Jim Rattigan (0-1), Martin Smith; Ray Byrne, Val McMahon; John Burke (0-1), Dónal Treacy (0-3), Jimmy O Rourke; Seán Moore, Tommy Troy (0-1), Paul Rattigan. Subs: Paul Byrne for P Rattigan, Seán McKenna (0-1) for O Rourke, Michael Jones for Burke.

1988: Junior Football Division 3

Final: Drumree 2-6 Kilmainham 1-4 at Páirc Tailteann
Dónal Carroll; Gerry Boyle, Michael Boyle, Ben Fitzpatrick; Jim Rattigan (0-1), Seán Walsh, Paul Molloy; Tony Gleeson, Larry McMahon; Shane Mahon (1-1), David O Brien (1-2), Paul Rattigan (0-1), Capt.; Michael Jones (0-1), Martin Wall, Jimmy Walsh. Subs: Dónal Treacy for Molloy, Dónal Wall, Martin Smith, John Boyle, Charlie O Brien, Alan Boyle, Macartan McGroder, Jimmy O Rourke, Martin Lynch, Philip Byrne, Liam Holton, Michael Rattigan, Trevor Doyle and Declan Troy.

1990: Junior Football Championship

Semi-Final: Simonstown Gaels 3-12 Drumree 1-8 at Trim
Dónal Treacy; Trevor Doyle, Martin Wall, Paul Mulloy; Seán Walsh (0-1), Jim Rattigan, Declan Troy; Michael Boyle, Larry McMahon; Shane Mahon, Tony Gleeson (1-1), Paul Rattigan; John Boyle (0-3), Peter Watters, John O Brien (0-2). Sub: Paul O Brien.

1991: Junior Football Championship

Semi-Final: Drumree 3-10 Duleek 2-8 at Kilmessan
Final: Carnaross 1-14 Drumree 0-5
Alan Boyle; Martin Wall, Michael Boyle, Willie Brennan; Martin Lynch, Seán Walsh, Patrick O Brien; Shane Mahon, Larry McMahon; John O Brien, Jim Rattigan (0-1), Declan Troy; Evan Kelly (0-2), Tony Gleeson, Paul Rattigan (0-2). Team Management: Liam Harnan, Seán Doyle, Johnny Lynch, Patsy Curley.

1993: All County Football League, Division 5

Final: Drumree 0-9 Kilmainham 0-7
James Walsh; Trevor Doyle, Martin Wall, Liam Holton; Seán Walsh, Paddy Doyle, Aaron Fitzpatrick; Michael Boyle (0-2), David Troy (0-1); John Treacy (0-3), Evan Kelly, Shane Mahon (0-1); Neil McCarrick (0-1), Peter Watters, Adrian Faherty. Sub: Emmet Downes (0-1).

1985: East Meath Football League

Final: Drumree defeated St. Vincents
Panel: Jim Rattigan, Patrick O Brien, Michael Jones, Martin Smith, Dónal Carroll, Val McMahon, Michael Boyle, Gerry Wall, Tom Donoghue, Gerry Boyle, Paul Rattigan, David O Brien, Joe Doran, Dónal Wall, Martin Wall, Ray Byrne, Macartan McGroder, Anthony Wall, Seán Walsh, Jimmy O Rourke, Ben Fitzpatrick.

1995: All County Football League, Division 4

Final: Drumree 1-11 St. Ultans 0-7
Team members, not in line out order: John Boyle, Dermot Doyle, Aaron Fitzpatrick, Declan Troy, James Walsh, Seán

Walsh, Jim Rattigan, Capt., Roy Sheridan, Evan Kelly, Michael Collins, Pat Doyle, John Cullinane, John Ryan, Shane Mahon, Neil McCarrick.

1996: Junior Football Championship

Semi-Final: Drumree 0-14 Meath Hill 0-14 at Páirc Tailteann

Replay: Meath Hill 1-14 Drumree 0-12 at Páirc Tailteann

Trevor Murphy; Seán Walsh, John Cullinane, Dermot Doyle; Roy Sheridan, Aaron Fitzpatrick (0-1), Shane Mahon; Willie Brennan (0-1), Patrick Doyle; Damien Fitzpatrick, Jim Rattigan, Ronan Curley; Michael Boyle (0-2), Evan Kelly (0-5), John Treacy (0-3). Subs: Paul Rattigan for A Fitzpatrick, Paul Gaughan for Doyle.

1998: Junior Football Championship

Semi-Final: Drumree 1-9 Moylagh 1-4 at Páirc Tailteann

Final: Drumree 1-11 St. Marys 2-5 at Páirc Tailteann

John Boyle; Dermot Doyle, Patrick Doyle, Aaron Fitzpatrick, Capt.; Gerard Troy, Declan Troy (0-1), Roy Sheridan; John Cullinane, Bobby Geraghty (0-1); James Walsh, Jim Rattigan (0-2), Paul Gaughan (0-1); Jim Hayes (0-3), Evan Kelly (1-3), Shane Mahon. Subs: Damien Fitzpatrick, David Troy, Pádraig Shanley, Gary Donoghue, Garreth Kelly, Seán Walsh, Gavin Kilbane, Christopher Doyle, Mark Rattigan, Aidan Walsh. Team Management: Pat Kelly, Stephen Wade, Joe Kelliher.

1998: Leinster Club Junior Football Tournament

Semi-Final: Drumree 2-14 Ballinamere, Offaly 1-5 at Tober

Final: Drumree 2-12 Ballyroan, Laois 1-10 at Dunshaughlin

John Boyle; Dermot Doyle, Michael Collins, Aaron Fitzpatrick, Capt.; Gerard Troy, Declan Troy, Roy Sheridan; John Cullinane (0-1), Bobby Geraghty (0-1); Shane Mahon (0-2), Jim Rattigan (0-1), Paul Gaughan (0-1); Jimmy Walsh (0-1), Evan Kelly (2-2), Jim Hayes (0-2). Sub: David Troy and Patrick Doyle (0-1). Team Management: Pat Kelly, Stephen Wade, Joe Kelliher.

2000: Intermediate Football Championship

Semi-Final: St. Patricks 0-15 Drumree 1-8 at Páirc Tailteann

Alan Boyle; Roy Sheridan, David Troy, Brian Kenny; George Troy, Dermot Doyle, Christopher Doyle; Aaron Fitzpatrick, John Cullinane; John Gilsenan, Michael Collins, James Walsh; Shane Mahon (1-0), Evan Kelly (0-2), Paul Gaughan (0-6). Subs: Declan Troy for Fitzpatrick, Gavin Kilbane for Sheridan, Paul O Rourke for Walsh. Team Management: Philip Phelan, Pat Kelly, Emmet O Callaghan.

2006: All County Football League, Division 5

Final: Curraha 0-7 Drumree 0-4 at Dunshaughlin

Christopher Dixon; James Gaughan, Ciarán Kenny, Stephen McGroder; John Gilsenan, Gavin Kilbane, Roy Sheridan; John Cullinane (0-1), David Troy; Emmet O Callaghan, Dermot Doyle, David McMahon; James Walsh, John Brennan (0-1), Christopher Doyle (0-2). Subs: Séamus Wallace for Dixon, Neil McCarrick for Doyle.

Hurling

1991: Junior Hurling Championship, Division 2
Final: Kilmessan beat Drumree

1992: Junior Hurling Championship, Division 2
Final: Athboy beat Drumree

1993: Junior Hurling Championship, Division 2
Final: Drumree 2-7 Boardsmill 1-4
Patsy Curley; Mark Rattigan, David Farrell, Trevor Doyle; Liam Holton, Willie Shanley, Paul Rattigan; Paddy Doyle (0-2), Michael Boyle; Aaron Fitzpatrick (1-2), Paul O Rourke, David Troy (0-3); Dermot Doyle, John Considine, Jimmy Walsh Snr. Subs: Tommy Troy (1-0) for Considine, Pat Kenny for M Rattigan, James Walsh, Jnr., Thomas Walsh, Adrian Faherty, Derek Doyle, Hugh McCabe, Wayne Cottrell, Charlie Leonard. Team Management: Patsy Curley, coach, Michael Boyle, Seán Doyle and Willie Shanley selectors.

1996: Junior Hurling Championship, Division 2
Final: Drumree 1-6 Ratoath 1-6
Final Replay: Drumree 2-5 Ratoath 0-3
Willie Shanley; Gerard Clarke, Charlie Leonard, Rory O Sullivan; Paul Doyle (0-1), Declan Troy, Pádraig Shanley; Dermot Doyle, Capt., Paul O Rourke; Paul Gaughan, David Troy (1-1), David Crimmins (0-3); Seán Curley (1-0), Patrick Boyle, Ronan Curley. Subs: Gary Donoghue for R Curley, Gerard Troy for S Curley. Trainer: Peter Mooney.

1996: Junior Hurling Championship
Final: Killyon beat Drumree

1998: Junior Hurling Championship
Final: Drumree 0-4 Trim 0-4
Final Replay: Drumree 1-6 Trim 1-5
Willie Shanley; Gerard Clarke, Trevor Doyle, Paul O Rourke; Paul Doyle, Declan Troy (0-2), Pádraig Shanley; Dermot Doyle, David Crimmins; Paul Gaughan, Gerard Troy (1-1), Gary Donoghue (0-1); Seán Curley (0-1), David Troy, Capt., (0-1), Shane Kennedy. Subs: George Troy for Kennedy, Kennedy for Curley.

1999: Under 21 Special Hurling Championship
Final: Drumree 3-5 Kildalkey 2-2.
John Gilsenan; Paul Doyle, Gerard Clarke, Capt.; Kevin Burke, David Crimmins (1-2), Brian Kenny; Christopher Doyle, Alan Kenny; Pádraig Shanley (1-0), Gary Donoghue, George Troy; Seán Curley (1-3), Shane Kennedy. Sub: Paddy Boyle.

2000: Intermediate Hurling Championship
Semi-Final: Drumree 1-8 Na Fianna 1-5 at Longwood
Final: Boardsmill 1-11 Drumree 2-3 at Páirc Tailteann
Mark Rattigan; Paul Doyle, Brian Kenny, Kevin Burke; Gerard Clarke, David Troy (0-2), Christopher Doyle; Dermot Doyle, John Gilsenan (1-0); Seamus Wallace, George Troy, Seán White; Shane Kennedy (0-1), Pádraig Shanley (1-0), Ronan Curley. Subs: James Walsh for C Doyle, S Smith for Kennedy, Seán Curley, Alan Kenny.

2003: Intermediate Hurling Championship
Final: Drumree 4-7 Clanna Gael 0-6 at Páirc Tailteann.
David Farrell (Capt.); Kevin Burke, Gerard Troy, John Gilsenan; Brian Kenny, Ronan Curley, Christopher Doyle; Caoimhín King, John Crimmins; David Wallace (0-1), Seamus Wallace (0-5), Dermot Doyle (1-1); Brendan Walsh, Paul Gaughan (1-0), Seán White. Subs: David Crimmins (1-0) for Curley, Curley for Walsh, David Troy (1-0) for White, Séamus Smith for Dermot Doyle, Gary

Donoghue, Gerard Clarke, Brian Walsh, Brian Coughlan, Ronan Gilsenan, Ciarán Kenny.

2010: Intermediate Hurling Championship
Semi-Final: Drumree 1-14 Blackhall Gaels 1-7
Final: Drumree 1-10 Boardsmill 2-6

Ronan Curley; Ciarán Kenny, Shane Troy, Stephen McGroder; Paul Walsh, Caoimhín King, Johnny Gilsenan, Capt.; Brendan Walsh, Brian Coughlan (0-1); Stephen Doyle (0-8), John Crimmins (0-1), David Wallace; Fearghal Delaney, Christopher Doyle, Liam Shanley. Subs: David Crimmins (1-0) for C Doyle, James Reilly for Delaney, Keith Rooney for Shanley, Daire Flanagan, Paul Kiernan, Robert Lyons, Peter Rattigan, Mark Devanney, Paul Hendrick, Andrew Kiernan, Martin Kelly, Robert Connolly, Brian Kenny, Bill Reilly, Conal O Sullivan, Dermot Doyle, James Gaughan, GT Troy, David Donoghue.

2010: Leinster Intermediate Hurling Championship
Delvin 1-10 Drumree 0-9 at Mullingar

Ronan Curley; Ciarán Kenny, Shane Troy, Stephen McGroder; Paul Walsh, Brian Coughlan (0-1), Johnny Gilsenan; Brendan Walsh (0-2), Fearghal Delaney; Stephen Doyle (0-4), Caoimhín King (0-1), David Wallace (0-1); Keith Rooney, David Crimmins, Christopher Doyle. Subs: Mark Devanney for Gilsenan, Peter Rattigan for Rooney, James Reilly for C Doyle.

2010: Junior Hurling League, Division 2
Final: Drumree 3-6 Kiltale 2-6 at Trim

Ronan Curley; Ciarán Kenny, Shane Troy, Stephen McGroder; Paul Walsh, Brian Coughlan (0-1), Johnny Gilsenan; Brendan Walsh, Fearghal Delaney; Stephen Doyle (0-3), Caoimhín King, David Wallace (0-1); Mark Devanney (1-0), David Crimmins, Christopher Doyle (1-1). Subs: James Reilly for Walsh, Keith Rooney (1-0) for Delaney, Daire Flanagan, Paul Hendrick, Conal O Sullivan, Andrew Kiernan, James Gaughan, Robert Lyons, Paul Kiernan, Brendan Walsh, Dermot Doyle, Peter Rattigan.

2012: Under 21 B Hurling Championship
Final: Drumree/Blackhall Gaels drew with Dunderry
Final Replay: Drumree/Blackhall Gaels 2-11 Dunderry 1-7

Paul Kelly; Gavin Byrne, Conor Delany, Co-Capt; Gareth Rooney, Shane Whitty (0-2), Conal O Sullivan, Co-Capt; Stephen Morris, James Rattigan (0-3); Stephen Doyle, Keith Rooney, Colm Whitty (0-2); Niall Mangan, James Reilly (2-0). Subs: David Reilly for Doyle, Niall Kelly for O Sullivan, Brendan O Malley for Mangan, Andrew Kiernan for Byrne. Team Management: Daire Flanagan, Christy Mangan, Dermot Doyle, and Ronan Curley. Four points unaccounted for.

2013: Under 21 A Hurling Championship
Semi-Final: Drumree/Blackhall 2-13 Kildalkey 1-13
Final: Drumree/Blackhall Gaels awarded the title as Kiltale refused to field due to two players' involvement with Summerhill.

2014: Intermediate Hurling Championship
Semi-Final: Kilskyre 2-11 Drumree 1-8

Christopher Doyle; Paul Walsh, Keith Rooney, Gavin Byrne; Conal O Sullivan, James Gaughan, John Gilsenan; Fearghal Delaney (1-0), Gareth Rooney; David Reilly, Caoimhín King, Shane Troy (0-8); Mark Devanney, Seán White, Liam Carey. Subs: Josh Wall for Devanney, Duncan Geraghty for Byrne, David Wallace for White, John Crimmins for King, James Reilly for D Reilly, Darren Lawless, Keith Commons, Niall Mangan, Liam Shanley, Brian Coughlan, Brendan Walsh, Robert Connolly.

APPENDICES

Under Age Hurling
1999-2014

From 2009 Drumree represented the parish at under age hurling and the successful under age teams in the 2009-14 period are detailed below. Corresponding under age football results will be found in Appendix 7 with Dunshaughlin results.

2009: Under 14, Div 2 Championship
Final: Drumree 5-8 Clanna Gael 5-7

Lorcán Casey; Darren Lawless, Diarmuid Christie; David Dunne, Gareth Rooney Capt., Darragh Nolan; Shane Gallogly, David Reilly (0-1); Josh Wall (1-3), Dan Ormsby (0-1), Killian Gavin (1-0); Liam Carey (1-3); David Moore (2-0). Subs: Alan Reilly for Casey, Darragh Walsh for Nolan, Stephen Farrell for Christie, Kevin Madden, Eddie Murphy, James Logan, Aidan McMahon, Andrew Doolan, Senan Ó Muirí. Selectors: Frank Bawle, Eamonn Dunne, Conor Gavin and Martin Wall.

2011: Under 12B
Semi-Final: Drumree 3-3 Longwood 1-4 at Drumree
Final: Drumree defeated Rathmolyon at Kildalkey

Panel: Conor Jones, Kevin Bawle, Pádraig Clinton, Alastair Philip, Liam Hanley, Luke Mitchell, David Fildes, Matthew Moyles, Daniel Fildes, Jamie Rattigan, Andrew Baggott, Ross McQuillan, Mathew Costello, Kevagh Slater, Andrew Leneghan, Aaron Lawlor, Ava Foley, Niall Gavin, Niall Hurley. Mentors: Frank Bawle, Conor Gavin, Willie Hanley.

2011: U16 B Championship
Final: Rathmolyon 3-16 Drumree 3-14 aet. in Trim.

Panel: Lorcan Casey, Darragh Nolan, Liam Carey (0-1), David Dunne, Edward Murphy, Jack Leonard, Martin Keane, Diarmuid Christie, Darren Lawless, Killian Gavin (0-1), Shane Gallogly (1-0), David Moore (1-7), David Reilly (0-5), Josh Wall (1-0), Gareth Rooney, Daniel McTigue, Alan Reilly. Selectors: Frank Bawle, Vincent Brennan, Conor Gavin.

2011: Minor B Hurling Championship
Semi-Final: Kildalkey 5-10 Drumree 1-7

Andrew Kiernan; Keith Rooney, C. Farrell; Gareth Rooney, Darren Lawless, Leon Everitt; James Reilly (0-3), Seán Gavin; Cathal Gavin (0-1), David Baggott, Josh Wall; David Moore (0-1), Liam Carey (1-0). Subs: David Reilly (0-2) for D. Moore, D Moore for C Gavin.

2012: Under 13 Hurling Shield
Final: Drumree 3-9 Ratoath 2-10

Conor Gavin, Edward O Riordan, Frank Bawle and Willie Hanley managed the following panel: Conor Jones, Conor Moyles, Jamie Rattigan, Liam Hanley, Niall Hurley, Ross McQuillan, Daniel Byrne, Paul Briody, Mathew Costello, David Fildes, Paddy Conway, Kevin Bawle, Pádraig Clinton, Andrew Leneghan, Niall Gavin, Ódhran O Riordan, Jonathan Pearle, Luke Mitchell, Josh Kallides.

2012: Under 16 B Hurling Championship:
Semi-Final: Na Fianna defeated Drumree

2012: Minor B Hurling Championship
Semi-Final: Drumree/Blackhall Gaels 3-11 Kilmessan 2-12 after replay
Final: Drumree/ Blackhall Gaels 1-16 Rathmolyon/Na Fianna 1-13 aet at Dunboyne

Paul Kelly, Darren Lawless, Diarmuid Christie, Gareth Rooney, Niall Kelly, Shane Whitty (0-10), David Reilly (1-3), Philip Carey, Seán Gavin, Josh Wall (0-2), Shane McGuinness, Liam Carey (0-1). Note: one player's name missing. Subs: Killian Gavin for McGuinness, Hugh Smith for Carey, Shane Gallogly for Seán Gavin, Colin Farrell, Darragh Walsh, Fergus Ryan, Pádraig Keane.

2013: Under 12B Hurling
Final: Drumree 4-11 Kildalkey 3-7

Team management: Ed O Riordan, Martin Wall and John Fraher.

2013: Under 13 Hurling Shield
Semi-Final: Clann na nGael defeated Drumree

2013: Minor Hurling Division 1 Shield
Final: Drumree 1-15 Ratoath 1-6

Paul Kelly; Darren Lawless, Diarmuid Christie, Killian Gavin; Fergus Ryan, Gareth Rooney, Alan Reilly; Josh Wall, Niall Kelly; Liam Carey, David Reilly, Darragh Walsh; Eddie Murphy, Hugh Smith, Andrew Doolan. Team Management: Frank Bawle and Conor Gavin.

Camogie Final Results

Until 2009 St. Martins catered for underage camogie. Since then teams have played in the Drumree name and colours

2008: Under 12 Shield
Final: St. Martins victorious by 3-0 to 2-1

Panel: Cliodhna O Riordan, Niamh Kennedy, Hannah O Brien, Marissa Horan, Muireann O Hora, Ciara Reynolds, Chloe Byrne, Brona Gavin, Shona Lynch, Niamh Gallogly, Ciara Jones, Sophie Mc Namara, Gráinne Hanley, Hayley Briody, Sarah Sweeney, Kerri Moran, Rebecca Farrell, Alannah Chalkley, Eimear Woods and Megan Pritchard. Team management: Nuala Gavin, Edward O Riordan.

2008: Under 14 B
Final: Dunboyne 3-2 St. Martins 1-4

Cliodhna O Riordan; Siobhán Scully, Jessica Wall, Rebecca Sweeney; Ciara Kennedy, Catriona Kennedy, Emma Connolly; Clíona Murphy, Orla Bracken; Rebecca Keane, Louise Griffin, Méabh Gallogly; Hannah McNamee, Emma Kennedy (1-0), Áine Brennan. Subs: Saoirse Conlon for Brennan, Marissa Horan for Catríona Kennedy, Catríona Keane for McNamee.

2009: Under 14
Final: Drumree 5-2 Killyon 0-2

2010: Under 12 Div 2B
Final: Drumree beat Dunderry.

2010: Junior Camogie Championship
Final: Boardsmill 2-4 Drumree 2-3

Cliodhna O Riordan; Catríona Kennedy, Aimee McQuillan, Sinéad Ennis; Leanne McMorrow, Gemma Flanagan, Sarah Keane; Róisín Ní Dhúshláine, Cliona Murphy (0-1); Cliona Ni Dhúshláine, Niamh Kelleher, Emma Kennedy; Áine Brennan, Kim Slater (0-1), Emma Doyle (2-1). Subs: Ciara Kennedy for Keane, Lisa Donnelly for Brennan, Aide Pritchard, Eleanor Troy, Saoirse Inge, Ann Marie Rattigan, Rita Weber, Louise Griffin, Patricia Monks, Melissa Leonard, Jessica Wall.

2011: Under 14
Final: Dunboyne 7-4 Drumree 4-0

Panel: Rebecca Farrell, Kerri Moran, Liadan O Riordan, Aisling Moyles, Sorcha Casey, Alannah Chalkley, Chloe Mahon, Ciara Jones, Siobhán Whitty, Juliette Wall, Kevagh Slater, Brona Gavin, Sadhbh Ó Muirí, Ruth Byrne, Shona Lynch, Caoimhe Rooney, Aisling Maye, Áine Maye, Niamh Gallogly, Emma Bannon, Beibhin O Hora.

2011: Junior Camogie Championship
Final: Drumree 2-5 Trim 1-1

Adrienne Pritchard, Leanne McMorrow, Maeve Scanlon, Jessica Wall, Louise Griffin, Cliona Murphy, Sarah Keane, Emma Doyle, Emer O Reilly, Cliona Ní Dhúsláine, Áine Brennan, Gemma Flanagan, Sinéad Ennis, Ciara Kennedy,

Annemarie Rattigan, Rosie Hand, Lisa Donnelly, Patricia Monks, Kim Slater, Noeleen Greally, Brenda Greally, Niamh Kellegher, Emma Kennedy, Saoirse Inge, Áine Lynch, Caitriona Kennedy, Catherine Rattigan, Shiobhra Delaney, Rita Weber. Team management: GT Troy, Maureen Doyle and Vincent Brennan.

2013: Under 16 B
Final: Drumree 6-9 Kildalkey 1-3

Rebecca Farrell; Ruth Byrne, Liadan O Riordan, Aisling Moyles; Hayley Reynolds, Siobhán Whitty, Caoimhe Rooney; Chloe Mahon, Niamh Gallogly, Capt.; Ciara Jones, Alannah Chalkley, Juliette Wall; Sabrina Kelly, Brona Gavin, Orlaith Moyles. Subs: Sorcha Casey, Saoirse Casey, Áine Maye, Aisling Maye, Beibhín O Hora, Éabha Ryan, Kevagh Slater. Team management: Ed O Riordan, Shane Mahon and Martin Wall.

2013: Junior Camogie Championship
Final: Dunderry 6-5 Drumree 2-7

Annemarie Rattigan; Jessica Wall, Rosie Hand, Eimear O Reilly; Muireann O Hora, Alannah Chalkley, Hannah O Brien; Louise Griffin, Áine Brennan; Gemma Flanagan, Cliodhna O Riordan, Cliona Murphy; Emma Kennedy, Cliona Ní Dhúshláine, Patricia Monks.

2014: Under 13 Division 2
Final: Kiltale 1-2 Drumree 1-1

Panel: Alannah Brennan, Ciara Fitzpatrick, Latisha Rattigan, Ava O Brien, Sonia Leonard, Orla Bannon, Ella Morris, Sinéad Moyles, Muireann Ryan, Emma Flynn, Jesse Prichard-Egan, Rachel Duke, Aoife Harrington, Shayla Rattigan, Joy Smith, Raina Byrne, Ciara Philip. Team management: Johnny Leonard, Nuala Gavin, Ettie Philip, Kevin Duke.

2014: Junior Camogie Championship
Final: Drumree 1-9 Donaghmore-Ashbourne 1-9
Replay: Donaghmore-Ashbourne 1-9 Drumree 0-6

Gemma Flanagan, Cliona Murphy, Juliette Wall, Annemarie Rattigan, Cliodhna O Riordan, Liadan O'Riordan, Brona Gavin, Ciara Jones, Chloe Mahon, Patricia Monks, Emma Doyle, Adrienne Pritchard, Louise Griffin, Capt., Alannah Chalkley, Marissa Horan, Sarah Keane, Jessica Wall, Áine Brennan, Lisa Donnelly, Niamh Gallogly, Emer O Reilly. Team management: Conor Gavin, Maureen Doyle, Ed O Riordan and Shane Mahon.

Appendix 10
Royal Gaels: Results of Championship and League Finals

1997

Under 14 FC
Final: St. Ultans 5-12 Royal Gaels 0-12 in Bective
Sarah Morgan; Deirdre Mooney, Sharon Tugwell, Gráinne Kelly, Maria Kealy, Caroline King, Sharon Mahon, Aileen Creavin, Karen Bowe, Fiona Murray, Fiona McCabe, Shona Donoghue, Donna Brennan. Subs: Orla Power for Brennan, Catherine McDonald for McCabe.

2001

Junior B FC
Final: Boardsmill 3-10 Royal Gaels 4-5
Ciara McHale; Olivia O Neill, Leona Gilchreest, Deirdre Kane; Jane Everard, Gráinne Kelly, Deirdre Mooney; Caroline King, Charlene McAuley; Shona Donoghue, Sorcha O Dwyer, Aileen Creavin; Blaithín Brennan, Karen Bowe, Maria Kealy.

Football League Division 3
Final: Navan O Mahonys 1-11 Royal Gaels 2-4 in Bective
Ciara McHale; Olivia O Neill, Leona Gilchreest, Deirdre Kane; Jane Everard, Aileen Creavin, Deirdre Mooney; Caroline King, Charlene McAuley; Blaithín Brennan, Gráinne Kelly, Karen Bowe; Shona Donoghue, Sorcha O Dwyer, Maria Kealy. Subs: Fiona Murray, Mary McHale, Katie Brennan, Fiona McCabe, Suzanne Colgan, Tracey Redmond, Gemma Flanagan, Orla Power, Siobhán Gogan, Aoife O Donoghue, Brenda McTigue, Anne Swaine and Sharon Mahon.

2002

Junior B FC
Final: Royal Gaels 3-12 Moynalty 0-4
Ciara McHale; Suzanne Colgan, Maria Kealy, Fiona Murray; Karen Bowe, Aileen Creavin, Deirdre Mooney; Charlene McAuley, Shona Donoghue; Sarah Weld, Fiona McCabe, Sorcha O Dwyer; Blaithín Brennan, Mary McHale, Caroline King. Subs: Gemma Flanagan, Katie Brennan, Tracey Redmond, Brenda McTigue.

Football League Division 2
Final: Royal Gaels 1-7 Boardsmill 0-4
Ciara McHale; Suzanne Colgan, Maria Kealy, Fiona Murray; Deirdre Mooney, Aileen Creavin, Karen Bowe; Shona Donoghue, Charlene McAuley; Gemma Flanagan, Fiona McCabe, Sorcha O Dwyer; Blaithín Brennan, Mary McHale, Caroline King. Subs: Sarah Weld, Katie Brennan, Tracey Redmond, Brenda McTigue.

2003

Under 14B FC
Final: Royal Gaels defeated Boardsmill

Under 16 B FC
Final: Royal Gaels defeated Boardsmill
Semi-Final team- Orlagh McLaughlin; Aisling Reilly, Ciara Byrne, Niamh Beagan; Lisa Redmond, Eanya O Brien, Laura McMorrow; Suzanne Colgan, Brenda McTigue; Sinéad Beagan, Lorna Duffy, Fiona O Sullivan; Niamh O Sullivan, Maureen Bowe, Kristina Troy. Subs: Zoe Baggott for McMorrow, Sinéad Murphy for Reilly, Leanne McMorrow for Redmond, Tara Ryan for S Beagan, Sinéad Kennedy, Lucy Shirren, Lorna O Connor, Sarah McBride, Carol Gregan, Leah Russell.

2004

Under 12 FC
Final: Royal Gaels defeated Moynalvey
Panel: Charlotte Coquet, Avril Tormey, Tara Matthews, Louise O Regan, Sarah Corrigan, Amy Ennis, Alex Swan, Jennifer Kelly, Kristina Troy, Sinéad Kelly, Aoife Moore, Capt., Megan Holohan, Mary Fitzmaurice, Niamh Donachie, Rebecca Considine, Laura O Toole, Claire Duffy, Shiobhra Delaney, Leanne McMorrow, Laura Ryan, Nicola Bowen, Rachel Lord, Shauna Moore, Finola Kane. Team Management: Stephen McMorrow, Pat O Regan, Michael Beagan.

Football League Division 2
Final: Royal Gaels 1-11 Donaghmore/Ashbourne 1-10

Junior A FC
Final: Na Fianna defeated Royal Gaels

2006

Under 13 Féile
Final: Oldcastle defeated Royal Gaels.
Team Management: Stephen McMorrow, Pat O Regan.

Under 14 Division 1 FC
Final: Oldcastle defeated Royal Gaels

Under 16 Division 1 FC
Final: Royal Gaels 4-7 Ratoath 1-7
Orlagh McLaughlin; Lucy Shirren, Laura McMorrow, Aoife Moore; Alex Swan, Rebecca Considine, Jenny Kelly; Tara Ryan, Leah Russell; Zoe Baggott, Áine Nestor (0-1), Shauna Moore (1-0); Niamh O Sullivan (0-4), Kristina Troy (3-1), Laura O Toole. Subs Gráinne Gallogly (0-1) for Baggott, Shiobhra Delaney for Swan, S McBride. Team Management: Michael Beagan, John O Brien.

Minor FC
Final: Dunboyne 4-11 Royal Gaels 2-3
Team Management: Michael Beagan, John O Brien.

2007

Intermediate FC
Final: Royal Gaels 1-15 Na Fianna 1-5
Orlagh McLaughlin; Cliona Ní Dhúshláine, Maria Kealy, Sorcha O Dwyer; Eimear O Sullivan, Aileen Creavin, Rebecca Considine; Blaithín Brennan (0-2), Karen Bowe (1-2); Róisín Ní Dhúshláine (0-1), Gemma Flanagan (0-1), Sinéad McGroder; Niamh O Sullivan (0-6), Charlene McAuley (0-1), Tara Ryan (0-1). Subs: Shona Donoghue for McGroder, Robyn Kinsella for Ní Dhushláine, Gráinne Gallogly for Ryan, Fiona Murray for Considine, Ciara McHale, Sinéad Ennis, Mary McHale, Ciara O Dwyer, Louise O Regan, Maureen Bowe, Bronagh Tinnelly, Aisling O Donoghue, Laura Ryan, Áine Nestor, Heidi Carty, Lisa Redmond. Team Management: Seán Walsh, Peter Mooney, Dan O Sullivan.

League Division 2
Final: Royal Gaels 3-8 Summerhill 0-9
Orlagh McLaughlin; Cliona Ní Dhushláine, Maria Kealy, Shona Donoghue; Róisín Ni Dhúshláine, Blaithín Brennan, Rebecca Considine; Gemma Flanagan, Niamh O Sullivan (0-4); Tara Ryan (2-2), Karen Bowe (0-1), Sinéad McGroder; Gráinne Gallogly, Robyn Kinsella (0-1), Maureen Bowe (1-0). Subs: Sinéad Ennis, Fiona O Sullivan, Bronagh Tinnelly, Ciara McHale. Team Management: Seán Walsh, Peter Mooney, Dan O Sullivan.

Under 14 FC
Final: Oldcastle 11-5 Royal Gaels 0-4.
Team Management: Colum Bracken, Stephen McMorrow, Pat O Regan.

2008

Under 16 FC
Final: Oldcastle defeated Royal Gaels
Team Management: Pat O Regan, Colum Bracken.

Under 19 FC
Final: Donaghmore-Ashbourne 1-14 Royal Gaels 2-5
Orlagh McLaughlin; Laura Murray, Laura McMorrow, Lousie O Regan; Laura Ryan, Orla Bracken, Rebecca Considine; Jenny Kelly, Niamh O Sullivan (2-5); Shiobhra Delaney, Gráinne Gallogly, Cliona Murphy; Heidi Carty, Sinéad Ennis, Leanne McMorrow. Subs: Karla O Callaghan for Ennis, Rebecca Keane for Leanne McMorrow, Catríona Kennedy for Gallogly, Tara Matthews for O Callaghan, Maeve Scanlon for Carty, Emma Connolly, Méabh Gallogly, Saoirse Conlon, Amy Ennis, Fiona Traynor. Team Management: Sean Walsh, Maria Kealy.

2009

Under 13 FC Division 2
Final: Clanna Gael defeated Royal Gaels.
Team Management: Pat O Regan.

Under 19 FC
Final: Royal Gaels 3-10 Clanna Gael 0-6
Orlagh McLaughlin; Leanne McMorrow, Aimee McQuillan, Gráinne Gallogly; Shiobhra Delaney, Laura McMorrow, Laura Ryan; Niamh O Sullivan, Rebecca Considine (0-2); Caitríona Kennedy, Jenny Kelly (0-1), Maeve Scanlon (0-2); Amy Ennis (1-0), Tara Ryan (0-5), Laura McMahon (2-0). Subs: Orla Bracken for Delaney, Louise O Regan for Bracken, Saoirse Conlon for Kennedy, Laura Murray, Fiona Traynor, Emma Connolly, Méabh Gallogly. Team Management: Colum Bracken, Maria Kealy.

2010

Under 11 FC Division 2
Final: Royal Gaels 4-7 Clanna Gael 0-1
Saoirse Carey; Molly Regan, Rachel Ennis, Orlagh Keane; Kevagh Slater, Caoimhe Rooney, Rachel Huijsdens; Eimear Traynor, Laura Quinn; Niamh Curtin, Kelly O Dwyer, Ava Fox; Georgie Benson, Orlaith Moyles, Hope O Dwyer. Subs: Caitlin O Neill, Sophie O Connor, Ciara Galvin, Shaughna Gibney, Lara Reynolds, Megan O Reilly, Ava Foley, Lauren Slater, Katelyn Doherty.

Under 12B
Final: Kilbride defeated Royal Gaels

Under 13 FC Division 2
Final: Royal Gaels 0-9 Skryne 0-2
Panel: Amy Mulvaney, Kate Hanley, Sarah Darby, Sadhbh O Muiri, Gemma Donoghue, Saoirse Patchel, Katie Usher, Niamh Gallogly, Cara Usher, Emma Murray, Tara Scanlon, Alannah Chalkley, Louise Nevin, Niamh Hetherington, Ailis Bruce, Juliette Wall, Sarah Kelly, Tara Hanley, Siobhán Duffy, Jessica May. Team Management: Ian Bruce, Tara Ryan.

Under 14 FC Division 2
Final: Royal Gaels 4-5 Clanna Gael 3-6
Amy Mulvany; Cliodhna O Riordan, Sarah Darby, Aisling Traynor; Niamh Gallogly (1-0), Alannah Chalkley, Gemma Donoghue (0-1); Róisín Bruce, Capt., Marissa Horan; Hannah O Brien (1-0), Niamh Kennedy, Ciara Murray; Aoife O Shea, Claire O Brien, Niamh Hetherington (2-3). Subs: Cara Usher (0-1), Hannah Duggan, Siobhán Duffy. Team Management: Ian Bruce, Mick O Brien.

2011

League Division 2

Final: Oldcastle 1-16 Royal Gaels 1-10

Orlagh McLaughlin, Cliona Ni Dhushlaine, Aileen Creavin, Laura Murray, Laura Ryan, Maria Kealy, Rebecca Considine, Blaithin Brennan, Gemma Flanagan, Fiona O Sullivan, Niamh O Sullivan, Maeve Scanlon, Tara Ryan, Róisín Bruce. One name unaccounted for. Subs: Aoife O'Shea, Alannah Chalkey, Laura McMorrow.

Won U10 Shield v Gaeil Colmcilles (Kells)

2012

Under 16 FC

Final: Skryne 4-11 Royal Gaels 1-7.
Team Management: Ian Bruce, Mick O Brien.

2013

Under 12 Division 1

Final: Dunboyne 3-2 Royal Gaels 1-5

Panel: Katelyn Doherty, Ciara Gorman, Mary McDonagh, Tara Hetherington, Petra Reilly, Ellie McCarthy, Megan McCarthy, Katie O Brien, Sarah Oliver, Michelle Sherry, Sarah McConnell, Rachel Byrne, Jane Larkin, Ava O Brien, Caitlin Power-King. Team Management: Hugh McCarthy & Kieran Doherty.

Under 12 Division 5

Final: Royal Gaels 4-9 St. Colmcilles 2-3

Panel: Shauna Summerville, Rebecca May, Kayleigh Fox, Katie Murphy, Sarah Benson, Méadhbh Reilly, Kay Gannon, Aoibhinn Bracken, Méadhbh Byrne, Maria Borgnolo, Katie Reilly, Gloria Flanagan , Caitlin O Dwyer, Jenny Reid, Clara McCanna, Eve Flanagan. Managers Colum Bracken, Alan Reilly.

Under 14 Division 2

Final: Royal Gaels 6-5 Na Fianna 5-4 in Martry

Lara Reynolds, Rachel Ennis, Rachel Huijsdens, Eimear Traynor, Orlaith Moyles, Caoimhe Rooney, Kelly O Dwyer, Ava Foley, Ava Fox, Shaughna Gibney, Olivia Flanagan, Orlagh Keane, Niamh Curtin, Michelle Jibowu, Laura Quinn, Lucy Kelly, Kyra Synnott, Ellen Byrne, Megan Reilly, Ciara Galvin, Caitlin O'Neill. Team Management: Teresa Ennis, Séamus Traynor.

Under 16 FL Division 2

Final: Royal Gaels 6-16 Gaeil Colmcille 5-0

Lara Reynolds, Sarah Kelly, Sarah Darby, Kate Hanley, Saoirse Patchell, Gemma Donoghue, Sadhbh O Muiri, Niamh Gallogly (1-10), Cara Usher, Rachel Huijsdens (1-2), Alannah Chalkley (1-0), Tara Scanlon, Louise Nevin (1-0), Ailis Bruce (1-3), Aideen McCabe (1-0). Subs: Niamh Curtin (0-1) for Nevin, Katie Usher for Kelly, Eimear Traynor for McCabe, Jessica May for Bruce, Laura Costello.

2014

League Division 3

Final: St. Michaels 4-10 Royal Gaels 0-9

Orlagh McLaughlin; Aisling Traynor, Gráinne Gallogly, Kate Hanley; Cara Usher, Rebecca Considine, Saoirse Patchell; Maeve Scanlon, Laura Murray; Tara Scanlon, Jenny Kelly, Alannah Chalkley; Ailis Bruce, Niamh Gallogly, Emma Kennedy.

Under 12 Division 1 Shield

Final: Royal Gaels 3-7 Simonstown 4-2 at Dunganny
Team management: Colum Bracken, Alan Reilly.

Under 13 Division 1 Cup

Final: Royal Gaels 4-5 Dunboyne 2-3

Panel: Ciara Gorman, Capt., Ellie McCarthy, Jane Larkin, Michelle Sherry, Sonia Leonard, Molly McNamara, Ava O Brien, Petra Reilly, Mary McDonagh, Katie O Brien,

Megan McCarthy, Katelyn Doherty, Sarah Oliver, Tara Hetherington, Katie Reilly, Méadhbh Byrne, Aoibhinn Bracken. Team management: Hugh McCarthy, Kieran and Caitriona Doherty.

Under 14 Reserve Cup
Final: Royal Gaels 4-6 St. Colmcilles 1-5 at Dunganny
Panel: Megan O Reilly, Capt., Ellie McCarthy, Megan McCarthy, Katie O Brien, Sarah McConnell, Michelle Sherry, Sarah Oliver, Caitlin Power-King, Liadan O Neill, Sonia Leonard, Petra Reilly, Áine Lawless, Mary McDonagh, Maria Borgnolo, Katie Reilly, Aoibhinn Bracken, Méadhbh Byrne, Sarah Benson, Méibh Reilly.

Under 16 Division 1 Shield
Final: Royal Gaels 2-11 Donaghmore-Ashbourne 2-4
Team management: Seamus Traynor, Teresa Ennis, Gemma Flanagan and Gerry Reynolds.

2015

Under 14 Féile na nGael Qualifier, Blitz
Semi-Final: Royal Gaels 3-5 Seneschalstown 2-1
Final: Royal Gaels 3-6 Dunboyne 1-0 at Dunganny
Panel: Ellie McCarthy, Jane Larkin, Michelle Sherry, Ava O Brien, Ciara Gorman, Sonia Leonard, Molly McNamara, Petra Reilly (1-0), Mary McDonagh, Katie O Brien, Tara Hetherington (1-0), Megan McCarthy, Sarah Oliver, Katelyn Doherty (0-5), Katie Reilly, Shauna Summerville, Aoibhinn Bracken (0-1), Méadhbh Reilly, Méadhbh Byrne, Áine Lawless, Liadan O Neill (1-0), Kayleigh Fox, Rebecca May, Sarah Benson, Maria Borgnolo. Team management: Colum Bracken, Hugh McCarthy, Niamh O Sullivan, Alan Reilly.

Under 14 Féile na nGael Finals in Wexford
Round 1: Royal Gaels 3-3 St. Patricks, Wicklow 0-4
Round 2: Royal Gaels 2-3 Seir Kieran, Offaly 2-3
Round 3: Royal Gaels 5-11 Kilmore, Wexford 2-2
Qtr-Final: Royal Gaels 2-4 St. Marys, Tyrone 1-2
Semi-Final: Royal Gaels 2-8 Taghmon, Wexford 2-0
Final: St. Patricks, Wicklow 3-5 Royal Gaels 2-7 aet.

Appendix 11
Titles won by Parish Clubs

Dunshaughlin

Football:	Hurling:
Leinster Senior Club Football Championship: 2002	Senior Hurling Championship: 1909, 1910, 1925
Senior Football Championship: 2000, 2001, 2002	Intermediate Hurling Championship: 1983, 1987
Feis Cup: 2002, 2011	Junior Hurling Championship: 1908, 1923, 1982
All County League Division 1: 2002	Junior Hurling B Championship: 1957
Intermediate Football Championship: 1977, 1997	
Junior Football Championship: 1950, 1958, 1967	
Junior Football B Championship: 1994, 2012	
Junior Football Div. 3 Championship: 1991	
Under 21 A Football Championship: 2000, 2004, 2007	
Reserve Football Leagues: 1989, 1992, 1999, 2003, 2008	

Under Age Football since 2009
Under 10, Community Games: 2009, 2010, 2012
Under 12, Leagues, various Divisions: 2010, 2011, 2012, 2013, 2014
Under 12, Reserve League: 2012
Under 14, Leagues, various Divisions: 2009, 2010, 2012, 2013, 2014
Under 14, Reserve League or Shield: 2009, 2010, 2012
Under 15, Division 2, Autumn League: 2013
Under 17, Division 3 League: 2011
Minor Football Championship: 2009
Minor Football Championship, Division 2: 2011
Minor Spring League: 2013

St. Martins

Football	Hurling
Under 10 Community Games: 2008	Under 11, B HC: 1987, 1995
Under 12, Championship, Division 1: 2002, 2004	Under 11 Shield: 2000
Under 12 Leagues, various Divisions: 1992, 1995	Under 13, B Championship: 1992, 1998
Under 13 Community Games: 1983	Under 14, Rural Championship: 1994
Under 13, Féile Qualifiers, Division 1: 2000, 2003, 2004, 2005	Under 14, B Championship: 1985 as Dunshaughlin, 1992, 1994, 2000
Under 13, League, Division 2, 2002	Under 14, Féile: Div. C, 1984 as Dunshaughlin; Div. 2, 1992, Div. 1, 1994; B Div., 2000, Div. 1, 2001
Under 14 Rural Championship: 1957, 1958, 1959	Minor, B HC: 1997, 2001, 2003
Under 14, Championship: 2001, 2005, 2006	
Under 14, Leagues, various Divisions: 1979 as Culmullen, 1987, 1989, 1995, 2001, 2006	
Under 16, Championship: 2003, 2008	
Under 16, League Division 2: 2002	
Under 17, League Division 2, 2005	
Minor Championship: 1987 as St. Martins-Ratoath	
Minor Championship, Division 2: 2002	

Drumree

Football	Hurling
Intermediate Championship: 1961, 1969	Intermediate Championship: 2003, 2010
Junior Championship: 1959, 1998	Junior Championship: 1998
Leinster Junior Club Tournament: 1998	Junior, Division 2 Championship: 1993, 1996
Junior Division 3 Championship: 1988	Under 21 Championship: 1999, Special; 2012, B Grade; 2013, A Grade.
All County League: 1993, Division 5; 1995, Division 4	
East Meath Football League: 1985	

Under Age Hurling 2009-14	Camogie
Under 12 B: 2011, 2013	Junior Championship: 2011
Under 13, Shield: 2012	Under 12 Shield: 2008, as St. Martins
Under 14, Division 2: 2009	Under 12, Division 2B: 2010
Minor B Championship: 2012	Under 14: 2009
Minor Division 1 Shield: 2013	Under 16 B: 2013

Royal Gaels

Adult Record:
Intermediate Championship: 2007
Junior B Championship: 2002
Football League: Division 2, 2002; 2004, 2007
Under 19 Championship: 2009

Underage Record:
Under 10 Shield: 2011
Under 11, Division 2: 2010
Under 12 Championship: 2004
Under 12, Division 5: 2013
Under 12 Shield: 2014
Under 13: Div. 2, 2010; Div. 1, 2014
Under 13, Féile Qualifiers, Division 1: 2015
Under 14 B or Division 2, Championship: 2003, 2010, 2013
Under 14, Reserve: 2014
Under 16 Championship, Division 1: 2006
Under 16 Championship: B Div. 2003; Div. 2, 2013, Shield, 2014

Dunshaughlin, Community Games Leinster Finalists, 2012

Front: Jared Rushe, Jack O Riordan, Aidan Fraher, Seán Walsh, Charlie O Connor, Evan Lawlor, Eoin Butler, Aaron Murphy, James Traynor, Cilian McCool.
Back: Kieran O Riordan, Team Manager, Jospeh Dunne, Cian Edwards, Colm Keane, Fursey Blake, Conor Gray, John McDonagh, Seán McConnell, Ruairi Kinsella, Tommy Toal. Missing from photo Cian McLaughlin.
Back on right: Ultan Blake, Kieran Rushe, selectors.

Appendix 11A
Dunshaughlin GAA Player Record in Meath Intermediate Football Championship, 1983-1997

Note: Records pre the 1983 IFC campaign are incomplete so those making their debut before that are listed as Pre IFC 1983 unless full details are known

	Started	Played as Sub	Total Scored	First Team Ch'ship Debut, IFC unless stated
Blake, Garbhán	25	1	0-0	Dunsany 1990
Bracken, Colum	37	--	4-24	St. Marys 1992
Byrne, Ciarán	41	--	0-2	St. Marys 1991
Byrne, Thomas	5	2	0-2	Duleek 1984
Carberry, Joe	1	--	0-0	Pre IFC 1983
Claire, Alan	4	--	0-0	Dunsany 1992
Claire, Stephen	14	2	4-9	Wolfe Tones 1988
Cummins, Alan	5	--	0-0	St. Michaels 1986
Curran, Noel	5	--	1-4	Pre IFC 1983
Darby, Francis	49	--	4-31	Dunsany 1987
Doherty, Kevin	10	--	0-3	Oldcastle 1983
Dowd, Ger	35	5	5-25	Pre IFC 1983
Dowd, Graham	11	--	1-38	St. Patricks 1996
Doyle, Barry	9	1	3-14	St. Patricks 1996
Duffy, Alan	18	2	1-42	Dunderry 1989
Duffy, Michael	10	--	0-0	St. Michaels 1986
Ennis, Mervyn	2	--	0-0	Castletown 1995
Fahy, Alan	9	--	1-2	Meath Hill 1989
Fahy, Pearse	11	3	1-4	Dunsany 1990
Farrell, Simon	34	3	3-96	St. Marys 1988
Finn, Tom	25	2	0-2	Moynalvey 1983
Flanagan, Pat	--	1	0-0	St. Marys 1988
Foley, Allen	1	--	0-0	St. Marys 1992
Foley, Niall	6	4	0-0	O Mahonys 1990
Gallagher, Pádraig	18	1	1-2	Meath Hill 1985
Geraghty, Donnchadh	5	--	0-0	Meath Hill 1989
Hall, Ken	1	--	0-0	Rathkenny 1985
Jennings, John	5	--	0-0	Pre IFC 1983
Jennings, Pat	20	--	0-0	Pre IFC 1983
Kane, David	25	1	0-0	Dunderry 1989
Kane, Trevor	27	--	1-18	Dunsany 1987
Kealy, Aiden	24	--	0-2	St. Marys 1992
Kealy, Brendan	25	2	1-50	Dunsany 1990
Kealy, Denis	5	1	1-2	Rathkenny 1996
Kealy, Dermot	33	1	2-16	Wolfe Tones 1988

Kealy, Kevin	27	11	3-14	St. Michaels 1986
Kealy, Pat	17	2	1-7	Meath Hill 1989
Kealy, Richie	24	--	3-27	Castletown 1993
Keane, Gerry	14	--	0-2	Pre IFC 1983
Keane, Michael	10	1	0-0	Moynalty 1995
Keane, Robbie	3	2	0-1	Drumconrath 1997
Kelly, John	8	--	0-2	St. Marys 1984
Kenny, Derek	1	1	1-0	Duleek 1985
Kenny, Paddy	16	--	0-0	Pre IFC 1983
Leen, Diarmuid	4	--	0-4	Donaghmore 1993
Magee, Seamus	7	1	0-0	Athboy 1986
Maher, Derek	43	2	0-0	Dunsany 1987
McEntaggart, Matt	29	1	0-0	Oldcastle 1983
McGrath, M	2	--	0-0	Meath Hill 1985
McLoughlin, Don	9	--	0-2	Pre IFC 1983
McTigue, Kenny	11	--	0-1	St. Patricks 1995
Melia, Derek	30	--	0-0	Wolfe Tones 1988
Mooney, Brendan	15	--	0-0	Moynalty 1995
Moran, Dominic	6	2	0-2	Pre IFC 1983
Moroney, David	1	--	0-2	Syddan 1997
Naughton, Colm	26	3	0-7	Dunderry 1989
O Brien, Michael	28	1	0-0	Trim SFC 1981
O Brien, Pat	40	2	1-16	Pre IFC 1983
O Donoghue, Jerry	19	--	3-13	Oldcastle 1983
O Dwyer, Pádraic	7	--	2-3	Drumconrath 1997
O Dwyer, Pearse	23	1	0-0	Rathkenny 1985
O Hare, Pat	4	--	0-0	Pre IFC 1983
O Keefe, Mick	7	--	0-0	St. Patricks SFC 1979
O Leary, Gerry	10	1	0-2	Colmcille Gaels SFC 1982
O Neill, David	1	1	0-0	Syddan 1997
O Rourke, Brian	5	--	0-0	Drumconrath 1997
O Rourke, Jimmy	8	--	0-1	Pre IFC 1983
O Rourke, Paul	7	2	0-0	Syddan 1990
O Rourke, Tiernan	27	1	2-21	Moynalty 1991
Rawdon, Mick	9	--	0-1	Martinstown-Athboy 1985
Sullivan, Dan	12	--	0-0	Pre IFC 1983
Summerville, Martin	12	1	0-0	Moynalvey 1983
Tonge, David	4	1	1-4	Donghmore-Ashbourne 1997
Walsh, Aidan	55	--	12-175	Colmcille Gaels SFC 1982
Walsh, Martin	20	--	1-21	Donaghmore 1983
Wead, Michael	7	1	0-0	Rathkenny 1985
Yore, Ronnie	8	2	0-0	Castletown 1995

Appendix 11B

Dunshaughlin GAA Player Record Meath, Leinster and All-Ireland Senior Club Football Championship, 1998-2014

	Meath Senior Championship		Leinster & All-Ireland Club Championship		Total Scored*	First Team Championship Debut
	Started	Played as Sub	Started	Played as Sub		
Ahern, Michael	42	3	--	--	0-1	Duleek, SFC, 2006
Blake, Garbhán	1	3	--	2	--	Dunsany, IFC, 1990
Bracken, Colum	3	--	--	--	--	St. Marys, IFC, 1992
Burke, Damian	12	8	1	3	0-5	Blackhall, SFC, 2002
Byrne, Ciarán	33	--	9	3	--	St. Marys, IFC, 1991
Byrne, Niall	-	1	-	-	-	Simonstown, SFC, 2014
Carey, Christopher	2	--	--	--	--	Dunboyne, SFC, 2003
Claire, Stephen	8	3	--	3	0-14	Wolfe Tones, IFC, 1988
Clusker, Ciarán	1	0	--	--	--	Oldcastle, SFC, 2013
Clusker, Stephen	3	--	--	--	--	Simonstown, SFC, 2012
Crimmins, David	70	3	12	--	15-52	Moynalvey, SFC, 1998
Crimmins, John	28	8	--	2	0-4	Seneschalstown, SFC, 2002
Darby, Francis	3	--	--	--	--	Dunsany, IFC, 1987
Delaney, Fearghal	9	4	--	--	0-1	Dunboyne, SFC, 2012
Devanney, Mark	2	2	--	--	1-0	Gaeil Colmcille, SFC, 2014
Devereux, Conor	25	5	--	--	3-53	Wolfe Tones, SFC, 2009
Devereux, David	9	9	--	--	1-7	Kilmainhamwood, SFC, 2005
Dowd, Graham	27	5	7	--	3-33	St Patricks, IFC, 1996
Dowd, Trevor	70	5	12	--	20-158	Trim, SFC, 1999
Doyle, Alastar	25	1	--	--	--	Seneschalstown, SFC, 2011
Duggan, Ben	5	--	--	--	0-4	Gaeil Colmcille, SFC, 2014
Dunne, David	--	2	--	--	1-0	Walterstown, SFC, 2014
Farrell, Simon	2	--	--	--	--	St. Marys, IFC, 1988
Farrelly, Ciarán	3	8	--	--	0-1	Summerhill, SFC, 2006
Finn, Cillian	11	7	--	--	0-5	Wolfe Tones, SFC, 2005
Foley, Oisín	--	1	--	--	--	Simonstown, SFC, 2014
Gallogly, Shane	1	1	--	--	1-1	Walterstown, SFC, 2014
Geraghty, Ronan	2	1	--	--	0-1	Seneschalstown, SFC, 2014
Gogan, Fearghal	64	2	11	1	1-3	Ballinlough, SFC, 1998
Gogan, Ronan	92	--	12	--	--	Blackhall Gaels, SFC, 2000
Hagarty, Eoin	14	7	--	--	3-4	Walterstown, SFC, 2010
Hoary, Ciarán	3	1	--	--	--	Dunboyne, SFC, 2012

APPENDICES

	Meath Senior Championship		Leinster & All-Ireland Club Championship		Total Scored*	First Team Championship Debut
Johnson, Anthony	27	6	--	--	0-2	Duleek, SFC, 2006
Johnson, Michael	5	6	--	--	0-5	Duleek, SFC, 2006
Johnson, Tommy	39	2	--	--	1-9	Ballinlough, SFC, 2007
Kane, David	2	--	--	--	--	Dunderry, IFC, 1989
Kealy, Aiden	36	1	7	1	0-5	St. Marys, IFC, 1992
Kealy, Brendan	14	8	9	2	2-7	Dunsany, IFC, 1990
Kealy, Denis	71	3	12	--	5-39	Rathkenny, IFC, 1996
Kealy, Dermot	30	3	12	--	0-21	Wolfe Tones, IFC, 1988
Kealy, Kevin	4	4	--	2	0-1	St. Michaels, IFC, 1986
Kealy, Richie	61	16	11	--	8-118	Castletown, IFC, 1993
Keane, Robbie	--	2	--	--	--	Drumconrath, IFC, 1997
Keane, Michael	--	1	--	--	--	Moynalty, IFC, 1995
Kelly, Niall	79	5	11	--	3-144	Moynalvey, SFC, 1998
Kelly, Shane	15	8	--	2	0-7	Dunboyne, SFC, 1999
King, Caoimhín	68	--	--	--	1-18	Kilmainhamwood, SFC, 2003
Maher, Derek	2	--	--	--	--	Dunsany, IFC, 1987
Maloney, Ray	74	8	5	--	11-40	Summerhill, SFC, 2002
McCormack, David	2	3	--	--	0-2	Ballinlough, SFC, 1998
McHale, Michael	43	18	11	1	2-21	Dunboyne, SFC, 1999
McHale, Paddy	15	6	2	1	0-12	Skryne, SFC, 2000
McNabb, Jude	12	4	--	--	0-1	Dunboyne, SFC, 2004
McTigue, Kenny	92	3	12	--	4-0	St. Patricks, IFC, 1995
Moroney, David	6	1	--	--	0-2	Syddan, IFC, 1997
Moyles, Kevin	2	3	--	1	--	Blackhall Gaels, SFC, 2002
Murphy, Niall	25	2	--	--	3-22	Walterstown, SFC, 2010
Naughton, Colm	5	1	--	--	0-1	Dunderry, IFC, 1989
O Brien, Joe	3	1	--	--	0-2	Walterstown, SFC, 2012
Ó Dúshláine, Tadhg	21	4	--	--	0-8	Rathkenny, SFC, 2010
O Dwyer, Cathal	66	2	--	--	1-155	Simonstown, SFC, 2004
O Dwyer, Ciarán	1	--	--	--	--	Dunboyne, SFC, 1999
O Dwyer, Pádraic	--	2	--	--	0-1	Drumconrath, IFC, 1997
Ormsby, Dan	5	2	--	--	--	Navan O Mahonys, SFC, 2014
Ormsby, Liam	1	5	--	--	--	Simonstown, SFC, 2013
O Rourke, Brian	11	--	--	--	--	Drumconrath, IFC, 1997
O Rourke, Tiernan	12	2	--	1	2-7	Moynalty, IFC, 1991
O Sullivan, Tom	--	3	--	1	0-2	Syddan, SFC, 2000
Quinn, Andy	--	1	--	--	--	Cortown, SFC, 2003
Reilly, Martin	61	13	7	--	1-138	Ballinlough, SFC, 2001

BLACK & AMBER

	Meath Senior Championship		Leinster & All-Ireland Club Championship		Total Scored*	First Team Championship Debut
Ryan, Mick	7	2	--	--	--	Summerhill, SFC, 2003
Staunton, Conor	30	5	--	--	12-35	Wolfe Tones, SFC, 2005
Tonge, David	48	4	8	2	2-41	Donaghmore-Ash, IFC, 1997
Toolan, Fergus	26	--	--	--	0-30	Seneschalstown, SFC, 2011
Ward, Kevin	21	5	--	--	1-4	Simonstown, SFC, 2004
Ward, Stephen	10	7	--	--	1-14	St Patricks, SFC, 2003
Yore, Ronnie	59	3	9	2	0-2	Castletown, IFC, 1995

Record Scorers, 1983-2014

Each of the following players has scored over one hundred points in Intermediate and / or Senior Championship Football, 1983-2014

	Intermediate, 1978-1997	Senior, 1998 -2014	Points Value
Trevor Dowd	--	20-158	218
Aidan Walsh	12-175	--	211
Richie Kealy	3-27	8-118	178
Cathal O Dwyer	--	1-155	158
Niall Kelly	--	3-144	153
Martin Reilly	--	1-138	141
Simon Farrell	3-96	--	105

*Between the years 1998 and 2013 it was possible to trace all scores amassed by Dunshaughlin in the Senior Football Championship apart from the clash with Gaeil Colmcille in 1998 when Dunshaughlin scored eight points. The scorers of those points cannot be established with any degree of certainty and consequently are not included in the tallies presented here.

Record Breakers

The three men pictured below hold the record for the number of adult first team championship appearances for Dunshaughlin.

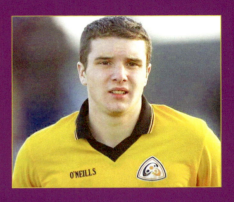

Kenny McTigue (118)

107 Senior and 11 Intermediate Championship appearances. Kenny played senior 1998-2014, v Simonstown and Skryne (10 each), Rathnew (Wicklow) and Trim (8 each), Blackhall Gaels (7), Dunboyne, Kilmainhamwood, Summerhill and Walterstown (6 each), Navan O Mahonys (5), Ballinlough and Wolfe Tones (4 each), Duleek, Gaeil Colmcille and St. Patricks (3 each), Cortown, Donaghmore-Ashbourne, Rathkenny and Seneschalstown (2 each), Dunderry, Moynalvey, Na Fianna, Oldcastle, St. Ultans, Syddan, Crossmolina (Mayo), Mattock Rangers (Louth), Moorefield (Kildare) and Rathvilly (Carlow) (1 each).

Kenny also made eleven Intermediate football Championship appearances in the Dunshaughlin colours, 1995-97 when the intermediate team was the club's first team. He played against Duleek (3 times) and once each against Athboy, Ballivor, Blackhall Gaels, Donaghmore-Ashbourne, Drumconrath, Moynalty, Rathkenny and St. Patricks.

Richie Kealy (112)

88 Senior and 24 Intermediate Championship appearances. Richie played senior 1998-2011 v Blackhall Gaels (9), Rathnew (Wicklow) and Skryne (8 each), Summerhill (7), Simonstown and Trim (6 each), Navan O Mahonys (5), Ballinlough and Dunboyne (4 each), Gaeil Colmcille, Kilmainhamwood, Rathkenny and Walterstown (3 each), Donaghmore-Ashbourne, Seneschalstown, St. Patricks (2 each), Cortown, Duleek, Duleek-Bellewstown, Dunderry, Moynalvey, Nobber, Oldcastle, St. Ultans, Syddan, Wolfe Tones, Crossmolina (Mayo), Mattock Rangers (Louth), and Rathvilly (Carlow) (1 each).

Richie also made twenty-four Intermediate football Championship appearances in the Dunshaughlin colours when the intermediate team was the club's first team. He played against Moynalty and St. Patricks (4 each), Castletown (3), Duleek, St. Ultans and Syddan (2 each) and Athboy, Ballivor, Carnaross, Donaghmore-Ashbourne, Drumconrath, Kilmainhamwood and St. Marys (1 each).

Ronan Gogan (104)

104 Senior Championship appearances, 2000-2014. Ronan played v Blackhall Gaels (10 times), Rathnew (Wicklow), Skryne and Simonstown (8 each), Trim (7), Kilmainhamwood, Summerhill and Walterstown (6 each), Navan O Mahonys and Seneschalstown (5 each), Dunboyne, (4), Donaghmore-Ashbourne, Rathkenny, Gaeil Colmcille and Wolfe Tones (3 each), Ballinlough, Cortown, Duleek, Nobber and St. Patricks (2 each), Duleek-Bellewstown, Na Fianna, Oldcastle, St. Ultans, Syddan, Crossmolina (Mayo), Mattock Rangers (Louth), Moorefield (Kildare) and Rathvilly (Carlow) (1 each).

Appendix 12
Winners of Leinster, All-Ireland Medals

Includes only those who were playing for Dunshaughlin or Drumree when they won a Leinster or All-Ireland medal or who played underage football or hurling with St. Martins 1956-2008.

Inter County Football Championship

All-Ireland

Senior:	Evan Kelly (2) 1996, 1999; Billie Rattigan 1954; Larry O Brien 1954; Noel Curran 1967; Jimmy Walsh 1967; Richie Kealy 1999.
Minor:	Brendan Kealy 1990; Aiden Kealy 1992; Brian O Rourke 1992.
Under 21:	Brendan Kealy 1993.
Junior:	Larry O Brien 1952; Jimmy Walsh, Capt, 1962; Trevor Kane 1988.
NFL:	Aiden Kealy, Div 1, 1993-94; Caoimhín King, Div 2, 2007.
Railway Cup:	Evan Kelly (2) 2001, 2002; Caoimhín King 2006.

Leinster

Senior:	Billie Rattigan 1954; Larry O Brien 1954; Jimmy Walsh (3) 1964, 1966, 1967; Evan Kelly (3) 1996, 1999, 2001; Richie Kealy (2) 1999, 2001; Noel Curran 1967; Niall Kelly 2001; David Crimmins 2001; John Cullinane 2001; Dermot Kealy 2001, Caoimhín King 2010.
Minor:	Pat Jennings 1972; Trevor Kane 1985; Brendan Kealy 1990; Aiden Kealy 1992; Brian O Rourke 1992; Richie Kealy 1993; Cillian Finn 2006; John Coleman 2006; Tommy Johnson, Capt. 2008. **Note:** John Jennings joined the Meath Minor panel in 1972 for the All-Ireland semi-final but wasn't on the panel for the Leinster final.
Under 21:	Brendan Kealy (2) 1991, 1993; John Cullinane (2) 1996, 1997; Jim Rattigan 1985; Derek Maher 1990; Dermot Kealy 1991; Richie Kealy 1996; Niall Kelly 2001; David Crimmins 2001.
Junior:	Richie Kealy (3) 1996, 1997, 2006; Trevor Kane (2) 1988, 1991; Aiden Kealy (2) 1995, 1996; Dermot Kealy (2) 1996, 1997; Jimmy Walsh, Captain, 1962; Val Dowd 1964; Derek Maher 1991; John Cullinane 1999; Trevor Dowd 2006.

Inter County Hurling Championship

All-Ireland

Railway Cup:	David Crimmins 2008.
Intermediate B:	David Troy 2001.
Junior:	Mick Clusker 1927; Christy Doran 1927; Tommy Troy 1970; John Davis 1998; David Troy, Capt. 2004; Christopher Doyle 2004; Ronan Curley 2004.
NHL, Div. 2:	Tommy Troy 1972.
Minor, Special:	Martin Walsh 1983; John Davis 1986; Vincent Moore 1986.
Under 21:	Gary Donoghue 1999.

Leinster

Junior:	Tommy Troy (2) 1961, 1970; David Troy (2) 2003, 2004; Chris. Doyle (2) 2003, 2004 Ronan Curley (2) 2003, 2004; Mick Clusker 1927; Christy Doran 1927; Jimmy Walsh 1970.
Minor, Special:	John Davis 1987; Vincent Moore 1987.

Ladies Football Inter County Championship Winners

All-Ireland

Under 16:	Maria Kealy, Capt. 2000; Caroline King 2000.

Leinster

Minor:	Maria Kealy (2), 2001, 2002; Caroline King (2) 2001, 2002.
Minor C:	Gemma Donoghue, Niamh Gallogly, Amy Mulvaney, 2015.
Under 16:	Maria Kealy (2), 1999, 2000; Karen Bowe 1999; Caroline King 2000; Niamh Gallogly, Capt, Under 16B, 2013.

Camogie Inter County Championship Winners

All-Ireland

Junior B, 2013:	Louise Griffin, Áine Brennan, Cliodhna O Riordan, Muireann O Hora, Sinéad Beagan.
Minor C, 2014:	Cliodhna O Riordan, Alannah Chalkley, Ciara Jones, Marissa Horan, Chloe Mahon, Juliette Wall.
Minor B, 2015:	Niamh Gallogly, Ciara Jones, Chloe Mahon, Juliette Wall.
Under 16 C: 2013:	Alannah Chalkley, Niamh Gallogly, Liadan O Riordan, Juliette Wall, Chloe Mahon, Ciara Jones.

Appendix 13
Senior Inter County Player Record, 1963-2014
Football Championship and National League

	Senior Championship				National League			
	Appearances				Appearances			
	Started	Substitute	Ch'ship Debut	Scores	Started	Substitute	League Debut	Scores
Michael Ahern	2	0	Carlow 2008	--	--	--	--	--
David Crimmins	8	2	Westmeath 2003	2-6	11	0	Mayo 2003	0-4
John Cullinane	4	9	Westmeath 2001	1-3	8	6	Sligo 2000	0-2
Noel Curran	10	4	Westmeath 1965	2-22	23	1	Westmeath 1964	6-30
Ger Dowd	--	--	--	--	1	0	Sligo 1975	--
Pat Jennings	--	--	--	--	1	0	Clare 1979	--
Trevor Kane	0	2	Louth 1989	--	3	0	Roscommon 1992	0-2
Denis Kealy	1	0	Waterford 2001	--	--	--	--	--
Dermot Kealy	1	0	Westmeath 2001	--	0	1	Cavan 2000	--
Richie Kealy	10	13	Wicklow 1999	1-10	24	4	Monaghan 1999	2-29
Evan Kelly	32	3	Offaly 1995	5-41	52	17	Derry 1994	7-50
Niall Kelly	4	4	Westmeath 2001	0-2	14	5	Laois 2002	2-11
Caoimhín King	30	0	Dublin 2005	0-5	29	2	Derry 2005	0-9
Jimmy Walsh	5	0	Wexford 1963	0-19	11	1	Sligo 1963	4-29

St. Seachnall's NS, Blake Cup Winners, 2007

Front: Shane Gallogly, Fergal Clery, Stephen McCarthy, Capt., Paul Mooney, Patrick Darby.
Back: David Doherty, Steven Kinsella, Laura Murray, Jack O Sullivan, Alan McEntee.

Appendix 14
HALL OF FAME AND OTHER AWARDS
DUNSHAUGHLIN GAA HALL OF FAME WINNERS 1995 - 2012

1995

Paddy Lynam

1996

Club Chairman Neil Halpin presents the 1996 award to Ben Lynam.

1997

Hughie McCarthy

1998

Club Chairman Neil Halpin presenting Joe Plunkett with his award.

1999

Club Chairman Paddy O Dwyer hands the 1999 award to Patsy McLoughlin.

2000

The Millenium Year award goes to Joe Smith.

APPENDICES

DUNSHAUGHLIN GAA HALL OF FAME WINNERS
1995 - 2012

2001
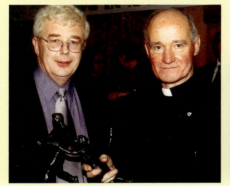
Fr. Eamonn O Brien accepts his 2001 Award from Cyril Creavin, club Secretary.

2002

Matt Daly with Patsy McLoughlin after being named to the Hall of Fame.

2003

Tommy Everard accepts his 2003 Award from Cyril Creavin, club Secretary.

2004

John O Sullivan the recipient of the 2004 Award with Cyril Creavin, club Secretary.

2005

Cyril Creavin, club Secretary presents Tommy O Dwyer with the 2005 award.

2006

Seamus Foley accepts his award from Patsy McLoughlin.

BLACK & AMBER

DUNSHAUGHLIN GAA HALL OF FAME WINNERS
1995 - 2012

2007

Club Chairman Jim Smith with Don Kane, the 2007 winner.

2008

Shaun McTigue accepts his 2008 Award from Mairéad Delaney, club Secretary.

2009

Club Chairman Jim Smith presents the 2009 award to Val Dowd.

2010

Club Chairman Jim Smith presents the 2010 award to Christy Purcell.

2011

Michael Walsh with his wife Kathleen receiving the 2011 award from club Secretary, Caroline Malone, on left.

2012

Noel Curran accepts his 2012 award from former winner and team mate, Val Dowd.

Awards at County or All-Ireland Level

Meath Hall of Fame:	Patsy McLoughlin, 2003
Meath Footballer of the Year:	Richie Kealy, 2000
All Star:	Evan Kelly, 2001
All Star Nominee:	Caoimhín King, 2007
Irish Compromise Rules Team v. Australia:	Evan Kelly, 2002
Meath Young Footballer of the Year:	Caoimhín King, 2003
Meath Hurler of the Year:	Neil O Riordan, 1976, with Kilmessan
Hogan Stand Meath Senior Club Player of the Year:	Cathal O Dwyer, 2011
Meath Ladies' Under 14 Player of the Year:	Niamh Gallogly, 2011
Meath Ladies' Minor Player of the Year:	Laura Murray, 2013
Leinster Club Footballer of the Year:	Niall Kelly, 2002
Senior County Final, Man of the Match:	Richie Kealy 2000
	Martin Reilly 2001
	David Crimmins 2002
All-Ireland Clubman of the Year:	Stephen Burke, 1988
Meath Referee of the Year:	Paddy O Dwyer, 1985, 1987
	Ollie O Neill 1995
	Jim Smith 2000
Club of the Year:	2001- shared with Blackhall Gaels, 2002
Club Grounds of the Year:	1988, 1990
Club Website of the Year, Leinster:	Dunshaughlin 2011

Referees of Meath Senior Finals and Leinster Minor Finals

Paddy O Dwyer: Meath Referee of the Year, 1985, 1987
Meath SFC Final: Navan O Mahonys v Skryne, 1985, 1987

Jim Smith: Meath Referee of the Year, 2000
Leinster MFC Final: Dublin v Westmeath, 2000. Stephen Burke, John O Sullivan, Ollie O Neill, Michael Walsh, Lally McCormack umpires.
Meath SFC Final: Wolfe Tones v O Mahonys, 2006

Ollie O Neill: Meath Referee of the Year, 1995
Meath SHC Final, Trim v Killyon, 1991
Leinster MH Final, Kilkenny v Offaly, 1995

Referees Ready

Jim Smith meets the Westmeath and Dublin captains prior to the Leinster Minor Football Final in 2000.

Paddy O Dwyer is the man in the middle for the 1984 Intermediate final between St. Colmcilles and Slane.

Frank Gallogly and his team of Con O Dwyer, Pat Herlihy, John O Sullivan and Dinny McCarthy are ready for action. Frank refereed the Feis Cup final of 2012 between Navan O Mahonys and Walterstown.

Appendix 15
Dunshaughlin Club Members as Officers of Meath GAA Boards

Meath County Board
Deputy Vice Chairman:	Patsy McLoughlin, 1979
Secretary:	Cyril Creavin, 2008-2012
Assistant Secretary:	Paddy O Dwyer, 1971-73
	Cyril Creavin 2003-07
	Mairéad Delaney 2013-15
Leinster Council Delegate:	Paddy O Dwyer, 1974-75, 2006-10
Development Officer:	Mairéad Delaney, 2009-2012

Meath Minor Board
Secretary:	Jim Gilligan, 1986
P.R.O.:	Jim Gilligan, 1991-1995

Meath Juvenile Board
Chairman:	Patsy McLoughlin, 1969-1972
Vice Chairman:	Tommy Downes 1958
	Val Dowd, 1976
Secretary:	Mairéad Delaney, 2001–2004
PRO:	Mairéad Delaney, 2000

Juvenile Hurling Board
PRO:	Paul Barry, 2001-2002
Assistant Secretary:	Conor Gavin, 2007-10

Ladies' County Board
Secretary:	Mary O Regan, 2010-15
Assistant Secretary:	Mary O Regan, 2009

Appendix 16
Gaelic Games in the Schools in Dunshaughlin Parish

St Seachnall's NS

Organized football competition at primary school level is a relatively recent phenomenon as Cumann na mBunscol, the Primary Schools' Board, wasn't set up until 1979. Prior to that, competition was confined to challenge games against neighbouring schools, usually in the summer in conjunction with festivals, carnivals and field days. Indeed organized juvenile football or hurling at club level was slow to take hold also. Nevertheless, there are occasional references to schools' football from time to time prior to the 1970s. As far back as 1912 the Drogheda Independent carried a report of the final game of a series of football matches between Dunshaughlin and Culmullen schoolboys. Each team was said to have 'a good many supporters, both young and old.' The passing, catching and combination of the Dunshaughlin youths proved a little too much for their less experienced opponents according to the report and Dunshaughlin recorded a 1-1 to 0-1 victory.

There was a concerted effort in the 1930s, supported by Leinster Council, to introduce underage competitions and in 1933 a hurling competition for National Schools in Meath began. The age limit was 15 years as many attended primary school well into their teens, there being little or no secondary education except for those who could pay for it. Dunshaughlin NS was paired with Athboy but nothing further could be traced. In 1939 an Under 14 competition for rural schools was proposed but attracted few entries from south Meath. The outbreak of the World War in 1939 finally played havoc with all fixtures due to petrol shortages.

Pupils of the school during the 1950s and 1960s state that little or no football was played in the school during Gerry Smith's Principalship. Charlie Gallagher replaced him in 1973 and promoted football among the boys. Games were played at the annual Pony Races and in 1975 Dunshaughlin won the cup presented by Brother O Sullivan of Warrenstown College, emerging victorious from an entry of eight schools. Games were often played against Rathbeggan NS at school sports' days while a challenge against a visiting team from the north of Ireland took place in 1974-75. At the time the school used a set of red jerseys, which were probably the original St Martins' set from the 1950s.

As explained in Chapter 8 when Jim Gilligan joined the staff in 1977 and Jimmy McGeogh was appointed to Rathbeggan NS the following year they promoted gaelic games within and between the schools. This friendly rivalry continued with the arrival of Mary Devine in Rathbeggan. The annual internal school leagues in Dunshaughlin NS began in 1980 and have continued since, with a Junior League for younger pupils added in 1985-86. The leagues were played after school during the third term in Dunshaughlin GAA grounds until the field behind the school was bought from the Murphy family. Senior captains usually came from sixth class and selected their teams from other pupils graded according to ability. The following article written by Shane Kelly for the School's Reunion Celebration in 2004, conveys very well the importance of the leagues.

School Days at Jim's Football Academy

Forget about playing for Meath, scoring a goal in an All-Ireland final or even winning a County Championship . . . the dream of any young lad interested in Gaelic football who attended Dunshaughlin National School was to win a Junior or Senior League.

Once in first or second class you could play in the Junior or Senior Leagues. Captains were chosen, teams picked - there could be up to ten teams with eight per side- it was straight down to the football pitch after school to see who would emerge victorious. The late, great Stephen Burke always had the pitches marked out and the posts ready to be put up.

Mothers and fathers would turn up to the league games to lend their support. During my time 'ever presents' included Celia Dowd who acted as Jim's independent scorekeeper, Mrs. Kealy- who by then was already a veteran of many campaigns- was always on hand with a bottle of water and a sympathetic shoulder to cry on when an unfortunate eight-year-old from second class happened to run into the path of a burly sixth classer. Catherine McHale patrolled many a sideline and Patty McCarthy was known for her words of encouragement to one and all.

Being part of the school team involved training in the pitch a couple of times a week. Away matches meant getting off school early at two o clock, piling into the back of parents' cars, there were no minibuses back then, as you headed for exotic far-flung places such as Oldcastle, Slane, Duleek or Athboy. Success in these matches could lead to a final in Páirc Tailteann and a victory would be rewarded with chips afterwards in McEntaggarts.

The finale of the school football year came in the month of June in the form of the popular seven-a-side tournament, The Blake Cup, named after Dunshaughlin GAA stalwart Paddy Blake. Teams from all over Meath travelled to the pitch and matches were run off all afternoon until the finals were played late in the evening. While the football was important, for many the highlight of the day was the feast of sandwiches, buns, crisps and drinks provided by the Dunshaughlin mothers for one and all at the end of the day.

The football education received at St. Seachnalls under Jim Gilligan laid the foundation for the recent successes achieved by Dunshaughlin GFC. The first fruits of Jim's toils came in the form of the 1997 Intermediate title and were followed in 2000 with the first ever winning of the Keegan Cup. On that historic day in 2000, fourteen of the fifteen players that started the final were alumni of St. Seachnalls. Further county championship successes followed in 2001 and 2002 with the pinnacle of these efforts being the Leinster Senior Club Championship victory in 2002.

Primary School for many will conjure up memories of alphabets, abacuses and art but mine will always be filled with great memories of football, football and football at Jim's Football Academy.

Shane Kelly, Pupil 1983-1991

St Seachnall's NS Record

	School Captain, Boys	School Captain, Girls	Senior League Winning Captain	Junior League Winning Captain
1979-80	Kevin Kealy		Michael Duffy	
1980-81	Trevor Kane		Trevor Kane	
1981-82	Simon Farrell		Pat Kealy	
1982-83	Dermot Kealy		Dermot Kealy	
1983-84	Thomas Walsh		Brendan Kealy	
1984-85	Ciarán O Dwyer		Tiernan O Rourke	
1985-86	David O Neill		Robert McCarthy	Aiden Kealy
1986-87	Aiden Kealy		Aiden Kealy	Kenneth McTigue
1987-88	Paul Baker		Richie Kealy	Clive Dowd
1988-89	Caoimhín Blake		Ian Caffrey	Gordon O Rourke
1989-90	Graham Dowd		Dessie Keane	Pádraic O Dwyer
1990-91	Shane Kelly		Shane Kelly	David Tonge
1991-92	David Crimmins		David Crimmins	Niall Kelly
1992-93	Niall Kelly		Niall Kelly	Trevor Dowd
1993-94	Trevor Dowd		Trevor Dowd	David McNerney
1994-95	Ray Maloney		Ray Maloney	Stephen Ward
1995-96	John Crimmins		John Crimmins	Caoimhín King
1996-97	Stephen Ward		Rory Bowe	Orla Power
1997-98	Caoimhín King		Caoimhín King	Cathal O Dwyer & David Devereux
1998-99	Paul Kennedy		Patrick Doohan	Shane Kelly
1999-00	Shane Kelly		Shane Kelly	Iain McLaughlin
2000-01	Iain McLaughlin		Iain McLaughlin	Edward Mac Sweeney
2001-02	Barry Jordan		Paul Barry	Niall Murphy
2002-03	Niall Murphy		Barry Jordan	Lee Duffy
2003-04	Eoin Hagarty		Conor Devereux	Keith Donoghue
2004-05	Frankie Lally		Frankie Lally	Fergal Cleary
2005-06	Keith Donoghue		Brendan Bowe	Paul Mooney
2006-07	Stephen McCarthy	Laura Murray	David Doherty	Shane Gallogly
2007-08	Shane Gallogly	Maeve Scanlon	Shane Gallogly	Ronan Geraghty
2008-09	Martin Nevin	Niamh Gallogly	Daniel Quinn	Conor Huijsdens
2009-10	Conor Mooney	Allahan Chalkley	Tom Boyhan	Paddy Maher
2010-11	Adam Kealy & Cian Gallogly	Tara Scanlon	David Carroll	Rachel Huijsdens
2011-12	Paddy Maher	Rachel Huijsdens	Paddy Maher	Matthew Moyles
2012-13	Matthew Moyles	Petra Reilly	David Fildes	Fionn Cummins
2013-14	Mathew Costello	Ciara Gorman	Fionn Cummins	John McDonagh

Former School Captains

Dunshaughlin NS, Cumann na mBunscol Winners, Boys' Division 2, 1981-82

Pictured in 1986 are
Front: Aiden Kealy, Captain 1986-87, David O Neill, Captain 1985-86.
Back: Dermot Kealy, Captain 1982-83, Simon Farrell, Captain 1981-82 and Trevor Kane, Captain 1980-81.

Front: Piaras O Connor, Ephrem Caffrey, Pat Kealy, Vinny Moore, Simon Farrell, Capt., Paul O Rourke, David Kane, Dermot Carey.
Back: Dermot Kealy, Karl Stoney, John Davis, Andrew Toole, Derek Melia, Philip McCarthy, Niall Foley.

Dunshaughlin NS, Cumann na mBunscol Winners, Boys' Division 2, 1991-92

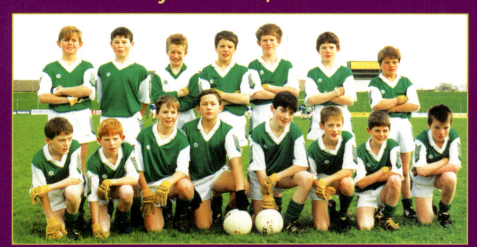

Front: Trevor Dowd, Paul Hendrick, David Tonge, David Crimmins, Capt., Denis Kealy, Alan Kenny, Kieran Lawlor, Stephen Moore.
Back: Stephen Morgan, Dessie McKeever, Michael McHale, Ronan Gogan, Paddy McHale, Niall Kelly, Darren Cottrell.

Dunshaughlin NS, Cumann na mBunscol, Division 3, Hurling Finalists, 1997

St. Seachnall's NS, Cumann na mBunscol Shield Winners 1999

Front: Cormac Delaney, Rory Bowe, Fergal Moore, Caoimhín King, Diarmuid Delaney. Back: Ciarán Staunton, Christopher McGuinnes, Ciarán Hoary, John Crimmins, Joseph McHale, Paul Faherty.

Front: Martin Cosgrove, Peter Gallagher, Shane Kelly, Richard Ryan, Kieran Murphy, Keith Byrne, Fearghal Delaney. 2nd Row: Cathal O Reilly, Timothy O Regan, Ian Hand, Simon Kennedy, Karl Kelly, Mark Caldwell, John Bedford. 3rd row: Ian Burnell, Duncan Geraghty, Andrew Brennan, Ciarán Farrelly, Tadhg Woods, Robert Robinson, Iain McLaughlin, Eddie McSweeney. Back: Conor Hegarty, Simon O Reilly, Joseph McGovern, Chris Farrell, Ciarán Dundon.

St. Seachnall's NS, Fingal Senior League Winners, 2009

Front: Laura Quinn, Siobhán Duffy, Tara Scanlon, Aoife O Shea Niamh Gallogly, Aisling Traynor, Kate Hanley, Emma Murray, Kevagh Slater.
Back: Gemma Donoghue, Alannah Chalkley, Amy Mulvaney, Siobhán O Riordan, Sarah Darby, Kaitlyn O Brien, Áine O Donoghue, Ciara Murray, Sophie McNamara, Cara Usher.

Successes in Meath Cumann na mBunscol and Fingal League Competitions

Dunshaughlin NS named St. Seachnalls NS from 1999

1981-82

Cumann na mBunscol, Michael Byrne Cup, Division 2.
Final: Dunshaughlin NS 4-7 Duleek 0-0
Derek Melia; David Kane, John Davis, Pearse O Connor; Karl Stoney, Dermot Kealy, Niall Foley; Simon Farrell, Capt., (0-2), Dermot Carey (1-0); Andrew Toole, Philip McCarthy, Vinny Moore (0-1); Paul O Rourke (1-1), Ephrem Caffrey (1-0), Pat Kealy (0-3). Subs: Brendan Kealy (1-0) for McCarthy, Michael Nixon for O Rourke, Adrian Faherty, Richard Corbett, Alan O Dwyer. Team Trainer: Jim Gilligan.

1982-83

Cumann na mBunscol, Michael Byrne Cup, Division 2.
Final: Duleek 0-8 Dunshaughlin NS 1-4
Stephen Lane; Conor Daly, Simon Conlon, Ciarán O Connor; Piaras O Connor, Karl Stoney, Garbhán Blake; Dermot Kealy, Capt., (1-3), Morty O Sullivan (0-1); Brendan Kealy, Thomas Walsh, Liam O Neill; David Forde, Noel McTigue, Fergus Summerville. Subs: Colm Naughton for Forde, Neal Drennan for Summerville, Fiachra Page, David Morgan, Gabriel Donnelly, Ciarán O Dwyer. Team Trainer: Jim Gilligan.

1986-87

Cumann na mBunscol, Michael Byrne Cup, Division 2.
Final: Dunshaughlin NS 0-3 Slane 0-2
Cathal O Connor; Hugh McCarthy, Gareth McQuaid, Alan Barber; Kenny McTigue, Paul Baker, Michael Keane; Aiden Kealy, Capt., (0-1), David Faughnan (0-1); Andrew Keane, Brian O Rourke (0-1), Richie Kealy; David Power, Alan Claire, Keith Wickham. Sub: Brian Murray for Keane, Terry Cullen for Power. Team Trainer: Jim Gilligan.

1987-88

Cumann na mBunscol, Michael Byrne Cup, Division 2.
Final: Dunshaughlin NS 0-6 Slane 0-2
Fionnán Blake; Simon Duffy, Kenneth McTigue, James Jones; Gerard Cassidy, Paul Baker, Capt., Caoimhín Blake; Brian Murray, Richie Kealy (0-1); Andrew Keane (0-1), Cathal O Connor, Clive Dowd (0-1); Terry Cullen (0-2), MJ O Rourke (0-1), Ian McTigue. Sub: Paul Morrin for I McTigue, Jerry O Sullivan, Gavin Daly, Cathal McQuaid, Ronan Delany, Graham Faughnan, Pádraig Herlihy. Team Trainer: Jim Gilligan.

1990-91

Cumann na mBunscol, Michael Byrne Cup, Division 2.
Final: Dunshaughlin NS 0-12 Slane 1-5
Niall O Connor; Pádraig McHale, David Crimmins, Brendan Killoran; Neil O Dwyer, Shane Kelly, Capt, Niall Kelly; Graham Dowd, Fearghal Gogan; David Tonge, Dominic Jones, Denis Kealy; Fintan Lawlor, Pádraic O Dwyer, Ronan Gogan. Subs: Paul Hendrick, Seamus Caffrey, Dessie McKeever, Trevor Dowd, David Ronan, Niall Barber, Ciarán O Dwyer, Stephen Morgan, Colm Kavanagh, John Delany, Stephen Moore, William Smith, Alan Kenny. Team Trainer: Jim Gilligan.

Meath INTO Seven a Side Finals

Final: Dunshaughlin NS 4-2 Castletown 2-1
Niall O Connor, David Crimmins, Niall Kelly, Dominic Jones, Fintan Lawlor, David Tonge, Ronan Gogan, Paul Hendrick, Pádraig McHale, Trevor Dowd. Team Trainer: Jim Gilligan.

1991-92

Cumann na mBunscol, Michael Byrne Cup, Division 2.
Final: Dunshaughlin NS 5-9 Oldcastle by 0-4.
Michael McHale; Stephen Moore, Pádraig McHale, Alan Kenny; Ronan Gogan, David Crimmins, Capt., Darren Cottrell; David Tonge (0-3), Niall Kelly; Paul Hendrick (0-4), Stephen Morgan, Denis Kealy (0-1); Trevor Dowd (1-0), Dessie McKeever (2-1), Kieran Lawlor (2-0). Subs: Marcus Maloney for Lawlor, JJ McDonnell for Dowd, Stephen West for Moore, Brian Faherty, Conor Power, Brian Murphy, William Smith, Kenneth Daly. Team Trainer: Jim Gilligan.

Meath INTO Seven a Side Finals
Final: Dunshaughlin NS defeated Lismullen in the final Michael McHale, Ronan Gogan, David Crimmins, Capt., David Tonge, Pádraig McHale, Paul Hendrick, Denis Kealy, Dessie McKeever, Stephen Morgan, Niall Kelly. Team Trainer: Jim Gilligan.

1997-98

Cumann na mBunscol, Michael Byrne Cup, Division 2.
Final: Duleek defeated Dunshaughlin NS.
Simon Kennedy; Niall McGuinness, David Hall, Derek Jordan; Paul Kennedy, Liam Barber, David Murphy; Caoimhín King, Capt., Cormac Delaney; Paul Cosgrove, Ciarán Hoary, Cathal O Dwyer; Shane Kelly, David Devereux, Eoin Hand. Subs: Thomas O Regan, Alan McLoughlin, Fergal Moore, Ian Hand, Ciarán Farrelly. Team Trainer: Jim Gilligan.

June 1997

Cumann na mBunscol, Division 3 Boys Hurling Final, 11 a side
Final: Rathbeggan NS defeated Dunshaughlin NS
Ciarán Hoary; Caoimhín King, Christopher McGuinness; Ciarán Staunton, Fergal Moore; John Crimmins, Capt., Joseph McHale; Diarmuid Delaney, Cormac Delaney; Rory Bowe, Paul Faherty. Subs: Paul Cosgrove, Michael Mangan, Mark Cannon, Gary Donnelly, Garret O Sullivan, Clive Cookson, Alan Carey. Team Trainers: Mairéad Delaney, Jim Gilligan.

This was the school's first ever appearance in a hurling final. It was due in the main to the work of John Davis, an ex-pupil, who coached hurling in the local schools in a scheme sponsored by Dunshaughlin, Drumree and St. Martins' GAA clubs, Meath County Board and Guinness as sponsors of the All-Ireland Championship.

November 1999

Winners Division 1 Shield, Boys Football
The following players represented the school: Peter Gallagher, Shane Kelly, Keith Byrne, Fearghal Delaney, Martin Cosgrove, Cathal O Reilly, Ian Hand, Simon Kennedy, Karl Kelly, Mark Caldwell, Duncan Geraghty, Andrew Brennan, Ciarán Farrelly, Iain McLaughlin, Robert Robinson, Richard Ryan, Kieran Murphy, Timothy O Regan, John Bedford, Ian Burnell, Tadhg Woods, Eddie McSweeney, Conor Hagarty, Simon O Reilly, Joseph McGovern. Team Trainer: Jim Gilligan.

The school withdrew from Cumann na mBunscol competitions in the early 2000s after Jim Gilligan was appointed Principal. This was due an inability to combine the running of a large school with coaching and training teams. As numbers attending the school increased new staff were appointed and the school applied for admission to the Fingal League, which had better and more fairly graded divisions than Cumann na mBunscol. Barry Slack, Paul Sheehy, Caoimhín King and Barry Murphy coached the boys' teams while Catherine McCormack, Sorcha O Dwyer and Fiona O Brien prepared the girls' teams with outstanding results.

St. Seachnall's NS, Winners, Senior Boys, Division 1 Fingal League, 2011-12

Front: Paddy Maher, Capt., Ben Hanley, Jack Caldwell, Andrew Gavin, Matthew Moyles, Conor Oliver, Ronan McMahon, Eoin O Connor, Daniel Fildes.
Back: Conor Jones, David Fildes, Mika Mikamibua, Conor Keena, Paul Kennedy, Eimhín Power, Mark Connolly.

St. Seachnall's NS, Winners, Division 1, Fingal League 2009-10

Front: Georgie Benson, Kelly O Dwyer, Tara Scanlon, Emma Murray, Laura Quinn, Alannah Chalkley, Cara Usher, Katie Usher, Louise Nevin.
Back: Georgia Dougherty, Siobhán Duffy, Jessica May, Alanna Bradley, Eimear Traynor, Kevagh Slater, Sarah Kelly, Kate Hanley, Sadhbh Morley, Rachel Huijsdens.

St. Seachnall's NS, Winners, Junior Boys Fingal League 2012-13

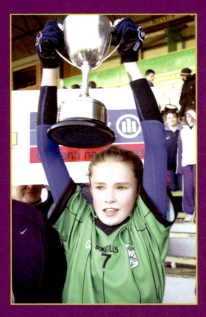

Petra Reilly holds aloft the Girls' Division 1 Cup after victory in the Cumann na mBunscol final in November 2012.

Front: Evan Butler, Liam O Connor, Harry Dunne, Seán O Connor, Capt., Aaron Murphy, Adam Territt, Cillian McCool, Cormac Curtin.
Back: Mathew Costello, Andrew Quinn, Colm Keane, Ethan Mahasé, Seán Walsh, James Traynor, Fionn Cummins.

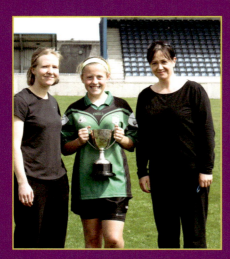

Team mentors, Catherine McCormack on left and Fiona O Brien on right, with Alannah Chalkley after victory in the 2010 Fingal League Final.

Pictured after double success in Parnell Park are Catherine McCormack, Fiona O Brien, Petra Reilly, Matthew Moyles, Barry Slack and Andrew Hennelly.

2004

Winners of the Meath INTO Seven a Side Finals

St. Seachnalls defeated Castletown in the final. Eoin Hagarty, Capt., Michael McCarthy, James Rattigan, Emmet Staunton, Conor Devereux, Lee Duffy, Eamon Bowe, Alan O Brien, Conor O Brien, Conal O Sullivan. Team Trainer: Jim Gilligan.

2006-07

Cumann na mBunscol, Girls, Division 1

Final: St. Seachnalls 1-3 St. Mary's, Ashbourne 0-3. Karen O Regan; Méabh Gallogly, Emma Connolly; Fiona Traynor, Rebecca Keane, Cliona Murphy; Laura Murray, Capt., (0-1), Maeve Scanlon; Jessica O Brien, Emma Kennedy (0-2), Niamh Gallogly; Saoirse Conlon, Sarah Keane (1-0). Subs: Bevin Usher, Laura McDermott, Áine Brennan, Gemma Donoghue, Aoife O Shea, Kaitlyn O Brien, Amy Mulvaney, Sarah Darby, Siobhán O Riordan, Kate Bradley, Alannah Chalkley. Mentors: Catherine McCormack, Sorcha O Dwyer.

Fingal League, Senior Girls, Division 2

Final: St. Marys Ashbourne defeated St. Seachnalls

2008-09

Fingal League, Senior Girls, Division 2

Final: St. Seachnalls defeated Airfield NS
Amy Mulvaney; Ciara Murray, Gemma Donoghue, Aisling Traynor; Sarah Darby, Alannah Chalkley, Kaitlyn O Brien; Niamh Gallogly, Siobhán O Riordan; Tara Scanlon, Áine O Donoghue, Aoife O Shea; Kate Hanley, Sophie McNamara, Siobhán Duffy. Subs: Cara Usher, Emma Murray, Laura Quinn, Kevagh Slater. Team management: Catherine McCormack, Fiona O Brien.

Fingal League Senior Boys, Division 2

Final: Sacr. Heart, Huntstown defeated St Seachnalls
William McCarthy; Cillian Hart, Aaron Keane, Anthony Fildes; Conor Huijsdens, Martin Nevin, Capt., Conor Mooney; Daniel Quinn, James Swan; Aaron Kealy, Ronán Geraghty, Sam Lavery; Gavin Maher, Cormac Fitzpatrick, Niall Swan. Subs: Cian Gallogly, Ben Conlon, Mark MacElhinney, Senan Ó Muirí, Conor Kiely, Kenneth Hand, Liam Donovan. Team management: Paul Sheehy, Caoimhín King, Barry Slack.

2009-10

Fingal League, Senior Girls Division 1

Final: St. Seachnalls defeated Bayside NS, Sutton
Kevagh Slater; Siobhán Duffy, Sarah Kelly; Kate Hanley, Tara Scanlon; Cara Usher, Alannah Chalkley, Capt., Eimear Traynor; Laura Quinn, Katie Usher; Emma Murray, Alanna Bradley. Subs: Louise Nevin, Jessica May, Georgie Benson, Sadhbh Morley, Kelly O Dwyer, Rachel Huijsdens, Georgia Dougherty, Sophie O Connor, Orlaith Moyles, Lara Reynolds, Michelle Jibowu, Emily Hetherton, Katie Kelly, Treasa Murphy, Niamh Curtin. Team management: Catherine McCormack and Fiona O Brien.

Fingal League, Senior Boys, Division 1

Final: Ratoath SNS defeated St. Seachnalls
William McCarthy; Darragh Quinn, Aaron Keane, Liam Donovan; Sam Lavery, Adam Kealy, Tom Boyhan; Conor Huijsdens, Conor Mooney, Capt.; Senan Ó Muirí, Niall Swan, Anthony Fildes; Cian Gallogly, Martin Keane, Adam McDermott. Subs: Ben Conlon, Daniel Kelly, Conor Kiely, David Carroll, Ciarán Malone, Paddy Maher, Mark MacElhinney, Adam Mahasé, Shane Claire, Eric Casserley, Dylan Dunne, Luke Shannon, Sam Butler, Conor Keena, Mika Mikamibua, Ciarán Quinn, Daniel Fildes, Cian Maher, Darragh O Meara, Andrew Gavin. Team management: Paul Sheehy, Barry Slack.

2011-12

Fingal League, Senior Boys, Division 1
Final: St. Seachnalls defeated Pope John Paul II NS
Jack Caldwell; Conor Oliver, Paul Kennedy, Ronan McMahon; Matthew Moyles, Eoin O Connor, Andrew Gavin; Mika Mikamibua, Conor Keena; Daniel Fildes, Paddy Maher, Capt., Ben Hanley; Conor Jones, Eimhín Power, Mark Connolly. Subs: Ciarán Quinn, Adam Summerville, Mathew Costello, Josh Kallides, David Fildes, Evan Butler, Ódhran O Riordan, Kevin Bawle, Alan O Connor, Aaron Lawlor, Cody Lynam-Costello, Oisín Caldwell, Liam Hanley. Team management: Paul Sheehy, Barry Slack.

Fingal League, Senior Girls, Premier
Final: Ratoath Senior NS 3-6 St. Seachnalls NS 2-5
Shaughna Gibney; Kyra Synnott, Lucy Kelly; Olivia Flanagan, Eimear Traynor, Ava Foley; Niamh Curtin, Rachel Huijsdens; Ava Fox, Lara Reynolds, Kelly O Dwyer; Michelle Jibowu, Katelyn Doherty. Subs: Ava Mangan, Alison Kean, Emily Hetherton, Treasa Murphy, Niamh Cowan, Aisling Flynn, Chloe Kelly, Ava O Brien, Maria Bradley, Michelle Sherry, Petra Reilly, Emily Madden, Arielle Gaughan. Team management: Catherine McCormack, Fiona O Brien.

2012-13

Cumann na mBunscol, Girls, Division 1
Final: St. Seachnalls 3-8 St. Oliv. Plunkett's, Navan 1-1
Michelle Sherry; Maria Bradley, Molly McNamara; Mary McDonagh (0-1), Ava Foley (0-1), Jane Larkin; Petra Reilly, Capt., Orlagh Keane (0-2); Ciara Gorman (2-0), Tara Hetherington, Katelyn Doherty (1-4); Ava O Brien, Katelyn O Brien. Subs: Emily Madden, Arielle Gaughan, Katie Reilly, Sarah Oliver, Aoife Duffy, Ellie McCarthy, Megan McCarthy, Caitlin Power-King, Alison Byrne, Alannah Brennan, Eve Flanagan.

Cumann na mBunscol Boys, Division 1
Final: Trim 3-5 St. Seachnalls 2-4
Ethan Mahasé; Ódhran O Riordan, Aaron Lawlor, Kevin Bawle; Cathal Sheehan, David Fildes, Josh Kallides; Matthew Moyles, Capt. (1-1), Mathew Costello; Evan Butler (0-1), Niall Gavin, Thomas Reilly (0-1); Liam Hanley, Harry Dunne, Darren Murphy (1-0). Subs: Oisín Caldwell (0-1), Alan O Connor, Paul Kean, Cian Hegarty, Andrew Quinn, Alastair Philip, Sam Fairbrother, Cillian Summerville, Christopher Varvari, Seán O Connor, Cormac Curtin, Liam O Connor, Josh Masterson, Gary O Connor, Conor Ogedegbe, Cormac O Connor-Flanagan, Tobi Balla. Team management: Barry Slack.

Fingal League, Senior Boys, Division 1
Final: St. Seachnalls 3-9 St. Patrick's NS Donabate 1-6
Ethan Mahasé; Ódhran O Riordan, Aaron Lawlor, Kevin Bawle; Cathal Sheehan, Josh Kallides, Cian Hegarty; Mathew Costello (0-4), Matthew Moyles, Capt.; David Fildes (1-0), Fionn Cummins (2-2), Evan Butler (0-1); Liam Hanley, Oisín Caldwell, Darren Murphy. Subs: Thomas Reilly (0-1), Alan O Connor (0-1), Alastair Philip, Niall Gavin, Harry Dunne, Cillian Summerville, Paul Kean, Sam Fairbrother, Seán O Connor, Andrew Quinn, Cormac Curtin. Team management: Barry Slack and Andrew Hennelly.

Fingal League, Senior Girls, Division 1
Final: St. Seachnalls 4-0 Holy Trinity, Donaghmede 0-4
Michelle Sherry; Maria Bradley, Molly McNamara (1-0); Tara Hetherington, Ava Foley, Sarah Oliver; Orlagh Keane, Petra Reilly (1-0); Katelyn Doherty, Mary McDonagh, Jane Larkin; Ava O Brien (1-0), Katelyn O Brien. Subs: Ciara Gorman (2-0), Arielle Gaughan, Katie Reilly, Aoife Duffy, Ellie McCarthy, Megan McCarthy, Emily Madden. Team management: Catherine McCormack and Fiona O Brien.

APPENDICES

Fingal League, Junior Boys, Division 1

Final: St. Seachnalls 2-12 Pope John Paul II NS, 2-9. Ethan Mahasé; Liam O Connor, Seán Walsh, Adam Territt; Colm Keane, James Traynor, Evan Lawlor; Mathew Costello (0-6), Fionn Cummins (0-4); Andrew Quinn, Seán O Connor, Capt., Harry Dunne; Cormac Curtin (1-1), Aaron Murphy (1-0), Cillian McCool. Subs: Mark O Brien (0-1), Tommy Toal, Conor Ogedegbe, Luke McCarthy, Josh Masterson, Matthew Synnott, Cormac O Connor-Flanagan, Michael Jibowu, Adam Ward, Olli Balla, Harry Magee, Josh McDermott, Joe Larkin, Conor Swan, Cian McLaughlin. Team management: Barry Slack, Sorcha O Dwyer, Andrew Hennelly.

Blake Cup Sevens

The Blake Cup is an inter schools invitational tournament named in honour of Paddy Blake, a Dunshaughlin player and official from the 1920s to the 1960s. St. Seachnalls has won twelve titles: 1987, 1988, 1991, 1992, 1994, 1998, 1999, 2004, 2007, 2012, 2013, 2014.

CULMULLEN NS

Culmullen first entered a football team in Cumann na mBunscol competitions in 1981 and first entered hurling competitions in 1990.

1983-84

Cumann na mBunscol, Boys, Division 3

Culmullen Runners Up

1984-85

Cumann na mBunscol, Boys, Division 3

Final: Culmullen 1-6 Bohermeen 1-4

David Troy; Paul Doyle, Dermot Doyle; Peter Rattigan, Patrick Doyle, Barry Walsh; Alan Boyle, Patrick Dunne; Emmet Downes, Kenneth McGuinness, Evan Kelly; Nigel Daly, James Walsh.

1991-92

Cumann na mBunscol, Hurling Div. 2

Final: Culmullen defeated Boardsmill

Gary O Donoghue; Gavin Kilbane, Philip Salmon; Gerard Troy, John McKiernan, Brian Kenny; Paul Doyle, Capt., Pádraig Shanley; Ronan Eagle, Kevin Burke, George Troy; Cathal Smith, Simon Maher. Subs: Justin Martin, Neil Mooney, John Gilsenan, Christopher Doyle, Myles Dunne, Patrick Hayes, Patrick Smith. Trainer: George Knightly.

1994-95

Cumann na mBunscol, Hurling Div. 3

Final: Culmullen 6-2 Oristown 3-1

Full team list unavailable. Among the panel were Ronan Gilsenan, Shona Donohoe (1-0), Christopher Doyle, Philip Doyle, D Murphy, J Coffey, D Mooney, C Gilsenan, E Doyle, T Spillane.

1998-1999

Cumann na mBunscol Hurling, Division 2, 11 a side

Final: Kilmessan NS 6-4 Culmullen 0-0

John Crosbie; Brian Coughlan, Stephen McGroder; Christopher Dixon, Paul Coffey; David Wallace, David Quinn; John Coffey, Robert Lyons; Eoin Reilly, Shane Troy. Subs: John O Callaghan, Emmet O Callaghan, Conor Staunton, Alan Moore. Team Trainers: Joe Geraghty, John Davis.

1999-2000

Cumann na mBunscol Hurling, Division 2, 11 a side.

Final: Kiltale v Culmullen

Christopher Dixon; Stephen Fox, John Coffey; Stephen McGroder, Conor Staunton; David Wallace, Brian Coughlan; Emmet O Callaghan, Shane Troy; Paul Coffey, Mark Coffey. Subs: Robert Crosbie, Bill Reilly. Team Trainer: Joe Geraghty.

2004-05

Cumann na mBunscol, Girls Division 4 Football

Final: Culmullen 2-7 Scoil Mhuire, Carlanstown 0-1

Leanne McMurrow; Aimee McQuillan (0-1), Rebecca Conlon-Trant, Melissa Leonard; Niamh Kelliher (0-1), Kristine Troy (2-3); Amy Crosbie, Lauren Lawlor (0-1), Laura McMahon (0-1). Subs: Emma Booth for Lawlor, Jessica Wall for Booth.

Culmullen NS, Winners Cumann na mBunscol, Boys Division 3, 1984-85

Front: Kenneth McGuinness James Walsh, Emmet Downes, Evan Kelly, Peter Rattigan, Barry Walsh, Dermot Doyle.
Back: Paul Doyle, Patrick Dunne, Patrick Doyle, Noel Burke, Nigel Daly, Alan Boyle, David Troy.

Culmullen NS, Winners Cumann na mBunscol, Girls' Division 4 Football, 2004-05

Front: Lauren Grall, Laura McMahon, Melissa Leonard, Niamh Kelleher, Laura Bannon.
Middle: Gráinne Boyle, Róisín Fulcher, Georgiana Flood, Anna Devey, Nikita Madden, Emma Booth, Jessica Wall, Amy Connolly.
Back: Aideen Treacy, Principal, Rebecca Sweeney, Rebecca Conlon-Trant, Lauren Lawlor, Kristina Troy, Ciara Nolan, Amy Crosbie, Joe Geraghty, Team Manager.
Insets: Aimee McQuillan, Christina Phelan, Leanne McMorrow.

Gaelscoil Na Ríthe

Gaelscoil na Ríthe was established in 1985.

1997-98

Cumann na mBunscol, Camogie Division 2

Final: St. Oliver Plunkett's, Navan 6-0 Gaelscoil na Ríthe 2-0
Niamh Ní Fheal, Natasha Nic Lámh, Bríghde de Faoite, Caitríona Ní Mhaidín, Sinéad Nic Canna, Lára Ní Fhlanagáin (1-0), Niamh Nic Domhnaill (1-0), Searon Ní Mhathúna, Aisling Ní Chearúil. Ionadaithe: Ailín de Faoite, Paula Ní Mhongáin, Clár Ní Ghríofa, Sorcha Ní Chasaide, Gillian Nic Ionmhainn. Bainisteoir: Annette Ní Mhuireagáin. B'í seo an chéad cluiche ceannais riamh do Ghaelscoil na Ríthe agus bhí an scoil fíor-bhuíoch do John Davis.

1998-99

Cumann na mBunscol, Camogie Division 2

Final: Dunboyne 6-1 Gaelscoil na Ríthe 3-0
Máire Nic Dara; Bláthna Ní Eabhróid, Nina Ní Mhaolbhuaidh, Amy Ní Chonsaidín; Ailín de Faoite, Paula Ní Mhongáin; Siobhán Ní Chiaráin (2-0), Clár Ní Ghríofa, Linda Ní Dhufaigh (1-0). Ionadaithe: Lisa de Paor, Katie Ní Mhásúin, Aisling Ní Chearúil, Erin Ní Chuilinn-Dhorchaí, Sorcha-Sinéad Ní Bhrádaigh. Bainisteoir: Deirdre Ní Fhiannachta.

Cumann na mBunscol, Hurling Division 3

Final: Dangan 2-2 Gaelscoil na Ríthe 0-0
S Ó Tuachair, Brian Mac Eoin, Cillian Ó Finn, Fionnán Ó Catháin, Domhnall Ó Dochartaigh, Ruairí Mac Dónaill, Roibeárd Caimpion, Darragh Mac Gréil, Luke Ó Fearaíl; Adrian Ó Tuathalann, Séamus de Faoite, Stiofán Mac Úistín, Colm Mac Lámh, Pól Ó Ciaráin, Val Mac Fhionnáin, Roibeárd de Búrca, Seán Ó Colmáin. Bainisteoir: Breandán de Bhál.

1999-2000

Cumann na mBunscol, Football Boys, Division 2

Final: Duleek 2-16 Gaelscoil na Ríthe 0-5
This was the school's first Cumann na mBunscol football final, the same year as Dunshaughlin's first senior final.
Val Mac Fhionnáin; Cathal Ó Mordha, Adrian Ó Tuathlainn, Ciarán Ó Ceallaigh; Sam Ó Tiarnaigh, Brian Mac Eoin, Seán Ó Colmáin; Ruairí Mac Domhnaill, Cillian Curnáin Ó Finn, Capt; Séamus de Faoite, Fionán Ó Catháin, Séamus Ó Horgáin; Stiofáin Mac Úistín, Séamus de Faoite, Pól Ó Ciarnáin. Ionadaithe: Daithí Ó Breacáin, Erin Ní Chuilinn Dhorchaí, Siobhán Ní Chiaráin, Alan Savage, Risteard Ó Cianaigh, Conall Ó Tuathail, Dónal Ó Cluabháin, Ciarán Ó Dufaigh, Seán Ó Maoildearg. Bainisteoir: Pól Ó hAoláin.

Cumann na mBunscol Hurling, Division 3

Final: Dangan v Gaelscoil na Ríthe
Cillian Ó Finn; Seán Ó Colmáin, Brian Mac Eoin; Val Mac Fhionnáin, Daithí Ó Breacáin; Adrian Ó Tuathalann, Capt., Fionnán Ó Catháin; Pól Ó Ciarnáin, Séamus de Faoite; Dónal Ó Leocháin, Dónal Ó Clúbháin. Ionadaithe: Alan Savage, Neal Ó Ceallaigh, Rónán Ó Breacáin, Diarmuid Mac Gréil, Ceiteach Ó Comáin, Risteard Ó Cianaigh. Bainisteoir: Breandán de Bhál.

2004-05

Cumann na mBunscol, Football Boys, Division 2

Final: Cannistown 5-6 Gaelscoil na Ríthe 3-4
Aindriú Ó Ciarnáin; Harry Ó Néill, Liam Ormsby, Gearóid Ó Flanagáin; Leoin Mac Eabhróid, Colm Ó Faoláin, Jack Ó Caomhánaigh, Seosamh Ó Briain, Aodán Boswell (0-2); Eimhin Cinseallach (0-1), Cillian Ó Súilleabháin, Dónal de Bhál (1-1); Pól Ó Conaill, Eoin Ó Cathail (2-0) Bainisteoir: Pól Ó hAoláin.

2005-06

Cumann na mBunscol, Football Boys, Division 2

Final: Cannistown 4-7 Gaelscoil na Rithe 1-2

Aodán Ó Marcaigh; Dara Ó Faogáin, Aindriú Ó Ciarnáin, Gearóid Ó Flanagáin; Cillian Ó Duinn, Colm Mac Suibhne, Niall Mac Liam; Pól Ó Conaill (0-1), Cillian Ó Suilleabháin (0-1); Leoin Mac Eabhróid, Oisín de Bhál, Dónal Mac Giolla Dé; Cathal Ó Casaide, Glen Mac Giolla Phádraig, Caoimhín Mac Raghnaill. Ionadaithe: Pól Ó Meachair for Mac Giolla Phádraig, Stiofán Ó Crualaoich for Ó Casaide, Ruairí Croke for Mac Raghnaill, Caoimhín Ó Banain for Croke. Bainisteoir: Breandán de Bhál.

2008-09

Cumann na mBunscol, Football Boys, Division 3

Final: Dangan NS 3-9 Gaelscoil na Ríthe 3-5

Liam Ó Ciardha; Lorcán Ó Cathasaigh, Cormac Ó Miacháin; Tom Cinsealach, Cillian Ó Dufaigh, Darragh Campion; Dónal Ormsby, Conchúr Mac Aodhbhuí; Lúcás Mac Uaid Slator, Aodh Ó Suilleabháin, Séamus Ó Leochain (1-0); Jordan Mac Giolla Dé (2-1), Conchur Mac Sheoinín (0-4). Ionadaithe: Marc Ó Gealbháin, Maitiú Bridgett, Eoin Mac Suibhne, Seán Ó Néill, Stiofáin Ó Tailliúir, Glen Mac Seain. Bainisteoirí: Pól Ó hAoláin, Rónán Mac Giolla Ruaidh.

Cumann na mBunscol Hurling, Division 3

Final: Gaelscoil na Ríthe 3-4 Gaelscoil na Bóinne 2-5

Tomás Cinsealach; Seán Ó Néill, Eoin Mac Suibhne; Roiberad Ó hUallacháin, Stiofáin Ó Gamhna-hAonghusa; Marc Ó Gealbháin Capt., Aodh Ó Suilleabháin (0-3); Darragh Campion, Cillian Ó Dufaigh (0-1); Lúcás Mac Uaid-Slator (1-0), Conchur Mac Seoinín (2-0). Ionadaithe: Maitiú Bridgett, Cormac Ó Miacháin, Lorcán Ó Raghallaigh, Michéal Ó Riain, Neil Mac Seain, Daithí Watté, Ferdia Ó Foghlú, Séamus Mac Raghnaill, Ian Ó Tailliúir. Bainisteoirí: Ailbhe Furlong, Rónán Mac Giolla Ruaidh.

2009-2010

Winners, Cumann na mBunscol Hurling, Division 3

Final: Bainisteoir: Rónán Mac Giolla Ruaidh.

2010-2011

Cumann na mBunscol Hurling, Division 3

Final: Gaelscoil na Ríthe 4-5 Rathbeggan N.S. 1-2

Luke Ó Mistéil, Ferdia Ó Foghlú, Seán Ó Néill, Pól Ó Brúaidí, Roibeard Ó hUallacháin, Niall Ó Hurthaile, Aodh Ó Súilleabháin (Capt.), Jack Hetherington, Ian Ó Táilliúir, Darragh Caimpion, Wesley Ó Goidín, Seán Ó hAonaghsa, Daithí Ó Máirtín, Tomás Ó Daltúin, Séamus Mac Raghnaill, Turlough Ó Maoileoin, JJ Mac Conmara, Séamus Ó Maoileanaigh, Rhys de Brús, Roibeard Mac Conaill, Naois Mac Suibhne. Bainisteoir: Rónán Mac Giolla Ruaidh.

Gaelscoil na Rithe, Buaiteoirí, Cumann na mBunscol, Craobh Peile Roinn 2, 2005-2006

Chun tosaigh: Colm Mac Suibhne, Seán Mac Giolla Phádraig, Cian Mac Conchoille, Dónal Mac Giolla Dé, Lorcán Ó Broin, Pól Ó Meachair, Cillian Ó Súilleabháin (Captaen), Ruairí Croke, Caoimhín Ó Banáin, Diarmuid Mac Críosta, Stiofán Ó Fearaíl

Ar chúl: Pól Ó hAoláin, Príomhoide Ionaid, Cathal Ó Casaide, Stiofán Ó Crualaoich, Criostóir Ó Táilliúir, Glen Mac Giolla Phádraig, Pól Ó Conaill, Gearóid Ó Flanagáin, Aindriú Ó Ciarnáin, Aodán Ó Marcaigh, Oisín de Bhál, Niall Mac Liam, Dara Ó Faogáin, Leoin Mac Eabhróid, Caimin Ó Duinn, Caoimhín Mac Raghnaill, Breandán de Bhál, Príomhoide agus Bainisteoir.

Gaelscoil na Rithe, Buaiteoirí, Cumann na mBunscol Craobh Iomána Roinn 2, 2010-2011

Chun tosaigh: Pól Ó Brúaidí, Daithí Ó Máirtín, Ferdia Ó Foghlú, Séamus Mac Raghnaill, Jack Hetherington, Seán Ó hAonaghsa, Wesley Ó Goidín, Niall Ó Hurthaile.

Ar chúl: Luke Ó Mistéil, Ian Ó Táilliúir, Roibeárd Ó hUallacháin, Seán Ó Néill, Aodh Ó Súilleabháin, (Captaen), Darragh Caimpion, Turlough Ó Maoileoin, Tomás Daltúin, Naois Mac Suibhne.

Dunshaughlin Community College

Due to the number of competitions and the paucity of records it has not been possible to compile a comprehensive listing of honours won by the school. What follows is a selection based on available sources.

Note re dating. Rather than use the school year, we have attempted to use the year in which the game was played.

Dunshaughlin Vocational School (VS) opened in the Workhouse, Dunshaughlin in January 1933 with Ciarán O Connell as headmaster and three other teachers. Night classes were also organized in Irish conversation, Irish dancing, Woodwork, Domestic Science and Rural Science. The average attendance in 1945 was 37 pupils in day classes and 30 in night classes. The school continued in the Workhouse, except for one year in the local courthouse in 1950-51, until a new two room Vocational School was opened on the site of the current Meath County Council offices. The attendance in 1951/52 was 38 day pupils. Gerard Commins replaced Ciarán O Connell as Principal and when Commins left in November 1958 John Holland replaced him, remaining as Principal until 1993. In 1967 the Intermediate Certificate was introduced followed by the Leaving Certificate in 1970-71 and this combined with the growth of Dunshaughlin led to the rapid expansion of the school. In September 1977 pupils moved into the current school which was designated Dunshaughlin Community College (CC). The latest extension opened in September 2013.

From the beginning, although numbers were small, the school participated in gaelic games.

1956

Meath Vocational Schools won the All-Ireland Vocational Schools Championship. John Holland, Principal of the College, 1958-93, then teaching in Nobber VS, was a selector. Christy Barry from Walterstown was the sole Dunshaughlin VS representative on the team. The following year, future Meath stars, Jack Quinn and Noel Curran were pupils of the school but the Meath team could not repeat the 1956 success.

Dunshaughlin CC Players on Meath VEC Leinster Final Winning Teams

2002

Leinster Final: Meath 2-11 Wicklow 0-6
All-Ireland Semi-Final: Donegal defeated Meath by 12 points.
It was Meath's first Leinster title in twenty-five years, with Ger McCullagh as captain and Caoimhín King, Robert Madden, Paul Faherty and Seamus Wallace also on the team while Pat Kenny was a selector.

2007

Leinster Final: Meath 1-18 Louth 0-4
All-Ireland Semi-Final: Meath 2-11 Galway 2-10
All-Ireland Final: Tyrone 1-12 Meath 0-9
Tommy Johnson, Fearghal Delaney.

2008

Leinster Final: Meath 2-12 Kildare 1-7
All-Ireland Semi-Final: Monaghan 2-6 Meath 0-11
Tommy Johnson, Stephen Clusker.

2009

Leinster Final: Meath 3-11 Kildare 0-5
All-Ireland Semi-Final: Galway 2-7 Meath 0-12
Conor Devereux, Eoin Hagarty, Eamon Bowe.
Pat Kenny selector.

2010

Leinster Final: Meath 2-15 Wicklow 0-6
All-Ireland Semi-Final: Cork 0-16 Meath 2-7
Alastar Doyle, Conor McGill, Paddy Kennedy.

2011

Leinster Final: Meath 0-10 Wicklow 0-8
All-Ireland Semi-Final: Donegal 2-6 Meath 0-6
Conor McGill, Capt, David Donnellan, Bryan Davis.

FOOTBALL HONOURS

The College has won six senior county titles since 1990 beating Oldcastle twice, Ashbourne twice, Nobber once and Navan once. Teams have also won two Leinster Senior B finals in 2003 and 2005 going on to claim the ultimate honour of All-Ireland victory in 2005.

1973

Meath VS Senior Final Dunshaughlin 3-2 Nobber 2-3

1977

Leinster VS Under 15

Final: Greenhills, Walk'town 3-8 Dunshaughlin VS 1-4
Dermot Reilly; Michael O Brien, Martin O Halloran, Dermot Rooney; John Eiffe, Stephen McInerney. Paul Everard; Martin Reilly, Aidan O Brien; John Forde, Dermot Browne, Joe Maguire; Dermot Finn, Paul O Shea, Paul Finn. Subs: Finian Ennis, Derek Conroy, Gerry Coss, John Ennis, Noel Whelan, Gerry Regan, Martin Summerville, Stephen O Connor, Declan Clusker. Team Trainer: Vincent Lane.

1978

Leinster Senior Final

Tullamore 2-12 Dunshaughlin 1-4
Dermot Reilly; Dermot Rooney, Michael O Brien, Derek Conroy; Paul Everard, Stephen McInerney, Anthony Wall; Noel Smith, John Forde; Stephen O Connor, Brian McCann, Martin Reilly; Dermot Browne, John Coyne, Paul Finn. Sub: Dermot Finn for O Connor.

1983

Meath VEC SFC Final

Dunshaughlin CC 3-4 Nobber VS 1-3
Kevin Crehan; Kevin Kealy, Pearse O Dwyer, Michael Duffy; Joe Bannon, David Brady, Bernard Wallace; Mervyn Ennis, (1-3), Niall McCarthy (0-1); Martin Walsh, Val McMahon, Damien Hobbs (1-0); John Faulkner, James Muldowney, Dermot Reilly. Subs: Robbie Moran (1-0) for Muldowney.

Meath VEC Under 15 Final

Dunshaughlin CC 3-4 Nobber VS 1-3
Panel: David Kane, Brian Rooney, Ciarán Byrne, Henry McQuaid, Kevin Nestor, Vincent Nestor, Alan Fahy, Derek Melia, Dermot Kealy, Alan Geraghty, Anthony McCabe, Morty O Sullivan, Martin Reilly, John Dollard, Vincent Donnelly, Capt., Vincent Moore, Pearse Fahy, Liam O Neill and Tommy Byrne.

Meath VEC Under 13 Final

Dunshaughlin CC 5-4 Navan VS 2-2
Fergus Smith; John Davis, Martin Lynch, Derek Maher; David Barker, Brian Duffy, Capt., Paul Stewart; Dessie Donnelly, Dermot White; Michael Walsh, Derek

Dunshaughlin CC, Meath VS Under 13 Winners, 1984

Front: Alan McCabe, Morty O Sullivan, Martin Reilly, John Dollard, Dessie Donnelly, Capt., Vinny Moore, Pearse Fahy, Liam O Neill, Tony Byrne.
Back: David Kane, Robbie Rooney, Ciarán Byrne, Henry McQuaid, Kevin Nestor, Vincent Nestor, Alan Fahy, Derek Melia, Dermot Kealy, Alan Geraghty.

Dunshaughlin Community College, Winners Leinster Senior VS, 2003

Front: Paul Cosgrove, Cathal Browne, Paul Kennedy, Michael Ahern, Kenneth Fitzmaurice, Tony McGunae, Diarmuid Brennan, David Devereux, Colm Kelly, Ciaran Kenny, David McMahon.
Back: Ciarán Hoary, Vinny McIntyre, Ronan Gilsenan, Cathal Flaherty, Jamie Minnock, James Everard, Dónal Kirwan, Alan Hogan, Cormac Dempsey, Kevin Carney, Caoimhín King, Pat Kenny.

Monaghan, Pat Kealy; Vinny Moore, Joey McLoughlin, David Hobbs. Subs: Niall Foley for Walsh, John Munnelly, Shane Thynne, Patrick Doyle, Trevor Bannon, Derek Melia, Fintan Barker, Alan O Dwyer, Anto McCabe, Michael Mangan, David Kane, Fergal Fewer.

1984

Meath VS Under 13 Final

Dunshaughlin CC 7-5 Nobber V 2-3

Derek Melia; Tommy Byrne, Dessie Donnelly, Capt., Alan McCabe; David Kane, Alan Geraghty, Kevin Nestor; Vinny Nestor, Dermot Kealy; David Hobbs, Alan Fahy (1-2), Vinny Moore (1-1); Morty O Sullivan (2-1), D Finlay, Martin Reilly (2-1). Subs: Ciarán Byrne (1-0), Robbie Rooney, Henry McQuaid, John Dollard, Pearse Fahy, Liam O Neill.

1985

Meath VEC U13 F Champions

Philip Burke, James Kelliher, Ciarán Byrne, Colm Naughton, Terry Rooney, Liam O Neill, Michael Nestor, Richard McCabe, Thomas Walsh, PJ Murray, Brendan Kealy, Garbhán Blake, Seamus Davis, Fiachra Page, Kevin Nestor, Conor Geraghty, Pearse Fahy, Colin Kennedy.

1987

Meath VS SFC Final

Dunshaughlin CC 1-9 Navan CC 1-0

Derek Melia; Ciarán Byrne, Liam Eiffe, Terry Rooney; John Davis, Simon Farrell, Stephen Claire; Dermot White (0-1), Liam Neville; Vinny Nestor (1-4), Joey McLoughlin (0-1), Dermot Kealy (0-1); Alan Fahy (0-1), Paul McCann, Nigel Fox (0-1). Subs: Kevin Nestor for V Nestor, Robert McGuinness for Fahy.

Leinster VS SFC

Semi-Final: Dunshaughlin CC 1-5 Ballymahon 0-3
Final: Tullow 1-9 Dunshaughlin CC 0-7.

Leinster Voc Schools U 15 Final

Dunshaughlin CC 1-8 Tullow 0-4

All-Ireland Semi-Final

Dunshaughlin CC 2-6 Killarney 2-2

All-Ireland Final

St. Pius, Magherafelt 6-11 Dunshaughlin CC 0-3

Team v Killarney: Bernard Whyte; David Collins, Barry Donnelly, Garbhán Blake; Colm Davis, Terry Rooney, Kevin Nestor; Ciarán Byrne (1-0), Colm Naughton (0-1); Steve Davis, John Naughton (1-2), Brendan Kealy; Ivor Reilly, Robert McGuinness (0-3), Liam O Neill. Subs: Dónal Coyne for O Neill, Eamonn Reilly, PJ Murray, David Moroney, Eddie McManus.

1988

Meath VS Junior Football Finalists

Philip Burke, Gavin Tierney, Seamus Davis, Brendan Kealy, Trevor Doyle, Ciarán O Dwyer, Brendan Gilsenan, David Moroney, Stephen Davis, Brian White, Colm Davis, Barry Donnelly, Ollie McLoughlin, Jason McAuley, Neville Monaghan, Darragh Smyth, Ivor Reilly, Patrick Stoney, Barry Drennan, Robert Ennis.

1989

Meath VEC Juvenile F Champions

Kenny McTigue, Martin Keane, Cathal O Connor, Fergal Rooney, Terry Cullen, Patrick Walsh, Joey Farrelly, Simon Duffy, Robert Bruton, Andrew Peat, James Walsh, Ronan Dardis, Paul Baker, Dermot Doyle, Mark Carberry, Richie Kealy, Darragh Cannon, Andrew Keane, Christopher Henry, Barry Bowens, Brian White.

1992

N Leinster C Juvenile Football Finalists

Martin Kelly, Denis Kealy, Conor Killian, Fintan Lawlor, Paul Kelly, Patrick Doyle, David McCormack, Shane Poleon, Martin Reilly, Vincent Cullinane, Conor Gorman, Ian Dowd, David Tonge, Paul Hendrick, David Moran, Ronan Gogan, David Crimmins, Paddy McHale, Brendan Thornton.

1993

Meath VEC, Juvenile Championship Final

Dunshaughlin CC 6-9 Oldcastle CC 1-4

Paul Kelly; Paddy McHale, Paul Doyle, Vincent Cullinane; Brian Faherty, David Tonge, Michael Reilly; Shane Poleon, Denis Kealy; David Moran, David Crimmins, Ronan Gogan; Paul Hendrick, Brian Geraghty, Ian Dowd. Subs: Alex Perry, Conor Gorman, Conor Killian, Brendan Thornton, Martin Kelly, David McCormack.

North Leinster VEC Juvenile C Final

Dunshaughlin CC runners up to Rochfortbridge

Paul Kelly; Paddy McHale, Fintan Lawlor, Capt., Vincent Cullinane; Michael Reilly, Paul Doyle, David Crimmins; David Tonge, Shane Poleon; Denis Kealy, David McCormack, David Moran; Ian Dowd, Dominic Jones, Paul Hendrick. Sub: Ronan Gogan.

1994

Meath Under 17 VS Final

Dunshaughlin CC 3-13 Navan CC 1-7.
11 a side competition.

Fearghal Gogan; Mark Henry, Ulick McDonnell; David McCormack (0-1), Fintan Lawlor; David O Sullivan (0-1), Dominic Jones; Justin Barron, Capt., John Kirwan (1-0); John Cullinane (1-0), Graham Dowd (0-8). Subs: Pádraic O Dwyer, Colin Walsh, Ciarán Keogh, Richard Quigley, Robbie Hetherton, Shay Sheridan, Johnny O Connor, Leonard Browne, Kris Murray, Damian Ryan, Denis Kealy.

Leinster Juvenile C Final

Dunshaughlin CC 5-5 Tallaght 5-4

Brian Faherty; Michael McHale, Vincent Cullinane, Pádraig McHale; Paul Kirwan (0-1), Conor Gorman, Emmet Ferguson; Denis Kealy (1-2), Niall Kelly; Paul Hendrick (2-1), David Tonge, Capt. (2-1), Neil Reilly; Martin Reilly, Stephen West, Kevin Lawlor. Subs: Gary Donoghue, David Tormay, Conor Killian, Paul Keane, David Tallant, Jason Keogh.

Meath VS Juvenile Final

Dunshaughlin CC 4-8 Longwood/Rathcairn 1-5

Brian Faherty; Conor Killian, Michael McHale, Mark Watters; Graham Cassidy, Vincent Cullinane, Jason Keogh; Niall Kelly (2-0), Emmet Ferguson (0-1); Kevin Lawlor (0-1), Neil Reilly (0-1), David Tormay (0-2); Martin Reilly (0-2), Gary Donoghue (2-0), Peter Smith (0-1). Subs: Brendan Thornton, Kevin Moyles.

North Leinster Juvenile C Final

Dunshaughlin CC 2-9 Maynooth PP 0-8

Brian Faherty; Michael McHale, Vincent Cullinane, Pádraig McHale; Paul Kirwan, Niall Kelly (0-1), Paul Hendrick; Emmet Ferguson (0-1) Denis Kealy (0-3); Neil Reilly, David Tonge (0-3), Conor Gorman; Martin Reilly, Stephen West (1-1), Kevin Lawlor (1-0).

Girls U 16 Final

Dunshaughlin CC 3-10 Longwood 3-6

Elaine Kavanagh; Glenda Faughnan, Deirdre Coleman, Margaret O Connor; Laura Morrissey, Ann McIntyre, Alison Kelly; Sandra Rooney (1-1), Elaine Reid (0-1); Edel Daly (0-1), Bridget Reilly (0-1), Sinead Cusack (1-2); Karen Ward, Róisín Grogan (1-3), Sandra Coleman (0-1).

Dunshaughlin Community College, Winners All-Ireland VEC Senior B, 2005

Front: Brian Coughlan, Gavin Moore, Ciarán Farrelly, Niall Clarke, Conor Staunton, Emmet O Callaghan, Stephen McGroder, John Coleman.
Middle: Pat Kenny, Aodhán McKeon, Cathal Moore, Diarmuid O Donoghue, Mark Caldwell, Alan O Keeffe, Terry Hetherton, Willie Mahady, Cathal Hennelly.
Back: Darragh Goodman, Shane Toher, Peter Durnin, David Keating, James Gaughan, Derek Jordan, Michael Ahern, Cillian Finn, Ian Davis.

Dunshaughlin Community College, Leinster Under 16 Finalists, 2009

Front: John Davis, Eoin Cahill, Colm McCullagh, Colin Farrell, Eoin Hannon, Pádraig Maguire, Sam Duggan, David Donnellen, Glen Fitzpatrick, James Kelly, Bryan Davis.
Back: Patrick Darby, Cormac Flaherty, Liam Ormsby, Colin Phelan, Jack Hogan, Andrew Smith, Capt., Niall Hannon, Eimhín Kinsella, Conor O Brien, Conor McGill, Seán Burke, David Baggott, Ian Gillett, Matt Sharp.

Andrew Smith receives the All-Ireland Under 16 Shield from Fergal Giles of Leinster Schools.

1995

Meath VEC Junior Final
Dunshaughlin 4-5 St Olivers Oldcastle 3-5

Brian Faherty; Michael McHale, Emmet Ferguson, JJ McDonnell; Paul Kirwan, Denis Kealy (0-1), Vincent Cullinane; Neil Reilly, Conor Gorman (0-1); Pádraig McHale (0-1), David Tonge (1-1), David Tormay (1-0); Paul Hendrick (0-1), Gary Donoghue (2-0), Kevin Lawlor.

Leinster VEC Junior Final
Tullow CS 3-7 Dunshaughlin CC 0-6

Aaron O Neill; Pádraig McHale, Darren Goodman, Emmet Ferguson; Conor Gorman, Fintan Lawlor, Paddy Coyne; Denis Kealy, Niall Kelly; Neil Reilly, Paul Kelly, David Tonge; Ian Dowd, David McCormack, Paul Hendrick. Sub: David Tormay.

Meath VEC Juvenile Football Final
Dunshaughlin 5-12 Navan CC 3-5

Gavin Lenihan; Seán Casserly, JJ McDonnell, Brian Kenny; Tomás Cunningham, Christopher Carey, Alan Spillane; Martin Reilly (0-2), Graham Cassidy; Trevor Dowd (1-0), Peter Smith (0-2), David Kelly; Oliver Nolan, Gavin Donnelly (3-6), Joe Hutchinson (0-2). Sub: Seán Ryan (1-0).

1996

Meath VS SFC Final
Dunshaughlin CC 5-16 St Olivers 3-4

Fearghal Gogan; Mark Henry, Shane Kelly, Michael O Reilly; Pádraic O Dwyer (0-2), Denis Kealy (0-1), Fintan Lawlor; Ciarán Keogh (0-1), Graham Dowd (1-4); Terence White (0-1), David Tonge (0-2), David McCormack (0-1); Paddy Coyne (3-3), Leonard Browne (1-1), Stephen Fox. Subs: David Moran, Aaron O Neill.

Meath VS Junior FC Final
Dunshaughlin CC 3-9 Athboy 0-10

Christopher Carey; Seán Casserly, Graham Cassidy, Alan Spillane; Tomas Cunningham, Michael McHale, Brian Kenny; JJ McDonnell (0-1), Peter Smith (1-2); Trevor Dowd, Gavin Donnelly, Martin Reilly (0-3); Joe Hutchinson (0-3), Thomas O Reilly (1-0), Jason Keogh (1-0). Sub: Kevin Moyles.

Leinster VS Junior A, Under 16, Championship
Final: Ard Scoil Clara defeated Dunshaughlin CC

1997

Leinster VS Junior A, Under 16, Championship Final
Ard Scoil Clara 1-6 Dunshaughlin CC 0-8

Christopher Carey; Alan Spillane, Michael McHale, Tomas Cunningham; Brian Kenny, Graham Cassidy, JJ McDonnell; Martin Reilly, David King; Trevor Dowd, Emmet Dalton, Austin McMahon; Joe Hutchinson, Peter Smith, Mark Brennan. Subs: Seán Casserly, Kevin Moyles, Conor O Sullivan, Seán Killian, Eoin McKee, Oliver Nolan.

Meath VS Juvenile U14 Final
Dunshaughlin CC runners-up

1999

N Leinster Junior C Final
Rathangan 2-10 Dunshaughlin CC 1-10

Panel: Robbie O Neill, Eoin Farrelly, John Clifford, Seamus Wallace, Bryan Duffy, Kieran Lawlor, Mark West, Austin McMahon, Conor Brennan, Paddy Maguire, Keith Mangan, Stephen Ward, David Everard, Ray Maloney, David O Neill, Mark Devanney. Donal Clynch, Daniel Finucane, Stephen Creagh, David Donoghue, Joseph McHale, Paul Sheehy.

2000

Meath VS Junior Girls Football Champions

2001

Leinster VEC Senior B Championship Final
Ballymahon VS 2-7 Dunshaughlin CC 2-6
Panel: Michael Ahern, Peter Kelly, David McMahon, Kenneth Fitzmaurice, Diarmuid Brennan, Tony McGuane, Keelan Fahy, Caoimhín King, Ger McCullagh, Dónal Kirwan, Owen Herlihy, Vincent McIntyre, Robbie Madden, James Geaney, Jamie Minnock, Ronan Gilsenan, Patrick Phelan, Diarmuid Delaney, Alan Hogan, Cathal Browne, Paul Cosgrove, James Whyte, Ciarán Hoary.

North Leinster Juvenile, U-14 C
Final: Dunshaughlin CC 6-8 Ardee CS 2-3

Leinster Juvenile, U-14
Final: Castlecomer CS defeated Dunshaughlin CC
Panel: Michael Ahern, Capt., David Devereux, Conor Staunton, Eldon Gavigan, Chris Kelly, Mark Caldwell, Ciarán Kenny, Cillian Finn, Brian Coughlan, Eoin Reilly, Alan McLoughlin, Robert Lyons, James Gaughan, Alan O Keeffe, David Wallace, Peter Durnin, Simon Kennedy, Paul Kiernan, Diarmuid O Donoghue, Derek Jordan, Oisín O Farrell, Paul Grimes, Colm Quinn, Daragh McGreal, Michael Synott, Martin Cosgrove, Stephen McGroder, Cathal O Reilly.

Ladies' Football League, 1st/2nd Year
Final Replay: Dunshaughlin CC 4-8 Longwood/Trim 2-3.
Deirdre O Donoghue, Tracey Redmond, Lorraine Herron, Sarah Flanagan, Suzanne Colgan, Aoife O Donoghue, Caitríona Brennan, Gillian Flanagan, Laura Glennon, Mary Rose McCann, Emma Fitzmaurice, Brenda McTigue, Alison Mannering, Anne Swaine, Elaine Connolly, C Grendon, Claire McGovern, Alison Eiffe.

2002

Meath VEC Senior Championship Final
Dunshaughlin CC defeated Ashbourne in Walterstown

North Leinster Juvenile, U-14 C
Final: Dunshaughlin CC 5-10 Bush PP, Carlingford 3-8

Leinster Juvenile, U-14 C Final
Sc. Conghlais, Balt'glass 3-10 Dunshaughlin CC 1-8
Semi-Final team: Chris Kelly; Stephen McGroder Cillian Finn, Emmet O Callaghan; Aodhán McKeown, David Wallace, Cathal Hennelly; Christopher Dixon, Conor Staunton; Diarmuid O Donoghue, Ciarán Farrelly, Niall Clarke; Alan O Keeffe, David Devereux, Mark Caldwell. Subs: David Goodman for O Donoghue, Martin Cosgrove, Paul Kiernan, Karl Kelly, Fionán O Kane, Ian Davis, Andrew Brennan.

2003

Leinster VEC Senior B Ch'ship
Semi-Final: Dunshaughlin CC 1-6 Ballymahon VS 2-2
Final: Dunshaughlin CC 1-10 Bridgetown VS 0-4
First Leinster Senior VS title
James Everard; Diarmuid Brennan, Michael Ahern, Ciarán Kenny; David McMahon, Cathal Flaherty, Ciarán Hoary; Caoimhín King, Capt., Tony McGuane; Cormac Dempsey (0-1), Dónal Kirwan (0-6), Kevin Ward (0-3); Colm Kelly (1-0), David Devereux, Alan Hogan. Subs: Jamie Minnock, Ronan Gilsenan, Kenneth Fitzmaurice, Vincent McIntyre, Paul Kennedy, Cathal Browne, Paul Cosgrove, Kevin Carney. Coach: Pat Kenny.

**Dunshaughlin Community College
Winners Leinster Senior VS**

Paul Cosgrove, Cathal Browne, Paul Kennedy, Michael Ahern, Kenneth Fitzmaurice, Tony McGuane, Diarmuid Brennan, David Devereux, Colm Kelly, Ciarán Kenny,

Dunshaughlin Community College, Leinster Senior Camogie Winners, 2012

Front: Emma Kennedy, Cliodhna O Riordan, Anna Fagan, Christine Grimes, Cheyenne O Brien, Cliona Murphy, Fia O Brien, Shannon Thynne, Megan Thynne, Nadine Doyle, Chloe Mahon, Juliette Wall, Ruth Fagan.
Back: Laura Lee, A. Wall, Tara Murphy, Alannah Chalkley, Emma McGill, Kelly Gorman, Áine Brennan, Lauren Gorman, Enya Flynn, Lauren McCann, Louise Griffin, Catherine Carroll, Catriona Bolger, Emer Keane, Mick O Keeffe, Team Manager.

Dunshaughlin Community College, Leinster Senior D Winners, 2013

Front: Eimear O Brien, Cheyanne O Brien, Laura Wall, Elizabeth Morland, Krystelle Clynch, Megan Thynne, Niamh Gallogly, Fia O Brien, Laura Quinn, Martha Ní Riada, Ailis Bruce, Sadhbh Ó Muirí, Róisín Hogan, Gemma Monaghan, Amy Duffy.
Back: Kevagh Slater, Sarah Kelly, Maria Power, Gemma Donoghue, Niamh Hetherington, Megan Lavery, Ingrid Ieremie, Amy Mulvaney, Emma McGill, Aoife Swan, Cara Usher, Marissa Horan, Aisling Kelleher, Áine Brennan, Niamh Keane.

David McMahon, Ciarán Hoary, Vinny McIntyre, Ronan Gilsenan, Cathal Flaherty, Jamie Minnock, James Everard, Dónal Kirwan, Alan Hogan, Cormac Dempsey, Kevin Carney, Caoimhín King. Coach: Pat Kenny.

Leinster VEC Ladies Junior C Final
Kilbeggan 1-13 Dunshaughlin CC 1-0

Panel: Suzanne Colgan, Tracey Redmond, Brenda McTigue, Aoife O Donoghue, Anne Marie Grogan, Áine Ryan, Caitriona Brennan, Deirdre Donoghue, Lyndsey Conway, Leanne Cuttle, Ciara Byrne, Niamh Hogan, Alison Eiffe, Siobhán Duffy, Catherine McMahon, Carol Gregan, Niamh Morgan, Lisa Redmond, Leah Russell, Sarah McBride, Fiona O Sullivan, Niamh O Sullivan, Niamh Marsh, Sinéad Kirwan, Laura McMorrow, Claire Murray, Laura Ryan.

2004

Meath VEC Senior Final
Dunshaughlin CC 3-13 O Carolan College 2-7

Derek Jordan; Gavin Moore, Brian Coughlan, Willie Mahady; Terry Hetherton (0-1), James Gaughan, Cathal Hennelly; Cillian Finn (0-1), Michael Ahern (0-1); John Coleman (0-1), Conor Staunton (0-5), Ciarán Farrelly; Alan O Keeffe, David Keating (0-1), Diarmuid O Donoghue (1-2). Subs: Mark Caldwell (2-1) for Farrelly, Eldon Gavigan for O Keeffe, Stephen McGroder for Mahady, Niall Clarke for Coleman.

Meath VEC Juvenile Final
Dunshaughlin CC 2-11 Dunboyne 0-7.

North Leinster Juvenile C Final
Dunshaughlin CC 4-4 Ashbourne CS 3-5

Leinster Juvenile Final
Coláiste Bríde, Carnew 0-9 Dunshaughlin CC 0-6

James Kelliher; Stephen Daly, Anthony Donnelly, Fearghal Delaney; Eddie McSweeney (2-0), Des Dolan (0-1), Stephen O Keeffe; Willie Mahady, Dara Devereux, Capt.; Conor Dempsey (0-1), Ciarán Clusker, Mark Smullen (0-2); Niall Murphy, Colm McLoughlin, Danny Logan (2-0). Sub: Francis Coyne, Niall Dundon. Team managers: Conor Brennan and Oliver Coogan.

2005

Meath VEC Senior Final
Dunshaughlin CC winners

Leinster Senior B Final
Dunshaughlin CC 1-12 Coláiste Eoin, Hacketst'n 1-8

All-Ireland Senior B Final
Dunshaughlin CC 2-7 McHale College, Achill 1-4

Derek Jordan; Emmet O Callaghan, Brian Coughlan, Gavin Moore; Aodhán McKeown (1-1), James Gaughan, Terry Hetherton; Cillian Finn, David Keating (0-1); Ciarán Farrelly (0-1), Conor Staunton, Capt., Mark Caldwell; John Coleman, Alan O Keeffe (0-2), Diarmuid O Donoghue (1-0). Subs: Peter Durnin for Keating, Keating for Durnin, Michael Ahern for Coleman, Stephen McGroder, Willie Mahady, Niall Clarke, Cathal Moore, Dave Goodman, Ian Davis, Shane Togher, Stephen Fox, Oisín McCóil, Cathal Hennelly. Coach: Pat Kenny.

2006

Leinster VEC, Under 16 A Final
Dunshaughlin CC winners.

2007

Leinster VEC, Under 16 A Final
Dunshaughlin CC 4-6 Gallen, Ferbane 2-6.

Included: Bryan Davis, Colin McCullagh, Eimhín Kinsella, Liam Ormsby, Conor McGill, Eoin Cahill, Conor O Brien, James Kelly, Sam Duggan, Niall Hannon, David Donnelan, John Davis, Seán Burke, Paudge Maguire.

2008

Leinster VS Junior, U-16 Final
Dunshaughlin CC 2-11 Bridgetown VS 3-5

All-Ireland Semi-Final
Dunshaughlin CC 3-9 Downpatrick De La Salle 1-12

All-Ireland Final
Athenry VS 4-8 Dunshaughlin CC 2-9

Leinster Final team: Michael McCarthy; Colm O Flaherty, Paddy Kennedy, Seán Joyce; Emmet Staunton, Conor O Brien, Alastar Doyle; Fergus McGorman (0-1), Niall Hannon; Bryan Davis (0-1), Eoin Hagarty (0-4), Danny Thynne (0-1); Eamon Bowe (2-2), Conor Devereux (0-2), James Rattigan. Sub: Alan O Brien for Davis, Niall Clusker, Shane Connolly, Conor McGill, Eoin Hannon, Ian Gillette, Sam Duggan, Eoin Cahill, Colin McCullagh, Andrew Smith, Seán Dunleavy, James Reilly, Joe Jordan, Tiernan Mahedy, Eoin Hogan, Cormac Flaherty, Conor O Sullivan. Team Managers: Mick O Keeffe, Conor Brennan.

2009

North Leinster Juvenile, U-14 FC, C
Dunshaughlin CC 5-17 Dundalk De La Salle 1-3

Leinster Juvenile, U-14 FC, C
Semi-Final: Dunshaughlin CC 2-11 Wicklow DLS 2-10
Leinster Final: Dunshaughlin CC 6-15 Portmarnock 3-4.

North Leinster Final team: Stephen McCarthy; Josh Wall, Aidan Wall, Michael Lennon; Seán Fitzpatrick, Glen Fitzpatrick (0-2), Conor Whelan; Jonathan O Connor, Paul Donnellan (0-2); Conor O Brien (1-2), Patrick Darby (0-3), Jake Harlin (1-0); Daniel Benson (0-4), Paul Clarke (1-2), Fergal Cleary (0-2). Subs: Ben Duggan, Stephen Kinsella, Emmet Jordan, David Reilly, Oisín Foley (1-0), Shane Gallogly (1-0), Daniel Aloba, Nathan Pleavin, Niall Thynne, Shane Lambe, Lorcan Byrne, Peter Butler, Josh Finnegan, Tom Sharp, Seán Doyle, Gareth Rooney, Michael McNally, Michael Montague, Dean Ryan, Jordan O Reilly, Lorcan Bannon, Cathal Burke. Team Manager Conor Brennan.

North Leinster Junior Colleges B
Final: Dunshaughlin 1-8 Scoil Dara, Kilcock 0-7

Andrew Smith; Pádraig Maguire, Conor McGill, Jack Hogan; Seán Burke, Conor O Brien, Eoin Cahill; Niall Hannon, Eoin Hannon; James Kelly, Colin McCullagh (0-1), Eimhin Kinsella (1-0); Ian Gillette, Bryan Davis (0-7), David Baggott. Subs: John Davis for Hogan, Sam Duggan for Baggott.

Leinster VEC Junior A Final
Dunshaughlin CC 4-6 Gallen CS Ferbane 2-6.

All-Ireland U-16 VEC
Semi-Final: Dunshaughlin CC 4-10 Athenry VS 0-5

Andrew Smith, Capt.; Pádraig Maguire, Conor McGill, Liam Ormsby; Eoin Cahill, Conor O Brien, John Davis; Seán Burke, Niall Hannon; Eimhín Kinsella (1-1), Colm McCullagh (0-2), Sam Duggan; David Donnellan (0-1), Bryan Davis (2-3), James Kelly (1-0). Subs: Ian Gillette (0-1) for Cahill, David Baggott for Duggan, Cormac Flaherty for Donnellan, Jack Hogan for John Davis, Colin Farrell for Ormsby, Patrick Darby, Colin Phelan, Eoin Hannon, Matt Sharp, Glen Fitzpatrick.

All-Ireland U-16 VEC
Final: St. Paul's Kilcrea 2-16 Dunshaughlin CC 2-4

2011

Leinster Schools Ladies D Final
Dunshaughlin CC 3-11 Loreto, Dublin 1-9

Niamh Carroll; Kate Whelan, Laura Murray, Aimee McQuillan; Niamh Keane, Leanne McMorrow, Emer Keane; Lauren McCann, Clíona Murphy; Cheyenne O Brien, Aileen O Sullivan, Emma McGill; Maeve Scanlon, Emma Kennedy, Laura McMahon. Subs: Adrienne McCann for McMahon, Catríona Kennedy for McQuillan, Róisín Bruce for O Sullivan, Róisín Hogan for Emma Kennedy, Rachel Whelan for Keane.

2013

N'th Leinster Post Prim. Schools, Under 14 B
Final: Dunshaughlin CC 3-9 Scoil Dara 3-7

Leinster Post Primary Schools, Under 14 B
Final: Dunshaughlin CC 4-8 FCJ Bunclody 2-13

Mark Foy; Tom Dalton, Adam Kealy, Capt., Robbie Clarke; Mika Mikamibua, Sam Butler, Jack Hetherington; Seán Irwin, Darragh Campion; Frank Carty, Ross McQuillan, Paddy Conway; Seán O Neill, Cathal Murphy, Cian Gallogly. Subs: Rian Kealy, Paddy Maher, Neil Byrne, Donagh Garvey, Ross Shivmangal, Michael Long, Dylan O Brien, Lee Lynch, Paddy McCabe, Cian Maher, Fionn Maguire, Ciarán Malone, Turlough Malone, Shane Claire, Andrew Slevin, Seán Byrne, Eoin Harkin.

Leinster Schools Ladies Juvenile
Final: Loreto SS, Kilkenny 5-10 Dunshaughlin CC 3-9

Lara Reynolds; Gemma Monahan, Laura Wall, Olivia Flanagan; Eimear Traynor, Martha Ní Riada, Orlaith Moyles; Sarah Kelly, Kelly O Dwyer; Niamh Curtin, Laura Quinn, Molly Regan; Megan Thynne (3-6), Rachel Huijsdens (0-2), Kevagh Slater (0-1). Subs: Diane Sauveroche, Ellen McGee, Aoife Sheridan, Blaithnaid O Brien, Kyra Synnott, Ava Fox, Lucy Kelly, Ellen Byrne, Ciara Hickey.

Leinster Schools Ladies Junior D Shield
Final: Dunshaughlin CC 8-19 Portarlington 4-3

Panel: Amy Mulvaney, Laura Wall, Ciara Hickey, Ellen McGee, Sadhbh Ó Muirí, Orlaith Moyles, Aoife Swan, Olivia Flanagan, Niamh Curtin, Gemma Donoghue, Niamh Hetherington, Rachel Huijsdens, Lara Reynolds, Gemma Monaghan, Eimear Traynor, Fia O Brien, Eimear O Brien, Cara Usher, Marissa Horan, Aisling Kelleher, Kevagh Slater, Blathnaid O Brien, Róisín Bruce, Ellen Byrne, Sarah Kelly, Laura Quinn, Krystelle Clynch, Niamh Gallogly, Elizabeth Morland, Megan Thynne, Martha Ní Riada, Kelly O Dwyer, Ava Fox, Lucy Kelly, Kyra Synnott. Team mentors: Róisín Ní Dhúshláine, Anne-Marie O Brien, Róisín Cousins.

Leinster Schools Ladies Senior D Final
Tullamore 5-6 Dunshaughlin CC 1-13

Amy Mulvaney; Gemma Donoghue, Eimear O Brien, Krystelle Clynch; Maria Power, Róisín Hogan, Sadhbh Ó Múirí; Fia O Brien (0-1), Niamh Gallogly (0-2); Cheyenne O Brien, Elizabeth Morland (0-4), Aisling Kelleher; Megan Thynne (0-3), Áine Brennan, Emma McGill (1-3). Subs: Laura Wall, Laura Quinn, Martha Ní Riada, Ailis Bruce, Gemma Monaghan, Amy Duffy, Kevagh Slater, Sarah Kelly, Niamh Hetherington, Megan Lavery, Ingrid Ieremie, Aoife Swan, Cara Usher, Marissa Horan, Niamh Keane.

2014

N'th Leinster Post Prim. Schools, Under 14 B
Final: Scoil Dara 4-15 Dunshaughlin CC 3-4

Aaron Lawlor; Ronan Hiney, Conor Keena, Paul Kennedy; Josh Kallides (0-1), Mika Mikamibua, Jarlath Jordan; Rian Kealy (1-1), Eoin Harkin; Matthew Moyles (0-1), Niall Hurley, Luke Thorpe; Conor Oliver (1-0), Paddy Maher (1-1), Wesley Goodwin. Subs: Colm Byrne for Thorpe, Jack Caldwell for Hurley, Seán Byrne, Shane Dowling, Cathal McIntyre, Seán Allen, Charlie O Donnell, Paul Briody, Daniel Fildes, Eoin O Connor, Aaron Gaynor, Cathal McCormack, Luke Mitchell, Jack Brady, David Fildes, Johnny Pearl, Chris Varvari.

HURLING & CAMOGIE HONOURS

1972

Under 14 Hurling Final
Dunshaughlin 4-1 Trim 1-0

Paddy Monaghan; Joey O Brien, Oliver Gannon, Dom O Neill; Eugene Hickey, Dónal Gaynor, Gabriel Hopkins; Martin Dolan, Pádraig Finnerty; Anthony McAuley, Tommy Ennis, Timmy O Connor; Vinny Byrne, Christopher Browne, John Watters.

1973

VS Hurling Final
Trim 1-4 Dunshaughlin 1-0

1974

VS Hurling Final
Dunshaughlin 3-1 Navan 2-2

Paddy Monaghan; JP Kelly, F Galvin, Gerard Eiffe; Brendan Carty, Oliver Gannon, Séamus Ennis; John Watters, Aidan Browne; Owen Clinch, Mannix Coyne, Eugene Connaughton; Anthony Gaughan, Pádraig Finnerty, Bernard Yourell.

2001

North Leinster Juvenile D Final
Dunshaughlin CC 4-7 St Josephs Drogheda 1-9
Semi-Final Team: John Crosbie; Brian Coughlan, Eoin Reilly; Robert Lyons, Paul Grimes, James Gaughan; Ciarán Kenny, David Wallace; Conor Staunton, Ciarán Farrelly, Peter Durnin; Diarmuid O Donoghue, Niall Clarke. Subs: Adam Kelly, Stephen McGroder, Darren King, David Bracken, Val Gannon, Darragh Dempsey, Paul Kiernan, Martin Cosgrove, Simon Kennedy, Thomas O Regan, Ian Hand.

2002

North Leinster Juvenile D Final
Dunshaughlin Winners

Team, not in positional order: Ciarán Farrelly, Diarmuid Donoghue, Stephen McGroder, Mark Munnelly, Daniel Murray, Darren Maguire, Niall Brennan, Seán Doyle, David Wallace, Niall Clarke, Conor Staunton, Christopher Dixon, Aodhán McKeown. Team Manager: Michael Wallace.

North Leinster Senior D Hurling League.
St. Patrick's Navan defeated Dunshaughlin CC

2003

North Leinster Junior C Final
Dunshaughlin CC 7-2 Clonaslee VS, Laois 2-3
John Crosbie; Eoin Reilly, Robert Campion; Robert Lyons, Ciarán Kenny, Paul Grimes; James Gaughan, David Wallace (2-1); Niall Clarke (0-1), Brian Coughlan (2-0), Conor Staunton; Peter Durnin (3-0), Anthony Donnelly. Subs: Diarmuid O Donoghue for Donnelly, Aodhán McKeown for Reilly, Christopher Dixon, Ciarán Farrelly, Niall Brennan, Stephen McGroder, Val Gannon, Thomas O Regan. Manager: Michael Wallace with Joseph Coffey and John O Callaghan.

North Leinster Juvenile Hurling D Championship
Semi-Final: Dunshaughlin CC 6-6 Kells CS 6-4
Final: Coláiste Rís Dundalk defeated Dunshaughlin CC
Semi-Final team: Darren Walsh; Mark Munnelly, Seán Doyle; Niall Clarke, Aodhán McKeown, Niall Brennan; Christopher Dixon, Diarmuid O Donoghue (1-2); David Wallace (2-4), Ciarán Farrelly, Conor Staunton (2-0), Darren Maguire, Daniel Murray (1-0). Subs: Stephen McGroder for Murray, Gerry King for Munnelly.

2004

North Leinster Juvenile Hurling D Final
Dunshaughlin CC 1-13 Killucan/Cas'pollard CC 3-3
Shane McCann; Pádraig Burke, Michael Lynch; Patrick Kelly, Willie Mahady, Shane Troy; Michael Gorman, Anthony Donnelly; Kevin Smith, Niall O Donoghue, Kelvin Doyle; Darren Maguire, Malcolm Doyle. Subs: Paul Walsh for K Doyle.

North Leinster Junior C Final
Dunshaughlin CC 3-9 Tullamore College 2-3

Leinster Semi-Final v B Winners
Dunshaughlin CC 1-12 Dunboyne 1-5

Leinster Junior B
Final: Borris VS 2-9 Dunshaughlin CC 1-3
Panel: Willie Mahady, Anthony Donnelly, Val Gannon, Darren Reilly, Mark Munnelly, Michael Lynch, Shane Vogelaar, Niall Brennan, Peter Mahady, Stephen McGroder, Seán White, Darragh Walsh, Thomas Kane, Niall Clarke, Diarmuid O Donoghue, David Wallace, Paul Kiernan, Aodhán McKeown, Darren Maguire, Conor Staunton, Ciarán Farrelly. Team Manager: Michael Wallace.

2009

Meath Camogie, 1st/2nd Years, Grade C
Final: Dunshaughlin CC beat Navan
Leinster Semi-Final: Dunshaughlin CC beat Johnstown, Kilkenny
Leinster Final: Dunshaughlin CC beat Kilbeggan
Capt. Cliona Murphy
Meath Senior Camogie Final: Dunshaughlin CC beat Trim
Leinster Senior Camogie: Johnstown, Kilkenny beat Dunshaughlin CC Capt. Fiona McGill

2012

Leinster Senior Camogie Final
Dunshaughlin CC 5-2 Col. Mhuire, Kilkenny 3-3
Cliodhna O Riordan; Christine Grimes, Anna Fagan, Emer Keane; Alannah Chalkley, Cheyenne O Brien, Emma McGll; Cliona Murphy (1-0), Kelly Gorman; Fia O Brien, Louise Griffin (1-1), Shannon Thynne; Emma Kennedy (1-0), Lauren McCann, Tara Murphy (2-1). Subs: Megan Thynne, Áine Brennan, Catherine Carroll, Catríona Bolger, Enya Flynn, Lauren Gorman, Chloe Mahon, Nadine Doyle, Juliet Wall, Ruth Fagan.

North Leinster Junior C Hurling Final
Dunshaughlin CC 2-15 Mercy, Kilbeggan 5-4
Lorcan Casey; Cormac Harkin, David Dunne, Niall Gorman; Alan Reilly, Michael Burke, (Capt.), Seán McCann; Josh Wall (1-6), Kyle Donnelly; Ciarán Casey (0-2), Josh Dennehy (1-0), Liam Carey (0-2); Colm Kiernan (0-1), Alastair Jackson, Eamonn McLoughlin (0-1). Subs: Seán Kiernan, for Donnelly, Shane Walsh (0-3) for Jackson. Team Mentors: Shane McGrath, Peter Durnin.

Dunshaughlin Community College, Leinster Under 14 B Winners, 2013

Front: Paddy Maher, Tom Dalton, Robbie Clarke, Frank Carty, Darragh Campion, Adam Kealy, Capt., Cathal Murphy, Lee Lynch, Seán O Neill, Dylan O Brien.
Middle: Jason Boland, Coach, Donagh Garvey, Ross Shivmangal, Jack Hetherington, Shane Claire, Fionn Maguire, Paddy McCabe, Ciarán Malone, Mika Mikamibua, Turlough Malone, Rian Kealy, Conor Brennan, Coach.
Back: Ross McQuillan, Mark Foy, Neil Byrne, Seán Irwin, Cian Gallogly, Sam Butler, Michael Long, Seán Byrne, Paddy Conway, Cian Maher, Andrew Slevin, Eoin Harkin.

Appendix 17
GAA Clubs in the Parish and Locality, 1886 -1900

The following is a list of various GAA clubs that existed in the parish since 1886. The prime source of the information is the local newspapers but it is not a comprehensive listing as clubs could exist but not have any details recorded in the press. In the early years of the GAA clubs appeared and disappeared with great regularity. The date given is the year the club is first mentioned and end dates are indicative only. Often clubs faded away and were rarely ended formally so clubs may have survived longer than the date given or may have lapsed between the dates shown. Further research might bring more clarity to the issue.

Dunshaughlin, initially **St. Seachnalls,** 1886 -91, 1894-99, 1901-04, 1907-11, 1913-31, 1923-29, 1933-present

Merrywell St. Martins, 1887

Warrenstown, 1887

Drumree Gaelic Athletic Club, 1891-92

Na Fir le Céile (The United Men), Dunshaughlin, hurling team linked to The Gaelic League, 1900s

Warrenstown Hurling Club, 1905-06, a team linked to The Gaelic League

Culmullen, 1901, 1904-05, 1914, 1924, 1934-1941

Bogganstown FC, 1914

Drumree Volunteer Club, 1915

Pelletstown, popularly known as the Pelletstown Reds, 1918-1924, 1929

Drumree, 1926-1931, 1947-1952, 1957-present

Salesian College, Warrenstown, 1932-1950s, mainly catered for minor football and hurling but won the Meath Junior Hurling championship in 1953

St. Martins, Drumree, 1942-45. An adult team.

Dunshaughlin Hurling Club, 1982-1990.

St. Martins Juvenile Club, 1956-1961 and 1983-2008.

Other Clubs in the Locality to 1900

1886

Ringlestown, Kilmessan
St. Patricks, Kilmessan
Corballis

1887

Black Bull FC
Ross, Tara
Rathfeigh Emeralds
Ratoath
Killana Shamrocks
Ballina Malachys, Tara
Grange Geraldines
Ratoath Shillelaghs

1888

Rathbeggan Sunbursts
Fairyhouse Gaels
William O Briens, Clonee
Dunboyne Volunteers, colours black and green
Home Rulers, Porterstown
Batterstown Bards
O Mahonys, Ardcath
Curraha Davitts
Moortown Independents, location uncertain.
Faugh a Beallach, Ashbourne, navy blue and white jersey, caps to match

1889

Ratoath Home Rulers
Rodanstown, near Kilcock
Macetown O Neills

1891

St. Patricks Hatchet FC, later O Connells

1894

Batterstown Wolfe Tones
Skryne Rangers

1898

Ardcath Slashers

1899

Killeen '98 FC

1900

Killeen Fingall Rangers
Clonee Tolka Rovers

1901

Corbalton